W9-BUN-760

Under the General Editorship of
Joseph W. Towle
Washington University, St. Louis
Houghton Mifflin Adviser in Management

To Walter F. Gast
A Professor's Professor and
Management Philosopher

Issues in
Business and Society

Readings and Cases

Second Edition

William T. Greenwood
Southern Illinois University

Houghton Mifflin Company • Boston

Atlanta • New York • Geneva, Illinois • Dallas • Palo Alto

Copyright © 1971 by Houghton Mifflin Company.

Copyright © 1964 by William T. Greenwood.

The selections reprinted in this book are used by permission of and special arrangements with the proprietors of their respective copyrights. All rights reserved. No part
of this work may be reproduced or transmitted in any form or by any means, electronic or mechanical, including photocopying and recording, or by any information
storage or retrieval system, without permission in writing from the publisher.

Printed in the U. S. A.

Library of Congress Catalog Card Number: 78–142819

ISBN: 0-395-11224-9

General Editor's Introduction

As the foundations of our economic system and traditional business morality are being challenged by the college student, as ecologists, minority groups and concerned citizens express dissatisfaction with the "order of things," leaders in the business community have become acutely aware of the new and pressing forces of change in our modern way of life. In this era of accelerated change our free enterprise system is being called upon as never before to respond to society's needs. In the light of this challenge, many businessmen are examining, evaluating, or even reformulating their business philosophy, ethics and standard practices.

In this well organized volume—consisting of text, readings and cases— Professor William Greenwood explores the major contemporary issues in business and society. The carefully selected articles included in this second edition express diverse and opposing points of view; the Part Introductions are insightful and provide an element of cohesiveness while the cases serve as a helpful analytical tool. Together, these three elements will help the student of business, as well as the business executive, to question and evaluate contemporary business challenges and business mores. In selecting and preparing the materials for this second edition, Professor Greenwood has provided a useful and provocative resource in the field of business management.

Joseph W. Towle
Washington University, St. Louis

Preface

Since the appearance of the first edition of this book in 1964, critics from the political Left and Right have become increasingly vocal in their observations about American society. The business community—as an integral part of society—has come under increasing scrutiny by groups advocating the end to poverty, the end to the war in Vietnam, the end to inadequate housing, the end to urban plight, and the end to inflation. Many observers argue that business—which has been responsibile for America's progress and prosperity—must now demonstrate more responsibility for America's social needs. Whether social responsibility is in accord with business responsibility or antithetical to the traditional goals of profit maximization is the dilemma which business now faces with increasing immediacy. Stockholders, employees, customers, government agencies, the unemployed, the recent college graduate and the high-school dropout, are all members of a general public to whom business must address itself. Whether the claims of these groups are answered negatively or affirmatively with action will be a function of the future role of the American corporation during the decade of the seventies.

As a reflection of widespread change that has occurred in the past six years, this edition represents a major revision of *Issues in Business and Society.* Less than fifty percent of the articles have been retained from the first edition, and four new cases have been selected. Of particular note are the articles in Part Eight, "Business and Its Environment," which deal with the immediate challenges to the business community and responsibilities for the future. The recent business-student communications gap, the potential threat of automation to white- and blue-collar workers, the active debate concerning the effectiveness of participative management as an alternative to "conformity," are all new to this edition. However, several topics representing a continuity of concern for the business community have been retained from the first edition, but more recent articles were selected to illustrate contemporary opinion about traditional business-society conflicts.

The eight Parts of the book are each subdivided into sections to highlight the issues. The Part Introductions are intended to serve as a framework for discussion and to provide an analysis of the issues and articles. The cases at the end of each Part are designed as a vehicle for practical application of each important issue treated in the Part Introductions and articles. An updated, selected Bibliography follows each Part.

This book presents a variety of contemporary opinion and should hopefully serve as a catalyst for debate. Whenever possible, both sides of controversial issues have been presented, and many of the articles within each section represent the best "pro" and "con" positions from the wealth of periodical literature that is available. With subject matter that is essentially interdisciplinary, such an approach is of value. It would be difficult for any one author to attempt to synthesize the great quantity of available information; and when issues are controversial, the reader should not be confined to one author's point of view. Therefore, this volume is intended to serve as a resource for courses in business and society, business ethics, and business and government and can be used either as a supplementary or basic text.

I would like to express my appreciation at this point for the contributions made by the case writers, the authors of the various articles, copyright-holding periodicals, and universities for granting their permission to reprint these materials. I would like to again acknowledge appreciation to Keith Davis at Arizona State University for initially assigning the responsibility for developing the materials for this new course some ten years ago, and for his assistance and editorial advice in the development of the original materials. My thanks go also to Charles McGinty and Lavon Carter who have been most helpful in their research assistance required to assimilate the materials and to Mrs. Loren Stephens of Houghton Mifflin for her extensive editorial assistance in this revision.

William T. Greenwood
Southern Illinois University

Contents

PART ONE

Our Free Enterprise Society

The number of issues and conflicts arising between business and society has increased dramatically over the past two decades, and we now regard the seventies as a period of even greater concern to business. The magnitude of issues and conflicts requires that management be better prepared to minimize and resolve these numerous conflicts in a manner advantageous to both business and society. The starting point for the businessman is an effective understanding of the free enterprise society in which he operates, the evolutionary nature of capitalism, and the interrelationships of business and society, especially the interrelationship of government and business.

A. The Evolution of Capitalism

Capitalism and freedom take on different meanings depending upon the context and environment within which they are applied. The businessman tends to equate freedom with free enterprise and an almost exclusionary interest in the freedom to make his business decisions. Capitalism—or free enterprise —is our chosen economic system, but it is a highly changing one due to the dynamic pressures of the private market and increasing social controls imposed by the government. In his article on "Business Philosophy" [1] Robert E. Moore traces the evolutionary stages of capitalism and the various philosophies of business. The author contends that in "this era of dynamic capitalism" the businessman has not yet developed a clear philosophy. If business is to inhibit society's enthusiasm for the ideas of socialism, and promote the value of the private market system, businessmen must become more aware of the inequities that exist between business and society in order to formulate a broad and flexible philosophy that is responsive to society's needs.

B. Business, Competition, and Government

Significant among the changing issues between business and society has been the debate between business and government. In the early 1900s the major emphasis was upon governmental anti-trust legislation against monopolistic and oligopolistic practices. Rapid technological and demographic growth over the last fifty years have created economic problems requiring the attention of business and government alike. In "Will Growth Increase Federal Control?" [2] Edward T. Chase interprets increasing governmental intervention at the federal, state and local level as a necessary response to problems created by accelerated growth. He strongly supports innovative, corrective action by the federal government in areas previously "controlled" by the forces of the private market. It is interesting to note that the problems cited in this article written ten years ago challenge the initiative of businessmen today. If these broad and pervasive problems of American society are to be resolved, some orientation must be taken toward national goals. The author prescribes centralized, economic planning as the only rational mechanism for coordinating the efforts of business and government to solve critical, economic problems in order to reach specific national goals.

A more moderate solution to the conflicts between corporate freedom and the public interest is cited in "A Changing Balance of Power: New Partnership of Government and Business" [3]. The article quotes leading businessmen who recommend that a voluntary partnership of business with government and labor will serve to reconcile and coordinate the interests of the public and the interests of the company. The article predicts that a new relationship is developing between business and government that will strike a balance between the extremes of centralized governmental control and corporate irresponsibility.

Illustrations of the need for the voluntary reconciliation of the conflicts between business, society, and government are offered in two cases. In the Nebbia vs. New York case, the court at the height of the depression decided in favor of states' rights to regulate the price and distribution policies for a milk producer. The significance of this case is that a business, regardless of type or size, that is vested or "affected with a high degree of public interest," is highly susceptible to extensive governmental regulation and control. This conclusion is based upon the presumption that the degree of dependence of the public upon this business is significant and, conversely, the amount of power and influence the business can have upon the public under particular economic conditions is extraordinary, and therefore must be restricted. In the U. S. Steel and the 1962 Price Increase case, we see a unique example of presidential influence and intervention into industry practices. When union requests for noninflationary wage-price guidelines were achieved through participation of the federal government in discussions with the steel industry and labor, labor and government expected that business would not raise the price of steel. When business did not voluntarily comply with the terms of the negotiations President John Kennedy brought extraordinary pressure to bear upon the steel industry. The relationship of public interest to concomitant social responsibilities is further illustrated in the Prairie Eye-Opener case wherein a relatively small newspaper is confronted with demands for greater responsibility in its identification of advertising, and its affiliation with, and influence over, other communication media in the area.

In general, we are forced to conclude that management must assume social responsibilities commensurate with the degree of power and influence they are capable of wielding, whether at the national, state, or local level. If this responsibility is not assumed, and if this power and influence are misused, whether intentionally or unintentionally, we know from the lessons of history that society, through government, will seek redress through some type of intervention or regulation. If business is to maximize its freedom for decision-making now and in the future, it must assume effective, socially responsible activities, especially in those areas where its influence and power may be felt.

C. Profits and Profit Sharing

Classical economic theory has emphasized profit maximization as the primary—if not exclusive—goal of the businessman in the American free enterprise system. Profits were understood by society as a means of providing the maximum allocation of scarce resources in the production of goods and services; they were also regarded as a reward for efficient risk-taking by investors through management. Today, we find opposing theories that substitute "reasonable" and "satisfactory" for maximum" when profit maximization is deemed inconsistent with the welfare and interest of society. However, in "What's Wrong with Profit Maximization?" [4] Charles F. Phillips, Jr. argues that profit maximization is consistent with and essential to society's well-being. Without maximum profits, management cannot achieve efficient utilization of resources to insure a greater variety of goods of high quality and at lower cost to the consumer, with high returns to investors, management and labor. For these reasons, the warning is voiced that social responsibility must not be a substitute for profit maximization, but that both goals may be achieved in the long run. The author argues, "Only by performing the economic function well is a business firm socially responsible."

The voluntary sharing of profits by business as incentives to the work force has had a highly variable record of success. The question of sharing profits as a right of labor and the customer gives rise to the philosophical question as to the source and extent of these rights. Traditionally, profits are the rewards for efficient risk-taking. Therefore, any rightful claim to them should be related to the respective types and degrees of risks assumed. If profit rights are lost to any degree at the bargaining table, business can blame itself for not developing a thorough analysis of, and philosophical framework for, the nature of profits. In "The Ethics of Profit Sharing" [5] the author tells us that business and society have reduced significantly the risks taken by the individual employee by offering him a fixed wage with a relatively high degree of job security and a great variety of unemployment and fringe benefits. As a result, the risk taken by the employee seems to be much less than that taken by the investor. However, the question of whether or not profit sharing can become a right of labor will eventually be decided by the National Labor Relations Board as it adapts its decisions to what can and cannot be included under the items of wages, hours and working conditions. The significant point is that in the future, if the risks are found to be high for the worker, the NLRB may make profits subject to collective bargaining. Presently, profits are shared at the discretion of management.

The three concepts of freedom, capitalism, and society have taken on new meanings and emphases. Freedom is not absolute, either for the businessman or any other individual or group in a democratic society. Contrary to the view held by particular groups, the determination of the operative limits of freedom are influenced by our total society rather than by any particular interest group. Capitalism is not a static system but one that has gone through and will continue to go through evolutionary changes. The causes of these changes and the role of the businessman will be of paramount significance now and in the future. The concepts of business and society require analysis in depth and in breadth. To be complete this analysis must identify the roles of the federal, state, and local governments, and particular interest and power groups in our democratic society, as well as the basic prerogatives of the individual.

Our free enterprise society is no longer a topic for debate reserved to legislative halls and academic classrooms. It is of direct concern to the individual business firm, regardless of size or location, and to its managers. The articles and cases presented in Part One emphasize the new meanings and dimensions of each of these concepts and their interrelationships. They also raise questions each businessman must face concerning his firm, his freedom, and his profits in a democratically determined society.

A. The Evolution of Capitalism

Business Philosophy **1**
Robert E. Moore

Business history reveals that business has been a major factor in the development of our present civilization. Business is the "core" of modern society. Consequently, business philosophy (an explanation of the phenomena of business) should logically be considered of extreme importance in the realm of ideas and thoughts which shape and guide our civilization.

The various types of business or phases of capitalism in history are conspicuous for the ideas and thoughts of businessmen that reflected necessity, but the development of a formulated system of thought or a philosophy is not always evident. On the other hand, economic thought or the economist's explanation of business has been well formulated. However, economic thought in most instances is too far removed from the realities of business to suffice as a philosophy of business or to serve as a reliable guide to the businessman in conducting his affairs. The explanation of this divergence between business and economic thought is twofold: (1) Economists have been reluctant to extend their inquiry down to the level of actual business administration. (2) As an aid to logical thinking, economists are prone to deal with just a few of the multiple considerations involved in business.

The explanation of the phenomena of business, which is a part of the society, must of necessity begin with a general understanding of the individuals who compose society. The recognition of "individual differences" is the basic concept to which we owe our present advances in the fields of psychology, psychiatry, and human relations. While the individual has many things in common with his fellow men, his peculiar needs must be taken into account at all stages of growth and development. Man is extremely heterogeneous, as opposed to the popular conception of homogeneity implied in the phrase "All men are created equal."

Reprinted with permission from the *Business Historical Society*, Vol. 24 (December 1950), pp. 196–209. Copyright © by the President and Fellows of Harvard College; all rights reserved.

Each individual inherently has fundamental drives or instincts, such as self-preservation, desire for power, desire for possessions, sexual gratification, and others. Society forces the individual to sublimate these inherent drives in accordance with its own mores and needs. Professor Spranger of Halle, Germany, made an analysis of the various value systems arising in individuals as a result of this sublimation. He isolated six ideal types of men: theoretic, economic, political, religious, aesthetic, and social. These types constitute an interesting attempt to describe and classify the heterogeneous composition of society.

The principal characteristics that Spranger attributed to these six ideal types can be summarized as follows:

1. *Theoretical man* lives in a realm of thought. He is devoted to systematizing his ideas. He values knowledge and truth.

2. *Economic man* aims at security through his own efforts. Material things are his interest. He values utility and efficiency.

3. *Political man* seeks power. He is interested in obtaining control over his fellow men.

4. *Religious man* is interested in the supernatural. He desires to understand ultimate reality, his position in a universe governed by a deity.

5. *Aesthetic man* is creative in an artistic sense. Beauty is his ideal.

6. *Social man* loves his fellow men. He seeks the approbation of others in serving them.

It should be recognized that only rarely do we find an individual who could be clearly confined to just one of these classifications. The six values are present to some degree in each individual. However, each person tends to accent a value in relating himself to society. These values are a part of man's environmental nature and heredity. History serves to prove that this value system of which mankind is composed is roughly enduring. There seems to be a relative constancy in percentages of our society which can be broadly categorized into each of the six classifications.

Each of the groups comprising these ideal classifications makes an essential contribution toward the civilization and society upon which business is dependent and which it in turn supports and develops. The extreme heterogeneity, exemplified in Spranger's analysis, highlights the difficulty of tying the members of each group to a common system of thought and opinion. This general acceptance of such a common system is the phenomenon which permits a society to exist; for the degree of acceptance is a measure of the completeness of the social union, and the nature of the common thought and opinion determines its kind. A unit in society which illustrates to some extent an ideal oneness of thought and opinion is the family.

Recognizing the concept of the heterogeneity of man, and that a common system of thought or opinion is necessary to complete social union, it is not hard to see that business has had and will continue to have difficulty in relating itself to a total society. Beyond this, however, the businessman has had a rather narrow philosophy which has not been adaptable to change.

Because, in general, knowledge and thought precede action, there is a close connection between the businessman's philosophy of business and actual business practices. Consequently, the historic narrowness and inflexibility of the businessman's philosophy has indirectly resulted in one system of business or capitalism which is predominant at one time giving way to another. Business history classifies these stages of capitalism as follows: Pre-Business, Petty, Mercantile, Industrial, Financial, and National Capitalism.

By exploring the philosophies of the various stages of capitalism we can see wherein they lacked the universality to provide for the heterogeneity of society. Perhaps in some measure we may relate the conclusions drawn to our present system of national capitalism where the requirement for a more complete social union is the order of the day.

PRE-BUSINESS CAPITALISM (BEFORE 1100 A.D.)

The long period in the development of civilization which is classified as the pre-business capitalism phase is characterized by the evolution of the cooperative collective economy. The cooperative collective economy evolved to its highest point in manorialism and feudalism during the tenth century A.D.[1] This phase in history was not barren of progress in economic activity. Regular work was developed, work was divided somewhat according to the particular skills of the individuals, and the feudal lords developed administrative and supervisory techniques to control production and consumption. Rudimentary accounting was also developed during this period. However, there was no business because the necessary elements for business were not evident: (1) The guiding plan of social activity was based on social status obtained by birth rather than by each individual's skills, efforts, and contributions. (2) Production was primarily for consumption and there was little if any producion for exchange. (3) There was no philosophy of advancing or progressing in material affairs.

We should note with interest this era of pre-business capitalism and collective economies, for it is a lesson in history that has present-day applications. Mankind since its inception struggled toward a collective economy and the security it provided. After many thousands of years of existence, the high point of feudalism was reached about 1100 A.D. only to give way to a new idea of social existence introduced by the petty capitalist. Petty capitalism arose because the philosophy of feudalism was too narrow and inflexible. It lacked the universality to appeal to the heterogeneity of man and his desire for progress. There was no place in the collective economy for the economic man,

[1] It should be noted that there had been a considerable development of private business capitalism in Ancient Times.

the group in society which emphasizes material progress and aims at security through effort directed toward economic advancement.

Today we again see the rise of collective economies under the banner of socialism—a type of social existence that has historically been rejected by mankind in spite of its long period of trial and development.

PETTY CAPITALISM (1100 A.D.–1300 A.D.)

Petty capitalism was the first type of private business capitalism. The petty capitalist introduced business to society. The economic man, who had largely been dormant in the collective economy of pre-business capitalism, arose to create the beginnings of a revolutionary new social order. In order to appreciate the significance of this event, we have only to compare the advances made in civilization in the last 900 years[2] to those made in the countless thousands of years during the era of pre-business capitalism.

When the petty capitalist introduced business to society, he laid the cornerstone of our present civilization. Business freed mankind from the almost completely absorbing task of providing directly for his own basic needs. By producing goods for exchange as well as consumption, non-perishable capital could be accumulated. This accumulation of work and effort in the form of capital permitted man the leisure to contemplate, plan, and specialize in those areas in which he could make the greatest contribution to society.

The direct putting-out system of capitalism was a contribution of the petty capitalist. In earlier times the usecapital system had prevailed; under this system capital was used by the owner and in no other way could it yield a return. The direct putting-out system presented a way whereby the owner of capital puts out directly to the user a certain amount of capital goods or money in return for a promise to pay interest or dividends. It made capital dynamic. By this device a businessman, clergyman, artist, or widow could derive sustenance by putting-out capital to work and receiving income from it. The three principal methods of getting an income from capital by direct putting-out under the system of petty capitalism can be summarized as follows: (1) investing in a business partnership; (2) loaning goods or money; (3) selling goods on credit but at a charge.

It is difficult to determine to what extent the petty capitalist, embodied in shopkeepers, storekeepers, and traveling merchants, formulated his thoughts and ideas in relation to himself, business, and society. However, by assuming a rather close connection between business thought and business practices we can reconstruct in a general way his guiding principles or philosophy.

The petty capitalist had the idea that status in the material world should be obtained through the individual's skills and efforts. This concept was in direct opposition to the feudalistic concept of status by virtue of birth. The petty capitalist was an individualist. He believed in economic independence. He

2 The developments of Ancient Times had then largely disappeared.

avoided control by other men except on an equal basis as within gilds. He offered apprenticeships to the able and industrious. Although the apprentice's wages were probably low, he had the opportunity to learn the trade and acquire a little capital with which he could become a partner or set up a shop of his own. Thus "opportunity knocked" for all who were willing and able. The petty capitalist's public policy can be summarized as democratic economic equality.

The petty capitalist recognized that his skill in the market place was the measure of his success. In order to fully utilize this skill, he confined his efforts primarily to the local market. He restricted the variety of goods and services offered to those with which he was intimately familiar so that his skill in exchange could be more effectively concentrated. He tried to buy his wares as cheaply as possible and sell them as dearly as possible.

To appreciate the atmosphere and the environment in which the petty capitalist conducted his affairs, it is well to consider the economic philosophy of the era. The economic doctrine of the church which culminated in the canon law was probably the first formulated body of economic thought. The canonist doctrine rested on theology or Christian ethics. It laid down certain principles of right and wrong in the economic sphere, and it was the work of canonists to apply these to specific transactions and to pronounce judgment on their permissibility. The two principal doctrines were those applying to "just price" and "usury."

The doctrine of "just price" was based on the fulfillment of the law of Christ, "Whatsoever ye would that men should do unto you, do ye also unto them." St. Thomas Aquinas, who summarized the doctrine of canon law, held that everything has one "just price," or what it is worth. He held that value was something objective, something inherent in the article which was outside the will of the individual purchaser. The marked difference between this point of view and the modern idea of "market value" is that "market value" includes a subjective measurement—what each individual cares to give for an article or service.

Aquinas contended that for every article, at any particular time, there was one "just price" that should not vary with momentary supply and demand, with individual caprice, or skill in the market. Included in his idea of "just price" was the desirability of trade. The distinction between licit and illicit trade depended on the motive of the trader. The exchange price should cover the "just price" paid by the merchant for the article together with such gain as would enable him to maintain his standard of living. If the price charged by the merchant for any article allowed him to improve his position, such trade was base. Clearly it was the desire for gain that impelled the merchant to trade.

There were two principal arguments by which theologians and lawyers of the time justified the prohibition of usury. The first was Aristotle's doctrine that money itself was barren, and that therefore fruit or payment cannot justly be demanded for the use of it. The second argument was more subtle and turned on the distinction in Roman law between consumptibles, such as corn, that are consumed or spent in use; and fungibles, such as a house, that are not consumed in use. Money, it was contended, belonged to the first class. To sell a thing, and then make a charge for the use of it, was unjust. The canonist argued that, when money passed into the hands of the borrower, it should be regarded as a sale of a fungible item in which payment of the price was deferred. No payment ought to be made for the loss of time in waiting for the price, because time was God's and ought not to be sold.

Let us not criticize too strongly this canonist economic thought. It consisted of logical reasoning based entirely on ethical considerations. The true nature of business and its role in society were not recognized. Rather, let us apply the lesson learned to present-day economic theories. Many of our present-day theories suffer from the same insufficient knowledge of business as did the canonist doctrine.

The petty capitalist did not suffer unduly because of the doctrine of canon law. The ways and means by which he evaded the penalties of the ecclesiastical courts are too numerous to be outlined here. Business progressed in spite of the doctrine of "just price," which if rigidly enforced would have curtailed all trade; for under that doctrine the merchant could not lose on one commodity of which there was a supply in excess of demand and hope to remain in business by charging a higher price for another commodity. As the benefit of trade began to be appreciated by society, the enforcement of the doctrine of "just price" and "usury" became more and more lenient even though canon law in its essential form lived on well into the sixteenth century.

When the petty capitalists were forced to give way to the mercantile capitalists, it was as a result of their own philosophy of business. As noted earlier, the petty capitalist believed the future of business was in selling a restricted line of goods and services primarily in the local market. Business became static. The town economy, which the petty capitalist had helped to create, could not grow. The populace was being deprived of many desirable goods and services.

The petty capitalist's public policy of democratic economic equality presupposed an almost universal equality of man which history and psychology have proved false. The petty capitalist fought against control from outside, yet such control was a key to the improvement of business and society. During the period of petty capitalism a certain amount of over-competition resulted, which the petty capitalist gilds tried to prevent; however, it took the industrial capitalists to prove the unworkability of extreme individualism in a heterogeneous society.

MERCANTILE CAPITALISM (1300 A.D.–1800 A.D.)

Mercantile capitalism replaced petty capitalism because it offered more to society than the old system had provided. The mercantile capitalist, in the form of the sedentary merchant, perceived that if business was to grow the market must be extended. Goods must be brought in from a wider area and

more goods must be sold to a vastly extended market. The mercantile capitalist believed that competition should exist primarily in the foreign market.
This over-all concept was a *priori* to the theory of mercantilism that gave
Europe its metropolitan economy. Accordingly the sedentary merchant adapted
administrative techniques, policies, and practices that would enable him to
fulfill this guiding principle of extending the market.

The mercantile capitalist introduced control to capitalism for good or evil. His
central policy was to remain at home in the countinghouse and take on the
role of an administrator. He exerted control over his agents who carried his
goods to the foreign market. In order to secure control over the type and quality of his merchandise, he tried to reduce the wholesale handicraftsmen to
economic subordination. Perhaps he was the first businessman to realize the
disruptive influence extreme individualism could have on society. At least he
recognized that further progress in business at that time was possible only
through some subordination of those engaged in economic activity to a better
informed central control.

The sedentary merchant had a constant problem of risk. He met this problem
by diversification and integration of functions. He commonly performed such
diverse functions as importing, exporting, wholesaling, retailing, transportation, storage, banking and insurance.

The height of recognition for mercantile capitalism came when the basis
of public wealth was seen to be private wealth, when the chief source of all
wealth was thought to be foreign trade, and when the nation was held to the
same limitations of policy as the merchant. Business thought and economic
thought were united. Contrast this with the present governmental economic
thought which is implied in many governmental activities: "The government
can do anything that business fails to do that is socially and economically
desirable, and it can do it better." Perhaps the politicians who advocate fiscal
suicide under the guise of a planned and stabilized economy have never
heard of mercantilism, or having heard are deaf to its logic.

Mercantile capitalism as a system in business lasted about six centuries.
No other system of business capitalism has flourished so long. Its philosophy
had a certain universality; it became part of man's thinking. The system was far
from perfect, but each ideal group of that period from the theoretic man to
social man apparently somehow made a workable adjustment to the society
which mercantilism and mercantile capitalism helped develop and support.

The system of mercantile capitalism gave way to specialization from within
and to the Industrial Revolution from without. As the volume of trade increased, the mercantile capitalist found it increasingly difficult to control and
administer his diverse functions. He began to specialize in exporting or banking, allowing other merchants who also specialized to do the importing or provide transportation. The sedentary merchant generally did not have the technical ability for developing factory production techniques that were needed with
the advent of the Industrial Revolution. Mercantile capitalism under mer-

cantilist public policy also became overburdened with regulations designed primarily to protect business and guarantee a favorable balance of trade. This over-regulation began to prevent the essential flow of goods necessary to maintain a high level of economic activity.

When the system of mercantilism which embodied the sedentary merchant's business philosophy disappeared, the sedentary merchant disappeared with it. The petty capitalist, on the other hand, is with us today, even though petty capitalism disappeared as a dominant system of business about 1300 A.D.

INDUSTRIAL CAPITALISM (1800 A.D.-1900 A.D.)

The industrial capitalist was a specialist. He used power machinery wherever possible, he drove his employees hard, and preferred paid workers rather than agents. The tendency toward specialization, however, was the fundamental characteristic of the industrial capitalist that differentiated him from the mercantile capitalist. The system of industrial capitalism gave the petty capitalists a new chance to seek dominance in the business world. Many petty capitalists, such as blacksmiths and craftsmen, had the technical ability for factory management and became successful industrial capitalists. For this reason, it is interesting to compare the similarity in the philosophies of the petty and industrial capitalists.

The industrial capitalist's guiding principle was to reduce costs—to reduce costs, and thus to reduce prices, providing more goods for all at cheaper and cheaper prices. He believed that as more goods were available at cheaper and cheaper prices, the general standard of living would be raised.

Classical economics added to the industrial capitalist's philosophy by providing for a business freedom to supplement the growing demand for social and political freedom furthered by the French Revolution. The political leaders in England recognized that complete freedom of trade would allow them to dominate the world market because of England's obvious margin in manufacturing facilities and techniques. Thus economic or business freedom was in fact incidental to the political and social freedom advocated in the doctrine of "laissez-faire." Although economic freedom was incidental to political and social freedom, it does not follow that social and political freedom can exist without economic freedom. "Laissez-faire" became a reality only after England proclaimed the desirability of business freedom. Today we face the same issue and it is phrased "opportunity or security." Let us not be fooled into believing that a true democratic system of government can be maintained if the ownership and control of business is not primarily in private hands.

The industrial capitalists, composed partly of petty capitalists, seized on the doctrine of "laissez-faire" as being akin to the previous doctrine of democratic economic equality. Industrial capitalism, in its brief period of approximately a hundred years, was to develop some of the essential weaknesses that forced petty capitalism to give way to mercantilism (i.e., over-competition and narrowness of distribution).

At first the industrial capitalists enjoyed profitable operations because their competitors were composed largely of businessmen using the old techniques. When the system of industrial capitalism advanced to the stage where competition arose between two firms having the same technical knowledge and equipment, the severity of competition led to bankruptcy or near bankruptcy. The industrial capitalist was commonly a poor financial manager. He capitalized his plant on a narrow base and plowed back earnings into more machinery and equipment and larger operations. Consequently, when he was faced with competition or the partial loss of the market due to depressed business conditions, he was hard pressed to survive.

The philosophy of industrial capitalism like classical economics overlooked the heterogeneity of man. Economic liberalism was based on the false premise that all men are economic men, and in a free society each individual would be able to satisfy his peculiar needs through his own efforts. Industrial capitalism failed in its complete lack of universality. It provided for only one segment of our total society—economic man.

The working class was exploited in the constant efforts to reduce costs, and the consumers were neglected in the emphasis on producers' goods. It might be said that, to the industrial capitalist, producers and sellers were persons, while workers and consumers were things.

FINANCIAL CAPITALISM (1890 A.D.–1933 A.D.)

Financial capitalism was a system of necessity. The industrial capitalists had become the victims of their extreme specialization and ruthless competition. Many industrial capitalists realized that further competition was not the answer to their financial distress, but it took the financial capitalists to restore order to the economic chaos that had been created during the brief period of economic liberalism.

Financial capitalism was so short-lived that it did not develop a formulated system of thought. However, in the ideas and thoughts that reflected necessity one may discern an arising neo-mercantilism or business economics. The beginnings of this unformulated philosophy can be deduced from the policies and practices of the investment bankers who took over the control of business to protect the interest of the investing capitalists.

The financial capitalist substituted diversification of products and multiple economic functions for specialization. He built up reserves to mitigate or prevent the bankruptcies that formerly resulted when demand or prices fell momentarily. Cut-throat competition was replaced by a new concept of cooperative competition. The growth of trade associations exemplified the financial capitalist's idea that policing and restraint should be accomplished from within.

Although these economic ideas and policies were not formulated, they are still evident in business thinking today and may form a base for a new philosophy of business with the breadth and flexibility to meet the needs of our changing society.

Financial capitalism was in a position to perform a true social service. Cooperative competition allowed for rises in prices and wages, whereas the philosophy of the industrial capitalists, with its emphasis on reduced cost, made no such provision. The system of financial capitalism had a flexibility with which a workable balance between the principal elements in our economy could have been achieved. The financial capitalist, however, did not realize he was in control of a system. He did not recognize the inherent potential of this system to correct the social inequities that had been created during the era of industrial capitalism. If financial capitalism had been allowed a longer period of time to operate effectively, this potential might have been recognized and exploited to the benefit of all.

Financial capitalists, however, were too preoccupied with the necessity of providing for the investing capitalists to develop the needed working balance between the three interest groups: the workers, the consumers, and the investors. The cry also arose that the financial capitalists through horizontal and vertical integrations were creating monopolies to the detriment of our economy. The petty capitalist found it harder and harder to get into the field and compete with big business. Of all the systems of capitalism that have existed, none have been so widely condemned as financial capitalism. "Industrial Absolutism" and "Money Trust" became popular everyday phrases describing the system.

The financial capitalists in the United States reached their greatest heights during the merger period, 1897–1903, and the recovery period, 1923–1929, following the postwar depression of 1920–1922. When excessive speculation resulted in the crash of 1929, and the subsequent depression of the 1930's, financial capitalism was through as the dominant system of business. Labor caught on to the old and outmoded idea of business "to get the most for the least" during the late 1920's and was instrumental in bringing on national capitalism in 1933, after the complete change in political administrations.

NATIONAL CAPITALISM (1933 A.D.–   )

National capitalism took over control of business, not on behalf of the industrial capitalists as did financial capitalism, but on behalf of labor and the petty capitalists. Ownership of business is still primarily in private hands, but the government uses its power of regulation over capital and credit to control business according to its policies. The underlying purpose of national capitalism is of a social character—to remedy the inequities created under industrial and financial capitalism.

We should recognize that national capitalism and social democracy are very likely transitional business and political systems. At the end of the road there are two unwelcome alternatives, socialism and fascism. Socialism substitutes public ownership of business for private ownership. Fascism retains private ownership but establishes a tight political control over business. Each of the two alternatives has the undesirable but inevitable consequence of sacrificing personal liberty for autocracy.

Each of the ideal groups which roughly comprise our society has been continually struggling to adjust to the various systems of business that have existed in our civilization. The most extensive adjustment was made under the system of mercantile capitalism. When adjustment was not possible under an existing system, it was replaced by a new system that promised more to certain elements in our heterogeneous society. Each diverse group has also recognized that if business could not serve their desires, they could obtain a certain measure of relief through political action. This pressure from many diverse sources has forced our government to expand its sphere of influence over business and society. The ultimate end of the constantly expanding government participation and control is socialism or fascism.

Many of the measures taken by government in the past seventeen years have been clearly labeled "socialistic," even though they have filled a need of society. Unfortunately, this indiscriminate labeling has given the theory of socialism a certain respectability which is undeserved, for these so-called socialistic measures have been largely dependent on private business capitalism for their success.

The theory and philosophy of socialism have a universality of appeal that to this date has not been matched by the theory and philosophy of private business capitalism. The principal reason for this discrepancy is that the proponents of private business capitalism have been notably inarticulate. However, socialism in practice lacks the universality to provide for a total society. Socialism fails in that it needs economic contributions to exist and ultimately uses control or force to obtain them. Men are herded together according to the existing needs of the state, and any semblance of individualism is ruthlessly submerged. The increasing number of reports received in this country concerning the slave labor camps in Eastern Europe is testimony to the reality of a socialistic state. Socialism does not allow the six ideal groups in society to make a workable adjustment. Certainly the needs and contributions of the economic man are completely overlooked, as are others as well.

Obviously no business and political system can be universal enough to provide exactly for each individual in society. For example, an aesthetic man who finds no market for his "second rate" art creations cannot continue indefinitely in this chosen line of endeavor. He must adjust and find some other way to make his essential contribution toward society while retaining art as a hobby. Private business capitalism and social democracy have the inherent flexbility to allow these adjustments to be made so that a close social union may prevail. The challenge of business today is to formulate a philosophy of business around this inherent flexibility.

The modern businessman has not formulated a businessman's philosophy of national capitalism. He is largely conducting his business today with the ideas and thoughts of earlier business systems. Some of these earlier ideas are applicable to national capitalism but many are not. For example, the old and unworkable idea of "economic liberalism" that characterized industrial capitalism is still given a place of honor in the businessman's thinking today. A hope to return to "economic liberalism" was the underlying rallying point of business in the 1948 Presidential election. It is not too soon for business to separate these old ideas into two categories and to discard all those that have no present-day applicability.

The neo-mercantile thought that is discernible in some business policies and practices today may form the base for a new philosophy that recognizes and provides for the heterogeneity of man. The philosophy of national capitalism must be structured on the idea that each individual makes his contribution toward the civilization on which business depends, and business in turn must help to create the economic and social environment in which each individual can make necessary adjustments.

The need to formulate and articulate at least the tentative principles of business in this dynamic era of national capitalism stems from two primary considerations:

1. Business should have a guide for establishing business policies and practices that are in accord with the requirements of our total society. A broad and flexible business philosophy can give direction and emphasis to the concepts of "business statesmanship" and "business responsibility."

2. Our present society does not recognize that business is the vital "core" of our civilization. Business is still regarded by many as being predatory. The economic explanation of business is incomplete and in many instances lacks reality. Unfortunately, public action in regard to business is governed largely by public opinion and economic theory. Therefore, a businessman's explanation of business or of business economics must become part of the fabric of social thinking so that a working balance between the various forces in society can be achieved.

B. Business, Competition and Government

Will Growth Increase Federal Control?

2

Edward T. Chase

It is clear that the highly charged debate over our economic growth rate and the integral question of private versus public spending will be the central domestic issue of the 1960s. The manner in which the Kennedy Administration attempts to resolve this problem will determine our governmental framework for a generation. In particular, it will establish the pattern of relationships between the federal government and our other great power system, free enterprise, or what economists call more precisely the price-market system.

It was Allen W. Dulles, director of the Central Intelligence Agency, who first predicted economic suicide if we did not change our ways. As the controversy evolves, there is an increasing realization that growth and private versus public spending—a polarity Americans had not thought about in twenty-five years—have to do with our very survival. Only recently, the chairman of the Council of Economic Advisers, Professor Walter W. Heller, suggested that government intervention in the economy may not need to be directing, but simply stimulating. "One of the chief arguments for a more positive program for economic growth," Dr. Heller stated, "is that it is far easier to achieve many of our common goals by enlarging the size of our economic pie than by transferring income and wealth from one group to another."

But Federal Reserve Board Chairman William M. Martin, Jr., differed with him over this point. He contended that, in the case of chronic unemployment, for example, general stimulation of the economy will not be enough. We have the modern paradox of employment and unemployment simultaneously

From the *Atlantic Monthly* (August 1961), pp. 32–36. Copyright © 1961 by the Atlantic Monthly Company, Boston, Mass. Reprinted with permission.

at record peaks. Affirmative government intervention in specific programs of training and job placement is needed to overcome the kind of persistent structural unemployment now so common. In effect, Martin was saying that a stepped-up economic growth rate alone, while desirable and even essential, is an incomplete solution. This hard lesson will have to be learned again and again, because it applies not only to unemployment but to a whole series of economic problems.

The consequences of our failure to learn are serious in the extreme; we can lose in the competition with Communism for the allegiance of the world's newly emerging nations, because our own example will prove unpersuasive. We can lose something even more precious—our sense of confidence that our own social institutions are both effective and serve worthy ends. In this latter respect, the morale of the younger generation is at stake.

The urgency of the growth debate is comprehensible only in the light of two basic forces: 1) our demographic change, by which I mean population growth, a change in the age complexion of the American population, and the population's massive shift into our urban and suburban centers; 2) technological progress. Take a vivid example fraught with political tension—medical care for the aged. Many readers, like the author, have parents over sixty-five. According to official government reports, 55 per cent of all people sixty-five and over (including those still working) have less than $1000 cash income per year. About a third have liquid assets up to $200, in case of an emergency. Only a tiny fraction have substantial assets readily convertible to cash. And illness strikes the aged two to three times more frequently than the rest of the population; their hospitalization is much longer—the costs run 120 per cent higher than those for the rest of us; and for drugs and medicines the disproportion is even greater. Meantime, medical costs, which have doubled since the war, continue to spiral, with hospital costs advancing relentlessly 5 to 6 per cent each year. Scientific progress has meant marvelous but very expensive new equipment, drugs, and procedures.

Technology has equipped medicine with the means to control the death rate and thus make those over sixty-five the nation's fastest growing population group, and at the same time it has made our industrial plant so productive as to eliminate the aged as an essential part of our work force. Thus, relatively few can earn even minimal annual incomes.

The elderly, increasing in number at the rate of one million every three years, while tolerably fed, housed, clothed, are largely unprotected by health insurance. Only about 40 per cent have even fragmentary health-insurance coverage, according to the Department of Health, Education, and Welfare. Even if the growth of health insurance continues at the booming rate of earlier years, still only about 56 per cent of the aged will be covered by 1965. Yet, after food, clothing, and shelter, medical care has come to be accepted as the fourth basic social right, a right regardless of income.

What bearing has this situation on the question of growth and private versus public spending? This much is clear: a rise in the economic growth rate by itself is beside the mark. Though economic growth is necessary for many reasons, we are learning that growth in a modern industrial society also can be dismayingly irrelevant. In the instance at hand, the bulk of the elderly lack the financial means to afford the health insurance they desperately require; whereas the insurance industry, operating in the market system, cannot hope to insure the aged at premium rates on which the companies can break even, let alone make a profit, for these rates are set by the costs of medical care in the first place.

What we witness, in short, is the spreading phenomenon that goes to the root of the growth debate: the incapability of the price-market system, for technical reasons beyond its purview, to supply an essential public need. The only recourse is government support or provision of the service. And, given the strapped financial situation of the states, the federal government usually must step in.

URBAN CONGESTION

Medical care for the elderly is by no means an isolated example of what the twin forces of technology and demographic change are doing to our society, and, more particularly, to our reliance upon the price-market system as the key determinant of how our wealth is allocated. Consider urban congestion and urban renewal. The problem of urban congestion has become a national nightmare, and its most critical aspect is the alarming decline in mass transportation facilities. As commuter railroad services are terminated, as whole lines fold, as transit companies founder under rising costs and declining patronage, automotive vehicles and the facilities encouraging them proliferate. America's fabulous technological achievement in mass-producing highways and private automobiles has made the giant, sprawling metropolitan complex possible. Here is the locus of the population explosion. At the same time, this accomplishment mortally threatens public transportation as a profit venture.

Can a "hands off, let private growth solve this" position succeed? Obviously not, because the market system simply cannot cope with such a mammoth deficit operation. Hence, substantial government subsidies, tax relief, and even outright takeover of mass transportation systems have become commonplace. And such measures alone do not remedy the situation. Substituting government financing for the market system is not a sufficient answer, since the proper planning of transportation facilities and of land use is the essence of the matter. Support without planning means wasting tax moneys on moribund or irrational organizations; for example, inefficient railroads, or authorities building highways which add to the traffic problems of cities. The congestion, air and land pollution, destruction of neighborhoods, and hideous disarray of our urban complexes are usually traceable to a lack of integrated planning from a central vantage point. The lesson has been made clear again and again that without government intervention, either by an authority transcending petty political jurisdictions or by some federal entity, the imbalance will grow between private automotive transportation and public mass transportation. If we intend to rescue our cities before this situation becomes irretrievable, we must come to accept more rather than less government "interference" in realms where the invisible hand of the market has hitherto held sway.

The same holds true in the closely related case of urban slum clearance and rehabilitation. Of all the domestic tasks confronting mid-century America, none has a higher priority than the physical renewal of our cities, where two thirds of our entire population live. Will an increase in our economic growth rate, even up to 5 per cent annually, benefit matters here? Precious little. The evidence shows that mere demand does not register in the tremendously costly and complicated task of rebuilding cities. Only with the intervention of the federal government through the clever mechanism of the "Title 1" program, which makes a profit incentive possible, can the forces of the market be brought to bear on the slum-clearance problem. Only the most hidebound conservatives would contend in 1961 that we should leave the survival of our cities up to the vagaries of market values. The role of government is as inevitable here as it is in regulating the natural monopolies of water, gas, electricity, and telephone service.

The controversy grows hotter in areas where it is only beginning to be appreciated that the market system is failing to fulfill the need. For instance, it is uncertain whether Americans will yet tolerate the principle of large-scale government participation in acquiring and preserving open land. Open land is disappearing at a rate of a million acres a year, for superhighways, airports, and suburban sprawl. We prosecute for food pollution, and even for air and water pollution. Yet, apart from local anti-billboard regulations, we have not begun to invoke comparable powers to prevent land pollution. Is there any doubt but that controls must be forthcoming, and would be, if they were not stigmatized as anti-business by vested business interests?

RESEARCH AND DEVELOPMENT

Now consider the specialized issue of air tranportation. It typifies a whole category of vital technical problems and poses a fundamental question about the government's part in financing industrial research and development. The government has recently announced that supersonic commercial airliners are coming in the immediate future. Their production cost is well beyond the capacity of the private aviation companies. No conceivable acceleration in their growth will render these corporations able to meet the burden of producing the supersonic commercial airliner. Also, it is estimated that the world market will be able to sustain only one producer. Therefore, the first nation to create an effective supersonic airplane will achieve monopoly. It will achieve something more—the national prestige that goes with such an achievement. What is essential again is not growth alone, but bold governmental decision on a matter of resource allocation.

This example raises the point that government intervention may be essential to achieve economic growth itself, besides accomplishing a given project. How big should government's role be in subsidizing industrial invention and innovation? These activites are at the heart of economic growth. There is evidence that the price-market economy is by no means sufficiently effective in seeing to it that we are devoting enough resources to "R and D" (as the knowing call research and development), to invention, to innovation. The fantastic success of government research and development in military technology is prompting economists to examine their potential in industrial areas as well.

The terrible gap between our actual economic productivity and our potential productivity is another reason why Washington economists contemplate a revolutionary research and development role for government. The gap in 1960 between actual and potential output was $30 to $35 billion, or 6 to 7 per cent of our total output. This amounts to two thirds of what we spend on national defense, almost twice what we spend on public education, and about one and a half times what we spent in 1960 on new homes.

The gap in mid-1961 between what we are producing and what we can produce is approaching $50 billion. A basic reason for this higher figure is that recoveries from recent slumps have been incomplete, never quite regaining previous peaks in employment and productivity. Steel and oil have been operating at hardly better than 50 per cent of capacity for a long period. This holds for several other major sectors of the economy. Small wonder that the President's Council of Economic Advisers testified to Congress that "Even the world's most prosperous nation cannot afford to waste resources on this scale."

Our leading economists are, therefore, considering radically broader applications of research and development. Inventiveness, knowledge, and highly technical skills are the crucial contributors to growth. The newest stress is upon the primary value of investment in people versus machinery. Large-scale federal subsidy and direction will be necessary in re-educating, retraining, and re-locating the victims of technological change, who range from unskilled farm laborers to skilled transport workers displaced by pipelines.

POLITICAL ACTION AND PUBLIC NEED

Paradoxically, at the height of its achievement in producing foods and services, the American price-market system is revealing alarming inadequacies, not only as a self-regenerating force for growth but as a rational allocator of our large but limited resources. Professional economists and political leaders and the educated public are becoming uncomfortably aware of this. The general public will remain ignorant and complacent for only a short time. In consequence, control of the economy is becoming a government concern, not because of subversion or ideological considerations but because the impersonal forces of technology and demography are requiring it.

The corporation, which is the work horse of the economy (four fifths of Americans work for corporations), increasingly will find its main endeavors directed by law instead of by the invisible hand of the competitive market. Now, so far as the corporation is concerned, intervention by law hitherto has been aimed strictly at keeping the market free, because the health of the free market has been judged primary to national well-being. Even today no one disputes the fact that the competitive price-market system founded on private property and the profit incentive remains our most effective instrument for distributing consumer goods and services.

But, because the market is failing to solve vital social needs, a completely new kind of intervention will occur. Corrective action will not mean simply a stepping up of the traditional kinds of government interference, such as trust busting, tariffs, and regulations. It will be something quite strange to Americans. There is one major precedent that illustrates this new kind of government role —the Full Employment Act of 1946. That act was the first instance where the national government stipulated by law that the goals of full employment and equitable income distribution were to be a federal legal concern and were not to be left up to the price-market system.

At that time, the end of World War II, all but a handful of economists predicted nationwide unemployment. This anticipated crisis stimulated passage of the law. But the crisis did not materialize, owing to the immense, underestimated backlog of demand created by the war. The thinking behind the act was not "radical" in the invidious sense of the term; namely, a socialistic demand that we scrap the American way and try something different. Rather, the philosophy was one of tacit acknowledgment of an essential role for the market system, supplementing it with political action in the interest of rational resource allocation and public need. The whole thrust of the growth debate is for extensive implementation of this principle.

A NATIONAL ECONOMIC BUDGET

The United States must develop a new kind of national economic budget, quite different from the federal budget as we have known it. The traditional budget has actually involved some limited planning and allocation of resources, but only on a short-term basis. In the future, the budget will have to embrace all our national resources viewed against national goals over a long term. Such a budget, goals oriented, would be more than a mere annual federal accounting. It would comprise an integrated, comprehensive, continuing plan for the entire nation. It would mean five- or six-year projections of the use of our national resources and output in terms of employment, growth, foreign policy objectives, housing, roads, welfare, and other such goals.

One of the appeals of such a budget (apart from the inexorable logic of the forces making it a necessity) is that, enunciated by the President, it would act as a means for rallying public opinion, for articulating a meaningful program for the American economy beyond the sheer aggrandizement of material wealth. In its broadest aspects, it would amount to a working agreement on the priorities for the use of our total resources. In its narrowest aspects, it would amount to national programming of explicit policies.

RATIONING OUR RESOURCES

Such a budget is not going to be achieved overnight, but it will come within the decade. It must come, because long-range blueprints and decisions on use of resources are an essential ingredient of the future. Though perhaps not a matter for jubilation, it certainly should not be a matter for dismay. Walter Lippmann hinted at such a conception of the budget in his commentary on President Kennedy's first budget. His remarks also indicated why even a tentative move in the direction of a goals-oriented budget will not be accomplished immediately. "It is a complicated thing," he wrote, "to explain that the Federal budget is not only an accounting of revenues and expenditures. It is also a great fiscal engine which as a matter of national policy has to be managed in such a way as to promote a stabilized growth of the economy. It is a makeweight which has to be swung from deficit to surplus and from surplus to deficit to compensate for the ups and downs of the business cycle. There is nothing sinister or mysterious in this idea. But it is a *new* idea." Lippmann went on to write that the notion of a budget covering a number of years, instead of just one year, will require that the President himself educate the people. For, "most of what he has promised to do, most of what for the long pull urgently needs to be done, depends on explaining this theoretical issue to the people."

THE TEST OF OUR INVENTIVENESS

Resistance to the idea can be expected. It will be charged that bureaucratic planning and reduced profit incentive will stifle the market system; that the public will be the victim of a noncompetitive, flaccid economy, with Communist-style suppression of cherished individual freedoms just around the corner. But this risk is justified by disagreeable facts: that we are operating drastically under our productive capabilities, slump or no slump, and have been for some time; that the imbalance between satisfying public needs and fulfilling private demands continues to worsen; and that the public already is victimized by noncompetitive, administered prices in industries making up a third to a half of our economy—basic industries like steel, electrical equipment, and autos—and by industry-wide union wages, combining to create a relentless wage-price rise that is the despair of economists.

There is an inherent possibility of a constitutional crisis. American political inventiveness, our justly famous instinct for freedom, is going to be put to the most difficult test it has had in a century. This is because any successful society must have a theory, a clear comprehension of principle, for what it is doing. Such an understanding is essential if a society intends to achieve great ends, and as the precondition for the kind of congressional action required. The Council of Economic Advisers serves as an example of the type of organization needed. This might well be made by law into a powerful agency for national planning.

The intense pressure for planning is building up from many directions. Presidential adviser Dean James Landis, for one, has suggested that the federal regulatory agencies, through better formulation and coordination of their policies, could be the key to revitalization of major sectors of the economy. But the most fundamental pressure of all is exerted by the fact that the United States now competes in a world of government-controlled economies. Meanwhile, our own economy remains substantially guided by disparate private corporate interests. The strategies of these corporations reflect their primary obligations to shareholders. No formal compunction exists to relate these obligations to the common interest. The American myth about the free, competitive system and its miraculously beneficient role runs counter to legal and political regulation of economic affairs.

Our hope must be that genuine public understanding of our true condition will do two things. It will act to eliminate the anxiety that comes from the unknown, and the resultant dangerous nonsense about subversion. It will thus release us to exercise to the full America's unmatched talent for combining individual freedom with optimum collective performance. In this light, President Kennedy's striking statement in his State of the Union Address, "Before my term has ended, we shall have to test anew whether a nation such as ours can endure. The outcome is by no means certain," can be appreciated as more than rhetoric. Survival is, indeed, the issue.

A Changing Balance of Power: New Partnership of Government and Business

3

Business Week

A new pattern is emerging in the relationship between business and government in the U. S. Its concrete manifestations can be spotted all over the map:

Reprinted with permission from *Business Week* (July 17, 1965), pp. 85–106.

In the area of wages and prices, the federal government seeks to get business and labor to stay within "noninflationary wage-price guideposts."

In race relations, business and government join in efforts to create more and better employment opportunities for Negroes.

In foreign trade, investment, and lending, "voluntary" programs by U.S. business and banking are helping government to eliminate the deficit in the nation's balance of payments.

In the war against poverty, government is drawing on the help of business to upgrade the knowledge and skills of the poor.

In science and technology, government depends on private industry to advance national interests in areas as wide-ranging as economic development, military power, and exploration of outer space.

In matters of taxation and public expenditure, government and business are working more closely together to shape fiscal policy in ways to promote full employment and more rapid economic growth.

Dilemma for Business. Caught up in the swirl of these rapidly changing business-government relations, businessmen are facing some tough decisions. The central problem is whether big business should accept "voluntarily" a new and closer relationship with big government—or whether they should oppose any such "partnership" lest it transform the traditional free enterprise system beyond recognition and obliterate what they consider to be their economic freedom.

Some leading business executives are moving toward the conclusion that the dangers to their own freedom, and to society's, will be reduced rather than increased if a new balance—involving elements of both cooperation and conflict—can be worked out between business and government. These men are already working to achieve such a balance of business and government functions and responsibilities.

Ending a "Cold War." Some put it in terms of ending what has been an almost traditional conflict between business and government in the U. S. One of these is Lammot du Pont Copeland, president of E. I. du Pont de Nemours & Co.

"It would be in the national interest, as well as our own interest," says Copeland, "to put an end to what at times has seemed like a cold war between business and government." He suggests a "conscious, determined effort on both sides to improve the relationship."

The University of Michigan's Kenneth E. Boulding describes the "cold war between business and government," which he traces back as far as 1880, as the most crucial problem facing the U. S. "I think we have now got to the point," he says, "where failure to come to some kind of resolution of this ancient conflict is our most serious handicap."

Pervasive. Whatever the attitudes of the two sides may be, the actual overlaps between business and government interests today are multiple; they embrace not only the areas already mentioned but also housing and urban redevelopment, communications, transportation, banking, power, farming, and other regulated or subsidized industries.

So pervasive are these overlaps that some observers feel the very nature of the U. S. economic system has already been changed from what used to be called capitalism to something that needs a new name.

Many names have been proposed for the present system: the mixed economy, the managed economy, the pluralistic economy, the garrison state, the welfare state. Whatever the system is called, however, it has become increasingly clear to businessmen that the role of govenment in their affairs has "changed drastically in our lifetimes," as Logan T. Johnston, president of Armco Steel Corp., puts it. "Government," says Johnston, "is now a partner of business—some even think the dominant partner. Whether or not business wants such a partner is academic. The partner is there.

"Whether or not this parner's advice is sought does not matter. He will offer it. If need be, he will enforce his views."

Here to Stay. This state of affairs deeply distresses—even infuriates—a great many businessmen. Many, as Johnston notes, "blame their partner for the majority of their problems—including their ulcers." And many ardently wish their government partner would just go away and let them run their businesses in peace.

"Yet," says Logan Johnston, "businessmen who are frank with themselves in their moments of introspection know that this partner is not going away, at least in the foreseeable future."

Whether they like it or not, practical businessmen know that the huge and changing role of government in the U. S. economy presents them with a critical managerial problem.

HOW BUSINESSMEN SEE THE BASIC ISSUE

The issue has uncovered differences within the U. S. business community that are both intellectual and emotional.

On one side, many businessmen strongly resist the contention that they should run their businesses in such a way as to serve not only their private interests but also "the public interest." Many condemn this motion that private business should seek to fulfill "social responsibilities" as—in the words of Professor Milton Friedman, an adviser of Barry Goldwater in the 1964 Presidential campaign—"a fundamentally subversive doctrine."

Friedman asks: "If businessmen do have a social responsibility other than making maximum profits for stockholders, how are they to know what it is? Can they decide how great a burden they are justified in placing on themselves or their stockholders to serve that social interest? Is it tolerable that these public functions of taxation, expenditure, and control be exercised by the people who happen at the moment to be in charge of particular enterprises, chosen for those posts by strictly private groups?"

He warns that if businessmen once begin behaving like civil servants, then sooner or later they will become nothing but civil servants—elected or appointed like any others.

The doctrine of "social responsibilities," traditionally minded businessmen fear, may lead to a highly centralized and controlled economy in which their freedom and independence as businessmen—or citizens—will be lost.

George Champion, chairman of the Chase Manhattan Bank, recently launched a heavy attack against the government's setting of guidelines for business behind "the facade of friendliness and partnership between business and government."

"In my judgment," said Champion, "the new trend toward government-by-guideline is one of the most insidious and dangerous on the national scene today, and one which businessmen should work to reverse with all the energy and dedication they can muster. The guideline approach represents a giant step away from self-reliance and personal responsibility, and toward federal domination of our national economy."

Balance of Interests.   On the other side of this emotional—and ideological—debate are businessmen who believe that, with corporations as big and important as they are today, there is simply no way for corporate executives to avoid affecting the public interest.

Hence, they contend that, if U. S. business leaders want to retain their private freedom and autonomy to make decisions, they must take cognizance of the effect of their actions on the public interest—with which their own basic corporate interests are inevitably bound up.

Some proponents of this view, in fact, assert that the most critical job facing the head of a major corporation today is to determine how best to coordinate a company's interest with the public interest.

One who holds the view that a businessman can take account of the public interest in his business decisions "and still be successful" is Thomas J. Watson, Jr., chairman of International Business Machines Corp. Watson says: "I would be the first to admit that it's a good deal easier to state this proposition than to put it into practice."

Yet he feels sure that one of the most important problems American management must face in the years ahead is "how we can strike a balance between what is sound business practice in the management of our large organizations and what is good for the national interest."

Profits and the Public.   Businessmen who take the position that corporations should seek to serve public as well as private interests do not think this means sacrificing profits—at least not in the long term. On the contrary, they insist that efforts to improve corporate earnings are wholly consistent with national interests.

Profits, these men contend, are both rewards for past efficiency and innovations, and incentives for future business achievement. They are a means of financing growth and of efficiently allocating human and material resources to uses that the public—the buying public—favors.

Thus, these businessmen refuse to concede that they are any less hard-headed or profit-oriented than their fellows. Indeed, they consider themselves more realistic in facing up to the hard facts of how to operate successfully in today's economy—an economy in which government has a big role to play and the public not only demands "socially responsible" behavior from business, but can enforce its demands politically if it grows dissatisfied with business action and policies.

CLASH OVER STEEL—AND A FRESH START

The critical issue in this debate is how to define the "public interest," a concept that many businessmen regard as foggy. One skeptic says: "On the most difficult issues, 'socially responsible' behavior is not obviously revealed to all or deductible from the Ten Commandments. It has to be enunciated by someone. In practice this usually means the President.

"I think the real issue is not whether individuals should do what is right," says this man, "but whether the President should tell them what is right, as distinct from what is legal, and whether individuals have any responsibility to do what he says."

But Joseph L. Block, chairman of Inland Steel Co., declares that those who deride the "public interest" as a "nonexistent will-of-the-wisp, a self-serving device used by politicians to cloak ulterior objectives," are speaking "utter nonsense." Block contends that they are denying not only the need for private businessmen to consider the public interest but even the right of government itself to define the public interest.

"Surely," says Block, "the greater good of the nation as a whole should be of paramount importance to everyone." He maintains that "while no one has an omniscient power to define 'public interest' accurately at any given time, and certainly not all of the time, it surely behooves all of us—and most particularly government—to endeavor to do so."

Moment of Truth. Block and his fellow executives at Inland Steel faced a moment of truth on this issue in April, 1962; it came during the confrontation between the Kennedy Administration and the steel industry over the hike in steel prices following labor negotiations with the United Steelworkers.

The refusal of eighth-ranking Inland Steel—strategically located in Chicago in the heart of a major industrial market—to go along with the steel price hike was probably the critical factor that forced other steel companies to rescind their across-the-board price increase.

The often-told story involved telephone calls by Under Secretary of Commerce Edward Gudeman to Inland's vice-chairman, Philip D. Block, Jr. (Joseph Block was in Japan), and to others in Chicago.

The upshot was that Inland held the price line, though the White House never specifically asked this. The White House did, however, threaten the steel industry with antitrust action, and it genuinely frightened businessmen by what they regarded as "police state" tactics.

Turning Point. Though the Kennedy Administration nominally won the steel battle, the confrontation was regarded as a fiasco by both sides. It left deep scars on relations between business and government, scars that President Kennedy—and Roger M. Blough, chairman of U. S. Steel Corp.—never succeeded in healing, despite efforts on both sides.

Yet that battle was a turning point in efforts to put the business-government "partnership" on a healthier basis.

Johnson's Moves. After President Kennedy's assassination, Lyndon B. Johnson quickly moved to establish closer and friendlier relations between Washington and the business community—and to "draw a veil" over the steel battle of 1962. He consulted not only with liberal businessmen who had been sympathetic to Kennedy but with conservatives as well, many of whom had strongly opposed the Kennedy Administration as "anti-business."

A combination of circumstances, in fact—the steel episode, a reported insulting remark of the late President's about businessmen, the "intellectual" tone of the Kennedy Administration, its reformist leanings—had united to awaken in these business circles the kind of intense hostility toward the Kennedy Administration that had marked conservative business thinking during Franklin D. Roosevelt's New Deal.

President Johnson was determined to allay this hostility. Shaken by the assassination, many business leaders were, on their side, eager to repair relations with Washington.

Era of Good Feeling. As Johnson pressed his program to gain business cooperation, many businessmen felt that he had succeeded remarkably in dispelling the once bitter atmosphere. Said one who had known Kennedy and liked him personally—David Rockefeller, president of the Chase Manhattan Bank: "Johnson has established much better relations with business. Kennedy wasn't terribly interested. Johnson has talked to more businessmen, and has shown his sincerity. He's put his relations with the business community on good strong footing."

These efforts bore political fruit. Johnson got the influential support of some top businessmen—led by Henry Ford II, of Ford Motor Co. and Stuart T. Saunders of the Pennsylvania RR—for his big tax cut (proposed at a time when the federal budget was running heavily in deficit).

Johnson even succeeded in attracting a sizable amount of big business support for his political campaign in 1964. The Republican candidate, Senator Goldwater, complained during the campaign about "the Eastern establishment" of businessmen and financiers who were supporting Johnson.

Johnson's cultivation of the business community was not aimed solely at getting votes or campaign contributions. Rather, it was intended to restructure business-government relations as a means of dealing with a number of crucial national problems.

JOHNSON'S MOVES: POLICY AND PRACTICE

Soon after winning his landslide victory over Goldwater, Johnson sought to define his concept of separate and joint business-government responsibilities. He did this in an address before the Business Council—a body of predominantly conservative chiefs of major corporations. The Business Council in 1961 had brawled with the Kennedy Administration and cut itself off from official government connections.

President's Aims. The President told the Business Council that government and business must "operate in partnership," not as antagonists, to solve many problems. He listed four as paramount:

Accelerating the rate of economic growth.

Maintaining price stability.

Strengthening the U. S. balance of payments.

Finding ways to reduce high rates of unemployment among teenagers and to assure "adequate economic opportunities for all our people"—obviously including Negroes.

Role of Government. In attacking all those problems, said Johnson, business and government had distinct roles. One of government's main jobs was to produce a tax system that would not overburden businessmen or consumers, and would maintain incentives for productive effort.

The big 1964 tax cut—totaling $14 billion—had clearly produced a major effect in accelerating growth and reducing unemployment. Johnson emphasized that the U. S. government would seek, through both fiscal and monetary policy, to create conditions of stable economic growth in which individual businesses could prosper.

The government's role should not be confined, said Johnson, to creating enough total money demand to keep the economy functioning at a high level.

Government should also shape expenditure programs to improve human and natural resources and make "social investments . . . to support private enterprise."

But the government, Johnson told the businessmen, should avoid trespassing on the proper area of private business; it should leave a "clear field" wherever competitive enterprise is the most efficient way of getting a job done.

. . . and Business. The major responsibilities of business, according to the President, were to produce high-quality goods, to innovate, to cut production costs, to sell vigorously at home and abroad, to offer workers both job security and incentives, and to invest in growth. For its own sake as well as the economy's, business should try to plan investments carefully and avoid hectic inventory building and dumping.

Solving some national economic problems, the President added, would require joint efforts by business and government. These included steps to cope with the nation's international balance-of-payments problem in such a way as to permit economic expansion to continue at home.

Prime Rate Story. On Nov. 23, 1964, shortly before the President went before the Business Council, the Federal Reserve had raised the discount rate from 3½% to 4%. This was done to guard against any rush of money out of the country in response to a hike to 7% of the British bank rate in an effort to protect the pound sterling.

President Johnson pleaded with U. S. bankers not to put up their interest rates to domestic borrowers just because the Fed had raised the discount rate; this, he said, might slow economic expansion. He was "sure," said the President, that bankers must realize their own long-term interests were inseparable from the nation's prosperity. And he warned that, if the economy slid into a recession, it might force him to increase government spending and increase the size of the deficit.

Soon afterward, three banks outside New York did boost their prime rate by ¼% to 4¾%. But they put the rate down as the President continued his jawbone campaign—and the New York banks held their prime rate at 4½%. An overwhelming majority of bankers—including even those friendly to the White House—grumbled that this was undue meddling in their business. But their public protests were muted.

Those Guideposts. Johnson has not interpreted his "era of good feeling" to mean that he should not try to guide or influence the lending, investing, price, or wage decisions of business.

On one of the most inflammatory issues—the "noninflammatory" wage-price guideposts that were first spelled out by President Kennedy's Council of Economic Advisers in 1962 and that were at stake in the Kennedy-steel confrontation that April—Johnson has continued to call for business and labor cooperation.

But his own criticisms have been muted when the guidelines—which would hold wage settlements to national productivity gains of 3.2%—were violated, as in the 1964 automobile and 1965 aluminum settlements.

Voluntary Gains. As the balance-of-payments problem persisted, President Johnson issued a strong call to U. S. bankers to participate in a "voluntary" program to curb the growth of lending abroad, and to industrialists heavily involved in foreign operations to handle their affairs in such a way as to reduce the U. S. payments deficit.

The small number of highly visible—and vulnerable—big banks heavily engaged in international lending (nine banks do 83% of all lending abroad) saw no alternative but to cooperate. Somewhat more surprising has been the degree of cooperation by the heads of a large majority of 600 major industrial companies.

What Business Did. Says Albert L. Nickerson, chairman of Socony Mobil Oil Co., the key business executive working with Commerce Secretary John T. Connor, on the voluntary balance-of-payments program: "We all felt that if top management of each company reviewed its specific programs for new plant, working capital, and cash balances overseas, some reductions and postponements could be made with only a slight adverse effect even on long-range profitability."

Neither from the nation's viewpoint nor that of business, said Nickerson, could companies be asked to forego market opportunities that would repay costs of expansion for many years to come, or to skimp on projects for modernization, new technology, or increased scale that would yield real efficiencies.

But he said top management was finding there are ways of economizing on cash that serve both corporate and national interests.

PARTNERSHIP, BUT NO "ESTABLISHMENT"

The Presidental pleas for business cooperation—and the willingness of business to cooperate—are founded on a fundamental but usually unstated assumption: That the free market does not necessarily provide satisfactory—or prompt—answers to many of the crucial economic and social problems facing the nation, including not only economic growth, price stability, and balance-of-payments equilibrium but also such vital—and interrelated—political issues as unemployment, poverty, and race relations.

Increasingly, executives of large corporations are coming to see that, if they are to keep their own company's sales and profits growing, and to operate in a healthy political and social environment, it is essential to work for the stability and development of the system as a whole.

Common Interests. Thus, in many important respects, executives see their corporate interests bound up with those of other groups:

With the interests of political leaders who are pressed to produce full employment, stable prices, and balance-of-payments equilibrium.

With labor leaders, who must strive to gain job security and rising incomes for the rank and file.

With other manufacturers and businesses, who want strong and rising demand for their own products or services, and are themselves customers of every major industry.

With financial institutions—banks, life insurance companies, pension funds, savings and loan associations—which want to be sure that savings continue to flow to them and that their investments will produce stable and rising returns.

Even with foreign governments and business institutions, whose political and economic decisions can mean life or death to a U. S. corporation.

In this interdependent financial and industrial system, the nation's business leaders begin to see more clearly a need to concert their aims with those of other important policy-makers, whether in business, banking, government, politics, labor, education, or other institutions.

Control—but Where? Indeed, many observers now contend that the U. S. corporate world—along with American society generally—is now controlled by some kind of interlocking directorate among business, government, and other national leaders—an "establishment" like the one that is thought to control Britain.

However, the pictures drawn of this alleged U. S. establishment vary greatly. The late C. Wright Mills of Columbia University called it a "power elite," which he saw as a conservative or reactionary force. Leaders of the civil rights movement refer to it as "the white power structure." Former President Eisenhower, in his farewell speech, warned about a "military-industrial complex," a group that was forcing the nation's economy toward excessive dependence on government defense spending.

Richard H. Rovere has suggested that this "American establishment" covers a political spectrum from slightly left to slightly right of center. It would thus apparently include such diverse personalities as the lawyer, banker, and public servant John J. McCloy; the Harvard professor, economist, and sometime ambassador to India, J. Kenneth Galbraith; and the head of the AFL-CIO, George Meany.

Religion seems to be a critical element to some observers. Professor E. Digby

Baltzell of the University of Pennsylvania calls it "the Protestant establishment." But William F. Buckley, Jr., and the editors of the right-wing *National Review* see it as a kind of liberal-big business conspiracy—a version that was apparently the basis of Senator Goldwater's "Eastern establishment."

Even a subcommittee of the U. S. Congress—the Celler subcommittee of the House Banking Committee—this year used such terms as "power elite" and "business establishment" to describe the men who allegedly are most influential in controlling U. S. economic life, and who sit on many corporate boards of directors.

No Central Group.   These differences in descriptions of the nature, composition, and role of the "U. S. establishment" strongly suggest that there is no such thing—at least not in any simple or literal sense.

The pluralistic U. S. society has many centers of power—in industry, government, politics, the foundations, the press, banking, labor, the intelligentsia—none of which has anything approaching absolute control. There are regional and local as well as national "establishments"—or power groups. Alliances among them are shifting and uncertain.

Both the nature of the political democracy and the still important forces of competition in the economy curb the power of any single group—or of any existing coalition of groups.

HISTORIC ROOTS OF THE PARTNERSHIP GOAL

Yet there are, of course, unmistakable signs that the entire U. S. system has become more centralized with the growth of big business, big government, and big labor. This trend has gone on for a long time—at least since the 1880s—with the rise of the large corporations.

Early political reform movements, such as Populism and Progressivism, failed in their aim to halt the growth of huge corporations, just as the early industrial empire builders foresaw.

James B. Dill, the lawyer who brought Andrew Carnegie and J. P. Morgan together to form the U. S. Steel Corp., once told the muckraker Lincoln Steffens: "Trusts are natural, inevitable growths out of our social and economic conditions. You cannot stop them by force, with laws. They will sweep down like glaciers upon your police, courts, and states and wash them into flowing rivers. I am clearing the way for them."

Psychic Split.   Despite the Sherman Antitrust Act of 1890—and continued popular concern over bigness in the decades that followed—it became clear that technological advance and the growth of a national market were making huge corporations inevitable. These in turn gave rise to huge labor and governmental institutions, in part meant to curb or oppose corporate power.

There was a major split in the American psyche over whether it favored conflict or cooperation among these powerful institutions. Businessmen themselves were split. So were liberals, some decrying "the curse of bigness" and some favoring socialism—which represented an acceptance of bigness but a turning away from competition toward state control.

Mark Hanna's Way. In 1912, Herbert Croly—a brilliant editor of *Architectural Record* (now a McGraw-Hill publication) who was soon to found the liberal journal, *The New Republic*—saw a third alternative in the career of the great Republican political boss, Mark Hanna. Croly saw Hanna's life as an effort to coordinate business and government interests for the public welfare. Hanna envisioned a kind of business-government partnership that would be cooperative, not compulsory.

"Of course," wrote Croly, "as a politician he could not help representing business because business was a part of himself—because business was in his eyes not simply moneymaking, but the most necessary kind of social labor."

Mark Hanna, said Croly, saw no evil in what he was trying to do. Rather, he sought to keep alive "the traditional association between business and politics, between private and public interest, which was gradually being shattered by the actual and irresistible development of American business and political life." Hanna, in Croly's view, saw an essential harmony between business interests and those of the whole American community, and sought to develop it.

Central Issue. But how could this be done? How avoid the danger that this harmony would be at the expense of the "common people"—the workers and farmers—and possibly at the expense of freedom itself?

This had been the central issue in U. S. politics from the beginning—from the classic debates between Alexander Hamilton, the proponent of a strong central government founded on the combination of business and government interests, and Thomas Jefferson, the advocate of a weak government and of extreme individualism.

Hamilton's opponents had accused him of being the enemy of liberty. But in fact, Croly declared in a book, *The Promise of American Life*—which had a major impact on the "New Nationalism" of Theodore Roosevelt—Hamilton wished, "like the Englishman he was, to protect and encourage liberty, just as far as such encouragement was compatible with good order."

Hamilton realized, Croly said, that genuine liberty "could be protected only by an energetic and clear-sighted central government, and it could be fertilized only by the efficient national organization of American activities."

Croly was somewhat ahead of his time in worrying about ways to concert business and government activities for national aims. World War I naturally focused the attention and energies of both on the same national cause. In the 1920s, business had no reason to complain of government, partly because the Republican Administrations were regarded as business' own creatures, partly because the role of government was of slight importance in that period of prosperity.

Depression Impact. The end of that era came with a bang in 1929. President Hoover sought to rally business support for government efforts to steady the economy and spur recovery—but the real problem was to determine exactly what government could or should do.

Looking back later in his Memoirs, Hoover insisted that "no President before had ever believed there was a governmental responsibility in such cases. No matter what the urgings on previous occasions, Presidents steadfastly had maintained that the federal government was apart from such eruptions; they had always been left to blow themselves out."

Any such idea of governmental laissez-faire ended dramatically with the New Deal. President Franklin D. Roosevelt began to intervene all through the business sphere, with his long list of "alphabetical" agencies, starting with NRA.

Both because of traditional business opposition to governmental intervention and because Roosevelt excoriated businessmen as "economic royalists" and virtually accused them of responsibility for Depression miseries, bitter hatred developed between business and government.

Pause and Revival. That conflict was adjourned by the exigencies of World War II, and the postwar boom obviated any need for business and government to go to the mat again during the Truman years. With the coming of Eisenhower, businessmen felt that at last they again had an Administration sympathetic to their interests.

The old issue was reopened, however, with the end of the "postwar era" in the recessions of 1957-58 and 1960, followed by the election of John F. Kennedy. It soon turned out that amid the harassments of slumps, unemployment, balance-of-payments problems, and slow growth, the long-standing issue of government-business relations in the U. S. needed a better solution.

New Start. Today some business leaders are sensing a fresh relevance in the Alexander Hamilton-Herbert Croly-Theodore Roosevelt philosophy. For this is a period in which government seeks the cooperation of business to achieve many ends, ranging from stable economic growth to advancement of Negroes and low-skilled workers. And these are ends difficult or impossible to achieve through legislation alone—and ends that Americans do not wish to achieve by radical change in the political-economic system.

To gain such objectives, some business leaders are turning away from their traditional version of the "Jeffersonian" creed, with its anti-government bias, its commitment to laissez-faire, its emphasis on "rugged individualism." They are wondering whether such doctrines have become inappropriate to the efficient operation of a modern industrialized society—and even to individual liberty and progress.

Constitutional amendments and civil rights laws may be insufficient, without conscious business cooperation, to promote the advancement of those left behind in U. S. economic and social development.

CAN CORPORATIONS ACT FOR SOCIAL ENDS?

These trends have brought a new focus to the business-government relationship.

Over a century ago a prophetic Virginia statesman, Benjamin Watkins Leigh, declared: "Power and property may be separated for a time by force or fraud —but divorced, never. For so soon as the pang of separation is felt . . . property will purchase power, or power will take over property. And either way, there must be an end to free government."

Business leaders today—and government and intellectual leaders as well— are searching for ways of forming a fruitful and healthy relationship between power and property—one in which neither side corrupts or abuses the other, and in which neither oversteps the appropriate limits of its own role. This is an incredibly complex and crucial problem—or series of problems, since it continuously presents itself in different guises.

Classic Case.   One already classic episode in the evolution of the problem affected U. S. Steel Corp. and its Tennessee Coal & Iron Div. in Birmingham, Ala., in 1963.

During that spring, Birmingham was gripped by racial tensions and violence. Under the urging of the U. S. Dept. of Justice, a group of Birmingham's leading citizens—industrialists, bankers, lawyers—formed a committee to work out some kind of settlement of the racial conflicts.

But this Community Affairs Committee had met only twice when four Negro girls were killed on Sept. 15 by a bomb planted in their Sunday school.

Pressures—from the federal government, civil rights groups, liberal newspapers, even from some Southern moderates—quickly built up for U. S. Steel to use its power to improve the racial situation in Birmingham. A young Birmingham lawyer, Charles Morgan, talking to the Young Men's Business Club, rhetorically asked, "Who is guilty?"—and replied that the "good people" of the city, its business, professional, and religious leaders, were as guilty as the perpetrators of violence.

"Birmingham," said Morgan, "is a city in which the major industry, operated from Pittsburgh, never tried to solve the problem."

Limits of Power.   Responding to these pressures and criticisms, U. S. Steel's chairman, Roger Blough, set forth his view of the limits of corporate powers and duties.

Blough declared that Arthur V. Wiebel, president of the TC&I Div., had been "working since 1946 developing understanding and strengthening communications between the races in Birmingham." Blough said that "as individuals we can exercise what little influence we may have as citizens, but for a corporation to attempt to exert any kind of economic compulsion to achieve a particular end in the social area seems to be quite beyond what a corporation can do . . ."

Indeed, such resort to economic compulsion by a private corporation would be "repugnant to our American constitutional concepts," said Blough, though U. S. Steel should and did provide equal opportunities in its own plants. It is the job of government, not business, he asserted, to seek to compel social reforms.

Controversial. Whether U. S. Steel—or any corporation—does have the power to change community behavior, and if it does, whether using it to promote better community racial relations would be a misuse of power, remain controversial issues.

Some Alabama businessmen thought TC&I would have been hit by a severe strike if it had gone further than it did; as one said, "the rank and file of the unions are rabid segregationists." But a leading Birmingham lawyer argued: "TC&I wouldn't have had a strike; not if everybody, the banks, other mills and power companies came in with them."

On whether the power should be used, if it exists, many businessmen feel that Blough correctly drew the important distinction between rights and responsibilities of individual company officials acting as citizens, and those of corporations.

Contrary View. Others—such as Rodman C. Rockefeller, 33-year-old vice-president of the International Basic Economy Corp.—feel this distinction is artificial and no longer meaningful. Today, Rockefeller argues, corporations are more than an extension of the property rights of their owners; they are "free participants in our society."

Rockefeller outlined his views in an address this spring at Dartmouth College—the institution whose dispute with the State of New Hampshire over the inviolability of its corporate charter established the basic freedoms of U. S. corporations in 1819.

Society, in recognizing the corporation's right to private property and tolerating the private ownership and use of the means of production, Rodman Rockefeller declared, expects the corporation in return to produce "the minimum socially and economically needed good."

"Other People's Money."   Other thoughtful men feel that corporate officials have no right to take such crucial moral or social matters into their own hands, or to use "other people's money" to achieve social ends. Some even doubt whether this would provide better answers to critical social questions than simply aiming to achieve the corporation's economic and financial objectives.

"For example," asks one skeptic, "would racial discrimination be greater or less if all employers operated in a coldly profit-maximizing way than if they operated in conformity with the moral standards of their own communities?"

A NEW STRUCTURE—AND NEW LEADERSHIP

In the American society today, no longer is there a simple division between power (meaning political authority) and property (meaning business interests). The concept of property itself has been drastically modified by the rise of the great corporation and the wide diffusion of ownership and control of the means of production, both through financial institutions and through the political process.

Many institutions—labor unions, racial and religious groups, the press, scientists and intellectuals, as well as political parties and their leaders—have some degree of power to influence the course of American life. The business corporation clearly does not bestride U. S. society like a top-hatted Wall Street banker in a cartoon in *Pravda* or *Izvestia*. Yet few would deny it has a crucial role to play.

The ancient cold war between business and government is breaking up—on both sides. The new partnership is still in process of evolution. There is always the possibility—some would say probability—that it will collapse under fresh political, economic, or social pressures. Certainly, the U. S. business community, which is far from unified, does not feel itself committed to any one party's, or to one man's, concept of the Great Society.

Yet there are reasons for thinking that the kind of restructuring of business-government power relations that is going on in the U. S. represents a genuine change in the workings of the system.

Worldwide. For one thing, what is going on in the U. S. is only a manifestation of changes at work in all modern industrial societies throughout the world. As Duke University's Calvin B. Hoover puts it:

> "The experience of all modern industrialized societies demonstrates that some sort of the new 'mix' of the responsibilities and functions of the state, of economic organizations, and of individuals essentially different from that of capitalism of the past is inevitable."

Every Western democracy is striving to discover for itself the means of achieving a better balance between private and public responsibilities in solving key problems. There are parallels between the President's Council of Economic Advisers and his Advisory Committee on Labor-Management Relations, and the new Dept. of Economic Affairs and the National Economic Development Council in Britain, or the Economic and Social Council in France.

The U. S. Way. No two nations are tackling these problems in quite the same way. The U. S. government still plays a less controlling role in industry than do governments in other countries. U. S. industry, says Thomas J. Watson, Jr.,

—whose IBM Corp. operates in many countries—is still "less fettered than in any other country, by a long, long shot."

This, he thinks, is a major reason why U. S. industry is so strong and innovative. U. S. industrial success, as he sees it, is closely related to "the speed of the decision process."

The willingness of private business voluntarily to work with government is, in Watson's view and that of a growing number of other business leaders, a way to retain their present degree of freedom and to avoid what they fear will be inefficient or wrongheaded government controls.

Formidable. The technical and operating problems facing businessmen who would measure up to the needs of the time are formidable. They may range from fiscal and monetary policy to urban renewal to race relations to problems of national defense and the uses of outer space—and, of course, a knowledge of how to run their own businesses successfully in a period of explosive technological change.

The education of tomorrow's business leaders will have to offer better preparation for such a wide range of problems than the education—and experiences—afforded the present generation of business leaders.

Models. Some business leaders of today, however, do provide models of how to serve the interests of private business and the broad society. One such man is Robert A. Lovett—banker, World War I Navy hero, World War II public official, Secretary of Defense under President Truman, and a leading candidate for inclusion in the mythical "U. S. establishment."

Says Lovett: "The corporation should not seek to replace public authority. Yet the corporation is endowed with the public interest—a bit. It is created by the state, and it must be responsible . . ."

Democracy, Lovett adds, requires that freedom be coupled with restraint. There is no simple formula for this, he concedes, but says: "I can't believe that there is not enough wisdom or wit in this country so that we can handle our problems within a context of freedom."

There is growing support within the U. S. business community for such views.

THE HARD CHOICE THAT FACES BUSINESS

It is becoming clear that what U. S. business faces today is a set of choices on the role it is to play in relation to the broad society. Business cannot avoid the necessity of choice, because the modern corporation has become the towering institution of today's society—and the problems of society have become its problems as well.

The society is demanding the achievement of a great many national objectives—national security (which inescapably involves the corporation), maximum employment, racial equality, rising living standards (especially for groups left behind in the growth race), improved education, better medical care, a healthier urban environment, the safeguarding of natural resources.

Two Roads. In attempting to achieve those ends, which involve overlapping business and government functions and responsibilities, there are two basic choices:

To increase the role of government and, where business is concerned, to make greater use of coercion or fiat to bring about the kind of business behavior desired.

To seek to develop more fruitful, voluntary cooperation between business and government.

Either approach has obvious dangers.

The first may involve excessive centralization of power in the government, posing genuine threats to the freedom and efficiency of business, and to society itself.

The second may be too loose and uncertain, and can scarcely avoid the problem of sanctions against "chiselers," or simply hard-pressed businesses that are not able to mesaure up to the standards of "social responsibility" assumed by large and prosperous corporations.

No "Either-Or."   But the choice is not a simple either-or decision.

Indeed, the success or failure of the voluntary approach in particular areas will largely determine whether the coercive role of government is to be closely limited or greatly expanded.

And how far government intervenes in the economy or in social relations will depend heavily on its ability to create conditions making for a healthy and growing over-all economy.

There are reasons to hope that thanks to progress in the understanding and use of fiscal and monetary policy by government, the detailed decisions on production, distribution, employment, location of industry, and such matters can on the whole be handled by business on its own.

Yet specific problems have emerged—and others will continue to develop —that require business and government cooperation, or legislative solution.

Today, some of these issues involve collective bargaining and strike threats in key industries, the nation's balance of payments, race relations, unemployment, poverty, urban decay. What specifically the critical issues of the future will be no one can know for sure.

Cautions. Just as they do today, viewpoints in the future are bound to differ on the gravity or nature of particular problems and on how to deal with them. These viewpoints will be colored in part by the interests of the parties that are involved and by their ideologies—including interests and ideologies of government officials and their academic or other allies, as well as those of business.

That means it will be vitally important to guard, on the one hand, against the notion that "the public interest" is always best defined and understood by public officials. The power of the state, as Calvin B. Hoover warns, "cannot automatically be assumed to be wielded in the public interest."

On a host of matters, businessmen must be free to make their own decisions, or society will suffer. They should not—as one of them recently told the President—be treated "like children."

At the same time, some businessmen point out, it cannot automatically be assumed that whatever the President, or other government policymakers, propose is damaging to business interests. Frederick R. Kappel, chairman of American Telephone & Telegraph Co., in thinking back over the forces that prompted the growth of his own giant corporation, has stressed that one of the most essential factors—besides technical innovation and entrepreneurial drive—was "the public consensus, the political decision . . ."

Leadership and Economics. The U. S. system puts heavy responsibility on the federal government, and the President in particular; and the American people have come to expect Presidents to exert leadership whenever and wherever national problems are serious—whether in matters of national defense, foreign affairs, race relations, or economic affairs.

The last is a relatively new area for Presidential leadership. But it emerged as a crucial area with the development of full-scale modern industrialism and came to crisis with the Great Depression—which the American people are determined never to let happen again.

Economics has persisted as an area of Presidential concern in a society in which some critical problems can better be solved by high-level decision makers, in government and business, rather than being left to the "marketplace"—or to accident or fate. Wherever possible, however, it makes good sense to let competition in the marketplace and consumers' choices determine economic activity.

How Tension Helps. One of the great advantages of a free society is that, though one respects one's political chief, one must not necessarily do what he says. Businessmen have a different perspective from government, and society's ends—"the public interest"—may often be best promoted by a tension between business and government. Tensions and conflicts may be as constructive for the broad society as within any single organization.

But they may sometimes become destructive. The endless problem, within an organization or society as a whole, is to find a balance—to permit tensions, but set limits on conflict lest it become ruinous.

Role for Business. The problems of avoiding excessive power for the business corporation are as worthy of concern as is limiting the power of government. There are inherent restrictions, however, for the corporation is not the only significant or powerful institution today. Labor unions in many respects provide a useful check on the power of both business and government. So do farm groups, universities, foundations, professional organizations, racial and religious groups, even the family.

The corporation may unavoidably be involved in moral issues, but it cannot presume to replace the churches, or the conscience of the individual. Nor can the corporation be mother and father to its employees. A free society is a pluralistic society—one in which no one institution (or one political party) can be all-powerful and controlling.

Yet businessmen today are increasingly coming to understand that they do have considerable power and that they can play—as heads of huge organizations—a major role in shaping the fortunes of a free society.

C. Profits and Profit Sharing

What Is Wrong With Profit Maximization?

4

Charles F. Phillips, Jr.

Corporate management must face up to a predicament that has crucial economic and social implications. On the one hand, many argue that business must assume social responsibilities, in addition to its historic economic and legal obligations, by becoming involved even more deeply in such activities as corporate giving, support of higher education, political participation, and representation in community affairs. In discussing the changing role of business in our economy, David Rockefeller, President of the Chase Manhattan Bank, argues:

> "In *social* terms, the old concept that the owner of a business had a right to use his property as he pleased to maximize profits has evolved into the belief that ownership carries certain binding social obligations. Today's manager serves as trustee not only for the owners but for the workers and indeed for our entire society. . . . Corporations have developed a sensitive awareness of their responsibility for maintaining an equitable balance among the claims of stockholders, employees, customers and the public at large."[1]

.On the other hand, an equally vocal group contends that management should adhere to its traditional economic function of producing goods and services at maximum profit. In the words of Milton Friedman, the University of Chicago's well-known economist:

> "Few trends could so thoroughly undermine the very foundations of our free society as the acceptance by corporate officials of a social re-

---

Reprinted with permission from *Business Horizons* (Bloomington, Ind.: The University of Indiana Press, Winter 1963) pp. 73–80.

[1] David Rockefeller, "The Changing Role of Business in Our Society," in an address before the American Philosophical Society, Philadelphia, Nov. 8, 1962.

sponsibility other than to make as much money for their stockholders as possible. This is a fundamentally subversive doctrine."[2]

Professor Friedman believes, moreover, that even business contributions to support charitable activities represent "an inappropriate use of corporate funds in a free-enterprise society."

The choice of a course involves far more than mere intellectual exercise. As challenging as that may be, management faces the grave prospect of undergoing a significant modification of its traditional role unless it faces decisively the issues raised by the present controversy. As a result of indecision, a solution may be forced upon management—perhaps against its best interests.

THE THESIS

In the past few years, some businessmen have tended more frequently to soft-pedal profit maximization and to emphasize the modern corporation's growing list of social obligations. But the phrase "social responsibility," rarely defined, remains a hazy concept. Sometimes it implies only a shift in emphasis, perhaps for public relations purposes, without modification of business goals or values. At other times, however, the implication is that corporations should step beyond their traditional economic and legal functions *even at the sacrifice of long-run profit.* This view of social responsibility is, to use Joseph W. McGuire's phrase, "a crude blend of long-run profit making and altruism."[3]

In the writer's opinion, both business and our private enterprise system would suffer if profit maximization were sought irresponsibly, but they would also suffer if uncritical philanthropy were introduced in the guise of social responsibility. Profit maximization must remain as the basic goal of business firms. In turn, the profit maximization approach can guide management in the area of social responsibility. Businessmen must be socially responsible insofar as social responsibility leads to higher profits, but they must possess a fine sense of double-entry bookkeeping! Argues Henry Ford II, Chairman of the Board of the Ford Motor Company:

> "Once 'business is business' meant dog-eat-dog, the devil take the hindmost, the law of the jungle. Today we need that phrase 'business is business' just to remind us that business is *not* first and foremost a social institution, a charitable agency, a cultural gathering, a community service, a public spirited citizen. It is an action organization geared to produce economic results in competition with other business."[4]

[2] Milton Friedman, *Capitalism and Freedom* (Chicago: The University of Chicago Press, 1962), pp. 133.

[3] Joseph W. McGuire, *Business and Society* (New York: McGraw-Hill Book Company, Inc., 1963), p. 144.

[4] Henry Ford II, "What America Expects of Industry," in an address before the Michigan State Chamber of Commerce, Oct. 2, 1962.

Why is it felt that management should be responsible to society as a whole rather than to its stockholders? What are the long-run implications of social responsibility? What is a socially responsible enterprise in a market economy? Finally, is the quandary regarding social responsibility and profit maximization real or illusory?

SOCIAL RESPONSIBILITY: ORIGINS

The traditional justification for a private enterprise economy rests on the assumption that rigorous competition will prevail. One of the basic tenets of competitive theory, as developed by Adam Smith and other classical economists, is that business firms will seek to maximize profits. By so doing, business will allocate society's scarce resources in the best possible manner, and serve the best interests of both their stockholders and the general public. A competitive market system thus reconciles private interests with the public good.

In 1932 Adolf A. Berle, Jr. and Gardiner C. Means questioned the relevance of these assumptions for modern capitalism and, in so doing, started a continuing debate over corporate responsibilities.[5] The authors noted that the ownership of corporate stock was becoming dispersed among society's members, while control of corporate capital assets was becoming concentrated in the hands of a relatively few salaried managers. The first trend tends to reduce the effectiveness of stockholder control and the second to increase the economic power of management.

Few today disagree with the conclusions of the Berle and Means study; statistics on the dispersion of ownership and the concentration of control of corporate assets are familiar. More important for present purposes are the problems raised by these developments.

The first arises from the fact that in our modern economy stockholders own property without effective control while management has power without substantial ownership. The classical economists assumed that ownership and management were synonymous; profits were the reward for successfully exercising this ownership-management function. The separation of ownership and control, therefore, raises a question: to whom is management responsible? To use Berle's phrase, the stockholder has become a "passive receptive" who cannot manage and who is thus functionless. But management has no legitimate claim on profits because it lacks ultimate ownership. On the matter of corporate control, Edward S. Mason writes:

"What Mr. Berle and most of the rest of us are afraid of is that this powerful corporate machine, which so successfully grinds out the goods we

---

[5] Adolf A. Berle, Jr. and Gardiner C. Means, *The Modern Corporation and Private Property* (New York: The Macmillan Co., 1932). See also Adolf A. Berle, Jr., *Power Without Property* (New York: Harcourt, Brace and Company, Inc., 1959).

want, seems to be running without any discernible controls. The young lad mastering the technique of his bicycle may legitimately shout with pride, 'Look, Ma, no hands,' but is this the appropriate motto for a corporate society?"[6]

The second problem is raised by corporate size. Economists generally believe that competition among large enterprises is different from competition among small decision-making units. This belief is reflected in the popular feeling that competition has declined in the United States and that prices are administered or institutionally determined. Management, the argument goes, has the freedom (within limits) to set prices and to determine the rate of technological change and economic growth. Competition, many feel, is not the strict disciplinarian it was once thought to be and, as a result, the goals of management have changed. Management is far more interested in the corporation as an institution and in its continued existence than in immediate, or even long-run, profits.

Because the irresponsible use of this immense power is unthinkable, management must become socially responsible; it has been suggested that management has no choice. The accumulation of power by any group in a democratic society has always been suspect. The tremendous economic power of Big Business, unless used justly, will be further restricted by Big Labor and Big Government. (Both of the latter have also been subjects of debate.) To maintain a private enterprise economy, so the argument goes, business must assume new social responsibilities.

SOCIAL RESPONSIBILITY: ITS IMPLICATION

If social responsibility becomes the dominant force in business decision making, three significant implications should be understood. In the first place, the idea of a corporate conscience assumes that management has the option of being socially responsible or not. While such an assumption may be vehemently denied by business leaders, the fact remains that vigorous competition and social statesmanship are logically imcompatible. In the words of Theodore Levitt:

". . . only businessmen who are free from the rigid demands of competition are free to practice the prerogatives of business statemanship. Statesmanship is a luxury of some degree of monopoly. Any business that habitually practices statesmanship must be presumed to have achieved the felicity of not having to keep its nose continuously to the competitive grindstone. If it can purposely hold prices down or freely raise them, if it can have extravagant employee welfare plans, make handouts to every solicitor for a supposedly good cause, make its headquarters a crystal

6 In Edward S. Mason (ed.), *The Corporation in Modern Society* (Cambridge: Harvard University Press, 1959), pp. 3–4.

palace of ankle-deep rugs and solid-gold water coolers—if it can do these, one may begin to question whether the industry is entirely competitive."[7]

Levitt may be pushing the argument to the extreme, but his point is valid; a business firm cannot have the best of two worlds. The first implication of social responsibility, then, is that competition in our economy has become so "imperfect" that the market is a poor regulator of corporate behavior.

In the second place, conscience requires that value judgments be made. Two questions immediately arise: does business know what is good for society and, even if it does, should business force its value judgments on society? One may properly question whether any interest group in the economy knows what society really wants or should want; clearly a consensus does not exist. Argues Ben W. Lewis:

> "Economic decisions must be right as society measures right rather than good as benevolent individuals construe goodness. An economy is a mechanism designed to pick up and discharge the wishes of society in the management of its resources; it is not an instrument for the rendering of gracious music by kindly disposed improvisers."[8]

In the third place, the acceptance of social responsibility may make it impossible for business to carry out its major function of economizing, that is, to be efficient in the use of the nation's scarce and limited resources. Responsibility or conscientiousness has nothing to do with economizing. Should society at large come to accept the idea of a corporate conscience, business may find it exceedingly difficult to make sound economic decisions with respect to prices, wages, and investment. Such decisions are often unpleasant—for example, the decision to move a plant from one community to another. Again, Professor Lewis' words are well worth considering:

> "Ponder the plight of the management of a giant firm producing a basic commodity, employing thousands of workers at good wages, making splendid profits, and presently facing a crippling strike unless it accedes to a demand for a wage increase. The increase can easily be passed along in higher prices. Workers want higher wages and no interruption in employment; consumers want continued output at an increasing rate and so do stockholders. The public does not want further inflation, and large numbers of small firms do not want further increases in wages. The White House, which wants high production, full employment, healthy wages, abundant profits, and low prices, now admonishes industrial statesmen to recognize their public responsibility and to adopt measures appropriate to

---

[7] Theodore Levitt, "The Mythological Potency of 'Peoples' Capitalism,' " in *The Corporation: Its Modern Character and Responsibilities* (Columbus: The Ohio State University, 1960), pp. 15–16. See also, by the same author, "The Dangers of Social Responsibility," *Harvard Business Review*, XXXVI (Sept.-Oct., 1958).

[8] Ben W. Lewis, "Economics by Admonition," *American Economic Review*, XLIX (May, 1959), p. 395.

the maintenance of equity, full employment, stability, and progress. The management—as allocator, distributor, stabilizer, trustee, conservator, prophet, and chaplain, as well as manager—consults its conscience. The diagnosis of the attending psychiatrist will be 'multiple schizophrenia': The management's personality will not be split. It will be shredded and powdered!'"[9]

One can sympathize with United States Steel's Roger Blough when, in the face of overwhelming governmental displeasure, he attempted to defend his company's 1962 price increase to the nation in terms of profits and investment needs. But it would be difficult to imagine his defense in terms of social responsibility: to maintain equity among the company's interested groups, higher wages were voluntarily granted to workers and increased prices to suppliers, which, in turn, necessitated higher steel prices to provide greater profits for stockholders' dividends and for new investment to satisfy consumer demand (all beneficial to society at large). Or consider the following reply by an executive of one of the country's largest corporations when asked by a stockholder to defend his firm's annual educational gifts: "We in the . . . Company believe in being good corporate citizens. We think the principle of corporate giving is well established. It is encouraged by our tax laws; it has been upheld in our courts; and the public has come to expect it of corporations."

Is not this the crux of the issue faced by management? Since bigness is frequently suspect and the level of existing profits as well as the need for higher profits often questioned, corporate actions are frequently defended in terms of responsibility. But such a defense will subject management's conscience to countless pressures, and the public will come to expect contributions, even when the corporation cannot expect either direct or indirect benefits. "A competitive establishment cannot be selfless in any genuine fashion. Selflessness, however, is what socially responsible behavior implies," writes Levitt.

If these implications are correct, management's attempt to justify both its size and its power in terms of social responsibility may end in gigantic failure. The corporation is an economic institution, not a welfare organization, and its real justification is profit maximization for the benefit of its stockholders. By stepping into the social arena where there are few, if any, acceptable standards of efficiency in the use of society's resources, business may invite restrictions on its freedom.

Social responsibility is a function of government, civic organizations, and business leaders as individuals. Public officials are responsible to the public at large, but "it is highly repugnant that a corporate manager, not publicly elected and hence not subject to popular recall, should have a special responsibility for what the managerialists call the process of government. At least a socialistic government can be defeated at the polls."[10] Benevolent man-

9 "Economics by Admonition," p. 396.
10 "Have Corporations a Higher Duty Than Profits?" *Fortune,* LXII (August, 1960), p. 148.

agement rule is not, I am confident, the intent of those advocating social responsibility.

THE CASE FOR PROFIT MAXIMIZATION

Eugene V. Rostow has succinctly stated the case for profit maximization:

"The law books have always said that the board of directors owes a single-minded duty of unswerving loyalty to the stockholders, and only to the stockholders. The economist has demonstrated with all the apparent precision of plane geometry and the calculus that the quest for maximum revenue in a competitive market leads to a system of prices, and an allocation of resources and rewards, superior to any alternative, in its contributions to the economic welfare of the community as a whole. . . . If, as is widely thought, the essence of corporate statesmanship is to seek less than maximum profits, post war experience is eloquent evidence that such statesmanship leads to serious malfunctioning of the economy as a whole."[11]

In short, according to Rostow, social responsibility will "sabotage the market mechanism and systematically distort the allocation of resources," thereby making "the task of monetary and fiscal authority in controlling general fluctuations of trade more expensive and more difficult," and perhaps making "it impossible to sustain high levels of employment save at the cost of considerable price inflation."

In everyday phraseology, profit assumes that management is responsible for running an efficient business organization, that is, performing its economic function. *In so doing, the organization is being socially responsible.* In making a decision, whether that decision concerns prices, investment, plant location, or an educational contribution, some criteria must be used as guides. Profit maximization is a criterion; social responsibility, emphasizing equity, is not.

"The corporate conscience is irrelevant to the corporate purpose. Conscience is not something you introduce as a piece of organizational decor, performing simply a decorative function. If it is allowed to influence the mechanism of economic decision-making, conscience automatically assumes a central role. Nothing could be worse. The stronger the conscience the harder it will be to make a businesslike decision and get the economic job done."[12]

Further, the primary of philosophy adopted by management—whether social responsibility or profit maximization—determines the decisions made. Should Firm X continue to operate in Community Y, where it is the largest employer, or should it move to Community Z where its profit potential is greater? Should corporations sponsor higher quality television programs at the risk of smaller

[11] Eugene V. Rostow in *The Corporation in Modern Society*, p. 63.
[12] "The Mythological Potency of 'Peoples' Capitalism,' " p. 15.

audiences in an attempt to get the industry out of the "vast wasteland," or should program content be aimed at capturing the largest possible audience? Clearly, social responsibility and profit maximization are two entirely different concepts involving different goals and values.

It might be argued that the traditional or orthodox justification for profit maximization is no longer suited to the needs of modern capitalism. One of the basic assumptions of those advocating corporate social responsibility is that the market mechanism no longer functions as effectively as was once thought and that corporations consequently have some degree of market power or choice over such variables as prices and the rate of technological innovation. My own opinion is that competition, whether in the price or nonprice dimension, exists in sufficient strength to limit the long-run area of choice open to the managements of most American corporations.

Let there be no misunderstanding. Competition is far from "perfect" and public policy could and should promote, to achieve maximum efficiency and personal freedom, a stronger pro-competitive policy (by eliminating trade barriers and fair trade laws, to name only two examples). Yet in most industries, the existing degree of competition is sufficient (in economic terms "workable") to protect the consumer interest. The danger in accepting the philosophy of social responsibility is that management will forget its economic function and will attempt to assume the functions that have traditionally been assigned to the market mechanism. (Just as dangerous are attempts by either government or labor to assume managerial functions.[13]) Concludes Ford:

> "I have deep faith in the stimulating power of competition and in the capacity of the free market to allocate resources and to bring us optimum growth and progress, if we will only let it work. And we will let it work if we can bring ourselves to accept a few very simple ideas about business: that business is a tool, and that the sharper its cutting edges are the stronger its motivating power, the better job it will be able to do for all of us."[14]

It has been suggested that a compromise is necessary to solve the issue of social responsibility. Thus, Richard Eells argues that "the root of the conflict over social responsibilities lies in the irreconcilability of two equally untenable theories of the corporation," namely, the "traditional corporation," which intends to maximize profits, and the "metrocorporation," which assumes limitless social obligations. He puts forward the "well-tempered corporation," a compromise between these two extremes, which regards profits as primary but also considers its social obligations in the decision-making process.[15]

---

[13] Charles F. Phillips, Jr. and Harmon H. Haymes, " 'Psychological' Price Control: Meddling or Masterstroke?" *Business Horizons*, V (Summer, 1962), pp. 99–106.

[14] Henry Ford, "What America Expects of Industry."

[15] Richard Eells, "Social Responsibility: Can Business Survive the Challenge?" *Business Horizons*, II (Winter, 1959), p. 37.

The editors of *Fortune* find it difficult to distinguish between the "well-tempered corporation" and the "metrocorporation." In their words:

"... it is impossible to attach a definite meaning to the expression 'profits are secondary' or even to 'profits are primary but coordinate with other functions.' If profits are secondary, then they can *always* be sacrificed for the sake of fulfilling obligations that are primary; but since profits are an indispensable condition of the corporation's existence, this is tantamount to saying that the corporation can sacrifice its existence and at the same time fulfill its obligations to the community. Again, to say that profits are a primary function, coordinate with other functions, amounts to saying that these other functions are also primary and hence of equal importance. So what does the corporation do in the event of a conflict?[16]

The management of a modern corporation may be a "self-perpetuating oligarchy" (Berle's phrase), but that management making inadequate profits will not survive for long. Moreover, social responsibility is a fair-weather concept; management cannot even think in terms of philanthropy unless profits are adequate.

SOCIAL RESPONSIBILITY IN A MARKET ECONOMY

The basic proposition, as every businessman knows only too well, is that profits are the indispensable element in a successful business enterprise. The role of profits may not be recognized or understood by as many of our citizens as would be desirable, but to duck the issue by hiding behind the cloak of "social responsibility" does not seem to be the answer. Management must operate at maximum economic efficiency to get rid of the evil connotations attached to the word "profit." The corporation that is efficient, that constantly strives to improve old products and introduce new ones, and that seeks to satisfy consumer demand in the most efficient manner and at the lowest possible price is the one with the strongest case for maximum profit.

Yet conscience is an integral part of management's everyday decision making and profit maximization functions. Responsible behavior requires scrupulous adherence to the spirit of the law as well as to its letter, avoidance of any misrepresentative advertising, and bargaining with labor in good faith. This point has been well stated by Frederick R. Kappel, Board Chairman of the American Telephone & Telegraph Company:

"... the purpose of business is not simply to provide the opportunity for making a fast buck. ... The fast-buck philosophy not only stands in the way of a good job, it also robs the individual of the feeling of accomplishment that he needs in his personal life. I don't mean that one needs to be a 'do-gooder' in the sense in which that phrase is often used. But *the person of character* will approach business life with the idea that

16 "Have Corporations a Higher Duty Than Profits?" p. 109.

he has obligations to fulfill. He will set his ethical sights high and hold himself strictly to account. He will act on the principle that good management, sound business practice, and balanced judgment are ideals well worth his best striving."[17]

Similarly, profit maximization does not imply that business leaders can be indifferent to the country's social system. Management has an interest in trying to maintain and aid the development of a social system in which firms can operate with maximum freedom, profitability, and longevity. However, *business should seek society's good in ways that are also good for business.* Philanthropic acts often have economic justification: gifts to a local school construction program may improve the company's labor force; matching employees' gifts to their universities or other philanthropies may increase both the stability and the effort of its labor force; and community gifts of many kinds may improve community relations in ways that admittedly are difficult to measure. For these reasons, insurance companies conduct safety education, banks employ agricultural specialists, and railroads promote area development.

Therefore, a contribution to a charitable organization should be made because it benefits the corporation and not because it is the thing to do or because it is expected. The executive who was quoted earlier concerning his company's policy of contributing money to educational institutions was asked to defend the policy again a year later. This time, however, his answer was quite different: "When we finally commit ourselves to an expenditure, we feel that within the limits of human fallibility we have done our best to be able to say: 'This expenditure, this investment, will be profitable and remunerative for the company and, through it, for the shareholders.' We devote exactly the same attention to our contributions for philanthropy and education." No longer is the emphasis upon responsibility; it is upon profits.

Would it not be ironic for management to lose the struggle for public recognition of the role of adequate profits, for which it has fought so long, just at a time when it appears that the chances of success may be at hand? It has been a long time since an administration has actively advocated and sought a tax cut to stimulate economic growth. And it has been an even longer time since a Democratic president has publicly argued that increased business profits are one means of achieving this goal. Many obstacles remain before words become deeds, but this hardly seems to be the time for a basic shift in management's philosophy.

What is wrong with profit maximization as management's basic decision making goal? Nothing, if properly understood. The choice between profit maximization and social responsibility is not an either-or proposition. As long as profit maximization is the dominant factor in corporate decision making, guiding management in the area of social responsibility, no problem exists. But

17 Frederick R. Kappel in an address at the commencement exercises of Michigan State University, June 9, 1963 (emphasis added).

if business adopts a dominant philosophy of social responsibility, our free, competitive, private enterprise system cannot survive.

A business firm is not a charitable or philanthropic organization. It is an economizing institution and its basic function is to economize; only by performing its economic function well is a business firm socially responsible. Nor is a business firm an instrument through which its management seeks to replace the functioning of the market with its value judgments as to what is good or bad for society. Business operates within a legal framework and is subject to market control. If the market does not adequately control business decisions, then the public can be expected to demand government control. Market control is the essence of a democratic, private enterprise system.

Many will disagree with the view being expressed. Some, such as McGuire, have termed profit maximization the "traditional" approach, one that does not permit business "to adapt to a changing world." Nothing could be further from the truth; business has changed and will continue to change. Certainly the public expects more from business today than it did fifty years ago and assumes that businessmen will be men of character with a high sense of what is right and wrong. But as executives of corporations, business leaders' major responsibility is to manage as efficiently as possible the allocation of that portion of society's resources that come within the corporation's control. Is this not, after all, the only economic, legal, and social justification for a business enterprise in a free society?

The Ethics of Profit Sharing   5

Benjamin L. Masse

In response to certain remarks of the writer on the moral aspects of profit sharing ("War or Peace in Detroit," *America*, March 1, 1958, pp. 626–629), a number of readers have written in to express a dissent. A few contended that I had aided and abetted a sinister plan to subvert the American system of private enterprise. Most of the correspondents, however, suggested that my approach had been too conservative. They argued that in the light of Catholic social teaching there was much more to be said in defense of a union demand for profit sharing than I had given the reader reason to believe. Obviously, a more extended treatment of this question is indicated.

Reprinted with permission from *America*, 106 West 56th Street, New York, New York (May 31, 1958) pp. 285–287.

In the article which stirred up this discussion, I stated that, so far as remuneration went, an employer who paid his workers a fair wage had fully discharged his obligation in justice to them. I wrote that such workers "cannot demand a share in profits as a strict right," or, as a consequence, resort to economic force to support a demand for profit sharing. In taking this stand I leaned heavily on the late Pope Pius XI, who upheld the justice of the wage contract against those who insisted that it must be replaced by a partnership contract. Though the Pope did commend profit sharing, as well as labor's sharing in management and ownership, he presented these modifications of the wage contract only as something "advisable." I therefore concluded that, although workers could submit a profit-sharing proposal to their employer, the employer was under no moral obligation to grant it, or even to consider it.

I gladly concede that this highly condensed statement of the case gives not only an inadequate but also a misleading impression of Catholic writing on the morality of profit sharing. It is, indeed, an easy task to cite writers who contradict it. Here are a few of them.

IN COMMUTATIVE JUSTICE

In the final revised edition of his well-known *Distributive Justice*, the late Msgr. John A. Ryan raises the question whether workers who are receiving just wages have any claim upon profits (p. 294 sq.). By profits in this context, Monsignor Ryan seems to mean the residue remaining after the payment of all costs of production, including dividends. He says that where the employer carries on his business in competitive conditions, workers who are already receiving just wages—what he calls the "equitable minimum"—have no strict right to any additional compensation out of the rare "surplus profits" which may develop. However, in companies that are monopolies or quasi-monopolies, all who work for the business have a right to share in its "surplus profits." In such companies, he writes, "the surplus profits should all be distributed among those who perform any function in the industry, from the president of the company down to the office boy."

The distribution of such profits, he adds, "should be in proportion to their respective salaries and wages"—a standard which reflects, presumably, the contribution of each employe to the success of the enterprise. Monsignor Ryan could find "no conclusive reason" for forbidding workers to use their economic power to gain a share in surplus profits.

Does not this division of the corporate income do violence to the rights of stockholders? No, answers the monsignor. So far as their contribution to the success of the enterprise goes, he could see no difference between bondholders and stockholders. Aside from providing capital, neither contributes in any way to the productive process. "Why," he asks, "should the non-working stockholders receive any part of the surplus to the production of which they have contributed neither time nor thought nor labor?" Therefore, he concludes:

If matters are so arranged that they are certain to receive the prevailing rate of interest each year, and if a sufficient reserve is set aside to protect them against losses, they are receiving all that seems to be fair and all that is necessary to induce men to invest their money in a concern of this sort (p. 337).

In the first edition of *Distributive Justice,* Monsignor Ryan had been somewhat more generous to stockholders. In *commutative* justice, which governs the claims of workers and owners on corporative income based on their contributions to the common enterprise, he allowed stockholders a dividend of one per cent above the prevailing rate of interest. In *social* justice, which governs the distribution of corporate income in the interest of the general welfare, he conceded them an additional four per cent return from the surplus profits.

Prof. J. Messner of the University of Vienna is another distinguished writer who holds that workers have a right in commutative justice to a share in profits, but he argues the case differently. In a capitalistic economy, he explains in *Social Ethics,* the employer is supposed to assume the risks of fluctuations due to market circumstances. In practice, however, the employer tries so far as possible to shift this risk to his employes by cutting their wages and laying them off. "The worker," he concludes, "is therefore in the right when he endeavors to gain a share in surplus profits" (p. 765). Professor Messner observes, however, that when the profit position of the firm is favorable, workers as a rule strive to compensate for past losses by demands for higher future wages.

IN SOCIAL JUSTICE

Like Monsignor Ryan, the Rev. Raymond J. Miller, C.Ss.R., in his commentary on *Quadragesimo Anno, Forty Years After: Pius XI and the Social Order,* distinguishes between small businesses, employing "less than 100 workers," and "the hundred-million and billion-dollar giants, which do the greater part of the business of the nation." The small employer, he holds, is entitled to whatever profit he can make. The stockholders in the big corporation, on the other hand, since he renders no service beyond providing capital, is entitled in commutative justice only to a fair return on his investment. Who, then, asks Father Miller, owns the undistributed profits—"that portion of the income of a business which remains after all the creditors and all the stockholders of the business have been paid off"?

At this point Father Miller parts company with Monsignor Ryan. The stockholders own these "surplus profits," he says, morally as well as legally. They are not free, however, to use them as suits their fancy, since they have the obligation "of allocating or distributing them in the way that will best serve the common good." That workers who have been paid just wages have no claim in commutative justice to surplus profits is clear, Father Miller believes, from Pius XI's defense of the justice of the wage contract. "It is of the essence of the wage contract," he argues, "that the workers give up any rights they might have to the profits in return for a fixed wage."

Granted this analysis of the problem, the only basis for a union demand for profit sharing lies in social justice. Father Miller holds that such a demand can be justified because "the common good will be served if both the capitalists and the workers get a share of the profits." To charges that union demands for profit sharing are an invasion of management rights, Father Miller replies that the same Pope who taught that the capitalist owns the profits and should have the "leading voice" in distributing them for the common good taught also that it would be advisable to give workers a share not only in profits but in management as well.

In a doctoral dissertation submitted to the Faculty of the School of Sacred Thelogy at Catholic University, *Distribution of Profits in the Modern Corporation*, the Rev. George F. Bardes likewise holds that stockholders in the big corporation have a claim in commutative justice "to no more than an interest rate somewhat higher than the pure and simple creditor." The profits remaining after the payment of fair dividends should be retained in the business or distributed as the needs of the enterprise and the general welfare of society suggest. Where surplus profits are foreseen, writes Father Bardes, who is a priest of the Archdiocese of New York, they "are aptly presented for discussion at a bargaining table." And he adds: "The worker is free to bargain at this time for a change from a pure wage-earning status to one of modified partnership whereby he may become a sharer in profits, ownership and management." Father Bardes holds that such a demand for a form of modified partnership "may be the subject of a strike."

From this sampling of the literature on the subject, it will be clear that there is a case for profit sharing on the grounds of both commutative and social justice. How strong is that case?

CONCLUSION

With all respect for the memory of John A. Ryan, whose friendship I cherished, *I do not see how workers have any claim in commutative justice to "surplus profits."* If we assume that all contractual obligations have been met and that the customers have not been overcharged, then these profits belong to the owners of the corporation, and they belong to them morally as well as legally. As Father Miller rightly says, by contracting for a fixed wage, the workers forgo any further claim on the corporation's income. Even if one grants that the status of the stockholder in big corporations is coming more and more to resemble the status of bondholders, and that they are amply compensated for the risks involved in this type of ownership by a somewhat higher return on their investment than bondholders receive, workers would still not acquire on that score any title in commutative justice to surplus profits.

As for Professor Messner, his argument is based on the assumption that the workers have not in the past received a just wage. In this case, he says, they rightly claim a share in future surplus profits. But such a claim resembles more a demand for compensation due and not paid than a demand for a share of profits in the strict sense.

With those who seek to find in social justice a basis for worker participation in profits, I am more in sympathy. I have no difficulty in accepting the proposition that the stockholders of a corporation fortunate enough to have excess profits—in practice, the board of directors—have an obligation to use these earnings to promote the general welfare. I am also persuaded that in many cases this could most effectively be accomplished by sharing the profits with the workers, as is being done now by an impressive and growing number of U. S. companies. My problem here arises in conceding to workers the right to force stockholders, by the threat and use of economic force, not only to discharge *their* obligation in social justice, but to determine as well *how* they are to do it. This right, it seems to me, resides in the community, whose well-beng is the object of social justice, and can in practice be legitimately exercised only by the supreme authority in the community, namely, the state.

With Father Miller I agree that a union may raise the question of excess profits at the bargaining table and try as best it can to convince the company that the common good would be fostered by sharing them with the employes. But I cannot see that it has a moral right—a right based on the natural law—to insist that the owners live up to their obligation of using surplus profits to promote the general welfare, or that they discharge it by sharing profits rather than in some other way. I must conclude, therefore, that workers would violate the rights of private property were they to employ economic force to oblige their employer to practice profit sharing. I am not sure that Father Miller would dissent from this conclusion.

What chiefly influences me to take this stand is the parallel between worker demands for profit sharing and worker demands for sharing in management. When a decade ago some Catholics argued that workers had a natural right to share in management, the Holy See felt obliged to issue a warning. While reiterating the teaching of Pius XI that some modification of the wage contract through profit sharing and sharing in management and ownership was advisable and to be commended, the present Holy Father warned against any exaggeration that would infringe on the rights of owners. In an address to the Ninth Congress of the International Union of Catholic Employer Associations on May 7, 1949, the Pope rejected the opinion that all the employes of a business enterprise have a right to share in its ownership or profits on the ground that the enterprise is a society wherein relationships are governed by the norms of distributive justice. However much he favored liberalizing employer-employe relationships, he insisted that "the owner of the means of production, whoever he be—individual owner, workers' association or corporation—must always . . . retain control of his economic decisions."

ADVISABLE, NOT MANDATORY

A little more than a year later, on June 3, 1950, in a talk prepared for an audience of Catholic social scientists, the Holy Father returned to the question of co-management. Discussing the threat to personal responsibility in business inherent in some postwar proposals for reform, the Pope wrote:

> A similar danger is likewise present when it is claimed that the wage-earners in a given industry have the right to economic joint-management. . . .
> As a matter of fact, neither the nature of the labor contract nor the nature of the business enterprise in themselves admit necessarily of a right of this sort.

The Pope is obviously talking here of a natural right, and he is talking in the context of Pius XI's treatment of the alleged moral inadequacy of the wage contract. Like his predecessor, he hails the "usefulness" of what has been achieved by giving workers some share in ownership, or profits, or management; but if he isn't making it clear at the same time that workers have no strict right to these features of partnership, I am at a loss to say what he is talking about. In other words, I agree with what Canon Brys, chaplain of the Belgian Christian Labor Movement, wrote about the Holy Father's June 3, 1950 address in the September, 1950 issue of the information bulletin of the International Christian Social Union:

> The Holy Father has no intention of disapproving or discouraging what is being done to make the worker participate in the property, management or profits of the enterprise. But he does not want us to go beyond a *certain limit,* nor will he admit *as rights* certain claims that have nothing to do with the sphere of natural right.

With due regard, then, for the opinions of others, and not without some diffidence, I incline to the belief 1) that those who in the name of the owners control our big corporations have a duty to use surplus profits to promote the common good; 2) that one highly desirable way of doing this is to share the profits with all the corporation's employes; 3) that workers receiving a just wage have no strict right to share in profits, either in commutative or social justice; and 4) that while workers may raise the question of profit sharing at the bargaining table, they cannot demand profit sharing in the sense that they may strike to bring the employer around to their way of thinking.

The last proposition assumes, obviously, that the objective sought through strike action must, if it is to be a just cause, have a foundation of some kind in justice. It must be based on something more, that is, than convenience, propriety, desirability or equity.

That this is a large assumption I willingly grant. Even those, however, who refuse to restrict the right to strike in this way would probably concede that where justice is not involved, "the accompanying circumstances more readily tend to make the strike illegitimate."

A similar warning seems appropriate to strikes for objectives due in social justice. As one highly regarded moralist informed this writer: "It may well be that one could seldom verify the condition of proportionate reason if the sole object of the strike were to obtain a share in profits." (So far as the negotiations in the auto industry go, the issue, fortunately, is not likely to arise in these difficult terms. In the improbable event that a strike should follow a breakdown in bargaining, its sole object will almost certainly not be profit sharing.)

Finally, it should be noted that workers may acquire a legal right to demand profit sharing. This could happen if the Government broadened the matter of collective bargaining, which is now restricted to wages, hours and conditions of employment, to include profit sharing. In that event workers would also have a moral right to demand and strike for profit sharing.

Cases

Nebbia v. New York

The Nebbia case arose over the attempt of the State of New York to control the price and distribution of milk within the state. In 1933, the New York State Legislature passed legislation setting up a Milk Control Board empowered, in addition to other things, to fix both minimum and maximum retail milk prices for milk consumed off the premises where sold. Nebbia, a Rochester grocer, sold two quarts of milk and a five-cent loaf of bread for eighteen cents, whereas, at the time, the Board had set the price of milk at nine cents a quart.

New York state had in 1933, at the time of the establishment of the Milk Control Board, a long list of legislative enactments affecting the milk industry of the state, prompting Mr. Justice Roberts, who delivered the majority decision in the case, to comment that, "Save the conduct of the railroads, no business has been so thoroughly regimented and regulated by the State of New York as the milk industry."

Nebbia took his case to the Supreme Court after two unsuccessful appeals to lower courts. By a 5–4 majority the Court affirmed the finding against him.

MR. JUSTICE ROBERTS DELIVERED THE OPINION OF THE COURT

Under our form of government the use of property and the making of contracts are normally matters of private and not of public concern. The general rule is that both shall be free of governmental interference. But neither property rights nor contract rights are absolute; for government cannot exist if the citizen may at will use his property to the detriment of his fellows, or exercise his freedom of contract to work them harm. Equally fundamental with the private right is that of the public to regulate it in the common interest. . . .

The Fifth Amendment . . . and the Fourteenth, do not prohibit government regulation for the public welfare. They merely condition the exertion of the admitted power, by securing that the end shall be accomplished by methods

291 U.S. 502 (1934). This material was prepared by Professor James H. Patterson, Indiana University, while a member of the faculty of the School of Business, Northwestern University, for *Individual Freedoms and the Businessman*, edited by Professor John A. Larson. Copyright © 1959 by Northwestern University. Reproduced by permission.

consistent with due process . . . And the guaranty of due process . . . demands only that the law shall not be unreasonable, arbitrary, or capricious, and that the means selected shall have a real and substantial relation to the object sought to be attained.

We may as well say at once that the dairy industry is not, in the accepted sense of the phrase, a public utility. We think the appellant is also right in asserting that there is in this case no suggestion of any monopoly or monopolistic practice. It goes without saying that those engaged in the business are in no way dependent upon public grants or franchises for the privilege of conducting their activities. . . .

. . . The private character of a business does not necessarily remove it from the realm of regulation of charges or prices . . . It is clear that there is no closed class or category of business affected with a public interest, and the function of the courts in the application of the Fifth and Fourteenth Amendments is to determine in each case whether circumstances vindicate the challenged regulation as reasonable exertion of governmental authority or condemn it as arbitrary or discriminatory. There can be no doubt that upon proper occasion and by appropriate measures the state may regulate a business in any of its aspects, including the prices to be charged for the products or commodities it sells.

If the law-making body within its sphere of government concludes that the conditions or practices in an industry make unrestricted waste harmful to the public, threaten ultimately to cut off the supply of a commodity needed by the public, or portend the destruction of the industry itself, appropriate statutes passed in an honest effort to correct the threatened consequences may not be set aside because the regulation adopted fixes prices reasonably deemed by the legislature to be fair to those engaged in the industry and to the consuming public . . . Price control, like any other form of regulation, is unconstitutional only if arbitrary, discriminatory, or demonstrably irrelevant to the policy the legislature is free to adopt, and hence an unnecessary and unwarranted interference with individual liberty.

Tested by these considerations we find no basis in the due process clause of the Fourteenth Amendment for condemning the provisions of (the law) here drawn in question.

The judgment is   Affirmed.

SEPARATE (DISSENTING) OPINION OF MR. JUSTICE REYNOLDS

Regulation to prevent recognized evils in business has long been upheld as permissible legislative action. But fixation of the price at which "A," engaged in an ordinary business, may sell, in order to enable "B," a producer, to improve his condition, has not been regarded as within legislative power. This is not regulation, but management, control, dictation—it amounts to the deprivation of the fundamental right which one has to conduct his own affairs honestly and along customary lines. The argument advanced here would support general prescription of prices for farm products, groceries, shoes, clothing, all the necessities of modern civilization, as well as labor, when some legislature finds and declares such action advisable and for the public good.

But plainly, I think, this Court must have regard to the wisdom of the enactment . . . Unless we can affirm that the end proposed is proper and the means adopted have reasonable relation to it this action is unjustifiable.

The court below has not definitely affirmed this necessary relation; it has not attempted to indicate how higher charges at stores to impoverished customers when the output is excessive and sale prices by producers are unrestrained, can possibly increase receipts at the farm. The Legislative Committee pointed out as the obvious cause of decreased consumption, notwithstanding low prices, the consumers' reduced buying power. Higher store prices will not enlarge this power; nor will they decrease production. Low prices will bring less cows only after several years. The prime cause of the difficulties will remain. Demand at low prices becoming wholly insufficient, the proposed plan is to raise and fix higher minimum prices at stores and thereby aid the producer whose output and prices still remain unrestrained! . . . Better prices may follow but it is beyond reason to expect them as the consequen(ce) of that order.

Not only does the statute interfere arbitrarily with the rights of the little grocer to conduct his business according to standards long accepted—complete destruction may follow; but it takes away the liberty of twelve million consumers to buy a necessity of life in an open market. . . .

The Legislature cannot lawfully destroy guaranteed rights of one man with the prime purpose of enriching another, even if for the moment, this may seem advantageous to the public . . . All rights will be subject to the caprice of the hour; government by stable laws will pass.

The judgment of the court below should be reversed.

Mr. Justice Van Devanter, Mr. Justice Sutherland, and Mr. Justice Butler authorize me to say that they concur in this opinion.

QUESTIONS FOR DISCUSSION

1. What is the constitutional source of the regulatory powers which the states have attempted to exercise in these cases?

2. What is the constitutional basis for appeal to the courts, by businesses seeking to escape regulation?

3. What is meant by the statement that a business is "affected with a public interest"?

4. Do you note a progressive change in the Court's attitude toward the right of the state to regulate?

5. What economic ills was the regulation in each case probably designed to alleviate? Does the regulation in each seem "economically sound"? Does such soundness or lack of it have anything to do with the validity of the legislation?

6. In the Nebbia case, how important is the emergency to this decision? How far would the court permit regulation if this case were followed, as it has been?

Prairie Eye-Opener

Frank Whittaker spent a week in Brownridge, Alberta on business. During this time he read the daily edition of the *Prairie Eye-Opener* published in Sagitawa, a major city about fifty miles from Brownridge. This had been the first time he had had the opportunity of reading the *Prairie Eye-Opener* for several consecutive days and he was somewhat disturbed by some of its articles. In particular, there was a series on automobiles during this week which seemed more like advertising than news, though the articles carried no indication of being ads. Each one was given about seven or eight column inches. Typical headlines were:

> "Dual Lights Plymouth Standard"
> "Dodge Tail Fins Reduce Steering Effort"
> "1958 Ford Features Complete Styling Change"
> "Wider Look Featured in 1958 Studebaker"
> "New Type Engine Featured in GM Trucks."

Mr. Whittaker felt an obligation to write the publisher of the *Prairie Eye-Opener* and make the observation that the paper was offering as news what was, he felt, advertising. He believed that a newspaper had a responsibility to the public to present news. Advertising and editorial opinion, he felt, should be clearly marked and should be kept separate, though these were properly an important part of any paper.

Mr. Whittaker wondered if he should write a letter, what good it might do, and what form it should take.

Reprinted by the courtesy of Emmett Wallace. Copyright © 1958. All names, places, and dates are disguised. Cases are prepared for educational purposes. They typically represent actual administrative problems and situations, but not necessarily the most effective methods of dealing with such matters.

EXHIBIT 1

1958 Ford Features Complete Styling Change

The 1958 Ford car featuring major styling changes will go on display at four Sagitawa dealers Thursday. Dealers showing the new Ford are: Sagitawa Motors, Ottawa Avenue and Main Street, Dominion Motors, 2739 Manitoba Avenue, Prairie Motors, 720 Church Street, and Alberta Motors, 6929 Center Avenue.

In making the announcement, P. G. Willey, General Manager, Ford-Edsel Division, Ford Motor Company of Canada, Limited, pointed out that historically auto companies have made basic changes in their cars over three years. "But in the 1958 models, Ford has actually created basic design and engineering changes just a year after the new 1957 model," he said.

DIFFERENT LENGTHS

Demonstrating the change are 20 models on two separate wheel bases, the Fairlane and Fairlane 500 with overall lengths of 207 inches and the Custom, Custom 300 and station wagon covering 202 inches.

New 332 and 352 cubic inch displacement engines are the result of more than 25 years sales and Ford engineering leadership in the V-8 engines. They combine new highs of efficiency, durability and economy with the added time and convenience of quick service accessibility.

Also new will be air suspension, optional for Ford Fairlane, Fairlane 500's and station wagons with V-8 engines and automatic transmissions.

REPLACE SPRINGS

Air domes made of specially strengthened rubber, reinforced with steel sleeves, replace springs on each wheel. Air pressure inside the domes is supplied by a compressor and air storage tank and varies according to the weight of the passengers and luggage to keep the car at a constant height and optimum springing for a "boulevard" ride.

The external appearance of the new car features Ford's sculptured-in-metal treatment in which styling lines are moulded into the sheet metal.

The distinctive Ford '58 styling is emphasized in the massive, wrap around one-piece bumper with anodized aluminum grille, dual headlights and power flow hood.

New sheet metal treatment incorporates reducing front fenders, new roof with seven front rear flutes or grooves and trunk lid and rear quarter panel innovations.

Ford also introduced the newest and most modern overhead valve V-8 engines. The "332" has a torque rating at 340-360 foot pounds at 4600 r.p.m. and horsepower ranging from 240 with two-barrel carburetor to 265 with four-barrel carburetor. The "352" engine is rated at 395 foot pounds at 2800 r.p.m. and horsepower at 300.

The economical six is available for most models and the 292 V-8 engine is standard on some series.

The new engines feature completely machined, wide-type combustion chambers, larger cooler running valves, new carburetion and exhaust porting and direct flow intake for peak performance at all engine speeds.

Each engine is electronically mass balanced while running at operating speed under its own power.

Brownridge, Alta.
November 8, 1957

Mr. David Dale, Publisher
The Prairie Eye-Opener
Sagitawa, Alberta

Dear Mr. Dale:

You may recall that we met one day when I was visiting the office of Charles Ormsby, your production manager.

During the past week I have been visiting Brownridge. I have had the opportunity to read the Eye-Opener nightly. I am writing you because it seems to me that some of your "news" articles do a dis-service not only to the public but to yourselves.

I refer specifically to the series of announcements re: new 1958—model cars, e.g., Friday night's paper carries articles titled "New Type Engine Featured in GM Trucks" and "American Motors Offers 'All-New' 1958 Model." These are advertisements and should be so labelled. Too often newspapers headline announcements which are merely ads, but the very fact that they are not so labelled provides, perhaps, better readership. Your articles indicate a blatant misuse of the trust and responsibility you bear towards the public to give *news*. I believe that such misuse invites public control. Please don't.

Sincerely,
Frank Whittaker

cc: C. Ormsby
(written by hand)

Putnam, Alberta,
December 3, 1957

Mr. David Dale, Publisher,
The Prairie Eye-Opener,
Sagitawa, Alberta.

Dear Mr. Dale,

On November 8th I wrote you from Brownridge concerning certain advertisements which purported to be news. Perhaps this letter never reached you, so I am enclosing a copy.

Sincerely,
Frank Whittaker

Encl.

Office of the Publisher
The Prairie Eye-Opener
Sagitawa, Alberta
December 4, 1957

Mr. Frank Whittaker
Putnam, Alberta

Dear Sir:

In the absence of Mr. Dale from the city, I am acknowledging your letter of December 3. You will no doubt be hearing from Mr. Dale on his return to the office some time next week.

Very truly yours,
Harriet Goodyear
Secretary to Mr. Dale

Office of the Publisher
The Prairie Eye-Opener
Sagitawa, Alberta
December 9, 1957

Mr. Frank Whittaker
Putnam, Alberta

Dear Mr. Whittaker:

I decided to ignore your letter of November 8.

Yours very truly,
David Dale

Putnam, Alberta
19th December, 1957

Mr. Gordon Parker
COCO-TV
Sagitawa, Alberta

Dear Gordon:

When I was in Brownridge in November I had the opportunity of reading the Prairie Eye-Opener over a period of two weeks. I became somewhat perturbed by the distortion in the newspaper. I wrote David Dale by hand concerning a series of articles about the new automobiles. These purported to be news, but were unquestionably advertisements. A copy of my letter is enclosed, enclosure #1.

I did not hear from Mr. Dale for three weeks and therefore sent a follow up letter to which I received a response from his secretary per enclosure #2. I then received a note from Mr. Dale per enclosure #3.

I had shown my original letter to Scotty Ingram[1] who expressed an interest in this problem. Upon my return to Brownridge I showed him the complete correspondence and he suggested that this might be a proper subject for debate on TV.

This can, of course, be a hot potato, but I should like to make an offer to you that I will debate this matter with Mr. Dale on your station for a period of 15 or 30 minutes.

In actual fact, I doubt if Mr. Dale would accept such an offer but I should like to be able to make it. I find this situation shocking. Mr. Dale is in a position of public responsibility.

I should appreciate it if you would keep this matter confidential for the moment. Then, if you should be good enough to grant me TV time, I can make the offer directly to him.

Sincerely,
Frank

F. Whittaker
Encls.
[1] A television executive.

COCO-TV
Sagitawa, Alberta
December 30, 1957

Mr. Frank Whittaker
Putnam, Alberta

Dear Frank:

It was very nice to hear from you again. I read your enclosures with interest and must say that I was amazed at Mr. Dale's reply to your letter.

I am sure that he would not accept your suggestion and I do not feel that we are in a position to make the offer since the Prairie Eye-Opener is a substantial part owner of the television station.

The only suggestion might be to discuss it with one or two appropriate people in Toronto next week. If I find an opportunity to put across your point of view effectively, I may do this. Otherwise, I haven't and won't mention it to anyone.

Sincerely,
Gordon Parker

U.S. Steel and the 1962 Price Increase

On March 31, 1962, congratulations were extended to the steelworkers and to the steel industry for their "early and responsible settlement," well in advance of the June 30 deadline, and the earliest settlement in the quarter-century relationship between the industry and the union. This early settlement contrasted with the 1959 negotiations, which included a 116-day strike. President Kennedy in a telephone message to David J. McDonald, President of the United Steelworkers, said:

> When I appealed to the union and to the industry to commence negotiations early in order to avert an inventory buildup—with consequences detrimental to the nation at large as well as to the industry and its employees—I did so with firm confidence that the steelworkers union and the industry would measure up to their responsibility to serve the national interest.
>
> You have done so through free collective bargaining, without the pressure of a deadline or under the threat of a strike. This is indeed industrial statesmanship of the highest order.
>
> The settlement you have announced is both forward looking and responsible. It is obviously noninflationary and should provide a solid base for continued price stability.

An industry statement said the new benefits would increase employment cost by about 2½ per cent during the first year. That compares with an

Copyright © 1962, by Northwestern University. Reprinted with permission.

average annual increase of 3½ to 3¾ per cent under the contract negotiated in 1960, and with 8 per cent a year in the period between 1940 and 1960. R. Conrad Cooper of U. S. Steel, chief industry negotiator, said that the settlement cost did not fall wholly "within the limits of anticipated gains in productive efficiency." The industry statement estimated the cost of the settlement exceeded by about fifty per cent its productivity gain. Cooper added that the accord represented real progress in the development of voluntary collective bargaining in the steel industry.

STEPS IN THE NEGOTIATION

The 1960 steel contract provided for several wage increases, the last of which was scheduled for October 1, 1961. Prior to that date, executives of major steel companies were hinting at a general rise in steel prices to coincide with that wage increase. On September 6, 1961, President Kennedy wrote the heads of twelve steel companies expressing his concern with stability of steel prices. Mr. Kennedy wrote: "The steel industry, by absorbing increases in employment costs since 1958 has demonstrated a will to halt the price-wage spiral in steel. If the industry were now to forego a price increase, it would enter collective bargaining negotiations next spring with a record of three-and-a-half years of price stability. It would clearly then be the turn of the labor representatives to limit wage demands to a level consistent with continued price stability. The moral position of the steel industry next spring and its claim to the support of public opinion will be strengthened by the exercise of price restraint now." He eventually received replies from all twelve companies. The reply from Roger Blough for U. S. Steel denied that the cause of inflation would be found in the levels of steel prices and profits. Blough's letter noted that the President's letter "does raise questions of such serious import, including the future of freedom of marketing, that I feel impelled to include a word on that score also, for whatever value it may be." He wrote of "the admittedly hazardous task which your economic advisers have undertaken in forecasting steel industry profits at varying rates of operation. . . . Moreover, it might reasonably appear to some—as frankly, it does to me—that they seem to be assuming the role of informal price setters for steel—psychological or otherwise."

In January, 1962, President Kennedy urged an early agreement to avoid the upsetting uncertainty of a possible strike, and especially the speculation which precedes the strike deadline, such as heavy buying by steel users. At his news conference on January 15, Mr. Kennedy said that Secretary of Labor, Arthur J. Goldberg, would be available "for whatever good offices he may perform." In reply to a question at the conference, the President stressed his desire for a settlement which would not force an increase in steel prices, i.e., the cost of the wage increase should not exceed the savings resulting from increased productivity. The President's economic report to the Congress released the following week went so far as to urge that average productivity gains for the general economy be used as guidelines for wage settlements. The report of the Council of Economic Advisers recommended that the overall increase in output per man-hour of 2½ to 3 per cent a year be taken as the measuring rod for higher wages and fringe benefits in any industry. If efficiency of a specific industry has been going up faster, this would call for price reductions. (On January 27, 1962, *The New York Times* estimated that if the Council's productivity gauge were to be applied, a package settlement of about 10 cents an hour "would meet the test of equity this year.")

One of the strongest statements about the role of government in collective bargaining was Secretary Goldberg's "definitive" statement of the Kennedy Administration's labor-management philosophy to the Executive Club of Chicago, on February 23. Goldberg said that in the past, when government officials assisted in collective bargaining, their only aim had been to achieve a settlement. But today, in the light of the nation's commitments at home and abroad, government and private mediators must increasingly provide guidelines to the parties in labor disputes. Such guidelines should insure "right settlements" that take into account the public interest as well as the interests of the parties. Goldberg said he did not mean that government should impose the terms of a settlement, but he claimed that "everyone expects the government to assert and define the national interest."

Anonymous steel industry sources took exception to the Goldberg position. "The moment the government goes beyond being a policeman or offering its service as mediator, it has an impact on the outcome of collective bargaining and converts it from an economic to a political process. From a broad philosophical standpoint, most businessmen feel that in a competitive system you serve the national interest in pursuing your private interest. Government exertion of its influence prevents the system from operating as it should. From a practical standpoint, labor represents more votes than businessmen, so businessmen feel that any settlement that is a political settlement is likely to be more pro-labor than pro-management."

George Meany, President of the American Federation of Labor and Congress of Industrial Organizations, also brusquely rejected Secretary Goldberg's "definitive" statement. Mr. Meany said: "I don't agree with it. The government's role is mediation, conciliation or anything else it can do to help industrial peace. When he says the role of the government is to assert the national interest, he is infringing on the rights of free people and free society, and I don't agree with him whatsoever. This is a step in the direction of saying the federal government should tell either or both sides what to do, and I don't agree with that."

Support for Secretary Goldberg came from Joseph L. Block, chairman of Inland Steel, who was at the speaker's table when Goldberg spoke. (Block is a member of President Kennedy's twenty-one man Advisory Committee on Labor-Management Policy.) "I heartily endorse Mr. Goldberg's concept. It is the government's function to elucidate the national objectives, to point out what the national needs are. Those guidelines should be taken into account in collective bargaining. A contest of strength where the stronger side wins doesn't prove a thing. Each side has to represent its own interest, but neither side must be unmindful of the needs of the nation. Who else can point out those needs but the government?"

A. A. Berle, Jr. also supported the Goldberg view and the work of the Council of Economic Advisors, contending that there is an unwritten "social contract" holding both sides to certain responsibilities as well as granting both the privileges that make this power possible, and that under this social contract the government can—and perhaps must—intervene when economic power in private hands threatens the economic community of the United States. Berle sees the "emerging relationship" as this: "When the wage and price levels markedly affect, or threaten to upset, the economy of the country, the government claims power to step in on behalf of the 'public interest.' " The difficulty is in telling what the words 'public interest' mean. Berle sees the Council of Economic Advisors as the future key agency here, for "its views on acceptable wage and price levels are, and should be, extremely important."

> The council can advise the President—and through his authority advise both big labor and big corporations—about where the peril points are. It can advise the President when the government should intervene to modify private decisions based on power, either of labor to tie up plants by strike, or of management to set prices by administration. It can and indeed does keep a close check on these allegedly private decisions, taken in company offices or union headquarters. It could communicate to either or both when it sees a peril point approaching. And it can advise the President when intervention is needed in the "public interest"—that is, when employment, production and purchasing power under free competitive enterprise are likely to be weakened, when inflation becomes a danger, when economic stability generally is likely to be threatened.[1]

U. S. Steel's annual report, released March 20, 1962, pointed to its holding of the price line in 1961. Mr. Blough's statement to stockholders said that in 1961 "the inexorable influences of the market place in our competitive free enterprise system continued to dictate the course of U. S. Steel's pricing actions." No reference to pricing plans for 1962 appeared in the report, but Blough indicated deep concern about competition and slack demand. Robert C. Tyson, chairman of U. S. Steel's finance committee, called "unsatisfactory" the idea that productivity is a criterion for setting wages. "The notion appears to be that if an enterprise or industry learns how to produce more efficiently, then it can pay more to its employees without raising its product's prices. If we can do this, it is proper to force us to do so." Mr. Tyson said this theory

[1] A. A. Berle, Jr., "Unwritten Constitution for Our Economy," *The New York Times Magazine*, April 29, 1962.

is unsatisfactory because if more money is paid to those with jobs, there is less available for rehiring those workers without jobs. Unemployment becomes chronic and the incentives for creating new jobs are stultified. Productivity, he went on, is useful as a method of describing economic facts, rather than as a measure for determining wage rates. It indicates only that a price increase or widespread unemployment must result if the average wage level rises faster than productivity. "No increase in employment costs in excess of the nation's long-term rate of productivity increase can be regarded as noninflationary." (At this stage in negotiations, the industry was holding out for employment cost increases not exceeding two per cent annually, coinciding with the annual productivity increase as figured by the companies for recent years.)

STEEL PRICES GO UP—AND COME DOWN AGAIN

U. S. Steel signed the labor contract agreed upon at the end of March on April 5. This contract provided for costs (not in direct wages but in other benefits) which were subsequently estimated at 10.6 cents an hour, or a total of $159,000,000 a year for the industry, with some 520,000 workers. On April 10, the company announced an average increase of $6 a ton in the price of steel, accompanying the announcement with a statement signed by Leslie B. Worthington, president, explaining this increase:

> Since our last over-all adjustment in the summer of 1958, the level of steel prices has not been increased but, if anything, has declined somewhat. This situation, in the face of steadily mounting production costs which have included four increases in steel-worker wages and benefits prior to the end of last year, has been due to the competitive pressures from domestic producers and from imports of foreign-made steel as well as from other materials which are used as substitutes for steel.
> The severity of these competitive pressures has not diminished; and to their influence may be attributed the fact that the partial catch-up adjustment announced today is substantially less than the cost increases which have already occurred since 1958, without taking into consideration the additional costs which will result from the new labor agreements which become effective next July 1.
> Nevertheless, taking into account all the competitive factors affecting the market for steel, we have reluctantly concluded that a modest price adjustment can no longer be avoided in the light of the production cost increases that have made it necessary.
> In the three years since the end of 1958, United States Steel has spent $1,185,000,000 for modernization and replacement of facilities and for the development of new sources of raw materials. Internally, there were only two sources from which this money could come: depreciation and reinvested profit. Depreciation in these years amounted to $610,000,000; and reinvested profit, $187,000,000—or, together, only about two-thirds of

the total sum required. So after using all the income available from operations, we had to make up the difference of $388,000,000 out of borrowings from the public. In fact, during the period 1958-1961, we have actually borrowed a total of $800,000,000 to provide for present and future needs. And this must be repaid out of profits that have not yet been earned, and will not be earned for some years to come.

During these three years, moreover, United States Steel's profits have dropped to the lowest levels since 1952; while reinvested profit—which is all the profit there is to be plowed back in the business after payment of dividends—has declined from $115,000,000 in 1958 to less than $3,000,000 last year. Yet the dividend rate has not been increased in more than five years, although there have been seven general increases in employment costs during this interval.

In all, we have experienced a net increase of about 6 per cent in our costs over this period despite cost reductions which have been effected through the use of new, more efficient facilities, improved techniques and better raw materials. Compared with this net increase of 6 per cent, the price increase of 3½ per cent announced today clearly falls considerably short of the amount needed to restore even the cost-price relationship in the low production year of 1958.

In reaching this conclusion, we have given full consideration, of course, to the fact that any price increase which comes, as this does, at a time when foreign-made steels are already underselling ours in a number of product lines, will add—temporarily, at least—to the competitive difficulties which we are now experiencing. But the present price level cannot be maintained any longer when our problems are viewed in long-range perspective. For the long pull a strong, profitable company is the only insurance that formidable competition can be met and that the necessary lower costs to meet that competition will be assured.

Only through profits can a company improve its competitive potential through better equipment and through expanded research. On this latter phase we are constantly developing lighter, stronger steels which—ton for ton—will do more work and go much farther than the steels that were previously available on the market. They thus give the customer considerably more value per dollar of cost. As more and more of these new steels come from our laboratories, therefore, our ability to compete should steadily improve. But the development of new steels can only be supported by profits or the hope for profits.

The financial resources supporting continuous research and resultant new products as well as those supporting new equipment, are therefore vital in this competitive situation—vital not alone to the company and its employees, but to our international balance of payments, the value of our dollar, and to the strength and security of the nation as well.[2]

President Kennedy was informed of U. S. Steel's price increase at a meeting requested by Roger Blough at 5:45 p.m. on April 10. Mr. Kennedy spoke at

2 *The New York Times,* April 11, 1962.

his news conference the next day in "a tone of cold anger," reading a long indictment of the steel company's actions:

> The simultaneous and identical actions of United States Steel and other leading steel corporations increasing steel prices by some $6 a ton constitute a wholly unjustfiable and irresponsible defiance of the public interest.
>
> In this serious hour in our nation's history when we are confronted with grave crises in Berlin and Southeast Asia, when we are devoting our energies to economic recovery and stability, when we are asking Reservists to leave their homes and families months on end and servicemen to risk their lives—and four were killed in the last two days in Vietnam—and asking union members to hold down their wage requests, at a time when restraint and sacrifice are being asked of every citizen, the American people will find it hard, as I do, to accept a situation in which a tiny handful of steel executives, whose pursuit of private power and profit exceeds their sense of public responsibility, can show such utter contempt for the interest of 185,000,000 Americans.
>
> If this rise in the cost of steel is imitated by the rest of the industry, instead of rescinded, it would increase the cost of homes, autos, appliances and most other items for every American family. It would increase the cost of machinery and tools to every American businessman and farmer. It would seriously handicap our efforts to prevent an inflationary spiral from eating up the pensions of our older citizens and our new gains in purchasing power. It would add, Defense Secretary McNamara informed me this morning, an estimated $1,000,000,000 to the cost of our defenses at a time when every dollar is needed for national security and other purposes.
>
> It will make it more difficult for American goods to compete in foreign markets, more difficult to withstand competition from foreign imports and thus more difficult to improve our balance-of-payments position and stem the flow of gold. And it is necessary to stem it for our national security if we're going to pay for our security commitments abroad.
>
> And it would surely handicap our efforts to induce other industries and unions to adopt responsible price and wage policies.
>
> The facts of the matter are that there is no justification for an increase in steel prices.
>
> The recent settlement between the industry and the union, which does not even take place until July 1, was widely acknowledged to be noninflationary, and the whole purpose and effect of this Administration's role, which both parties understood, was to achieve an agreement which would make unnecessary any increases in prices.
>
> Steel output per man is rising so fast that labor costs per tone of steel can actually be expected to decline in the next twelve months. And, in fact, the Acting Commissioner of the Bureau of Labor Statistics informed me this morning that, and I quote, "employment costs per unit of steel output in 1961 were essentially the same as they were in 1958." The cost of major raw materials—steel scrap and coal—has also been declining.

And for an industry which has been generally operating at less than two-thirds of capacity, its profit rate has been normal and can be expected to rise sharply this year in view of the reduction in idle capacity. Their lot has been easier than that of a 100,000 steelworkers thrown out of work in the last three years.

The industry's cash dividends have exceeded $600,000,000 in each of the last five years; and earnings in the first quarter of this year were estimated in the Feb. 28 Wall Street Journal to be among the highest in history.

In short, at a time when they could be exploring how more efficiency and better prices could be obtained, reducing prices in this industry in recognition of lower costs, their unusually good labor contract, their foreign competition and ther increase in production and profits which are coming this year, a few gigantic corporations have decided to increase prices in ruthless disregard of their public responsibility.

Price and wage decisions in this country, except for a very limited restriction in the case of monopolies and national emergency strikes, are and ought to be freely and privately made. But the American people have a right to expect, in return for that freedom, a higher sense of business responsibility for the welfare of their country than has been shown in the last two days.

Sometime ago I asked each American to consider what he would do for his country, and I asked the steel companies. In the last twenty-four hours we had their answer.

Question: Is the position of the Administration that it believed it had the assurance of the steel industry at the time of the recent labor agreement that it would not increase prices?

Answer: We did not ask either side to give us any assurance, because there is a very proper limitation to the power of the Government in this free economy.

All we did in our meetings was to emphasize how important it was that . . . there be price stability. . . and to persuade the union to begin to bargain early and to make an agreement which would not affect prices. . . .

We never at any time asked for a commitment in regard to the terms— of the agreement from either Mr. McDonald or Mr. Blough, because, in our opinion, that is—would be passing over the line of propriety. . . .[3]

A great many actions were taken by governmental agencies during the 72 hours between U. S. steel's announcement of its increase on the afternoon of April 10 and its rescinding of this increase at 5:28 p.m. on April 13. In addition to the governmental actions, three companies made no move to increase prices in line with U. S. Steel's announcement—Inland, Armco, and Kaiser. After consulting with Joseph L. Block, who was vacationing in Japan, the directors of Inland issued the following statement on the morning of the 13th:

Inland Steel Co. today announced that it will not make any adjustment

---

[3] *The New York Times,* April 12, 1962.

in existing prices of its steel mill products at this time. The company has long recognized the need for improvements in steel industry profits in relation to capital invested. It believes this condition, which does exist today, will ultimately have to be corrected. Nevertheless, in full recognition of the national interest and competitive factors, the company feels that it is untimely to make an upward adjustment.

The following week, after the prices had come back down, the joint Senate-House Republican Leadership issued a statement summarizing nine governmental actions used by the White House, and deploring their use:

1. The Federal Trade Commission publicly suggested the possibility of collusion, announced an immediate investigation and talked of $2,000 a day penalties.

2. The Justice Department spoke threateningly of antitrust violations and ordered an immediate investigation.

3. Treasury Department offcials indicated they were at once reconsidering the planned increase in depreciation rates for steel.

4. The Internal Revenue Service was reported making a menacing move toward U. S. Steel's incentive benefits plan for its executives.

5. The Senate Antitrust and Monopoly subcommittee began subpoenaing records from twelve steel companies, returnable May 14.

6. The House Antitrust subcommittee announced an immediate investigation, with hearings opening May 2.

7. The Justice Department announced it was ordering a grand jury investigation.

8. The Department of Defense, seemingly ignoring laws requiring competitive bidding, publicly announced it was shifting steel purchases to companies that had not increased prices, and other Government agencies were directed to do likewise.

9. The F.B.I. began routing newspaper men out of bed at 3:00 a.m. on Thursday, April 12, in line with President Kennedy's press conference assertion that "we are investigating" a statement attributed to a steel company official in the newspapers.

Taken cumulatively these nine actions amount to a display of naked political power never seen before in this nation.

Taken singly these nine actions are punitive, heavy-handed and frightening.

We condone nothing in the actions of the steel companies except their right to make an economic judgment without massive retaliation by the Federal Government.

Temporarily President Kennedy may have won a political victory, but at the cost of doing violence to the fundamental precepts of a free society.

This nation must realize that we have passed within the shadow of police state methods. We hope that we never again step into those dark regions whatever the controversy of the moment, be it economic or political.[4]

James Reston, writing of the steel-price dispute, concludes that the reason for all the friction lies in a little known fact:

> This is that the Kennedy Administration is dissatisfied with the labor-management collective bargaining process and has set out to change it. The process, as the Administration sees it, is now having a profound effect on the nation's economic growth, on its ability to achieve full employment, to compete against foreign goods, to sustain the heavy burden of arms and foreign aid, and is therefore too serious a business to be left to labor and management alone.
>
> The President is insisting not only that paralyzing labor-management disagreements, but even labor-management agreements at the cost of higher noncompetitive prices, are not in the national interest and that something, therefore, must be done to strengthen the public's voice in the collective bargaining process. That the Administration does not quite know yet what that "something" should be is clear enough from its savage lurch into the U. S. Steel price dispute.
>
> The movement now is toward a series of experiments in tripartite discussions, with the Government taking a more active part in asserting the natonal interest. As the President sees it, this is merely the common sense of the new industrial, scientific and commercial revolution of the world. But as Roger Blough sees it, the President is moving toward the substitution of a managed for a free economy. This is why feelings have been running so high on both sides.[5]

WHAT COMES NEXT?

The new wage contract went into effect on July 1 with no change in steel prices. Both Kennedy and Blough were at considerable pains to explain their actions further and to demonstrate, after a further private meeting on April 17, that both sides were seeking much the same things. President Kennedy told the U. S. Chamber of Commerce, on April 30, that his administration was seeking "an economic climate in which an expanding concept of business and labor responsibility, an increasing awareness of world commerce and the free forces of domestic competition, will keep the price level stable and keep the government out of price-setting." He acknowledged that "many of you" wanted much more liberal tax allowances than the administration was planning to grant for writing off the costs of modernizing plant and equipment, but explained that greater allowances would cut the government's revenue too much, and would hamper efforts to balance the federal budget. It was

[4] *The New York Times,* April 20, 1962.
[5] James Reston, "Why Not A Summit Meeting on Wages and Prices?", *The New York Times,* April 18, 1962.

reported that the reception of the President's talk was cool, in contrast to the talk of Richard Wagner, outgoing president of the Chamber, who was interrupted by applause several times. Mr. Wagner said that business earnings are inadequate "because too much is siphoned off" for government spending and for excessive wages. "Business leadership must make certain that both business and labor remain free to make their decisions without government intervention." Departing from his prepared address, Mr. Wagner said he was "very much comforted" by the President's attention to tax write-offs, but suggested that the loss-of-revenue argument was not convincing.

When Roger Blough faced his stockholders on May 7, he was greeted by a round of applause after his initial comment: "It has been sort of a warm spring." The next wave of applause was triggered by the comment that "I do not believe the public interest can ever be served by hostility between government and business." He said that government and business had to gain a better grasp of each other's needs in the national interest, an interest that could never be served by direct or indirect peacetime price controls. After the unsuccessful effort to raise prices, the most important need was to build "a better understanding of the economic problems and of the profit needs of the entire business community." Mr. Blough said he was encouraged by President Kennedy's Chamber of Commerce address, since Kennedy had said that if business did not earn a fair profit, the government could not earn sufficient revenues to cover its outlays. U. S. Steel's own profits had slipped from $304,000,000 in 1960 to $190,000,000 in 1961. Later, in answer to a stockholder's question, Blough added, "In Washington we have had some very interesting indications that this whole incident has acted as a catalyst to thinking" on the profit-squeeze plight of industry.

When U. S. Steel released its report of better first quarter 1962 earnings, Chairman Blough had said at a news conference that at the moment the company did not contemplate any price changes in the future. He did add that the company would do everything possible to improve earnings, but that the government could help by revising depreciation regulations. He made it clear that the company's capital spending plans were definitely under a "damper" because it could not raise prices. The following day, April 25, when Inland Steel reported its first quarter earnings, which were also up, Chairman Joseph L. Block welcomed limited government intervention to protect economic stability. Mr. Block did assail direct price-setting and said that this and other administrations had used the steel industry as "a whipping boy." When asked whether Kennedy had overstepped his bounds in his blitz against a steel price increase, Mr. Block said:

> I think any president is well within his rights in pointing out the national interest with regards to costs and prices or anything that affects the welfare of the people. The methods used, however, are subject to individual criticism. I for one, don't think that F.B.I. men and subpoenas and grand juries should be part of these methods.

Block also revealed that his concern intended, if financial and market conditions allowed, to go ahead with an expansion program previously set.

The day after Chairman Blough had spoken to U. S. Steel's stockholders, President Kennedy addressed the convention of the United Automobile Workers, and called on labor to exercise restraint and responsibility in its bargaining demands:

> This Administration has not undertaken and will not undertake to fix prices and wages in this economy. We have no intention of intervening in every labor dispute. We are neither able nor willing to substitute our judgment for the judgment of those who sit at the local bargaining tables across the country.
>
> We can suggest guidelines for the economy but we cannot fix a single pattern for every class and every industry. We can and must under the responsibilities given to us by the Constitution, and by statute and by necessity, point out the national interest and, where applicable, we can and must and will enforce the law on restraints of trade and national emergencies.
>
> But we possess and seek no powers of compulsion, and must rely primarily on the voluntary efforts of labor and management to make sure that their sense of public responsibility, their recognition of this dangerous and hazardous world, full of challenge and opportunity, that in this kind of world fulfilling our role that the national interest is preserved. . . .
>
> This country has the world's highest real wages and living standard simply because our output per man-hour is the highest in the world. No financial slight of hand can raise real wages and profits faster than productivity without defeating their own purpose through inflation.
>
> And I need not tell the members of this union, with its constructive history and policies, that unjustified wage demands which require price increases and then other demands and then other price increases are equally as contrary to the national interest as unjustified profit demands which require price increases. But when productivity has been raised by the skills of better management, the efficiency of labor and the modernization financed by investors, all three groups can reap the rewards of that productivity and still pass lower prices on to the consumer.

When the American Iron and Steel Institute met late in May, Chairman Blough again spoke in conciliatory terms about the need for better government-business relations. The next day, on May 24, Allison R. Maxwell, Jr., President of Pittsburgh Steel, gave a sometimes bitter speech about the "route to socialism" which "drew a standing ovation from some 1000 steel industry executives and technical personnel." This response suggests that there was more resentment smoldering in the steel industry. Mr. Maxwell, like Mr. Blough, called for cooperation with government, despite the "effrontery" of some administration comments questioning the patriotism of steel leaders. He said he was disturbed when U. S. Steel and others were treated as "transgressors." "We may decry specific power tactics, but these are merely symptoms of an issue far more dangerous. It would be an error to dismiss these actions as merely anti-business, when the real issue is that 'Big Government' is anti-individual rights. The obvious direction of all its policies is toward a form of socialism in which the pretense of private property is retained, while in fact prices, wages, production and distribution are dictated by bureaucrats."

As July 1 approached, the steel companies were continuing to stress the squeeze on capital fund sources, due to continued rising-cost pressure on profits, and to cash-generating depreciation charges that fall short of equipment replacement costs. Although the industry was pursuing cost-reduction programs and expanding research activities, much hope was expressed about a reform of "woofully inadequate" depreciation laws. Some authorities have suggested that capital expansion funds could be raised through new sales of stock or debt issues. Most steel men contend, however, that a low profit potential is hardly an inducement for further investments. Avery C. Adams, Chairman of Jones and Loughlin, said, "If the Kennedy Administration really wants to assure us that this is a pro-business administration, the most electrifying statement would be that the administration would work for giving our country the best depreciation policies in the world, instead of the worst." The contention is that with shorter depreciation periods, the cash set aside for depreciation, or the wear and tear of old equipment, would tend to match more closely the capital outlays considered necessary for replacing, expanding, and modernizing industrial plants. This would encourage more capital spending.

Industry insiders still expect a price rise eventually, barring the "miracle" of a national business boom rich enough to ease the cost squeeze that has narrowed steel profits. Steel is reported to have begun a major selling campaign to convince President Kennedy's key aides of the case for a price rise. Stress has been laid on the fact that steel profits have "backslid" while taxes, wages and other major cost ingredients have been advancing. Steel, it is emphasized, needs profits to modernize and expand plant and equipment for a growing economy in world competition. Often quoted is Labor Secretary Goldberg's estimate that some $90 billion of U. S. industrial plant and equipment is obsolete today. But whether President Kennedy will see it steel's way next time is the industry's major headache. A humorous sign in one steel vice president's office says in large letters: "I miss Ike." In much smaller printing it adds: "I even miss Harry."

Bibliography

A. The Evolution of Capitalism

Gregory, G. "Capitalists of Communism," *Duns Review* (April 1968) pp. 42–44.

Keezer, Dexter M. "The Score Against Capitalism," *Harvard Business Micro Review* (September–October, 1968), pp. 158–174.

Meany, G. "Labor Looks At Capitalism," *American Federationist* (December 1966), pp. 1–4.

Monsen, R. Joseph, Jr. "Can Anyone Explain Capitalism?" *Saturday Review* (December 14, 1963), pp. 13–15, 26.

Romney, G. "We Need a New Capitalism in America," *Nation's Business* (July 1966), pp. 34–35.

Stigler, G. J. "Private Enterprise and Public Intelligence" *Duns Review* (October 1966), pp. 17+.

Walton, C. C. "Critics of Business: Stonethrowers and Gravediggers," *Columbia Journal of World Business* (Fall 1966), pp. 25–37.

B. Business, Competition and Government

Austin, Robert W. "Who Has the Responsibility for Social Change—Business or Government?" *Harvard Business Review* (July–August, 1965), pp. 45–52.

Blake, Harlan M. and William K. Jones, "In Defense of Antitrust," *Fortune* (August 1964) pp. 135, 171–172, 174–176.

Bork, Robert H. and Ward S. Bowman, Jr. "The Case in Antitrust," *Fortune* (December, 1963), pp. 138–140, 192, 197–201.

Kintner, Earl W. "How Much Control Can Business Endure?" *Journal of Marketing* (July, 1961), pp. 1–6.

Marcus, Sumner. "New Weapons Against Bigness," *Harvard Business Review* (January–February, 1965), pp. 100–108.

McGuire, Joseph W. "How Much Freedom Does Business Really Want?" *Business Horizons* (Summer 1965), pp. 73–78.

Ways, Max. "Antitrust in an Era of Radical Change," *Fortune* (March 1966), pp. 128–131, 214, 216, 221–225.

C. Profits and Profit Sharing

Bedolis, R. A. "The Kaiser Sharing Plan: 2nd Year," *Conference Board Record* (July 1965), pp. 37–39.

Childs, J. J. "Profit Goals for Management," *Financial Executive* (February 1964), pp. 13–17.

"Corporation Profits: 'Economic Bulwark' " *Financial World* (August 10, 1966), pp. 3–4.

"Have Corporations A Higher Duty Than Profits?"*Fortune* (August 1960), pp. 108–109, 146–153.

Konopa, Leonard J. "Is Profit A Dirty Word?" *Banking* (April 1964), pp. 112–118.

Schofield, J. J. "Is Profit Bad?" *Controller* (September 1962), p. 434.

Speagle, Richard E. and Hugh R. Chace. "The Corporate Profit Equation," *Harvard Business Review* (March 1963), pp. 116–127.

Vickers, D. "Profitability and Reinvestment Rates," *Journal of Business* (October 1966), p. 17.

"What Is A Fair Profit?" *Duns Review* (April 1964), p.31.

Weisman, I. "I Believe in Profit Sharing," *Office Executive* (July 1961), p. 29.

PART TWO

Business and
Its Publics

As business operates in a free enterprise society, it forms interdependent relationships with specific groups. In terms of society at large, the general public is the regulator of the system and of the individual firms composing it. The actions of businessmen individually and collectively are constantly appraised by society and the various institutions operating within it. Good community relations have always been important to the individual business firm, and for the larger business firm, the community may well become the state, the nation, if not the international community.

Business deals with many publics, and in these relationships oftentimes "wears many hats." That is, business tends to assume a different posture toward various interest groups while developing a coherent public image that reflects its objectives and policies. The publics to whom business most frequently addresses itself are its stockholders, customers, related business firms with whom it deals, employees, influential interest groups, organizations and government agencies at the local, state and national level. In dealing with these various publics business must perform a vast array of voluntary tasks such as giving financial assistance and managerial leadership to civic drives and programs.

A. Public Relations and the Corporate Image

It has been contended that business often loses as much as it gains in performing its various public relations functions. Many large-scale firms have engaged in public relations activities on an extensive basis for many years and for all their efforts have often been accused of misuse of this function by creating and perpetuating artificial images to attract public support. In "The Price of Corporate Vanity" [6] David Finn enumerates the dangers inherent in the misuse of public relations techniques. Frequently, a new corporate image is a substitute for much needed corporate change. Public relations is used as a panacea for corporate ills, and false images are created to satisfy management's desire for popularity. The author recommends that the genuine opinions and actions of management should stand as the true corporate image, and he suggests that the most important function of the public relations expert is to "help businessmen themselves respond constructively to critical opinion."

Business is perennially concerned with a variety of interest and pressure groups in society because of their influence upon the environment in which the corporation must operate. In order to deal effectively with these groups business has attempted to develop a complex and integrated corporate image. This image provides a means of maintaining uniformity and consistency in those basic company practices and policies which affect the success of the firm in the eyes of its publics. In "The Corporate Image in Public Relations" [7] Richard Eells advocates the development of a many-faceted corporate image that would relate the corporation to its social environment while serving corporate objectives. This would entail the assignment of priorities to corporate goals and the formulation of policies to insure their achievement. To accomplish this task, management must identify and establish a hierarcy of important—or "key"—publics and identify the variety of roles, interests and pressures they represent. The function of defining the corporate image then becomes a process of formulating policies and statements that effectively interrelate corporate objectives and key publics.

Public relations experts often advise that the corporate image represent the philosophy, character and personality of the corporation. By-and-large the real image of the corporation will be determined by its standard business practices, not by official speeches, or published statements on company policy. However, this does not diminish the value of company policies to the process of decision making. Company policies exist as control guides over delegated decisions within the firm and provide managerial control over actions and decisions made by individuals within each department throughout the organization.

A composite of the various publics to whom a company may respond is presented in the Heartland Gas Company case. In this case, a public utility systematically relates its overall company objectives to the programs and activities of each department, and each component to its various publics. This case illustrates the necessity of formulating corporate policies to insure consistent action among departments in order to create an integrated corporate image.

B. Corporate Philanthropy

Today's community organizations frequently enlist the support and expertise of business managers. Conversely, businessmen often volunteer their services in support of community projects. As an integral part of the community, business management has a legitimate place in defining and supporting community goals. Business managers have a unique contribution to make to community projects by providing managerial know how and experienced leadership.

Community needs are articulated in an ever-increasing number of ways. Among the paramount appeals made to business by the community are requests for financial contributions to public and private programs relating to community welfare. Recently community solicitation for funds are increasing as the number of sponsoring organizations and programs grow. While the legality of corporate philanthropy has already been resolved in court, the question of business giving or philanthropy as a legitimate and advisable corporate act is debatable. Criteria for selecting recipients, the determination of appropriate amounts and types of gifts, and the relationship of corporate giving to overall corporate objectives and policies must be resolved by corporate managers.

Starting from the premise that philanthropy is a normal business function, Harold R. Bowen in "Charity and the Corporation" [8] provides some basic principles for resolving these issues. He emphasizes the interdependence of the corporation and society and, therein, the legitimacy of corporate giving, and attempts to classify corporate donations as gifts, business expenses and informal taxes. In making corporate donations, Bowen points out that business must carefully weigh its obligation to society, the financial progress of the corporation and the interests of its stockholders. He argues that the single most compelling reason for corporate giving is the protection and preservation of pluralism in our society. If the private sectors of our economy in such areas as education, welfare and the arts are to survive, they must depend upon private contributions. "Without private philanthropy," says Bowen, "the entire load would be shifted to government, with a corresponding centralization of power, reduction in imaginative variation, limitation on experiment, and avoidance of risk." If we are to avoid a monolithic society in which government is responsible for all social needs, private institutions, such as the corporation, must continue to give increasing financial support.

Contrary to Bowen's concept of philanthropy, Richard Eells in "A Philosophy for Corporate Giving" [9] contends that corporate giving must be directly related to corporate objectives. He argues that responsible managers must provide a sound rationale for donative decisions, and he recommends that professional, donative management follow a "prudential" theory of corporate giving. He rejects the concept that corporate giving be based solely on philanthropic principles and argues that good business practice—or prudential decision making—guide managers in their donative policies. By relating financial contributions to the long-term goals and profits of the business, business can then more effectively justify these contributions to stockholders. Eells recommends that each donative proposal be considered in the light of specific company objectives.

The Hanley Engineering Corporation case provides a complex example of the practical problems involved in corporate, donative decision making. The relationship of a community adult education program to the long-range goals of the corporation as well as the influence of a personal friend conducting the fund drive are factors that must be considered. The priority of different public appeals made to the corporation for donations and the ability of the corporation to commit itself to future donations must also be carefully weighed in the decision to support the drive. These questions require an explicit and complete corporate policy that can be applied to all community appeals. If a policy is not formulated, the company will be subject to inconsistencies in making donative decisions in the future.

In conclusion, the variety of requests and demands from the many publics require business to define an array of corporate policies for handling these demands consistently and equitably over time. These policies represent the many facets of the corporate personality, character, and eventually its philosophy. In fact, the basic set of policy statements of most corporations serve as their philosophies. These policies will provide the means of recognizing the many publics and evaluating the significance of their claims in relation to corporate objectives.

A. Public Relations and The Corporate Image

The Price of Corporate Vanity
6

David Finn

The experience of American business in recent decades has clearly established the fruitfulness of making a good corporate impression. But it has also become clear that corporations (and perhaps governments and other human institutions) can go overboard in the effort to make other people like them and that this can do considerable harm. The exaggerated prominence which the word "image" has achieved in our vocabulary suggests that we may be going too far in our practical concern for external appearances and that sound business considerations (as well as human, moral, and cultural considerations) warrant a re-evaluation of the basic approach to public relations as practiced in our society.

DANGERS CREATED

I believe that three types of danger may result from an overweening interest in one's corporate image:

1. When facing business reverses, management can deceive itself about its real weaknesses by believing that the only thing wrong is a bad public image. This deception has emerged as a national tendency in government and has provoked criticism from those who feel that we should be less concerned about whether we "project *an image* of vitality" to the world and more concerned with making a straightforward examination of just what our vitality as a people and as a culture actually is.

Some economists are similarly upset by the idea that a business recession can be reversed by slogans aimed at building positive attitudes rather than by concrete measures to alleviate the sources of economic distress. As one journalist said recently, we are beginning to behave like fat

Reprinted with permission from the *Harvard Business Review* (July-August 1961), pp. 135–143. Copyright © 1961 by the President and Fellows of Harvard College; all rights reserved.

old ladies primping ourselves in front of the mirror. We are attracted by the Idea that we can look beautiful at all times whether we really are beautiful or not.

2. We are also misled if we define wisdom as that policy which wins the widest approval rather than that policy which creates the highest values. Such a view holds that management should do things because they are popular, not because they are right. This can make us a people without principle, without morality, without faith in ourselves—a people whose primary gratification is an approving pat on the back. Businessmen become, then, not a force for progress in society, but a mirror reflecting existing tastes and deflecting any effort to work toward a better world.

.3. Our passion to establish a good public posture may lead us into a third danger. We may destroy the process of free public debate which is both the most prized characteristic of a democratic society and the essential mechanism by which a competitive business economy can work and prosper. A free press is one in which editors may write as they please and criticize even the most powerful groups in society. To the extent that business interests seek a favorable press through special pressures or inducements, they deny themselves the value of constructive public criticism of their affairs. What is more, are not scientific research, educational policy, and theological judgments most fruitful when they are directed by the experts in the field rather than by vested interests seeking third-party endorsement for their points of view? How much do we damage the foundations for our long-term success as a culture by seeking the immediate public support we believe necessary for the success of our individual enterprises?

These three areas of risk necessitate a careful re-examination of the means by which public relations practitioners are trying to help corporations deal with their public images. It is important to learn in what ways these efforts may be harmful or helpful.

THE FALLACIOUS IMAGE

On the face of it, the basic notion of public relations image-making does not seem potentially dangerous to the corporation. To the contrary, it seems plausible that the idea should be a great help in making it easier to do business with the multiplicity of companies operating in a mass society. The reasoning goes as follows:

1. By definition, images are impressions and mental pictures about things.

2. If management has publicly stated its corporate philosophy and expressed a consistent point of view in its trademark, its advertising, and its public service works, the public will have the feeling that it knows what the company stands for.

3. If people like what the company stands for, then they may choose to do business with it rather than its competitors.

4. This seems particularly true when it is impossible to know at firsthand the management running a company or the manner in which its products are made; impressions or images are useful substitutes for concrete knowledge.

Significantly, no one individual claims to have originated the phrase "corporate image." Industrial designers introduced the idea of "corporate identity" programs just a few years ago. At the same time, opinion researchers were working on "image studies," and public relations practitioners were trying to cope with the problems of what they called "faceless corporations." When the phrase "corporate image" appeared, it was quickly adopted as describing exactly what they all had in mind. The need for some unified approach to developing company reputation seemed to have been answered by the coining of a phrase.

Has the need really been answered? Or have we just deluded ourselves?

MIXING-BOWL APPROACH

Some executives believe a corporate image can be created for anybody who wants one by mixing together a standard set of ingredients without regard to what any particular company really is like. Such executives will ask their public relations adviser to recommend a good image and then get to work to create it. The inexperienced or insensitive practitioner proceeds to do so "by the numbers." He produces a trademark that may not express the corporate personality at all, yet which is thought to qualify because it is a compelling design by an outstanding artist. He produces articles and speeches which tend to sound alike because they are ghostwritten by the same person, but which are excused if they have some kind of theme and get exposure. One public relations program can look frighteningly like any other, and images may differ only in the extent of the "treatment" that companies have received.

But here is the rub. If an image fails to be individual and distinctive, it will have no relation to reality, i.e., the actual corporate personality. It will be only a fabrication. As such, it negates one major premise of its existence—that an offered image can make up for the public's lack of firsthand knowledge of the corporation. It exploits, rather than compensates for, the public's lack of direct contact and represents an attempt to make people think what the corporation wants them to think, rather than to give them a grasp of what the corporation actually is like.

More basic still, how valid is the notion that there *is* such a thing as an actual corporate personality? While certain characteristics may be attributed to present and past managements, it is a grave mistake to view a corporation as a monolithic entity. All its employees do not think alike about any issue. The idea that a single pattern of thought differentiates one entire company from another is an unforgivable presumption. It suggests that a corporation is or can be made an amalgam of stereotyped human beings, and does not consist of a group of individuals thinking for themselves.

Finally, as this corporate haberdashery mushrooms, one must ask: Is the whole idea of image-making nonsense? Can any kind of public relations activity really create or change images in people's minds? The research done to date on this question is inconclusive, and much of it suggests that efforts to persuade the mass only reinforce the opinions of those already persuaded. Most opinions, it seems, are formed out of a multiplicity of influences, and no one image-making scheme can be so powerful as to overcome all contrary opinions just by the sheer brilliance of its technical virtuosity. The best one can do (practically, as well as idealistically) may be to get the truth as one sees it on public record and let images be hanged!

IMPULSE TO DISGUISE

Recently a professor of philosophy at a large university reviewed the work that was done by a public relations firm for one of its clients over three years. He examined all correspondence as well as other written material produced as part of the program. Then he led a series of discussions with ten members of the staff who had worked for this client. He attempted to determine if there was any difference between what everybody thought they had been doing and what they actually had been doing.

The stated goals of the campaign were: (a) to establish a nonprofit educational foundation through which an industry association could attempt to combat negative attitudes toward its product and, through this effort, (b) prevent restrictive legislation, and (c) help build sales. In the course of the discussions, the group became aware that:

> The client actually did not represent the industry but only a few individual members of the industry who happened to be especially sensitive to public opinion.

> There was no evidence that the public's opinion was negative, or at least negative in such a way as to affect sales or legislation; anxiety about public opinion seemed to be entirely subjective.

> The foundation was not truly educational and, while it did not make money, its true purpose was the profit of the industry. The program could have served its purpose just as well by using a perfectly straightforward commercial name like "association" instead of assuming an educational guise.

> Legislative interest seemed to be based on a technical evaluation of the tax levies imposed on the product. This was a question which deserved legitimate public debate. Everybody in the public relations firm assumed uncritically that the client's arguments were valid, and no real effort was made to check the facts presented by the opposition.

Published comments on the fine values of the product were made in the press as if they were the opinion of the editors, when actually the stories were written by the public relations specialists in the employ of the companies making the product. The comments would have been just as effective if their source had been openly identified.

Nobody really believed that the program could succeed in changing attitudes.

Everybody agreed that the real, though unspoken, value of the program probably was to provide the client companies with the subjective satisfaction of seeing a positive evaluation of their product made in public.

Thus, this campaign was carried out through a technique of disguise which might have made sense in terms of the supposed goals but was silly and unnecessary in terms of the real goals. The activities of the client, the PR practitioners, and the press were all characterized by a series of disguises which were both misleading and unnecessary. This made the whole campaign one of play acting rather than truthtelling, when telling the truth seemed to be the real objective of the campaign.

PLACEBOS FOR MISMANAGEMENT

When business is bad, or at least does not live up to expectations, management tries to do everything it can to find the cause of the trouble and provide the remedy. On such occasions, however, many executives seem to have a weakness for patent medicines. They tend to look for ready-made solutions as described in the latest issues of the "how to" trade publications. These cures often work, partly because of the mental therapy involved in taking any medicine, and partly because the formulas contain some ingredients which are of real value. But sometimes they can do great harm. If the ailment is serious, something drastic may be required to save the business; and wasting time on faddist measures may prove fatal.

Image-making can be one of the more dangerous types of management panaceas. It gives the false impression that a fundamental change is being made, for creating a new image of oneself seems deceptively like creating a new self. This looks like the ultimate step in solving the most difficult of management problems—the deficiency of management itself. And yet of course it is not. Management needs to do more than change its image to change itself. Recognizing its blind spots and learning useful new skills are essentials.

Trying to project a new or improved face for oneself in such situations is like undergoing plastic surgery to correct a basic personality disorder. For a while everything seems beautiful, but the remedy is only skin-deep. A Pagliacci suffers behind the smiling mask.

Businessmen are particularly inclined to mask their shortcomings. They tend to measure their achievements (to the extent that they can measure them at all) in terms of the popular notions of success. Since the purposes of business are served by promoting and catering to mass appeal, it is natural for the businessman to respond to them in his own life. And then, when something goes wrong, he may feel he can cope with it if he keeps up the appearance of success. From this it is a short step to believing that the appearance of success *is* success.

There are several classic situations in which this tendency shows itself, and most experienced public relations practitioners have encountered conditions similar to those that follow.

INCOMPETENCE AT THE HELM

First and most common, there is the case of the inadequate company president who thinks himself better than he really is. Inadequate leadership radiates from this kind of top executive like spokes in a wheel.

If the hub is weak, the company's public relations will be weak and no amount of professional ingenuity can make it otherwise. But if, in addition, the president considers himself a really dynamic manager and thinks the fault is elsewhere, he is prone to believe that public relations can solve his problems. He suspects that the only thing wrong is the "spirit" of the company or its "look" to others, and that the arts of persuasion can change all this. The more strongly he believes this, the less likely he is to face the truth. If he is lucky (and his company unlucky), he can go on for years believing that in the long run and with the right kind of public relations, his fate will change.

Is it an exaggeration to suggest that public relations is ill-used or harmful in such a case? If the practitioner is at all sensitive, he feels, at best, that his tactics are diversionary and, at worst, that he is perpetuating a lie. A sensitive PR man realizes that the president who purrs at the minor acclaim he receives should instead be mourning his failures. There is no future in such a publicity assignment or in any firm that employs public relations under such conditions.

IMAGINARY TEAM

A contrasting case is that of the strong company president who wants to build public confidence in his second- and third-level management because too many people believe he is running a one-man company. Usually people believe this because it is true, but the president once again does not want to see the truth. He hires good executives to work under him to disprove these accusations and asks his public relations specialists to spotlight the depth of the management team.

The appointment of the executives is itself a public relations move, calculated more to influence opinion than to strengthen management. What the president does not do, of course, is actually delegate authority, so the public relations effort turns out to be unavailing. A continuous turnover of executives is proof that the president does not take the idea of management in depth seriously, and that he is trying to use public relations as a cover-up for a weakness that he will never overcome. All this is bad not only because the public relations does not work but also because everybody involved is clearly making a fool of himself in acting out the farce.

THE DYING PRODUCT

What is perhaps even more serious is the use of public relations to create fanfare for a product that is losing its market because of basic deficiencies in design, quality, pricing, or marketing. Any PR man knows that his skill cannot be of value unless the product has *natural appeal* (a quality that no one knows quite how to analyze, but that is clearly a necessary ingredient for success), can stand up to competition, and has an effective selling machinery behind it.

Many industries have run into major problems because of a deterioration of, say, their dealer setup through uncontrollable price cutting, the inroads of other more profitable items, or lack of effective sales help from manufacturers. But too often management decides to sponsor a public relations program to reintroduce the element of glamour in the product instead of correcting the structural defects. Everybody works hard and perhaps some glamour does get created, but sales continue to slump. Those who realize what is happening get the feeling that the industry "is fiddling while Rome burns"—making lovely images while the market is falling apart instead of spending its energy first to put out the fire. If the situation is not calamitous, both can be done simultaneously. However, to consider public relations alone as a cure for so basic an illness is self-deception.

THE FAILING COMPANY

Another classic situation is the case of the company which has a bad financial record and counts on public relations to make it look good. But if the record is bad, can any amount of hullabaloo change it? To be sure, there are frequently special circumstances which may put the failures in a better light, and it is perfectly legitimate to attempt to highlight these circumstances. Yet sometimes companies go much further than this. They convince themselves that because of their great dreams for the future, the record should be virtually ignored. The public relations assignment then is to try to make the dreams look real. This, unfortunately, may succeed, and then management, the stockholders, and the business community all believe what is actually no more than a fairy tale. When the truth comes out, the company may be too far gone to save.

In all such cases as those mentioned, the conscientious public relations practitioner abhors the sense of working on a mask rather than on reality. He knows that management is dealing with mirages, not images, and that this cannot do any good. He feels obliged to help the executives look inward rather than out-ward and see what is really wrong, rather than try to create the impression that everything is right. If he is successful, he finds himself acting like a con-sultant to management on management rather than on public relations; his hope is that self-knowledge and self-improvement will take place so that a more natural and positive form of public relations can evolve.

MIRRORS INSTEAD OF IDEAS

Even when business is good, too much concern for a company's public im-age can sap the company's energy, weaken its leadership, and ultimately destroy its capacity for self-generation of new ideas and new directions. Most execu-tives who expose themselves to this danger are unaware of what they are do-ing; they feel that they are sensibly examining their profiles in a mirror and making adjustments which can further improve their business. But it is unfor-tunately too easy to step over the line and begin to run a company as one thinks others want it run rather than following one's own best judgments as a manager.

COURAGE OR POPULARITY?

Philosophers and critics in many fields have for some time been complain-ing about the excessive desire to be liked which seems to characterize many administrative tendencies of our time. One prominent educator has maintained for several years that public relations specialists should be kept out of all board meetings of universities lest the courage to support unpopular ideas be under-mined. His favorite comment is that any new idea which immediately wins majority support is years behind its time. Good administrators must dare to be wrong, and the willingness to be unpopular is a test of this strength.

Again, statesmen have become increasingly concerned with government officials who are preoccupied with the image they project. Americans have been told many times that they have the wrong idea of public relations when they point out the negative attitudes that a particular move might provoke. Action should be based on inner conviction, not on a concern for public sentiment.

In marketing, the battle has raged even more fiercely. Should automobiles be designed according to public taste or according to principles of safety and good engineering? Should T.V. programming give the people what they want (the programs that get the highest rating) or what is good in terms of deeper cultural values? Should foods be sold which are flavored and colored to appeal to the largest number of people, or which have the best natural taste and high-est nutritional value?

Similar dilemmas face management in other areas of decision making. To mention a few:

How should humanitarian interests in employees and the community be balanced against high production costs when a particular plant becomes unprofitable?

Should a generous community relations program be maintained because of public pressure in spite of poor business conditions?

Should a missile be fired in a way that will gain the most public applause or in a way that can most advance the state of knowledge—especially when the latter choice might result in what would publicly be called a failure?

A REASONABLE BALANCE

The wisest approach to these questions involves striking a balance between conflicting interests. Making products that will not sell, broadcasting programs no one will listen to, or firing missiles in a way that loses public confidence and Congressional appropriations is impractical. On the other hand, concentrating exclusively on the most popular products, programs, and missile shots can also lead to public stagnation.

Long-range values (e.g., possibilities for sales tomorrow as well as for today) and the satisfaction of personal ideas (e.g., producing a product of which one can be proud) are needs which cannot be met with popularity ratings. Seeing ourselves in the mirror may at times help us work toward these goals, but we must not worry too much about outward appearances. Albert Einstein never chose to dress up, even for the most formal occasions, and there are corporations which are also successful even though they don't particularly care about their public image. What we look like is important only when it expresses how we feel and what we are.

The "dress up" programs of corporations can well be evaluated on this basis: Do they represent what management feels is most important or are they slick masquerades designed only to entice public interest? This standard should be applied, I believe, across the board—to the architectural design of company offices and of plants; to the graphic design of trademarks, letterheads, and packages; to the design of products; to speeches of top executives; to company house organs; to advertisements; and, finally, to corporate policy.

THE ULTIMATE CONCEIT

It has long been argued that healthy, vigorous criticism is an important spur to creativity. The personal histories of many artists bear this out. Critics train themselves to be brutally honest in their reactions rather than to be tactful and politely complimentary. It is a widely held proposition that criticism is often a more effective means of provoking creative effort than applause, and that failure and frustration often breed success.

A corollary to this proposition is that success breeds failure. An artist who achieves acclaim and recognition may find the spark which drives him to greatness extinguished by the pleasures of flattery. Accomplishment in life seems to be a product of inner tension, and circumstances that make one self-satisfied can easily dissolve the basis for initiative, drive, and, above all, the daring to be original.

This is hardly a universal truth, but it applies quite widely, I think, to businessmen as well as to artists (though the criteria are quite different for judging if success has taken its toll). For the executive, the test is not in the works, as with the artist, but in the manner and the attitude with which work *is done*. Also, the businessman may not suffer personally from his overdose of success, but almost certainly his firm, and society, will have to bear the burden of any conceit that comes with his power.

In the world of art, the critic is ever present. Thus, the too-successful artist can be cut down to size when the quality of his work diminishes. But the businessman has no such watchman. If he loses touch with reality through an over-inflated ego, no one is there to cut *him* down to size. His employees and business associates may bewail his exaggerated sense of importance and his pretension to infallibility, but there is little they can do about it.

Can the business press serve the businessman as the critic serves the artist? Management fights this possibility with all its strength. In fact, as I have suggested, the assignment of the public relations specialist often is to see to it that negative criticism is kept out of the press, thus warding off the jolt that would bring the executive to his senses. Management's *ultimate* conceit is to imagine that it should be above public criticism, that its power and self-sufficiency give it the right to utilize a technique which is designed to banish unpleasant controversy from executive life.

This self-destructive conceit operates on many levels. Let us look at some examples now.

SELF-GLORIFICATION

A legitimate function of public relations is to help an executive take a position in his industry or in public life which is in keeping with his background, his ability, and his ambitions. The same is true about helping companies become better known for achievements of which they can be justly proud. But too often the public relations approach to such an undertaking is out of proportion to the facts. The businessman is encouraged to look at his achievements as events unequaled in human history and to feel that his public relations goals will be reached only when the rest of the world looks at his success with equal reverence.

Fortunately, most businessmen have better sense than to believe that all the praise that comes their way is entirely justified. But there *are* those who insist

on looking at themselves as Horatio Algers. And there *are* public relations practitioners who think it is part of their job to encourage this hallucination, or
even (in some cases) to foist it on an executive who would otherwise have
better sense. And there are *many* who, while not so extreme in their views, are
sometimes influenced by these attitudes.

It is unfortunate for the business community, and, in the long run, even for
the public relations practitioner and his client, that such programs are ever
launched. Few people are as impressed with personal glorification as the subject of it, and the sad truth—as every experienced public relations man knows
—is that the impression doesn't last very long. The executive is pleased momentarily, but then he discovers that he is the same person he always was and is
disappointed. If he has the "bug," as the saying goes, he wants to feel a little
more than mortal through his public relations program. Thus he always wants
more, hoping that the next honor he gets will do the trick. And, in the process,
his delusion gets greater, his capacity to manage the business wisely and with a
sense of balance diminishes, and, sooner or later, he becomes frustrated.

SELF-RIGHTEOUSNESS

Occasionally in the life of any corporation something happens which leads
the press to report unfavorably on something dear to the heart of management.
This may be in connection with labor problems, selling methods, a proxy fight,
product failures, or the successes of a competitive product. If it is bad enough,
the public relations specialist may get a spanking for letting such a "distortion
of the facts" get into print. The battalions then are brought out (advertising
pressure, meetings with publishers, counterattacks against "the other side,"
etc.) to turn back the tide.

How amazing it is that management cannot realize the self-deception involved in the notion that it alone has "all the facts;" and that if reporters would
only learn to "get their facts straight," the problem of an unfavorable press
would be solved. Unhappily the sad truth is that sometimes management is
wrong and deserves to be brought to account by a responsible press. There is
no reason why this should be done with kid gloves. The press has a right (some
think an obligation) to speak its mind if it has the damning facts. These facts
admittedly may not be enough for a final judgment. However, the purpose of a
critical press is not to assess corporate values for the "Good Book," but rather
to be an instrument by which an alert society can make progress more rapidly
and fruitfully.

A sturdy, self-confident management responds to criticism with action, not
with public relations, when it is under attack. This does not mean that the public relations specialist is not consulted, but it does mean that his job is to help
management learn and respond to criticism rather than fight like a bully or hide
behind a smoke screen.

SELF-PERPETUATION

Many executives have a keen interest in public affairs and feel rewarded in their public relations efforts if they gain the opportunity to express their opinions forcefully or even play a strategic part in obtaining social action which they support. There is no reason to hide the connection between one's business interests and the social, economic, or political position one publicly supports. The integrated individual who holds the same beliefs in both his business and his private life is certainly better off than the individual who leads a double life. Expressing one's convictions effectively and working toward a better society as a busnessman and as a citizen lead to personal fulfillment.

But this impulse can go awry if an executive loses the capacity to look at opposing opinions as being just as worthy of a public hearing as his own. If he denies that public argument should be a fair battle between competitive ideas and may the best man win, he finds himself waging a no-holds-barred crusade in which he believes management's point of view is a holy cause. All ideas which serve to perpetuate the business are right; all values which may be in conflict with these ideas must be sacrificed.

This, of course, is shameful and entirely inconsistent with the principles of democracy. People are entitled to think that peace is more important than the perpetuation of business, that public health is more important than the perpetuation of business, and that freedom of opportunity is more important than the perpetuation of business. I do not mean that business interests are opposed to these worthy causes, but the fact is that they *may* be (or that harried managers may *think* they are).

To discover the truth, the market place must provide a free and effective exchange of *all* points of view. Every time business interests become intolerant of the opposition and, through public relations efforts, fight a secret or underhanded battle to stifle public expression of contrary convictions, they strike a blow at the foundations of the system which permits their own enterprises to thrive. At a time when the system of free enterprise is facing its most serious challenge, this is indeed a dangerous course to follow.

CONCLUSION

Now, more than two decades after the dramatic definition of public relations as "the engineering of consent" was conceived[1]—and subsequently discredited—the time has come for the self-destructive, anti-social tendencies of public relations to be separated from the constructive and useful contributions it can make.

[1] Edward L. Bernays, "The Engineering of Consent," *The Annals of the American Academy of Political and Social Science: Communication and Social Action*, March 1947, p. 113.

PR practitioners know that mass persuasion through some elaborate form of brainwashing is an illusion, primarily for the reasons Abraham Lincoln made famous and which still hold true. But practitioners also have learned that self-promotion has important limitations; it cannot take precedence over the natural processes by which society corrects and improves itself in a dynamic culture. The main instrument of those natural processes is free and independent criticism, the very institution which public relations so often seems bent on destroying. It is not the job of public relations to secure public support for a cause any more than its function is to mold or evolve public opinion. Its purpose instead is to make management's opinion public and to present the case for causes that the managers believe in.

CONSTRUCTIVE PROMOTION

The destructive tendencies of public relations are a product of vanity in business. This conceit leads to false images which deceive no one, but dissipate the energy and dull the talent to manage well. Public relations has no business promoting illusions. Its business should be to help the businessman gain the kind of personal satisfaction from his work that stimulates the drive to greater achievement.

Artificiality, disguise, subterfuge, pressuring, manipulation—all these can play a part in public relations if it is employed by businessmen whose power and success have gone to their heads. How can these tendencies be checked? Not by moralizing, for this leads people in the business to think that "our" kind of public relations is always right, and that the transgressions are only committed by "the rascals," whoever they may be! And not by self-restraint, for this is not in the nature of men with strong promotional instincts.

What *is* vitally needed is a strengthening of all those institutions which have a potential for criticizing business or even for fighting actively against destructive business interests. These critics include editors who sometimes find it difficult to cope with pressures from the companies which they write about, scientists and scholars who may feel impelled to tread carefully on subjects of interest to their industrial sponsors, and government officials and legislators who are aways conscious of the commercial interests of their constituents. If these groups were stronger, the job of the public relations practitioners would be to make straightforward appeals to the independent judgment of "third parties," and to help businessmen themselves respond constructively to critical opinion. What I am saying, in other words, is that the constructive role of public relations cannot be secured by good will, but only by the effective workings of a healthy democratic society.

DEVELOPING CRITICISM

The best way in which a strong institution of criticism can be developed is through education in the specialized schools which train the critics (particularly the journalists), the businessmen, and the public relations practitioners. Cooperative efforts by these schools can help clarify what the most effective relationships should be among those in each field. There is need for workshops in which students practice reacting to opposition, and seminars which explore mutual responsibilities in a world of conflicting ideas and interests.

Since many successful men in these fields do not graduate from the schools of their specialty, some means should also be found to create a mature and sophisticated understanding of business-community relationships in general colleges and universities. The primitive concept of "the public" as a receptacle for all sentimental notions about life must be dispelled. Every educated individual must learn that whenever he expresses an opinion in public, he *is* the public. His primary obligation as a citizen is to make sure he is expressing his own opinion and not that of some others who are trying to use him for their own purposes. If he decides to support their cause, fine; if not, he must have the courage to speak out against them. And all those who accept the democratic idea must learn to hold this independence inviolable.

Most important, businessmen must accept the fact that free, vigorous, constructive criticism helps improve the course of human enterprise. They must recognize that the job of public relations should be to further this process, not impede it. Only in this way can the professional practice of public relations avoid becoming a corrupting influence in our society and instead become a force for continuous social betterment by performing the useful task of giving public expression to dynamic leadership.

The Corporate Image in Public Relations
Richard Eells

7

Despite huge dollar outlays for corporate public relations, many public-relations programs designed to serve long-range corporate goals fall far short of the mark. Usually the basic reason is that corporate managers tend to think of public relations as a peripheral matter—rather than a major function of management. They do this because they fail to understand that the way in which a corporation relates itself to society is vital to its existence.

Copyright © 1959 by The Regents of the University of California. Reprinted from the *California Management Review* (Summer 1959), pp. 15–23, by permission of The Regents.

The recognition of public relations as a major *function* of management, along with such well-established functions as engineering, manufacturing marketing, and finance, is fairly recent. As a unique kind of work, public relations has become specialized both as to personnel and as to major staff and operating units. In the past, unlike specialists in other functions, public-relations specialists often have had no exclusive claim on the kind of work they performed. Today their responsibilities cover specific areas which have begun to be defined by a special literature and special skill and techniques.

BROAD CONCEPT OF PUBLIC RELATIONS

The purpose of this article is to examine certain problems which the public-relations function poses for management and to suggest approaches to their resolution. Basic to this discussion is a broad concept of public relations. From the viewpoint of the board and executive management, who must conduct the corporation's affairs as more than just a profitable business operation, a broad concept of public relationships is indispensable. The institutional character of the concern, its long-range goals, its essential role in the society that nourishes it, its contributions to many different groups which, in turn, contribute to its welfare—all these are compelling reasons for thoughtful inquiry into the public-relations function of the twentieth-century American corporation.

By public relations I mean the communication of the corporate image to key groups, both inside and outside the corporation, for two purposes: (1) to relate the corporation to its social environs, and (2) to serve the corporate objectives. This is much more than publicity through the press, radio, and television, although this is certainly a valid, if limited purpose in itself. This broad definition of public relations has many implications, of course; but two in particular have special significance for the subsequent discussion.

The first is that in order to "relate the corporation to its social environs," public-relations work must be reciprocal. A company should listen as much as it talks—perhaps more so. When the company limits itself to *sending* messages, it is engaging in but one phase of the communication process.[1] For communication means also that messages are received and responded to, and that the responses get back to the original sender, who adjusts further messages in light

---

[1] See James G. Miller, "Toward a General Theory for the Behavioral Sciences," in L. D. White (ed.), *The State of the Social Sciences* (Chicago: University of Chicago Press, 1956), pp. 29–65, on the "diffusion function" and "information transfer"; Colin Cherry, " 'Communication Theory'—and Human Behavior," in Ayer, Haldane, *et al.*, note (1) above; B. L. Smith, H. D. Lasswell and R. D. Casey, *Propaganda, Communication and Public Opinion: A Comprehensive Reference Guide* (Princeton: Princeton University Press, 1946), with four essays on the science of mass communication; and Warren Weaver, "Recent Contributions to the Mathematical Theory of Communication," in C. E. Shannon and W. Weaver, *The Mathematical Theory of Communication* (Urbana, Illinois: University of Illinois Press, 1949).

of these responses. Moreover, this listening needs to be continuous and systematic since both the audience responses and the media are constantly changing as a result of social and technological dynamics.

Even though a company can demonstrate a near-total recall of its messages through opinion surveys, it may not be getting its true message across. Moreover, aside from the practical necessity of knowing how its specific messages have been received, the corporation's image of itself as a social institution depends in large part upon two-way communication, as will be shown later in this paper. For the time being, however, suffice it to say that it is an egregious error on the part of management to assume that it is "adequate" communication to achieve the apparent conversion of the listener.

The second implication is that a company's public-relations program must do more than relate the organization to its social environs; it must serve the corporate objectives. In order to do this, management must define the corporation's own broad economic and political goals as concretely as possible. Thus, a broad concept of public relations must unfold in a two-step process:

1. Identifying the *real* corporate goals in their order of priority; and

2. Translating these goals into effective policies and programs that will communicate and relate the corporation to the Greater Society in terms of these goals.

Without these two steps, taken sequentially, public-relations work will inevitably continue to be either haphazard, or in accordance with preconceived personal notions of corporate public-relations managers, or of external public-relations agencies.

There are many possible ways of stating a company's objectives.[2] When well done, the objectives will take into account all the major groups of people— or "publics"—with which a company carries on relations, and the major purposes of its relationships with those publics.

Public-relations and executive managers should keep in mind, however, that the published objectives of a company will never reflect all of the goals and values of the corporation as an institution nor of its management as human beings. For example, the goals of influence and strength are never explicitly mentioned objectives. These, however, are objectives of every going concern as basic as are wealth, well-being, skill, enlightenment, respect, rectitude, and affection. (This list of goals, incidentally, is representative of the goals that men hold universally, though of course with considerable variation in priority from person to person, place to place, and from one point of time to another.)

For every business organization, then, a key purpose should be to translate corporate goals into realistic public-relations policies that successfully project the desired corporate image to all the company's publics.

[2] See Stewart Thompson, *Management Creeds and Philosophies* (New York: American Management Association, 1958).

DEFINING THE CORPORATE IMAGE

One major problem in projecting a favorable and consistent corporate image is the difficulty corporate managers themselves have in perceiving the corporation in terms of twentieth-century social beliefs, expectations, and promises. Thus the image they themselves have and the image they project is anything but clear and meaningful. Frequently the managers' inability to see themselves and their company as people on the outside see them, compounds the difficulty.

Each manager sees his corporation in terms of his own "operational code," which includes his system of values (i.e., what he wants, what he believes is good, and what he wants to achieve). More importantly for his view of the corporation, his code includes how he sees the world in which his company operates. Unfortunately, as Herbert Simon points out, "The limit of human understanding of complex social structures leads human beings to construct simplified maps (i.e., theories or models) of the social system in which they are acting, and to behave as though the maps were the reality."[3]

The complex social structure, of which one's company is a part, cannot be seen or felt directly in all of its implications; the manager must rely upon inherited maps, models, and theories. From these, the manager forms his own image of the corporation as a social institution. Some of the maps, and thus the corporate image in the managerial mind, are exceedingly realistic and usable for short excursions into the immediate corporate environment and for specific functional tasks, such as marketing a product or recruiting equity capital. For the wider-ranging journeys which public relations entails, the maps may be disastrously misleading. Long-term planning for the company and assessment of the social, political, and economic trends of the human environment require models different from those managers are likely to have at their disposal.

For example, the notion that the "proper" relationship between the corporation and its socio-political environment is one of laissez-faire, as defined in classical economics, has long persisted. Such models have permeated the literature which businessmen were taught to respect in their college courses. Today, these models are probably more widely accepted among corporate executives than the more recent and more realistic models proposed by contemporary economic theorists who deal with changed conditions, both in public and in business administration.

Many policy-makers have inherited and try to apply time-bound concepts not only of the nation-state and of public government, but also of private enterprise itself. This makes for unrealistic and often inconsistent perception of the corporation on management's part; and, since the policies of management affect the public's image of the corporation, it is not surprising to find that the corporate image held by the corporation's key publics may also be

---

[3] Herbert A. Simon, "Comments on the Theory of Organizations," *American Political Science Review*, Vol. 46, No. 4, December, 1952, p. 1135.

confused. Their image of business is confused because it mirrors inconsistencies in the minds and behavior of the men who manage the business enterprise.

For example, the attitude "no other world but our company" may lead to *company policies* opposed to *national policies* of tariff abatement, even though such national policies may make for firmer alliances with countries oriented toward the West and nations still uncommitted in the world struggle. In the same vein of internal inconsistencies, there are those who claim that the sole and exclusive purpose of the corporation is economic, so that management is apparently obliged to maximize profits to the exclusion of all other considerations. Some managers, however, who take this position with great zeal will exhibit equal zeal in undertaking defense contracts that yield little or no profit to the company on the ground that such is the duty of a good corporate citizen. These apparent inconsistencies can be resolved, but not without a philosophy of business on which to formulate a realistic theory of public relations.

This emphasis on the necessity for management to be aware of its social role and of the publics' view of that role should not be construed to mean that all companies are duty-bound to identify with larger spheres of interest—community-wide, national, or international. On the contrary, in a system such as ours, in which diversity is regarded as a necessary condition of a free society, a business corporation, no matter how large, cannot permit its image to become frayed at the edges and fused with the image of society as a whole.

The business corporation must maintain a distinct individuality, a high degree of integrity, and great flexibility in order to withstand the constant pressures on its growth which, if unrelieved, so frequently and so easily lead to state intervention and finally, state control. Accurate knowledge and realism in evaluating the goals, aspirations, needs, and activities of others outside the corporate "island" are consistent with a forthright stand in favor of corporate self-interest and indeed are essential to managements' realistic perception of the corporate image. Diffuse and equivocal policy-making arises in part from lack of such knowledge.

If management is to project an image that is unique, timely, internally consistent, and meaningful to the publics at which it is directed, it must itself have such an image.

In short, management's own image of the corporation must rest ultimately on an accurate and penetrating analysis of the corporate environment. Thus the two-way communication mentioned earlier is important not only for testing the effectiveness of specific public-relations programs, but also for formulating the basic corporate image which guides policy.

PUBLICS SHAPE THE CORPORATE ENVIRONMENT

The large corporation has many publics with which communication must be maintained. To identify these publics and determine their characteristics is important to management for two reasons: (1) the publics shape the corporation's attitudes and dynamics which should affect management's own image of the corporation; and (2) in order to project this image effectively, once management had defined it, corporations must know the predilections of the groups with which they maintain relations. Selecting the publics is an important element of public-relations policy. Too narrow a view of corporate interests in the complex environment may impair the effectiveness of public-relations programs by unduly limiting the publics. Yet, some lines must be drawn. Occasionally there may be a tendency to exclude certain publics for budgetary reasons with the plausible argument that those excluded are too remote from the affairs of business. Or there may be confusion as to the meaningful categories of publics for public relations as distinguished from other kinds of functional work within the organization as a whole.

There are three possible approaches which management can take in trying to pinpoint its publics. The *first* would be to identify and separate internal and external publics or groups. The *second* would be to identify the publics or groups by the roles individuals play in their life situations. The *third* would be to identify the publics or groups by their direct or indirect contributions to the corporation and their claims upon it.

If we classify publics by the first method (internal and external groups), certain difficulties arise. In our classification scheme we would include such typical groups as employees, unions, management, customers, share owners, suppliers, competitors, distributors, dealers, and so on—groupings that obviously bear directly on the nature of the enterprise. Obviously, the membership of some of these groups overlap. For example, employees are members of the internal company "team," but they are also members of an external organization that bargains collectively with management. As the latter, they may sometimes be identified in the minds of some managers with an adversary interest, but, as employees, elaborate efforts are made to identify them with "the company." Does their union constitute a public for the purpose of public-relations work? And how is this kind of work to be integrated with "union relations"?

Special problems with wide social implications and with very immediate implications for public-relations programs arise when employees are regarded as a part of the formal organization of the company. It has been argued that the company's demands upon them, as a part of the formal organization, may be quite out of line with their needs as well-integrated and healthy persons, as individuals.[4] The formal organization itself, as well as directive leadership by management (as distinguished from "democratic leadership"), tight management controls, and "human-relations" programs are said to be devices that managers use to heighten the employees' feeling that they are part of the "team" in order to increase their productivity.

In its relations with unions, on the other hand, management hardly seeks

[4] See Chris Argyris, *Personality and Organization* (New York: Harper, 1957), p. 233.

identity of interests, at least not in the same sense. It will seek a common ground for determining policies as to wage structures, working conditions, benefits, and the like; but it will resist attempts on the part of a union to encroach upon "management prerogatives" and thus to identify itself with the company as an institution.

To some extent, the second approach (identifying publics by listing roles that people play), is an improvement on simply separating internal and external publics. An inventory of publics by this method would include people in their roles as: members of the national community; citizens, voters, and constituents; customers, share owners, employees, and suppliers; members of the press; members of educational groups; leaders and members of religious groups; members of governmental agencies; members of industry and trade organizations; members of service organizations; members of professional and scientific societies; members of fraternal, cultural, and ethnic associations.

This listing makes the assumption that a company may have a relationship with the same individual in various ways, through the various roles he plays in his life situations. Every person plays many roles and each of these roles carries with it definite attitudes, beliefs, customs, codes, manners, aspirations. In order to communicate successfully with its publics by reaching people in their various roles, a company must acquire a working knowledge of the characteristics of these roles. To be able "to listen" to people, as well as "to speak" to them through media, a corporation must direct its antennae in a number of directions. Role listing provides a clue to these directions.

The third approach identifies the publics in terms of their contributions to and claims on the enterprise. Many directly or indirectly contribute their effort, time and substance to the establishment and growth of the corporation. For this reason, many lay claim to the fruits of its productivity.

Four general categories of *direct* contributor-claimants can be identified, and these are almost universally recognized as such in current thought about the modern business corporation. They consist of the corporation's security holders, its customers, its employees, and its suppliers. Each of these groups expects the corporation to meet specific kinds of responsibilities and each, in turn owes specific duties.

Four *indirect* claimant groups can be identified: competitors in the business community; local communities; the general public; and governments (local, state, and federal).

This third approach to defining publics has great merit because it is the only one which permits management to identify and evaluate specific contributions and claims made by the various groups. By such identification and evaluation, management can sharpen its perception of its responsibilities to these various publics. Once corporate social responsibility has been established, it becomes integral to the goals of the corporation, thus taking on more tangible meaning for those who must portray the corporate image in terms of corporate goals.

In practice, an eclectic approach—taking the best from all three approaches to fit existing company organization—would probably be the most effective way for companies generally to identify their various publics and thus to modify and supplement the "social maps" which in such large measure affect management's own images of their companies.

COORDINATION OF "COMMUNICATING-ACTIVITIES"

Another important aspect of relating the corporation to its social environment is that relationships with key publics are maintained in countless ways other than through publicity releases from the public-relations department. Thus, if the corporate image in the public eye is not to be confused and contradictory, all those activities which establish relationships with any group must be coordinated. So extensive and complex are the relationships of a corporation with publics that a more nearly accurate term (if we exclude relationships with groups of people within the corporation) would be "external relations" —one variation of the term that nation-states use to distinguish problems of foreign policy from those of domestic policy. Why would it not be wise for the large corporation to have a "Department of External Affairs" which would be responsible for all activities establishing relationships with the outside?

The idea is tempting. But it overlooks the hard fact that external relations are infinitely varied, complex, and comprehensive. They involve marketing, supply, legal relations, financial relations, and a host of others. To merge all of these functional kinds of external relations into a single organizational unit is manifestly impossible. Nation-states are not able to do it, as witness the corps of attachés in foreign embassies—each of the attachés being responsible not to the foreign office but to some other department of the home government. One might add that, in this age of pressure toward people-to-people contacts across international frontiers, the attempt by governments to funnel all such contacts through state departments and foreign offices becomes increasingly impracticable.

Foreign policy, the cynics say, is the art of influencing other nations to your own nation's ends. Corporation public-relations policy, by analogy, could be said to be the art of influencing external groups of interest to corporate ends.

Neither the policies of states nor those of corporations may be so cynical as all this, but the instruments of policy remain the same and they do exhibit striking similarities. The instruments of foreign policy include arms, economic measures, diplomacy (negotiation and agreement), and communication through mass media and other channels (government-to-people). The instruments of corporation policy—in its external relations with various groups in the environment—include legal measures, economic measures, negotiation and agreement, and communication through mass media and other channels (corporation-to-people). The application of all these instruments contributes to the corporate image held by the world outside.

To get an overview of the entire range of external relations of the corporation (on which there is practically no literature today) would require a systematic survey of all the ways in which particular companies use all these instruments. Such a survey would undoubtedly show that some companies make inadequate use of some of these instruments and that few indeed coordinate their application with singleness of purpose. This coordination is a top-management responsibility and can be called the "relations" function in its broadest sense.

But the question arises whether top management is properly equipped to undertake this coordination. Usually it is not, for top management often lacks the information necessary for it to adjust its own corporate image to the needs and wants of its social environment and to see the cause-and-effect relationships between that environment and the instruments of policy. It is not sufficient to insist, as is often done, that the necessary staff exists, but is distributed among various departments and committees. It is undoubtedly true that every specialized department has its own antennae out to the pertinent environmental forces that affect its particular kind of work. What is often lacking, however, is a synthesis. Even in the larger corporation there is no systematic effort made to synthesize public-relations "intelligence" with all corporate activities. Such a synthesis would present a unified picture to executive management of the *changing role of the company as seen from the outside.* After the synthesis, the next step would be a follow-up to determine whether the appropriate policy decisions had been made throughout the company. Instead, there is usually a mass of unrelated reports on external relations of all sorts that are circulated to many desks at various times. The mass of reports is never processed as a whole or acted upon as a whole, nor indeed is it ever intended to be acted upon as a whole.

This problem is not peculiar to the corporation. The intelligence operations of governments also appear to fail notoriously in the critical act of integrating the necessary information needed by policy-makers at top-executive and legislative levels. Continuous failure to solve this problem for any nation could mean a national disaster. Failure to solve it in the corporation could have a direct bearing upon its survival as an institution.

Where, then, do the public-relations specialists fit into this broad concept of public relations? Public-relations specialists should properly be the specialists on communication as a potent instrument in all aspects of corporate policy, and not just specialists in the use of mass media. As specialists, their task should be both to counsel executive management in the work of coordinating all the relationships which the corporation has with various publics and to advise company specialists (in marketing, finance, legal work, manufacturing, etc.)

on adjusting to the corporate environment in the interest of advancing such types of work.

In order to accomplish these tasks, public-relations specialists should be knowledgeable in:

1. The identity and characteristics of all the key publics toward which company messages are to be directed and from which messages are to be received.

2. The content and purpose of these messages, with special attention to the things that should be said and done in public view by persons and components acting on behalf of the company.

3. The corporate image, not only as it appears in the minds of the key publics toward which company messages are directed and from which messages are received, but also as it operates upon the minds of company personnel in their decision making in all kinds of external relations.

4. The most effective media or channels to be used for communicating with the key publics, not excluding the possible effect of unintended messages sent out from the company in the form of activities that are not usually considered to be public-relations work.

5. The effects of outwardly directed messages upon these key publics, measured not only in terms of their verbal responses, their opinions and attitudes, but also their actions with respect to matters of concern to all decision makers in every kind of functional work throughout the company.[5]

Since some decisions in public relations obviously deal with highly technical matters (e.g., choice of media, content analysis, etc.) there is always danger that public relations, for this reason, will be regarded as peripheral to the central issues of business policy. This is far from the truth. The choice of key publics, for instance, may profoundly affect the growth and even the survival of the corporation. To cite a single illustration: to exclude government officials from a list of key publics could be a vital error, especially in an age of mounting governmental regulation of business at every level of public government.

Because the "fit" of the corporation into the prevailing social norms depends upon managerial decisions in all functional fields and not just upon the activities of the public-relations department, a corollary function of public-relations departments, then, would be to keep a watchful eye upon relationships of the

[5] The literature of this field is growing rapidly, as indicated in the bibliographical works: Bruce Lannes Smith, Harold D. Lasswell and Ralph D. Casey (eds.), *Propaganda, Communication and Public Opinion* (Princeton: Princeton University Press, 1946) and Bruce Lannes Smith and Chitra Smith, *International Communication and Political Opinion: A Guide to the Literature* (Princeton: Princeton University Press, 1956). A concise diagrammatic statement of the elements in the communication process by W. Phillips Davison and Alexander L. George is available in "An Outline for the Study of International Political Communication," in Wilbur Schramm (ed.), *The Process and Effects of Mass Communication* (Urbana: University of Illinois Press, 1954), pp. 433–443, applying the general principles expounded by Schramm in his article on "How Communication Works" in the same volume, pp. 3–26.

entire organization with the public. The specialists would alert the entire organization to public-sensed deviations from standards of performance set by general company objectives. Feedback of opinion polling may be highly useful in developing a new set of premises for future policy decisions in various functional areas. It may be used also, of course, for policy-making in public-relations work with respect to informational output, or "selling" the company.

Some may object that this is too comprehensive a function to require of the public-relations specialist. Perhaps this is asking too much because of the way public-relations work is sometimes organized and staffed, and, especially, in view of the relatively subordinate role the public-relations specialist plays in the operation of many firms. But the answer is simple. The function is of vital importance to the large corporation. If one prefers to attach the public-relations label only to those who perform the more modest role of proclaiming the virtues of the company, then another name must be found for this broader function.

To summarize briefly, then, in order to communicate a meaningful image of the corporation to its key publics, somewhere in the organization someone must perform the broad "intelligence" function of sensing the social climate in which the corporation operates. This is necessary both to management's defining a realistic corporate image and to the effective communication of that image. The success of the projection of that image depends also on how well management is able to coordinate company activities that produce an image in the public eye as a by-product with the specific public-relations function which has as its major goal the projection of the corporate image.

Once executive management appreciates this broader view of public relations as an aspect of communication and as an instrument of corporate policy, many of the current public-relations practices and programs of corporations may well be headed for the junk-pile.

B. Corporate Philanthropy

Charity and The Corporation

8

Howard R. Bowen

The corporation has long been regarded in the law as a *person*. This person, as originally conceived, was not a very humane creature. In recent decades, however, the corporation has been taking on some of the nobler aspects of personality. It is becoming concerned with citizenship and accepts community responsibilities. It is becoming involved in the welfare of those whose lives it touches, and occasionally rises to something approaching love of neighbor. And it has accepted the obligations of charity and has become an important philanthropist. If the present trend continues, the corporation may at last acquire what it has long been accused of lacking, namely, a soul.

These changes in the character of the corporation are of course controversial. Some argue that the extent of humanization is greatly exaggerated or is only a coverup for selfish and exploitative corporate behavior. Others hold that the alleged humanization of the corporation is really a cynical public relations campaign designed to bolster the political strength of private enterprise. Still others hold that it is wrong for the corporation to try to "do good" with other people's money, and that managers should confine their aims to the interests of stockholders. As against all these views is the opinion that a genuine and welcome humanization of the corporation is taking place. I am one of those who believe that corporations are becoming more human, and that it is a good thing. True, business motives are often the prime cause of corporate "virtue" and rationalizations are easy to fabricate. (If corporations are human enough to acquire the virtues of personality, they are human enough to practice the vices as well.) Yet it seems to me incontrovertible that a pronounced transformation has occurred in the spirit of business enterprise.

Reprinted with permission from *Management Record* (February 1962), pp. 28–33. Copyright © 1962 by the National Industrial Conference Board.

Actually, it should not be surprising that the corporation could acquire the attributes of personality. The corporation consists not merely of shares of stock, ledgers and balance sheets, or plant and machinery; the corporation is above all a group of people, very human people, organized for collective decision making. There is no reason to suppose that an organized group of people should behave less humanly or should be less concerned about obligations to follow men than an individual person. The astonishing thing is that the theory could ever have been seriously accepted that ordinary moral principles are less applicable to the business enterprises than to individuals.

Though it would be possible to consider many aspects of corporate personality, I shall confine myself to charity (i.e., charitable giving).

THE NATURE OF CORPORATE DONATIONS

For purposes of analysis, corporate donations may be separated into three categories: (1) gifts, (2) business expenses, and (3) informal taxes. Most actual donation are a complex mixture of these, yet the three categories are analytically distinguishable.

Many corporate donations are outright *gifts*. Money is provided voluntarily for socially useful purposes and little or no direct benefit accrues to the corporation itself.

Some donations are wholly or partly intended to produce benefits to the corporation. For example, if a donation to a college is expected to create good will, it is comparable to institutional advertising. If a donation to a local hospital is expected to raise worker morale, health, or productivity, it is comparable to expenditures for employee cafeterias or plant physicians. If a donation to vocational education is expected to increase the supply of skilled labor available to the company, it is comparable to wage payments. If a donation to a law school is expected indirectly to lessen the rigors of public regulation, it is comparable to the payment of legal fees. To the extent that donations are for the benefit of the company, they should be considered ordinary *business expense*.[1] That a corporation can derive benefit from donations does not imply that such donations are undesirable. If a corporation can generate good will, or good labor relations, or better employee morale, or other benefits by donating to hospitals or colleges or community chests, that may be much more desirable socially than generating the same benefits through advertising or selling or lobbying. The corporation is helped while valuable social benefits are

[1] Business expense and donations are in practice difficult to distinguish and merge into each other. For example, if a company gives money to a local hospital or school, the payment will be charged to charitable donations. If the same company builds a school and hospital for its employees in a remote area where these facilities do not exist, the payment will be charged to business expense. In both cases, the purpose may be to improve the corporate environment.

produced. A dollar of giving creates two dollars' worth of benefits, one dollar's worth to the corporation and one dollar's worth to society.[2]

As the practice of corporate giving becomes more widespread, donations tend to take on some of the characteristics of *taxes*. In earlier times, when the prevailing opinion held that corporations exist only to make profits, corporate giving aroused the wrath of stockholders as the "squandering of other people's money." Social pressures were then opposed to it. But today the prevailing opinion holds that the corporation should be a "human" institution, a good citizen, and a good neighbor. Strong social pressure is exerted in favor of corporate giving, and a company that does not give gets black marks against it. In this sense, the community has come close to imposing on the corporation a kind of informal taxation which requires the corporation to give in order to retain public approval. This public attitude perhaps reflects ingratitude toward the earlier generous impulses of corporate managers, but it nevertheless places on the corporation an obligation which the community enforces through moral sanctions. This social pressure is simply another instance of the ancient principle that a privilege of long standing becomes accepted as a right.

In practice, few corporate gifts can be regarded exclusively as gifts, business expenses, or informal taxes. Most gifts include all three elements. They are partly true gifts made without thought of benefit to the company and in the spirit of good citizenship. They are partly business expenses made in the expectation that something of value will be returned to the company. They are partly informal taxes paid in response to powerful social pressure.

WHOSE MONEY?

It has usually been assumed in legal opinions and in other discussions of corporate philanthropy that the money donated belongs to the stockholders— that the effect of donations is to reduce the net income or assets of stockholders. My analysis of the nature of corporate donations casts some doubt on this simple theory.

To the extent that the donations are *gifts*, in the sense that no benefit to the company is expected and that they are not made under social pressure applicable to many companies, the traditional theory is valid. Such gifts are surely a charge on funds that would otherwise eventually belong to the stockholders'

---

[2] To create conditions in which companies can achieve corporate goals through supporting needed social services may well be in the social interest. The motive of self-interest is thus harnessed to the social welfare. The advocate of pure competition may argue that enterprises should compete for customers by lowering prices and should compete for labor and capital by raising wages and returns to capital, and that they should not be concerned about good will and public relations. In practice, however, every company must be concerned about the protection and enhancement of its position as a corporate entity, and it must allocate funds to this end.

income but expenses designed to enhance that income. To the extent that donations are made as a result of social pressures applicable to bring returns to the corporation, they are obviously not charges on stockholders' that donations are made as a result of social pressures applicable to most or all companies, they become a regular cost of doing business which may in the long run be shifted to consumers in the form of higher prices (or possibly to workers in the form of lower wages). The final incidence of donations made under social pressure may be comparable to that of the corporation income tax. Economists disagree sharply on the question of who ultimately pays that tax. Most business men and many economists (I among them) believe that the corporate income tax is at least partially shifted to consumers in the form of higher prices.[3] It may be that corporate donations are also borne, at least in part, by consumers rather than by stockholders. As the practice of corporate giving becomes more general and as social pressure in favor of it becomes more insistent, the likelihood of such shifting becomes greater. A reasonable hypothesis is that a substantial portion of corporate donations are borne by members of the community other than stockholders. If this hypothesis is valid, it means that when company officials make corporate donations, they are acting not only as agents of stockholders but also of the community generally.

UNDISTRIBUTED PROFITS

One of the peculiar characteristics of a corporation is that it is, in a sense, an ultimate recipient of income. I refer to undistributed profits or retained earnings. Retained earnings belong nominally to the stockholders; yet stockholders have only the most tenuous control over the use of these funds. They represent a large block of income, averaging for the entire country perhaps $10 billion a year, that is received by no individual and no part of which can flow to philanthropic purposes unless corporate officials elect to make donations from it.

I would argue that in a pluralistic society dependent upon private giving for many of its most important institutions and social services, a portion of every dollar of income generated should be accessible to charitable purposes. Our institutional arrangements should not block the flow of charitable giving with reference to any part of the national income. For this reason, it seems to me that the power of the corporate officials to retain income should carry with it a special right and duty to make charitable contributions from this income. In advancing the proposition that the case for corporate giving is especially compelling with reference to retained earnings, I do not imply that corporate giving should be limited to these particular dollars. I would suggest, however, that the amounts contributed from these dollars should be proportionally

---

[3] My views on this subject were expressed in two articles, "Taxation of Net Income from Business," *Bulletin of the National Tax Association*, December, 1945, pp. 72–80; "Incidence of the Corporate Income Tax," *American Economic Review*, March, 1946, pp. 146–147.

greater than the amounts contributed from dollars otherwise intended for dividends. The conclusion from this principle is that a corporation which retains a large share of its earnings should contribute a larger portion of its net income to charitable purposes than a corporation which pays a large share of its income in dividends.

HOW MUCH?

The good causes to which corporate funds might be given are virtually unlimited. In the disposition of these funds, a reasonable balance must be struck between the obligations to society, the progress of the corporation itself, and the interests of stockholders. There are few recognized criteria to guide corporate officials in these decisions.

In recent years, all United States corporations combined have given about $500 million annually or about 1% of their net income before taxes. This amount and percentage represents the combined judgment of the officers of all of America's companies as to their corporate responsibility and perhaps also as to the strength of the social pressure being exerted upon them.

I shall present several tentative suggestions regarding possible or desirable future amounts.

One solution might be based on the reasoning that the corporate share of the nation's total philanthropic bill should be measured by the ratio of corporate net income before taxes to total national income. This ratio is about 11%, and voluntary giving from all sources is about $10 billion. On this theory, then, all corporations should together contribute about $1.1 billion (or 2.4% of net income before taxes).

A second solution might proceed on the theory that corporations have a special responsibility to give from retained earnings since these cannot otherwise be tapped for philanthropic purposes. Retained earnings in the last decade have averaged about 40% of corporate net income after taxes. The relevant base on which the corporate obligation might be measured would then be 40% of net income before taxes, or about $18 billion. Since total philanthropic giving from all sources is about 2.5% of national income, I assume then that corporations should give about 2.5% of $18 billion, or $450 million. Add to this contributions from the remaining 60% of net corporate income at, say, the rate of 1%: a reasonable total of corporate giving might be $700 million (about 1.5% of corporate income before taxes).

A third solution would assume that the corporate share of the philanthropic bill would be equal to the corporate share of the tax bill. The underlying theory would be that society might expect corporations to bear a philanthropic load roughly proportional to their share of the tax load. Corporations pay about 35% of all taxes (federal, state, and local); thus, corporations would bear about 35% of the philanthropic bill, or $3.5 billion. This would represent about 7.7%

of corporate net income before taxes, and would exceed the 5% limit provided in the Internal Revenue Code.

Still another solution would be to assume that corporate giving should be related to the rule permitting contributions of up to 5% of net income before taxes. Since the 5% rule is intended as a maximum limit, not an average, and since the minimum of 0% is clearly too small, the midpoint of 2.5% of net income before taxes might be a reasonable figure. The contributions would then be about $1.1 billion, or about 2.4% of net income before taxes.

I do not place great importance on these calculations except as they may be suggestive of general orders of magnitude, and may possibly provide some slight rationale for what is otherwise likely to be a wholly arbitrary judgment. Most of these calculations result in figures between roughly $700 million and $1.1 billion or between 1% and 2.5% of net income before taxes. In general, they suggest that the present level of giving of 1% of net income before taxes is minimal and that an average level more comparable to that already achieved by the leaders in corporate philanthropy would be possible and appropriate.

The level of corporate giving should probably be higher than the present level because part of the donations counted in published data could be viewed as business expenses, and not strictly as gifts. For example, some donations to technical education or research yield direct returns in employee recruitment or in product development. Some are in effect wholly comparable to institutional advertising, etc.

Another perhaps more pertinent approach to the question of how much a corporation should give relates to the extent of the need. Presumably the corporation has an interest in maintaining the private sector of our educational and social welfare establishment. In view of the present rapid growth of population, it is likely that private hospitals, schools, colleges, and social welfare agencies will occupy a progressively smaller proportion of the field unless resources flow increasingly to them in pace with the growth of the country. To cite the field I know best, there is danger that the private sector of higher education will occupy a diminishing role in our national life. Corporate officials and stockholders generally share my view that a relative decline of the private sector of our educational and social services and a relative increase in the public sector would be unwholesome in a society that values decentralization of power and diffusion of initiative. It would seem then that corporations have an interest in increasing their donations at this time to help in the preservation and extension of pluralism in our society. In my opinion, the average level of corporate giving might advantageously grow in the next few years from the present 1% of net income to 2%, 3%, or 4% of net income.

Still another approach to the level of corporate giving relates to the amount that corporate officials can give without serious stockholder opposition. This amount obviously varies with the general climate of public opinion and the particular circumstances of each company. In my opinion, most corporate officials have been rather timid and conservative on this point. With a few notable exceptions, they have tended to follow rather than to lead public opinion and have been swayed by traditional views of the powers and obligations of corporate officers. While I would not advocate lavish squandering of corporate resources, I do feel—as I believe the great majority of the public and the stockholders feel—that corporate officials are in good position to make wise philanthropic investments. So far the trust has seldom been abused and the record of corporate giving is, I think, not only defensible but brilliant.

In my present position as president of a private college, I can scarcely claim disinterest when I recommend increased corporate giving. Yet, in reaching this conclusion, I have tried to rise above my personal interests.

WHAT TO SUPPORT?

Every company that engages in charitable giving has the problem of deciding what charitable objectives to support and in what proportion funds should be allocated among them. There are no simple rules or formulas to ease the pain of these decisions. At present, corporate officials collectively direct about half their contributions to health and welfare, about a third to education (mostly higher education), and the remainder to civic, cultural, and business purposes. The proportion to education is apparently increasing. I have no basis for criticizing this allocation or for suggesting that more or less should be directed toward any particular undertaking. I should like, however, to offer several observations that might be of use to corporate officials who are faced with decisions on what charitable objectives to support.

The Investment Approach. Philanthropic giving, whether intended for so-called capital purposes or current operations, is basically *investment*. It is investment in human beings intended to produce future returns in the form of knowledge, skills, strength, character, or morale. The returns may be reaped in the form of higher productivity, better citizenship, or greater personal welfare. Just as a company attempts in its business operations to find those lines of investment which will yield the highest possible future returns in money income, so in its philanthropic operations it should try to find those lines of investment which will yield the highest returns in human values. The same care and prudence that goes into ordinary investment decisions of the company must go into philanthropic investment decisions if the money is not to be wasted.

A Policy. A company that gives should have a policy regarding its support program. Such a policy should of course grow out of deliberation and should be followed consistently (though not blindly or inflexibly). Without a policy, the company is unlikely to attain a balanced charitable program and its giving is likely to be guided by adventitious pressure from the outside rather than by planning from within. Money is likely to be used to relieve the pressure of solicitation rather than to gain the highest possible returns. With a defensible and consistent policy, a company is in a position to say "no" to solicitations for excluded purposes without embarrassment and without loss of good will.

Concentration of Giving. A company should concentrate its giving on a limited range of projects. Otherwise, it cannot adequately investigate the various organizations or projects to which money is given and it cannot achieve the satisfaction of having a significant influence on any philanthropic objective. This advice is particularly relevant to smaller companies which cannot devote much staff or money to investigation.

Some corporate officials believe that their giving must be spread among many projects so that all are treated "fairly." This argument is weak because contributions are made by many corporations with differing emphases. The biases of one, based upon the particular interests and judgments of its officials, will be counteracted by the different biases of others. If one company emphasizes health, another symphony orchestras, another colleges, and another the Boy Scouts, the total result may be a well-balanced program for society at large, even though the giving of each donor is biased in the direction of one or the other project. The total effect will be good, provided each donor is reasonably conscientious in seeking those philanthropic investments that in his considered judgment will produce the highest return.

The Human Touch. Giving is a very human activity through which deep personal values are expressed and from which great personal satisfactions are derived. There is no reason for corporate officials to be denied the pleasure of being humanly involved in and personally moved by the objects of their corporate giving. Only if they are so involved are they likely to have a keen interest in exploring philanthropic opportunities or in judging the returns from their charitable investments. This does not imply that funds should be channeled exclusively into the pet projects of corporate officials. What is needed is a reasonable balance between personal interest and broad social obligation. But there need be no conflict between these two. Indeed, philanthropy without personal interest and involvement is a cold and sterile thing.

Supporting Success. A tendency of many donors, especially corporate donors, is to support success, i.e., to give to those institutions and projects that have already achieved an outstanding record of service and progress. This policy is understandable and to a degree defensible. No one, particularly no business man, wants to bet on a failure or to support mediocrity. Yet caution is needed in following such a policy, in that it tends to make the rich richer and the poor poorer—even to the extent of giving an embarrassment of riches to some institutions or projects while starving others. There are presently many new or neglected undertakings that are of great potential importance. Some of these offer potentially higher returns than can be gotten by adding to the resources of already well-established and excellent institutions or projects. In some cases, if investments in the weaker enterprises are to pay off, gifts must be supplemented by technical services, advice, and motivations through which the potential return may be realized. Philanthropy directed toward the less successful is risky and involves time and attention but may be highly fruitful and satisfying.

Provincialism.   Most corporate officers feel, rightly, that they owe major obligations to the local communities in which they operate; that they are in a posi-investments in them may be made intelligently; and that donations invested tion to know something about nearby institutions and projects so that their in the local area are likely to produce returns of immediate benefit to the company. Because of the obvious attractions of local giving, there is perhaps a tendency to view philanthropic obligations and opportunities rather too narrowly. The purpose of corporate philanthropy is not merely to do something of immediate benefit to the company, and the money given is not solely stockholders' money. Companies operate in an interdependent nation-wide or world-wide economy and society. Their stockholders, customers, and suppliers are often widely dispersed. The source of their labor is often nation-wide. For example, a company operating in Chicago may have more long-range interest in and responsibility for education in Mississippi than it has for education in Evanston or Winnetka. Similarly, the fact that officials of national companies tend to be concentrated in New York, Detroit, Chicago, and other big cities does not necessarily give them more responsibility for charitable enterprises in metropolitan areas than they owe to charitable enterprises elsewhere. In this era of international interdependence and of growing obligations of Americans toward underdeveloped nations, a case can be made also for corporate donors to look beyond the borders of the United States. To cite one personal example, in my visit to Thailand this past summer, the ambassador and I discussed the possibility that the acute shortage of business talent in that country might be alleviated if American corporations could lend some middle-management personnel to Thai business enterprises.

Restricted Gifts.   Corporate givers have generally been very enlightened in their willingness to forego detailed control over the uses of their gifts. Their gifts are often completely unrestricted as to use, or restricted only to very broad categories of use. Businessmen know that the restriction of gifts to narrowly specified purposes tends to be defeated in the long run. Recipients eventually compensate by withdrawing unrestricted funds from those activities that are relatively oversupplied with restricted funds. For example, when corporate gifts tend to pile up in science departments of universities, university administrators will eventually try to redress the balance by providing relatively larger unrestricted funds for the humanities and social studies. Nevertheless, there is a lingering tendency for funds to concentrate in certain parts of an institution, and corporate givers should be sensitive to the problem.

A related issue pertains to gimmick-giving, by which I mean donations for highly restricted and novel purposes which may or may not contribute to the activity being supported. Every administrator of recipient organizations occasionally feels the pain of accepting a gift for some inconsequential purpose while important programs languish for lack of funds. In general, the trustees and administrators of a recipient organization, if they are worthy of gifts at all, know their high priority needs. I would repeat, however, that the record of corporate donors in avoiding the practice of gimmick-giving is relatively very good.

Social Audit. In its philanthropic activity, a corporation is attempting to contribute to the progress of society at large. It would seem reasonable that periodically the corporation might arrange for its philanthropic activities to be confidentially reviewed by outsiders who represent the social point of view. For example, the corporation might at five-year intervals engage a board of consultants consisting of community leaders, officials of public foundations, social workers, university professors, etc., to review the philanthropic activities of the company. This board would report its confidential appraisal and recommendations to the board of directors and management. This procedure would be analogous to a management survey or an accounting audit. It would assist the company in keeping in touch with social needs wherever they exist and in gearing the philanthropic program to these needs.[4]

Cooperation. Because corporate philanthropy, when well conducted, is a difficult and time-consuming activity, might there be a place for cooperative effort? I have in mind the creation of foundations to which several or even many corporations would assign part or all of their donations for administration. By the pooling of contributions from several corporations, the administrative cost per dollar of contribution would be reduced, and the social returns from corporate philanthropy might be increased. Indeed, companies might turn over funds to existing foundations like Ford, Carnegie, or Rockefeller which already have the administrative organization and know-how. I offer this suggestion tentatively with the thought that it might be of special assistance to smaller companies. I emphatically do not offer this suggestion as an implied criticism of present corporate philanthropy which I consider to be on the whole socially enlightened and constructive. I offer the suggestion as a way of

---

4 A similar idea was presented in my book "Social Responsibilities of the Businessman," (Harper, New York, 1953), pp. 155–156. I suggested a "social audit" in which the social performance of the corporation in all areas would be reviewed.

reducing a heavy administrative burden that American companies are increasingly being asked to carry.[5]

CONCLUSION

One of the most remarkable revolutions of recent times has been the change in the attitudes of the public, of company officials, and of judges toward corporate philanthropy. Only a few decades ago, corporations were legally without the right to give unless the gifts could be shown to be in the direct terests of stockholders. Today, corporations not only have the legal right to give to a wide range of charitable purposes, but are subjected to compelling moral pressure to do so. The revolution has been reflected not only in attitude, but also in practice, with the result that corporations have become major philanthropists.

The new role of the corporation as philanthropist has thrust upon corporate officials a new range of interests and responsibilities, and has required considerable adjustment in their view of themselves and their corporations. In my conversations with corporate officials (usually in the role of solicitor) I have been impressed by the complexity of their problem as they try to balance the interest of stockholders, of the corporation itself, and of society, and I have been equally impressed by the skill and vision which they apply to their new task. It is clear, however, that many officials—perhaps most—are still searching for philanthropic policies that will be equitable to the several interests involved and that will be personally satisfying to the officials themselves. A generally accepted philosophy of corporate giving has not yet emerged, and the solutions reached by various companies are far from uniform.

DIVERSITY IS THE KEY

The searching, I think, is entirely beneficial. And so is the diversity of solution. Diversity is the essence of philanthropy. It is the element that makes philanthropy a desirable and necessary part of the support of educational and social-welfare activities in a free society. Without private philanthropy, the entire load would be shifted to government, with a corresponding centralization of power, reduction in imaginative variation, limitation on experiment, and avoidance of risk. So long as philanthropy continues to be the vigorous expression of indvidual values that it now is and should be, there will never be a single uniform solution to the problem of corporate giving.

[5] The cooperative idea has already been partially implemented through such organizations as the community chests and the various state-wide organizations of private colleges. These institutions, however, distribute funds on the basis of set formulas and do not attempt to seek out investment opportunities and to make basic decisions on the allocation of funds.

A Philosophy for Corporate Giving
Richard Eells

9

Why do we need a rationale for corporate giving? A rationale is presumably a reasoned argument, and argument—it has been said—is a discussion that has two sides and no end. Heated argument, moreover, is something the other fellow starts. Why not avoid it all in the case of corporate giving, simply by going ahead with the giving and stopping all the argument?

The trouble is that corporate giving involves the exercise of a legal corporate power—the donative power—by directors and executive managers who are responsible for their acts, including the act of corporate giving. Individual philanthropists may be able to reject debate about their case for giving. Responsible managers are expected to explain their use of this power. The corporate donor may be an artificial person, but these managers are the real persons who decide who gets what from a corporation's funds, and they must be ready with reasons for a donative decision. The reasons constitute a rationale that is more than an explanation.

As we look back over the past decade, I think it is possible to chalk up some progress toward the development of a sound rationale for corporate giving. Today, we have a corpus of juristic rationale that pretty well settles the old argument about the donative power. For legal purposes in most jurisdictions in the United States, corporate managers do not have to show a "direct benefit" to the donor company to justify a corporate gift. In some jurisdictions, the door is in fact open to corporate philanthropy in the best sense of that term. As one lawyer put it:

> "In the name of social need and institutional responsibility, the remnants of greed have been swept aside and the law has proclaimed that the business 'corporation may love humanity. Indeed, it may express its love in a most practical way—with dollars."

I do not mean to imply that the legal argument is entirely settled. Corporate counsel must always be consulted for an acceptable rationale of corporate giving as well as for specific donative programs. But in general, the donative power in corporations is well established. There are, of course, other legal questions besides corporate power to make donations, and one in particular should be noted. The famous 5% clause represents a long-standing policy of

Reprinted with permission from *The Conference Board Record* (January 1968), pp. 14–18. Copyright © the National Industrial Conference Board.

the national government that corporate giving is to be encouraged through the offer of deductions in the corporate income tax. In practice, this amounts to a 1% clause since corporations have never come through with much more than this small part of their pretax income. It had been hoped that they would do far more to aid philanthropic giving in this country. Think what it would mean if they were to do this. In 1964, the total at 5% would have come to something like $3.15 billion. Corporate pretax income that year was reported to be $63,059,000,000. Properly distributed, such an amount could aid impressively in meeting some of this nation's most serious domestic problems.

The original and continuing grounds for this Federal tax policy in favor of corporate giving have always had an important influence on the rationale of corporate giving. A company is certainly justified in insisting that the corporate sector is expected to do its part in the nation's total philanthropic effort. Stockholders can be shown that the tax-deductible gift is a relatively inexpensive way to achieve some business objectives. This is not, of course, a strong element in the rationale. If corporate gifts are a good thing, the "tax bargain" does not enhance their essential wisdom and virtue. The more important argument from the stockholders' point of view is that a corporate gift affects their equity favorably—or at least not adversely.

While these juristic developments have not been the most important developments during the past decade, since most of the legal aspects of corporate giving rationale were settled by 1957, the steps taken by legislatures and courts did open the way to the most important development in the decade past.

Professional donative management has now become the order of the day in leading companies. The whole activity of corporate giving has now become an accepted part of good corporate management. The donative decision, as we are now coming to appreciate more and more, is part and parcel of the whole decision process in managing a business. It ought to be considered in that context. (Corporate giving, in other words, is now properly regarded as one of the functional kinds of work that managers do on behalf of a corporation as a business unit.) If the donative decision is an integral part of the managerial decision process in business corporations, then one must expect a rationale for corporate giving that measures up to the reasoning used for all good management practice. One of the things we expect in reasoned management is the use of observation and induction as much as possible and intuition as little as possible.

A professional attitude toward donative work has become more and more evident in recent years. This observation applies to medium-sized as well as large companies, even to some that are relatively small. Expertise is sought and insisted upon to an extent that was not generally observable ten years ago. There are specific assignments of personnel to the donative task, and this fact alone has had a lot to do with progress toward sound rationale. Assignment of the donative task to specialized company managerial or staff components is not rare. And there are, of course, the company-sponsored foundations. Altogether, there has been a rather formidable growth of professionalism in this field that is without parallel in any other country.

Volume of giving is another factor of significance to be noted during the past decade. But there has not been any great upward trend. In fact, corporate giving has been of quite modest proportions for a nation that is more prosperous than any other, is presumably the leader of the free West against the oppressive East of communism, and is expected to practice in the world arena what Professor George Liska has called "the international politics of primacy."[1]

The actual figures for corporate giving are in dispute and cannot be stated with certainty. The officially reported amount for 1964 was $729 million, but it is arguable that business giving came to a good deal more than that. Total private giving in the United States for all causes in 1966 probably came to $13.6 billion. Reported and direct corporate giving was probably 6% of that, or over $800 million. To be nearer the mark, one must add certain undisclosed and indirect non-cash corporate contributions such as gifts-in-kind, the lending of company personnel, and all the relevant administrative and other internal expense in disaster relief, and good will expenditures for charitable local causes in the course of business. If this were done, business donors would then stand higher among those who are often classified as the major philanthropic donors. Individuals' gifts for religion always overshadow all the rest. But if these individual donors for religious purposes are set to one side it is probable that corporations and company-sponsored foundations provide from a fourth to a third of the remaining national philanthropic outlay.

A notable change during the past decade has been the *shift in corporate giving from traditional toward new fields*. There was a shift toward higher education a few years ago, and now there seems to be one toward cultural fields, notably the arts. Interpretation of the facts about this shift (admittedly we all need a better empirical basis for these judgments, but statistical methods are improving) leads to varying results. We may or may not be headed toward a basic shift in fields of corporate support. But there may turn out to have been, in retrospect, another kind of basic shift—one away from fields that draw more and more public support. Federal support of the arts is a case in point. Will the rationale of corporate giving, in view of the new national foundations in the arts and the humanities, now weaken on the necessity for strong private-sector support of these fields by corporations? My own view is that public support of the arts, now begun at last and on a most modest scale, should in no way disparage the corporate effort to strengthen this vital aspect of the corporate milieu.

But it is too soon to tell what the effect will be. One thing does seem fairly certain. The waxing and waning of public support in given fields—such as the arts, education, housing, the attack on poverty, and so on—may have a decided

---

[1] George Liska, *Imperial America: The International Politics of Primacy*, Baltimore, The Johns Hopkins Press, 1967.

effect on both the trends and the rationale of corporate giving. Unless business giving is guided by wisdom, the effect could be disastrous in the vital field of education. We are headed toward the necessity of massive public financial support of the universities, for example, and here both corporate and governmental (especially Federal) support will be indispensable. The tendency to rest the case for corporate support on an attempt to prevent Federal support must therefore be resisted.

All of these major events and trends of the past decade point to the necessity of a thorough review of the whole philosophy of corporate giving.

THE "PRUDENTIAL" THEORY OF CORPORATE GIVING

During the past decade, there have been two different approaches to this philosophy of corporate giving. Some say that the real motivation for corporate giving is and should be entirely philanthropic—done, that is to say, for the love of mankind alone, and completely as a public service. Others say that corporation giving is a matter of straight business expediency and therefore a completely self-regarding act. There are variations of these extreme positions, as well as modified views in between. There is a good deal of truth in some of these positions, but probably the whole truth in none of them.

The prudential basis of the donative rationale has always appealed to me as the most reliable one in the long run. By the prudential theory I mean that managerial reasoning for *good donative decision-making has to do with good business practice far more than with philanthropy.* Corporate giving should not, I think, be governed mainly by philanthropic principles but rather by the principles of prudent corporate management. Managers should certainly take every deduction that the law allows for gifts made from corporate funds, but these gifts are justifiable mainly because there are good reasons for such expenditures in the pursuit of a company's business objectives. The business objectives of corporations must not, of course, be narrowly limited to profit-maximization alone.

There are similarities between this theory and a general theory of prudential investment of corporate assets. Long-term benefits from wise investment—say in research and development—are certainly within the range of good and rational business practice by responsible corporate managers. Yet this term "prudential" as applied to corporate giving has been questioned on the ground that it calls up antiquated economic theory. To base corporate giving on prudential grounds, it has been argued, is to elevate the pursuit of corporate gain erroneously to the level of noble action in the public interest, much as the conventional wisdom in economics had seen the wondrous work of the invisible hand in an economy of shopkeepers.

This allegation of wrong-headed economics as the basis for a prudential theory of corporate giving is of course misdirected. A prudential theory of corporate giving is not rooted in an economics of corporate selfishness. It must be conceded, furthermore, that there is a substantial corpus of legal reasoning to substantiate managerial donative action on straight philanthropic grounds. We should all welcome this happy development. This legal reasoning can very well form a part of the rationale of corporate giving. But not the most important part. For corporate giving, which I believe to be far below what it ought to be both in dollar amounts and the things supported, ought to stand logically on its own feet. It needs to be justified in its own terms as an appropriate *corporate* function, and should not merely follow on the tail of public policy.

From this point of view, the most significant addresses of the rationale of corporate giving are the most influential sectors of the business community itself, and not public officialdom. Congress may possibly change its mind on the 5% clause. Legislators and judges might some day renege on their presently liberal views of corporate powers. But whatever happens in those quarters, corporate directors and managers must hold on to a prudential position and not let themselves back down one inch from their own businesslike reasons for extensive corporate support programs.

The prudential position, as I view it, makes no extreme claim for corporate support policy that is narrowly self-regarding, or for procedures that require a showing of probable pecuniary benefits from every corporate gift regardless of the public interest. It was never intended, when the 5% clause was introduced 30 years ago, that businessmen would forsake the profit motive and turn themselves into philanthropists. Nor was it intended, on the other hand, that they should get deductions only if they blinded themselves to any possibility of benefits. It was assumed that public interest and corporate benefit were simultaneous and reasonable ends of donative policy in corporations for profit.

There is today a rising demand for support from the private sector for urgently needed social measures in the public interest, many of which cannot be fully supported by public governments. For example, neither public support nor private investment alone can turn the trick in meeting educational needs or the needs of our cities. In a fundamental sense, the prudential theory of corporate giving necessarily merges corporate interest with public interest in a basic conception of the modern corporation and its role in our free society. There is no necessary conflict in principle between the pursuit of long-term returns to a company as a business institution in a free society, and the pursuit of public interest. "Benefit" to a company under a modern reading of the old common-law rule certainly does not exclude concurrent and long-term returns shared by business institutions generally and the environing society.

One of the most important benefits of wise business giving is the strength it lends to free institutions in the corporate environment. It seems now to be widely recognized that this is so, and I doubt that this was so ten years ago. Corporate donors are well prepared to counter the charge that we have what collectivists call a "riot of pluralism" in the American capitalistic system. Rationalization of a nation's economy that merges public and private sectors completely, so that the private sector disappears, carries with it a threat of statism that has to be guarded against. For this reason, corporate giving has correctly been justified as a preventive measure, aiding the vital private institutions of our society to survive and prosper. The principle has, of course, wide application—in education, in the arts, in the sciences, in social services, in recreation, and in many other humane fields. The pluralist principle urges dispersal rather than concentration of decision centers and insists upon private-sector as well as a public-sector attack on social problems. Corporate giving on these grounds can now be brought under a rule of prudential action that yields benefits to a company through its social milieu.

As business has come to be regarded as a profession and the corporation as a major social institution of our time, there is also a strong trend toward the idea that corporate "social responsibility" demands corporate giving. It is sometimes said that this responsibility theory competes with the view of corporate giving on prudential grounds.

The prudential approach requires those who do donative work to begin with the company's purposes, its aims as a business, and to consider each donative proposal as a means toward one or more of these ends. Corporate giving can sometimes be shown to be a very good, often the very best, way to achieve a company's *business* objectives. Nor must it for one moment be conceded that this linkage necessarily means pursuit of corporate self-interest at the expense of public interest. Both can be served.

But under the responsibility theory of corporate giving, one is likely to begin with completely exterior considerations—with reference, for example, to those on the outside to which a company presumably owes responsibilities—and then to seek a linkage of logic with company interests, if indeed any such linkage is sought at all. It is quite appropriate to begin and end the logical process with reference to the external institutions in foundation philanthropy. But not, I think, in the donative work by a company component. (A foundation is a non-business entity.)

So far as donative work by a company component is concerned, the objection is sometimes made that in linking company interests with donative effects one runs the danger of losing tax and other advantages because the philanthropic motive in all its purity is said to be absent. But I see no harm in the linkage between business purpose and donative efforts so long as there is no quid-pro-quo transaction. What is given must be a gift with no strings attached; but that does not preclude giving for firm-related purposes. An automobile manufacturer can reasonably support research on highway safety. Who could properly question a company's support of local community funds merely because its employees may benefit thereby, or a local art center because business today has got to offer a rich cultural environment if it hopes to recruit and hold able employees?

I hope no one will think that the prudential approach rules out very long-range and incommensurable benefits. On the contrary, I believe that corporate giving has been on the cautious side in the past. I think that the goals of the future should be quite far-out. In fact, some long-headed managers of corporate donative work today are already reaching very far out indeed, and properly so, for donative objectives that would hardly have been regarded as company-related at all just a few years ago.

Support of the arts is a case in point. A new corporate ecology has taken hold in the business community; I mean by this that there is emerging a new science of the corporation as an institution within its milieu, and even a technology of application that seeks the right balance in what Professor Boulding has referred to as the ecosystem of our highly organized society. Now it is beginning to be understood that the goals of giving and the goals of business converge at novel and distant points. As Dr. Frank Stanton, President of CBS, put it recently in remarks before the Arts Council in Columbus, Ohio:

> "We are all becoming parts of each other's world, and business is learning, along with every other sector of society—it may be slowly, but I believe surely—that it is not an island unto itself and that it both nourishes and is nourished by all those other activities that give any society character, richness, variety and meaning."

Dr. Stanton pointed to the recent history of the support of higher education by business as sufficient evidence of its "broadened horizons and increased awarenesses." As to the arts, he asked whether they were not "ultimately the meeting ground were liberal education and progressive business come together." For it is "the aim of a liberal education to give significance and nourishment to the individual human life," and it is "the arts, especially, that remind men of their humanity and of the sustaining values of our culture." So the first place to worry about American life losing its vitality of individualism, he thought, was in the arts. "If this happens, no liberal education will save our kind of society, and no business enterprise will long endure in what is left of it."

This, I think, is a succinct statement of the prudential theory of corporate giving. I do not believe that it is a crass rationale of expediency. Nor is it one that lays an inescapable duty on companies to give. Every company must decide for itself whether and how to do that. But I do think that with a good corporate ecology to stand on, and with good organization and procedure within every company or able outside consultants to look after donative work, the probability of a sound expansion of effort in this field is good.

During the past decade, we have moved toward that goal. I believe that during the next one—say by 1980—we shall see some very hard-headed giving (prudent, prudential, or responsible, as you please) that will move into radically new areas that we do not anticipate today. It will be done because business and other leaders of our society will find it both good and necessary: good for society, good for the corporate donor, and necessary to both.

Cases

The Heartland Gas Company

THE ORGANIZATION

The Heartland Gas Company is a privately owned gas utility company. The company's operating area embraces approximately two-thirds of one state and includes retail distribution of natural gas to over five hundred communities. It has over 800,000 retail customers. In addition, it serves approximately 300,000 customers indirectly through wholesale sale of gas to thirty-one other utility companies in adjoining areas. The annual sales volume exceeds 300 billion cubic feet.

Heartland is an integrated gas company. The distribution function described above is but one phase of the total operation. The company has production, storage, and transmission operations which rival the distribution phase in importance. They operate approximately 1800 producing wells, purchase gas from about 3800 other local producing wells which are independently owned, operate about 1500 storage wells and thirty-three compressor stations. These facilities are all connected into a complex piping system which ultimately delivers the gas to the consumer. The company has approximately 17,200 linear miles of pipeline in its system. The total plant investment is approximately $360,000,000.

The production, storage, and transmission phases of this company are very important from the standpoint of assuring an adequate supply to the ultimate consumer, and it is conceded that the conduct of employees in these departments have a bearing upon public relations but its over-all effect is minor when compared with the effect of the distribution department. This is due to the fact that the distribution department is responsible for all company functions after the gas has been delivered to the "city gate" or central measuring and pressure regulating station on the outskirts of any community the company serves. Assuming an adequate supply is made available to this point, this analysis will be limited to the organization of the distribution department and the relationship of various functions to the over-all public relations activity.

The Heartland Gas Company is organized on a line and staff principle. Top management consists of a board of directors, a president, a vice president and

Reprinted by the courtesy of Dr. Richard T. Rudduck, Professor of Management and Dean K. Seizert, M.B.A., The University of Toledo.

general manager, a secretary, a treasurer, a vice president in charge of engineering and planning, a vice president in charge of production and storage, a vice president in charge of distribution, a vice president in charge of rates and regulation, a vice president in charge of transmission, and a vice president in charge of wholesale. The organization chart in Exhibit 1 illustrates the top management's line of authority. It also shows the administrative level of such specialized functions as director of information, director of employee relations, and the manager of purchasing and stores.

The distribution department is organized under the vice president in charge of distribution on a line and staff basis. He has a staff in the headquarters office which are experts in each of the distribution functions. These include a service manager, a plant manager, an office manager, a business promotion manager, and an industrial sales manager. The operating area of the company is divided into six districts with each district's operations administered by a district manager. The district manager also reports to the vice president, distribution.

The organizational chart in Exhibit 2 shows the line of authority of the company's "middle management."

The management of each district is separated into five major functions under the district manager in a manner similar to that under the vice-president, distribution. In most cases, the district covers such a large geographical area that it is necessary for the area to be further sub-divided into divisions with a division manager in charge of operations in several communities. The division managers also report to the district manager.

The division managers are responsible for all functions within their area and have local managers working directly for them. On a local level, the manager is in charge of all operations. The separate functions of service and plant are sometimes consolidated if the community is relatively small so that the individual responsible for plant operations may also be responsible for services. In some cases, the office function is handled directly by the local manager. The business promotion activities are not delegated below the division level. In most cases, there is a business promotion representative in each division who reports to his counterpart in the district office. Industrial department activities remain at the district level.

To simplify the organization chart, the writer has chosen a consolidated district structure without a division manager level for illustration purposes. Exhibit 3 shows the line of authority in such a district operation.

Because public relations, good or bad, stems from the words and deeds of district personnel dealing directly with the customer, it is advisable to examine the district structure in greater detail.

The District Manager.   The district manager is responsible for the over-all conduct of the company's affairs within his operating area. He is the man who must administer top management's broad policies at the point where the customer and the company get together. Harold Young, a partner in the invest-

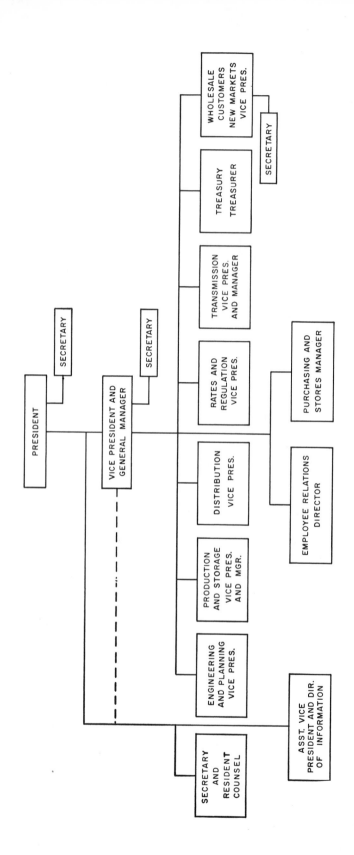

Exhibit 1   Organization Chart

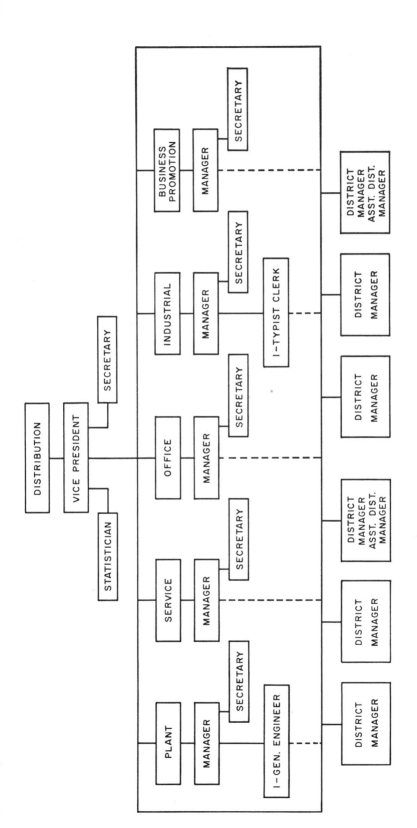

Exhibit 2   Organization Chart

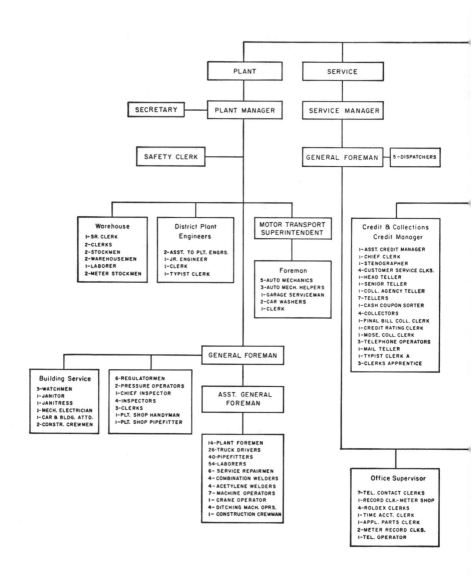

Exhibit 3   Consolidated District Structure

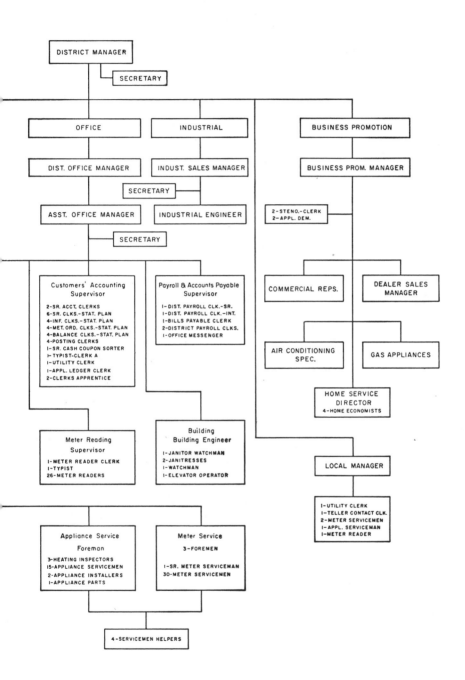

ment firm of Eastman, Dillon, Union Securities & Company, pointed out in an article on utility management that, "A district manager can 'make or break' a company at the grass-roots level."[1]

From a standpoint of public relations as well as operations, the district manager is the central figure. Although Young's article was devoted to the utility business district manager in general, his description of the district manager's public relations function is very appropriate for this specific company.[2]

> The District Manager, so far as most of the customers are concerned, is the man out front. If something goes wrong, the average customer does not think of the President, the General Manager, or any other of the "big brass." He thinks of the District Manager and makes a beeline for his office or gets him quickly on the telephone. Hence, the man who sits behind the District Manager's desk must have patience, tact, and a super-abundance of ability to get along with people. He must be prepared always to present and defend the case of the company and still send a customer away with ruffled feathers smoothed.
>
> However, it would be unfair to paint a picture of a District Manager as a glorified fireman who goes into action when something is wrong. The situation is quite the contrary, and because a good District Manager is always on the job, the task of hearing and settling complaints is often pretty well minimized. One of the big success secrets is that the District Manager, if he is worth his salt, is an integral part of the area for which he is responsible. His position in the community, or communities he serves, is usually an outstanding one. It is rare to find a District Manager who is not only a good citizen but also a reasonably prominent one.

The district manager is expected to take an active interest in community affairs. It is extremely desirable that he become well acquainted with other business leaders and civic officials. These contacts are very valuable in the never-ending job of "keeping a finger on the public pulse." The job of keeping informed requires an awareness and sensitivity which are best cultivated with the willing assistance of people who feel they know the manager well enough to offer criticism and information regarding public attitudes. The district manager in each of Heartland's distribution districts is expected to belong to the Rotary Club in the district headquarters town. He is expected to belong to a country club and join in other local club activities which offer opportunities to meet people and cultivate friends for himself and the company.

Everyone agrees that the public relations responsibility is of prime importance in the public utility field but so are the many basic operating functions which are the essential foundation upon which the public relations program is built. The district manager has many responsibilites, therefore it is important that all phases of the job be kept in their true perspective to avoid too much emphasis being placed on one phase at the expense of another.

[1] Harold H. Young, *The District Manager—Unsung Hero* (Washington, D.C., Public Utilities Fortnightly, Oct. 22, 1953), 4.
[2] *Ibid.*

The Heartland Gas Company's district organization is designed to serve as a balance wheel in this respect. Each of the major functions is supervised by a member of the district manager's staff. It is the department head's duty to keep him advised if a problem arises or if changing conditions make it apparent that a problem will result if a present operating procedure is continued. This element in the operation of each department cannot be neglected. Each department head must maintain vigilance and a genuine interest in public relations as well as his routine operating functions if the program is to be successful. The district manager or a higher managerial level make the ultimate decision to change policies and procedures, but the department head must operate each department in an efficient, productive manner. It might be said that, with the district manager's guidance, the department heads are accountable for keeping the company moving forward and the conduct of its employees.

The Service Department. The service manager is in charge of meter service, appliance service, customer's service records, and the telephone contact personnel who answer all routine customer inquiries or complaints. In metropolitan areas, these assignments are carried out by personnel with specific job classifications, whereas in small communities, the various service functions may be performed by one or two individuals who capably handle all types of service orders. In a metropolitan area, the work is divided among meter servicemen, appliance servicemen, heating specialists, installation men, and helpers. A radio dispatching system is used with a group of dispatchers communicating with the service trucks when necessary throughout the work shift.

The service manager is assisted by a general foreman. The supervisory staff is than broken down to the foremen level with foremen in charge of meter service and appliance service. In addition to the service foreman reporting to the general foreman, he has an office manager who directly supervises the keeping of customer service records and the personnel answering customer telephone calls.

The service department plays a very important roll in public relations. Exclusive of bill payments, the serviceman and the telephone contact men are the only contact the average customer has with the company except for a possible contact with a meter reader.

The training the servicemen receive to quickly and efficiently adjust or install appliances is a continuous process. As new models and design changes are introduced, the men must be schooled in the proper adjustment of the appliance. This is done by the service manager keeping informed of all changes and arranging for factory representatives to explain and demonstrate. The serviceman's attitude as well as skill has a bearing on the impression he leaves with a customer. For this reason, all personnel in this department must be reminded frequently of their key position in the over-all public relations program of the company.

The Plant Department. The plant manager is in charge of all distribution piping and construction. In addition to the construction and plant operations, he is in charge of plant engineering, warehousing, motor transport, and building services. In a typical district, each of these functions is supervised by an individual who reports directly to the plant manager.

Construction is supervised by a general foreman who is aided by several assistant general foremen. The assistant general foremen each have a specific branch of construction work to supervise. One is in charge of maintenance and repair, two for line extensions, one for service connections, and one for pressure regulation. The crew foremen who directly supervise the construction crews report to the assistant general foreman. This line type organization is very successful in fixing responsibility and avoids having too many people reporting to one individual for him to perform effectively. It also keeps the general foreman and the plant manager from becoming too involved in rather insignificant details and allows them to devote their time and thought to the overall planning and administration of the construction program.

Efficient construction crews providing gas service by extending piping to new customers when it is required with a minimum of inconvenience and delay can very favorably impress the public. Opinions are also based upon the general conduct of the construction personnel in their daily work assignments. Foremen must constantly strive to reduce inefficiencies and waste to gain public respect. This problem is not peculiar to utilities, however, it is more apparent to the public because all work is carried on under the public's eyes whereas private industry is not under such close scrutiny. It is also important that they remain "housekeeping" conscious on the job and leave open construction areas well barricaded and lighted to protect the public.

Plant engineering works very closely with the construction department. It is their duty to design and plan new plant facilities and piping to keep abreast of a constantly increasing market. As new housing developments are erected and new factories are built, it is necessary to expand the existing piping system. This department is supervised by the senior engineer who has several distribution engineers, assistant distribution engineers, corrosion engineers, and a clerical supervisor under his leadership. Besides planning plant construction, they prepare all necessary paper work and maintain records of pipe locations, pressures and other pertinent information to operate an extensive distribution system properly. Distribution planning affects the adequacy of the supply to the customer, therefore, it is a vital factor in the opinion each customer has of the company.

Warehousing is controlled by a supervisor who has a senior clerk, and several clerks, stockmen and warehousemen working for him. This department maintains an inventory of construction material as well as appliances, appliance parts and meters for use by all operating departments. The maintenance of an adequate supply of tools and material is a very important factor in the successful completion of a construction project or the prompt servicing of customers' appliances. From this standpoint, the manner in which this department's affairs are conducted has a bearing on public relations.

The motor transport department is headed by a superintendent who is assisted by a foreman on each of two work shifts. The foremen supervise the activities of the auto mechanics, auto mechanics helpers, garage servicemen, car washers and clerical personnel. Motor transport is responsible for the maintenance and repair of all company vehicles and general tools. In addition to the repair of cars and trucks, the mechanics must be well versed in the servicing of all types of internal combustion engines, compressors, and heavy duty construction equipment such as tractors, cranes, bulldozers, and side booms. The general appearance of the company's rolling stock has a bearing on public opinion. If cars and trucks are allowed to remain in service with dented fenders or are always dirty, it can create a bad impression. The same impression can be created by having to tow heavy equipment back to the garage through heavy traffic because it cannot be started at the job site. The company is aware of these possibilities and has a scheduled service and preventative maintenance program. They also strive to keep the equipment free of dents, well painted, and frequently washed for appearance sake.

The building services section reports directly to the construction department's general foreman. This group is composed of building watchmen, janitors and building maintenance personnel. The security and maintenance of company property is the responsibility of this group. Naturally, the appearance and cleanliness of company buildings is important from a public relations standpoint.

The Commercial Department. The office manager is in charge of meter reading, customer's accounting, credit and collections, payroll and accounts payable, and a building services section. Each of these specific departments within the commercial department is supervised by individuals who report directly to the office manager.

The meter reading department's supervisor is in charge of the reading of customers' meters each month. Meter reading must be conducted in a business-like, well mannered fashion to avoid criticism of the action of employees on customers' premises. The supervisor must thoroughly train new meter readers so their actions will be a credit to the company. The accuracy of the readings they obtain is also of major consequence. The customer expects to be properly billed each month. Billing errors resulting from incorrect readings are very irritating to the customer and reduce his confidence in the company. These reasons illustrate the importance of a public relations consciousness in this group.

The customer's accounting department prepares the customers' bills each month based upon the meter readings provided by the meter reading department. This is principally a clerical operation which has become highly automated in recent years, through the use of IBM billing equipment. The meter reading is recorded on a card with a special pencil by the meter reader. This card is then introduced directly into the IBM equipment which senses the reading at the beginning of the billing period, the reading at the end of the billing period, calculates the consumption and the amount of money owed by the customer, and finally records the consumption and dollar amount on the bill. This equipment has substantially reduced the human errors which occasionally caused incorrect bills in the past. The installation of this system resulted in both time and labor savings. Needless to say, it also had a very desirable effect upon public relations by insuring greater accuracy.

The credit and collection department is headed by the credit manager who is assisted by an Assistant Credit Manager and a head teller. The Credit Manager is in charge of the collection of bills. This entails the supervision of the tellers, numerous clerical employees and collectors. The credit department is also in a key public relations position because of its direct customer contact activities. The average customer that pays his bill over the company's counter expects prompt courteous treatment. Some come directly to the company's offices to apply for service or to request adjustment of appliances. In this case, they are greeted and their needs cared for by members of the credit department staff. In some cases, they are there to request an extension of time in the payment of bills. Regardless of the reason for their visit, it is very important that they leave completely satisfied and favorably impressed.

The payroll and accounts payable department performs the internal functions of paying bills incurred by the company and dispensing the company payroll. They also maintain employee records for life insurance, hospitalization and other employee benefits. The prompt payment of invoices received has a favorable effect upon suppliers' relations which is another factor in the over-all public relations program.

The Business Promotion Department. The business promotion manager is in charge of most of the company's promotional activities within the district. His chief function is to elevate the position of gas in relation to all competitive fuels and forms of energy. Although the company does not merchandise appliances directly to the public, they do have an extensive program established to facilitate their sale through other sources. The ultimate objective is to increase the acceptance of gas equipment by the public and subsequently increase the consumption level. The business promotion department personnel are separated into specific branches of the activity in metropolitan areas to provide expert assistance to home builders, appliance dealers and heating and air conditioning contractors. In districts that are widespread, it becomes necessary for one business promotion representative in each division of the district to provide this specialized service in all phases of promotional activity. To provide a better understanding of the various activities, the writer has chosen to examine each specific function as a separate job and point out its public relations significance.

Dealer sales activities are those cooperative activities which pertain directly to appliance dealers and are under the direction of a Dealer Sales Manager. The dealers vary in size from the small independent appliance merchant to the large national chain department stores. The company encourages them to promote the sale of gas appliances through sales campaigns and increased advertising. The assistance given to dealers takes many forms. If a dealer has a special promotional event planned, the company's dealer sales manager will gladly arrange for the home service department to have a home economist present to demonstrate gas appliances and explain the virtues of gas cookery. The dealer sales manager will also enter into cooperative newspaper advertising of gas appliances in conjunction with the event. In this case, the company will pay a portion of the advertising expense. Special floor display material, window displays, or point of sale displays may be furnished by the company. During special sales campaigns, the dealer sales manager may also offer special sales inducements to the appliance salesmen in each store. This usually is in the form of a small bonus paid by the company and gives each salesman an opportunity to supplement his normal commission on an appliance sale. It is expected that he will emphasize the sales features of the gas equipment under these circumstances in an effort to influence his prospect toward a gas equipment purchase because he will benefit more by its sale.

All of the cooperation given to appliance dealers is intended to improve the company's relations with this group and to increase gas appliance sales. Naturally, the owner of such a business is receptive because he is able to increase his advertising coverage, improve the quality of his displays, and offer special attractions to customers. In addition, his salesmen are grateful for the extra compensation resulting from sales. As a further sales aid, the company cooperates with dealers by offering free adjustment service on new appliances sold by him.

One other important public relations function performed by the dealer sales manager is his placement of gas appliances in the public schools. Under this program, the company provides the most modern gas ranges and refrigerators available for use in the high school and grade school home economics departments. This equipment is replaced every two years at no charge to the schools. This is done to acquaint future homemakers with gas cookery and to maintain a desirable relationship with the school system.

The home service department is a segment of business promotion which deals directly with the homemaker. This department is composed of several home economists who conduct demonstrations, explain new equipment and advise customers on the latest cooking and baking techniques.

One phase of this department's work is tied directly to the sale of appliances through dealers. After a gas appliance is sold, the dealer advises the home service department who sends a representative to the home to demonstrate the operation of the appliance to the lady of the house.

Group demonstrations are conducted for various women's club groups, girl scouts, boy scouts and others. These demonstrations offer an excellent opportunity to show off new equipment innovations as well as teach the younger groups to cook on gas.

The department also works directly with the schools to provide future home-makers with information about gas equipment and its proper use and care.

The home economists working in this department can have a very desirable effect upon future business because they devote much of their time to working with young people who will be tomorrow's customers. This program not only affects the opinion of those directly involved but also that of their friends and families.

Builder sales activities are conducted to increase the number of gas appliances installed in new homes. Gas advisors work directly with building contractors who are involved in new home construction. To this market the company does merchandise equipment. The dealer can buy appliances for installation in new homes at a rather attractive price. In addition to the sale of appliances, the Gas advisors are responsible for the development of several promotions each year with various builders. The object is to get gas appliances featured in homes that are open for public inspection. Each year the company features a "House of Enchantment" which is an all-gas equipped home complete with gas actuated air conditioning. The house is promoted jointly by the builder, the furniture dealer that has decorated and furnished the house, and the company. The house usually offers many intriguing features and is highly publicized. During the period it is open for public inspection, it is visited by thousands of people interested in new homes. This offers an ideal way to show the latest gas equipment to an interested public.

From a public relations standpoint, the builder sales program affects both the builder and the customer public. If a closer relationship with a builder results in his installing gas equipment in speculative homes rather than competitive equipment, the desired result has been achieved. He will do so only if he is convinced that the equipment he buys will make that house easier to sell than it otherwise would be. The program is designed to favorably impress the public by displaying to them the modernity of gas appliances and thus increase their acceptance.

The field of residential air conditioning is handled by an air conditioning specialist. It is his duty to work with heating and air conditioning dealers, architects and customers in the promotion of residential and small commercial air conditioning. In most cases, this involves direct customer contact to interest them in air conditioning and then designing an appropriate system. The air conditioning specialist must be well versed in the application of residential heating and air conditioning equipment and duct layout techniques.

The company is dedicated to the sale of high quality air conditioning systems. They are not interested in competing in the low-priced, low quality air conditioning market. It is felt that a high equipment standard must be maintained, and the quality of service must be higher than that offered by competitive air conditioning if the acceptance of gas actuated air conditioning is to improve. For this reason, the air conditioning specialist must be qualified to select equipment which will capably fill the needs as well as design a system which will give the customer complete satisfaction.

Although this function affects a relatively small number of customers and contractors in the trade directly, their reaction to the results has definite public relations significance. The best recommendation a product can get is the testimonial of a satisfied customer.

Commercial sales activities are directed toward another segment of the company's business. This phase of promotion is confined to commercial customers, restaurant equipment dealers, plumbers and large volume space heating contractors. Primarily this phase is a combination of cooperation directly with the customer and his contractor. Because of the size of most commercial projects, the company's commercial representative frequently becomes involved early in the planning stage through inquiries made by an architect, a contractor, or perhaps, the owner, into the availability of gas for the intended uses. In most cases, the size of the project is large enough that the planner realizes that some preliminary checking must be done to assure an adequate source. This is true whether the project requires gas for space heating only or if a quantity of gas is to be used for processing, such as would be found in a restaurant, bakery or laundry. It is the commercial representative's job to see that gas is used wherever practical in such instances. He will work directly with the planner to advise him of any specific requirements or aid in the planning by advising him of the size of gas lines to be installed, the meter location, size and piping details, or help in determining the proper type of equipment to install. In addition to serving the planners of new projects, he also must contact existing customers to determine their future needs and aid them in the correction of any service problems they may have. Direct customer contact through follow-up and canvassing is a very important element of success in this portion of the business. For this reason, the personnel selected for this assignment must be well grounded in gas application fundamentals as well as have the desirable characteristics of a good salesman. The advice he gives must be accurate or the company's public relations will suffer. The assistance and recommendations rendered may result in the expenditure of large sums of money. If his judgment has been poor, the consequences can be disastrous to the company's prestige in the eyes of the parties affected.

The commercial representative works directly with school boards, their administrative staffs, church councils, and municipal officials, as well as individual owners of commercial enterprises. For this reason, he is a key figure in our relations with the community public as well as the customer public. He is active in outside organizations such as the local restaurant association, the Chamber of Commerce, or perhaps technical groups such as the National Association of Power Engineers. Contacts made at meetings can be helpful because they are made on a semi-social basis. This allows the commercial representative to become better acquainted with the people he is dealing with. In turn, it allows them to know him better which can be good or bad depending upon his "words and deeds" under these circumstances. It is hoped that to know him better means that they will increase their respect for his judgment and call him whenever a fuel application problem arises. His conduct may influence a school board's decision to use gas or a competitive fuel in a new school, or it may lead a consulting engineer to recommend another fuel for a large project. For these reasons, the company must select qualified people for this job. The impact on public relations as a result of selecting the wrong man can be very severe.

The Industrial Department. The industrial sales manager is in charge of four principle functions: industrial development, the promotion and retention of industrial processing loads, the promotion of large volume air conditioning, and the promotion of gas in competitive large volume space heating situations. Depending upon the district's size and the number of accounts to be handled, the industrial sales manager may be assisted by one or more industrial engineers and industrial representatives. To qualify for a position in this department, the candidate must be a graduate engineer with a desirable personality. He must be aggressive and display a "sales outlook." Because of the technical nature of the work and the importance of contacts made, the management, by necessity, is very selective in the placement of personnel in this department. In each district, the industrial department operates on the district level rather than assigning individuals to the divisions. In widespread districts, this is modified by locating the industrial engineers in strategic locations in the district and making them responsible for a given area, but they still report to the industrial sales manager and remain a part of the district organization.

In the field of industrial development, the industrial department actively encourages new industries to settle in the area. This activity is not confined to merely contacting prospective industries but includes many other facets although this contact is an important part of the program. In addition, the industrial department cooperates with all other local agencies interested in industrial development. This is done through membership in the local Chamber of Commerce Industrial Development Committee, attendance at seminars and clinics devoted to industrial development which are sponsored by state organizations, cooperation with local governmental agencies such as planning commissions, and with other companies and organizations who are working with prospects. The company also engages in some national advertising directed to industries interested in expanding or relocating. This advertising outlines the many desirable features of the company's operating area. They also prepare brochures for direct mailing to prospects. The over-all program is a comprehensive system to help the economic growth of the communities the company serves.

From a community relations standpoint, the industrial development program is very important and should have very desirable results. The company benefits not only through the addition of a new industry but through the many desirable side effects created through increased employment in the community. Every new industrial plant not only creates jobs within the plant but also generates the increased buying power which supports many additional commercial businesses which are responsible for services. This also strengthens the banking interests and the general prosperity of the community.

The promotion and retention of industrial process loads is also an important phase of the industrial department's business. Many industries require large volumes of gas as an integral part of their conversion of raw materials into finished products. The proper application of heat requires the maximum flexibility possible combined with precise control methods. In many cases, the properties of gas have made it an indispensable tool. The industrial department personnel must be experts in the field of heat application in order to serve as consultants to industry as specific utilization problems arise. The assistance they offer their customers in the solution of such problems helps increase the acceptance of gas as a product. To further qualify industrial engineers for this type of work, the company sends them to the Institute of Gas Technology at the Illinois Institute of Technology where they receive an extensive concentrated course on gas utilization. The company realizes that there are occasions when the selection of a competitive fuel is the most practical solution to a problem. In this case, the company representative frankly advises the customer that the competitive fuel is the best choice. Although this does not sell gas for this particular process, it does earn the respect of the customer because he feels he has received an unbiased, honest answer. He will more quickly accept the representative's judgment when the next heat applicable problem comes up.

To be effective in this job, the department personnel must keep up to date with technological changes in all phases of fuel utilization. In addition to the numerous applications of gas to form heat for such operations as forging, heat treating, baking, drying, metal melting, glass melting, and many others, the representative must be familiar with processes which require gas as a raw material. Practically all modern heat treating techniques employ the use of a protective atmosphere prepared from natural gas or ammonia. Natural gas is also being used as a raw material in the petrochemical industry to provide the hydro-carbons which ultimately become synthetic fibers, fertilizer or some other wondrous product. The industrial department's goal is to be recognized by its customers as being technically qualified to answer all of their questions concerning processes requiring heat. This is a valuable sales tool as well as a favorable public relations factor.

Along with the service rendered directly to the customer, one should consider the effect of having satisfactorily completed the proposed project. The assistance rendered in the creation of new processes within an existing industry has the same desirable effects as the establishment of a new industry.

The promotion of the use of gas actuated large volume air conditioning is another function performed by the industrial department. Large volume air conditioning to the Heartland Gas Company means an installation requiring twenty-five tons of capacity or more. This criteria establishes the size project that will be handled by industrial department personnel instead of the air conditioning specialist of the business promotion department. This is the logical point in sizes to change the sales responsibility, because residential style and size equipment is normally used for smaller tonnage jobs and the smallest commercial type equipment available is in a twenty-five ton size. Buildings large enough to require twenty-five tons of air conditioning capacity or more are normally designed by an architect rather than from private plans. This is the reason the program entails scheduled contacts with local architects, mechanical engineering consultants, and installing contractors as well as calling on prospective owners. Because this field is highly competitive, the relationship cultivated with the architects and consultants has a definite bearing upon the success of the program.

Industrial department personnel help the architect and consultant by sizing and laying out the necessary gas piping and meter setting for them as well as providing them with complete information regarding the availability of gas for the project. Due to the fact that the use of gas for air conditioning is not a widely accepted practice, it is necessary for the industrial department personnel to try to educate the architect and consultant by providing him with information concerning the types of equipment available, the sizes, and the advantages of each type. In many cases, this also leads to the preparation of an owning and operating cost analysis for his use in comparing gas equipment with competitive equipment. The gas industry is hopeful that as architects and others interested in specifying air conditioning equipment become familiar with what is available and realize that dependable equipment is obtainable from several manufacturers, they will specify gas equipment. Until 1959, the gas industry had a very limited amount of equipment available for large tonnage systems. Until that time, only one manufacturer made an absorption air conditioning machine larger than fifty tons capacity. Since that time, two other prominent manufacturers with fine reputations in the air conditioning field have entered the absorption market. This has changed the attitude of many architects and consultants concerning absorption equipment because they had always been hesitant about specifying equipment available through only one manufacturer. As a result, the contact job performed by the industrial department has become more rewarding.

From a public relations standpoint, this phase of industrial department business is significant because of the influence this relatively small group of architects and engineers has over the customer who is investing in a new building. If product acceptance can be obtained through large volume air conditioning, the residential market will also become more penetrable.

Competitive large volume space heating is the fourth facet of industrial department responsibility. Space heating has always been a competitive market due to the difference in price of various fuels. In each case, an evaluation must be made of the facts other than the direct fuel costs. Large volume space heating normally involves the use of industrial type space heaters or steam generators depending upon the building design and the use to which it will be put. Many installations can be as adequately heated by one fuel as another. Many times the selection of fuel is based upon the degree of refinement of the system, the ease of control, the amount of maintenance required and the dependability of the fuel source. Industrial department personnel are qualified to evaluate all of the factors to be considered and to prepare a complete owning and operating cost study for consideration by the prospective building owner before his final decision is reached.

It is the company's policy to present a completely factual cost study without favoring gas except where the facts justify it. Some companies do not follow this policy and attempt to deceive the prospect by presenting him with a series of half-truths which favor their fuel or equipment. A utility company cannot afford to practice deceit. It would have the worst possible public relations effect. The company feels that it must maintain the highest possible integrity in competitive situations if it is to preserve its respected corporate image in the community.

The Company Reviews Its Program.   It can be seen from the description of the company organization that each department has a public relations obligation. Periodically, it is necessary to review the current standing to be certain that the public relations program is being effectively handled. For this reason, the management occasionally analyzes its position to see if changes are required to implement further improvement.

The current review and many of the pertinent facts disclosed therein are described to point out the necessity for developing a dynamic program which receives a reappraisal at frequent time intervals.

Performance Review.   During the course of a day, the Heartland Gas Company switchboard handles eight hundred fifty telephone calls from customers. The calls primarily pertain to service requests and inquiries concerning all phases of the business. Normally all calls of this nature are channeled into the telephone contact section of the service department. Eight men are assigned to receive calls of this nature and to answer the customers' questions. In the past ten years, the telephone contact section has been progressively expanded from a complement of four employees to the number now on the job. These additional employees were added because of the increased number of calls which were being handled daily. To a degree, this was brought about by the addition of approximately 3000 new customers to the lines each year. The average number of telephone calls handled per man per day was eighty in 1950. The number of calls received per customer per year was 0.91 in 1950. The year end tabulations for 1960 revealed that the average number of calls handled per man per day was ninety-five and the number of calls per customer per year was 1.42.

This increased telephone activity causes overloads in the system at times during peak hours. The company is aware that such an increase could cause problems and wants to completely evaluate the condition. To determine what could be done to correct this situation, the company requested the telephone company to conduct a survey over a prolonged period and to make their recommendations. After the telephone company had carefully checked the number of calls being placed into the company daily for six weeks and had monitored calls to each department, the following recommendations were made:

1. Reduce the amount of time spent on each call.

2. Answer the telephones more promptly.

3. Increase the number of people available to take calls during peak periods.

4. Increase the number of trunk lines into the company to accommodate more calls simultaneously.

5. Attempt to improve the personnel's telephone answering technique.

The company is constantly striving to improve its telephone service to customers because they realize the importance of this vital customer contact. After receiving the results of the telephone company's survey and its recommendations, the management decided to make a more thorough evaluation of the system to ascertain where changes should be inaugurated to make further improvements. To do this, calls were monitored to determine how well the contacts were being handled from the standpoint of information given to the customer and how delays occur which tie up the switchboard.

The supervisor in charge of the telephone contact section relayed the following cases to point out how public relations problems can develop from the use and abuse of a telephone.

Mr. Smith's Lost Meter. Mr. Smith, a customer, called to advise the company that he had recently purchased a different home and planned to move in three days. He requested that the service to his existing home be terminated on Friday and service be established at his new address the same day. The telephone contact man wrote down both addresses and asked Mr. Smith to hold the telephone while he checked the records. After a considerable lapse of time, the telephone contact man returned to the telephone and advised the customer that service could be terminated at the present address on Friday but there would be some delay in receiving service at the new house because the records showed that no gas was installed there. He further explained that the customer would have to install a gas pipe to the property line and the company would have to make a connection to its main before the meter could be installed. The customer told the employee that he was certain that a gas meter was in the basement of the new home. The employee responded by telling the customer that he must be mistaken.

Mr. Smith said he would check and call back. He then drove over to the new house, went into the basement and found a gas meter installed. Mr. Smith again called the telephone contact man and told him there was a meter in the basement. The telephone contact man told him there couldn't be because there was no record of such an installation in the service files. To convince him, Mr. Smith resorted to saying, "If you want me to, I'll bring the meter down and put it on your desk to prove it." Service was established in his name on Friday as he originally requested.

To further complicate the company's relationship with this customer, he didn't get a bill for the first three months at the new location. One day he was home for lunch and happened to see a gas company meter reader leave the house next door. When the meter reader started to pass his house without stopping, Mr. Smith called to him and asked why his meter was not being read. The meter reader told him that there wasn't any gas service in the house so he always passed it by. Mr. Smith straightened out this problem by leading the meter reader into his basement and showing him the meter. Since that time, the records for the Smith account have been brought up to date and no further diffculty has occurred.

Mr. Jones' High Bill.   Another customer, Mr. Jones, called to inquire about the amount of his gas bill. He explained that the current bill represented the largest gas bill he has ever received, yet the weather during the month was no more severe than previously and he had made no changes which would affect his consumption. The telephone contact man in this case politely asked Mr. Jones to wait until he could check the Accounting Department records. While Mr. Jones held one line, the telephone contact man then used a second line to call the accounting department for information concerning the account. After some delay obtaining the necessary information, he returned to the call from Mr. Jones and advised him that the records showed that a meter reading had been taken and the bill was not an estimate. He further explained that because of the size of the bill, he would gladly issue a service order to have a second reading taken to confirm the bill. Mr. Jones was pleased with the treatment he received from the courteous contact man but was disgruntled over having to wait several minutes to receive satisfaction.

Mr. Thomas' New House.   Mr. Thomas, a prospective customer, had recently been transferred here by his company and had just purchased a new home from a local builder and wished to get gas service as quickly as possible because he wanted to start heating the home to dry it thoroughly before moving his family from another city. His first impression of the company was created by receiving a "busy" signal when he called. His second was created when, after getting the company operator and stating what he wanted, the lines into the telephone contact section were busy. After waiting for a line to be available, the telephone rang numerous times before it was answered. Mr. Thomas then explained that he wanted to apply for service for a newly constructed home. He waited while the telephone contact man checked the service records to see if a service connection had previously been made in the name of the builder. He was then advised that because no connection had been made, he would have to talk with the engineering department. Mr. Thomas' call was then transferred to the engineering department where he was informed that they would mail him the necessary application for him to fill out and mail back. When the completed application was returned, the connection would be made as quickly as possible; however, he should anticipate about a two-week delay because of a backlog of such applications. Mr. Thomas explained the urgency of his request and was given special consideration so that he could avoid moving his family into a hotel until the work was completed.

Cases of these types were uncovered as a result of the section's supervisor monitoring calls. The supervisor quickly added that bad contacts do not occur very often when the total number of calls handled daily are considered. The cases described are not typical contacts but are examples of extremes. A great percentage of all telephone calls are expeditiously carried to a quick, concise conclusion to both parties' complete satisfaction.

Simultaneously, the management conducted a survey of customers' opinions of the quality of service offered by servicemen in their homes to see if this area contributed to the higher number of telephone calls received. The service manager relayed several cases which were brought to his attention which had interesting public relations results.

Mrs. James' New Range. Mrs. James was delighted with her recent purchase of a new gas range from her appliance dealer. The dealer explained at the time of her purchase that the Gas Company would gladly adjust the range after it was installed if she would call and advise the company when she wished service. Mrs. James had the new range delivered and installed, then called to have it adjusted. Arrangements were made for a serviceman to visit her home the following day. When the serviceman arrived, Mrs. James asked him how he liked her new range. He promptly told her that he didn't like it and that she should have purchased a different make which would give her better results and fewer maintenance problems. The serviceman adjusted the equipment without further comment. The mechanical part of his job was perfect but he left a different impression with Mrs. James. Mrs. James called the appliance dealer and accused him of selling inferior merchandise. After hearing the story, the dealer called the gas company and "commented" on the serviceman's "diplomacy."

The Politician's Pride. One serviceman was called to the home of a customer to calibrate an oven the day after a local election. The serviceman arrived in apparent poor spirits. He was polite to the lady of the house and performed as a model employee as he lit the oven and started to check the thermostat.

Then the lady of the house made the mistake of asking him what he thought of the election results. The serviceman then gave her his very complete opinion of the persons that had won the election including a description of the last horses they stole. He didn't know that the lady's husband was the campaign manager of one of the successful candidates.

Mr. Richards' Faulty Furnace. Mr. Richards called the gas company one morning to report that he had detected an odor of gas in his basement and wished to have it checked. Within a half hour, a serviceman was at Mr. Richards' home to investigate for leakage. Instead of greeting the customer with "good morning" when he opened the door, the serviceman's comment was, "You picked a fine day to have a gas leak." He then proceeded to shut the gas off to test the customer's lines to determine whether or not they were pressure tight. When Mr. Richards asked him what he was doing, his only reply was "I'm checking for leaks." After putting air pressure on the piping, he told the customer that the automatic valve on the furnace was defective and that a plumber would have to replace it before service could be restored. When asked how long it would take to get him back after repairs were made, he merely said, "I don't know." Fortunately, a plumber did replace the defective valve early in the same afternoon and Mr. Richards did get service restored the same day—by a different serviceman.

The first serviceman did a very efficient job of handling the mechanical part of his job; however the customer was less impressed by his mechanical ability than by his "bed-side manners."

The service manager maintains a training schedule which keeps all service employees acquainted with all technical developments in appliances. They are thoroughly schooled in the latest changes so they will be equipped with the "know how" to do a complete and efficient job of servicing on the customer's premises.

In order to measure the opinion of the commercial segment of the business, they, too, were surveyed. This survey included both customers and the tradesmen and professionals most frequently involved in large projects.

The business promotion manager interviewed architects, consulting engineers and piping contractors specializing in large commercial work. His conclusions were as follows:

> Our main problem is trying to educate the people interested in bidding large jobs so they will understand our requirements. It seems that every time a large shopping center or other commercial job is being constructed, the commercial representative has to go over every small detail with the bidders. If we don't do this, the owner doesn't get two bids back on the same basis. When this happens, the owner is unable to evaluate the bids. Usually the contract is then awarded on the basis of price only. Later, the owner is subjected to extras which cost more than he anticipated.

This problem is frequently caused by the architect's lack of detail in his specifications. He leaves it up to each bidder to work out his own details with the gas company or bid the job without any instruction. Because of this common practice, we are occasionally accused of being inconsistent in our requirements. There may be some foundation for this accusation because each job may have five or six contractors submitting bids. When they inquire about the details, perhaps they talk to different people in the department. Of course, many times there is more than one way to do the job; therefore, they may get slightly different information. Contractors also claim that we are too slow in providing the information at times so they don't wait but bid without our recommendations.

When such problems occur and the installation is improper, it becomes necessary for the contractor to change the installation to conform with the company's specifications. If any additional expenses are incurred, the contractor passes this additional cost on to the customer. The customer feels that this charge which increases the cost of his total project is unnecessary and usually holds the gas company responsible instead of his architect, the consulting engineer or the installing contractor.

The company also decides to review its relationship with the community. In this case, in reviewing the record, they found that the company was held in reasonably high regard by both local government and the community agencies. The local press has reacted favorably to the publicity relases offered by the company and has not opposed the company in rate applications or any other company function requiring public support. In all, the company's relationship could be considered favorable.

After reviewing the problems revealed by the close check on customer telephone contacts, by the survey of service performance, the interviews conducted in the commercial field, and the general community attitude, it was decided action was warranted to improve its public relations in all phases of its business.

Hanley Engineering Corporation

Byron Dobie, a 1959 graduate of the Amos Tuck School, was administrative assistant to Mr. Lincoln Lashton, President of Hanley Engineering Corporation. Byron had joined the training program of Hanley in June 1959 and was appointed Mr. Lashton's administrative aide in August 1960.

Reprinted by the courtesy of Professor John W. Hennessey, Jr., Dartmouth College. Copyright © 1962. This case has been disguised where feasible to permit its use for instructional purposes.

The Hanley Engineering Corporation was located in Pittsburgh, Pennsylvania, where it was founded in 1878. The Company provided engineering services of various kinds and had gradually built a national reputation for excellence in its consultations on such large construction jobs as bridges, dams, and hydroelectric installations. Nearly all of the executives of Hanley had engineering or technical degrees from university engineering schools. The stock of the Hanley Corporation was publicly subscribed; forty per cent of it was held by the family of George Hanley, the company's founder.

On September 19, 1960 the following conversation took place between Mr. Lashton and Byron Dobie.

Mr. Lashton: Byron, in the morning mail I got a leter which I want you to read. It raises an issue that I plan to put on the agenda of the October meeting of the Executive Committee. I want you to write a memorandum to me in preparation for that meeting. But first read the letter.

[Byron read the letter, attached here as Exhibit 1.]

Byron: Mr. Stokely is a personal friend of yours, isn't he, Mr. Lashton?

Mr. Lashton: Yes, we've been rather close friends for more than twenty-five years. I'm sure you know Stokely as one of the most respected men in Pittsburgh. He is practically Mr. Public Service, and he has done immeasurable good for Pittsburgh. Also, of course, we do a lot of work with Pioneer.

Byron: What kind of memo do you want me to put together?

Mr. Lashton: Our executive committee meeting is October 14th. I want to discuss Stokely's letter at that time, and prior to the meeting I will circulate his letter and some material on the activities of the Fund for Adult Education.

What I want you to do is this: give me by noon on October 8th a memo telling me what issues you think are involved for Hanley in considering our proper reaction to Mr. Stokely's letter. Also, I want you to include a brief discussion of your personal definition of "liberal education" and what relevance this concept has to the operation of Hanley Engineering Corporation.

Your memo will be a help to me. I may not agree with it and I'll tell you if I don't. I'm not going to talk with you about it at all because I want your views undistorted by my predispositions. I know you can't possibly make any recommendations and I don't want you to. But you can give me a comprehensive idea of the issues which are involved in thinking about what decision the executive committee must make.

Byron: Will you show my memo to other people?

Mr. Lashton: Probably not. I'll have to see it before I decide that. It is primarily for my own use in preparing for the executive committee meeting.

(End of dialogue)

Exhibit 1

Office of the President
Pioneer Steel Corporation
Pittsburgh, Pennsylvania
September 16, 1960

Mr. Lincoln R. Lashton, President
Hanley Engineering Corporation
Carnegie Building
411 Federal Street
Pittsburgh 3, Pennsylvania

Dear Lincoln:

As you know I am serving on the Board of Directors of the Fund for Adult Education. The Fund was established by the Ford Foundation in 1951 as an independent organization to advance and improve "that part of the educational process which begins when formal schooling is finished." The Directors of the Fund defined "its special task as that of supporting programs of liberal adult education which will contribute to the development of mature, wise, and responsible citizens who can participate intelligently in a free society." For the period 1951 through 1961, the Fund received from the Ford Foundation a total of $47,400,000.

The Fund has supported the development and offering of a wide variety of formal and informal programs of liberal adult education through institutions of higher learning; national organizations; fellowship awards and special training programs; public understanding; fact-finding, research, and evaluation; and educational television. The impact of these programs has been broad, and the Board has felt special gratification at the response to these efforts on the part of the business community.

At the end of 1961 the Fund's financial backing from The Ford Foundation will come to an end, and we are making plans to replace Ford support with that of a wide variety of institutions and persons interested in continuing liberal education for adults.

My own special interest is to develop support from my colleagues in Pittsburgh industry to provide a financial cornerstone, as it were, for the contributions other sectors of the Greater Pittsburgh community will want to make. As I told you recently, Lincoln, we see the promise of substantial rewards to our metropolis in such projects as expanding the power and influence of WPEX, our educational TV channel, giving grants to the local universities to offer programs and conduct experiments in the adult education field, and sponsoring public colloquia to promote liberal education among adults.

It is time for us to be concrete. I am asking the presidents of one hundred prominent business organizations in Pittsburgh to provide the leadership we need, by declaring what types and amounts of contribution they will make on behalf of their companies for the continuing support of this vital program. I think you agree, Lincoln, that we need to act; and the sooner the better.

The initial meeting of our group of one hundred Pittsburgh presidents will be on Thursday, October 20th, at 12:00 noon in the Duquesne Room at the University Club. At that time, I would like to discuss detailed plans with you, propose a $200,000 annual budget, and ask you each for (1) your reactions to the whole program and (2) what amount of support your company is prepared to give, in terms both of financial aid and executive time.

Please call me, Lincoln, if there are any questions you would like to discuss before October 20th.

Cordially,
James T. Stokely
President

Bibliography

A. Public Relations and the Corporate Image

Burns, Leland S. "Is Babbitt Dead?" *Harvard Business Review* (October 1967), pp. 14–54.

Henry, Kenneth. "Perspective on Public Relations," *Harvard Business Review* (July-August, 1967), pp. 14–18.

Newman, William H. and Thomas L. Berg. "Managing External Relations," *California Management Review* (Spring 1963), pp. 81–86.

Palmer, H. B. "Education-Industry Statesmanship," *Conference Board Record* (August 1965), pp. 21–24.

Petit, Thomas. "Imagery as a Management Skill," *Business Horizons* (Summer 1964), pp. 23–28.

Stephanson, T. E. "The Prismatic Image of the Organization," *California Management Review* (Spring 1963), pp. 67–72.

Wernette, J. Phillip. "The Image of the Businessman," *Michigan Business Review* (November 1962), pp. 26–31.

Wise, T. A. "Hill And Knowltons World of Images," *Fortune* (September 1967), pp. 98–102.

B. Corporate Philanthropy

"The Company and the Arts," *Duns Review* (July 1965), pp. 40–41, 62–64.

Johnson, Orace. "Corporate Philanthropy: An Analysis of Corporate Contributions," *Journal of Business* (October 1966), pp. 489–504.

Scheinfield, Aaron, "Social Investment: A New Concept of Corporate Philanthropy," *Management Review* (July 1968), pp. 2–7.

"Seven Rules for Corporate Giving," *Business Management* (March 1963), pp. 43–48.

Smith, George Alan. "Business Investment in the Arts," *Conference Board Record* (July 1966), pp. 23–26.

Watson, John H., III. "Corporate Contributions Policy," *Conference Board Record* (January 1967), pp. 12–14.

Weingarten, Jaala. "Some Company Answers to the Growing Problem of Corporate Giving," *Duns Review* (August 1967), pp. 31–32, 61–62.

PART THREE

Business and
The Individual

The conflicts that arise between business and groups in our society can usually be traced to the basic rights of the individual. Many conflicts fall into the categories of human relations, leadership, and conformity. Philosophically, the basic issue involves the fundamental ends versus the means of work accomplished by persons in our society. Should business consider individual employees as means to the economic-productive ends of our economy, or should business reorganize for and around the employees, with goals for their satisfaction primary to the efficient accomplishment of work? The dilemma posed by these two points of view is far from reconciled, but significant efforts have been made toward its resolution. In general, management has been condemned for a purely scientific approach to business which has ignored the sociological, psychological, esthetic, and physical value-needs of individual employees.

A. Business and Youth: Conformity
or Individualism

The hostility toward the business world among many recent graduates from top-ranking colleges and universities may be traced to the notion that business functions solely in the interest of efficiency and profit and at the expense of human needs and goals. In the selection, "The Private World of the Class of '66" [10], this unpopular image is characterized. Graduates are contending that "business isn't where the action is" and to many students, motivated by the desire to make a contribution to human betterment and social welfare, business is "for the birds." This unfavorable impression of business can, in part, be attributed to the novels of the past generation, if not half century, that have stereotyped the businessman as the unethical autocrat. The majority of students only read critiques of business practices and are unexposed to the business periodical literature. The task of the businessman to present a more effective image to the youth of today and the leaders of tomorrow is therefore difficult and complex. The businessman must be prepared to identify those areas in which business has made a significant contribution to the improvement of human welfare. Unfortunately, business has often been represented by campus recruiters offering the hard sell or the slap on the back, rather than by effective speakers who are able to represent business at its best.

A most effective spokesman for the business world, Roger M. Blough, argues that "Business Can Satisfy the Young Intellectual" [11]. In his article, he emphasizes that business provides an individual with the opportunity to translate free inquiry into effective action. Corporations have the resources—in money and manpower—for "getting ideas off the ground" and "into the marketplace." Contrary to the image of business as a breeding ground for conformity, Blough claims that individual initiative and creative thinking are the primary requisites for success in the business world.

B. Participative Management: Opportunity for Individualism

The conflicts between conformity and individualism underlie all philosophies of organization and human relations. If authority in industrial organizations creates perennial conflicts between individuals, work groups, and the total social system and business, the question will necessarily be raised whether or not the individual has been relegated to the role of an "organization man." On the one hand, business asks greater employee adaptation to organizational needs and goals. On the other hand, society discourages any business requirements which may create "organization men." It appears that the extremes of conformity or individualism must be avoided. Unacceptable forms and degrees of nonconformity create intolerable conflicts both in the achievement of organizational goals and in the working harmony of the organization itself. However, excessive managerial domination over employees through overt or subtle pressures to conform to organizational practices often stifle initiative and adversely affect work performance necessary to achieve economic goals.

Essential to the achievement of economic-production-work goals and human relations goals has been the analysis and formulation of business leadership philosophy. Our democratic heritage, the participation needs and values of individuals within democratic organizations, and the maximum development and utilization of human potential have served as goals for an ideal leadership theory. The process of maximizing individual human potential meets the dual objectives of effective resource utilization in our economy and the enhancement of human dignity in the development of employees as individual personalities. But the problem is not so easily resolved by defining ideal objectives. For example, participative management as an ideal of democratic leadership within business organizations has been promoted and argued for over a decade. In theory, managers and employees jointly establish work goals and share responsibility in broad areas of economic decision making. In "The Case for Participative Management" [12] Keith Davis describes the potentials of this technique for improving production and morale within business firms. He points out specific conditions necessary to insure maximum effectiveness such as open communication between manager and employee, and ample time for discussion. He cautions managers against adopting this technique without an understanding of its philosophy and an appreciation of the social science skill required to function as a dynamic discussion leader. With these caveats in mind, he encourages managers to "proceed."

An indepth analysis of participative management is presented in the selection "Participative Management: Time For A Second Look" [13]. A review of this leadership style reveals that it does not have universal application, but instead is essentially situational. It is generally known that this leadership theory has emphasized the communication and motivation skills of management in dealing with their subordinates. But this "second look" includes other factors such as the delegation of responsibility for decision making, the formulation of goals and performance standards, and the definition and application of managerial controls. When the responsibility aspects of these decisions and problems are defined, a more realistic analysis of the application of participative management is afforded. We now know that participative management is certainly not just a process of "keeping people happy," or allowing them to participate solely on the basis of their whims or inclinations.

The human relations, leadership, and conformity problems will not be easily reconciled. In fact, it is important to realize that these problems will be perennial. The varying types and degrees of leadership and human relations must be effectively reconciled with the legitimate needs of the organization, the individual, the work group, and society. These leadership issues are illustrated by the cases within this section. The Ralph Bennett case portrays the human-relations problems of an employee adjusting to an organizational environment in a foreign country. Distance and foreign environment compound the normal communications and organizational problems, and re-emphasize the necessity for defining responsibility and accountability procedures. The effects of different types of leadership upon an existing organization are examined in the Ball Wholesale Drug Company case. The problems involved in making a transition from two distinctive styles of leadership are detailed. The goals, accepted practices and philosophies of both subordinates and leaders in this case emphasize the effects of different types of leadership. While the theory of "ideal" types of leadership are constantly debated, a leadership style must always meet the pragmatic test of effective operation, given a particular environmental structure of personnel and organizational goals.

A. Business and Youth: Conformity or Individualism

The Private World of the Class of '66

10

Duncan Norton-Taylor

When President Barnaby Kenney of Brown was asked what he thought of the flock of students under his wing, he observed: "I'd like to wring their necks"—which might have been the response of any number of exasperated elders involved with today's undergraduates. Know-it-all airs, an inordinate amount of clamor, and a derisive attitude toward authority have appeared to mark a whole generation. But Keeney admits that they are "able and very sensitive people," distinguished from other generations by "the intensity and spread of their concern," a fact businessmen trying to hire these young people have discovered. Touching on a subject that has corporate management disturbed, Keeney adds disconcertingly: "They are very concerned with the stereotyped life of the businessman and I don't blame them. I don't think I could tolerate it either."

Some 526,000, the best of them kindled with idealism and actually very well informed about many things, will graduate this June. A lot of them will be captured by U.S. corporations, of course. But this does not mean that business doesn't have to worry about a disaffection that is widespread among these young fry. It is not only prevalent, it has been accumulating for some time. Some of it may diminish, as this year's graduating class grows older; or idealism may turn to cynicism. But this rejection of business is strong now, and many of those with the highest scholastic ranks will go into teaching, passing on their moral and intellectual disapproval. Management, for its part, can affect a concern about the stereotypes of teaching that have produced the mythology of the "stereotyped life of the businessman." But it cannot overlook

Reprinted with permission from *Fortune* (February 1966), pp. 128–132, 166, 168, 170, 172.

the current attitudes of the young—in its campus recruiting, its training programs, or in its public relations.

The large number of students going on to graduate school is cited as proof of the fact that they are shunning business. Actually, statistics for the whole U.S. show that graduate-school enrollment comes to only about 10 percent of the number in undergraduate schools, and that percentage has not increased very much in the past four years. But this figure is misleading, and obscures the real problem that business is up against. For the anti-business sentiment is strongest in the schools that have the highest academic standards, where U.S. business in the past has carried on its most ardent solicitation of recruits. And in these top-ranking colleges from 60 to 85 percent of last June's seniors reportedly decided to go on to graduate school, proclaiming as they went, "Business is for the birds."

THE HARVARD PATTERN

It will be some comfort to recruiters to know that the top percentages are a little exaggerated. Harvard College is a case in point, and a good one because it has at hand, as not many colleges do, a quite comprehensive survey of the class of '65. Surveys of the class of '66 at this date could only tentatively reflect students' intentions: many of them have not yet made up their minds as to what they are going to do in June; and a sudden change in the draft rules disallowing deferment for graduate work would alter many plans. But as of now the class of '66 can be expected to follow the pattern of '65.

The Harvard men's response to the questionnaire put out by the Office for Graduate and Career Plans was close to 100 percent. There were 1,091 men in the class (an extraordinary 67 percent of whom graduated with honors); 71 percent said they intended to go immediately into graduate schools; 16 percent into jobs; 8 percent into the military (in a less hazardous 1962, 14 percent of the class decided to discharge their military obligations immediately); 5 percent said they were going to travel, didn't know what they were going to do, or didn't answer.

The 16 percent who were job-bound hardly represented a triumph for company recruiters: a quarter of the jobs turned out to be in social-service work (e.g., the Peace Corps, Vista); a total of only fifty-one men in the whole class were clearly headed for corporate life: twenty-eight into general management, twelve into banking and finance, eleven into sales. Perhaps another dozen, technical men, would go immediately into some company. Half of the job-bound and those going into military service looked on this employment as only temporary; they planned to go back to school eventually for graduate study, the majority of them in the arts and sciences. If it all works out the way the report shows, then 85 percent of Harvard's class of '65 will indeed end up in graduate school.

In their final career plans, however, business stood higher than these figures would indicate. Thirteen percent of the 1,091 said definitely they intended to end up in "businesss"—i.e., manufacturing, transportation, banking, merchandising, insurance, utilities. And adding a number of masters and doctors (in scientific research, engineering, and the liberal arts) who will ultimately land in a corporation might well produce, Harvard's people think, something around 25 percent. It would be the largest percentage figure in the list of intended careers.[1] But it still did not alter the fact that U.S. corporations were losing out on a very large number of talented men. The report made the dry observation that the lower a man's academic standing the more likely he was to choose business as a career.

The Harvard pattern would most certainly be repeated at other high-ranking privately endowed colleges. Even in some of the tax-supported colleges, where the question of finances weighs more heavily than in the Ivy League, the high-ranking students are going on to graduate school in remarkab:y large numbers. At Rutgers, New Jersey's state college, some 50 percent of the 1965 class had plans for graduate study; so did about 50 percent at the College of the City of New York, where financial resources are often desperately low (and academic standings exhilaratingly high). There are, however, plenty of scholarships around that a smart young man can pick up. At Columbia, almost a third of those going into graduate school last June received one or another kind of award. The U.S. Government last year put out an estimated $262 million in grants that would see a man wholly or partially through two years of graduate work; there are also numerous private foundations passing out funds.

There are other factors in the graduate-school trend that actually have nothing to do with disliking American business. One of them is the growing conviction that a master's degree is a necessary piece of equipment in an increasingly competitive business world. A man who stops with a bachelor's degree is considered by some of his colleagues to be virtually a dropout. Students are exposed to a faculty bias in favor of academe as a permanent way of life. Another factor is the sellers' market the students find themselves in. Business recruiters falling all over themselves to offer them jobs is a phenomenon that the boys think will continue for some years. They also feel that two or three years of graduate work will give them more time to compose their thoughts and decide which of the large number of job offerings they want to choose.

And finally, once again, there is the draft. They are not always candid about admitting it is a factor, but it unquestionably is with many of them. Between going to graduate school and going into military service is an easy choice. It would be unjust to overlook a large number who consider military service an obligation every young American must take on with his maturity. A vocif-

[1] Some of the others: higher education (18 percent), law (18 percent), medicine (15 percent), creative arts and journalism (4 percent), secondary education (3 percent), government (3 percent).

erous minority, of course, are violently opposed to involvement in Vietnam both for the U.S. and for themselves. Others look on their impressment into military service as a misuse of superior manpower. "My friends don't say so," Terry Eakin, a Princeton engineering major, confided, "but their attitude is, 'We're the elite. Our talents can be used better somewhere else.'" It is safe to say that most of them are resigned to the possibility of being drafted sooner or later, but do not consider it either unreasonable or unpatriotic to avoid if they can.

"JACK KENNEDY TURNED US ON"

All these factors can be used to discount the significance of the figures on graduate-school enrollment. They add up to the fact that the motivations stirring the class of '66 are various and complex. But none of the foregoing diminishes the need for American management to understand the salient fact that a *Wall Street Journal* writer, Roger Ricklefs, turned up more than a year ago: the prejudice against business is undeniable, and permeates the country's highest-ranking colleges.

Their morbid view of things is not confined to business. In their narrow campus vista they don't see much about American society to encourage them; business is only a part, if a large and looming part, of a whole society that badly needs doing over. Obviously, there must be some background to this line of thought. Interviews with college administrators, faculty members, and the students themselves produced some insights into the private world of the class of '66.

President Buell Gallagher of C.C.N.Y. calls it the "dysphoric generation." Although their disgruntlement with the state of the world is shared by a lot of older people, their generation, they feel, has been confronted from the outset with an almost exclusively outrageous set of events. When asked to try to recall the first event they became aware of outside their own childhood, they answered, "Korea." Their boyish confidence in their own country was shaken by the orbiting of the Russians' Sputnik. They recall the TV quiz-program scandals. Mother and father may have liked the Eisenhower Administration but twelve-year-olds found nothing to enthuse over: "A government of old men." The 1960 presidential election caught their interest: "Jack Kennedy turned us on." But the sky fell in when he was slain in Dallas. Nor did the pall lift with Lyndon Johnson and his Great Society, which they view with skepticism. Now in the short span of their life so far their country has moved from Korea to Vietnam.

Could they had done any better? That's not the point. It is they, please, who intend to do the questioning. True, the young are always disposed to question authority—for one thing, to find out if it knows what it is talking about. This college generation is more disposed than most to question authority, because they have an unusual lack of confidence in it.

Their questioning is not always direct. Where the assault on authority is overt it usually comes from a small group, while the rest watch interestedly. The questioning may take the form of mockery. President Keeney of Brown could trace a good deal of his exasperation to one M. Charles Bakst, a wispy youth with an abundant crop of hair falling down to the top of his large spectacles. As editor-in-chief of the Brown *Daily Herald,* Bakst launched attacks on such conventions as the parietal rules, which regulate the hours when male undergraduates can entertain girls in their dormitory rooms. Bakst wanted all strictures lifted. "After all, we're adults." One of his favorite causes (which also inspires undergraduate agitators on other campuses) was the need for more communication between students and the administration, not to say the businessmen members of the corporation. In the interest of better communication Bakst had one of his editors phone the members of the Brown corporation and demand to hear their views on the parietal rules. Thomas J. Watson, Jr., who besides being on Brown's executive and advisory committee is chairman of I.B.M., replied in effect that he couldn't listen to every file clerk at I.B.M. who might have an idea about how the company should be run; and if *he* were president of Brown he would make the rules more, not less, strict.

Bakst was his own undoing. He published a report in the *Herald,* a complete hoax, to the effect that the administration was going to let some Brown coeds maintain their own apartments off campus. The president and the deans decided Bakst had gone too far, and his career as a college editor came to an end. Bakst, incidentally, expects to go into journalism after he graduates: "I don't see any satisfaction in a business career. I'm too egotistical."

There was never any "Berkeley incident" at Brown. The majority of students accepted as inevitable the rules of the university and of society, one professor thought. But precisely what this college generation is doing is questioning what rules of this society *are* inevitable. And while few students on any campus would rise and march with Bakst, they would agree with the spirit of his published harangues. Why can't they have more freedom? The answers, when forthcoming, don't satisfy them. They trust faculty members, but not presidents, deans, parents—all those conspiring to frustrate them. In the end they retire behind their own defenses: they confront their elders (who include businessmen offering them jobs) with a seemingly formidable self-confidence. It shines in the candid faces on these pages, almost hiding their apprehensions.

"WE DON'T HAVE TIME TO THINK"

One must keep reminding oneself, talking to them, that they are still adolescents, even though they are old enough to go to war, and sometimes large enough to get offers to play professional football. They have qualms about the leap into adulthood and into a career, and what they say they think is sometimes a way of rationalizing their misgivings. Now what is it, specifically, that they think of business, apart from what they think of the world at large? They measure business subjectively: how does business' purpose in society connect with *my* purpose in life?

Discussion with them took place at nine colleges: in the job placement office at Columbia (while outside along College Walk two partisan groups manned rival posts—for and against the war in Vietnam—and small knots of students stood arguing in the rain, although most of the people abroad on the campus hurried by purposefully with books); at the Colonial Club, in Princeton; at Brown in the John D. Rockefeller Jr. Library (which students call "The Rock" since the administration begged them not to call it "The John"); at sobersided Rice, in the library of one of the women's colleges (Rice is divided into colleges like Oxford); at Rutgers, at the University of Texas, at U.C.L.A., at Northwestern, at C.C.N.Y. The settings would change, and some of the costumes, but the same somber, surprisingly humorless voices would be heard at each place.

In a sense they are in rebellion against the cliché, which business leaders like to expound, that they are a national asset. They think that the idea takes away their individuality, that they are being served up wholesale to some cause they don't acknowledge and don't sympathize with. Meanwhile they are prevented from making certain choices of their own, which might have included not going to college at all. They feel curiously that they are a deprived group. At U.C.L.A.: "We've been herded along. We don't have time to think of what's really important." At Rutgers: "You have to go to college for the opportunities. It's all laid out for you." . . . "My father says, 'You've got to make a choice on how you're going to earn a living.' He climbed on my back for being a history major." At Brown: "Some of my friends in the Peace Corps feel a definite tension with their parents. But this generation completely rejects parents having any say in our choice of careers."

The idea of making a significant contribution to human welfare is a strong motivation everywhere. It is, of course, one urge that has taken so many of them into the Peace Corps. It also accounts for the considerable turning of backs on business, since students see few opportunities there to serve mankind. They feel that corporations more often than not have fallen down in their responsibilities to the public welfare. Where, they inquired at U.C.L.A., was business leadership in such matters as installing safety devices in cars and in cleaning up air pollution in Los Angeles? How did Houston businessmen justify building the Astrodome stadium and various cultural centers, one young man inquired at Rice, while overlooking "terrible hospitals, air pollution, fantastic slums?" His indictment did not go entirely unchallenged, however, by Rice students well aware of the amount of oil and cattle money invested in Rice.

But the theme, "I'm concerned with doing something significant," ran through every discussion. "I've given thought to business only as a last resort," said Mario Polese, an economics major at C.C.N.Y. "Business and the sale of products are what make the U.S. what it is. But what I'd like to do is improve the lot of people. I'd like to say I've made a change, no matter how small, in the United States, Africa, somewhere."

The bulletin board outside the placement office at Columbia carried posters advertising job opportunities with the Peace Corps, Department of Labor, the Foreign Service, CIA, NSA, AID. San Francisco and the Tennessee Civil Service reached out for the men on Morningside Heights. New York City offered an "exciting career as an Investigator"—i.e., helping the city's authorities to detect tax frauds, bring to book outfits that were unlawfully soliciting public funds, circumvent unworthy people who were trying to get free hospital care. This was only part of the job market. Numerous other government agencies were after the class of '66, not to say the graduate schools, which overtly recruit and, of course, hundreds of corporations. The very multiplicity of jobs, along with the plenitude that accounts for the confidence that a job will always be waiting, distracts them. Seniors are like chameleons on a plaid, said one placement officer. A history major at Rutgers mourned: "I want to do something but I don't know what so I don't want to decide on anything."

MONEY JUST DOESN'T FIGURE

The idea of making money appealed to very few young men and women with whom the question was discussed. In fact, at the Colonial Club in Princeton there was some questioning as to whether the whole profit system was to be trusted, any more than a lot of other ideas previous generations had believed in. The discussion took place in the dining room before the students moved into the lounge for coffee and cigars.[2]

That they are happy heirs of a well-developed profit system seemed momentarily to have escaped the attention of the men at the Colonial Club. They are not unique in this respect. Few other campus groups found the benisons of the profit system a particularly arresting thought. Naturally they are aware of living in an affluent society. There's plenty of money around, but so what? Does it contribute very much to personal happiness?

At the University of Texas, Kaye Northcott decided: "I've had comfort and security all my life and I know what it's like—it's dull." Money is not necessarily evil, it just doesn't figure. At Rice: "People aren't talking about money any more. They take it for granted. Money is almost a by-product." At Rutgers, a possibly more pragmatic attitude: "I want lots of money or not any. I don't want any temptations that get you into a lot of petty bickering, time payments,

---

2 Some readers will recall Mrs. Blaine writing to her son Amory at Princeton, circa 1920, and urging him to go into finance. "You start as a messenger or a teller, I believe, and from that you go up—almost indefinitely"; and Amory's—or F. Scott Fitzgerald's—Corybantic revolt and peroration: "Socialism [is] the only panacea I know." And some readers will wonder if things have changed very much at Princeton. Reassuringly, Whig Hall still stands.

and all that." At Northwestern: "I'm not completely oblivious to money but I'm not so concerned with it as with doing something significant."

Meanwhile, business and industry show up in various shades of gray, turning the wandering chameleon into complementary colors of dejection:

John Meier, of Brown, gloomily reported: "I had a summer job with a corporation—every morning 150 guys arriving at the same office, all carrying briefcases and wearing neckties!" Also at Brown: "I don't know where my antipathy to business comes from but I can't get excited about boosting the G.N.P. or even continually raising the country's standard of living." Frank Kretzer, of U.C.L.A., had this conviction: "In a university laboratory you can pursue whatever interests you. In business mostly you crank out answers for some pharmaceutical company." At Columbia: "We're taught in college to act as individuals. We get a sense of pride out of an academic product we turn out. In business we won't be creating anything. We'll just be helping to maintain the corporation." Said Steve Raskin, a history major: "Do I have to learn to live in a rat race, working nine to five and commuting from some little house in the suburbs? Is that all I have to look forward to?" And he added, "I know when I've got it good. I'd like to stay right here."

There were a few voices raised above this general *Angst:* At Rice: "You don't have to get lost in a corporation. Goodness brings its rewards. If you work hard enough someone will see you." . . . "Business can be a way of influencing our society." At Northwestern, Peter Mattingly, who is majoring in business studies and is in the top 10 percent of his class, observed: "A lot of kids in our class are a bunch of pansies." (He meant craven.) And he added bravely: "I look forward to getting out without anxiety." But such voices were infrequent.

IT'S NOT WHERE THE ACTION IS

Business has been in bad repute before on the campuses, most notably in the days of the depression. But by the fifties certainly it had acquired considerable aura, so that there is an irony about its sinking from favor now, at a time of unprecedented prosperity and in the midst of all its splendid technological adventures. It became clear in the discussions that the students were almost completely ignorant of what has been going on in modern business: they can discern no bright and challenging aspects—only dark ones.

But where do they get their ideas? Some of them came from businessmen themselves—from fathers who brought their office woes home with them. (They were not treated to the sight of father zestfully arriving at the office next morning.) They read almost nothing in the business press, which is probably to be expected. Edward Dauber, president of the Student Council at Rutgers, registered his impression that there is no excitement in business, no great entrepreneurs, no leaders to attract a young man's interest, and dismissed business journalism with a wave: "Only businessmen read business magazines."

In a recent speech Lawrence Kimpton, vice president of Standard Oil of Indiana, complained of the novels, movies, and TV programs "which have exhibited a truly remarkable lack of realism in their treatment of business, coupled with a generally hostile viewpoint." Though dated, *The Organization Man* and *The Man in the Grey Flannel Suit* are still widely influential source books. But let the young men help explain where their ideas come from:

At Texas: "We're all products of the 1930's liberal intellectual criticisms of business." At Northwestern: "A lot of our ideas come from the professors. We hear a lot of condemnation of business practices in the last century. There is praise, too, but it's never as resounding as the condemnation. We idolize our top professors." At Brown: "The faculty has no remarkable attitude toward business. Their attitude is rather a remarkable unconcern." At Rutgers: "Actually they don't give us much of anything about business history, mostly just about the Robber Barons and the munitions manufacturers who started the First World War."

Is the class of '66 simply seized of clichés? Have they been "brainwashed," as Kimpton put it? To some extent. But it is fairer to let several of them sum up how it all looks to them:

"We've never seen war, no bad depression, we've been shielded from death," said Richard Abrahams, a history major at Northwestern. "Our generation probably has more ability, time, wealth than any in a long time. It's natural that there should be a tendency toward idealism. We are more aware of things. Each of us expects to do at least as well as our parents but there is a concern about non-fulfillment. We want to be part of the changing attitudes of the world."

"Our parents wanted to make the world a better place too and business was their way of doing it," said John Sennhauser, of Brown. "Our minds are more open. We're interested in the chance to make ourselves felt, to put our own ideas into effect, to be decision makers. We don't object to business but we feel that business doesn't need us. *It's* doing all right."

"Business isn't where the action is," said John Durham, an anthropology major at Rice.

$636 FOR A CHEMICAL ENGINEER

Business has to take these young men and women seriously. And obviously it does. Talent scouts representing the biggest corporations and some not so big ones are now tracking across the campuses, competing for recruits with government men and highly skilled counselors from graduate schools. Company recruitment in the graduate schools themselves and among bachelors of science (chiefly engineers) takes place in the fall; the second-semester search, which is not as avid, is for bachelors in the liberal arts.

Du Pont will have as many as fourteen full-time, forty part-time recruiters at work. Last year Du Pont interviewed 10,000 students at 230 colleges and hired some 1,500. Humble Oil will have six full-time men, backed by some 175 line organization people spending part of their time in the campaign. Last year Humble held some 15,000 interviews, made 1,800 offers, and hired 675. Equitable Life used 117 recruiters, five of them full time, held some 2,700 interviews on campuses, made 232 offers, and hired 101. Interestingly enough, Equitable does not recruit for salesmen at the colleges; it goes after older men.

A top-ranking engineering student may get ten to twelve offers. At Rice they tell of one youth who had twenty-two offers, encouraged everyone to feel he was interested in that particular firm (which he no doubt was), and spent most of his last year being flown around the country for a firsthand look at various headquarters and plants. Students know pretty much what they can expect in the way of salary. Average starting monthly salaries offered C.C.N.Y. students in 1965 are typical (they are running about 5 percent higher this year). They range from $636 for a chemical engineer to a low of $320 for a liberal-arts major. Some liberal-arts majors hired for management training programs were offered as much as $550.

A master's degree in the technical fields is good for an extra $100 a month, a Ph.D. $200 to $300—a consideration not overlooked by those students who are trying to make up their minds whether to go on to graduate school. Nor is it overlooked by graduate-school recruiters, who also stress that the advanced degree, with its broadening effect, will enable a man to grow laterally through a company in any number of directions, like a tree, while the fellow with only a bachelor's degree and a company training program behind him is inching along in some narrow divisional groove. The point is open to some argument.

Government starting pay scales will run below corporations', but not enough to make much difference among social-welfare-conscious students who take money matters so lightly. The Peace Corps, which enlisted upwards of 5,000 college students last year, pays $75 a month plus room and board (such as it is).

"THAT'S A LAUGH"

For all the time and effort they expend, corporations don't always put their best foot forward when they go out to recruit. This is too bad, since it is in the college placement officers' interview rooms that business and the new generation come face to face. Many college administrators (and students) think recruiting policy needs to be revised. Some revisions are suggested by the criticisms made of recruiting.

"Too many of the recruiters," said the placement officer at one eastern college, "are crew-cut, sharp fellows who aggravate the bad image business already has." The dean of another college contrasted them with Dr. Raymond Saalbach of the Wharton School of Business—a "real pro who can interview twenty-five students in a row and remember each one perfectly without taking a note. Business often just sends a man who will clap the kids on the back."[3]

The hard-sell recruiter is no more effective with the students than the clap-on-the-back man if they suspect he isn't giving them straight answers, and suspicions are always high: "Ford and I.B.M. come here and try to get us all psyched up—tell us we're going to do scientific things." . . . "They always talk in terms of superlatives, like we're going to be the James Bond of the business world. At a company like Du Pont that's a laugh. Everybody knows everything is done by committees." . . . "Recruiters can't talk on a technical level. Why don't they send somebody who knows something about it." . . . "Their brochures feature us sitting in big offices with good-looking secretaries. *That's* a laugh."

The brochures, on which corporations spend much money and creative talent, do feature the words "growth" and "challenge," and show very small groups of predominantly youthful men (often without coats) in obviously important conferences. Many of those boys who have had summer jobs in industry, like John Meier at Brown, have come back to the campus to contribute their experience to the general skepticism about such pamphlets: "It's not like it says in the book."

The task of creating an appealing image of business requires a sophisticated kind of public relations—e.g., using the tool of education itself. One idea along this line might be to have the Council for Economic Development sponsor some chairs, underwritten by corporations that now spend millions of dollars for research at the colleges, for the undergraduate teaching of business history and modern corporate operations. Many young men are attracted to the Peace Corps because it offers a chance to run something; the idea of being a big frog even in some faraway puddle strikes their fancy. An education in modern business methods might show them just how effective a young executive can be inside a corporation, with large resources to work with. They would discover that in many modern corporations committees are part of the art of good management, and far from smothering initiative they encourage it. Then undergraduates might start believing the brochures.

Training programs ("internships" is now the word for it) are themselves part of public relations. But too often they flatten out youthful spirits. "I doubt if businesses have overhauled their training programs to accommodate the quality of the current graduating senior," says Frank Endicott, director of placement at Northwestern. "Companies are giving these college men jobs that

---

[3] Not that employee-relations departments don't urge their recruiters to do better than that. From the instruction manual of a major oil company: "The task of the interviewer is to listen actively and to keep the information flowing. He does this by conveying to the applicant the feeling that he is interested in him as a person. The interviewer should demonstrate that he is following attentively what the applicant is saying. An occasional 'hmm' or 'uh uh' or 'I see what you mean' will help to accomplish this."

high-school graduates could handle. When these kids come back to the campus they never say they were given too much responsibility—always too little. This is the worst image business could get."

One dean recalled a recent graduate who went into training at Armstrong Cork and wrote one of his old professors after a short time, "Get me out of here." Others have come back from summer jobs at I.B.M., said the dean, vowing, "I can't possibly put up with a life like that."

NOT MUCH FOR AN ENGLISH MAJOR

Recruiting has recently taken a turn that disconcerts those who believe in the importance of business' whole role in the world. A corporation's divisional needs have always determined to a great degree the kind of men recruiters go looking for. Currently, of course, industry has a seemingly limitless need for engineers, and probably will have for a long time to come. The demand has been inflated by the defense buildup. In any case, the recruiting effort has turned more and more avidly on the engineers, and away from the liberal-arts majors.

Two points can be made here. First, it is a situation that the liberal-arts students' own attitude has helped produce, particularly at the privately endowed colleges in the East. Newell Brown, director of Princeton's Career and Study Services, says, "Companies that have been coming here for a long time now say they hear so much anti-business talk they aren't coming back." Robert Canning, director of college recruitment at G.E., reports, "Less than ten years ago, a G.E. recruiter's visit to Dartmouth would produce fifty interviews. Now we're lucky to get five or six to show up." According to Eastman Kodak's Marion Folsom, that company makes no attempt at all to recruit any more at the eastern colleges at the undergraduate level. Virtually all the new men for sales, administration, industrial relations, and Eastman's various training programs are recruited from a score of small colleges and the state universities.

Some there are who applaud this development. They are glad to see companies getting away from "the eastern-college syndrome"—an infatuation with the academic prestige of the eastern group and a few other great schools in the U.S. It is true that business has tended to overlook much of the talent to be found in less famous colleges. It has also overlooked other sources of young recruits—for example, the government itself. But it would be a sad thing for both sides if business should turn away from those colleges that still jealously nourish rich academic traditions. Neither business nor the vital centers of humanistic culture in the U.S. can afford to become isolated one from the other.

The second point grows out of that. Business is currently putting a low priority on the man who has majored in the humanities. This will be denied; but the evidence lies in observable hiring polices. Sitting in his office overlooking the booming landscape of Houston, Harry Taylor, who is in charge of recruitment for Humble, said matter-of-factly:"The poor liberal-arts majors. We are looking for them but mostly for sales. There's not much of a job market for an English major."

At Princeton last fall a seminar of businessmen and educators met to discuss "The Liberal Arts Graduate and the Business Community." It was a pity that more representatives of U.S. industry were not there, as well as some undergraduates. For several of the speakers described very well the challenges that are inherent in business, and made some familiar arguments, but with new passion, to the effect that the men most competent to meet the challenges were in fact men trained in the humanities.

WHERE SHAKESPEARE COMES IN

Ormsbee Robinson, director of educational affairs at I.B.M., spoke of the changing nature of American corporations and the corporate world; of the increasingly multinational character of U.S. firms, of how decisions made in home offices can affect the economies of whole nations.

James F. Oates, Jr., chairman of the board of Equitable Life, spoke of the "simultaneous" task of management to serve the best interest of employees, owners, and customers to their satisfaction. For example, what should management do about aging and no longer useful employees, whose problem must be weighed against the interests of other employees, the continuing efficiency of the company, and the public's investment? "This is a human saga and the heart is touched by such responsibility," he said. "Certainly, the solutions require imagination, vision, and humanity."

Business must search out men with curiosity and open minds; men with a taste for adventure; men with an understanding of human nature who have learned to live with ambiguities, uncertainties, and stubbornly held opinions, and can distinguish between what is important and what is not, and answer the question, "What god do I choose to serve?"—the question, said Oates, toward which a study of the humanities leads a man "inexorably." These qualities must be developed by formal disciplines, said Princeton's dean of the faculty, J. Douglas Brown, through history that lays out perspectives, through literature that reaches into the minds and emotions of other people: "No one should have power over others who has not been exposed to Shakespeare's explorations of human tragedy."

And yet Taylor of Humble was, to a degree, right. An English major is not very marketable in today's world—if the poets are the limit of his passion. One cannot deny that technology has risen as a force that is changing society and human character as well. And a highly marketable man in modern business is the man trained in the humanities *and* in technical disciplines—in accounting or mathematics, or law or engineering or chemistry or physics. A man forsooth for all seasons. A challenge indeed for the country's educational system and a stimulus to undergraduates who are sitting around moping because business careers seem so purposeless and they themselves so little understood. Within their generation lie the potential of what could be a remarkable development in history: a highly technological world with a conscience—a realizable proposition if the idealism of the current college generation doesn't turn sour on exposure to inevitable frustrations.

The heaviest obligation in repairing the alienation between business and scholarship falls on business. One cannot expect twenty-year-olds to know exactly what direction reforms should take. They have splurged their discontent, and business has received some jolts from its young critics, which may be in its ultimate interest if management can find the way to respond.

Business Can Satisfy the Young Intellectual
11
Roger M. Blough

Where will the young intellectual go in search of a career? Is the currently graduating collegian shunning the opportunities of the marketplace? Or is all the talk about business being "for the birds" an unsupported conclusion built on inadequate data?

These questions are debatable, for the data are indeed inadequate, but they suggest a number of even more basic questions which can and should be answered:

> Does business have a realistic offer to make to the intellectual? Does it have a desired place for him? Does it offer a worthwhile choice? Can it provide meaningful work? Will it require him to "stretch" his native capacities to the utmost? May he comment, criticize, and dissent in the environment of business, and can he induce constructive change?

> Or, contrarily, will the work he finds in the business world constitute dull drudgery? Will it mean stagnating conformity and lead to a gradual ossification of the intellect?

NEEDED: BRAINS

The matter is of serious import because twentieth-century business needs the young intellectual today more than it ever needed him before. The scope of

Reprinted with permission from the *Harvard Business Review* (January-February 1966), pp. 49–57. Copyright © 1966 by the President and Fellows of Harvard College; all rights reserved.

operations, multiplication of environmental factors, accelerating technological change, complexity of products, and intangibles and imponderables that constantly arise in the marketplace, all call for the best brains available.

DESIRABLE ATTRIBUTES

The thoughtful and disciplined intellectual of whom we speak has a restless spirit of inquiry and an idealistic desire to improve the society in which he lives. He has some knowledge of history, economics, and literature, as well as current affairs. He has an understanding of the environmental forces and activities that affect his fellowman, and he can appreciate the importance of some of the questions which are daily tossed up to his intellectual level. He has a two-way antenna. He knows how to be receptive but also how to communicate. He has some grounding in basic sciences and mathematical techniques. He has—or eventually will acquire—some knowledge of the art of management.

And if he goes into business, he may well need all these attributes, and a few more. For the business units which operate in today's competitive world have no easy, nonintellectual time of it.

A cursory examination of the topics covered in any recent issue of HBR and other business publications will demonstrate this point. The list includes plant-community problems, government-business relations, public affairs, stockholder relations, internal management problems which range all the way from installation of information systems and centers to new products and product obsolescence, competitive pricing, investment and marketing analyses, union-company viewpoints, internal communications, public relations, diversification, international variables, status symbols, and many others—all requiring intense attention, careful analysis, and decisions that constantly test the soundness of executive judgment.

If he has time to contemplate, the intellectual in business may also wish to ponder the competitive effect of the revisionist economics of Communist countries, the balance of payments deficit, or a dozen other matters, all of which will have a bearing on his large or small business in this tightly woven world, and any one of which can engage his attention indefinitely.

But if it is true that some youthful intellectuals of today are rejecting the challenging opportunities of the marketplace, where are they actually going?

NONBUSINESS COMPETITION

It has been reported that only 40 of the 1,064-man class of 1964 at Harvard had signed up with corporate recruiters by the time of graduation. Most of the others, it is said, favored careers in such fields as teaching, scientific research, law, and public service, while 31 signed up with the Peace Corps.

Dartmouth, on the other hand, reported that out of 640 men who graduated in 1964, 200 looked toward business careers in accounting, advertising, finance, industrial administration, and insurance. Another 227 were headed for related careers, such as architecture, aviation, forestry, journalism, and corporate law. The remaining 213 planned nonbusiness careers.

The data are fragmentary, but there does not appear to be adequate evidence that there is any substantial increase in the percentage of current graduates who are bypassing business in favor of other occupations.

GOVERNMENT SERVICE

An inquiry at the U.S. Civil Service Commission yields the following information:

> Results of thousands of college recruitment interviews conducted with those expressing an interest in federal government service as a career demonstrate no pronounced trend away from business. Business recruitment appears to be just as competitive with government service now as it has ever been.

> Despite the extensive new emphasis on college recruitment by the Civil Service Commission, the federal government (excluding what are known as temporary agencies, such as the Peace Corps and Poverty Program, which are not under the Civil Service Commission) has hired diminishing numbers from the Federal Service Entrance Examination in recent years, as these figures show:

> 1962—10,000
> 1963— 9,000
> 1964— 6,000
> 1965— 6,000 (projected)

> Recruitment by so-called temporary agencies has been greatly accelerated, but it is apparent that those entering such programs are generally not making a career decision. In many cases they are seeking an "unusual experience" before choosing a career. The Peace Corps, since its inception in 1962, has in fact placed only approximately 10,000 college graduates in the field out of a total first attraction of 70,000.

TEACHING PROFESSION

The National Education Association, on the other hand, reports that the recruitment of teachers is steadily increasing. This is credited to the following four factors: (1) a great national concern for education, and a rapidly rising demand for teachers; (2) the improved status of teachers; (3) the rapid increase in teaching salaries; and (4) the employment of a larger number of graduates in the arts and sciences as teachers, without the requirement of extensive undergraduate work in education as such.

There does not appear to be a significant number choosing education on the negative basis of "flight from business." As a corollary bit of information, the National Education Association's Higher Education Series reports that about the same number—approximately 2,000 biennially—have left business to enter college or university teaching in the academic years 1957 through 1965. Of the total number of new teachers in institutions of higher learning from all sources, the percentage of those coming from the world of business has decreased from a high of 11.1% in 1957 to 8.2% in the 1964–1965 academic year.

ADVANCED EDUCATION

The most intense competition business faces for college seniors of today, however, seems to come from the colleges and universities themselves in their recruitment of candidates for their graduate schools. Studies indicate that nationwide about 33% of those receiving bachelor's degrees in June 1965 applied for advanced schooling, while in the Ivy League colleges the number is reported to have run as high as 80%. Furthermore, many of them receive financial assistance. At Harvard, for example, it is said that 60% of the students now enrolled in the university's graduate schools enjoy scholarship stipends of some form.

So marked has this trend toward advanced education become, in fact, that the graduate who resists it may almost pride himself on being a nonconformist. But the mere fact that a young intellectual who receives his bachelor's sheepskin decides to work for an advanced degree instead of seeking an immediate job in business does not necessarily mean that he has renounced business as an ultimate career.

Inquiry in educational circles sheds some interesting light on this point. For example:

Every graduate school of business in the United States is filled to capacity, and the Educational Testing Service reports that the number of students taking admissions tests for graduate study in business was 30% greater in the 1963–1964 academic year than in the previous year. The comparable figure for law schools was 23%.

E. C. Arbuckle, Dean of the Graduate School of Business at Stanford University, feels that the on-campus attitude toward business is improving, not deteriorating. He reports an increase of 29% in the number of applications received in the 1964–1965 academic year and says that when this increase in the *number* of applications was compared with that for the graduate schools of law, medicine, and engineering, only the law school showed a comparable gain. Moreover, 96% of the 1965 graduating crop of MBA's (excluding those with military obligations) took jobs in industry, while 80% to 90% of those receiving master's degrees in engineering also turned to industrial careers.

Business school deans also report that industry is making starting salaries so attractive to the holders of advanced degrees in business, engineering, the sciences, and other disciplines that undergraduates increasingly feel the need to enter graduate school. It is interesting to note that business and industry currently employ more Ph.D.'s than all of the liberal arts colleges in the country combined.

Certainly the usefulness of a graduate degree to those who seek to reach the higher echelons of management is not to be denied. The Council for Financial Aid to Education recently reported the findings of a study it had made of the backgrounds of the two top executives in each of America's 100 largest corporations.[1] This study revealed that, in 1955, 61% of these executives were college graduates, with 17% having earned advanced degrees. By 1961 these percentages had risen to 68% and 22% respectively. And by 1964 the figures had risen to 75% and 26% respectively. This is an increase of nearly 23% in college graduates and of about 53% in those holding advanced degrees—all in a period of ten years. In the light of this evidence it would be unwise to jump to the conclusion that the college senior who goes on to graduate school has necessarily renounced a business career in perpetuity.

However, it is of course possible—and even probable—that a number of young intellectuals who might otherwise have embraced a career in the marketplace will continue their pursuit of knowledge indefinitely and thus remain in the academic world as teachers or as scholars. But before we go to the wailing wall, let us note that it would be a very unhappy day indeed if many of our intellectuals did not choose the path of the scholar, go into the ministry or medicine, become writers or artists, or engage in the work of government or the cause of charity. There is no substitute for teaching, for example. Knowledge is not transmitted from generation to generation biologically.

As for our own recruitment efforts at U.S. Steel to attract high-potential college graduates, recent experiences indicate that while competition is increasing markedly, the resources of the campus for providing suitable candidates are apparently in proportion to our needs.

To sum up the available evidence, therefore, it seems that (a) college graduates are entering the marketplace in satisfactory numbers to meet current manpower requirements, and (b) of those bypassing the marketplace now, a growing proportion of them are seeking advanced degrees in business administration and other disciplines designed to equip them for eventual leadership-career roles in business and industry.

STUDENT "VALUES"

At the same time, however, the evidence also indicates that the world of business enjoys less than unalloyed prestige among those on the campus who regard themselves as the intellectual elite and who would seek acclaim among their fellow intellectuals.

[1] See Fact Sheet entitled "Study of College Backgrounds of Top Two Executives in America's Largest 100 Business Corporations" (New York, 1965).

PERSONAL HEROES

Searching for insight into a student's "scale of personal values," the admissions committee at Antioch College has, for the last three years, asked candidates this question: "What prominent human being who has lived during the twentieth century do you most admire?"

The 450 freshmen who entered Antioch in the 1964-1965 academic year named 104 personal heroes. The top 10 were Mohandas Gandhi, John F. Kennedy, Winston Churchill, Franklin D. Roosevelt, Dr. Martin Luther King, Dr. Albert Schweitzer, Bertrand Russell, Eleanor Roosevelt, Albert Einstein, and Woodrow Wilson—in the order named. But not one of the 104 personalities named by the young students was a businessman or industrialist; nor, incidentally, was a single military leader cited by the Antioch freshmen.

Evidently the unique qualities of a Dwight Eisenhower or a Douglas MacArthur, like those of an Andrew Carnegie or Thomas Edison, are not the ones most admired by the budding intellectuals at Antioch. The great contribution such men have made to the preservation of human freedom, on the one hand, and to the advancement of man's material welfare, on the other hand, does not seem to satisfy the idealistic urge of many of today's young collegians for selfless service to humanity.

The ideological gap between the intellectual and the marketplace thus still remains as it was in the days of ancient Greece, and it is best summed up in modern colloquy by the jesting collegian who said he had nothing against businessmen—he just wouldn't want his daughter to marry one.

PRACTICAL CO-EDS

Fortunately for the perpetuation of mankind, this collegian's view is not universally embraced on the co-ed side of the campus. John Chamberlain, author and columnist, appeared last summer as a panelist at a "forum on economics" in which the participants were 50 "college queens" chosen from leading universities on the basis of classroom standing, campus popularity, extracurricular achievements, and personality.[2]

He reports that most of the girls disavowed any prejudice against businessmen as prospective mates. Nevertheless, one U.C.L.A. co-ed, who concurred in this unbigoted view, reported that a majority of students on that campus resented business. She attributed this antipathy to the "myths" that were circulated there about the profit system.

A girl from the University of Florida, who was personally pro-business, noted that the business courses in her college seemed to attract the "stupidest people." A campus queen of the University of Connecticut, who was

[2] This "Forum on Economics" was held at the Hall of Free Enterprise at the New York World's Fair. Mr. Chamberlain's column, syndicated by King Features, Inc., appeared in the the *New York Journal-American* on June 19, 1965.

among the minority, did not want a businessman for a husband—on the grounds that he would be away from home too much and, besides, the big corporations "put too much pressure on the executives' wives." She and others said that their ideas of business had been gained chiefly from plays, movies, television, "and Vance Packard."

All of the foregoing commentary led panelist Chamberlain to conclude not only that this reflected badly on college faculties, but that business had done "an abysmally rotten job for more than 30 years in justifying its own existence to the high school and college students of America."

ESCAPISM REALITIES

In the face of this indictment from such a respected source, it is only small consolation to note, in passing, that the young intellectual who would shun the marketplace may not always succeed in doing so, since some 80% of the American people are engaged in some phase of business activity. Occupational America is mostly business America.

Choosing the worthy occupation of priesthood, the intellectual may, for example, find himself a bishop of a diocese but with vast real estate interests to oversee. If the intellectual chooses public service and is successful, he may become responsible for one of the already too many businesses now owned or controlled by government. If he chooses medicine, he is likely to find himself in contact with the business aspects of his own establishment, and sooner or later he may go on a bank board or head the local school board.

If he chooses journalism, he may eventually find himself the publisher of a successful magazine. He will then definitely be in business in a big way. If he confines his activities to authorship or is a columnist, between the income-tax collector, the syndicates, or the hard-cover book houses and the paperback publishers, he will find himself more or less in business even if he wants no part of it and tries to leave these "sordid" details to his literary agent.

So with the odds four-to-one against him, the business-scorning intellectual will not always find it easy to escape the maelstrom. But the fact that he may wish to do so must prompt every thoughtful businessman to inquire: Why?

STRANGE ASSUMPTION

From the campus come many answers. Business, it is said, is dull and routine. It is a place where conformity rules—where men in gray flannel uniforms indulge in gray flannel thinking, and where people cease to be flesh-and-blood individuals and become mere numbers, lost in the unfathomable depths of electronic computers. It is a jungle where acceptable standards of ethics are readily compromised by corner cutting in the drive to meet competitive pressures. And nowhere in the business world is there to be found the freedom which is so greatly cherished by the intellectual—the freedom to comment, criticize, and dissent.

MAJOR COMPLAINTS

But these uninformed indictments of business can hardly be regarded as the basic motivation of any serious intellectual who actively seeks to avoid a career in the marketplace. Some, no doubt, are excuses rather than reasons. The three major complaints of the intellectual, perhaps, are that (1) business is crassly materialistic—i.e., the selfish goal of those who serve in business is money and the security that money provides; (2) business affords none of the inner satisfactions which come from selfless service to society; and (3) those who seek accomplishment, fame, and glory will not find these elusive rewards in the marketplace.

The assumption here is that material service to mankind is somehow incompatible with the idealistic goals to which the young intellectual of today is dedicated. On the one hand, to bring knowledge, cultural opportunities, spiritual comfort, and charitable aid to one's fellowmen is laudable and meritorious, as indeed it is. But, on the other hand, to serve the material wants and needs of society is somehow different, selfish, and meretricious.

To me, this assumption is utterly incomprehensible when service to the material needs of man is so clearly a prerequisite to the satisfaction of his intellectual and spiritual needs. To illustrate:

> It is told that one winter during the Civil War an itinerant preacher came upon a group of soldiers who were suffering greatly from chilblains as they huddled around a small fire. Instead of offering them spiritual comfort, however, he took a more practical tack. "Men," he said, "try soaking your feet in a poultice of soft soap; and when I pass this way tomorrow night, you'll be much more receptive to the word of God."

Similarly, the inspiring magnificence of a Pieta or Mona Lisa will provide solace, only sparingly to the beholder who is homeless and destitute. While a masterpiece may often be created in hunger, it is seldom enjoyed in starvation.

MISSING INGREDIENT

So while the intellectual who becomes a great statesman or a leader of humanitarian causes may enjoy a richly earned sense of achievement, and may even be included in the select list of individuals who are most admired by the college freshmen of 30 years hence, there is one deep satisfaction he will never know; namely, the rewarding feeling of fulfillment that comes from having produced some material, tangible thing which serves to feed, warm, house, or clothe his fellowman—to free him from drudgery, to emancipate him from a life-long battle for survival, and thus even to make it possible for him to engage in purely intellectual pursuits.

This is not to denigrate the importance of the contribution that is made to society by the intellectual who serves outside the productive sector, as the term is used here, in the fields of government or academic life. Rather, it is to emphasize that man's material, intellectual, and spiritual progress are insepa- rable parts of the whole. None of the three can be despised or denied if civili- zation is to develop and flourish.

It is also to expose the fallacy of the assumption that money and security are the sole rewards of a successful career in the marketplace. There are in the world of business, without doubt, as many dedicated men as can be found in government, medicine, education, or in any other field—men who find their greatest personal reward in the knowledge that they have performed a worthy economic service to society.

Accordingly, the thoughtful intellectual, in choosing a career, will be wise to turn to whatever occupation may most excite his interest, thus assuring himself that his work will never be dull and routine. If history is his forte, he may derive great satisfaction from teaching rising generations to avoid the pitfalls of the past, and he may even have hopes of preventing our present civilization from collapsing as other great civilizations of the past have done.

Again he may prefer to make history instead of teaching it, in which case he may well turn to a career in business and industry, for, it has always seemed to me, the progress of man has been influenced far more by the invention, development, technology, production, and distribution of the products of industry than it has been by the succession of wars and the passing parade of governments to which the pages of history are so largely devoted.

CAPITAL OPPORTUNITY

Certainly the challenges of the marketplace today must appeal to a wider variety of interests than do those of any other single field, for nowhere in this kaleidoscopic world of ours is change occurring so rapidly as it is in the produc- tive sector.

The collegian of today may reasonably expect to see the dawning of the twenty-first century, when it is estimated that the population of the United States will itself have increased to 330 million souls, let alone the enormous world increase in population, particularly among the less developed countries.

CHALLENGE AREAS

If all of these people are to be supplied with food, shelter, clothing, heat, transportation, and all the other material amenities of life that they will re- quire, new and revolutionary methods of production must be discovered and developed. The horticulturist must find new hybrids. The chemist must discover new fertilizers and pesticides. Deserts must be transformed into Edens. And even the seas must be more fully utilized.

Lakes and streams must be freed from contamination. The air must be purified of polluting substances by methods that are not yet known and by equipment that today does not even exist. New forms of energy must be found as our commonplace fuels grow scarce. New sources of fresh water must be created synthetically. And new metals with properties as yet only dreamed of must be discovered, developed, and produced.

These are but a few of the challenges that confront the intellectual in the world of business. This is but a glimpse of the inner satisfactions which the young idealist may find in serving the material needs of the man of tomorrow. This, in short, is Opportunity with a capital O for any intellectual in the marketplace.

So if we turn back at this point to the basic question we posed earlier, and ask ourselves what business has to offer to the intellectual, the most compelling answer I can think of is: *he is needed.*

It is commonplace to point out that the human animal likes to be where he is wanted and needed, and in the growing complexities of modern business there is no substitute for his intellect. Moreover, in any given group, he will find so many of his fellow intellectuals that his natural aptitudes will be sharpened by rubbing elbows with his associates.

INQUIRY AND MOVEMENT

But what about freedom of inquiry—the choicest possession of the intellectual and rightly so? This search for the better way is especially viable and rewarding in business. Let it be quickly said that a business unit whose work is related to bookbinding, for example, may have little stimulation for the intellectual whose interest is in the development of a better fertilizer. By and large, however, there is no barrier in business to prevent the intellectual who is interested in bookbinding, electronics, space, food preservation, or shipbuilding from gravitating in the direction of his interest.

Transferability of intellectual interests from one type of work to another is usual in business. Moving from engineering to operations or sales, or from research to management, is commonplace within a company. Also, it is always possible, though sometimes hazardous, to transfer to a different type of business. If the intellectual enters business with a basic professional training, he can end up in almost any activity he chooses. In fact, this freedom of inquiry and movement may even lead him back to the institution from which he was graduated or to one like it. This, as indicated, happens many times.

If we postulate an intellectual finding a home in a field which is congenial to his makeup and style, he will have an opportunity not only to inquire but to influence the results of the work of the group with which he is associated.

Freedom of inquiry is one thing; getting something done as a result of that inquiry is quite another. Business can be a happy combination of both.

On reflection, corporate groups are the most adaptable and useful vehicle yet discovered for effective human action. In fact, when it comes to manufacturing, transportation, or the many other forms of business, group action is indispensable. The job simply cannot be done, or done as effectively, in any other way. Within a corporate group, the intellectual will find not only a ready-made market for his thinking if he proves himself, but also an opportunity for getting his idea off the ground and into use.

ETHICAL STANDARDS

Perhaps one of the largest single deterrents for the intellectual who shuns a career in business is related to what he supposes is the standard of ethics inherent in the marketplace. From hearsay, the market may appear to him to be operating at lower moral standards, which are not necessarily unethical but possibly untenable to an ethically sensitive person. And even though the future ethics of business will be whatever today's graduates will ultimately make them, the question for the present is: Must the collegian sacrifice the tenets of his intellectual world, including its ethical base, or does an ethically acceptable world also exist in business? I think that it does.

FREEDOM TENETS

The heart of the matter lies in such things as principles of freedom. For example, our market-oriented economy is based on freedom of contract—to buy or not to buy, to sell or not to sell, to commit or not to commit. And with this freedom of contract goes the inescapable obligation to perform on one's agreement even when it hurts. It is true that in almost any form of human endeavor circumstances may provide some elements of coercion. But coercion is the antithesis of freedom to contract. It is not within the ethical boundaries of a free market. Nor is it likely to be present where there are many buyers and sellers, where there is a choice of serving or not serving, and where the state is not the sole producer or the single customer.

But will the young intellectual have to abide by policies he does not like or did not originate? Sometimes he will, but this is true even in university life on occasion. Consider, too, the dissidents in the churches of today, one or two of whom for all we know may be budding Martin Luthers.

Asking for business to be ethically based is a "natural." It is part of the urge to benefit one's fellowman—an urge which is recognized as of the highest order.

But what better way is there to bring benefits to others among us, whether here or abroad—as a deep-seated matter of ethics or as a matter of effectiveness—than to engage in a productive, profitable, creative business?

To be effective in serving human needs, business must be creative, and that creativity must justify itself in the marketplace. That creativity necessarily has an ethical base, for those who produce add rather than subtract from human welfare. They multiply so that all may have more, rather than merely divide what exists until no one has enough.

Another concern of the intellectual is that business is said to cater to the public taste, however uncultured that taste may be, and that it creates consumer desires for gadgetry. My view, on the contrary, is that an expression of freedom takes place daily and broadly in a market economy.

Let the intellectual cock an inquiring eye at some of the products or some of the advertising which may seem to him to border on the childish. But let him also realize that if people like soft drinks in steel cans or a special hair tonic, or do not like low-calorie foods, they have the opportunity of choosing. They may buy what they like and what they need. There is certainly nothing unethical about maintaining full freedom of choice.

Supplying the free market is seldom thought of as an ethical matter. But if there were no free market, the foundations of personal freedom would collapse about us. If we can be told what to buy, we can be told what to believe. If we can be told where to work, we can be told where not to work. If we can be told what to make because that is what the people are permitted to have, then we become a pawn in a gigantic chess game where there is little freedom for the individual.

PRODUCTIVE MIRACLE

Production is concerned with such things as automobiles and books and penicillin and hospitals and airplanes and computers, and 1,001 other things which enable people to do what they want to do and to go where they want to go. And this, no doubt, is all "good" in the sense of adding to personal freedom and not subtracting from it.

A few would probably prefer to turn the matter of production over to the state in the supposition that this would somehow increase efficiency and avoid social waste. But one wonders if they have ever tried to comprehend, for instance, all the things that 8 million people buy daily from all the shelves, counters, and display rooms in New York City.

If government had to produce, distribute, and supply all of these things to the merchants who sell them, if it had to time their transportation and arrival so that the supply and the demand would always be kept in balance, if it never created a glutted market in some commodities with a consequent loss of taxpayers' money or dislocation of jobs, if it never caused a scarcity of some essential items (thus either forcing prices to skyrocket or requiring people to queue up with ration cards to share in the available supply), and if it simultaneously wrought this miracle for the remaining 186 million people in all of the cities, towns, villages, and farms in the land—this would certainly require the full-time services of all of the intellectuals in America, and the odds would still be heavily stacked against success.

Yet this miracle occurs every hour of every day in the free market system, and it is so commonplace that it is taken for granted. The late President John F. Kennedy, in a talk before the business editors in September 1962, took note of this when he said:

> "It is well to remind ourselves from time to time of the benefits we derive from the maintenance of a free market system. The system rests on freedom of consumer choice, the profit motive, and vigorous competition for the buyer's dollar. . . .
>
> "The free market is a decentralized regulator of our economic system. The free market is not only a more efficient decision maker than even the wisest central planning body, but even more important, the free market keeps economic power widely dispersed. It thus is a vital underpinning of our democratic system."[3]

INTELLECTUAL EXERCISE

The collegian who seeks a challenge that will tax his talents and resources to the utmost can hardly turn to a more likely area than the world of business. When a competitor produces a new or a better product, all of his innovative skills may be required to avert disaster. When the intellectual comes face to face with the serious problems of employee relations, he may find himself in a dilemma that will test his balance of judgment to the nth degree.

He may think well of union representation of his employees as a matter of conscience, and he may recognize that if unions did not exist, it might be necessary, perhaps, to create them as the most effective means of resolving the complex problems which arise continually in the employee relations of a large corporation. But he may also see his business unit being overwhelmed by the irresistible force and power of an industrywide labor organization.

It will require no slight intellectual exercise on his part, therefore, to distinguish between the freedoms which he would cherish for all of his fellow-men—between the freedom, on the one hand, to join unions and to gain mutual economic benefits, and the freedom, on the other hand, to have the group produce and to operate continuously without the disturbance of nation-wracking strikes.

The intellectual in business will also learn, sometimes to his dismay, how government can help or hinder progress. Recognizing fully the necessity for government, the intellectual may at the same time realize that the freedoms he so deeply cherishes are diminished or denied as the process of decision making

---

[3] The President's Special News Conference with Business Editors and Publishers, September 26, 1962, in Washington, D.C.; *Public Papers of the Presidents of the United States, January 1 to December 31, 1962* (Washington, Government Printing Office, 1963), pp. 710–711.

moves from his individual business unit to the multiple collection of bureaus in Washington or in state capitals. President Kennedy was correct: "The free market is . . . a more efficient decision maker than even the wisest central planning body."

So there is plenty of intellectual exercise ahead for one who enters business. Likewise, there will be plenty of companionship with his colleagues, for many of them will have tastes and avocations that run the gamut from authorship or collecting rare books to art, music, citizenship service, or what have you. And their originality and dedication will border on the astonishing.

CONFORMITY FOLLY

Also, astonishing as it may seem to the young intellectual in the light of some of the things he has doubtless read, success in business is not born of conformity. As a business manager, he will instantly see the disastrous folly of surrounding himself with yes-men.

Around him he will want, above all, men who possess individuality—those with creative ideas, original concepts, and a wide variety of backgrounds, knowledge, and experience—whose judgment he respects and whose counsel he finds useful primarily because it often differs from his own views and first-blush inclinations. Only with that type of organization can he and his associates examine from every facet the serious problems which confront him, and develop the best-reasoned solutions to them. Only men with inventive minds, original ideas, and unrutted patterns of thought can meet the challenge of change in the business establishment of today and the greatly multiplied challenges of change that are on the business horizon.

Conformity is a provocative word that has proved to be not without profit to a number of distinguished authors, but it is only wisdom not to confuse system and effective work with authoritative conformity. Probing into space, operating a university, or winning a baseball game requires teamwork, and so does a well-organized business. But teamwork does not mean becoming a number or losing one's individuality. When Mickey Mantle celebrates his emergence from a batting slump by poling a grand-slam homer, do the newspapers report that "Number 7" knocked one out of the park? And who, outside of the brotherhood of Giant fans, remembers the number worn by Willie Mays?

In business, as in any other form of teamwork, it is individual initiative, energy, innovation, and drive that count. The possessor of these qualities will win recognition and advancement without regard to so-called office politics, without having to marry the boss's daughter, and even if tailors stop making gray flannel suits altogether!

The unadjusted, ineffective, or congenital idlers may need to turn to other fields to rekindle their interests, but for the intellectual who can face up to accountability and is willing to put his own thinking on the line and have it tested in the marketplace by the everyday buyers of products or the intellectual buyers of ideas, business will never be dull or routine.

CONCLUDING NOTE

For the benefit of those intellectuals who may have had the patience to read this piece, and who may question the reliability of the picture of business that has been painted here by one who can hardly claim to be wholly unprejudiced in the matter, let me conclude with an observation and a challenge.

The hallmark of the true intellectual is his restless spirit of inquiry, his unflagging search for truth, and his willingness to reject any preconceived idea or theory—no matter how popular or pleasant it may be to him—when it does not square with the facts. Likewise, the hallmark of the true scholar is his unwillingness to turn to secondary sources of information, and his desire to seek original sources wherever they may be available.

So the intellectual and the scholar who *truly* is an intellectual and a scholar will not glean his "image" of the marketplace from books, plays, movies, television shows, or any of the other secondhand sources which those campus queens were forced to rely on. He will seek the truth at its source and weigh his findings with due and unprejudiced deliberation. And when he arrives at the truth as he sees it, the intellectual will find that in the world of business the latchstring and the welcome mat are always out for him—and rewardingly so.

B. Participative Management: Opportunity for Individualism

The Case for Participative Management

12

Keith Davis

Participation is an overworked word in business and government, but an underworked activity. The idea sounds good to most managers, but they are frequently unsure of what to do with it. Some grossly misinterpret what it is, so that when they say, "Participation is great," they are really talking about something else; others are not sure when to apply it or how far to go with it.

One reason for the slow growth of participation is that it is a difficult philosophy to understand, and even more difficult to develop in a group. Genuine social science skill is required to make participation work. Many supervisors get in over their heads in a burst of enthusiasm and, after experiencing a rebuff, tend to withdraw from further efforts at participation. It appears that improperly applied participation may be worse for productivity and morale than simply doing nothing. Ineffective attempts to secure participation may make a group feel manipulated, resentful, confused or lacking in objectives.

In spite of the difficulty of developing participation, it does have enormous potential for raising productivity, bettering morale, and improving creative thinking. The need of people to participate is not a passing fancy. It is rooted deep in the culture of free men around the world, and it is probably a basic drive in man.[1] Because of its significance and permanence, participation is a

Reprinted with permission from *Business Horizons* (Bloomington, Ind.: The University of Indiana Press, Fall 1963), pp. 55–60.

[1] Comparative studies in England and the United States suggest that participation is a basic human drive rather than a cultural acquisition. See N. R. F. Maier and L. R. Hoffman, "Group Decision in England and the United States," *Personnel Psychology*, XV (Spring, 1962), p. 86.

method to which leaders need to devote long-range efforts. Means of tapping this source of creativity and of using its cohesive power for teamwork need to be developed. Participation affords a means of building some of the human values needed in a group. It can create an asset in morale so that when necessary orders are given, people will respond more cooperatively because they are participating in their group, although they did not participate in determining the instruction they have most recently received. The importance of participation has been described as follows:

"Two thousand years ago we put participation in the religion which has come to dominate the Western world. Two hundred years ago we put this essential element in our political and social structure. We are just beginning to realize that we ought to put participation in business as well."[2]

CLASSICAL EXPERIMENTS

Classical experiments by Roethlisberger, Bavelas, and Coch and French confirm our belief that participation is extremely valuable. Roethlisberger and his associates originally sought to show the relationship of physical change in environment and output. In the course of their experiments, new relationships, many of them involving participation, developed between workers and supervisors, and workers and experimenters. The results convincingly showed that these social changes improved both productivity and morale. Although participation was not the whole cause of these improvements, it seemed to be a significant cause.[3]

Bavelas worked with a group of women performing a sewing operation on a group incentive basis. For his experiment, he chose a superior group whose production averaged about 74 units hourly, with a range of 70 to 78. He asked them to set their own production goal. After considerable discussion they agreed unanimously on a goal of 84 units hourly, which they exceeded within five days. A goal of 95, set at a later meeting, could not be met. The goal was then reduced to the relatively permanent level of 90 units. During the next several months, the group's output averaged about 87 units with a range of 80 to 93. The net increase after participation was about 13 units hourly.[4] Coch and French achieved similar results in experiments with sewing machine operators.[5]

[2] Ralph M. Besse, "Business Statesmanship," *Personnel Administration,* XX (January-February, 1957), 12.

[3] F. J. Roethlisberger, *Management and Morale* (Cambridge: Harvard University Press, 1941), p. 14.

[4] Norman R. F. Maier, *Psychology in Industry* (Boston: Houghton Mifflin Company, 1946), pp. 264–66. Lawrence and Smith have since repeated Bavelas' experiments with similar results. See Lois C. Lawrence and Patricia Cain Smith, "Group Decision and Employee Participation," *The Journal of Applied Psychology,* XXXIX (October, 1955), pp. 334–37.

[5] Lester Coch and John R. P. French, Jr., "Overcoming Resistance to Change," *Human Relations,* I (No. 4, 1948), pp. 512–32, and John R. P. French, Jr. and Alvin Zander, "The Group Dynamics Approach," in Arthur Kornhauser, ed., *Psychology of Labor-Management Relations* (Champaign, Ill.: Industrial Relations Research Association, 1949), pp. 73–75.

The benefits of participation are evident in the experience of a large air-craft manufacturer, who employed from 5,000 to 20,000 shopworkers during the decade following World War II. The company used a safety committee system in which each department was represented by one worker. During these ten years, not one person suffered a disabling injury while serving as safety committeeman. This record was made despite the facts that hundreds of workers served on the committee during the decade, and accident-prone workers sometimes were appointed to the post in order to make them safety conscious. Although some committeemen probably returned to work earlier than they should have after an accident in order to preserve their record, the facts still show a significant difference between committeemen and other workers. Part of the difference was surely due to the fact that the committee-men were participating in a safety program.

Participation is especially important in encouraging people to accept change, a persistent pressure on all of us in our dynamic society. Participation is help-ful both in planning and installing change, because when employees under-stand the objectives and content of a change, they are confident that manage-ment is not trying to "pull a fast one" on them. Participation may actually im-prove carefully devised management plans, because it elicits the ideas of the persons who are most thoroughly acquainted with the working effects of those plans. It may cancel a poor plan and thus save management many headaches. In any case, it broadens the outlook of those involved and helps them feel that they have an active part in what is taking place.

When a change is within management's control, such as the determination of a new work method, best results are realized when the group participates in the recognition of the need for change. Participation is less effective if it begins only after management has decided that a change is necessary.

KEY IDEAS IN PARTICIPATION

Participation is defined as an individual's mental and emotional involve-ment in a group situation that encourages him to contribute to group goals and to share responsibility for them. This definition contains three important ideas.

First, participation means mental and emotional involvement rather than mere muscular activity. The involvement of a person's *self,* rather than just his skill is the product of his mind and his emotions. The person who partic-ipates is ego-involved instead of merely task-involved.[6] Some managers mis-take task-involvement for true participation. They go through the motions of participation, but it is clear to employees that their manager is an autocrat who does not really want their ideas. Employees cannot become involved in this kind of situation.

[6] Gordon W. Allport, "The Psychology of Participation," *The Psychological Review,* LII (May, 1945), p. 22.

A *second* important characteristic of participation is that it motivates contribution. Individuals are given an opportunity to direct their initiative and creativity toward the objectives of the group. In this way, participation differs from consent,[7] which uses only the creativity and ideas of the leader who brings his idea to the group for their approval. Participation requires more than mere approval of something already decided. It is a two-way psychological and social relationship among people rather than a procedure imposing ideas from above.

A *third* characteristic of participation is that it encourages people to accept responsibility for an activity. Because they are self-involved in the group, they want to see it work successfully. Participation helps them become responsible citizens rather than non-responsible automatons. As individuals begin to accept responsibility for group activities, they become interested in and receptive to teamwork, because they see in it a means of accomplishing a job for which they feel responsible. A person who is actively involved in something is naturally more committed to carrying it out. Of his own free will, he creates responsibility rather than having it forced upon him by delegation. By making himself responsible, he gains a measure of independence and dignity as an individual making his own decisions, even though these decisions are heavily influenced by his group environment.

Managers often ask, "If I share decisions with my personnel, don't I lose authority? I can't afford to give up authority because I'm responsible." This is a perfectly normal worry of an executive who is considering the values of participation for the first time, but it is hardly a justifiable worry. The participative manager still retains his authority to decide. He shares his problems with the group by means of a process that may be called social delegation. Social delegation in the human relations domain is comparable to formal delegation in the organizational domain. Neither type of delegation weakens a manager's organizational authority. No manager of the future—say twenty years hence—will object to a certain amount of social delegation through participation under normal conditions. It will be as much his stock in trade as formal delegation is today.

PRACTICE LIMITATIONS

These experiments (and the conclusion drawn from them) have a number of limitations that managers cannot ignore. Their success is no guarantee that all similar practices will be successful. The experiments described were performed by professional men skilled in human relations; similar efforts by ordinary supervisors undoubtedly would not produce such consistent results. The step from experimentation to practice is a long one indeed. The experi-

[7] Mary P. Follett, "The Psychology of Consent and Participation," in Henry C. Metcalf and L. Urwick, eds., *Dynamic Administration: The Collected Papers of Mary Parker Follett* (New York: Harper and Brothers, 1941), pp. 210–12.

ments were mostly one-shot efforts in a narrow work situation, using small groups who were doing repetitive work and undergoing changes. Participation in large work groups may be more difficult. In any case, managers should not go overboard for participation as they once did for scientific management. The latter was a worthwhile development, but managers' failure to recognize its uses and limitations in particular situations nearly ruined it.

In developing participation, we must be able to strike a precarious balance between counterfeit participation, which would arouse distrust, and excessive participation, which would consume valuable work time and destroy unified direction. Many issues are involved. Counterfeit participation may be tinsel and ribbon to make people happy, or it may be a more insidious tool handled by skilled social scientists, the engineers of consent.

Another danger of participation—as was true of scientific management—is that practitioners will get lost in the procedures of participation and overlook its philosophy. The substance of participation does not automatically flow from its procedures; there is no such mechanistic connection. Rather, when procedures are used at the right time and in the right circumstances, they enable it to develop.

Another issue concerns a person's right not to participate. There is no evidence that advanced participation is required for everybody; there is evidence that many persons do not want to be bothered with participation. Shall we force them into a mold merely because we think it is good for them? Some persons want a minimum of interaction with their supervisor and associates. The role expectation of many employees is to work for an autocratic supervisor, and consequently they produce effectively with this type of leadership. Research shows that the more authoritarian personality derives less benefit from participative methods, while the more equalitarian personality is more favorably affected.[8] Sometimes a group can be kept participating only by pressure from above. When that pressure is released, the group reverts to patterns of less participation.[9]

PREREQUISITES FOR PARTICIPATION

Finally, it should be emphasized that the success of participation is directly related to how well certain prerequisites are satisfied. Some of these conditions occur in the participants; some exist in the environment. Taken together, they mean that participation works better in some situations than others—and that in certain situations, it works not at all.[10]

[8] Victor H. Vroom, "Some Personality Determinants of the Effects of Participation," *Journal of Abnormal and Social Psychology*, LIX (November, 1959), pp. 322–27.

[9] Robert N. McMurry, "The Case for Benevolent Autocracy," *Harvard Business Review*, XXXVI (January-February, 1958), pp. 82–90.

[10] For further explanation, see Robert Tannenbaum, Irving R. Weschler, and Fred Massarik, *Leadership and Organization: A Behavioral Science Approach* (New York: McGraw-Hill Book Company, Inc., 1961), pp. 88–100.

The first prerequisite is that ample time must be allowed to participate before action is required. Participation may not be appropriate in emergency situations. Second, the financial cost of participation should not exceed the values, economic and otherwise, that it produces. Third, the subject of participation must be relevant to the participant's organization, something in which he is interested, or he will regard it as mere busy work. Fourth, the participant should have the abilities, intelligence, and knowledge to participate effectively.

Fifth, the participants must be able to communicate in order to be able to exchange ideas. Sixth, no one (employee or manager) should feel that his position is threatened by participation. Seventh, participation for deciding a course of action in an organization can take place only within the group's area of job freedom. Some degree of restriction on subunits is necessary in any organization in order to maintain internal stability; subunits cannot make decisions that violate company policy, collective bargaining agreements, or similar restraints.

Since participation is a deep-seated need of man, it is worth trying: (1) if the manager understands what he is doing; (2) if he has developed some social science skill; (3) if he will meet the prerequisites; (4) if he will respect the role expectations of his people; and (5) if he will begin in a small way, rather than shooting for the moon in the first few months. Managers should proceed with caution, building each improvement upon past successes—but by all means, they should proceed.

Participative Management: Time for a Second Look 13
Robert C. Albrook

The management of change has become a central preoccupation of U.S. business. When the directors have approved the record capital budget and congratulated themselves on "progress," when the banquet speaker has used his last superlative to describe the "world of tomorrow," the talk turns, inevitably, to the question: "Who will make it all work?" Some people resist change. Some hold the keys to it. Some admit the need for new ways but don't know how to begin. The question becomes what kind of management can ease the inevitable pains, unlock the talent, energy, and knowledge where they're needed, help valuable men to contribute to and shape change rather than be flattened by it.

Reprinted with permision from *Fortune* (May 1967), pp. 166–170, 197, 198, 200.

The recipe is elusive, and increasingly business has turned to the academic world for help, particularly to the behavioral scientists—the psychologists, sociologists, and anthropologists whose studies have now become the showpieces of the better business schools. A number of major corporations, such as General Electric, Texas Instruments, and Standard Oil (N.J.), have brought social scientists onto their staffs. Some companies collaborate closely with university-based scholars and are contributing importantly to advanced theoretical work, just as industry's physicists, chemists, and engineers have become significant contributors of new knowledge in their respective realms. Hundreds of companies, large and small, have tried one or another formulation of basic behavioral theory, such as the many schemes for sharing cost savings with employees and actively soliciting their ideas for improved efficiency.

For forty years the quantity and quality of academic expertise in this field have been steadily improving, and there has lately been a new burst of ideas which suggest that the researchers in the business schools and other centers of learning are really getting down to cases. The newest concepts already represent a considerable spin-off from the appealingly simple notions on which the behavioral pioneers first concentrated. The essential message these outriders had for business was this: recognize the social needs of employees in their work, as well as their need for money; they will respond with a deeper commitment and better performance, help to shape the organization's changing goals and make them their own. For blue-collar workers this meant such steps as organizing work around tasks large enough to have meaning and inviting workers' ideas; for middle and upper management it meant more participation in decision making, wider sharing of authority and responsibility, more open and more candid communication, up, down, and sideways.

The new work suggests that neither the basic philosophy nor all of the early prescriptions of this management style were scientifically sound or universally workable. The word from the behavioral scientists is becoming more specific and "scientific," less simple and moralistic. At Harvard, M.I.T., the University of Michigan, Chicago, U.C.L.A., Stanford, and elsewhere they are mounting bigger, longer, and more rigorous studies of the human factors in management than ever before undertaken.

One conclusion is that the "participative" or "group" approach doesn't seem to work with all people and in all situations. Research has shown that satisfied, happy workers are sometimes more productive—and sometimes merely happy. Some managers and workers are able to take only limited responsibility, however much the company tries to give them. Some people will recognize the need to delegate but "can't let go." In a profit squeeze the only way to get costs under control fast enough often seems to be with centralized, "get tough" management.

Few, if any, behaviorists espouse a general return to authoritarian management. Instead, they are seeking a more thorough, systematic way to apply participative principles on a sustained schedule that will give the theory a bet-

Diagnose Your Management

	SYSTEM 1 EXPLOITIVE AUTHORITATIVE	SYSTEM 2 BENEVOLENT AUTHORITATIVE	SYSTEM 3 CONSULTATIVE	SYSTEM 4 PARTICIPATIVE GROUP
LEADERSHIP				
HOW MUCH CONFIDENCE IS SHOWN IN SUBORDINATES?	NONE	CONDESCENDING	SUBSTANTIAL	COMPLETE
HOW FREE DO THEY FEEL TO TALK TO SUPERIORS ABOUT JOB?	NOT AT ALL	NOT VERY	RATHER FREE	FULLY FREE
MOTIVATION				
ARE SUBORDINATES' IDEAS SOUGHT AND USED, IF WORTHY?	SELDOM	SOMETIMES	USUALLY	ALWAYS
IS PREDOMINANT USE MADE OF 1 FEAR, 2 THREATS, 3 PUNISHMENT, 4 REWARDS, 5 INVOLVEMENT?	1, 2, 3, OCCASIONALLY 4	4, SOME 3	4, SOME 3 AND 5	5, 4, BASED ON GROUP SET GOALS
WHERE IS RESPONSIBILITY FELT FOR ACHIEVING ORGANIZATION'S GOALS?	MOSTLY AT TOP	TOP AND MIDDLE	FAIRLY GENERAL	AT ALL LEVELS
COMMUNICATION				
HOW MUCH COMMUNICATION IS AIMED AT ACHIEVING ORGANIZATION'S OBJECTIVES?	VERY LITTLE	LITTLE	QUITE A BIT	A GREAT DEAL
WHAT IS THE DIRECTION OF INFORMATION FLOW?	DOWNWARD	MOSTLY DOWNWARD	DOWN AND UP	DOWN, UP, AND SIDEWAYS
HOW IS DOWNWARD COMMUNICATION ACCEPTED?	WITH SUSPICION	POSSIBLY WITH SUSPICION	WITH CAUTION	WITH AN OPEN MIND
HOW ACCURATE IS UPWARD COMMUNICATION?	OFTEN WRONG	CENSORED FOR THE BOSS	LIMITED ACCURACY	ACCURATE
HOW WELL DO SUPERIORS KNOW PROBLEMS FACED BY SUBORDINATES?	KNOW LITTLE	SOME KNOWLEDGE	QUITE WELL	VERY WELL

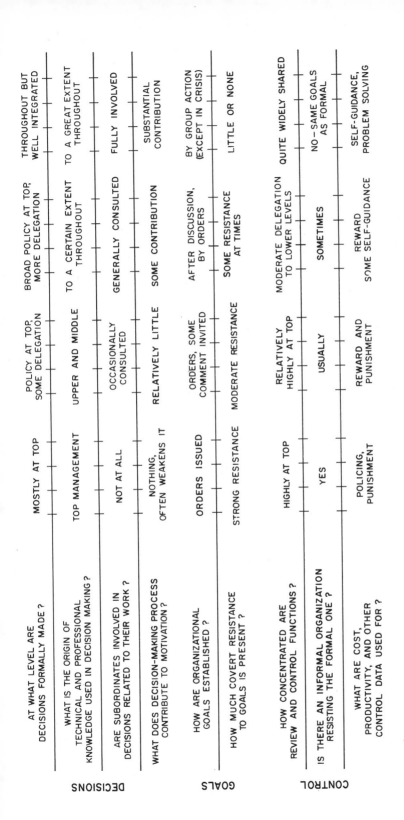

DECISIONS	AT WHAT LEVEL ARE DECISIONS FORMALLY MADE?	MOSTLY AT TOP	POLICY AT TOP, SOME DELEGATION	BROAD POLICY AT TOP, MORE DELEGATION	THROUGHOUT BUT WELL INTEGRATED
	WHAT IS THE ORIGIN OF TECHNICAL AND PROFESSIONAL KNOWLEDGE USED IN DECISION MAKING?	TOP MANAGEMENT	UPPER AND MIDDLE	TO A CERTAIN EXTENT THROUGHOUT	TO A GREAT EXTENT THROUGHOUT
	ARE SUBORDINATES INVOLVED IN DECISIONS RELATED TO THEIR WORK?	NOT AT ALL	OCCASIONALLY CONSULTED	GENERALLY CONSULTED	FULLY INVOLVED
	WHAT DOES DECISION-MAKING PROCESS CONTRIBUTE TO MOTIVATION?	NOTHING, OFTEN WEAKENS IT	RELATIVELY LITTLE	SOME CONTRIBUTION	SUBSTANTIAL CONTRIBUTION
GOALS	HOW ARE ORGANIZATIONAL GOALS ESTABLISHED?	ORDERS ISSUED	ORDERS, SOME COMMENT INVITED	AFTER DISCUSSION, BY ORDERS	BY GROUP ACTION (EXCEPT IN CRISIS)
	HOW MUCH COVERT RESISTANCE TO GOALS IS PRESENT?	STRONG RESISTANCE	MODERATE RESISTANCE	SOME RESISTANCE AT TIMES	LITTLE OR NONE
CONTROL	HOW CONCENTRATED ARE REVIEW AND CONTROL FUNCTIONS?	HIGHLY AT TOP	RELATIVELY HIGHLY AT TOP	MODERATE DELEGATION TO LOWER LEVELS	QUITE WIDELY SHARED
	IS THERE AN INFORMAL ORGANIZATION RESISTING THE FORMAL ONE?	YES	USUALLY	SOMETIMES	NO—SAME GOALS AS FORMAL
	WHAT ARE COST, PRODUCTIVITY, AND OTHER CONTROL DATA USED FOR?	POLICING, PUNISHMENT	REWARD AND PUNISHMENT	REWARD, SOME SELF-GUIDANCE	SELF-GUIDANCE, PROBLEM SOLVING

Adapted with permission from *The Human Organization: Its Management and Value* by Rensis Likert, published in April 1967 by McGraw-Hill.

ter chance to work. Others are insisting that management must be tailor-made, suited to the work or the people, rather than packaged in a standard mixture. Some people aren't and never will be suited for "democracy" on the job, according to one viewpoint, while others insist that new kinds of psychological training can fit most executives for the rugged give-and-take of successful group management.

As more variables are brought into their concepts, and as they look increasingly at the specifics of a management situation, the behaviorists are also being drawn toward collaboration with the systems designers and the theorists of data processing. Born in reaction to the cold scientism of the earlier "scientific management" experts with their stopwatches and measuring tapes, the "human relations" or behavioral school of today may be getting ready at last to bury that hatchet in a joint search for a broadly useful "general theory" of management.

WHY EXECUTIVES DON'T PRACTICE WHAT THEY PREACH

Before any general theory can be evolved, a great deal more has to be known about the difficulty of putting theory into practice—i.e., of transforming a simple managerial attitude into an effective managerial style. "There are plenty of executives," observes Stanley Seashore a social psychologist at the University of Michigan's Institute for Social Research, "who'll decide one morning they're going to be more participative and by the afternoon have concluded it doesn't work."

What's often lacking is an understanding of how deeply and specifically management style affects corporate operations. The executive who seeks a more effective approach needs a map of the whole terrain of management activity. Rensis Likert, director of the Michigan Institute, has developed a chart to assist managers in gaining a deeper understanding of the way they operate. A simplified version is on pages 196–197.[1] By answering the questions in the

---

[1] The chart on pages 196–197 is adapted from a technique developed by Rensis Likert, director of the Institute for Social Research at the University of Michigan, to help businessmen analyze the management style used by their companies. Anyone—executive or employee—can use it to diagnose his own company or division. Check the appropriate answers, using the guide marks to shade your emphasis. After the first question, for example, if your answer is "almost none," put the check in the first or second notch of the "none" box. Regard each answer as a sort of rating on a continuous scale from the left to the right of the chart. When you have answered each question, draw a line from the top to the bottom of the chart through the check marks. The result will be a profile of your management. To determine which way management style has been shifting, repeat the process for the situation as it was three, five, or ten years ago. Finally sketch the profile you think would help your company or division to improve its performance. Likert has tried the chart on a number of business executives. Most of them rated their own companies about in the middle—embracing features of System 2 and 3. But nearly all of them also believe that companies do best when they have profiles well to the right of the chart, and worst with profiles well to the left.

left-hand column of the chart (e.g., "Are subordinates' ideas sought and used?"), an executive sketches a profile of the way his company is run and whether it leans to the "authoritative" or the "participative." Hundreds of businessmen have used the chart, under Likert's direction, and many have discovered a good deal they didn't realize about the way they were handling people.

Likert leads his subjects in deliberate steps to a conclusion that most of them do not practice what they say they believe. First, the executive is asked to think of the most successful company (or division of a company) he knows intimately. He then checks off on the chart his answers as they apply to that company. When the executive has finished this exercise, he has nearly always traced the profile of a strongly "participative" management system, well to the right on Likert's chart. He is next asked to repeat the procedure for the least successful company (or division) he knows well. Again, the profiles are nearly always the same, but this time they portray a strongly "authoritative" system, far to the left on the chart.

Then comes the point of the exercise. The executive is asked to describe his own company or division. Almost always, the resulting profile is that of a company somewhere in the middle, a blend of the "benevolent authoritative" and the "consultative"—well to the left of what the executive had previously identified as the most successful style. To check out the reliability of this self-analysis, Likert sometimes asks employees in the same company or division to draw its profile, too. They tend to rate as slightly more "authoritative" than the boss does.

Likert believes that the predominant management style in U.S. industry today falls about in the middle of his chart, even though most managers seem to know from personal observation of other organizations that a more participative approach works better. What accounts for their consistent failure to emulate what they consider successful? Reaching for a general explanation, Likert asks his subjects one final question: "In your experience, what happens when the senior officer becomes concerned about earnings and takes steps to cut costs, increase productivity, and improve profit?" Most reply that the company's management profile shifts left, toward the authoritarian style. General orders to economize—and promptly—often result in quick, across-the-board budget cuts. Some programs with high potential are sacrificed along with obvious losers. Carefully laid, logical plans go down the drain. Some people are laid off—usually the least essential ones. But the best people in the organization sooner or later rebel at arbitrary decisions, and many of them leave.

At the outset, the arbitrary cost cutting produces a fairly prompt improvement in earnings, of course. But there is an unrecognized trade-off in the subsequent loss of human capital, which shows up still later in loss of business. In due course, management has to "swing right" again, rebuilding its human assets at great expense in order to restore good performance. Yet the manager who puts his firm through this dreary cycle, Likert observes, is often rewarded with a bonus at the outset, when things still look good. Indeed, he may be sent off to work his magic in another division!

Likert acknowledges that there are emergencies when sharp and sudden belt-tightening is inescapable. The trouble, he says, is that it is frequently at the expense of human assets and relationships that have taken years to build. Often it would make more sense to sell off inventory or dispose of a plant. But such possibilities are overlooked because human assets do not show up in the traditional balance sheet the way physical assets do. A company can, of course, lose $100,000 worth of talent and look better on its statement than if it sells off $10,000 worth of inventory at half price.

A dollars-and-cents way of listing the value of a good engineering staff, an experienced shop crew, or an executive group with effective, established working relations might indeed steady the hand of a hard-pressed president whose banker is on the phone. Likert believes he is now on the trail of a way to assign such values—values that should be at least as realistic as the often arbitrary and outdated figures given for real estate and plant. It will take some doing to get the notion accepted by bankers and accountants, however sophisticated his method turns out to be. But today's executives are hardly unaware that their long payrolls of expensive scientific and managerial talent represent an asset as well as an expense. Indeed, it is an asset that is often bankable. A merely more regular, explicit recognition of human assets in cost-cutting decisions would help to ensure that human assets get at least an even break with plant and inventory in time of trouble.

Likert and his institute colleagues are negotiating with several corporations to enlist them in a systematic five-year study, in effect a controlled experiment, that should put a firmer footing under tentative conclusions and hypotheses. This study will test Likert's belief that across-the-board participative management, carefully developed, sustained through thick and thin, and supported by a balance sheet that somehow reckons the human factor, will show better long-run results than the cyclical swing between authoritarian and participative styles reflected in the typical middle-ground profile on his chart.

CONVERSION IN A PAJAMA FACTORY

Already there's enough evidence in industry experience to suggest that participative management gets in trouble when it is adopted too fast. In some cases, an authoritarian management has abruptly ordered junior executives or employees to start taking on more responsibility not recognizing that the directive itself reasserted the fact of continuing centralized control. Sometimes, of course, a hard shove may be necessary, as in the recent experience of Harwood Manufacturing Corp. of Marion, Virginia, which has employed participative practices widely for many years. When it acquired a rival pajama maker, Weldon Manufacturing Co., the latter's long-held authoritarian traditions were hard to crack. With patient but firm prodding by outside consultants, who acknowledge an initial element of "coercion," the switch in style was finally accomplished.

Ideally, in the view of Likert and others, a move of this kind should begin with the patient education of top executives, followed by the development of the needed skills in internal communication, group leadership, and the other requisites of the new system. Given time, this will produce better employee attitudes and begin to harness personal motivation to corporate goals. Still later, there will be improved productivity, less waste, lower turnover and absence rates, fewer grievances and slowdowns, improved product quality, and, finally, better customer relations.

The transformation may take several years. A checkup too early in the game might prove that participative management, even when thoroughly understood and embraced at the top, doesn't produce better results. By the same token, a management that is retreating from the new style in a typical cost squeeze may still be nominally participative, yet may already have thrown away the fruits of the system. Some research findings do indicate that participation isn't producing the hoped-for results. In Likert's view, these were spot checks, made without regard to which way the company was tending and where it was in the cycle of change.

A growing number of behaviorists, however, have begun to question whether the participative style is an ideal toward which all management should strive. If they once believed it was, more as a matter of faith in their long struggle against the "scientific" manager's machine-like view of man than as a finding from any new science of their own, they now are ready to take a second look at the proposition.

It seems plain enough that a research scientist generally benefits from a good deal of freedom and autonomy, and that top executives, confronted every day by new problems that no routine can anticipate, operate better with maximum consultation and uninhibited contributions from every member of the team. If the vice president for finance can't talk candidly with the vice president for production about financing the new plant, a lot of time can be wasted. In sales, group effort—instead of the usual competition—can be highly productive. But in the accounting department, things must go by the book. "Creative accounting" sounds more like a formula for jail than for the old behaviorists' dream of personal self-fulfillment on the job. And so with quality control in the chemical plant. An inspired adjustment here and there isn't welcome, thank you; just follow the specifications.

In the production department, automation has washed out a lot of the old problem of man as a prisoner of the assembly line, the kind of problem that first brought the "human relations" experts into the factories in the 1920's and 1930's. If a shop is full of computer-controlled machine tools busily reproducing themselves, the boy with the broom who sweeps away the shavings may be the only one who can put a personal flourish into his work. The creativity is all upstairs in the engineering and programing departments. But then, so are most of the people.

"Look what's happened in the last twenty years," says Harold J. Leavitt, a social psychologist who recently moved to Stanford after some years at Carnegie Tech. "Originally the concern of the human-relations people was with the blue-collar worker. Then the focus began to shift to foremen and to middle management. Now it's concentrated in special areas like research and development and in top management. Why? Because the 'group' style works best where nobody knows exactly and all the time what they're supposed to be doing, where there's a continuous need to change and adapt."

DEMOCRACY WORKS BETTER IN PLASTICS

One conclusion that has been drawn from this is that management style has to be custom-designed to fit the particular characteristics of each industry. The participative approach will work best in those industries that are in the vanguard of change. A Harvard Business School study has compared high-performance companies in three related, but subtly different, fields: plastics, packaged food, and standard containers. The plastics company faced the greatest uncertainties and change in research, new products, and market developments. The food company's business was somewhat more stable, while the container company encountered little or no requirement for innovation. The three achieved good results using markedly different management styles. The plastics firm provided for wide dispersal of responsibility for major decisions, the food company for moderate decentralization of authority, and the container company operated with fairly centralized control.

Less successful enterprises in each of the three industries were also examined, and their managements were compared with those of the high-performance companies. From this part of the study, Harvard researchers Paul Lawrence and Jay Lorsch drew another conclusion: not only may each industry have its own appropriate management style, but so may the individual operations within the same company. The companies that do best are those which allow for variations among their departments and know how to take these variations into account in coordinating the whole corporate effort.

Both the sales and the research departments in a fast-moving plastics company, for example, may adopt a style that encourages employees to participate actively in departmental decision making. But in special ways the two operations still need to differ. The research worker, for example, thinks in long-range terms, focusing on results expected in two or three years. The sales executive has his sights set on results next week or next month. This different sense of time may make it hard for the two departments to understand each other. But if top management recognizes the reasons and the need for such differences, each department will do its own job better, and they can be better coordinated. On the other hand, if top management ignores the differences and insists, for example, on rigidly uniform budgeting and planning time-tables, there will be a loss of effectiveness.

It seems an obvious point that sales must be allowed to operate like sales, accounting like accounting, and production like production. But as Lawrence comments, "The mark of a good idea in this field is that as soon as it is articulated, it does seem obvious. People forget that, five minutes before, it wasn't. One curse of the behavioral scientist is that anything he comes up with is going to seem that way, because anything that's good *is* obvious."

PEOPLE, TOO, HAVE THEIR STYLES

Other behavioral scientists take the view that management style should be determined not so much by the nature of the particular business operation involved, but by the personality traits of the people themselves. There may be some tendency for certain kinds of jobs to attract certain kinds of people. But in nearly any shop or office a wide range of personality types may be observed. There is, for example, the outgoing, socially oriented scientist as well as the supposedly more typical introverted recluse. There are mature, confident managers, and there are those who somehow fill the job despite nagging self-doubt and a consuming need for reassurance.

For a long time, personality tests seem to offer a way to steer people into the psychologically right kind of work. Whether such testing for placement is worth while is now a matter of some dispute. In any case, the whole question of individual differences is often reduced to little more than an office guessing game. Will Sue cooperate with Jane? Can Dorothy stand working for Jim? Will Harry take suggestions?

The participative approach to management may be based upon a greatly oversimplified notion about people, in the view of psychologist Clare Graves of Union College in Schenectady, New York. On the basis of limited samplings, he tentatively concludes that as many as half the people in the northeastern U.S., and a larger proportion nationwide are not and many never will be the eager-beaver workers on whom the late Douglas McGregor of M.I.T. based his "Theory Y." Only some variation of old-style authoritarian management will meet their psychological needs, Graves contends.

Graves believes he has identified seven fairly distinct personality types, although he acknowledges that many people are not "purebreds" who would fit his abstractions perfectly and that new and higher personality forms may still be evolving. At the bottom of his well-ordered hierarchy he places the child-like "autistic" personality, which requires "close care and nurturing." Next up the scale are the "animistic" type, which must be dealt with by sheer force or enticement; the "ordered" personality that responds best to a moralistic management; and the "materialistic" individual who calls for pragmatic, hard bargaining. None of these are suited for the participative kind of management.

At the top of Grave's personality ladder are the "sociocentric," the "cognitive," and the "apprehending" types of people. They are motivated, respectively, by a need for "belonging," for "information," and for an "understanding" of the total situation in which they are involved. For each of these levels some form of participative management will work. However, those at the very top, the unemotional "apprehending" individuals, must be allowed pretty much to set their own terms for work. Management can trust such people to contribute usefully only according to their own cool perception of what is needed. They will seldom take the trouble to fight authority when they disagree with it, but merely withdraw, do a passable but not excellent job, and wait for management to see things their way. In that sense these highest-level people are probably not ideal participators.

Graves believes most adults are stuck at one level throughout their lifetimes or move up a single notch, at best. He finds, incidentally, that there can be bright or dull, mature or immature behavior at nearly all levels. The stages simply represent psychological growth toward a larger and larger awareness of the individual's relationship to society.

If a company has a mixture of personality types, as most do, it must somehow sort them out. One way would be to place participative-type managers in charge of some groups, and authoritarian managers in charge of others. Employees would then be encouraged to transfer into sections where the management style best suits them. This would hardly simplify corporate life. But companies pushing the group approach might at least avoid substituting harmful new rigidities—"participate, or else!"—for the old ones.

THE ANTHROPOLOGICAL VIEW

Behaviorists who have been studying management problems from an anthropological viewpoint naturally stress cultural rather than individual differences. Manning Nash, of the University of Chicago's business school, for example, observes that the American emphasis on egalitarianism and performance has always tempered management style in the U.S. "No matter what your role is, if you don't perform, no one in this country will defer to you," he says. "Americans won't act unless they respect you. You couldn't have an American Charge of the Light Brigade." But try to export that attitude to a country with a more autocratic social tradition, and, in the words of Stanley Davis of Harvard, "it won't be bought and may not be workable."

Within the U.S. there are many cultural differences that might provide guides to managerial style if they could be successfully analyzed. Recent research by Lawrence and Arthur N. Turner at the Harvard Business School hints at important differences between blue-collar workers in cities and those in smaller towns, although religious and other factors fog the results. Town workers seem to seek "a relatively large amount of variety, autonomy interaction, skill and responsibility" in their work, whereas city workers "find more simple tasks less stress-producing and more satisfying."

In managerial areas where democratic techniques *are* likely to work, the problem is how to give managers skill and practice in participation. The National Education Association's National Training Laboratories twenty years ago pioneered a way of doing this called "sensitivity training" (see "Two Weeks in a T-Group," *Fortune*, August, 1961). Small groups of men, commonly drawn from the executive ranks, sit down with a professional trainer but without agenda or rule book and "see what happens." The "vacuum" draws out first one and then another participant, in a way that tends to expose in fairly short order how he comes across to others.

The technique has had many critics, few more vocal than William Gomberg of the University of Pennsylvania's Wharton School. Renewing his assault recently, he called the "training" groups "titillating therapy, management development's most fashionable fad." When people from the same company are in the group, he argues, the whole exercise is an invasion of privacy, an abuse of the therapeutic technique to help the company, not the individual. For top executives in such groups, Gomberg and others contend, the technique offers mainly a catharsis for their loneliness or insecurity.

"PSYCHING OUT THE BOSS"

Undoubtedly the T-group can be abused, intentionally or otherwise. But today's sensitivity trainers are trying to make sure the experience leads to useful results for both the individual and his firm. They realize that early groups, made up of total strangers gathered at some remote "cultural island," often gave the executive little notion of how to apply his new knowledge back on the job. To bring more realism to the exercise, the National Training Laboratories began ten years ago to make up groups of executives and managers from the same company, but not men who had working relationships with one another. These "cousin labs" have led, in turn, to some training of actual management "families," a boss and his subordinates. At the West Coast headquarters of the T-group movement, the business school at U.C.L.A., some now call such training "task-group therapy."

Many businessmen insist T-groups have helped them. Forty-three presidents and chairmen and hundreds of lesser executives are National Training Laboratories alumni. U.C.L.A. is besieged by applicants, and many are turned away.

Sensitivity training is supposed to help most in business situations where there is a great deal of uncertainty, as there is in the training sessions themselves. In such situations in the corporate setting there is sometimes a tendency for executives to withdraw, to defer action, to play a kind of game with other people in the organization to see who will climb out on a limb first. A chief ploy is "psyching out the boss," which means trying to anticipate the way the winds of ultimate decision will blow and to set course accordingly.

The aim of sensitivity training is to stop all this, to get the executive's nerve up so that he faces facts, or, in the words of U.C.L.A.'s James V. Clark to "lay bare the stress and strain faster and get a resolution of the problem." In that limited sense, such therapy could well serve any style of management. In Clark's view, this kind of training, early in the game, might save many a company a costly detour on the road to company-wide "democracy." He cites the experience of Non-Linear Systems, Inc., of Del Mar, California, a manufacturer of such electronic gear as digital voltmeters and data-logging equipment and an important supplier to aerospace contractors. The company is headed by Andrew Kay, a leading champion of the participative style. At the lower levels, Kay's application of participative concepts worked well. He gave workers responsibility for "the whole black box," instead of for pieces of his complex finished products. Because it was still a box, with some definite boundaries, the workers seized the new opportunity without fear or hesitation. The psychological magic of meaningful work, as opposed to the hopelessly specialized chore, took hold. Productivity rose.

VICE PRESIDENTS IN MIDAIR

But at the executive level, Kay moved too quickly, failing to prepare his executives for broad and undefined responsibilities—or failing to choose men better suited for the challenge. One vice president was put in charge of "innovation." Suspended in midair, without the support of departments of functional groups and lacking even so much as a job description, most of the V.P.'s became passive and incapable of making decisions. "They lost touch with reality—including the reality of the market," recalls Clark. When the industry suffered a general slump and new competition entered the field, Non-Linear wasn't ready. Sales dropped 16 percent, according to Kay. In time he realized he was surrounded with dependent men, untrained to participate in the fashion he had peremptorily commanded. He trimmed his executive group and expects to set a new sales record this year.

Sheldon Davis of TRW Systems in Redondo Beach, California, blames the behavioral scientists themselves for breakdowns like Non-Linear's. Too often, he argues, "their messages come out sounding soft and easy, as if what we are trying to do is build happy teams of employees who feel 'good' about things, rather than saying we're trying to build effective organizations with groups that function well and that can zero in quickly on their problems and deal with them rationally."

To Davis, participation should mean, "tough, open exchange," focused on the problem, not the organizational chart. Old-style managers who simply dictate a solution are wrong, he argues, and so are those new-style managers who think the idea is simply to go along with a subordinates proposals if they're earnestly offered. Neither approach taps the full potential of the executive group. When problems are faced squarely, Davis believes, the boss—who should remain boss—gets the best solution because all relevant factors are thoroughly considered. And because everyone has contributed to the solution and feels responsible for it, it is also the solution most likely to be carried out.

One of the most useful new developments in the behavioral study of management is a fresh emphasis on collaboration with technology. In the early days of the human-relations movement in industry, technology was often regarded as "the enemy," the source of the personal and social problems that the psychologists were trying to treat. But from the beginning, some social scientists wanted to move right in and help fashion machines and industrial processes so as to reduce or eliminate their supposedly anti-human effects. Today this concept is more than mere talk. The idea is to develop so-called "socio-technical" systems that permit man and technology *together* to produce the best performance.

Some early experimentation in the British coal mines, by London's Tavistock Institute, as well as scattered work in this country and in Scandinavia, have already demonstrated practical results from such a collaboration. Tavistock found that an attempt to apply specialized factory-style technology to coal mining had isolated the miners from one another. They missed the sense of group support and self-direction that had helped them cope with uncertainty and danger deep in the coal faces. Productivity suffered. In this case, Tavistock's solution was to redesign the new system so that men could still work in groups.

In the U.S. a manufacturer of small household appliances installed some highly sophisticated new technical processes that put the company well in the front of its field. But the engineers had broken down the jobs to such an extent that workers were getting no satisfaction out of their performance and productivity declined. Costs went up and, in the end, some of the new machinery had to be scrapped.

Some technologists seem more than ready to welcome a partnership with the human-relations expert. Louis Davis, a professor of engineering, has joined the U.C.L.A. business-school faculty to lead a six-man socio-technical research group that includes several behaviorists. Among them is Eric Trist, a highly respected psychologist from the Tavistock Institute. Davis hopes today's collaboration will lead in time to a new breed of experts knowledgeable in both the engineering and the social disciplines.

"IT'S TIME WE STOPPED BUILDING RIVAL DICTIONARIES"

The importance of time, the nature of the task, the differences within a large organization, the nature of the people, the cultural setting, the psychological preparation of management, the relationship to technology—all these and other variables are making the search for effective managerial style more and more complex. But the growing recognition of these complexities has drained the human-relations movement of much of its antagonism toward the "super-rationalism" of management science. Humanists must be more systematic and rational if they are to make some useful sense of the scattered and half-tested concepts they have thus far developed, and put their new theories to a real test.

A number of behaviorists believe it is well past time to bury the hatchet and collaborate in earnest with the mathematicians and economists. Some business schools and commercial consulting groups are already realigning their staffs to encourage such work. It won't be easy. Most "systems" thinkers are preoccupied with bringing all the relevant knowledge to bear on a management problem in a systematic way, seeking the theoretically "best" solution. Most behaviorists have tended to assume that the solution which is *most likely to be carried out* is the best one, hence their focus on involving lots of people in the decision making so that they will follow through. Where the "experts" who shape decisions are also in charge of getting the job done, the two approaches sometimes blend, in practice. But in many organizations, it is a long road from creative and imaginative decision to actual performance. A general theory of management must show how to build systematic expertise into a style that is also well suited to people.

The rapprochement among management theorists has a distinguished herald, Fritz J. Roethlisberger of Harvard Business School, one of the human-relations pioneers who first disclosed the potential of the "small group" in industrial experiments forty years ago. He laughs quickly at any suggestion that a unified approach will come easily. "But after all, we are all looking at the same thing," he says. "It's time we stopped building rival dictionaries and learned to make some sentences that really say something."

Cases

Ralph Bennet

Ralph Bennet arrived in the Near East in October, 1955 to work in the personnel department of a large oil company. He had formerly been employed in the States by several large manufacturing companies. In his most recent job he served in the capacity of training supervisor. Prior to leaving the States, arrangements had been made for his wife and two children to join him before Christmas. Arrangements were also made for picking up, crating and shipping his household effects the latter part of November. The lease on his apartment had been terminated and arrangements made to vacate the apartment by the end of November.

Ralph and his family had approached the new job with great enthusiasm. He regarded it as a real challenge and considered it an opportunity to make an important contribution to life. He visualized helping native workers improve their lot, both within the company and the community. The pay was better than he had ever received before and he was told that there was ample opportunity for advancement. His wife had never been out of the States before. She realized that living standards would differ from those to which she had been accustomed. Even so, she was quite anxious to go and tended to regard the whole affair as an adventure. This attitude was shared by the two children.

Shortly after his arrival Ralph was notified that the company was contemplating transferring him to one of its districts as the training supervisor. Because of a lack of housing in this district the company indicated that it would not pick up and ship his household effects until such time as field housing could be assigned. It was requested that his family not join him until adequate housing was available. Thus, their arrival might be delayed for as long as nine months, perhaps even one year.

Ralph was naturally distressed by this turn of events, especially since it had been understood clearly at the time of his employment that he could bring his family and their effects to the Near East shortly after his arrival. He there-

All names and organizational designations have been disguised. Northwestern University cases are reports of concrete events and behavior prepared for group discussion. They are not intended as examples of "good" or "bad" administrative or technical practices. Written by Harper Boyd. Copyright © 1956 Northwestern University.

fore notified the company that if it did not fulfill the terms of his employment he would resign. Within a few days the company granted his request. The Bennet family arrived before Christmas and their household goods were picked up on December 14 and placed in storage until a final destination could be assigned.

In January, 1956 the company decided to locate Ralph at headquarters. Its offices in the States were given notice to ship his furniture. His job assignment was to assist all district field training supervisors in production training. This meant that he would spend considerable time in the field helping the various district supervisors with their programs. His time at headquarters would be spent working up course materials and preparing training aids.

About the middle of May, Fred Ackerman, a field training supervisor at District A, told Ralph that he was being recommended as his vacation replacement for the months of July and August. In the subsequent weeks Fred and Ralph discussed the work which was to be done during Fred's absence. Arrangements were also made for Ralph to use Fred's house and car. Ralph discussed all these matters with his headquarters supervisor who indicated that upon receipt of the district's request he would give a favorable answer. On or about June 1, Fred notified Ralph that the district superintendent had agreed to the plan and that an official request for his services was to be sent.

At about the same time, the headquarters personnel manager discussed with Ralph the possibility of being permanently assigned to District B. The subject was to be reviewed with the production department to obtain housing clearance. The training job at this camp had been vacant for almost a year. It was the job the company had initially wanted him to take, but housing had not been available. Ralph was willing to accept this "permanent" job, especially since it meant a promotion to the next higher grade. His supervisor informed him that the attempt to obtain for him a permanent transfer had complicated the temporary assignment. Ralph was informed, however, that there was to be a meeting in the field during the week of June 11 at which time his status would be decided. It was stated that he should know what was going to happen by June 15.

While waiting word on his future assignment Ralph learned that the company was considering transferring Richard Clueman, the training supervisor at District D, to take over a vacancy in the headquarters office. Ralph also learned, unofficially, that the district superintendent had stated that he would not release Clueman unless an adequate replacement could be obtained. Ralph immediately saw the possibility that he might be considered as Clueman's replacement. He became upset when he learned via the grapevine that he was being considered for this job. He felt that he should have been consulted during these discussions. A few days later he heard from an "informed but unofficial source" that headquarters had not only talked about him as a replacement but had, in fact, nominated him for the job and had received an official acceptance from District D.

In presenting the job to Ralph, the personnel manager apologized for the switch and then explained the reasons "why." He reviewed the background of the change and said, "We'd like to have you go to District D as Clueman's replacement. It's a great opportunity because not only will you be promoted but you'll get more and better experience. Your new assignment means supervision over one of our special craft schools in addition to your other training work. It's a nice area too—not nearly as hot as some of the other districts. Besides, there's no housing problem, since you can have Clueman's house. It's very adequate."

Ralph replied, "I've moved around a lot and I'm accustomed to making my own decisions about where and when I go. Besides, I'm not so sure I want to work for the district superintendent. From what I hear he's a rough character and a lot of fellows have trouble working for him. I'm supposed to be a training supervisor and morale's my business; yet I'd have a rough go of it with such a boss."

The personnel manager replied that he knew the superintendent well and, while he wasn't all peaches and cream, he was really a nice guy who wouldn't give Ralph any trouble. Also, he said that the morale problem was greatly exaggerated.

Ralph finally closed the discussion by requesting permission to visit the district and see the situation firsthand. He was particularly interested in meeting and talking with the district superintendent. His request was granted and the following day he left by plane.

In discussing the job with the district superintendent Ralph was surprised to find the job referred to as a developmental assignment holding the same rating as he now held. The explanation given was that it was hoped the present job rating would be upgraded and that when this did occur the individual on the job would be promoted. The superintendent thought this job change might come along "any time now." Ralph replied that he thought it wiser to have the rating changed before he took the job. The matters of the job level were left open and the superintendent said he would radio headquarters shortly as to their decision about the assignment. While Ralph was waiting to hear whether the district still wanted him and whether the job would be upgraded, he discussed his problem with an associate.

In talking about this situation Ralph reflected the feeling that his refusal to accept the transfer quickly had been resented. He indicated he was not sorry he had come to the Near East but added that if a similar situation had occurred in the States he would "probably be with another company by now." He expressed anxiety about how his wife might come to feel about the company and the work environment. He said that all this experience had taken some edge off his enthusiasm and that if the company behaved toward other employees in this way, its human relations in general must be bad. He expressed the opinion that the company disliked anyone to question a decision made by a department manager. He felt that the company had not outgrown its old concepts sufficiently to recognize that employees need to be consulted when their future is involved.

He also pointed out that he was not sure what his alternatives were. The other jobs had by then been filled. He guessed he could stay on doing coordination work at headquarters (the job he had held since January), but he was not sure where this job would lead. He was convinced that management had not considered the possibility that he might not accept the job in District D, were it offered, regardless of whether a promotion were involved.

Ball Wholesale Drug Company

Early in 1954 the Third Area office of the Ball Wholesale Drug Company advertised for an Assistant Chief Accountant. Sales volume in the area had expanded considerably over the past year and Mr. Paul Donovan, Area Manager, had secured the agreement of the home office to make this addition to his staff. Mr. Donovan had felt for some time that the accounting department needed improvement. He had been criticized by the home office for the lateness of various weekly reports and for the seeming inability of his area to submit monthly data to the home office on time.

As a result of the advertisement and referrals from several employment agencies, fourteen applicants were interviewed and tested over the next month. The field was narrowed down to two men on the basis of the interviews and test results. One of the applicants was Henry League, a man who had had three years' experience in accounting in an area related to the kind of work done by the accounting department at Ball. He had an extremely pleasing personality and made a good appearance. Mr. Fred Wright, Jr., the Chief Accountant, recommended the hiring of Mr. League.

Paul Donovan, however, preferred Russell Phillips, a man with even more outstanding accounting aptitude who had scored at the very top in all of the tests. Mr. Phillips was extremely tall, seemed rather shy and unsure of himself, and, although dressed neatly at the time of his interviews, did not present as impressive an appearance as Henry League. Mr. Donovan and Mr. Wright had several discussions on the subject of which man to hire. Wright felt that, since the position would involve the supervision of six girls in the bookkeeping department, Mr. League should be chosen. He argued that League, despite his

Prepared by Robert J. Agnew for the School of Business Administration, University of Pittsburgh, and reprinted with his permission.

slightly lower test results, would make a better supervisor because of his more outgoing personality and more forceful manner.

Mr. Donovan was more concerned with the speed and accuracy of the accounting department and he felt that the position required an accountant of great ability. In his opinion, the supervisory aspects of the job were only secondary. He advised the hiring of the less dynamic and personable Mr. Phillips in consideration of his superior accounting aptitude, better test performance and equal experience.

Wright was persuaded, somewhat reluctantly, to offer the position to Mr. Phillips who accepted and assumed his duties on the first day of the next month.

There was an almost immediate improvement in the performance of the Accounting Department. After only two weeks of Phillips' tenure, fewer errors were being committed and allowed to reach the home office. Within only a few months the deadline dates for the weekly and monthly reports began to be met and within six months the "on time" performance of Mr. Donovan's area became the best in the Central Region.

Mr. Donovan also sensed an improvement in the morale of the bookkeeping office. The girls seemed to be less tense. Mr. Donovan attributed this to their no longer being under such pressure to meet deadlines. Overtime work in the department was reduced almost to the vanishing point and employees of that department were able to join other members of the office force in coffee breaks. The section members became, for the first time in years, really a part of the office society.

In his first semiannual review of Phillips, Mr. Wright gave him excellent ratings and recommended a salary increase. Mr. Donovan agreed with enthusiasm and the raise was approved by the New York office. Privately, Mr. Wright commented repeatedly to Mr. Donovan on the fact that Phillips was doing an excellent job and indicated complete satisfaction with the choice of Phillips over Mr. League. Wright confessed that he was somewhat puzzled by the fact that the performance of the department as a whole had improved so remarkably. He reported that Phillips appeared to be doing very little real "supervising" of the girls in terms of organizing their work, arranging coverage for the office telephones during coffee breaks, assigning definite responsibilities to the girls, etc. The work, however, was getting done and Wright told Mr. Donovan that he hesitated to interfere. He did report that Phillips had not followed through on several suggestions for system improvements that Wright himself had made and which he felt would serve to reduce some of the confusion he could see in the department.

Mr. Donovan agreed with Mr. Wright that Phillips did not appear to be "on top of the job" but felt that the greatly improved accuracy and outstanding "on time" record more than compensated for the minor deficiencies of Mr. Phillips as an organizer.

In thinking about this situation after one of his talks with Wright, Mr. Donovan came to the realization that there had been some marked changes in

Russell Phillips. It seemed to him that most of the girls in the department had taken an almost personal interest in Phillips' appearance. His manner of dress had become much neater and his bearing and self-assurance had improved.

Mr. Donovan overheard a conversation one morning in the bookkeeping section where he had gone to check on a delinquent account. Two of the girls were chiding Phillips about his choice in neckties. "You shouldn't wear that tie with your brown suit, Russell. It makes you look like the janitor," one of the girls had said. "Yes," said the other, "you have the dignity of the Department to uphold." The three of them had then laughed but Mr. Donovan noticed that Phillips had returned from his lunch wearing a different necktie. Donovan had laughed at the incident at the time, but could not help but feel that much of the improvement in Phillips' appearance had resulted from the personal attention of the girls in his office.

Some months later the Third Area Accounting Department won an annual award given by the home office to the Area scoring highest in a contest, which included an examination of all the records and accounts kept in each area office from the point of view of accuracy and current status, as well as "on time" performance on the weekly and monthly reports.

The Third Area had never before won this award. Mr. Donovan provided a dinner party at company expense for the entire Accounting Department and their escorts. Mr. Wright and his wife joined Mr. and Mrs. Donovan at the head of the table while Mr. Phillips and a young lady from the order department whom he had invited presided at the other end.

Mr. Donovan was struck by the easy air of camaraderie which prevailed at the dinner and the ease with which Phillips conducted himself. He remarked to Wright that Phillips had "come a long way in a little over a year and a half." The party was made even gayer when Russell Phillips and June Larson, the young lady from the order department, chose the occasion to announce their engagement.

Several months after his marriage, Mr. Phillips requested an interview with Mr. Donovan. Donovan was prepared to grant Phillips an increase in salary but was not prepared for Phillips' announcement that he was leaving the company.

In the interview Donovan learned that Mrs. Phillips who had originally come from the West Coast, had expressed to her husband a keen desire to return, and convinced him that they should move to California. Mr. Donovan expressed his disappointment but recognized that this was not a bargaining tactic. The Ball Company had recently absorbed a smaller drug wholesale firm in California. Mr. Donovan was able to arrange a transfer to California for Phillips, whom he regarded as a valuable employee worth keeping in the Company. The Accounting Department held a farewell party for Mr. and Mrs. Phillips and Mr. Donovan and his wife were honored guests.

The problem of replacing Phillips had been considered before his departure. Mr. Wright reported that Mr. League, his original choice for the position, had taken other employment as an accountant but at a lower salary than that offered by Ball. It was agreed that Wright would approach Mr. League and that the position would be offered to him rather than to go through the time consuming routine of interviewing a new lot of applicants. In his interview, League again impressed Mr. Wright very favorably but Mr. Donovan still held a few reservations. He was not able to point to any specific fault and ascribed his impression to his previous preference for Phillips. However, in view of League's excellent performance on the tests some two years before and his support by Wright Mr. Donovan did not make an issue of the hiring and the position was accepted by Mr. Henry League.

The excellent performance of the accounting department continued and Mr. Donovan and Mr. Wright agreed that they had been extremely fortunate in securing so able a replacement. Mr. Wright felt that, if anything, there had been an improvement in the operation of the bookkeeping function directly under Mr. League's control. He indicated his belief that discipline had improved and that there was less time wasted under Mr. League than there had been under the more informal supervision of Mr. Phillips. Wright also indicated that Mr. League was much more willing to adopt suggestions and had improved and simplified various aspects of the work flow.

Mr. Donovan received a friendly letter from Mr. Phillips a month or two after his arrival in California expressing enthusiasm for his new position and also thanking Mr. Donovan for having arranged the transfer. Donovan learned from the New York office that Phillips had made a very favorable impression upon his superiors in the California office.

About six months after Mr. League had taken over, errors and incomplete reports began to appear. The "on time" performance of the accounting department became less than perfect. Mr. Donovan was chided by the home office for this fall from grace, but agreed with Mr. Wright that Mr. League was in no way to blame. The poorer performance was blamed on an increase in the work load and an additional girl was hired for the bookkeeping section.

However, the record of the department failed to improve. Mr. Wright was still unwilling to hold Mr. League responsible for the poor performance, even when the record of the department fell to the level it had been before the hiring of Phillips. Mr. Wright indicated that he felt that Mr. League perhaps needed more time to get his feet on the ground in the job and that they owed him that time because Ball had hired him away from his former position.

Mr. Donovan agreed that they had a certain responsibility to Mr. League but became increasingly concerned about the poor performance and the criticisms directed at his area by the home office. Overtime in the department and particularly in the bookkeeping section became the rule, rather than the exception. The New York office, in no uncertain terms, ordered Mr. Donovan to reduce this item of cost.

Later in the same week in which the order relating to the reduction of overtime arrived, Mr. Donovan received a letter from Mr. Phillips. Mr. Phillips expressed his satisfaction with the California position and with the company. He did not like the location, however, and stated that the climate had proved detrimental to the health of his wife. He also said that an old sinus condition of his own had been aggravated and that he would like to move. His wife's parents had died and she no longer felt the attraction to the area which had taken them there in the first place. His letter concluded:

> I know that my old job in Prenticeburg has been filled and I do not expect the company to make another place for me. I would like to ask you, however, to keep your ears open around town for any opening you think I might be able to fill. Both you and Mr. Wright are familiar with my record and abilities and I would much appreciate your doing what you can for me in this connection.

Bibliography

A. Business and Youth: Conformity or Individualism

Baumhart, Raymond C. and George D. Fitzpatrick. "Can Business Attract the Young," *Personnel* (September–October, 1967), pp. 30–35.

Bond, Edward L., Jr. "American Youth—Why They Avoid Involvement With Business," *Public Relations Journal* (May 1966), pp. 8–11.

Drucker, Peter F. "Is Business Letting Young People Down?" *Harvard Business Review* (November–December, 1965), pp. 49–55.

Habbe, Stephen. "Business and the College Student," *Conference Board Record* (September 1967), pp. 18–26.

Lynn, Richard. "Getting the Bright Boys into Business," *The Director* (June 1967), pp. 440–443.

Schein, Edgar H. "The College Graduate's First Job: What He Wants, What You Want and How to Have it Both Ways," *Management Review* (May 1967), pp. 56–59.

St. John, Jeffrey. "Business Management—Where the Action Is," *Michigan Business Review* (June 1967), pp. 28–32.

B. Participative Management: Opportunity for Individualism

"Everyone Wants a Hand in Management," *Business Week* (April 9, 1966), p. 89.

Leavitt, Harold J. "Unhuman Organizations," *Harvard Business Review* (July–August, 1962), pp. 53–61.

Newport, M. Gene. "Participative Management: Some Cautions," *Personnel Journal* (October 1966), pp. 532–537.

Rosenfield, Joel M. and Matthew J. Smith. "Participative Management: An Overview," *Personnel Journal* (February 1967), pp. 101–105.

"The Whole Staff Has a Voice in Running Sentry," *Business Week* (July 30, 1966), pp. 112–114.

"When Workers Manage Themselves," *Business Week* (March 20, 1965), pp. 93–94.

PART FOUR

Labor-Management Relationships

Of the many business-society relationships, the one which has been most publicized is that between business, as a dominant institution in society, and labor, as represented by organzed labor unions. Among the vast array of issues that fall within this realm are the controversies over the collective bargaining process, nationwide bargaining issues, and the organizing activities of unions.

A. Collective Bargaining, Full Employment and Inflation

The general success of labor-management relations depends for the most part on the collective bargaining process. Society recognizes the desirability and necessity for maximum freedom in collective bargaining agreements that include both labor and management. In spite of this necessity, the feasibility and long-run success of the collective bargaining process have been seriously questioned. In "Crisis in Collective Bargaining" [14] Benjamin L. Masse notes that European critics are disillusioned with the American collective bargaining process and feel that it has not responded effectively to technological changes and increased foreign competition. They argue that collective bargaining contributes to continuing inflation because labor and management tend to engage in "collusion" for higher wages which are passed on to the consumer in the form of higher prices. In spite of these problems, both labor and management insist that collective bargaining remain as free as possible and that government remain aloof, especially in any form of arbitration.

Another major criticism of collective bargaining is its emphasis upon the adversary rather than cooperative aspect of the process, since both parties are opposed to each other and seek to maximize their own gains at the bargaining table. The question of whether or not the process can be made more "cooperative" is the major challenge. The idea of summit meetings, federal coordinators, or regional groups working for some form of cooperation appear to exist only in the literature today, rather than in practice.

While it may be true that collective bargaining contributes to inflation, inflation and the rate of joblessness—two indices of a nation's economic climate—may affect the bargaining positions of labor and management. Solutions to disputes are often inhibited by economic realities. For example, labor's "right to work" may be undercut by avowed national policy to cut inflation.

The full employment versus inflation trade-off problem is presented in article 15, "GOP Is Thrown a Price-Job Curve." In the short-run economists predict that a reduction in unemployment will generally result in increased inflation. A trade-off policy may also be aimed at decreasing inflation with a natural rise in unemployment. We find that in the early 1960s the reduction of unemployment received greater attention as a national priority; in the latter half of the 1960s, as today, the reduction of inflation has been emphasized by policymakers. However, we now find that *both* unemployment and inflation are increasing, and this development is, by definition, contrary to the goals of a trade-off policy.

Most economists recommend that the natural unemployment rate of between four and five and one-half per cent should, in the long run, be reduced. They contend that only through government action will joblessness be lessened. Control of the unemployment rate has traditionally taken the form of wage-price guidelines implemented by the executive branch of the federal government. However, the Nixon administration, despite recommendations to the contrary, has not established wage-price guidelines or wage-price controls. The President has made appeals to business groups to take responsible action in view of present economic difficulties, and he has recommended productivity studies, but he has refused to propose any form of direct economic control.

As unemployment and inflation increase, the cost of freedom in the collective bargaining process will certainly be a major issue in the seventies. The degree to which businesses should take "responsible" action, as recommended to them by the President, must be viewed in the total context of what "responsible actions" labor will also take, and what guidelines and overt action the federal government, especially through the executive branch, might take. At this time, uncontrolled inflation, the fear of a recession and the possibility of a depression raise serious questions as to what responsible action must be taken by the federal government, labor and management. If the collective bargaining process is to remain free, it must be handled in a responsible manner. Otherwise, it will become necessary for citizens through their legislators to bring their influence to bear. Historically, action taken by the executive branch has sought to influence negotiations. However, it appears that other means must be found to increase the effectiveness and responsiveness of the collective bargaining process to the needs of society.

B. The Right-To-Work Controversy

Although collective bargaining became the law of the land in 1935, recognition of unions, and of employees seeking to form unions, is still being contested in many states. In spite of the law protecting the right of the individual employee to bargain collectively with his potential or actual employer, numerous managers, companies, and business and industry associations have systematically fought the unionization of employees. These battles contributed to the inclusion of Section 14(b) in the Taft-Hartley Act of 1947 which delegated to the states the right to pass the so-called right-to-work laws. These laws gave to the individual employee the right to join or not to join, and also the right to leave, a union. Ever since this law was passed, the labor unions have sought its repeal.

In seeking repeal of Section 14(b) of the Taft-Hartley Act, the labor unions have sought to return control of labor policy to the federal government. This controversy is presented in article 16 "The Battle Over 14(b)." Since almost half of the states have passed right-to-work laws, unions are concerned about the problems caused by these laws. In particular, unions claim that most attitude polls have revealed that workers definitely prefer union shops, which preclude an individual from leaving the union. Unions maintain that, as in our democratic form of government, the minority must go along with the majority decisions of union workers. They contend that the ability to leave the union arbitrarily serves to encourage free riders who do not want to pay or participate in the strikes that have led to increased wages and benefits, or to participate in union programs protecting their rights. Union leaders argue that many states have used the right-to-work laws as a means of attracting unionized industries out of heavily unionized states into states where union influence might be minimized or precluded.

Business has supported the retention of the right-to-work laws. The arguments presented in "Dangers in More Forced Unionism" [17] indicate that businessmen are apprehensive of more union power, and expectant of increasing strikes if union power is not curtailed. They contend that right-to-work laws provide a necessary check upon union power because they give individual workers the right to resign from a union. In what we might call philosophical terms, business seeks the protection of any individual's freedom to join or leave any organization within society, especially the labor union.

When we review the extensive arguments for and against the repeal of Section 14(b), we find ourselves reduced to the fundamental issue of collective bargaining. That is, collective bargaining was created to offset the serious and overwhelming imbalance of power between the individual employee as he bargained with the employer. Given the massive resources in the hands of the manager, the individual employee, unless holding unique technical and professional skills, has little bargaining power. The argument that corruptive and dictatorial tactics on the part of labor union leaders jeopardize business, might be offset by reference to the Landrum-Griffin legislation, which provides for the prosecution of labor leaders misusing the power of their office. For these and other reasons, we must carefully consider the means available for maintaining some equality of bargaining power between labor and management.

In conclusion, there are two important questions to consider. If the corruptive practices of labor union leaders can be checked by the Landrum-Griffin bill, what methods—other than collective bargaining via organized trade unions—are available in order to strike a balance of power between individual employees and managers? And if the individual employee is free to leave the union and deny it his active and financial support, will the labor union survive as an effective instrument in providing some equality of bargaining power with management now and in the future?

C. The Employment Responsibilities of Business

Among the many goals sought by labor in its collective bargaining agreements with management are the primary ones of job security and seniority. These goals particularly relate to the intent of the Full-Employment Act of 1946. Given the present trend of technological innovation resulting in employment problems such as job dislocation, the goal of full employment will most probably entail greater emphasis on employment stabilization, as well as the creation of new job opportunities. As society depends upon our economy and free enterprise system for economic growth, preservation of buying power, and full employment, the trustee concept of management and business is reemphasized.

If the individual in our society must exercise his right to life, liberty, and the pursuit of happiness through his job, his job rights will inevitably increase in importance in our highly specialized economy. It is often said today that a man's "right to life" is his "right to a job." This is emphasized by the fact that employment of the individual worker in industry or business has vastly increased since the turn of the century. In 1900, approximately 15 percent of the population was dependent upon business and industry for employment. A much larger percentage found employment in agriculture. Today approximately 85 percent of the employable members of our society depend upon business for a job.

The problems of unemployment and full employment, as affected by automation and technological innovation, are highlighted in article 18, "Machines Do It Better Than Humans: An Assessment of a Workless Society and Proposals for Action." Written as a memorandum to President Lydon B. Johnson in 1964 by a group of economists, labor leaders, publishers and others, this article predicts the effects of cybernetics upon the economy in the seventies. The expectation is that the rate of automation will be so high that our economy will be virtually a cybernetic one, that is, one virtually self-operating and controlled by machines. Based upon these projections, it is expected that the technological displacement of employees and jobs will be so great that there will be a massive segment of our society without employment or buying power. This group of unemployed will become "the workless society." Without other employment opportunities, they will rely upon welfare for survival. If this prediction is realized the shift from the traditional emphasis upon work as a major source of income to the maintenance of buying power by government subsidy will become an integral part of our life. It is interesting to note that this is already partially true in the plans and programs for the indigent presently on welfare. The government is much more inclined now toward providing direct monetary payments to the unemployed in the form of negative income taxes. Extensive efforts must be made to transfer workers from industry to industry as some jobs become obsolete and new and different jobs and skills are required. The committee recommends that the United States take a direct approach to planned cybernation and managed change. This would require action and planning at all governmental levels to include citizen participation. As a result of planning, employment would shift from industry to other areas of activity such as teaching and public welfare programs.

According to the predictions in "Machines Won't Take Over After All [19]" we find that the employment level for different jobs in various industries will remain reliatively stable through 1975. No drastic displacement of jobs or persons as a result of technological innovation or automation is expected. Demand for less skilled persons will continue, but employment will grow fastest in the professional and technically skilled areas. The problems for minorities and youth will continue unless significant inroads are made to increase job opportunities. It is noted that the extent of automation will vary significantly from industry to industry. Therefore, provision for occupational shifting from industry to industry, and job to job must be considered.

The problem of unemployment amidst abundance in our society does not appear as drastic as defined in the cybernetic revolution. While employment in manufacturing industries will decline—and it is in these industries that we have achieved and maintained our highest rate of productivity increase—we do find an extensive and emphatic shift toward service industries. The expected abundance of automated or cybernetic productivity will be seriously offset by the declining productivity in the increasing employment areas of service industries; for instance, in 1969, productivity declined in these industries.

Even though the final responsibility for full employment has been placed upon the federal government in the Full-Employment Act of 1946, business and industry have demonstrated in the last ten years a strong interest in maintaining full employment. Extensive experimentation has been conducted to create new jobs, and train uneducated and unskilled persons for employment. Such responsibility must continue because it is in the long-run interest of business. Without business support job training and the creation of jobs will become the exclusive responsibility of the federal government, and the cost of these programs will be passed on to the businessman in the form of higher taxes.

While many businessmen have been seeking ways to increase employment and have initiated on-the-job training programs—some of which have been partially supported by federal funds—greater attention and ingenuity on the part of management are demanded if the problem is even to be contained. Although an unemployment level of three percent is hoped for by mid-1970, economic indicators for 1970 do not point to that level. Even if the rate of inflation can be checked, we may be forced to reorder our national priorities and seek a less ambitious level of employment perhaps between four and five percent or between five and six percent. The simultaneous developments of inflation with unemployment will probably require a more effective partnership in the future between business and government to include labor. More joint planning and planned action may well be a requirement of the seventies, especially if full employment is specifically adopted as a national goal. Management would then be forced to assume the particular responsibility for achieving full employment, or full productivity within the firm. Society in turn must then provide effective incentives and rewards for innovations and efforts made by management and labor. Only through a commitment to these goals and actions can we achieve the increased levels of economic activity and the concomitant maintenance of adequate employment levels.

D. Civil Rights and Fair-Employment Practices

Labor-management or employer-employee relationships are probably most important in the day-to-day, face-to-face contacts between superiors and subordinates in all organizations, large and small. The highly varied and extensive number of personnel policies formulated for the handling of these problems in large organizations attest to their complexity and frequency. Since each individual employer-employee problem appears to contain many variables, efforts to achieve justice and equity in resolving these problems require careful analysis. Personnel policies attempt to prevent arbitrary management decisions which could result in grievances and inequities in relationship with employees. This type of problem solving and decision making is illustrated in the Seabrook Manufacturing Company case where the inconsistency of management decisions resulting from the lack of clear-cut personnel policies affects employee specifications required for the job. Management can, through the tools of job evaluation, merit rating systems, and job specifications, clearly delineate those factors most common to employee-company conflicts and thereby help to resolve internal personnel problems.

Where management's arbitrary decisions result in discrimination based on race, color, or creed, the records show that social opposition will be forthcoming eventually. An example of this action is the legislation by the Fair

Employment Practices Commission prohibiting discriminatory decision-making in many states. The Well-Run Oil Company case illustrates the degree to which pressures may be brought to bear in the form of economic boycott as retaliatory action against management's hiring decisions involving race or color of applicants. If these grievances and conflicts are to be reconciled, management must establish a basic framework of principles, objectives, and policies which will be compatible with prevailing social mores.

An overview and suggested approach to the problem of fair employment are presented in "Equal Employment Opportunities: Company Policies and Experience" [20]. Industry can adopt a number of measures to attack the problem of unfair employment practices by opening entry into more jobs, and by demonstrating honest concern for the employment needs of Blacks and other minority groups. In particular management must provide leadership to insure that both equality of employment opportunities and knowledge of these opportunities are available. Since the critical factor is one of job qualification, Blacks and other minority groups must be trained in company programs not only for semi-skilled, but also for managerial jobs. A more widespread effort must be made in our society to give equal opportunities to Blacks and other minority groups in education, and in all spheres of social and economic life.

The reform of employment practices to extend opportunities to black and other minority groups may create difficulties for many firms. These difficulties are specifically noted in article 21, "Where Civil Rights Law Is Going Wrong." The author points out that many businessmen are concerned that reverse discrimination will preclude opportunities to the well-qualified candidate who is not a member of a minority group. With the Civil Rights Act of 1964 guaranteeing equality of opportunity between the sexes, businesses are again being forced to reappraise their hiring practices as more women are demanding access to jobs traditionally reserved for men.

Many problems that fall under the broad umbrella of equality of job opportunities may take time and experience to resolve, and management faces a difficult job of resolving these new pressures, conflicts, and problems. Managers must adopt new attitudes that are appropriate to present-day social reform. Patience, understanding and education alone will not serve to change ingrained attitudes. New attitudes develop as a result of close association and shared experiences with black and other minority groups. Given management's attitudinal bias, management is concerned that aggressive recruitment of minority employees will result in reverse discrimination; yet, alternatives for achieving some semblance of equity and justices to offset past discrimination in jobs and education are not often proposed. While management is certainly a target of criticism and pressure, the pervasiveness and long history of discrimination requires that justice be served immediately. In effect, management must now adapt to changes being rapidly, and belatedly, imposed on our society's mores.

A. Collective Bargaining, Full Employment and Inflation

Crisis in
Collective Bargaining

14

Benjamin L. Masse

After the war European industrialists and trade-union leaders streamed across the Atlantic to learn the secret of our industrial relations. They are not coming to these shores any more. Whatever the reason may be, people from advanced industrial countries, as Solomon Barkin, research director of the Textile Workers, noted in the November *Fortune,* have ceased to regard collective bargaining, American style, as the answer to modern labor-management relationships.

What has gone wrong with our 25-year-old national policy that survived the shock of war and looked so promising in the late 1940's? Why has a feeling of frustration spread widely through the AFL–CIO? Why do the meetings of management men rumble with dissatisfaction over the course of industrial relations? Why did such a knowledgeable man as Victor Borella, who keeps industrial relations at Manhattan's Rockefeller Center humming smoothly, write recently that "we find our nation's labor-management set-up is not only an unhappy but an unfortunate stance to meet the truly great challenges of our time"?

As a curious, and concerned, reporter digs around for answers to those questions, several themes keep recurring. They are, though not necessarily in order of importance, the Cold War, inflation, foreign competition and automation. In one or the other of these, or in some combination of them, must be sought the causes of the growing doubts about collective bargaining.

Reprinted with permission from *America,* 106 West 56th Street, New York, New York (January 14, 1961), pp. 469–471.

In a typically thoughtful address at Roosevelt University last August 17, Senator Kennedy's popular choice for Secretary of Labor, Arthur J. Goldberg, bore down heavily on the disruptive effects of the Cold War and automation:

> We live in an age of revolutionary technological change and in an age of extraordinary international tension.
> Traditional practices, which have served us so well, and which would continue to do so if we were really at peace, must be adapted to a period where our whole way of life is being challenged. Traditional practices, which served us so well, must be adapted to an age when our industrial society is being transformed by technological advance.

In the *Fortune* article referred to above, Mr. Barkin, though approaching the problem somewhat differently, arrives at conclusions strikingly similar to Mr. Goldberg's. "The machinery of industrial relations is at dead center," he writes, "bogged down in costly and irritating parochial bickering." Neither labor nor management, he says, is dealing in a creative, dynamic way with the growing threat of foreign competition. Unions tend to meet the danger by fighting stubbornly for the security of a declining labor force. Equally traditional in their approach, employers strive to cope with the threat by slashing payrolls. The clash between these short-term, self-interest approaches, Mr. Barkin believes, "is at the heart of the current high tension in industrial relations."

Mr. Barkin argues, furthermore, that traditional methods of collective bargaining are proving no more adequate to cope with inflation and the forces of industrial change than they are with foreign competition. Probably every responsible union leader in the country would echo his lament on inflation:

> Union leaders have been perplexed as to how to proceed responsibly in wage negotiations in order to minimize the possibility of price increases. They have had no guarantee that, if they adopted wage restraint, management would make a parallel commitment for price restraint.

The Textile leader, one of the most stimulating intellectuals in the labor movement, sadly concludes that collective bargaining as we have known it cannot deal with this great issue—in which the public is so keenly interested—because management "has refused to discuss price and production policy with union representatives."

The crisis in collective bargaining was given an exhaustive airing last summer at a conference sponsored by the Fund for the Republic's Trade Union Project. This informal seminar assumes special importance because among the thirty participants who assembled during the week of July 17 at Santa Barbara, Cal., were men prominent in industry, labor, government and education. The following paragraph from the summary of the discussions—which Paul Jacobs, director of the project, kindly made available to the writer—emphasizes the importance the seminar attached to technological change:

Thus, it is fair to say that the entire conference agreed that a re-thinking of traditional collective bargaining practices was required. The world market, the Cold War, union structure, these and other factors were mentioned as affecting, and being affected by, this crisis. But the central factor which occupied the conference discussion was that of technological change. The rate and range of this process in recent years was seen as creating problems which were so serious and extensive as to require the United States to go beyond its old, familiar way of doing things.

Industry views of the strains in industrial relations tend to place the emphasis elsewhere. Fairly typical were the advertisements which the steel companies published during the long strike in 1959. Over and over again, these statements, stressing the dangers of inflation and foreign competition, proclaimed the need for wage restraint on the union's part and a willingness to accept changes in working rules dictated by considerations of effciency. The wage and work-rule issues also preoccupied the rail transportation industry in its protracted struggle last year with the railroad brotherhoods. (There was a complete breakdown of collective bargaining on the rules issue and this problem, at the instigation of the White House, has now been handed over for study to a special Presidential panel.)

To many management men, the Cold War, automation, foreign competition and the rest are not so much causes of the crisis in industrial relations as occasions which have revealed ingrown weaknesses in our system.

On the one hand, they explain, unions have come to believe that workers are entitled to an annual increase in wages and fringe benefits. On the other, they have curbed management's freedom to effect the changes in production methods that would make higher wages economically possible. So long as demand was strong and foreign competition negligible, management found it expedient to acquiesce in most union demands. Now that foreign firms have become aggressive and the American public will no longer stand for inflationary price increases, management has been obliged to reassert its rights to direct the business as it thinks best. This means that it must be solicitous, not only for employes, but for the company's stockholders, suppliers and customers as well.

Very much to the point, according to management men, was the sermon which the National City Bank of New York preached to its audience in its *Monthly Letter* for December. In the context of an economy faced with intensified competitive pressures and a balance-of-payments problem, the bank exhorted:

> In exercising their power in collective bargaining, union leaders as well as managements must face up to the fact that prices can no longer be raised each time that big wage raises are negotiated. They must recognize that they defeat their own cause when they demand pay increases that outrun gains in efficiency and wipe out profitable return on new investment.

Prescriptions for handling the crisis in collective bargaining reflect the different evaluations put on it by management and labor. If the machinery is breaking down because inflation, foreign competition, technological change and the pressures of the Cold War have overburdened it, then one kind of medicine is indicated. Another kind entirely might be called for if the pressures of the times have not caused the breakdown but only revealed old defects in the machinery.

Management believes that whatever is wrong with collective bargaining would soon be righted if 1) unions stopped challenging and impeding its function of managing, and 2) union "monopolies" were prohibited by law. What the government should do is attack labor's monopoly power by outlawing all types of union security, as right-to-work legislation does, and by subjecting unions to the nation's antitrust laws. Presumably if this were done, most unions would no longer be in a position to challenge management control.

These are the key reforms in management's programs. In addition to them the National Association of Manufacturers feels that the atmosphere surrounding collective bargaining would be much improved if secret ballots were required for strikes and if union political activities were even more restricted than they are by the Taft-Hartley Act.

As for labor, which regards the industry solution as no solution at all, it has officially endorsed the proposition, first advanced by Arthur J. Goldberg, that the problems besetting industrial relations are too far-reaching for resolution at the bargaining table. By its very nature, Mr. Goldberg contends, the bargaining table emphasizes the adversary rather than the cooperative aspect of industrial relations. It is, consequently, a poor mechanism for discussing questions that go beyond individual companies and unions. Such questions should first be discussed, he says, by a small group of top men in labor and industry in circumstances free of the pressures of bargaining. Accordingly, he suggested a union-employer "summit meeting" under the aegis, but not the domination, of the White House.

After some hesitation President Eisenhower, at the insistence of AFL-CIO President George Meany, accepted the idea. Early last year he asked the NAM and the AFL-CIO to sit down together and chart an ascent to the summit. Although some meetings have been held, there has been as yet no report of any progress.

This silence may be significant. Generally speaking, management has no desire to go to the summit. That was obvious enough even before Ford and General Motors rejected an invitation from Walter Reuther, head of the United Auto Workers, to discuss matters of common interest on an industry level. Since Mr. Reuther sent his invitation under the patronage, so to speak, of President Eisenhower—in a speech in Detroit on October 17 the President had urged such a meeting—the intensity of management opposition to the summit idea can easily be imagined.

On the other hand, the AFL-CIO has little confidence in joint meetings with the NAM. When the idea of a summit meeting was first broached, President Meany warned that it would accomplish nothing unless industry was represented by the heads of companies actually engaged in bargaining with AFL-CIO unions.

The Fund for the Republic conferees split over remedies for the collective-bargaining crisis. One group was so impressed by the complexity of today's problems that it despaired of any exclusively labor-management approach to them. In dealing with issues like inflation, foreign economic policy and the rate of technological change, collective bargaining, they insisted, is only one of many factors involved—and a subordinate one at that. This group called, therefore, for a national, coordinated approach in which the Federal Government would have a substantial role. They recommended the creation in the Executive Branch of a council composed of government officials and leaders of management and labor that would thresh out problems too big for the bargaining table and seek to reach agreements on broad policies.

Another group felt that traditional methods of collective bargaining were not so inadequate that they could not be adapted to the changing times. They conceded that some place had to be made today for public representation in labor-management affairs, but they believed that this could be provided for without involving the government. It was suggested, for instance, that the role of arbitrators might be enlarged, so they could act more creatively and energetically than is now the case, or that labor-management meetings on a regional or industry level be held in which the public would be represented.

All the conferees agreed that in any event both labor and management had to abandon some of their cherished positions, and that a new spirit of cooperation for the common good was urgently required.

In an account of this kind, dealing with such a vast field, there must be room for a minority report or two.

Some management and labor men wonder what all the wringing of hands is about. They don't perceive any crisis in industrial relations.

The management men who feel this way are likely to be found in big business circles, where the most recent negotiations in autos, steel and electrical manufacturing have been a source of considerable satisfaction. On the other side, the old AFL unions, though still bitter over some provisions of the Taft-Hartley and Landrum-Griffin Acts, seem not to be conscious of any crisis in their affairs. Inventions and new processes have caused some jurisdictional troubles, but then these are an old story in the building trades unions. As for the Teamsters, the only crisis they know about is the one involving Jimmy Hoffa. Over the past few years, this scandal-scarred union has greatly prospered.

On the question of a summit meeting, a few industry people have publicly supported the proposal. Presumably they are as aware as their colleagues that a meeting of this kind would lend prestige to the labor movement and help to offset the damaging effects of the McClellan committee hearings. They probably suspect that Arthur Goldberg's original proposal was partly motivated by a desire "to get labor off the hook." Even so, they say, the proposal itself is sound and statesmanlike. Mr. Goldberg didn't start the Cold War. He didn't create the inflationary pressures of what is, in fact, a semi-war economy. He is certainly not responsible for the swift pace of technological change and the unemployment it is causing. No one suggests that he fostered foreign competition or invented the balance-of-payments squeeze. These are all real life problems; and when Mr. Goldberg, pondering them and noting the growing polarization of hostile management-labor attitudes, calls upon both sides to attack them in a cooperative, public-minded spirit, what is wrong with the proposal?

But, as I say, this is a minority sentiment in industrial circles. That is why some observers doubt that a summit meeting will be held, or if it is held— under White House pressure—that any good will come of it. They fear that all it may do is dramatize the gulf which has come to exist between management and labor thinking on the great issues of the day.

As this survey was being completed, news arrived that President George Romney and Vice President Edward Cushman of American Motors have suggested a variant of the summit approach. They want a clergy committee representing Protestants, Catholics and Jews to invite top industry and labor leaders to meet with them in some secluded spot and there together, without a formal program, talk out their problems. The formula is not new, and it certainly promises no miracles. If, however, labor-management relations continue to deteriorate, it may offer an acceptable alternative to some head-cracking by a tough and impatient government.

GOP Is Thrown a Price-Job Curve 15
Business Week

So far, Republican economists have walked fairly happily in the never-never land of a new Administration. Yet they have embarked on a strategy that could, in the long run, put them in the kind of doghouse the Democrats just vacated.

Reprinted with permission from *Business Week* (March 22, 1969) pp. 60, 62, 64.

In 1961, the Democrats set out to cut unemployment, and they did—from 6.7% that year to a 15-year low of 3.6% in 1968. Now, the rate is down to 3.3%. But with the speedup in growth and employment came the biggest price rise to hit the U.S. since the Korean war. The Consumer Price Index (CPI) rose more than 4.5% last year, and is still steaming ahead.

DILEMMA

Now, the GOP has taken a blood oath to reduce inflation. And no one really doubts it will succeed—if the growth rate slows. Ironically, though, the GOP is walking smack into a mirror image of the Democrats' dilemma. When inflation slows, unemployment rises—but policymakers simply do not know how high the jobless rate must go. Moreover, they do not know how much inflation they should allow to remain in the economy to keep unemployment as low as possible in the years ahead.

To economists, both questions revolve around a fashionable analytical device called the Phillips Curve (named for economist A. W. Phillips, who first charted the curve for Britain in 1958). This curve attempts statistically to measure the inverse relationship—the trade-off—between changes in prices and unemployment.

The problem for 1969 and 1970 turns on the nature of this trade-off in the short run. But the experts have not been able to produce a firm estimate of what this trade-off really is. The U. S. Phillips Curve seems to alter its shape in response to changes in other economic forces, such as profits and over-all growth rates.

In short, if the Administration is aiming at less than 2% inflation by 1970, say, economists can't tell whether this will mean unemployment of 4%, 6%, or more. The last time consumer prices moved this slowly was 1965, when the index rose 1.7%; unemployment that year was 4.5%. But no one expects the same result now.

LONG-RUN WORRY

If this short-run problem perplexes Washington, the long-run dilemma is just as bothersome: Would employment benefit over the next few decades if the U. S. accepted a steady rate of moderate inflation? Or can the jobless rate be held down only by ever-faster inflation—as in the past few years?

Some analysts—including the University of Chicago's Milton Friedman, Yale's Henry Wallich, and the research and policy panel of the Committee for Economic Development—claim there is no trade-off at all—in a sense, no Phillips Curve—over the long haul. The economy, they insist, has a long-run jobless rate that is quite unaffected by inflation. No matter what rate of steady price increase the government allows, they say, unemployment will wind up at its "natural" rate, which they currently estimate at 4% to 5½%.

Moreover, these economists assert, if the government squeezes unemployment below this natural rate—and it's below it now—the only way to maintain such an artificially low job level is to allow ever-faster inflation to batter the economy.

CHOICE OF PRIORITIES

Though this view seems to be gaining among economists, there is still a large and vocal group—including many New Economists, like Harvard's Otto Eckstein, and most analysts working on poverty or urban problems—who contend that the U. S. can lower long-run unemployment by accepting some inflation. They argue that 2% to 2½% inflation would keep joblessness lower than a return to the nearly flat price levels of the late 1950s or early 1960s. And they think that such small, steady price increases are the price the country must pay to keep more unskilled workers employed, and to keep unemployment rates generally at low levels.

The Administration hasn't tackled the long-run issue yet, but its short-term decisions are clear. Paul McCracken, head of the Council of Economic Advisers, told a Congressional committee last month: "Sometimes one [goal] is more pressing and urgent than the other." In the early 1960s, he said, unemployment had priority; now, the price level has it.

COMMITMENT

The Republicans do not treat this choice lightly—especially after the recessions and unemployment of the Eisenhower years. And a sharp increase in unemployment today—particularly in the nation's ghettos—would be social dynamite. But the best McCracken could offer the Joint Economic Committee was a "hope that the impact [on unemployment] won't be large" and a promise that Washington would "actively" pursue manpower programs to keep joblessness as low as possible while the economy slows to squeeze out inflation.

Actually, the new Administration will surprise most experts if it really gets inflation down to 1% or 2% over the next few years without triggering a recession. This would be a first in post-World War II economics. "It's going to be a very delicate operation," says one economist close to the Administration. McCracken uses words like "careful," "gradual," and "sensitive" to describe the administration's intended use of monetary and fiscal restraints.

The hope in Washington is that somehow unemployment will average under 4% for 1969, which means it could top that level on a monthly basis by yearend. But McCracken concedes it's impossible to judge what the trade-off will be.

GUIDEPOST IMPACT

In the mid-1960s, some economists thought federal wage-price guideposts had reduced the trade-off. As unemployment began to drop in 1964 and 1965 prices and wages seemed to be moving up less rapidly than in similar periods of low unemployment in the 1950s.

George L. Perry, economist at the University of Minnesota, whose work on the Phillips Curve helped to generate that optimism, is still not sure how much credit the guideposts deserved. But as they were abandoned in the last few years, he reports, the country seemed to get back on its old, more inflationary trade-off path.

Still, the Nixon team has no intention of restoring the guideposts—only a little bit of jawbone restraint. Says one Washington economist: "If we start tossing out specific numbers now, people wouldn't think we were serious about getting rid of inflation."

AWARENESS

Optimists in Washington are hoping that the short-term trade-off has improved somewhat from business' awareness of the nation's social problems. Arthur F. Burns, counsellor to the President, believes companies will try to cut working hours as demand subsides rather than lay off employees. And the government thinks high-skill workers will be hoarded during the slowdown, as they were in the mini-recession of early 1967.

The trade-off could also benefit from the nation's shift toward service employment—a category less vulnerable to cyclical changes than manufacturing.

THE CURVE'S LONG SHADOW

So far, of course, there is little evidence that the long-awaited slowdown has even begun. But if Washington succeeds—if unemployment begins to rise and inflation to ebb—the next big question will be how far to go. And this is where the long-run Phillips Curve casts its confusing shadow over policy.

If Friedman and like-minded economists are correct, the government would be foolish to accept any steady rate of inflation as a long-run target. Instead, the policymakers should let unemployment rise to its natural level, which could be 5½%. At this level, theoretically, wages would tend to rise at the same rate as productivity. Thus, the economy could operate with virtually no inflation.

The only reason unemployment is now below its natural rate, say these economists, is the inflation of past years. And the only way to keep it low, they add, is more inflation, which means failure or disaster for any policy that attempts to maintain unemployment below its natural rate.

GRAND ILLUSION

The key to this view of the economy is the major role supposedly played by people's expectations. Last year, for example, everyone expected prices to rise—but not by a big 4.5% in the CPI. Because of this error, which economists call a "money illusion," workers thought their paychecks would buy more than they did. And some unemployed persons accepted jobs they would have shunned if they had known in advance how much of their wages would be swallowed by inflation.

Businessmen also operated under false premises, failing to realize how much of the country's booming demand was just a money illusion. So they hired more workers than they really needed. The result: a drop in unemployment from 3.8% in 1967 to 3.6% last year. And the process of mistaken expectations continues to keep unemployment low, this theory says.

NEW MATH

If the government allowed price increases of 1968 dimensions to continue several more years, people would learn the arithmetic of inflation, the theory goes. Eventually, expectations would catch up with reality, and unemployment would move up to its natural rate, where it is governed by real wages and real prices rather than inflated values. But, say the analysts, if the government generated ever-faster inflation, expectations would forever be in error.

Although this gloomy scenario is still just a theory, it seems to have found some support in the new CEA. One member, Herbert Stein, wrote recently in the Brookings Institution's Agenda for the Nation that a "credible case" can be made for the proposition that steady rates of inflation have no long-term payoff in lower unemployment.

SOLVING A HUMAN EQUATION

Nonetheless, there's a ray of sunshine for those who argue that a little inflation may be good for the long haul. Once inflation throws expectations out of whack, the economy takes its sweet time returning to the natural rate of unemployment; indeed, some experts argue that people never entirely shed their money illusions about the real value of their own wages.

Friedman estimates that it may take 10 to 20 years for people to catch up with reality, if inflation persists at a steady rate. During this lag, many more workers—and particularly the less-skilled—would be employed, which would be enough to satisfy some economists.

AREA OF AGREEMENT

But more importantly, the lag gives Washington a chance to improve the trade-off and lower the natural jobless rate. All economists—no matter what they think of the virtues of inflation—agree that government policy must move in this direction.

Suggestions on how to do it are numerous: Use computers to speed the matching of men and jobs; upgrade and educate unskilled labor; use anti-trust policy more actively to sharpen competition; get rid of fair-trade laws; repeal government floors on transport rates.

Obviously, some of these moves are political hot potatoes. Says Harvard's Eckstein: "I'm afraid the growing confusion about the trade-off is providing a lot of intellectual background noise to justify very orthodox employment policies. We cannot let inflation continue at current rates, but we can't let unemployment jump to 4½% or 5%."

RUNNING SCARED?

Some economists are more radical. They don't believe that inflation would have to gallop to keep unemployment where it is; nor do they believe inflation now is so bad—not even for the balance of payments.

Charles Holt, labor economist at Washington's Urban Institute think tank, is dismayed with current policy. "They're running away from a problem that doesn't exist," he says. Holt points to data that show a strong correlation between rises in the jobless rate and increases in crime and suicides. "How quick and glib they are," he says, "to push up unemployment."

And R. G. Hollister of the University of Wisconsin's Institute for Research on Poverty thinks the country is running too scared. "Just what is this monkey that we're so anxious to get off our backs by letting the poor pay?" he asks.

MYTHOLOGY

Hollister asserts it's a myth that inflation hurts the poor. Indeed, his studies show that the poor benefit from inflation: Prices they pay go up more slowly than general price levels; their incomes rise more rapidly, because labor markets tighten and more jobs become available; and fixed-value assets—the great losers in inflation—provide very little of the average poor person's income.

Moreover, Hollister thinks a long period of tight labor markets is just what business needs to learn to employ the country's least able or wanted workers. "If we loosen up now," he says, "we'll lose all the momentum we've built. Businessmen will never be convinced it's worth the trouble."

B. The Right-To-Work Controversy

The Battle Over 14(b)   16

Pro-Repeal
Clair M. Cook

Should section 14(b) of the Taft-Hartley Act be repealed? My answer is a firm Yes. However, before I present specific reasons for my answer, let me sketch a bit of the background of the issue.

Many strikes by labor unions in the past 150 years have grown out of the refusal of members to work alongside nonunionists. In 1890 the newly formed American Federation of Labor put it succinctly: "It is inconsistent for union men to work with nonunion men." This is one of the American labor movement's strongest traditions. As Andrew J. Biemiller, legislative director for the A.F.L.-C.I.O., said in testimony on June 23 before the Senate labor subcommittee in hearings on the repeal of 14(b): "A worker who refuses to join the union weakens it, and to that extent weakens the collective effort to win the terms that all should enjoy. That is why union workers feel so deeply about this matter of union security."

"CLOSED" AND "UNION" SHOPS

Until about 1900 the term "union shop" simply meant a workplace where all employees were union members. The National Association of Manufacturers in its 1903 "Declaration of Labor Principles" proclaimed its "unalterable antagonism to the closed shop"—one of the earliest uses of that phrase. Remarked Samuel Gompers in 1907: "Those who are hostile to labor cunningly employ the term 'closed shop' for a union shop because of the general antipathy which is ordinarily felt toward anything being closed, and with the specious plea that the so-called open shop must necessarily be the opportunity for freedom."

Copyright © 1965 by the Christian Century Foundation. Reprinted by permission from the July 28, 1965 issue of *The Christian Century*, pp. 937-940.

But nothing could prevent usage of the term and so "closed shop" now refers to a work situation in which an employer may hire only persons who are already union members. This practice is expressly forbidden by the National Labor Relations act of 1947, commonly called the Taft-Hartley act. "Union shop," on the other hand, has come to mean a situation in which union membership is required as a condition of continued employment— an employer may hire anyone, but the new employee must join the union within (usually) 30 days if he wishes to remain on the job. This requirement is a part of the union contract and therefore bears the signatures of both management and labor as a joint decision arrived at through collective bargaining.

A SOURCE OF CONFLICT

Just as "closed shop" was a phrase "cunningly" advanced by antiunionists, so "right to work" is an expression which has won advocates on the strength of its misleading phraseology. Banning the right to bargain collectively for the union shop form of security does not bestow any "right" to work; only an employer, in making a job offer, can extend that right, and a union shop clause in a contract does not limit his freedom to do so.

Far more accurate is "compulsory open shop," a phrase which I coined in an article in *The Christian Century* (January 1, 1958) and which has gained some currency in labor circles. A "right to work" law compels employer and union to permit any worker to remain outside the union, while at the same time requiring that he be given all wage increases and other benefits won by the union. Thus "right to work" laws encourage "free riders" to evade responsibility. For this reason leading churchmen of all faiths have condemned such laws.

The question before us here and before Congress, however, is not whether the open shop should be compulsory; neither is it a question of requiring a union shop, for, contrary to what the defenders of 14(b) contend, its repeal would not make the union shop mandatory. In fact, repeal would accomplish precisely what the National Council of Churches' General Board advocated some eight years ago: "Union membership as a basis of continued employment should be neither required nor forbidden by law: the decision should be left to agreement by management and labor through the process of collective bargaining." As Secretary of Labor Willard Wirtz declared in his June 22 Senate testimony: "The issue underlying the question of whether Section 14(b) should be repealed is not, therefore, whether there is to be a 'right to work.' It is whether there is to be a *right to decide.*"

Now for the reasons which in my opinion dictate the wisdom of repeal.

First, 14(b) is internally inconsistent both with the purposes of the law of which it is a part and with our total national legislative policy. The U. S. Supreme Court itself has noted that this section allows the states "to carry out policies inconsistent with the Taft-Hartley Act itself." The act in other respects decrees a uniform labor policy for the entire nation, recognizing the need for national controls in a time when business and manufacture are nationwide even for a single company. While outlawing the closed shop and preferential hiring of union members, Taft-Hartley specifically authorizes contracts requiring workers to join the union within 30 days after being hired (the requirement has been cut to seven days in building and construction trades). It states that the union cannot refuse membership to a worker thus hired so long as he pays "uniform" dues and initiation fees ("excessive" fees are forbidden), and it requires only payment, not attendance at meetings or any other duties. If the union members wish, they may request an election supervised by the National Labor Relations Board in order to determine by majority vote whether a union shop arrangement is to be retained. Thus the federal law both allows for the union shop and establishes sufficient controls to regulate it.

But 14(b) negates all this. It enables the states to ignore Congress' specific sanction of union shop contracts—the built-in restrictions notwithstanding —if they have a more restrictive statute of their own. In effect the federal government says to the states, "We have a national set of standards, but we will allow you to break them if you decide you want to be tougher on unions."

This odd provision is not, however, a two-way street. New York and California have laws explicitly permitting the closed shop—but here national law supersedes and invalidates state law. As the Supreme Court has noted, "There is thus conflict between state and federal law; but it is a conflict sanctioned by Congress." In no other area does the federal government preempt an area for regulation and then permit the states to override national policy. Section 14(b) should be repealed in order to restore the basic control of national labor relations policy to the federal level of government.

TO STRENGTHEN DEMOCRACY

Second, retention of 14(b) is inconsistent with Congress' 1951 amendments to the Railway Labor act. The basic railway act (1926) preceded by several years the federal government's first general labor regulations of the 1930s, and railway labor relations have always been conducted under the act's own separate formulas. Though the 1951 amendments took the union security provisions of the Taft-Hartley act as their model, they uniformly authorized the union shop without provision for state restrictions. Thus even the 19 states forbidding the union shop have a union shop in the railroad industry. Here federal law takes precedence. As Secretary Wirtz has pointed out, in this action Congress "expressed its policy on this point in clear and firm language." It should be consistent and do the same in regard to the basic national labor law in other industries.

Third, repeal of 14(b) will strengthen, not undermine, democracy in the workplace. The 1947 act stipulated that in states permitting a union shop contract, approval must be voted by the workers for such a contract to become effective. Some legislators thought that opponents of the union shop agreement might be right in claiming that it did not reflect the true wishes of the workers and was only a tool by which union officers could build membership. Between 1947 and 1951, 46,119 polls to determine worker sentiment were held among *all* workers in bargaining units, not merely among union members. Out of the 5.5 million voters, fewer than one worker in ten voted against the union shop; 97 per cent of the elections resulted in ratification. Congress in 1951 saw the pointlessness of this expensive procedure and eliminated the requirement. As Secretary Wirtz notes: "There is no violation of freedom in a minority's having to accept a majority's fair judgment fairly arrived at."

TO REDUCE CONFLICT

Finally, repeal of 14(b) would reduce conflict both in internal industrial relations and among the states. It is noteworthy that the opponents of repeal and the proponents of "right to work" laws are seldom workers themselves. The cry of "freedom for the worker" is most often raised by employers. For example, heading the list of 34 signatories in the Citizens Committee to Preserve Taft-Hartley full-page advertisement in the May 4 *Washington Post* was A. D. Davis, president of Winn-Dixie Stores, Inc.—a company which has been found guilty by the N.L.R.B. on four charges of unfair labor practices. (The sixth circuit court of appeals on February 27 sustained the N.L.R.B. findings— among them, a refusal to bargain.) Too often support for "right to work" and for 14(b) has been a convenient cover for attacks on unionism itself.

Within the workplace, the requirement that the union's services be extended to workers who refuse to join it inevitably causes conflict, diversion of energies and even lower production. Frequently employers prefer a union shop for this very reason, but as long as 14(b) stands, *their* freedom to achieve better harmony through collective bargaining is curtailed.

States which have adopted "right to work" laws have used them to try to lure companies away from the more industrialized areas. And some companies have been receptive. General Electric president Ralph Cordiner told a group in Richmond, Virginia, on October 11, 1956: "We believe that we should go to states that have right-to-work laws. That's where we feel we should invest our shareholders' money." And G.E. vice-president Lemuel Boulware informed the Phoenix chamber of commerce on May 21, 1958: "A very important factor in G.E.'s decision favoring Arizona . . . was the fact that you do have a right-to-work law." The nation cannot afford the kind of low wage competition between states which 14(b) encourages.

Perhaps the best summary of the argument for repeal of 14(b) is to be found in the conclusion of the House report issued June 22 by the committee on education and labor and titled "Repeal of Right-to-Work Provisions." In recommending repeal the committee declared:

> The Federal labor code has been carefully constructed over a long period of years pursuant to the sound principle that the Nation constitutes an economical and integrated whole. Experience with the impact of these State laws in this area of union security has satisfied the committee that there is no longer any justification for permitting this single statutory departure from the principle of Federal supremacy. In the committee's judgment, the time has come for removing this issue from the political arena and returning it to the bargaining table where it belongs.

With this I concur. And I have no doubt that the Senate committee and the majority of both houses of Congress will also concur. Then sometime before Labor Day or soon after, President Johnson will sign the repealer he has requested and "right-to-work," with its long history of controversy, will become a dead issue. The industrial health of the nation should be considerably improved as a result.

Pro-Retention
William Jones Fannin

This is the year in which we decide whether the principle of civil rights is to be applied consistently in our nation. Just last year Congress enacted legislation to guarantee the rights of individuals of any race, color or creed in reference to public establishments, employment and schools. Currently before Congress are two more bills pertaining to civil rights. One would eliminate the requirement, still existing in several southern states, that an individual pay a poll tax to vote in state elections. Contrastingly, the other would establish a national labor policy in favor of agreements requiring an individual to pay union dues in order to work. This paradox is before Congress because labor union officials have listed repeal of section 14(b) of the Taft-Hartley act (National Labor Relations act) as their number one legislative goal.

The repeal bill would remove the following provision of the Taft-Hartley act:

> Nothing in this Act shall be construed as authorizing the execution or application of agreements requiring membership in a labor organization as a condition of employment in any State or Territory in which such execution or application is prohibited by State or Territorial Law.

This part of the act affirms the right of a state to protect its citizens by a law making illegal the requirement that a worker be compelled to join a union in order to continue his employment.

To understand the significance of the effort to repeal 14(b), one must understand the terms "closed shop" and "union shop." A closed shop is one which requires that a man be a union member before he can be hired. The only difference between a closed shop and a union shop is that in regard to the latter a worker is permitted a grace period—usually 30 days—before he must join a union. The Taft-Hartley act makes closed shops, but not union shops, illegal.

Section 14(b) of the act, on the other hand, provides that a state may make the union shop illegal—may outlaw compulsory unionism by a right-to-work law. Thus a right-to-work law declares illegal any agreement which makes membership or nonmembership in a labor union a condition of employment. Repeal of section 14(b) would nullify the right of a state to pass laws to protect workers from being compelled to pay union dues.

The First amendment to the U.S. Constitution guarantees freedom of association. Congress cited this fundamental right in the policy declaration of the Taft-Hartley act, stating that the act's purpose is to be achieved "by protecting the exercise by workers of full freedom of association." Repeal of section 14(b) would violate this basic American principle of freedom of association. No one should be required against his will to pay dues to a private organization whether it be church, civic club, chamber of commerce or the A.F.L.-C.I.O. If this section of the Taft-Hartley act is repealed, ours will be the only country in the free world which sanctions compulsory union dues.

The effort to repeal 14(b) is a salient example of special interest legislation which can be harmful to the public. If the proposed repeal is successful, union treasuries will receive millions of dollars from workers forced to pay dues. Labor officials, not union members and other workers, are the ones who would benefit from repeal; though their unions would experience a tremendous increase in membership, they would not have to worry about losing members for lack of satisfaction.

Section 14(b) is designed to protect the individual worker, whether union or nonunion. To dispel the claims of union officials that right-to-work laws are detrimental to the employee, let us analyze the status of a union member who happens to be employed in a state having such a law.

First, the union member laboring in a right-to-work state need not fear that his employer will discriminate against him because he belongs to a union. Section 9(a)(3) of the Taft-Hartley act specifies that it is an unfair labor practice for an employer to discriminate against union members in either hiring or firing practices. Thus the union member is protected against discrimination in a right-to-work state just as in other states.

Second—and more importantly—the union member in a right-to-work state is *free to choose* whether to belong to the union. This is important because he may not want to belong if the union is not providing a service or if its officials are corrupt or espouse beliefs contrary to his own. In a right-to-work state he can resign his membership but still keep his job.

The National Labor Relations act protects the workers' right to organize in a right-to-work state. If a majority of the employees of a company so vote, the union can enter into negotiations with the employer for higher wages, better working conditions, fringe benefits—in other words, it can fulfill the very purpose for which unions were created. The only aspect of bargaining which right-to-work laws prohibit is compulsory membership agreements. Such agreements are for the benefit of labor officials rather than that of the workers. Protection of an individual is not unusual in legal contracts. The courts limit the freedom of contract whenever there is coercion or duress or where they find that an agreement is contrary to the public interest.

The chief argument of advocates of repeal is that all workers should be union members if they are to receive the benefits of collective bargaining. This is known as the "free rider" argument. It assumes that it is better for a worker to be forced to join the union than for the union to be deprived of his dues. It should be remembered, however, that a substantial portion of union dues is spent on civic, political and promotional activity having no relation to the service of collective bargaining—a fact which seriously weakens the "free rider" argument.

In the battle of statistics, union officials claim that the southern states which have right-to-work laws are among the lowest worker income states. Their opponents often answer that wages in southern states have increased at a faster rate than in union shop states. Both statements are half-truths. Owing to economic factors, southern states had lower wages than northern states long before right-to-work laws were enacted. As for wages increasing at a faster pace in the south than in union shop states, this is a consequence not of right-to-work laws but of the recentness of industrialization in the south.

Secretary of Labor Willard Wirtz acknowledged the fallibility of statistics before the special subcommittee on labor on May 24 while testifying in favor of the administration bill to repeal section 14(b):

> I could give the committee, if I felt confidence in it, a whole stack of studies which purport to show, translated into economic results, the effect of having right-to-work laws or not having right-to-work laws. I have no confidence in them. What it comes to is this: If you take a percentage impression or picture of what has happened in the last 18 years, the right-to-work states show gains, large percentage gains, economically during that period, because they start from a lower base.

Advocates of repeal also charge that right-to-work laws are to blame for an increasing movement of industry from north to south. It is true that some industries have moved to the south—but for reasons having to do with climate, water, transportation and power. No one has claimed that industry has been stolen from industrial states such as Minnesota by the right-to-work states of North Dakota, South Dakota and Kansas, or from California by Arizona, Nevada, Utah. It is both erroneous and unfair to generalize on the basis of developments in some but not all of the right-to-work states.

For the benefit of better labor-management relations, union officials should heed the words of a former labor union attorney, Supreme Court Justice Arthur Goldberg, when as secretary of labor he told the American Federation of Government Employees in 1962:

> We want to preserve the merit system for entry and retention in the federal service. I had my share of winning the union shops for unions in private industry, but I know you will agree with me that the union shop and the closed shop are inappropriate to the federal government. . . .
>
> In your own organization you have to win acceptance not by an automatic device which brings a new employee into your organization, but you have to win acceptance by your own conduct, your own action, your own wisdom, your own responsibility and your own achievements.
>
> Let me say to you from my experience representing the trade union movement that this is not a handicap necessarily.
>
> Very often even the union that has won the union shop will frankly admit that people who come in through that route do not always participate in the same knowing way as people who come in through the methods of education and voluntarism.

Voluntary unionism is in the best interest of the worker because it does not force him to support a union which is corrupt or which espouses political and social beliefs with which he does not agree; in the best interest of the public because it helps to safeguard the concept of freedom of association as set forth in the Constitution; and in the best interest of the union because it makes for a healthier, more responsible and efficient organization.

Dangers in   **17**
More Forced Unionism
Nation's Business

The most inflamed issue before Congress in years involves a four-line paragraph in the Taft-Hartley labor law—Section 14(b). It allows states to have right-to-work laws.

Reprinted with permission from *Nation's Business* (March 1965) pp. 31-33.

A right-to-work law forbids any labor contract that makes a worker join a union to get or hold a job.

Nineteen states now have these laws. All could be wiped out in one swoop by repeal of Section 14(b).

Organized labor has made repeal its primary target in the Eighty-ninth Congress. With President Johnson on their side and a Congress that stacks up as the most partial to their views since the New Deal, union lobbyists have high hopes of achieving their goal.

Opposing repeal of Section 14(b) are many of the 52 million workers— about three fourths of the labor force—who have not joined unions, most businessmen, many who are concerned about individuals' rights, and many members of Congress and other public officials and leaders in the 19 states which prohibit compulsory union membership.

To understand the full impact that repeal of Section 14(b) would have on your business and on labor-management relations in general, an editor of *Nation's Business* interviewed labor expert Sylvester Petro, professor at New York University Law School for the past 15 years.

Professor Petro has written many books and articles based on his studies of major strikes, union violence and other labor-management problems. He was a member of several unions before entering law practice.

Mr. Petro, how would repeal of Taft-Hartley's Section 14(b) affect the businessman?

For one thing, it would increase the imbalance of power in his relations with unions, an imbalance which already is in the unions' favor. Unions would gain more bargaining power and get more control over jobs and the operation of his business.

Repeal of Section 14(b) would give the National Labor Relations Board a virtual monopoly over labor law developments, with unfortunate results from a public and business viewpoint. It would accelerate the Board's tendency to intervene in collective bargaining and to impose its judgment over that of the union and employer as to what is best for them.

In the 19 states with right-to-work laws great numbers of employees would lose the right they have to work without joining a union—and many would have to join almost immediately to keep their jobs.

At the same time, of course, repeal of 14(b) would prevent other states from passing right-to-work laws and giving employees in their states the same protection against compulsory union membership.

Would this lead to more strikes?

It could mean more strikes. Unions armed with additional power are likely to get more arrogant, to make more demands. The more they ask for, the less possible it's going to be for employers to give it. Then unions may be driven to calling strikes which they might not call if they didn't feel so powerful.

When some employees are not in the union, they can't be relied upon to participate in a strike. This induces unions to be a little more cautious about calling strikes. So it stands to reason that the effect of 14(b) repeal would be to encourage strikes.

Of course, supporters of compulsory unionism contend that it makes unions more responsible and labor relations more stable.

Stability can always be purchased at the expense of freedom, at least for the short run. You take communist states. From a certain point of view they are more stable than this widely divergent, dynamic, complex society we have where freedom prevails to so much greater an extent.

I'm sure that businessmen would find their lives much less complicated and much more stable if they never had to worry about pleasing their customers and competing with each other.

In this same way industrial relations would be more stable if unions had absolute control over the workers and did not have to worry about keeping them satisfied, too.

The quest for stability must be harmonized and balanced by our interest in freedom without allowing either to destroy the values inherent in the other. We must, in short, tolerate a certain amount of instability if the elimination of that instability would involve us in a sacrifice of one of our extremely important values—namely, freedom.

A substantial reduction in freedom is much too high a price to pay for a dubious return in stability.

Have you seen evidence of corruption connected with compulsory unionism?

All of the vivid examples of union corruption turned up by the McClellan Committee (the 1957-61 Senate investigation of corrupt labor practices) involved the traditional closed shop unions. It's logical. (You give any man absolute control over another man and you're likely to produce corruption.)

Compulsory unionism conveys to a union pretty near absolute power over a worker's livelihood. As I see it, the most important—maybe the only—check of any significance on union corruption that we have today is the right of employees to resign from a union when they feel that they are being abused by their leaders.

Encouraging the growth of compulsory unionism, which repeal of 14(b) would do, would reduce significantly, if not eliminate entirely, this most important check on the abuse of union power.

Would repeal of Section 14(b) give unions a special privilege which would further stimulate corruption?

It clearly would add to unions' special privileges. The more special privileges that anyone gets, whether it be a child, an adult or a group in society, the more likely they are to consider themselves above and beyond the law and act accordingly. When you think of the large spectrum of special privileges that unions now have, you should pause and consider very carefully what it would mean to repeal 14(b). Keep in mind the significance this special privilege would have. Unlike any other organization in our society, unions, even without the privilege of compulsory union membership, act as agents for people who have purposefully rejected them as their agents.

How is that, Mr. Petro?

This is a consequence of the majority rule, exclusive bargaining principle that has existed in labor relations law since the enactment of the original Wagner Act. Under this principle, a union becomes the exclusive bargaining representative of all employees in a bargaining unit even though vast numbers of the employees in that unit may have voted against the union.

This is a remarkable special privilege, especially in a society which prides itself upon personal freedom and freedom of choice.

Would you call this a denial of individual rights?

To tell a working man that, even though he has expressed his will vigorously to the contrary, he must nevertheless accept a union as his bargaining representative, is to tell him that he does not have freedom of contract in this most important area of his life.

This creates a situation which, while distinct in some ways, has points in common with slavery. For that which distinguishes a free man from a slave is that a free man has a right to contract freely for his labor while, a slave does not.

Are you saying, Mr. Petro, that individual liberties would be sacrificed on the altar of labor stability?

Individual liberty has been sacrified on some altar or other. The principal rationale of our labor relations policy grows out of an outmoded and often refuted theory—that working men are helpless unless they have union representation.

In the face of the quite obvious fact that many nonunion workers are treated very well by their employers, and that in many areas of this economy nonunion workers are far better off than union workers, it remains to be proved that workers are helpless without a union.

It is competition for workers among employers themselves that leads to better wages and working conditions. The income of workers relates directly to their productivity. The real source of worker benefits is capital investment, which is the main source of increases in productivity. If you want to improve the conditions of workers, the thing to do is to encourage the growth and wise investment of captal.

Don't unions have special privileges under the antitrust laws?

Yes. Whenever trade unions act in their own interest they are exempt from the antitrust laws. They can restrain trade without fear of prosecution. An employer who restrains trade in the same way becomes subject to antitrust penalties.

But the special privileges granted unions by law are less significant than those they enjoy from the double standard of law enforcement which prevails.

The NLRB applies the Taft-Hartley Act very vigorously if employers are involved, but it is infinitely ingenious in the discovery of loopholes when union conduct is an issue.

Our police officials act as though violence and intimidation in labor disputes is to be expected and should not evoke the same stern measures that intimidation and violence evoke when they are used by a private citizen.

Judges usually go much easier on pickets who intimidate workers who prefer to continue working during a strike than they do on nonunion workers who may commit similar acts of violence and intimidation.

Mr. Petro, unions contend that workers in a unionized plant should pay dues for services the union provides, otherwise they are free riders. Do you agree?

No. The statement presupposes that unions do perform services for workers. I am not sure that they do and even if they do I'm not sure that they perform services for all the employees.

I know workers who have been directly and quite seriously harmed by union representation, rather than helped. More than that, it remains to be proved that unions are capable of even so simple a service as raising wages.

There is a very respectable school of economic thought which holds that wage raises come about as a consequence of productive capital investment, not of union action. But beyond that, even assuming that unions perform a service, I do not believe that anyone has a right to force his services on anyone. The union charge of free riders is a semantic trick. The truth is that in many instances the employees who don't want to be union members are forced riders—not free riders.

Now as to the rights that a worker gives up when he must join a union— he gives up the right to bargain for himself. An individual worker has more bargaining power than most people think. I know of cases where workers were forced to take pay cuts because the union ordered the employer to quit paying wages higher than the union scale.

A worker who has a grievance against an employer may not take it up himself. He must go through the union. If the union refuses to prosecute his grievance, he's out of luck.

Able and efficient workers are sometimes penalized by the tendency of unions to restrict production to the lowest common denominator. There have been recent cases in which unions have fined workers because they exceeded union production quotas. This is a pretty situation when a worker, because he's joined a union, is compelled to earn less than he otherwise would earn.

A worker represented by a union forfeits his right to decide whether he wants to strike. I doubt that there is a union which doesn't penalize members who cross a strike picket line to go to work.

A union member can be compelled to picket and to engage in other activities at the union's direction.

Every union that amounts to anything, I'm sure, has in its constitution and by-laws the power to penalize a member for conduct detrimental to the best interest of the union, which can be anything.

Mr. Petro, what effect would the repeal of 14(b) have on the use of union dues for political purposes?

In a country which prides itself on being a free political democracy it's peculiarly shocking to think that we're going to compel people to contribute to political causes to which they may be opposed. There's no doubt that if we repeal 14(b) we're going to have to provide a way for employees to "opt out," as the British do. British law gives employees the right to refuse to have their dues used for political purposes.

Doesn't the Taft-Hartley law say that union dues shall not be used for political purposes?

It says it, but I doubt that anyone informed in this field thinks that this prohibition has been effective. It was doomed to ineffectiveness from the very beginning because in a political democracy of our kind it's vital that all organizations be free to engage in political activities.

Would repeal of 14(b) increase the use of union dues money for political uses?

That's quite predictable. There are too many ways in which unions engage in political conduct that the law and law enforcement just can't touch.

If we want to preserve political freedom, we should not prohibit political expenditures by unions, but we should prevent unions from imposing membership on people who do not want to become members. The way to do that is to reinforce rather than repeal Section 14(b) by passing a national right-to-work law so that no worker may be forced into a union in any state.

In other words, rather than repeal 14(b), we should repeal the prohibition on political contributions and expenditures and prohibit compulsory unionism.

If we do these things we preserve the liberties of all involved.

We preserve the right of unions as voluntary associations to participate in political action.

We also preserve the right of employees to join or not to join unions, and we free employees of the repugnant obligation to contribute to political causes, political parties and political candidates to whom they are very often quite vigorously opposed.

C. The Employment Responsibilities of Business

Machines Do It Better Than Humans: An Assessment of a Workless Society and Proposals for Action

18

Ad Hoc Committee on the Triple Revolution

This statement is written in the recognition that mankind is at a historic conjuncture which demands a fundamental reexamination of existing values and institutions. At this time three separate and mutually reinforcing revolutions are taking place:

The Cybernation Revolution. A new era of production has begun. Its principles of organization are as different from those of the industrial era as those of the industrial era were different from the agricultural. The cybernation revolution has been brought about by the combination of the computer and the automated self-regulating machine. This results in a system of almost unlimited productive capacity which requires progressively less human labor. Cybernation is already reorganizing the economic and social system to meet its own needs.

The Weaponry Revolution. New forms of weaponry have been developed which cannot win wars but which can obliterate civilization. We are recognizing only now that the great weapons have eliminated war as a method for resolving international conflicts. The ever-present threat of total destruction is tempered by the knowledge of the final futility of war. The need of a "warless world" is generally recognized, though achieving it will be a long and frustrating process.

Reprinted with permission from *Advertising Age* (April 6, 1964), pp. 121–122, 124, 126. Copyright © 1964, by Advertising Publications, Inc.

The Human Rights Revolution. A universal demand for full human rights is now clearly evident. It continues to be demonstrated in the civil rights movement within the United States. But this is only the local manifestation of a worldwide movement toward the establishment of social and political regimes in which every individual will feel valued and none will feel rejected on account of his race.

We are particularly concerned in this statement with the first of these revolutionary phenomena. This is not because we underestimate the significance of the other two. On the contrary, we affirm that it is the simultaneous occurrence and interaction of all three developments which make evident the necessity for radical alterations in attitude and policy. The adoption of just policies for coping with cybernation and for extending rights to all Americans is indispensable to the creation of an atmosphere in the U.S. in which the supreme issue, peace, can be reasonably debated and resolved.

The Negro claims, as a matter of simple justice, his full share in America's economic and social life. He sees adequate employment opportunities as a chief means of attaining this goal: The March on Washington demanded freedom *and* jobs. The Negro's claim to a job is not being met. Negroes are the hardest-hit of the many groups being exiled from the economy by cybernation. Negro unemployment rates cannot be expected to drop substantially. Promises of jobs are a cruel and dangerous hoax on hundreds of thousands of Negroes and whites alike who are especially vulnerable to cybernation because of age or inadequate education.

The demand of the civil rights movement cannot be fulfilled within the present context of society. The Negro is trying to enter a social community and a tradition of work-and-income which are in the process of vanishing even for the hitherto privileged white worker. Jobs are disappearing under the impact of highly efficient, progressively less costly machines.

The U.S. operates on the thesis, set out in the Employment Act of 1964, that every person will be able to obtain a job if he wishes to do so and that this job will provide him with resources adequate to live and maintain a family decently. Thus job-holding is the general mechanism through which economic resources are distributed. Those without work have access only to a minimal income, hardly sufficient to provide the necessities of life, and enabling those receiving it to function as only "minimum consumers." As a result, the goods and services which are needed by these crippled consumers, and which they would buy if they could, are not produced. This in turn deprives other workers of jobs, thus reducing their incomes and consumption.

Present excessive levels of unemployment would be multiplied several times if military and space expenditures did not continue to absorb 10% of the gross national product (i.e., the total goods and services produced). Some 6 to 8 million people are employed as a direct result of purchases for space and military activities. At least an equal number hold their jobs as an indirect result of military or space expenditures. In recent years, the military and space budgets have absorbed a rising proportion of national production and formed a strong support for the economy.

However, these expenditures are coming in for more and more criticism, at least partially in recognition of the fact that nuclear weapons have eliminated war as an acceptable method for resolving international conflicts. Early in 1964 President Johnson ordered a curtailment of certain military expenditures. Defense Secretary McNamara is closing shipyards, airfields, and Army bases, and Congress is pressing the National Space Administration to economize. The future of these strong props to the economy is not as clear today as it was even a year ago.

HOW THE CYBERNATION REVOLUTION SHAPES UP

Cybernation is manifesting the characteristics of a revolution in production. These include the development of radically different techniques and the subsequent appearance of novel principles of the organization of production; a basic reordering of man's relationship to his environment; and a dramatic increase in total available and potential energy.

The major difference between the agricultural, industrial and cybernation revolutions is the speed at which they developed. The agricultural revolution began several thousand years ago in the Middle East. Centuries passed in the shift from a subsistence base of hunting and food-gathering to settled agriculture.

In contrast, it has been less than 200 years since the emergence of the industrial revolution, and direct and accurate knowledge of the new productive techniques has reached most of mankind. This swift dissemination of information is generally held to be the main factor leading to widespread industrialization.

While the major aspects of the cybernation revolution are for the moment restricted to the U.S., its effects are observable almost at once throughout the industrial world and large parts of the nonindustrial world. Observation is rapidly followed by analysis and criticism. The problems posed by the cybernation revolution are part of a new era in the history of all mankind but they are first being faced by the people of the U.S. The way Americans cope with cybernation will influence the course of this phenomenon everywhere. This country is the stage on which the machines-and-man drama will first be played for the world to witness.

The fundamental problem posed by the cybernation revolution in the U.S. is that it invalidates the general mechanism so far employed to undergird people's rights as consumers. Up to this time economic resources have been distributed on the basis of contributions to production, with machines and men competing for employment on somewhat equal terms. In the developing cybernated system, potentially unlimited output can be achieved by systems of machines which will require little cooperation from human beings. As machines take over production from men, they absorb an increasing proportion of resources while the men who are displaced become dependent on minimal and unrelated government measures—unemployment insurance, social security, welfare payments.

These measures are less and less able to disguise a historic paradox: That a substantial proportion of the population is subsisting on minimal incomes, often below the poverty line, at a time when sufficient productive potential is available to supply the needs of everyone in the U.S.

INDUSTRIAL SYSTEM FAILS TO PROVIDE FOR ABOLITION OF POVERTY

The existence of this paradox is denied or ignored by conventional economic analysis. The general economic approach argues that potential demand, which if filled would raise the number of jobs and provide incomes to those holding them, is underestimated. Most contemporary economic analysis states that all of the available labor force and industrial capacity is required to meet the needs of consumers and industry and to provide adequate public services: schools, parks, roads, homes, decent cities, and clean water and air. It is further argued that demand could be increased, by a variety of standard techniques, to any desired extent by providing money and machines to improve the conditions of the billions of impoverished people elsewhere in the world, who need food and shelter, clothes and machinery and everything else the industrial nations take for granted.

There is no question that cybernation does increase the potential for the provision of funds to neglected public sectors. Nor is there any question that cybernation would make possible the abolition of poverty at home and abroad. But the industrial system does not possess any adequate mechanisms to permit these potentials to become realities. The industrial system was designed to produce an ever-increasing quantity of goods as efficiently as possible, and it was assumed that the distribution of the power to purchase these goods would occur almost automatically. The continuance of the income-through-jobs links as the only major mechanism for distributing effective demand—for granting the right to consume—now acts as the main brake on the almost unlimited capacity of a cybernated productive system.

Recent administrations have proposed measures aimed at achieving a better distribution of resources, and at reducing unemployment and underemployment. A few of these proposals have been enacted. More often they have failed to secure congressional support. In every case, many members of Congress have criticized the proposed measures as departing from traditional principles for the allocation of resources and the encouragement of production. Abetted by budget-balancing economists and interest groups they have argued for the maintenance of an economic machine based on ideas of scarcity to deal with the facts of abundance produced by cybernation. This time-consuming criticism has slowed the workings of Congress and has thrown out of focus for that body the inter-related effects of the triple revolution.

An adequate distribution of the potential abundance of goods and services will be achieved only when it is understood that the major economic problem is not how to increase production but how to distribute the abundance that is the great potential of cybernation. There is an urgent need for a fundamental change in the mechanisms employed to insure consumer rights.

FACTS AND FIGURES OF THE CYBERNATION REVOLUTION

No responsible observer would attempt to describe the exact pace or the full sweep of a phenomenon that is developing with the speed of cybernation. Some aspects of this revolution, however, are already clear:

The rate of productivity increase has risen with the onset of cybernation.

An industrial economic system postulated on scarcity has been unable to distribute the abundant goods and services produced by a cybernated system or potential in it.

Surplus capacity and unemployment have thus co-existed at excessive levels over the last six years.

The underlying cause of excessive unemployment is the fact that the capability of machines is rising more rapidly than the capacity of many human beings to keep pace.

A permanent impoverished and jobless class is established in the midst of potential abundance.

Evidence for these statements follows:

1. The increased efficiency of machine systems is shown in the more rapid increase in productivity per man-hour since 1960, a year that marks the first visible upsurge of the cybernation revolution. In 1961, 1962 and 1963, productivity per man-hour rose at an average pace above 3.5%—a rate well above both the historical average and the postwar rate.

Companies are finding cybernation more and more attractive. Even at the present early stage of cybernation, costs have already been lowered to a point where the price of a durable machine may be as little as one-third of the current annual wage-cost of the worker it replaces. A more rapid rise in the rate of productivity increases per man-hour can be expected from now on.

2. In recent years it has proved to increase demand fast enough to bring about the full use of either men or plant capacities. The task of developing sufficient additional demand promises to become more difficult each year. A $30 billion annual increase in gross national product is now required to prevent unemployment rates from rising. An additional $40 to $60 billion in-

crease would be required to bring unemployment rates down to an acceptable level.

3. The official rate of unemployment has remained at or above 5.5% during the Sixties. The unemployment rate for teen-agers has been rising steadily and now stands around 15%. The unemployment rate for Negro teen-agers stands about 30%. The unemployment rate for teen-agers in minority ghettoes sometimes exceeds 50%. Unemployment rates for Negroes are regularly more than twice those for whites, whatever their occupation, educational level, age or sex. The unemployment position for other racial minorities is similarly unfavorable. Unemployment rates in depressed areas often exceed 50%.

UNEMPLOYMENT IS FAR WORSE THAN FIGURES INDICATE

These official figures seriously underestimate the true extent of unemployment. The statistics take no notice of underemployment or featherbedding. Besides the 5.5% of the labor force who are officially designated as unemployed, nearly 4% of the labor force sought full-time work in 1962 but could find only parttime jobs. In addition, methods of calculating unemployment rates—a person is counted as unemployed only if he has actively sought a job recently—ignore the fact that many men and women who would like to find jobs have not looked for them because they know there are no employment opportunities.

Underestimates for this reason are pervasive among groups whose employment rates are high—the young, the old, and racial minorities. Many people in the depressed agricultural, mining and industrial areas, who by official definition hold jobs but who are actually grossly underemployed, would move if there were prospects of finding work elsewhere. It is reasonable to estimate that over 8,000,000 people are not working who would like to have jobs today as compared with the 4,000,000 shown in the official statistics.

Even more serious is the fact that the number of people who have voluntarily removed themselves from the labor force is not constant but increases continuously. These people have decided to stop looking for employment and seem to have accepted the fact that they will never hold jobs again. This decision is largely irreversible, in economic and also in social and psychological terms. The older worker calls himself "retired"; he cannot accept work without affecting his social security status. The worker in his prime years is forced onto relief: In most states the requirements for becoming a relief recipient bring about such fundamental alterations in an individual's situation that a reversal of the process is always difficult and often totally infeasible. Teen-agers, especially "drop-outs" and Negroes, are coming to realize that there is no place for them in the labor force but at the same time they are given no realistic alternative. These people and their dependents make up a large part of the "poverty" sector of the American population.

Statistical evidence of these trends appears in the decline in the proportion of people claiming to be in the labor force—the so-called labor force participation rate. The recent apparent stabilization of the unemployment rate around 5.5% is therefore misleading: It is a reflection of the discouragement and defeat of people who cannot find employment and have withdrawn from the market rather than a measure of the economy's success in creating jobs for those who want to work.

4. An efficiently functioning industrial system is assumed to provide the great majority of new jobs through the expansion of the private enterprise sector. But well over half of the new jobs created during 1957-1962 were in the public sector—predominantly in teaching. Job creation in the private sector has now almost entirely ceased except in services; of the 4,300,000 jobs created in this period, only about 200,000 were provided by private industry through its own efforts. Many authorities anticipate that the application of cybernation to certain service industries, which is only just beginning, will be particularly effective. If this is the case, no significant job creation will take place in the private sector in coming years.

5. Cybernation raises the level of the skills of the machine. Secretary of Labor Wirtz has recently stated that the machines being produced today have, on the average, skills equivalent to a high school diploma. If a human being is to compete with such machines, therefore, he must at least possess a high school diploma. The Department of Labor estimates, however, that on the basis of present trends, as many as 30% of all students will be high school drop-outs in this decade.

6. A permanently depressed class is developing in the U.S. Some 38,000,000 Americans, almost one-fifth of the nation, still live in poverty. The percentage of total income received by the poorest 20% of the population was 4.9% in 1944 and 4.7% in 1963.

Secretary Wirtz recently summarized these trends. "The confluence of surging population and driving technology is splitting the American labor force into tens of millions of 'have's' and millions of 'have-nots.' In our economy of 69,000,000 jobs, those with wanted skills enjoy opportunity and earning power. But the others face a new and stark problem—exclusion on a permanent basis, both as producers and consumers, from economic life. This division of people threatens to create a human slag heap. We cannot tolerate the development of a separate nation of the poor, the unskilled, the jobless, living within another nation of the well-off, the trained and the employed."

NEW CONSENSUS NEEDED

The stubbornness and novelty of the situation that is conveyed by these statistics is now generally accepted. Ironically, it continues to be assumed that it is possible to devise measures which will reduce unemployment to a minimum and thus preserve the over-all viability of the present productive system. Some authorities have gone so far as to suggest that the pace of technological change should be slowed down "so as to allow the industrial productive system time to adapt."

We believe, on the contrary, that the industrial productive system is no longer viable. We assert that the only way to turn technological change to the benefit of the individual and the service of the general welfare is to accept the process and to utilize it rationally and humanely. The new science of political economy will be built on the encouragement and planned expansion of cybernation. The issues raised by cybernation are particularly amenable to intelligent policy-making: Cybernation itself provides the resources and tools that are needed to ensure minimum hardship during the transition process.

But major changes must be made in our attitudes and institutions in the foreseeable future. Today Americans are being swept along by three simultaneous revolutions while assuming they have them under control. In the absence of real understanding of any of these phenomena, especially of technology, we may be allowing an efficient and dehumanized community to emerge by default. Gaining control of our future requires the conscious formation of the society we wish to have. Cybernation at last forces us to answer the historic questions: What is man's role when he is not dependent upon his own activities for the material basis of his life? What should be the basis for distributing individual access to national resources? Are there other proper claims on goods and services besides a job?

Because of cybernation, society no longer needs to impose repetitive and meaningless (because unnecessary) toil upon the individual. Society can now set the citizen free to make his own choice of occupation and vocation from a wide range of activities not now fostered by our value system and our accepted modes of "work." But in the absence of such a new consensus about cybernation, the nation cannot begin to take advantage of all that it promises for human betterment.

PROPOSAL FOR ACTION

As a first step to a new consensus it is essential to recognize that the traditional link between jobs and incomes is being broken. The economy of abundance can sustain all citizens in comfort and economic security whether or not they engage in what is commonly reckoned as work. Wealth produced by machines rather than by men is still wealth. We urge, therefore, that society, through its appropriate legal and governmental institutions, undertake an unqualified commitment to provide every individual and every family with an adequate income as a matter of right.

This undertaking we consider to be essential to the emerging economic, social and political order in this country. We regard it as the only policy by which the quarter of the nation now dispossessed and soon-to-be dispossessed by lack of employment can be brought within the abundant society. The unqualified right to an income would take the place of the patchwork of welfare measures—from unemployment insurance to relief—designed to ensure that no citizen or resident of the U. S. actually starves.

We do not pretend to visualize all of the consequences of this change in our values. It is clear, however, that the distribution of abundance in a cybernated society must be based on criteria strikingly different from those of an economic system based on scarcity. In retrospect, the establishment of the right to an income will prove to have been only the first step in the reconstruction of the value system of our society brought on by the triple revolution.

The present system encourages activities which can lead to private profit and neglects those activities which can enhance the wealth and the quality of life of our society. Consequently, national policy has hitherto been aimed far more at the welfare of the productive process than at the welfare of people. The era of cybernation can reverse this emphasis. With public policy and research concentrated on people rather than processes we believe that many creative activities and interests commonly thought of as non-economic will absorb the time and the commitment of many of those no longer needed to produce goods and services.

Society as a whole must encourage new modes of constructive, rewarding and ennobling activity. Principal among these are activities such as teaching and learning that relate people to people rather than people to things. Education has never been primarily conducted for profit in our society; it represents the first and most obvious activity inviting the expansion of the public sector to meet the needs of this period of transition.

We are not able to predict the long-run patterns of human activity and commitment in a nation when fewer and fewer people are involved in production of goods and services, nor are we able to forecast the over-all patterns of income distribution that will replace those of the past full employment system. However, these are not speculative and fanciful matters to be contemplated at leisure for a society that may come into existence in three or four generations. The outlines of the future press sharply into the present. The problems of joblessness, inadequate incomes, and frustrated lives confront us now; the American Negro, in his rebellion, asserts the demands— and the rights—of all the disadvantaged. The Negro's is the most insistent voice today, but behind him stand the millions of impoverished who are beginning to understand that cybernation, properly understood and used, is the road out of want and toward a decent life.

THE TRANSITION[1]

We recognize that the drastic alternations in circumstances and in our way of life ushered in by cybernation and the economy of abundance will not be completed overnight. Left to the ordinary forces of the market such change, however, will involve physical and psychological misery and perhaps political chaos. Such misery is already clearly evident among the unemployed, among relief clients into the third generation and more and more among the young and the old for whom society appears to hold no promise of dignified or even stable lives. We must develop programs for this transition designed to give hope to the dispossessed and those cast out by the economic system, and to provide a basis for the rallying of people to bring about those changes in political and social institutions which are essential to the age of technology.

The program here suggested is not intended to be inclusive but rather to indicate its necessary scope. We propose:

1. A massive program to build up our educational system, designed especially with the needs of the chronically undereducated in mind. We estimate that tens of thousands of employment opportunities in such areas as teaching and research and development, particularly for younger people, may be thus created. Federal programs looking to the training of an additional 100,000 teachers annually are needed.

2. Massive public works. The need is to develop and put into effect programs of public works to construct dams, reservoirs, ports, water and air pollution facilities, community recreation facilities. We estimate that for each $1 billion per year spent on public works 150,000 to 200,000 jobs would be created. $2 billion or more a year should be spent in this way, preferably as matching funds aimed at the relief of economically distressed or dislocated areas.

3. A massive program of low-cost housing, to be built both publicly and privately, and aimed at a rate of 700,000-1,000,000 units a year.

4. Development and financing of rapid transit systems, urban and inter-urban; and other programs to cope with the spreading problems of the great metropolitan areas.

5. A public power system built on the abundance of coal in distressed areas, designed for low-cost power to heavy industrial and residential sections.

6. Rehabilitation of obsolete military bases for community or educational use.

---

[1] This view of the transitional period is not shared by all the signers. Robert Theobald and James Boggs hold that the two major principles of the transitional period will be (1) that machines rather than men will take up new conventional work openings and (2) that the activity of men will be directed to new forms of "work" and "leisure." Therefore, in their opinion, the specific proposals outlined in this section are more suitable for meeting the problems of the scarcity-economic system than for advancing through the period of transition into the period of abundance.

7. A major revision of our tax structure aimed at redistributing income as well as apportioning the costs of the transition period equitably. To this end an expansion of the use of excess profits tax would be important. Subsidies and tax credit plans are required to ease the human suffering involved in the transition of many industries from man power to machine power.

8. The trade unions can play an important and significant role in this period in a number of ways:

a. Use of collective bargaining to negotiate not only for people at work but also for those thrown out of work by technological change.

b. Bargaining for perquisites such as housing, recreational facilities, and similar programs as they have negotiated health and welfare programs.

c. Obtaining a voice in the investment of the unions' huge pension and welfare funds, and insisting on investment policies which have as their major criteria the social use and function of the enterprise in which the investment is made.

d. Organization of the unemployed so that these voiceless people may once more be given a voice in their own economic destinies, and strengthening of the campaigns to organize white-collar and professional workers.

9. The use of the licensing power of government to regulate the speed and direction of cybernation to minimize hardship; and the use of minimum wage power as well as taxing powers to provide the incentives for moving as rapidly as possible toward the goals indicated by this paper.

These suggestions are in no way intended to be complete or definitely formulated. They contemplate expenditures of several billions more each year than are now being spent for socially rewarding enterprises, and a larger role for the government in the economy than it has now or has been given except in times of crisis. In our opinion, this is a time of crisis, the crisis of a triple revolution. Public philosophy for the transition must rest on the conviction that our economic, social and political institutions exist for the use of man and that man does not exist to maintain a particular economic system. This philosophy centers on an understanding that governments are instituted among men for the purpose of making possible life, liberty, and the pursuit of happiness and that government should be a creative and positive instrument toward these ends.

CHANGE MUST BE MANAGED

The historic discovery of the post-World War II years is that the economic destiny of the nation can be managed. Since the debate over the Employment Act of 1946 it has been increasingly understood that the federal government bears primary responsibility for the economic and social well-being of the country. The essence of management is planning. The democratic requirement is planning by public bodies for the general welfare. Planning by private bodies such as corporations for their own welfare does not automatically result in additions to the general welfare, as the impact of cybernation on jobs has already made clear.

The hardships imposed by sudden changes in technology have been acknowledged by Congress in proposals for dealing with the long- and short-run "dislocations," in legislation for depressed and "impacted" areas, retraining of workers replaced by machines, and the like. The measures so far proposed have not been "transitional" in conception. Perhaps for this reason they have had little effect on the situations they were designed to alleviate. But the primary weakness of this legislation is not ineffectiveness but incoherence. In no way can these disconnected measures be seen as a plan for remedying deep ailments but only, so to speak, as the superficial treatment of surface wounds.

Planning agencies should constitute the network through which pass the stated needs of the people at every level of society, gradually building into a national inventory of human requirements, arrived at by democratic debate of elected representatives.

The primary tasks of the appropriate planning institutions should be:

To collect the data necessary to appaise the effects, social and economic, of cybernation at different rates of innovation.

To recommend ways, by public and private initiative, of encouraging and stimulating cybernation.

To work toward optimal allocations of human and natural resources in meeting the requirements of society.

To develop ways to smooth the transition from a society in which the norm is full employment within an economic system based on scarcity, to one in which the norm will be either non-employment, in the traditional sense of productive work, or employment on the great variety of socially valuable but "non-productive" tasks made possible by an economy of abundance; to bring about the conditions in which men and women no longer needed to produce goods and services may find their way to a variety of self-fulfilling and socially useful occupations.

To work out alternatives to defense and related spending that will commend themselves to citizens, entrepreneurs and workers as a more reasonable use of common resources.

To integrate domestic and international planning. The technological revolution has related virtually every major domestic problem to a world problem. The vast inequities between the industrialized and the under-developed countries cannot long be sustained.

The aim throughout will be the conscious and rational direction of economic life by planning institutions under democratic control.

In this changed framework the new planning institutions will operate at every level of government—local, regional and federal—and will be organized to elicit democratic participation in all their proceedings. These bodies will be the means for giving direction and content to the growing demand for improvement in all departments of public life. The planning institutions will show the way to turn the growing protest against ugly cities, polluted air and water, an inadequate educational system, disappearing recreational and material resources, low levels of medical care, and the haphazard economic development into an integrated effort to raise the level of general welfare.

We are encouraged by the record of the planning institutions both of the Common Market and of several European nations and believe that this country can benefit from studying their weaknesses and strengths.

A principal result of planning will be to step up investment in the public sector. Greater investment in this area is advocated because it is overdue, because the needs in this sector comprise a substantial part of the content of the general welfare, and because they can be readily afforded by an abundant society. Given the knowledge that we are now in a period of transition it would be deceptive, in our opinion, to present such activities as likely to produce full employment. The efficiencies of cybernation should be as much sought in the public as in the private sector, and a chief focus of planning would be one means of bringing this about. A central assumption of planning institutions would be the central assumption of this statement, that the nation is moving into a society in which production of goods and services is not the only or perhaps the chief means of distributing income.

THE DEMOCRATIZATION OF CHANGE

The revolution in weaponry gives some dim promise that mankind may finally eliminate institutionalized force as the method of settling international conflict and find for it political and moral equivalents leading to a better world. The Negro revolution signals the ultimate admission of this group to the American community on equal social, political and economic terms. The cybernation revolution proffers an existence qualitatively richer in democratic as well as material values. A social order in which men make the decisions that shape their lives becomes more possible now than ever before; the unshackling of men from the bonds of unfulfilling labor frees them to become citizens, to make themselves and to make their own history.

But these enhanced promises by no means constitute a guarantee. Illuminating and making more possible the "democratic vistas" is one thing; reaching them is quite another, for a vision of democratic life is made real not by technological change but by men consciously moving toward that ideal and creating institutions that will realize and nourish the vision in living form.

Democracy, as we use the term, means a community of men and women who are able to understand, express and determine their lives as dignified human beings. Democracy can only be rooted in a political and economic order in which wealth is distributed by and for people, and used for the widest social benefit. With the emergence of the era of abundance we have the economic base for a true democracy of participation, in which men no longer need to feel themselves prisoners of social forces and decisions beyond their control or comprehension.

Machines Won't Take Over After All   19

Business Week

Reports of the death of the U.S. worker—supposedly slain by automation—have been greatly exaggerated. Even the comparatively unskilled worker, in the popular view automation's sure victim, will survive the technological developments of the next decade.

While industry will undergo some major employment shifts by 1975, over-all demand for workers will grow sharply, with white-collar workers extending their numerical dominance over blue-collar employees and with professional and technical workers in the heaviest demand.

These are the major conclusions of a new manpower survey, America's Industrial and Occupational Manpower Requirements 1964-75, issued by the Labor Department's Bureau of Labor Statistics. Many of the conclusions reinforce earlier estimates of the employment needs of the next 10 years, but the report also offers some surprises.

HOLDING FIRM

The most significant undoubtedly is the prediction that automation in a growing economy will create no drastic displacement of men by machines.

"The major conclusion of this study, which takes into account every technological change in American industry that can be identified and makes a careful appraisal of its potential effect on employment, is that the over-all demand for less-skilled workers will not decrease over this 11-year period," the Labor Department says.

This contradicts past predictions by union economists that automation would destroy up to 40,000 jobs a week. Automation's destructive potential has been a constant of union theorizing in this field.

Another union worry—that employment will grow fastest in areas where union organization is weakest—is confirmed by the report.

Reprinted with permission from *Business Week* (October 8, 1965), pp. 93–94, 96.

The BLS estimates that white-collar workers will form 54% of the work force by 1975. The blue-collar sector, where unions are most heavily represented, will shrink to 33%, although even in this sector job needs will increase 17%. The need for service workers will increase 35%.

Where the Jobs Will Be in 1975

	Millions of Jobs		Percent Change 1964-75
	Actual Employment 1964	Projected Requirements 1975	
Government	9.6	14.8	+54%
Services	8.6	12.3	+43
Contract construction	3.1	4.2	+37
Trade	12.1	16.2	+33
Finance, Insurance and Real Estate	3.0	3.7	+26
Manufacturing	17.3	19.7	+14
Transportation and Public Utilities	3.9	4.4	+12
Mining	0.6	0.6	− 2
Agriculture	4.8	3.7	−21
Total	62.9	79.6	+27%

Data: Labor Department

PICKING UP SPEED

The report's projections are for the acceleration of trends that have been in effect since 1947. For instance, BLS statisticians project labor-force growth at the rate of 1.7-million persons annually, compared with an annual rate of 1.1-million between 1960 and 1965. The increase was actually 1.8-million in 1964-65.

On this basis, the economy should show a net gain of 18-million jobs by 1975, produced by adding 19-million non-farm jobs and subtracting 1-million farm jobs.

LONG-TERM FORECAST

In making public its estimates, the Labor Department emphasized that they were based on assumptions of long-range economic growth provided by the National Commission on Automation and Technological Progress. The commission asked BLS to make the study.

The basic assumption was existence of a 91.4-million work force by 1975, with 88.7-million workers actually employed. This would mean an unemployment rate of 3%, virtually full employment.

The commission also assumed:

That peacetime conditions, similar to those prior to the Vietnam buildup, would exist in 1975. This would mean 2.7-million in the armed forces, roughly the 1964 level.

That no sharp changes would take place in economic and social patterns or in patterns of consumption.

That scientific and technological advances would proceed as in the past and that research and development expenditures would continue to grow, although at a slower rate than during the past 15 years.

The Labor Department warned that its projections will be affected to the extent that actual events modify the commission's assumptions. The projections will be "off" to a greater or lesser degree if defense expenditures rise or fall, if patterns of consumption or levels of income change, if unforeseen technological developments occur, or if the decade produces other surprises.

Assuming their accuracy, some of the Labor Department projections have obvious social implications.

For instance, although less-skilled workers will continue to be in demand (partly because of rapid growth in the service industries) the heaviest demand will be for highly trained workers. This suggests a substantial change in the social makeup of the work force.

MINORITY GROUPS

The report also predicts that heavier-than-average unemployment will continue for nonwhite workers unless "they gain access to white-collar and skilled jobs at a faster rate than they have in recent years."

With the supply of younger workers growing at a faster-than-average rate, youngsters will continue to experience high unemployment unless industry takes such steps as "lowering the minimum age at which they hire workers for certain occupations, using younger workers as aides or assistants to the relatively more scarce mature and experienced workers, or promoting them faster to more skilled jobs."

Women should find ready employment, thanks to the rise in white-collar jobs, even though their numbers will increase faster than those of the work force as a whole. On the other hand, the report warns, women can expect to encounter increasing competition from men in such traditionally female jobs as teaching, social work, and library work.

SPOTLIGHTING SKILLS

As expected, the sharpest increase predicted for any single category was for professional and technical workers. The BLS expects 4.5-million more of them to be needed by 1975—54% above current requirements.

An increasingly technological economy plus expanding research and development programs will create additional needs for engineers and even greater demand for scientists. Technological innovations in teaching—teaching machines, and mass instruction by television—won't diminish the need for teachers but will greatly increase the need for writers, researchers, electronic technicians, and broadcast engineers.

In manufacturing, where the rate of job growth will be less than in other categories, employment needs will increase annually by 1.3% or more than double the growth between 1947-64. The increase will be due primarily to continuing economic growth and to a rising population.

In manufacturing, use of computers and instrumentation in production will bring an increase in employment among maintenance, technical, and supervisory workers. The need for production workers, however, will continue the decline of recent years.

COUNTER MOVES

Some industries will be less susceptible than others to automation advances. Because of the small size of real estate firms, for example, little change in employment is anticipated. Automation, however, is expected to have a sharper impact on banking and insurance, on air transportation and communications, among other industries.

Most industries will show job growth, despite the job-shrinking effects of automation. Construction employment, for example, will experience a projected one-third increase in manpower to more than 4-million. But it would grow even faster were it not for anticipated improvements in tools and building techniques.

In a breakdown on construction by trades, the report predicts a gain of more than 40% among workers who use road machinery, due primarily to anticipated highway construction. But here the gain would have been even greater were it not for more efficient earth-moving equipment and machinery. However, the need for painters will advance by a relatively low 10%, because of the increase in pre-finished wood products coming from factories.

Some 200,000 more electricians will be needed by 1975, the report reckons, owing to increased use of appliances and air conditioning.

But, carpenters, plumbers, and pipefitters will show relatively slow gains because important technological advances came earlier in those trades.

Employment of carpenters actually declined by some 220,000 between 1950 and 1964, in the wake of the rising use of pre-fabricated building components.

The report noted that technological change, in some cases, had caused severe unemployment within industries, and it cited railroading, lumbering, wood products, baking, and telephones. But the effects have been limited by occupational shifts in those industries or by rising employment elsewhere.

D. Civil Rights and Fair-Employment Practices

Equal Employment Opportunities: Company Policies and Experience

20

Effects on the Economy
G. William Miller

The challenge to provide equal job opportunities is urgent business. It is urgent because America cannot afford the economic danger of discrimination or ignore the moral obligation to the fundamental principle on which our nation was founded and has prospered.

The cadence of change has quickened, and with it American business has become increasingly aware of its special responsibility in this area.

Equal employment opportunity has an important bearing on our national economy. There is a wide economic gap between the white and the non-white American. Income for a Negro family averages about 60 per cent of that for other Americans. Unemployment rates for Negroes and other minorities run twice the national average.

The cost to our economy is estimated at some thirty billion dollars. A recent study by a nationally known economist determined that more than half the differential is due to discrimination, rather than to lack of individual qualification or training.

Translated into today's economic environment, the importance of recouping the loss is apparent. Our gross national product has been expanding at an average rate of about 3 per cent. We need to accelerate this growth rate in order to overcome the effects of technological change, to be increasingly competitive in world markets, and to assure the strength essential for national security. A more rapid, noninflationary growth is urgently desired. So for American business the need for equal opportunity is not academic. It has a real and immediate bearing on national economic progress.

Reprinted by permission of the publisher from *Management Review* (April 1964), pp. 5–23. Copyright © 1964 by the American Management Association, Inc.

If the gap of thirty billion dollars is closed over a five-year period, it would be more than a 30 per cent increase in the growth rate of the economy. If done over ten years, it still would be more than a 15 per cent increase. No other factor offers the opportunity for a contribution of this magnitude.

American businessmen have direct experience with the cost of discrimination. They pay the cost of bias every day, in the form of higher unemployment rates, the cost of crime and delinquency, higher taxes to pay for spiraling welfare expenditures, or indirectly for public housing and redevelopment of slum areas. Whatever the form, the payments represent a real cost of doing business, imposed at a time when profit margins have been shrinking.

In addition to higher costs, discrimination deprives American industry of the potential for expanded markets. With equal job opportunities, the purchasing power through increased earnings would create a larger market for every American business.

Thus we have a dual effect: increased costs, and lost markets. In an effective free-enterprise system, industry is able and willing to play a new role in overcoming these obstacles. In striving to provide equal job opportunities, the concern is not only with present discrimination. It is possible to offer employment immediately on the basis of individual merit, but this will not automatically erase generations of deprivation, which have precluded the development of skills that Negroes and other minorities are capable of attaining. This requires remedial action in depth. A broad and continuing affirmative program is necessary.

Equal opportunity may be the most important issue that this nation faces for many decades not only because of its effects on business, markets, and economic growth, but also because the American system itself is being tested. Unless we assure equal rights and equal justice for all, our form of government will be in jeopardy.

It is encouraging that American business is responding. For example, many of our largest employers have taken the initiative through voluntary efforts. About 150 major firms, representing more than six million employees, have developed equal employment programs under Plans for Progress. The response is reassuring, for it indicates the strength of American free enterprise.

Each generation is called to a task of protecting and furthering the cause of individual liberty. That cause will fail if freedom of opportunity is for a few rather than for all. In the American tradition, business will do its best to provide equal opportunity. To do so is good business—and it is right.

What Industry Can Do
Harold Mayfield

Various minorities suffer from being different—American Indians, Spanish Americans, Orientals, and so on. But their problems involve only a few localities, whereas the Negro is a large and underprivileged segment in nearly every industrial community. When we speak of equal employment opportunities, therefore, we tend to concentrate on the problems of the American Negro —problems that are widespread and pressing at this time.

The Negro in America will have some special problems ,for a long, long time to come. Educational equality, for example, cannot be achieved in a day or even in a generation, since so much of it depends on the home environment and the example of adults. Ideals and aspirations may be largely shaped by the time a child is six. Hence, it is only as this generation achieves the qualities needed for a richer home life that the next generation will come up with a full measure of the attitudes and abilities that most of us take for granted.

JOBS AND HOPE

Many of these achievements will be a long time coming, but a crucial part of the remedy seems to rest with us who are employers. Dr. Gunnar Myrdal, the distinguished Swedish social scientist, pointed out more than thirty years ago in the classic study, *The American Dilemma,* that among those things the American Negro wanted most, *jobs* headed the list. More recently, it has become apparent that whatever else the Negro may need, he can never become a first-class citizen and the father of first-class citizens until he holds a first-class *job.*

It has become apparent also that there is another requisite the Negro must have if he is to fix his eyes upward and rise through his own efforts. He must have *hope.* If we expect the Negro to carry his full load in our economy and our society, it is not enough that we promise him and his wife jobs as porters and housemaids. His sons will never go to college with just these expectations dangling before them. Nor is it enough to point to Jackie Robinson and Dr. Ralph Bunche. Abilities of this order do not seem attainable to the ordinary boy. He must see what has been possible for his neighbors and uncles.

Coupled with a fair opportunity for work, we in industry must give Negroes a fair opportunity to rise through work to positions of dignity and substantial pay.

These things are within our power—to provide Negroes with a fair opportunity for jobs, and to provide them with a fair opportunity to move upward according to their abilities.

RACES AND MEN

There are real difficulties in providing opportunities to Negroes. One of the most serious is the shortage of well-qualified people in the race. Like other underprivileged groups, they have been hurt by discrimination and deprivation, and they come to the employer with the damage done. As a group, they lack the education, experience, and other qualities required for some occupations. On the average, they do not measure up in some respects to people who have had better opportunities for a lifetime.

This is a sad fact. But is it relevant in the hiring situation? When we are hiring a man for a job, we are not hiring a race. We are not hiring a man's relatives or neighbors. We are hiring one man, and the only relevant question is *his* ability. If he can do the job, that is all that ought to matter.

Another difficulty faced by the Negro is his problem of getting decent housing. Ordinarily, a company would regard this as a personal problem of an employee and therefore not a matter that should involve the company. But sometimes, as when a technical or managerial recruit is brought into a strange town, the move cannot be accomplished unless satisfactory housing can be found. Then the company cannot ignore the problem.

PROPERTY VALUES?

Here a major part of the difficulty stems from a widespread misconception. It is an almost universal belief among white people that property values go down when a Negro moves into a white neighborhood. Indeed, this can happen if the residents panic and many of them throw their property onto the market. But actual study of a large number of such neighborhoods shows that in the majority of instances it does not happen. In some elite neighborhoods today there is a hint of the opposite: The white neighbors are proud of the Negro lawyer or doctor who has settled in their midst and regard this new family almost as a prestige symbol. Many thoughtful people want their children to have the experience of association with a variety of citizens as a preparation for life in a pluralistic society.

NOT SO HARD

From the experience of Owens-Illinois and other companies in recent years, several lessons about the employment of Negroes can be learned. First, with regard to the social obstacles (that is, the attitudes of fellow employees, supervisors, and customers), *it is easier than anyone thought it would be.* Any proposed step toward equal opportunity is usually greeted by dire predictions of probable consequences. The cautious businessman invariably says, "This is dynamite!" Yet none of the predictions seem to materialize. The hard core of resistance to full equality on the job among white citizens is not nearly so large nor so hard as it was even a few years ago. Times have changed. As shown by a recent survey in *Newsweek* magazine, the one privilege the man on the street in all sectors of America is most willing to grant the Negro is equality on the job.

Second, to make worthwhile progress toward giving the Negro a fair deal in employment takes effort. You do not just announce your policy, lean back, and let nature take its course. You have to search for good candidates; you may have to offer special training; you will certainly have to argue strenuously to convince individual supervisors that a candidate has the potential if not the experience to do a job well.

Third, we have learned that the typical manager will take no significant action on this matter unless he is told to do so by his own boss. There is no more classic illustration of the social conservatism of the professional manager—or perhaps it should be called monumental single-mindedness to the task at hand, namely, the making of nuts and bolts—than the reluctance of the typical manager to upset traditional practices of human relations, even when these are clearly wrong. Few managers will press the special measures required to meet this problem until the order to do so comes down from the top.

Providing equal opportunities for all is one of the great problems of our time. It is one of the great opportunities—and responsibilities—of our lifetime to take part in the solution of this problem.

Training and Development
G. Roy Fugal

Those of us who are seeking for people to conduct and expand our businesses recognize the need for increasing the flow of qualified applicants, particularly from minority groups. Most of us would be only too happy to recruit from these groups, if we could find candidates with the qualifications we need. It is true that this sometimes presents difficulties—but there are many people yet undiscovered who are capable or potentially capable of doing the jobs that we have in our places of business, if we but seek them out. One of the first things we must do, therefore, is to utilize the flow that already exists.

At General Electric, for example, we have made a careful analysis of prospective applicants on the graduate level. We know the schools that are graduating Negroes—those that are strictly Negro schools, those that are predominantly Negro schools, and those that have some Negro graduates. We know where this year's 189 Negro graduates in engineering are coming from; where the 81 EE graduates are coming from; where the 44 ME graduates will come from; where the 417 bachelors or masters in mathematics can be acquired; where the 28 physics bachelors and masters will come from; where the 263 bachelors and masters in chemistry will be. We know the schools that will graduate an equivalent or perhaps a gradually increasing number of Negroes year by year, out of a total of some 36,000 college graduates in a year. (These figures may change somewhat as the result of later surveys become available.)

In fact, we were the first large company to recruit on a national scale from Howard University—starting the year that that school became accredited.

There still exists in this country today a vast army of underemployed minority-group people. It is encouraging to note that the ranks in that under-employed army are diminishing because of the aggressive and positive efforts that American business is now exercising.

In the area of apprenticeship, particularly on the level of professional and technical skills, we can also do much more than we have in the past. More than twelve years ago, GE graduated its first Negro apprentice from a four-year tool-and-dye-making course, and since that time we have graduated many other four-year apprentices. This program is conducted in our own facilities, with related training generally being obtained from local community institutions. When local institutions cannot provide the required related training, it is our practice to organize our own program and pursue it until the community is able to provide the required supplementary training. Most companies will find that they can contribute a great deal at the community level by promoting and supporting community programs that will promote training in the skills required by that community.

Efforts in recruiting, training, and development of minority-group members should not be limited to such areas as engineering, skilled jobs, or the salaries jobs classified as nonexempt. Industry should make an investment in providing opportunities for capable minority-group people to get the training necessary for them to rise to management positions in such areas as finance, engineering, manufacturing, marketing, and employee relations. At GE we recruit nationally for candidates for our training programs in those five areas. This climate of opportunity makes equal employment opportunity a reality over the complete scale of our industrial jobs, and we have found that these people compete favorably with other employees in the managerial and professional categories.

Companies will also find it worthwhile to cooperate with the Urban League and other organizations that are trying to provide educational and developmental opportunities for members of minority groups. In the New York area, for example, GE and five other companies got together to sponsor a secretarial training program. This community-based program consists of four consecutive 11-week courses with 40 girls in each class, recruited almost entirely from minority groups. Participants are carefully selected; the first group was chosen from more than two hundred people. The fact that most of the graduates are now favorably placed is the best testimony to the efficacy of a community-based program that offers the opportunity to learn new skills and obtain employment.

Equal opportunity means *equal preparation,* and that just doesn't happen overnight. Our task is not alone to raise the skill level of those already in the work force, but to take affirmative action to help those still in school to prepare for tomorrow's competition.

With this in mind, GE has established a summer course for high school and junior high school counselors. For the past several years, these groups have met at Syracuse University, and another group is now being set up at the University of Louisville. The course is designed to demonstrate to these school counselors—many of them Negroes—exactly what is required in the business world. They get professional, formal instruction and practical, everyday courses, and at the end of this training, we feel they are better prepared to encourage the children in the sixth and seventh and eighth grades to do what they must do, on their own, to be prepared—to be able to take advantage of equal opportunity.

This kind of program, which reaches the children who will be tomorrow's adults, may in the long run prove to be one of the most important steps to be taken toward providing equal opportunity for all.

In the meantime, we owe it to the nation and to all its people to seek out presently qualified individuals, regardless of race, creed, or color, and place them in available job opportunities strictly on the basis of merit.

The Community Approach
Eugene G. Mattison, Jr.

Last summer, the Advisory Council on Plans for Progress to the President's Committee on Equal Employment Opportunity was established. Within that council, the Community Relations Community was created to provide guidance and assistance in the development of community attitudes that promote the implementation of Plans for Progress. Specifically, the committee is searching out successful techniques in working with the changing attitudes and conditions within the community.

TAILORING SOLUTIONS

Many situations require tailor-made solutions to suit local problems. In the presence of unfavorable factors in the community, efforts to provide equal employment opportunity may be impeded, and companies are finding techniques to alter or influence such unfavorable factors. In other cases, favorable factors exist in the community, on which companies may capitalize in order to better implement their policies of providing equal employment opportunties. There are many examples of success in various geographical areas, some under most difficult conditions.

Many groups and organizations, both formal and informal, may play a part in developing favorable community attitudes. Some of these are the Urban League; the NAACP; churches; youth organizations; chambers of commerce and industry associations; unions; newspapers, radio, and television; and schools, colleges, and universities. In working with these groups, companies have developed techniques of particular value in solving community-relations problems. They help to communicate the aims and advantages of equal opportunity at the local level. These techniques include:

1. Talks to local groups by company representatives.

2. Private meetings with community and group leaders to discuss problems and their solution.

3. Plant tours to familiarize interested people with the particular industrial situation or problem.

4. Visits to schools and agencies.

5. Carefully planned publicity, showing real-life success stories of minority individuals.

6. Participation, including membership, on local boards, committees, etc.

COMPANY EXPERIENCES

The experiences of a number of Plans for Progress companies illustrate some of the practical problems that have been encountered—and their solutions.

A large defense contractor, for example, endeavoring to further its Plan for Progress to provide equal employment opportunity, was having difficulty communicating with the Negro community, and this was manifesting itself in inadequate response to the company's recruiting efforts. The company launched a positive program to encourage Negroes to apply for jobs by instituting three concurrent courses of action: (1) meetings were held with ministers; (2) appropriate employment advertising was run in the local Negro press; (3) a committee of large local companies was formed to jointly promote equal employment opportunity in the community. As a result of this effort, there was a considerable increase in Negro applications, and this led to the employment of substantially increased numbers of qualified Negroes.

A large utility company in the Northeast was having difficulty in getting adequate response by qualified Negroes to its recruiting advertising. They made contacts with the local president of the NAACP and subsequently arranged a meeting with a number of Negro ministers. This effort produced twelve candidates, but only two of the twelve were qualified and hired. The ministers expressed surprise and disappointment at these results, and it was felt there was some doubt about the sincerity of the company's program. In an effort to erase the suspicion and doubt, the company invited the ministers to its employment office to discuss standards and employment practices. This was followed by a visit to a nearby work location to enable the ministers to associate selection criteria with job operations. This technique established confidence and rapport that has resulted in the parties' working closely together and has substantially increased the referral of qualified applicants.

A large defense contractor in the East, finding inadequate response by qualified Negroes to its recruiting efforts, made a special contact with the social director of a local Negro group to explain their program and needs and to solicit its cooperation in finding qualified applicants. This resulted in the development of a line of communication into the Negro community that produced results.

A large northern utilities company with a very extensive Plans for Progess program, in an effort to stimulate qualified Negroes to apply for openings, established a rather extensive program of community relations: (1) The company made contact with local minorty groups, held meetings and dinners with local leaders, and conducted plant visits by these individuals in order to fully communicate the extent of the program and the sincerity of the company in its efforts to carry it out. (2) The company supported memberships of its representatives throughout the state in local Urban League chapters. (3) The company provided representatives to serve on various city, county, and state equal employment opportunity committees. (4) Company representatives attended work-shops and special meetings in various government, minority group, and private organizations. They report that these techniques have resulted in considerable improvement in their relationships within the community and a substantial increase in applications from qualified Negroes in response to their recruiting advertising.

Another large defense contractor, in an effort to encourage youth to stay in school and adults to prepare themselves for the increased complexities of positions in the aerospace industry, organized, with the assistance of the Urban League, two special equal employment opportunity programs: Students' Day and Ministers' Conference. This has resulted in considerable enthusiasm among the participants, who have voiced their intention to communicate their newfound knowledge and enthusiasm throughout the local Negro community.

A large eastern industrial company has helped set up "YMCA Industrial Service Teams" to make slide presentations in Negro homes (for three or four families at a time) on a personal, informal basis to carry the message that jobs are opening up rapidly in the area but an education is needed to take advantage of the opportunities. The repeated theme of the slides is that race is ceasing to be a barrier to employment, but qualifications are absolutely essential.

A large defense contractor located in the southern region made very careful preparations in establishing a new facility in an area known for strict state and local segregation laws and deeply rooted segregation customs and attitudes. Careful attention was given to pace and timing of integration steps, with a full appreciation of the community situation as it existed at the given moment. Management alerted and solicited the cooperation of state and local officials regarding company plans and progress at all steps. Close liaison was also maintained with key and influential business and community leaders, as well as organizations such as the Urban League, YMCA, State Department of Labor, and state and private school officials.

Several large corporations operating on a national basis have prepared booklets or pamphlets to describe their company's policy and program to employees, and to organizations and groups interested in furthering employment for minorities.

THE CRITICAL FACTOR

The experiences of these companies, and many others, has proved that attaining the goal of equal job opportunities for all is not beyond our reach —even in areas where discrimination has long been a way of life.

The critical factor is one of qualifications. We have found over and over again in our experience in Marrietta, Georgia, where we employ 18,000 people, that qualified Negroes are accepted readily by their fellow workers. If the company's policy is understood and is firmly observed, and if people are selected strictly on the basis of qualifications, the employment of minorities can work—and work well.

A Company Case History
H. W. Wittenborn

In industry, especially for companies that have been involved in government contracting for any period of time, equal opportunity in employment is not a new policy. In 1941, President Roosevelt issued an Executive Order (No. 9001) establishing the requirement that government contractors provide equal employment opportunities without regard to race, creed, color, or national origin. This concept was continued through the Truman and Eisenhower Administrations and on into the Kennedy-Johnson Administration.

The discrimination that does exist in industry has been a product of nonpolicy rather than policy. In most cases, the pattern has simply evolved, growing out of custom, habit, fear, or some similar factor. The general attitude of industry has been to let sleeping dogs lie, while community customs remained static or changed slowly.

Today, however, community customs are changing fast, and the business executive is faced with a dilemma: More and more he is feeling the squeeze between the external pressures demanding change (the government, racial groups, interracial groups, and the community) and the internal, structured customs within his organization demanding status quo.

BUMPS IN THE ROAD

Instead of merely yielding to pressures, a growing number of companies are seizing the initiative. Unfortunately, change does not come easily. The road is sometimes a little bumpy, and past practices are often tied to seniority rules or job assignments and are closely linked to job security and status.

The experience of the Cook Electric Company provides a good example of some of the bumps—and of the type of action that is being taken in many companies in spite of them.

Cook has always had an official policy that tied employment and post-employment practices to ability and performance rather than to color, race, creed, or national origin. Nevertheless, in 1951 the only Negroes we had were in service jobs: janitors, matrons, degreasers. Shortly after I transferred to manufacturing, personnel hired a young Negro to fill a janitorial position in my department. He was tall, well mannered, nice looking, had some high school education, and did a good job—and he also was ambitious. There seemed to be no advantage, to the company or to the man, in allowing his ambitions to become frustrated or his abilities to stagnate, so I initiated a transfer for him to the classification of wirer and solderer. When the transfer went to the plant superintendent for approval, he hit the ceiling. He used that well-worn line, "You can't do this; you'll stir up a hornet's nest in the department." I countered with, "But the company has a policy—." You see, I wasn't aware of the fact that even though the company had a policy of nondiscrimination, in practice there was discrimination by custom. In this case, however, the superintendent told me I could see the president if I wanted to, since he was the one who made the policy. In the end, the transfer was approved; the young man did go on the production line; no hornet's nest was stirred up; the young man did a good job; he was accepted by his fellow workers; and he is still working for our company.

Four important factors are pointed up by this story:

1. Management's attitude.
2. Management's concern or fear.
3. Management's communications.
4. Management's affirmative action.

MANAGEMENT ATTITUDE

Primary to the success of any program dealing with equal job opportunities is the attitude of top management. Unless top management is behind the program, it is difficult, if not impossible, for the operating personnel to achieve any degree of success in offering employment opportunities and postemployment advancement to members of minority groups. Top management must mean what they say about equal opportunity.

MANAGEMENT CONCERN

Most company officers can honestly say they hold no principle or prejudice that would prevent them from subscribing to a program of equal employment opportunity. But they deterred from taking any action because of concern lest this action disrupt their organization. Our former plant superintendent typifies this concern—and, in most cases, fear of adverse reactions are as groundless as his.

Recently, a clerk-typist opening developed in one of our plants. This plant has had Orientals on its clerical staff, but they had never had a Negro. One of the girls in the personnel office learned that a forty-year-old Negro woman employed as a matron in the plant was attending a business college and learning to type. She had previously bid on a number of factory jobs in higher labor grades, only to be rejected because a senior employee also bid.

SMOOTH ADJUSTMENTS

The woman was offered the job, although it was understood that she was not a trained typist or clerk, because those with whom she was to work agreed to cooperate in her training. A short time ago, the personnel manager of the plant reported: "Insofar as acceptance by other employees is concerned, I can honestly say I have not heard one word of criticism or resentment reflecting on the employee's race or personal conduct, and my observations are that she has been accepted by the other employees with no reservations. Similarly, she herself does not appear uneasy or uncertain as to her relations with or status among them. I feel the adjustment for all concerned has been accomplished."

In another recent situation, a Negro floor inspector making $2.50 per hour was considered the best-qualified man for promotion to the position of quality-control engineer at a rate of $145 per week.

Three months after his promotion, he was evaluated to determine his progress and suitability for his new job. His evaluation read: "Outstanding in enthusiasm, cooperates well with others, makes sound decisions, uses good judgment, exceptional administrative ability"—and so on. The director of quality assurance commented, "He has been extremely effective in working with the Air Force. In production quality-control areas he is firm but reasonable and cooperative. He is highly regarded by his co-workers." And the personnel manager reported, "The fact that he is a Negro has neither helped nor hindered his progress. It simply hasn't made any difference. He is a hard-working, capable, and well-liked employee." This man is currently attending Illinois Institute of Technology Evening School under the Cook Electric Company tuition reimbursement program to pick up the extra credits he needs to attain his B.S. in physics.

In many other cases, within our company and others, Negroes are now being placed in jobs that were heretofore not open to them because management was afraid of what might happen. Undoubtedly, this kind of fear is the greatest stumbling block in the path of the equal employment opportunities program.

MANAGEMENT COMMUNICATIONS

Good communications downward are important to any management program, but they are vital to a program dealing with corporate practices as they relate to minority groups. The president of a large corporation may wholeheartedly subscribe to a program of equal employment opportunities as he sits in his plush Chicago office, but unless the word comes down to the division manager in the Detroit plant in terms he can understand, he may continue to "let sleeping dogs lie." And it is not sufficient for the management personnel to understand the company policy. It must be understood by every employee, by the community, by the employment agencies, and by other recruitment sources. It must be clear to everyone that the policy is one of affirmative action.

MANAGEMENT ACTION

Presidential Executive Order No. 10925 relating to government contractor states, "the contractor will take affirmative action to ensure the applicants are employed, and that employees are treated during employment, without regard to their race, creed, color, or national origin." This means that government contractors are expected to do more than just *not discriminate*.

Cook Electric Company, in policy, has always been in compliance with the previous executives orders. We did not discriminate. If a Negro came to us to apply for a job, and he was qualified for an opening available at that time, he would be hired. However, Executive Order No. 10925, issued by President Kennedy, differs from all others by requiring affirmative action. Under this concept, our former policy was not sufficient. We could not sit back and wait for the Negro to come to our office, to answer our newspaper ad, or to come from the employment agency. It hadn't happened that way in the past, and we had no reason to believe it would happen now.

EXTRA EFFORT

Now, when we need a group of wirers and solderers, we contact the minority-group representative at the Illinois State Employment Service. We have reviewed the personal history files of our present Negro employees to determine skills or training that could be used to up-grade them. Our recruitment advertising has been extended to include Negro community newspapers. Our employment agency contacts have been advised that whenever possible we want a mix of races and colors in the applicants they provide. We utilize the various organizations devoted to assisting the Negro in his quest for employment, such as the Urban League. Our college recruitment program has been extended to include the Negro colleges. We are using every available means to get our message across to prospective applicants of all colors or races or creeds.

As a result of this stepped-up effort, we have increased our non-white population from 6.16 per cent of the workforce in December, 1962, to 9.71 per cent in December, 1963. But our job is not finished; we are committed to a Plan for Progress, and we intend to carry out our commitment. Because we are an organization dedicated to social work? No—just because it makes good economic sense.

What Cook Electric Company has done will not necessarily produce the same results in every company. No two companies or communities or groups are quite alike, and discrimination itself takes many different forms. A successful program for your company will require a careful assessment of the situation, followed by management's determination to act and to see it through. The road to success may be hard, but the goal is attainable.

Breaking the Bias Barrier
George A. Spater

One of the toughest problems to be faced in 1964—the need for opening more skilled jobs to Negroes—has been in the making for a long time. Back in 1936, Dr. Alba M. Edwards asked this question:

If, with the further mechanization of industry, the machine takes over much of the unskilled work [Negroes] are now doing, will they be able to rise to higher pursuits, or will they replace white workers in the remaining unskilled pursuits, or, finally, will they largely fall into that permanently unemployed class certain writers have prophesied that we shall have in the future?

The intervening 27 years have seen further mechanization and the steady loss of jobs by unskilled workers, both white and Negro. The remaining unskilled jobs are rapidly decreasing. As a result, the issue has been simplified. There now appear to be two choices: Will the Negro be able to rise to "higher pursuits," or will he largely become permanently unemployed—a constant drain on the economy, a constant threat to domestic peace, and a constant burden on our consciences?

It's easy to say that good Negro job candidates will be hired, and if they demonstrate ability, they can rise to positions of responsibility. The sober fact is that there are relatively few good Negro job candidates for "higher pursuits." There are fewer qualified applicants than there are jobs. Perhaps the chief reason for this is that Negroes have not been educated to take advantage of some of the new opportunities that are becoming available.

Dr. Stephen Wright, President of Fisk University at Nashville, has said:

> No one who has ever taught in a Negro public school in the South would fail to observe the built-in sense of futility that stems from a lack of access to opportunity, the absence of high aspirations, and the extensive poverty which imputes a certain sense of reality to both the futility and the absence of aspirations.
>
> The low aspirations were not limited to students in the public schools. They extend to the college level. I have personally known, for example, engineering graduates from M.I.T. who could not secure jobs as engineers. It was not surprising, therefore, that few students could be persuaded to pursue this demanding field which held no promises for them.
>
> Until very recently, the Negro college student could prepare, in the main, only for those occupations reserved, in a sense, for Negroes.

As a consequence of this history, there are today only an insignificant number of Negroes attending the better law schools, business schools, or engineering schools from which businesses draw their principal candidates for the "higher pursuits."

This presents a tight, vicious circle: Since there are few examples of Negroes in the more attractive jobs, it is difficult to persuade young Negroes to undertake the rigorous and expensive education necessary to attain jobs that may exist only in theory.

BREAKING THE CIRCLE

Much of the effort that is being exerted today in the equal employment opportunity field is to break this vicious circle. And it is fairly well agreed by those who have studied the problem that *motivation* is the key.

Without going into too much detail, we know enough about people to be able to say confidently that motivation is a very subtle thing. Children at an early age will decide they want to become doctors or lawyers or engineers because they have relatives or neighbors in those professions, or because in some other way they gain the impression that the profession is an attractive one. Even very young children have a way of knowing what jobs are or are not thought to be within their competence.

If a company accepts a policy of complete equality of opportunity in employment, this is very good. But it is not very likely that this will be enough to cause a Negro child eight or ten years old to try to get the long formal education required to be an accountant or a statistician in order to get a job with your company. Something else will have to happen first: The Negro child will believe that accounting and statistics are within his competence when he sees Negroes getting jobs as accountants and statisticians. He will exert himself to get the education and his school will exert itself to provide the education when they see that the job opportunity is real.

MORE THAN HALFWAY

Enlightened employers can make the job opportunity real, and can provide motivation, by doing a little more than any law or Executive Order requires. During the past twenty years, almost every major employer has hired Negroes whose inherent abilities are greater than the jobs to which they are assigned. If, from these present employees, we select those who would be most likely to benefit by some additional formal education and see that they get this education, we will have made a major contribution toward breaking the vicious circle.

If, for example, you have a man who would make a good accountant, induce him to go to night school, or continue him on your payroll while he takes a day course to acquire the education he needs to become an accountant. When he completes the education, give him a chance at an accountant's job.

This is the only way there can be any immediate breakthrough for greater opportunity. Few Negroes today are trained to assume "higher pursuits," and there is very little tangible motivation for young boys to undertake long training. If major businesses make the extra effort that is needed, we can establish some believable evidence of job opportunity. When there are examples of Negroes holding management jobs, boys will have the motivation to educate themselves for comparable positions—and schools will have the motivation to furnish the education.

REVERSE DISCRIMINATION?

There are those, of course, who express concern about the dangers of doing a little more for Negroes than you do for whites. But is it really inequitable to practice what some have called "reverse discrimination?" Perhaps the best answer was expressed by Anatole France when he sardonically remarked, "The law in its majestic equality forbids both the rich and the poor to sleep under bridges." This tells the whole story in one short, sarcastic sentence. Let's not fall under the illusion that people are treated equally when no recognition is given to three hundred years of deprivation of opportunity.

This does not mean that we should lose our heads in romantic notions. We must look at the problems realistically, as citizens and businessmen. Providing "greater opportunity" does not benefit only the employee—it also means benefits to the employer. A recent survey of leading university economists indicates that more than two-thirds believe that discrimination against minorities constitutes a serious obstacle to economic efficiency. When you provide greater opportunity, you not only provide a means of filling future jobs, you also create a new consumer and assist in removing the economic blight that would result from supporting a permanently unemployed class. This is the objective of equal employment.

One of the greatest teachers of all time taught by parable: by stating a principle, then illustrating it—making it believable—by a story involving real people. Those who accept the principle of equal opportunity must make it believable by illustrating it with real people. Everyone who is in a position to do so can do a little more than the law requires and create tangible proof of job opportunity by making it possible for existing employees to move into more responsible management jobs.

Where Civil Rights Law Is Going Wrong
Nation's Business

21

Few businessmen in America today even suspect that an agency of the federal government would:

Send out teams of investigators with authority to go through your company's files without telling you exactly why.

Write out tests for every job in your organization and pressure you to use them as a basis for hiring.

Deny you the right to put your son in a training program in your own company.

Encourage your employees to lodge complaints of discrimination in your company, but refuse to tell you who your accusers are.

Require you to exhibit "proper" social attitudes as defined by a board of government appointees.

Receive unsworn complaints about you and then threaten to make them public if you refuse to do what the agency wants you to.

Tell you to hire a man instead of a woman as your personal secretary.

Force you to hire persons who are not qualified for a job and make you educate them.

Reprinted with permission from *Nation's Business* (November 1965) pp. 60–62, 64, 66, 68, 70, 73.

Make you put young women in expensive executive training programs, even though experience shows many will quit.

Require you to give back pay to anyone the agency thinks has been denied advancement in your firm in the past because of his or her race, sex, color, religion or national origin.

Further require you to put some persons in the positions they would have been in today if discrimination had not occurred and to give extra money to the rest of your employees to soften the impact on them.

Preposterous?

These are just some of the suggestions being seriously considered by a U.S. government agency which is gathering momentum since being set up four months ago and already has indicated that it intends to step beyond the letter of the law to achieve its purposes.

Called the Equal Employment Opportunity Commission (EEOC), it is a creature of Title VII of the Civil Rights Act of 1964 which forbids discrimination in employment because of race, color, religion, sex or national origin.

DISTORTION FEARED

Few Americans oppose the basic objectives of the Act. Certainly reasonable citizens today want their fellow citizens to have equal opportunity, whatever their race, creed, color or sex. But there are unmistakable signs that implementation may now be distorted through bias or economic ignorance of those charged with administering it.

The commission is supposed to receive complaints and oversee compliance with the law. It consists of five commissioners and a staff plucked from the ranks of unions, civil rights groups and the Peace Corps.

While the group is still organizing and deciding how to carry out its charge, there are strong movements in Congress to give it even more sweeping power.

There is, for example, a bill sponsored by Rep. Augustus F. Hawkins (D., Calif.), officially called the Equal Employment Opportunity Act of 1965 (H. R. 10065). The bill, which was rushed through the Education and Labor Committee, would transform the commission from an agency designed mainly for conciliation into one that would act largely as prosecutor, judge and jury.

The Hawkins bill would allow the commission, which now can seek its aims only through the courts, to issue "cease and desist" orders to employers, unions and employment agencies.

The Hawkins bill, which counts the activist Student Non-Violent Coordinating Committee among its chief supporters, also would—for all practical purposes—eliminate state fair employment practices commissions and substitute federal control.

The powers outlined at the beginning of this article were among recommendations made in August during a two-day White House Conference on the new commission. And most of these recommendations can be implemented under the current law.

The conference started with a general session in the State Department's auditorium and then broke into seven "workshops." The 300 conferees included many sociologists, civil rights proponents and representatives of unions, women's organizations and state fair employment commissions.

DISSENT STIFLED

There was also a group representing employment agencies and employers. A few from this group spoke out indignantly at suggestions being made. But many sat silent fearing accusations of bigotry from a confused public or in a few cases even retaliation by the federal government when government contracts are let.

Government officials have put pressure on many large employers to hire more Negroes, even though a number of business firms have been making special efforts to seek out qualified employees and even quietly giving preference to Negro applicants over whites.

News of the White House conference has now spread, and businessmen are beginning to voice their dismay. *Nation's Business* has talked confidentially with dozens of executives. Many requested that their names and firms not be mentioned.

A typical reaction came from E. J. Shroedter, assistant industrial relations director of Evinrude Motors, Milwaukee.

The reports of the White House conference workshop panels are "disturbing," he said. "In many instances it will disrupt the basic philosophies upon which hiring, promotion and other practices have been established.

"Certainly, no one is advocating that discrimination against minority groups continue, nor should practices that foster discrimination be retained. However, the reverse should not happen either. Preference and greater consideration should not be given to less competent applicants regardless of race or color, because this would be discrimination in reverse."

DANGER IN NUMBERS

The vice president of a major phone company commented on one important phase of the conference this way:

> "I would strongly urge that the EEOC not automatically assume a pattern [of discrimination] exists because of statistical evidence indicating a high proportion of minority employees in specific jobs. They must carefully ascertain the facts and recognize that 'pockets' of minority employees may not only exist, but may also be inevitable, due to the qualifications of the individuals. They certainly should not reason that numbers per se indicate discrimination."

Some conference participants urged a complete merger of seniority lists according to dates of entrance in firms. This would put everyone, no matter what his duties or qualifications, on one big list.

"Such a rule would be onerous to follow," argues a steel executive, "and, in the case of hundreds of applications filed with a large operation in a day or a week, would create countless problems in filing and processing."

It was further suggested at the workshops that something be done to soften any impact that realigned seniority lists might have on members of the majority group, since they were not directly responsible for any discrimination.

"This type of relief," says the Commission's official report on the workshops, "might be the use of the back-pay provision which would cause the employer to bear the burden of the readjustment."

The president of a Midwest manufacturing firm argues that this approach would result in "nothing short of chaos." He suggests that instead of expending effort "correcting" the past, the commission concentrate on building for the future.

"The notion that back pay might be paid employees discriminated against in the past is highly objectionable," says a railroad vice president. "It assumes that they can be identified and that the extent of the discrimination can be defined in monetary terms. It would penalize employers as the result of the unsound presumption that they are responsible for every instance of past discrimination.

"The elimination of present and future discrimination is a more than adequate task for the commission—and is clearly the assignment given it by the law."

Thomas J. Hogan, executive vice president of Eastern Express, Inc., of Terre Haute, Ind., fears the commission will order "some careless general merger" of seniority lists which would place unqualified drivers on city and road units.

One workshop at the White House conference took up the problems of complaint procedures and the relationship between federal, state and local regulations regarding discrimination in employment.

Representatives from some civil rights groups at the workshop expressed "serious and severe distrust" of the Federal Bureau of Investigation and of the ability of present federal and state agencies to protect persons complaining about discrimination. They suggested that EEOC commissioners file charges without naming the complaining parties.

"My blood curdled when I read suggestions that the employer be denied rights that are granted to criminals in the matter of discovery according to the rules of the court," said Claire T. Grimes, executive secretary of the Hollywood, Calif., Chamber of Commerce.

"Why must a complaining witness be completely protected in an accusation against an employer who is contributing to the advancement of society, whereas a criminal in a dope arrest—even though the evidence is found on him—cannot be convicted unless he is informed as to who the informer is? This is a double standard of the worst order and makes me indignant beyond all comprehension that such absurdities can be proposed."

A New York corporation lawyer says he can't believe the power of the federal government is "so weak and inadequate that it is unable to protect an individual who files a complaint with a governmental agency." Withholding the name of the charging party from the accused employer, he adds, would deprive the employer of the opportunity to develop his defense.

The burden of proof should be borne by the accuser, another businessman insists. Requiring an employer to furnish all the proof that he is innocent of any charge would place him at a severe disadvantage, he says, because of the adverse publicity usually connected with cases of this type.

HARASSMENT MADE EASY

"Ignoring the legal principle of the accused being confronted by his accuser," another maintains, "makes it both attractive and safe to fabricate trial cases or otherwise harass the employer."

One executive said the commission should reject the suggestion to take information in any form, sworn or unsworn. Instead, he said it should follow the National Labor Relations Board safeguards of requiring sworn complaints with criminal penalties for perjury.

"I read the workshop report without getting the idea that EEOC was going to do anything special to protect the employer," says Frank C. McAlister, director of personnel and labor relations of the Indiana State Chamber of Commerce. "I feel the employer should have some protection from harassment and unfounded charges that could be filed promiscuously against him."

Another businessman takes issue with the suggestion made at the workshop that a state agency should be allowed to discuss a case with the commission prior to the state's decision on it.

"It would, in effect, deprive an employer of his fundamental right to an unbiased appeal," he says. "In essence the state agency's decision would be the commission's decision." Still another claims that the commission's duty to act as a conciliator would be destroyed if it adopted a workshop suggestion that investigators' reports be made available in future cases.

"If statements and comments of an employer could possibly be used against him in subsequent litigation," he says, "he would have no other course open than to take a legalistic and cautious approach at the very inception of an investigation by the federal agency."

Regarding a proposal that any failures in conciliation be made public routinely, George T. Heaberg III, employment manager of Smith Kline & French Laboratories, argues: "Even though failure to conciliate is due to reasons other than discrimination on the part of the employer, we believe publicity in several of these cases would very likely damage the employer's reputation as an equal opportunity employer. Therefore, we question the advisability of unnecessarily risking damage to the employer's reputation."

COERCION CHARGED

The vice president of a large manufacturing firm calls the proposal "a blatant attempt to coerce an employer into accepting any solution the commission might suggest regardless of its merit." It verges on compulsory mediation, he adds, and is obviously contrary to the spirit and intent of the law.

"It implies," says an Oregon executive, "that the employer is automatically resisting conciliation if he stands on his convictions."

The civil rights law generally provides that states with satisfactory fair employment practice laws have jurisdiction for 60 days before cases go to the federal authorities.

Theoretically, businessmen complain, a single company could find itself involved with the new commission, the NLRB, the Community Relations Service, the Justice Department, the President's Committee on Equal Employment Opportunity and the Labor Department in addition to numerous state and local fair employment commissions.

"The area of jurisdiction between individual states and the federal government needs to be cleared up very quickly," says M. E. Berthiaume, manager of industrial relations for the Arrow Co., Troy, N.Y. "This is particularly important for a company that does business in many different states.

"For example, we have had a civil rights commission in New York State for a good many years and are familiar with its method of operation and can appreciate that there will be no areas of conflict between the federal government and the state. However, in Alabama, where we also have plants, the area of agreement between federal and state is not so clear and it tends to leave an employer under difficulties as to how to operate under the law.

"It is, therefore, important that this area be cleared up completely before an employer is held liable for any error on his part."

Workshop No. 3 concerned discrimination because of sex. The word "sex" was put into the civil rights legislation to delay passage of the bill. Once it was in, congressmen were afraid to speak out against including the word for fear of ruffling the hair-dos of half of their constituents. So the commission is faced with the problem of determining what is meant by discrimination because of sex.

HIRE MALE BUNNIES?

Title VII says the only time you can't hire people of either sex is when there is a "bona fide occupational qualification," an oft-used term reduced by commission staffers to "BFOQ." The search for a definition of BFOQ took up a good part of workshop No. 3.

Some refer to this as "the bunny problem." What, they ask, do you do when a knobby-kneed male waiter shows up at a Playboy club seeking a job as a bunny? Or a woman wants to be an attendant in a men's Turkish bath? Or a man has an urge to clerk in a woman's corset shop?

Suggestions were made at the workshop that only the narrowest interpretation be given to BFOQ.

"The burden is on the employers," said one commission staffer. "If they can't think of any reason not to hire women for jobs traditionally held by men, then they better do it."

Commission Chairman Franklin D. Roosevelt, Jr. said his agency "should be alert to distinguish those situations where it is merely a convenient extension of tradition and those where sex appears to have a stronger tie to the requirements of the job or other basic values."

One speaker at the workshop said women and men should be allowed any job except where only one sex could reasonably be expected to do the work or where "national mores" would require selection of one sex over the other —as in the case, for example, of a washroom attendant or a fashion model.

The workshop suggested that most jobs are interchangeable between sexes and that, for example, weight lifting would be no problem, assuming adequate mechanical handling equipment.

But an electric executive says:

"Unfortunately, I envision accelerated physical, if not emotional, failure and increased claims for compensation. What assurance does the employer have that—in exchange for accepting any instabilities of women, interruptions for child bearing, earlier retirement and the ever present possibility that a woman will quit to let her husband be the breadwinner—he will get undivided attention to the job, loyalty and a fair return on his investment?"

Another suggests that the commission force only new plants to provide facilities for women.

A widespread hope among businessmen who are aware of commission plans is that the commission will use panels of experts, including responsible representatives of industry, to advise it in establishing bona fide occupational qualifications and in setting a course where federal law conflicts with state laws.

Commission staffers also believe business should not favor men as candidates for executive training programs.

Industry representatives point out that women are a greater risk in such situations because when they marry, they usually leave a company.

This is not a valid defense, commission representatives counter. They said no BFOQ could be based upon "such broad propositions as an assumed or actual increased cost of employing women due to higher turnover, higher sick leave or other alleged generally high cost of employment."

The director of industrial relations for a large manufacturer argues: "The suggestion that the commission be empowered to extend state labor laws to both sexes where the law relates only to one is on its face unconstitutional.

Obviously, no federal regulatory agent has any authority to alter, amend or vary a state statute."

On record-keeping and reporting, it was recommended that employers be made to keep secret records on each employee, indicating his race, sex, religion, national origin and source of referral.

Industry men at the conference argued that this could conflict with state or local laws prohibiting such records and that trained investigators do not need such written records to determine validity of a complaint.

RECORDS FOSTER BIAS

"We are color-blind rather than color-conscious in our record-keeping and other personnel operations," comments S. Lester Block, labor attorney for R. H. Macy & Co., Inc. "I believe that recorded information on an employee's race would be a disservice to employees and could actually abet discriminatory practices.

"Further, the proposal that a record indicating the employee's race should be 'kept only under circumstances where it would not be available to those responsible for personnel decisions' is unrealistic and unworkable.

"It is significant that states having long experience with fair employment practice regulations, such as New York and California, have frowned upon racial indicators on employment records."

John E. Stark, vice president of industrial relations, Westinghouse Air Brake Co., says, "The completing of forms is becoming a major task. As time goes by, employers are required to complete increasingly more forms, particularly governmental. We would like to see some controls established to exert a diminishing effect on this practice."

Title VII gives the commission access to any records required by it or any state or local fair employment practice agency and makes it unlawful to interfere with agents of the commission.

The commission's attitude toward unions seems to differ from that toward industry. The commission staff proposed that unions be exempted from the record-keeping requirement except in hiring halls and apprentice programs.

Employer representatives pointed out that Title VII of the Civil Rights Act specifically covers labor unions as well as them. Certainly unions have been criticized widely for discrimination in employment policies.

LUNACY IN APPRENTICESHIP

It was suggested in workshop No. 5 on apprenticeships and the general upgrading of skills, that the commission consider Title VII violated if members of minority groups are not selected in apprentice programs.

M. E. Lantz, manager of industrial relations for Perfect Circle Corp., Hagerstown, Ind., contends that hiring as apprentices minority group members who do not have the capacity to advance beyond the trainee stage would be "sheer lunacy."

There's also concern over the prospective problem of an owner-father who has spent, say, 25 years building up a business to pass on to his son and then is denied the privilege of hiring him as an apprentice.

"According to present interpretations of the equal opportunity law he could hire his son only if he were at the top of the eligibility list," one executive says. "I am not convinced this is reasonable or, frankly, the American way of doing business."

Workshop No. 6 of the conference concerned hiring, promotions and dismissals. Preferential treatment for nonwhites was put forth as a way to correct past inequalities in hiring.

"Title VII forbids preferential treatment of any type," the commission said in its report on this workshop. But it added that, "After much discussion it was determined that the question was not whether we are meeting the letter of the law, as pertains to Title VII, but whether we are meeting the spirit of the law in going an extra step to provide sufficient means to enable Negroes to obtain jobs on a basis equal with whites."

A West Coast labor relations executive argues that industry already has adequate means to assure merit employment practices "without a government agency—insulated as it often is from an understanding of a free, competitive economy—entering the arena."

Representatives of industry and private employment agencies today complain of the lack of qualified Negroes to fill many present job vacancies.

"We have run into government competition for qualified Negro personnel on several occasions where Negro applicants in whom we have shown an interest have taken government jobs," says Donald S. Frost, vice president of Bristol-Myers Co. "In one particular instance a Negro research scientist left the company to take a government position. It is our feeling that if government is trying to encourage industry to train and hire Negro employees, the various agencies should be instructed not to compete actively against industry in this area."

NEGRO EMPLOYERS LOSE

"From the viewpoint of a Negro employer," says A. T. Spaulding, president of North Carolina Mutual Life Insurance Co., "I am convinced that I have more difficult problems now, because of the loss of trained manpower to white employers. Segregation no longer is a protective tariff for the Negro employer."

Another issue in the race discrimination question involves job descriptions and job qualifications.

Several White House conferees called on industry to train "occupational analysts" to perform job audits, rewrite job specifications and insure that personnel tests are geared to find the right kind of employee. Sometimes, it was said, job specifications are designed to find an employee who can perform a job without training even though it might take only a little training for an unskilled person to do the same job.

Some civil rights advocates argue that testing is discriminatory per se and that it has been the chief device by which many minority group workers have been denied equal opportunity in the job market.

Some say that tests, instead of being abandoned should be redesigned to meet "realistic requirements" for jobs, putting the accent more on the ability of a person to learn rather than on his technical knowledge.

They contend also that some tests are discriminatory because they contain cultural questions which many nonwhites do not have the background to answer.

"Complete elimination of tests would be terrible," maintains Sherry D'George, owner of a personnel agency in Altoona, Pa. "It would leave us with no way of evaluating an applicant.

"As for the suggestion that the federal government step in and decide what questions should be on tests, we'd then be like the Soviet Union. It would be a catastrophe. The government would be in complete control, telling us whom to hire and whom to fire."

EMPLOYERS DEFEND TESTS

Many employers insist that the use of tests is extremely important in hiring, not as a tool of racial discrimination but as a means for determining skills, abilities, interests and attitudes.

"Testing programs should not be discarded just because some firm abuses them," argues an Indiana industrialist. "The idea of different 'acceptable minimums' for 'culturally deprived groups' is in itself discriminatory and has no place in our society."

The commission should not attempt to force employers to lower hiring standards that employers have determined are pertinent to the job, businessmen argue.

"Industry should strive to cooperate with local school systems to insure that students are trained properly in skills which industry needs," the commission says. "Industry should be more willing to accept persons for employment who lack required skills but have the ability and desire to learn. . . .

"It is the responsibility of industry and the unions to provide the climate in which equal opportunity to train for employment and to compete for employment exists for all. It is especially incumbent on industry to make known to the schools and the unemployed the needs of industry. It is not enough to obey the technical letter of the law. We must go a step beyond in order to assure equal employment opportunity."

Some businessmen will question whether industry should be forced to train people if the job market can produce the applicants needed.

Most businessmen believe that promotions and dismissals should be a function of management rather than subjects for unwarranted scrutiny by the commission.

Management is charged with the responsibility of operating an efficient and profitable organization; every employee's job future depends on this.

"In today's labor market there is an acute shortage of qualified and technically competent people," notes one business executive, "and I can't believe that management would destroy its chance for survival by denying promotion to minority groups."

One of the workshops of the White House conference was entitled "Affirmative Action." Civil rights lawyer Herman Edelsberg, chairman of the panel, defined affirmative action as activity beyond the letter of the law.

Among affirmative actions suggested for employers were:

Voluntary group deeds to create a "climate of welcome for previously disadvantaged minorities."

Aggressive recruiting to counteract any minority group feelings of defeatism or timidity.

Display of commission posters and distribution of information on equal job opportunities.

Contributions to the Negro College Fund.

Spending "idle funds in the development of integrated suburban housing."

BUSINESS ROLE LIMITED

Influencing community attitudes can be accomplished only in part by employers, most businessmen believe. "Patience, understanding and education will do more to move the citizenry than any corporate action which to many people has implications of being politically motivated," declares one executive.

"Aggressive recruiting of minority employees for promotion is segregation in reverse which will lead to dissension within groups where a climate of welcome may once have existed," points out another.

Many businessmen express the fear that the vaguely worded Title VII will be administered according to prejudices of members of the commission. They compare the commission in this respect with the National Labor Relations Board.

James B. O'Shaughnessy, of the Labor Relations Committee of the Illinois State Chamber of Commerce, urges the immediate appointment of a citizens advisory committee to the commission. Composed of business and union representatives, it could act unofficially, suggesting procedures and approving or disapproving rules as made.

"Employers need to know the new ground rules—the procedural regulations under which they will have to operate," emphasizes Howard E. Eades, vice president of research and personnel for W. T. Grant Co., New York.

Rep. Glenn Andrews (R., Ala.), member of the full Committee on Education and Labor, cautions:

"When an individual risks his own capital and employs people, his capital, and his alone, is at stake and it is not a matter of public concern that he fail or not fail. The prerogative should be entirely his and whoever he hires is an important part of his success or failure. The proprietor of a business is entitled to full responsibility for his business venture.

"It is wrong that a public fair employment commission sit with him on his executive board and direct his employment. They are not a stockholder in his enterprise simply because he might have borrowed from a national bank or government directly, or may manufacture a product and paint it with a lacquer which has traveled once across a state line.

"Most responsible Americans, and absolutely including the decent and responsible citizens of my state and region, believe in fair employment practices. We may be a long way from that goal—in New York as well as in Alabama—but attempts at compulsion which reach into the private lives and businesses of our citizens harvest more rancor and resentment than equality of employment opportunity."

Cases

Seabrook Manufacturing Company

"All we need now is a strong man to complete the side show!" exclaimed Joe Larson, purchasing manager of the Seabrook Manufacturing Co., as he entered the office of Dale Wolff, personnel representative for the purchasing department.

"What do you mean, Joe?" asked Dale.

"You know that we have a lot of visitors and suppliers through here, and that old bag isn't doing much to doll up the area. These secretaries have a good deal to do with the impressions people get of our outfit, and they should be at least presentable! We spend thousands of dollars for carpeting and pictures and now this!"

"Who are you talking about?"

"I don't know what her name is, but you know damn well who I'm talking about! The Blimp! Take care of it, will you?"

The purchasing department of Seabrook Manufacturing Co. occupied the major portion of the third floor of the headquarters building of the company. The main working force was located in a large open area at several rows of desks. Executives of the division, all of whom were under the general control of Mr. Larson, were located in private offices that extended along the outer edge of the general working area. The secretary for each executive was situated at a desk directly in front of the office of the executive for whom she worked, but was separated from the rest of the workers by a wide aisle. This aisle was the main passage used by visitors and personnel from other divisions of the company to get from the reception lobby to the executives' offices. The secretaries' desks were finished with a walnut stain as contrasted with the lighter-colored finishes used on other desks in the open area, and the space between secretaries' desks was significantly greater than the space between other desks on the floor.

Mary Lampson, the secretary in question, had just been promoted to her

From *Human Elements of Administration* by Harry R. Knudson, Jr. Copyright ©1963 by Holt, Rinehart and Winston, Inc. Reprinted by permission of Holt, Rinehart and Winston, Inc.

new position as Jack Henderson's secretary and had moved to her new location while Mr. Larson had been away on a business trip. After his former secretary had submitted her resignation, Jack Henderson had selected Mary Lampson as his new secretary after reviewing the personnel files and talking with several individuals currently employed in the department whom Dale Wolff had recommended as candidates for the position.

Mary Lampson was forty-eight years old, and had been with the Seabrook Manufacturing Company for seventeen years, ten in the Purchasing Department. She had started work at Seabrook shortly after her husband had died. Prior to her assignment as Mr. Henderson's secretary, she had performed secretarial duties for several units in the department, but had always been located in the open area with the general employees of the division. She had two grown sons who had completed college and had moved to other parts of the country, and one other son, twenty years old, who was a sophomore at Eastern State University. Her record at Seabrook was unblemished. She had created favorable impressions wherever she had worked, and her former supervisors were unanimous in their praise of her abilities.

Mary Lampson was 5′ 4″ tall and weighed 225 pounds. Although her weight had been a continuing problem for her, she was very pleased with her recent progress on a weight control program, and had lost sixty pounds in the last two years by following her doctor's orders very closely. She was enthusiastic about her new job, for she could use the increase in salary to help put her youngest son through college, and, as she put it, "keep the creditors a little farther from my door."

While not knowing quite how to "take care of it," Dale Wolff decided that his first step should be to talk with Jack Henderson, Mary's boss.

After Mr. Wolff related his conversation with Mr. Larson, Jack Henderson replied: "What a hell of a way to run a railroad! You do what you want to, Dale, but things are in pretty miserable shape when looks are more important than ability. I'm certainly not going to mention this to Mary!"

The Well-Run Oil Company

Robert Jackson, President of The Well-Run Oil Company of Philadelphia, was faced with a decision to make concerning the hiring of additional Negro employees in his company.

Reprinted with permission of Professor Larry E. Greiner, Harvard University. Copyright © 1961 by the University of Kansas.

During the previous month, Jackson had been meeting with a group of four Negro ministers who, according to their spokesman, represented the combined Negro church population in the Philadelphia area. The first meeting found the ministers politely urging Jackson to hire more Negroes for positions of "greater responsibility" in the company. In reply, Jackson balked at what he regarded to be an "intrusion on management's rights," contending that the Well-Run management reserved the "right to make any employment policy it saw fit." "After all," Jackson continued, "we're in business to make a profit and not to solve the city's social problems." The ministers restated their request, after which Jackson concluded the meeting by saying, "I understand your problems, but frankly, it's not ours to solve."

Three weeks passed without further action being taken. Then the ministers returned with a more specific request. They asked that, "Well-Run hire twenty-eight Negro employees; twenty-two additional office workers, four permanent truck drivers, and two motor products salesmen within one month." And, "if Well-Run failed to comply," the ministers told Jackson, "we have no other choice but to call a city-wide Negro boycott of company products until there has been a change in company policy."

Jackson was amazed at their request. He resented what he termed, "a complete disregard for the free enterprise system." On the other hand, he realized that the ministers "meant business"; consequently, he attempted to remain courteous and objective about the matter. In doing so, he carefully pointed out to them that the company already had hundreds of Negro employees working in a nearby refinery, some of whom were in responsible supervisory jobs. In addition, he mentioned that the company had recently decided to include three Negro colleges in its yearly talent search. To this, the ministers replied, "we aren't interested in the number of Negroes working in the refinery. Negroes have always held jobs like that. You hired three Negro clerks a year ago, but none since. Three in an office force of fifteen-hundred isn't much, is it? And even though you plan to include Negroes in your talent search, you haven't actually hired any." Not wishing to prolong the discussion, Jackson adjourned the meeting, saying that he'd take their advice under consideration.

Immediately afterwards, Jackson began to think about the decision he would have to make. In doing so, he came across this comment in a recent issue of The Reporter[1] magazine:

> When four hundred ministers in one city advise their congregations not to buy something, a lot of whatever that something may be goes unbought and the company that makes it is quickly made aware of the fact. For a month and a half, starting March 19th, the congregations of four hundred Negro churches in Philadelphia have not bought Sunoco gas or

[1] Lees, Hannah, "The Not Buying of Philadelphia's Negroes," The Reporter (May 11, 1961), p. 33.

oil for their cars or trucks or Sun fuel oil to heat their homes. Last January for exactly one week they were not buying Gulf gas or oil. Last October for two weeks they were not drinking Pepsi-Cola. And last summer for two months they were not eating any cakes or pies made by Tasty Baking Company.

. . . With the Tasty Baking Company, the second firm they visited and the first one where they encountered opposition, the ministers asked the company to hire two Negro driver-salesmen, two Negro clerical workers, and three or four Negro girls in the icing department, where the workers had traditionally been all-white. They were not interested in the fact that the Tasty Baking Company already had hundreds of Negro employees. What they are interested in is placing Negro workers in positions of dignity and responsibility. Their aim is to change the public image of Negro workers. The Tasty Baking Company did not have any Negroes driving trucks or working in its office.

When Mr. Pass, the personnel manager of the company, and Mr. Kaiser, the president, pointed out that they had no need, just then, for more driver-salesmen or clerical workers, the ministers said politely but firmly that they still hoped these people could be hired within two weeks. If not, the four hundred ministers they represented would have to advise their congregations on the Sunday following not to buy any Tasty cakes or pies until they were hired.

Mr. Kaiser understandably felt pushed and resistant. The Negro driver-salesmen and clerks and icers were not hired within two weeks, and the ministers did tell their congregations not to buy any Tasty cakes or pies until further notice. Printed advertisements to this effect mysteriously appeared in bars, beauty parlors, and barbershops. Nobody knows how many thousand dollars' worth of sales the Tasty Baking Company lost during those summer months, but there are 700,000 Negroes in Philadelphia and a large proportion have some connection with those four hundred churches. When the boycott was officially called off two months later from four hundred pulpits, the Tasty Baking Company had in its employ two Negro driver-salesmen, two Negro clerical workers, and some half-dozen Negro icers.

Bibliography

A. Collective Bargaining, Full Employment and Inflation

Curtin, Edward R. and James K. Brown. "Labor Relations Today and Tomorrow," *Conference Board Record* (August 1968), pp. 46–55.

Seeger, Murray. "The Unions Versus the Conglomerates," *Duns Review* (February, 1968), p. 47.

"The Changing Face of Collective Bargaining," *Management Review* (May 1968), pp. 50–54.

Thompson, Arthur and Irwin Weinstock. "Facing the Crisis in Collective Bargaining," *MSU Business Topics* (Summer 1968), p. 37.

Ways, Max. "Labor Unions are Worth the Price," *Fortune* (May 1963), pp. 108–113, 238–240, 245–254.

"Will Organizing Be Made Easier?" *Business Week* (May 29, 1965), p. 111.

B. The Right-To-Work Controversy

"AFL-CIO Opens Fire on Right-To-Work," *Engineering News-Record* (December 3, 1964), p. 75.

Barton, Sam B. "The Economic Myth of 'Right-To-Work,'" *AFL-CIO American Federationist* (August 1967), pp. 15–18.

Blocker, C. E. and R. C. Graham. "Do Right-To-Work Laws Impair Labor-Management Relations?" *Personnel* (November–December, 1965), pp. 39–44.

Kopkind, Andrew. "Congress and the Right-To-Work," *The New Republic* (June 5, 1965), pp. 11–12.

Lens, Sidney. "The Fate of 14(b)," *Commonwealth* (September 17, 1965), pp. 662–665.

Skibbins, Gerald J. and Caroline S. Weymar. "The Right-To-Work Controversy," *Harvard Business Review* (July-August, 1966), pp. 6–17, 162–164.

C. The Employment Responsibilities of Business

Burck, Gilbert. "Must Full Employment Mean Inflation?" *Fortune* (October 1966), pp. 120–124, 259–260, 264–268.

Clague, E. and L. Greenberg. "Technological Change and Employment," *Monthly Labor Review* (July 1962), pp. 742–746.

"Easing the Hard Core Into the Workforce," *Management Review* (July 1968), pp. 17–20.

"Full Employment and Inflation: A Trade-Off Analysis," *Conference Board Record* (December 1966), pp. 17–27.

Michaels, Donald N. "Cybernation:" The Silent Conquest," *Computers and Automation* (March 1962), pp. 26–42.

"New Look at How Machines Make Jobs," *Nation's Business* (September 1965), pp. 58–64.

Snyder, John, Jr. "Automation and Unemployment," *Management Review* (November 1963), pp. 4–15.

D. Civil Rights and Fair-Employment Practices

Goeke, Joseph and Caroline S. Weymar. "Barriers to Hiring the Blacks," *Harvard Business Review* (September–October, 1969), pp. 144–152.

Haynes, Ulric, Jr. "Equal Job Opportunity: The Credibility Gap," *Management Review* (August 1968), pp. 44–51.

Lunardi, Vivian E. "Sex Discrimination In Industry—What Title VII Means to Your Company," *Factory* (April 1966), pp. 112–116.

Perry, John. "Business—Next Target For Integration?" *Harvard Business Review* (May–June, 1965), pp. 104–115.

Schwartz, Eleanor. "Does Title VII Widen the Personnel Door?" *Atlanta Economic Review* (September 1967), pp. 6–8.

Silberman, Charles E. "The Businessman and the Negro," *Fortune* (September 1963), pp. 97–99, 184–186, 191–194.

Viot, Van H. "The Corporation and Title VII," *Conference Board Record* (April 1966), pp. 16–17.

"What Business Can Do for the Negro," *Nation's Business* (October 1967), pp. 67–70.

PART FIVE

Ethics,
Religion and
Business

Business ethics, the predecessor to the "social responsibility" concept which has dominated business literature for the last twenty years, has actually continued as an underlying concern for business managers. In recent years, business has been criticized for practices involving half truths, and legal-but-unethical activities. As a result of the 1962 price-fixing conspiracies comments have been made that business appears interested in a free and unmanaged economy only until opportunities arise in which it is able to exert managerial influence itself. Evidence of planned business espionage and the establishment of departments of trade relations to exert influence, and in some cases coercion, for reciprocity of buying in the "free market" have also been recorded. Public opinion condemns business for its moral failures in many of its operations today.

This concern with ethics is not exclusively related to management. For example, practices of labor unions leading to monopolistic controls, restrictive work practices of featherbedding, and prolonged strikes with the underlying absence of good faith in bargaining having serious and costly effects on society also fall into the same ethical framework.

A. The Ethical Aspects of Business

Even though there is widespread public demand for higher levels of ethical performance by business (often supported by business groups themselves), there are, nevertheless, conflicting positions in this debate. For example, in Robert Freedman's article, "The Challenge of Business Ethics" [22], it is recommended that management confine its responsibilities to the efficient allocation of resources in our economy to the exclusion of any social responsibilities. In short he says, there is no obligation beyond profits. Following this mandate, business would leave the righting of social wrongs to society and government, even if this should conflict with the individual manager's personal code of morality. Contrary to Freedman's analysis, Glenn Gilman in "The Ethical Dimension in American Management" [23] argues that businessmen are becoming increasingly aware of ethical questions in the decision-making process. This awareness results from an acknowledgment of the interdependence of business with many group in society. The recent popularity of the marketing concept with its emphasis upon consumer behavior attests to this concern for business ethics. Moreover, the tactics of Ralph Nader, the active crusader for consumer welfare, have persuaded many business managers of their ethical responsibilities. Gilman speculates that a pragmatic sense of morality is indeed developing among businessmen today. Therefore, a code of ethics entailing effective ethical commitments to individuals and groups must be sought as management becomes increasingly professionalized.

Businessmen in general admit that they are aware of conflicts between economic and ethical goals and that many unethical practices occur daily in business practice. On the other hand, they disagree on the morality of specific acts. These businessmen would have the solution come from the chief executive in the organization in the form of written codes of ethics which contain "teeth" for enforcement. Robert W. Austin goes a step further in "A Positive Code of Ethics" [24] when he appeals not only for a code of ethics, but for a positively oriented one. He believes that a listing of "shalt nots" is incapable of meeting managerial needs and must be supplanted by a positive code of ethics that fulfills the professional requirements of management with a commitment to social responsibilities.

B. Business and Religion

The businessman's position is complicated by the absence of a specific body of ethics to which all individuals and groups could refer for the resolution of conflict situations in which morality is involved. For example, the moral and ethical norms as practiced today vary significantly by community, area, and institutional group. Since religions are the major value-forming influences in our society, their impact in particular regions will tend to emphasize differences in the ethical codes. Business, therefore, faces the problem of harmonizing its operations and objectives, particularly those that come into conflict with other groups, by recognizing the prevalent ethical code, estimating its relative legitimacy, and somehow establishing priorities for any areas of conflict. While reference may be made to the Ten Commandments, the Judaeo-Christian ethic, and the religious values contained in the Declaration of Independence and the Constitution, it is extremely difficult for business to bridge the gap between these many statements and their application to current problems.

Attempts have been made to resolve these problems by relating them to religious values and precepts. On the other hand, in the minds of most operating business managers, the chasm existing between business and religion is often regarded as infinite. While the businessman is often reluctant to discuss religion and, in particular, to attempt to relate it in any direct way to business, his need for an operating code of ethics must be met in some degree by value structures finding their roots in religious principles. If business and religion are discussed in the same context, one basic unresolved problem is always present. That is, is there not an essential and inherent conflict between the businessman, his system of capitalism and Christianity or our Judaeo-Christian ethic? Author Thomas C. Campbell, Jr. in "Capitalism and Christianity" [25] refutes this contention. He refers in one example to the number of demands made for a complete separation of business and religion, much like the demand for separation of church and state. Since it is difficult to speak of ethics without having recourse to specific principles identified wth a particular religion, the sectarian problem rears its head. O. A. Ohmann would resolve the sectarian issue in article 26, "Skyhooks," by emphasizing the spiritual principles common to all religions in our society. In his article, he advocates a direct and intimate relationship between religion, business, the individual, and work. Religious values not only will be served but also will be actively related to the workday process by assigning higher priorities to human than to material values. Also, a work environment will be provided in which the individual can relate his work situation to his spiritual aspirations.

Regardless of one's attitude or philosophy about the relationship of religious principles and values to business, there is an overwhelming concern for the development of a philosophy of business more comprehensive in scope and universal in application than now exists. This philosophy would include a consideration of attempts to relate business to the ideals of religion as they affect our society. It would also define the structure of a code of ethics to guide business in conflict situations. Both implicitly and explicitly, this philosophy and code of ethics would serve the needs of the emerging profession of business managers. When the businessman asked for a positive code of ethics with enforcement teeth, they were asking that business management be raised to the level of the other professions in our society.

The call for a code of ethics with enforcement teeth is not an easy undertaking. As is seen in the Nikipoulis Grocery case, the need for a code of ethics is vital in many areas where ethical businessmen are at a serious disadvantage because of the practices of their competitors. Without enforcement teeth in a code of ethics for business groups within communities, only governmental regulations can force the resolution of these conflicts. The other alternative is to join in those practices considered competitively necessary but ethically questionable by our society. The Anatomy of a Price-Fixing Conspiracy case brings us face to face with the realistic pressures in a competitive economy. To impugn the motives of the businessman, particularly in the gray areas of business operation, is not a realistic solution to the problem. Within a freely competitive society and economy, the problems of individual and group conflicts will be perennial, and any easy and automatic resolution of these will not be achieved by a simple formula or statement of an ethical code. This means then that the need of business to develop a code of ethics carries with it a concomitant responsibility for individuals and other groups in society to appreciate the inherent complexities of any free society and, in particular, those conflict areas in the economic realm. It is highly probable that these problems are often created as much by distrust and lack of understanding of motives, complexities, and practices of individuals and groups in our society as by actual unethical intent.

A.   The Ethical Aspects of Business

The Challenge of Business Ethics
22

Robert Freedman

Judging by the outflow of articles, books, and speeches by businessmen and business writers on the subject of business morality, it appears certain that there is a growing concern for the moral responsibilities which the power and the prestige of today's businessmen demand.

In all of the books and articles the refrain is the same—the businessman should accept responsibilities beyond that of profit maximizing. He should be a statesman, concerning himself with the problems of the nation and, indeed, the entire world. He should make decisions on behalf of employees, customers, and stockholders which are judicious and right. Finally, he should cleanse himself of narrow self-interest and devote his energy to the improvement of the individuals with whom he comes into contact.[1]

The contention of this writer is that this is a dead-end approach to the problem of business morality. For many reasons, to be spelled out below, the kind of uneasy compromise which the businessman is being asked to make between his role as administrator of society's physical and human resources and his humanistic goals can never be satisfactory. The businessman must live in an imperfect world and make choices, none of which can be ultimately satisfying. This essay seeks to illuminate the conflict between the businessman's role and his moral goals and to suggest the direction which a resolution of this conflict could take.

The view of social responsibility sketched out above is, according to

Reprinted with permission from the *Atlanta Economic Review* (May 1962), pp. 7-12. The author is grateful to the Lucius N. Littauer Foundation for its aid.

[1] Some books are: B. M. Selekman, *A Moral Philosophy for Management* (New York: McGraw-Hill, 1955); Dan H. Fenn, Jr., *Management's Mission in a New Society* (New York: McGraw-Hill, 1959); Sylvia and Benjamin Selekman, *Power and Morality in a Business Society* (New York: McGraw-Hill, 1956).

business writers, a radical departure from the ideology inherent in the economic model of Adam Smith and his followers which, along with Social Darwinism, formed the attitudes of nineteenth century businessmen.[2] It is my contention that, while this claim is to some extent true, the new morality is essentially a continuation and a refurbishing of the nineteenth century doctrine of trusteeship which demands an attitude of noblesse oblige on the part of the wealthy and powerful.[3]

The nineteenth century world was a simpler one of owner-operated firms in a society whose main problem was widespread poverty and whose economic goal, accordingly, was maximum production. Businessmen, in this world dominated by an ideology derived from Adam Smith and Charles Darwin, had to be ruthlessly competitive. This meant that they saw their roles primarily as administrators of resources and, in general, left social questions to religionists (such as bearers of the Social Gospel) and philanthropists. The imperatives of the economic system did not permit the businessman to concern himself with larger moral issues. He did tend to invoke the Puritan doctrine of hard work and thrift as a goad to himself and his workers, to accept Social Darwinism to justify ruthless competition, and to appeal to Adam Smith (really the Manchester School) to legitimize laissez faire. His rule was to "buy cheap and sell dear." By and large, the ethics of the businessman were subordinated to the necessity to survive.

MORAL CONCERN

A RESULT OF AFFLUENT CORPORATE SOCIETY

A few of the larger business firms and more successful business magnates such as Andrew Carnegie were freed by their monopolistic position to concern themselves with the moral implications of their position. The nineteenth century doctrine of trusteeship grew from the firm conviction that God or nature had not only provided the businessman with success and wealth but had made him responsible for the administration of this wealth in the interests of those less fortunate.[4] The marriage of Social Darwinism and the Protestant Ethic produced in certain affluent nineteenth century businessmen attitudes quite similar to those now widely held by twentieth century businessmen, if the literature to which I have earlier alluded accurately reflects the modern climate of opinion. The connection between the nine-

---

2 W. G. Sumner, *The Challenge of Facts, and Other Essays*, ed., A. G. Keller (New Haven: Yale Press, 1914).

3 Andrew Carnegie, "Wealth," *North American Review*, June 1889.

4 This is different from A. Smith's total conception in *A Theory of Moral Sentiments* and *The Wealth of Nations*. In *A Theory of Moral Sentiments* the doctrine of trusteeship is suggested by man's inherent "fellow feeling," but in the more famous work fellow feeling is strongly supported by the dispersion of power through competition.

teenth and twentieth century business ideology is this: the widespread affluence of modern corporate society protected by large size from the immediate pressures of the market has made it possible for a large number of business executives to be concerned not simply with the profits of their firms, but the morality of their actions. What is new is not the doctrine of trusteeship, which was held by certain affluent nineteenth century Puritan businessmen such as Daniel Drew, Rockefeller, and Henry Ford, but the degree to which it is now spread throughout our society.

Today, big business, because of the general affluence of our society and the size of the economic unit, has surpluses to distribute. The question which businessmen are asking themselves is, "How shall these surpluses be distributed?" What the businessman seeks to find out is what constitutes moral action under conditions of affluence.

I have no quarrel with this question. The world is certainly better because corporations now attempt to treat generously and humanely employees and executives on all levels who have lost their usefulness by keeping them on salary by various featherbedding devices. Also, there seems to be a clear social gain as business firms continually increase their contributions to worthy charities such as universities,[5] the Community Chest, and so forth. Class conflict is reduced to the extent that businessmen believe that wages should be "fair" rather than competitive; profits should be "reasonable" rather than exorbitant; and prices should be noninflationary. International relations can be served (and also the long-run interests of the firm) when business firms can be successfully reminded of their moral obligation to pursue the goals of American foreign policy while conducting business abroad.

A DEPARTURE FROM THE TRADITIONAL MANDATE OF BUSINESS

But what proponents of this view of business morality have never adequately shown, and I doubt that such a demonstration is possible, is that the businessman, whose clear mandate (derived from the intellectual tradition of Adam Smith and his successors) is to allocate society's scarce resources in accordance with individual and social demand, has either a moral right or obligation to take upon himself the righting of social wrongs according to his own view of this matter or as a special agent of society.

My reasons for holding this view are these: In the first place, the theory which justifies private property and free enterprise, limits the role of the businessman to that of allocator of physical and human resources. The businessman receives his income from providing these services to society. In a

[5] For a particular business firm to contribute to a particular university or group of universities may not be economically rational even though it appears to be an investment in human capital. The reason is that the "return" to the firm cannot be calculated and, given the diffuse consequences of education, is probably less than the outlay.

highly competitive economy, he simply reacts to or anticipates successfully the desires of consumers. Where competition is perfect, there is no corporate economic surplus for social purposes. If wages are "too low," it is because of low worker productivity, poor organization on the part of the worker, poor management, or small demand for the product. If wages in a particular industry cannot adequately meet some "basic" standard of income, it is the obligation of society through the tax system or other devices to redistribute income in socially desirable ways. It is neither the prerogative nor the responsibility of the businessman to decide these issues in his corporate role. *Since, in the theory of free enterprise, the individual businessman does not create social problems, he, in his role as businessman, is not responsible for their solution.*

INHERENT PROBLEMS

Criteria for Judgment? It may be objected that whatever may be said of the origin of surpluses, they do exist and the businessman must distribute them in some way. I agree. But it remains true, nevertheless, that the fact that the businessman *must* act does not make any specific action morally defensible. The most important reason for saying this is that *the businessman has no generally acceptable criteria for judging the relative worth of different individuals or different groups.* Since there is no way in which the businessman can be moral with respect to the nation, world, employees, stockholders, and the public at the same time, he must make choices based on some criteria and according to some hierarchy of values. For this decision, only his intuition, prejudices, or class attitudes are available.[6]

The Morality of Power Itself? Another point, which is not often considered in the writings on this subject, relates to the morality of power itself. By what right do some men order the lives of others—even for good? What right has the soap manufacturer to use the profits earned in selling soap to influence social life according to his personal outlook? The problem of the right to the use of power is either evaded or ignored by business writers. Even those whom I shall presently refer to as conservative critics —nonbusiness leaders such as theologians and economists who generally accept the buiness civilization as it is but opt for marginal improvement— generally would reduce the abuse of power rather than challenge the businessman's right to power.

[6] Two interesting collections of essays, one edited by H. F. Merrill, called *The Responsibilities of Business Leadership,* and another by T. V. Houser, *Business and Human Values,* exhort the businessman to be responsible in all areas of social life. Unfortunately there is no hint as to what responsibility consists of, and there is no suggestion for determining a priority system of values between the various claimants.

The Morality of Business Itself?   Finally, a standpoint which is entirely overlooked in the discussion of business morality is that of the morality of the system taken as a whole. Can any business system be moral? The businessman, in dealing with problems of moral action, usually takes the business system as given and never raises the question of whether an individual can act morally in a system which itself may be inherently immoral.

Before businessmen can begin to deal adequately with the problem of business morality they must delve into the questions raised above. The literature on business morality, for the most part, shows no insight into these issues.

THE LITERATURE ON BUSINESS MORALITY

In the literature on business morality, the businessman is exhorted to act morally for three general reasons, the lesser of which concerns the matter of prudence. It is sometimes argued that the misuse of power could lead to the loss of the free enterprise system, to socialism or other forms of governmental intervention.[7] Sometimes the misuse of business power is decried in terms of America's world position.[8] Our prestige as a good society is at stake.

But the most important concern is the purely moral one. Business power is to be used wisely for its own sake, as a matter of commitment to moral responsibility. A large number of articles appearing in *Fortune, Harvard Business Review, Rotarian, Dun's Review, Nation's Business,* and *America* exhort businessmen to act morally. But rarely do writers deal with the basic issues raised above. The clear implication of the literature is that the businessman can become morally responsible simply by the process of self-examination and character training. Most of these writers appear to be unaware of the fact that the businessman's capacity for autonomous action is limited by the requirements of maintaining a profitable concern. The businessman is by no means free to do what is "right." Failure to understand that there may be a conflict of what is "right" and what is "necessary" leads many of these writers to the view that outside social checks on the businessman are unnecessary. For implicit in the argument is that once the businessman sees the true meaning of morality, he will reform himself.[9]

[7] For example: C. B. Randall, "Free Enterprise Is Not a Hunting License," *Atlantic Monthly,* March 1952; W. K. Jackson, "Citizen Heal Thyself," *Nation's Business,* December, 1946.

[8] For example: B. M. Selekman, "Cynicism and Managerial Morality," *Harvard Business Review,* September 1958.

[9] See: "The Moral History of U. S. Business," *Fortune,* December 1949; "The Transformation of American Capitalism," *Fortune,* February 1951; Frederick Meyers, "Dual Standards for Corruption," *The Nation,* March 1, 1958; Bernard DeVoto, "Why Professors Are Suspicious of Business," *Fortune,* April 1951; W. A. Orton, "Business and Ethics," *Fortune,* October 1948; L. Finkelstein, "Businessmen's Moral Failure," *Fortune,* September 1958.

CONSERVATIVE CRITICS

It is only this last aspect of the problem of business power that is widely criticized outside of business circles by conservative critics. Conservative critics limit their concern to the reduction of the degree of arbitrary power rather than the morality of power itself. What conservative critics find wrong with concentrated power is that it might be misused.

Most academic economists are conservative critics who derive their critical view of the economic order from the politico-economic model of perfect competition inherited from Adam Smith and his followers. Adam Smith's model of perfect competition solves the twin problems of optimum resource allocation and arbitrary power by the device of removing the power of decision from the businessman. The businessman simply reacts to prices and costs provided impersonally by the market. In Adam Smith's monopoly-free model, the businessman is provided no leeway for autonomous action.

Reduce, Not Remove, Business Power. Conservative critics are, above all, "realists" who, recognizing that perfect competition cannot and perhaps ought not be achieved, compromise the issue of business power by advocating policies to reduce rather than eliminate it. Antitrust prosecution and governmental regulation are the basic policies of this group. Most economists recognize and defend the fact that such policies fail to eliminate business power. They would prefer to leave some power in the hands of large firms in the interests of "progress," which Schumpeter assures them requires some degrees of monopoly.

J. K. Galbraith[10] solves the problem of excessive power by elaborating a theory of "countervailing power" which also limits power without eliminating it. This doctrine of checks and balances starts with the assumption that there is a tendency to monopoly in modern large-scale society. Galbraith declares as virtually a natural law that "original" power begets countervailing power. The existence of power itself brings about its own check.

Whatever the device, economists seem generally satisfied to deal with only one aspect of the moral problem—the problem of the excessive concentration of power.[11] The only argument between economists and businessmen is that businessmen believe that they don't require checks to power and the economists believe that they do. But conservative programs leave economic surpluses in the hands of business firms, unlike Adam Smith's perfectly competitive order, which does not. Thus the modern economist is content to leave this surplus for distribution by the businessman so long as these

---

[10] J. K. Galbraith, *American Capitalism* (New York: Houghton Mifflin Co., 1952).

[11] Of the economists, Sylvia and Benjamin Selekman are the only ones in the literature reviewed who see that the problem of power goes beyond that of market power. Sylvia and Benjamin Selekman, *Power and Morality in a Business Society* (New York: McGraw-Hill, 1956).

surpluses are not used to the detriment of other groups such as consumers and laborers.

Even modern Protestant theologians are content with the conservative formula. In the entire series of books sponsored by the Federal Council of Churches of Christ in America (now merged with the National Council of Churches of Christ in America) nothing is added to the criticism of the conservative economists. Howard Bowen, an economist rather than a theologian, has written the most complete statement of position in the entire series of books.[12]

Control Through Law and Organized Groups.   Bowen notes that since individuals cannot be trusted to have selfless motives, social control through law is justified. He also recommends the countervailing power of unions and cooperative organizations. As religiously oriented people do, he tries to place the burden of morality upon the businessman by stipulating the following responsibilities: the businessman should recognize the dignity of the worker and should show compassion toward him. He should deal justly with customers, suppliers, and everyone else with whom he deals. He should not discriminate on the basis of race and color; he should provide opportunity for the self-development of the young, provide safer and healthier working conditions, pay just wages, and recognize human need as one of the criteria for compensation.

This position, although it compromises the issue of power, takes him somewhat further than Galbraith. It leaves unsolved the question of priorities among recipients, leaves unanswered the question of the right of the businessman to make decisions as to the comparative values of different persons, and leaves entirely alone the question of the morality of the business system as a whole.

Even one of America's most perceptive theologians, Reinhold Niebuhr, has little to add. His pessimistic view of human nature leads him away from radical or utopian solutions. The best that he can suggest is that men of affairs turn to religion, affirm the law of love, become aware of the persistent dangers of self-love, and develop a sense of responsibility toward others. Niebuhr, the realist, then goes on to suggest that power be reduced by creation of a system of balance and equilibria of power.[13]

Thus, the real distinction between conservative critics and the businessman is simply that the conservative critics doubt that the individual businessman by soul-searching can be depended upon to act with moral restraint.

---

[12] H. R. Bowen, *Social Responsibilities of the Businessman* (New York: Harper, 1951). Other books not cited elsewhere in this series have such titles as A. D. Ward, *Goals of Economic Life;* K. Boulding, *The Organizational Revolution;* J. C. Bennett, et al., *Christian Values and Economic Life.*

[13] In J. M. Hughley, *Trends in Protestant Idealism* (New York: Columbia University Press, 1948), p. 151.

They compromise the *in principle* problem of the right of the businessman to exert social power beyond that which is mandated by his social role as an administrator of society's resources, and then evade the other moral issues.

THE CONFLICT: BUSINESS SYSTEM VS. MORALITY

Ever since the Industrial Revolution there has been a drumfire of radical criticism of the business system. Socialists, Christian Socialists, Christian Democrats, medievalists, humanitarians, humanists, radical agrarians, and others have always made the argument that the business system is immoral in principle. It is neither possible nor necessary in this short space to develop the arguments of all of these groups in detail. Essential characteristics bind the arguments together.

A society which puts material things ahead of spiritual values, a society which treats individuals as if they were commodities on the market, a society which places the individual on a level above that of the group, a society which builds greed and avarice into its social system, which coops men up in factories, which fights wars for profit, which substitutes competition for brotherhood is, according to this criticism, clearly undesirable.[14] In the business literature reviewed, virtually no one deals with the morality of the system as a whole.

Protestant theologians do, of course, see the conflict between acquisitive and Christian values; but with Reinhold Niebuhr, they tend to despair, accepting this as the only world they are likely to be able to get, denying the optimistic view that man can create the Kingdom of Heaven on earth, being grateful for small reforms.

In the modern idiom Frank Knight, the great economist-philosopher, has provided the most incisive, devastating, and relevant evaluation of the morality of the business system to be found anywhere.[15]

WHOSE WANTS ARE TO BE SATISFIED?

In his classic article Knight argues that the only legitimate function of the system of free enterprise is to satisfy consumer wants. However, such a view leaves unanswered certain important and sticky questions related to values. *Whose* wants are to be satisfied is a question of prime importance in judg-

---

14 Although much of this criticism has been voiced since the inception of the industrial revolution, not all of it represents criticism relevant for modern capitalism. Some of it is romantically nostalgic for a long-lost primitive ideal. Some is simply anti-industrial. But the point is that they ask a basic question, "Is this a good society?" Business writers invariably assume the basic morality of the industrial system itself.

15 Frank Knight, "The Ethics of Competition," *Quarterly Journal of Economics,* 1923 pp. 579–624. This is a basic article, echoes of which can be found in W. H. White, *The Organization, Man;* David Reisman's writings; and most all sophisticated social criticism today.

ing the morality of the system. The question of whose wants are to be satisfied is related to the entire question of distribution of income, which is in turn related to the great issues of social justice. Why should the highest income go to the economically productive? Why not to the most virtuous, the most needy, and so forth? The economy may require as an operating principle a close connection between work and rewards. But this is a prudential rather than a moral argument.

WHICH WANTS ARE TO BE SATISFIED?

Second, the question of *which* wants are to be satisfied has been raised by Knight. Our economy satisfies whatever wants individuals in our society prefer, with certain exceptions such as habit-forming drugs. But this does not mean that simply because the wants we have are not damaging, they are desirable. Articles of conspicuous consumption, for example, may not be destructive of the character of the user, but they may bring about envy in others.

HOW ARE WANTS CREATED?

A third point is that the economic system is the *creator of wants*, although it is supposed to be simply the satisfier of wants. It creates wants both in the sense of *goods* and in the sense of *activity*, which help mold human personality. By producing and distributing the goods which some people want, the system helps to create a desire for emulation on the part of others. Whether emulation is a desirable human characteristic may be debated.

As an activity, Knight shows that the business system creates the kind of personality necessary for business success. In the era of laissez faire the inner-directed, frugal, work-oriented, self-centered, money-oriented, shrewd are more likely to succeed. In the milder climate of today's world, William Whyte tells us that the other-directed, security-minded, adaptable, gregarious conformist is best suited to business success. In either event, the issue is raised by Knight as to whether the personality types created by the economic system are ethically desirable.

IS BUSINESS A GAME?

Finally, although he goes much further than this, Knight evaluates business as a *competitive game*. Knight says "the good man has given way to the good sport." And what is the good sport? A man who plays the game and accepts its outcome. Whether the game is ethically defensible or whether the contest is in some sense noble is not to be questioned.

Knight's position raises basic issues. Economic life cannot be separated from social life, and to some extent the kind of a man you are depends upon the kind of thing that you do. There are moral consequences to work as well as to other human activities. Ultimately, according to Knight, the businessman must face up to the fact that the economic system has its own logic. The businessman who wishes to be a moral being is faced by the dilemma of having to participate in an economic order whose morality is itself in doubt.

IN SUMMARY

This article has sketched out with extreme brevity the wide areas which have been left untouched by the businessman in his search for moral standards in his role as a businessman. I contend that the businessman has not begun to understand the complexity of the problem which faces him and, until he does, can make no certain progress in his quest. The largest obstacle to progress is, I believe, that he does not understand that the problem of doing right cannot emerge from introspection and developing the habits of "right thinking." He must understand first that moral action is always restrained and conditioned by the environment in which the individual acts. Thus the businessman qua businessman should realize that there is often no escape from compromising what is right and what is necessary. In the end the business role demands that the businessman protect his business and encourage its growth. Attempts to compromise may only lead him away from his prime responsibility as allocator of society's resources toward the custodianship of social power which, I have argued, is not within the businessman's province of capacity.

The psychological burden of social power and responsibility is, I am sure, the force which compels the businessman to go beyond this role and seek to legitimize through good works the power which he exerts. Were he divested of this power, the burden would disappear. He needs to understand that it is society's job to ensure social justice, not his.

Society, as a practical matter, means government. But to substitute government ownership or regulation of business for private is to change the cast of characters who are burdened with moral problems of power. Therefore the solution is not found in governmentalizing society.

To prevent the exercise of power of man over man, each individual must be provided with adequate and roughly equal power. No man should depend on the good will of another for his protection. The difficulty with any kind of paternalism—business or governmental—is not only that it depends on the moral sense of the powerful (which may be faulty), but that it degrades the recipient. Business ethics as evidenced by what businessmen and their spokesmen write and say seem to suggest that, as a solution to the problem of power, businessmen become more paternalistic. This point of view ought to be rejected out of hand.

However, any imaginable society is likely to contain hierarchies of responsibility and therefore have a tendency toward differential power. It is therefore concluded that it is the *moral* responsibility of the businessman to demand no more than that power which is clearly relevant to his role as businessman, to reject the paternalistic solution, and to welcome social checks in the form of countervailing power as one device to prevent the misuse of power to which most human beings are prone. In the policy sense this "solution" is quite conservative. It simply suggests that marginal rather than radical change in the social structure be made. It appeals to policies such as countervailing power. It is conservative partly because there is much of value to conserve and partly because radical social change is often more damaging than the evil it intends to correct.

In another sense it is conservative because it does not attempt to deal with the more general and difficult issues raised by those who deny that any business (or even industrial) system can be moral. This writer tends to the view implicit in the position of conservative theologians that while a business society cannot maximize the moral life, it can at least minimize the immortality of arbitrary power.

In an ideological sense this solution is radical. It affirms that the businessman face up to the necessity for conducting himself by one set of rules in his capacity as businessman and by another in his capacity as citizen.

This essay has argued that the businessman with moral concerns should not attempt to bridge the gap by refusing to fulfill his commitment as businessman. To commit oneself to be a businessman is to agree to follow rules which may conflict with one's social sense. If an individual cannot accept the commitment to act as a businessman, he should seek a more congenial career.

It may be that it is psychologically unsatisfactory, if not impossible, for thoughtful people to be five-day sinners and two-day saints. However, so long as it remains true that the mandates of the business system are often in conflict with the moral imperatives of the Judeo-Christian tradition, and so long as the business system is thought to be the best realistic alternative, the businessman has no option but to follow the rules of his occupation. In his role as citizen, the morally responsible individual should direct himself to the improvement of the general climate of social life.

When the businessman learns to give up the personal quest for standards of moral action in his role as businessman and permit society its proper role in this area, he may then be freed to go about the task which justifies his control of society's resources—the creation of wealth.

The Ethical Dimension in American Management

23

Glenn Gilman

The intense public interest in the electrical company conspiracy trials of 1961 is but one instance demonstrating that the ethical behavior of management in our society is a matter of current concern to the American public. This has not always been true. As a business society we have always been interested in business behavior, good or bad, but until the last few decades our attitude toward the latter has been generally the same as our attitude toward bad weather: it is regrettable but inevitable, of no more than local concern, and apparently beyond our control.

It was not until the 1930's that we had even indirect evidence that sporadic national interest had changed to continuing national concern. Beginning with the Norris-La Guardia Act and extending through every administration since, an increasingly complex network of legislation and government control has established boundaries within which business practices must be contained. We can draw only one of two conclusions from this phenomenon. Few of us accept the possibility of one of the alternatives: that continuously for more than thirty years, in one of the most important sectors of our society, our democratic processes have broken down to the extent that government at the national level has failed to represent the will of the people. The other alternative is that society has concluded that:

1. Business morality is a matter of national rather than merely local importance.

2. It can be controlled.

3. Businessmen themselves cannot be depended on to control their own morality in the national interest.

More recent developments have been the implicit acceptance by the business community itself of the first two assumptions and its efforts to disprove the validity of the third. Those developments are reflected by an unmistakable trend in the literature tending to foreshadow changes in the managerial philosophy underlying business policies and practices. A casual glance through the journals that are read by upper and upper-middle management in our society—*Business Horizons*, the *California Management Review*, *Fortune*, the *Harvard Business Review*, the *Journal of Business*, for

Reprinted from the *California Management Review*, Vol. III, No. 1 (Fall 1964), pp. 45–52.
Copyright © 1964 by the Regents of the University of California.

example—discloses that during the last decade a significant and increasing proportion of their papers and articles deal with business ethics.

For the most part these papers criticize, admonish, or advise. Very rarely do they attempt to defend the existing state of managerial morality. None of them are laudatory. Titles such as "The Businessman's Moral Failure,"[1] "Can Management Afford to Ignore Social Responsibilities?"[2] "Moral Hazards of an Executive,"[3] "Toward a New Moral Philosophy for Business,"[4] and "The Apologetics of Managerialism"[5] are typical. We must add to these a respectable output of recent books directed toward the public as well as toward businessmen carrying such titles as *Ethics in a Business Society,*[6] *Big Business and Human Values,*[7] and *The American Business Creed.*[8] We cannot overlook the popular magazines. Even *Playboy* devoted 360 column inches in its November 1962 issue to a panel discussion on "Business Ethics and Morality"!

CONCERN OVER MORALITY

Why this current concentration of concern with the ethical character of modern business shared alike by the general public, by spokesmen for business, and by business educators? Are the managers of our enterprises so much less concerned for others than were their predecessors that a crash reform program is needed? Are they so insensitive to the expectations of our society as to the ethical and moral implications of their business decisions that we have no choice but to restrain them by legislative and administrative decrees?

Restraint may be eventually required. We certainly are not justified in ruling it out as a possibility. But let's look a little further before making a final judgment. There may be other considerations that encourage our concern over managerial morality.

A MASS SOCIETY

The United States has not been a great mass society for very long: in some respects, it still fights desperately to deny that it now is. For most of our history we have been a related group of folk-regional societies made up in turn of folk communities, dotted here and there with unassimilated concentrations (mostly urban) of immigrants. These concentrations had very little

[1] Louis Finkelstein, *Fortune*, September 1958, p. 116 ff.

[2] Keith, Davis, *California Management Review*, Spring 1960, pp. 70–76.

[3] Louis W. Norris, *Harvard Business Review*, September-October 1960, pp. 72–79.

[4] Henry M. Oliver, *Business Horizons*, Spring 1958, pp. 33–43.

[5] Edward S. Mason, *Journal of Business*, January 1958.

[6] Marquis Childs and Douglass Cater (New York: Harper and Brothers, 1954).

[7] Theodore Hill (New York: McGraw-Hill Book Co., 1957).

[8] Francis X. Sutton, *et al.* (New York: Schocken Books, 1956, paperback edition 1962).

to do with the development of social consensus anywhere, either directly or through being "taken into account." The business decisions that affected those within the significant units of consensus were mostly local or regional. To a considerable degree we could depend on local and regional mores to contain them within the bounds of expected propriety.[9] Once in a while, national issues arose, such as labor difficulty on the railroads or the threat of a combine that might raise the price of sugar or tobacco or steel, but these had the appearance of random phenomena that intruded into the local scene without really threatening to displace it as the center of our lives.

However, we can no longer confine our concern to the possibility that rail service may be halted or that a combine may raise commodity prices in a limited area of the market. Ours has become a complex mass society, particularly in its economic structure. The business decisions of managers far beyond the reach of local mores may have important and lasting consequences for every one of us.

ECONOMIC INTERDEPENDENCE

Yet this economic interdependence, significant though it is, is perhaps less important than our evolution from merely a business to a corporate society.[10] A tremendous concentration of power, extending well beyond the simply economic, has evolved to rest with a relatively few great enterprises. At any given time their managerial decisions can affect our political climate, the cultural tone of our society, even the opportunities for aesthetic choice open to us. We have become their "publics" in the truest sense of the word. That is, we may choose between the alternatives they offer us, but in the short run we have no power to affect the range of choice.

But it is not the ethical implications of top management decisions alone that concern most of us today. Few of us enjoy even that shadow of economic independence that many of our fathers rejoiced in as many farmers, small proprietors, independent craftsmen, or professional men. We have become a nation of employees. When this change is equated with the change in the basic structure of our society from folk to mass, from rural culture to urban civilization, the resultant has important economic as well as ethical connotations.

For all practical purposes, many of us are committed to employment with a single company for the balance of our lives. We must look to the accumu-

---

[9] See Glenn Gilman, *Human Relations in the Industrial Southeast* (Chapel Hill: University of North Carolina Press, 1956), especially chapter IX, for a discussion of the influence of regional mores and folkways on business decisions. See also W. Lloyd Warner and J. O. Low, "The Factory in the Community" in W. F. Whyte, ed., *Industrial and Society* (New York: McGraw-Hill Book Co., 1954) for an example of its operation in the Northeast.

[10] See, for example, W. Lloyd Warner, *The Corporation in the Emergent American Society* (New York: Harper and Brothers, 1962), especially chapter 2.

lated seniority benefits resulting from unbroken service for the security that even fifty years ago existed in the three-generation family charged to "look after its own" by the still powerful mores of our folk heritage. We can no longer afford to change jobs to escape a ruthless supervisor or an arbitrary department manager. We must hope for equity in compensation and promotion where we are. The ethical behavior of every official in the organization above us becomes a matter of personal concern if changing jobs is no longer a practical way to deal with inequitable treatment.

CONTROL OF ETHICS

The last statement can be generalized to cover the whole range of managerial behavior as it affects us personally. When the decisions, the policies, and the practices of someone over whom we have no effective personal control have personal meaning for us, our first hope is that he will "do the right thing" on the basis of his own convictions. Even the possibility that formal pressure in our behalf can be brought to bear on him from some direction is not a satisfactory substitute. Such pressure can at best be no no more than intermittent; it tends to have mainly long-run effectiveness in situations where short-run relief is needed.

We feel this not only as employees but as consumers. Under a simpler economy the range of consumer products offered to us did not include many whose complexity or highly technical nature put them beyond our capability to evaluate their quality. The policy of "let the buyer beware" was neither unrealistic nor necessarily unethical. But many of the products we regard as necessities today—such as automobiles and television sets— can be judged a to quality and fairness of price only by experts with laboratories at their disposal. As consumers we have to depend not only on the integrity of dealers and manufacturers but on the personal standards of each production supervisor. We can only hope, for example, that he has had sufficient moral fiber to resist taking short-cuts that may reduce quality merely to meet his production quota. As consumers we have an intuitive appreciation for what Quality Control tells the people on the line: "We can't *inspect* quality into this product. You've got to *build* it in!" We cannot escape dependence on the ethics of management even for such simple products as our foodstuffs. For many products modern packaging denies us the opportunity for personal inspection. We take on faith what it says on the label.

THE GREATEST GOOD

Our increasing personal stake in managerial behavior could not become really influential were it not for a second factor. The significant unit of consensus within our society believes it can afford to be considerably more critical of managerial behavior today than in the past. Until recently we saw our principal problems as those of production. How could we turn out enough goods to meet the effective demands of our expanding population? Fifty years ago we forgave our managers a great deal so long as they "delivered the goods" in a quite literal sense. Our tolerance for the methods they used to supply us with capital tools and consumer goods was based neither on greed nor on a cynical philosophy of materialism. For the first time in man's history we sensed that there was some real hope for freeing most of the citizens of a great society from the dehumanizing clutch of sheer physical want. With this greater goal in sight we were not inclined to hamper the managers who were carrying us toward it by insisting that they contain their efforts within formally defined channels of ethical behavior. And very few of those whose opinions made up the significant unit of consensus were affected adversely by the behavior of those managers.[11]

Pragmatically and perhaps unconsciously, we subscribed to the doctrine of the greatest good for the greatest number. If a minority of us were hurt in the short run in the process of advancing the interests of the majority in the long run, it was part of the price we had to pay. We were willing to accept the immediate social cost of economic progress when it foreshadowed the possibility of immeasurably more valuable social gains in the long run.

AN AFFLUENT SOCIETY?

Today the three-fifths of us who have family incomes greater than $6,000 a year or individual incomes greater than $3,000 a year have come to take production for granted. (These income figures are important, since they establish roughly the lower limits of the significant unit of consensus of our society, which in turn generates the assumptions that "we" hold as a society.[12]) Those of us who make up this unit have come to take production for granted. We assume that in general our productive capacity exceeds our ability to distribute its product. We find it easy to believe that we are indeed an affluent society. We feel there is sufficient margin of productive capacity to afford our concern with the short-run ethical implications of economic development. We see no reason why we cannot now insist that managerial practices be ethical in all directions and respects even though our insistence might limit the maximum volume of production possible at any one time. Having bought economic progress at the expense of certain concessions to social justice, we

---

11 See chapter III, "The Contending Forces," in Childs and Cater, *op. cit.*

12 See Gunner Myrdal, *Challenge to Affluence* (New York: Random House, 1962), pp. 46–49. His data are from *Poverty and Deprivation in the United States* (Washington: Conference on Economic Progress, 1962). He makes the point, substantiating my own judgment that the 40 per cent of our citizens who live below the level of deprivation play little or no part in establishing consensus in our society. Their voices, when they are heard at all, are the voices of protest and disillusionment.

feel in position to afford social justice even though it may entail some economic cost.[13]

It is characteristic of human behavior that neither our need nor our ability to act will move us to action unless we see a chance that action will be effective. In this case, our conviction that ethical business behavior is important to us and our belief that we can afford it are not enough by themselves to explain the rising flood of exhortation and appeal for ethically right conduct directed toward managers. Since the flood exists and gives every indication of continuing with unabated vigor, a third causative factor is suggested—that we believe management can behave ethically.

THE LAW OF THE JUNGLE

We have not always thought so. Until well into the present century, most of us accepted as a matter of course that Spencer's doctrine of the primacy of the law of the jungle was applicable to the business community. Given our premises, there was some degree of logic in our conclusion. Ethical behavior, we were taught, required that we take no thought for ourselves in our concern for others. But we recognized that no business could survive on this basis. Its managers had to concern themselves first of all with their own interests—with the interests of firms to which their own where inextricably tied. It followed therefore that since businesses could not operate on ethical principles as we defined them, its managers could not be expected to take ethical principles into account in their business decisions.[14]

Following this line of reasoning we accepted what we assumed to be inevitable. All we as a society could do was chain this amoral beast, the enterprise, with restrictive legislation and be thankful that once outside their offices its managers could be faithful husbands, kind fathers, and worthy members of the community. We resigned ourselves to what we felt was a fundamental law of nature—that when they entered their offices, they were required to check their ethical principles outside the door.

FALLACIOUS CONCLUSIONS

We now recognize some fallacies in this dismal conclusion of earlier generations. In the first place we realize that this toleration of unethical business behavior was in part a rationalization as long as "Production at any cost!" was the slogan. However, after a century of intensive and reasonably objective study of social processes, including an examination of the actual role of

---

[13] But while we may tend to assume that social justice carries an economic price tag, Myrdal says (*op. cit.*, pp. 64–65) "*Never in the history of America has there been a greater and more complete identity between the ideals of social justice and the requirements of economic progress.*" The italics are Myrdal.

[14] See chapter IV, "Modern Man and Modern Dogma," in Childs and Cater, *op. cit.*

ethical systems and values in a society, we are now inclined to believe that these businessmen of the past were not operating outside the boundaries of ethical constraint as we had assumed. They were outside a set of ethical principles to which the society they served gave lip service. There is no evidence that the society itself actually lived by them.

We think of the Victorian age, for example, as a time when a double standard prevailed for many areas besides sexual behavior. Formal obeisance was paid to an impossibly high ethical code, based mainly on philosophical and theological speculation rather than the realities of human existence; but at the same time its day-to-day decisions in all phases of human activity were being made on the basis of a pragmatically developed sense of morality that reflected somewhat more accurately the actual needs and conditions of a particular society at a particular time and place in the flow of history.[15]

When we examine what we might call the "ethics in action" of any society we find they provide effective control over business as well as non-business relationships. If managers appear to ignore formally stated moral criteria in their business dealings, it is because their enveloping society has implicitly granted them a waiver in this respect, rather than because business affairs are by nature outside the bounds of moral judgment. There is, in other words, no real evidence to substantiate the opinion that business decisions by their nature must ignore the ethical expectations of the society in which they are made. The evidence points the other way. Business decisions reflect the practical ethical system by which a society lives.

The assumption that managerial behavior can be contained within a working system of ethics is based on a somewhat more modest definition of ethical practice. So long as we were a federation of folk-regional societies we could live fairly comfortably under a dual system of ethics. Informal, and for the most part unconsciously held, understandings about the degree and kind of deviations from the formally stated code that were permitted were shared by the membership of our significant social units. These units were organized more effectively and more extensively by their informally shared understandings than by their formally stated precepts.

GUIDING PRINCIPLES

But a great mass society such as we have now become cannot operate effectively on the basis of informally shared and for the most part unexpressed understandings. It must look mainly to formal and explicit statements for practical guidance. Consequently our understanding of the nature of ethical concepts has had to be revised. We now expect them to be guiding principles that will help us to retain a sense of our own identity and our self-respect

[15] See Samuel H. Miller, "The Tangle of Ethics," *Harvard Business Review,* January–February 1960, pp. 59–62.

while at the same time we live in peace and harmony with our fellow men. It is no longer enough for them to serve principally as remote, perhaps unattainable, goals toward which we all agree we ought to strive.

This rethinking about the nature of ethical behavior has nearly eliminated the idea that it must necessarily be selfless, that it always requires one to put the interests of others ahead of one's own. Instead, we think it requires us to take the interests of others into account while we serve our own; and that our emphasis be on seeking an accommodative solution for divergent or conflicting interests rather than either meek surrender or callous ignorance of other's interests.

To put it another way, we think of ethical behavior as an operative sense of responsibility and accountability to those who may be affected by what we do.[16] In this day of fragmented ownership of large corporations, when it is difficult to exercise effective positive control over the short-run actions of top managements through formal lines of responsibility and accountability, we are especially sensitive to the need for managers who have a built-in sense of responsibility and accountability to the public.

Not only are we inclined to believe that, contrary to former opinion, managements have always operated within the actual (though not necessarily the ostensible) ethical systems of their society. We also feel that ethical behavior, defined in realizable terms, presents no barrier to the successful operation of a business. We feel that a sense of responsibility and of accountability to the public is a necessary qualification for the practical pursuit of managerial success.

REDUCED SENSITIVITY?

Now we can return to the first possibility mentioned in explanation of the current concern for managerial morality. Has management actually become less ethical in its behavior since the 1920's? Has the increasingly secular nature of our society, which has made us more sensitive to the need for managerial morality, actually reduced management's sensitivity to our need? While this is not an impossibility either from a common-sense point of view or in terms of social theory, a better explanation may be that we now expect so much more from our managers because our exhortations are more a function of our own anxiety than of their failure.

There is some rather suggestive evidence that the latter is the case and also occasional and well-reported instances to the contrary. Our judgment ought

---

[16] For example, the following comment on the philosophy of H. Richard Niebuhr, one of our great modern theologians, is found in Paul Ramsey, *Nine Modern Moralists* (Englewood Cliffs, N.J.: Prentice-Hall, Inc., 1962), p. 153. "Of all ethical notions none is more congenial to Niebuhr's main perspective on man and morals than the concept of 'responsibility.' In brief, to be ethically responsible means to be a responding being in relation to other beings."

to be based on an appraisal of broad, significant, and well-defined trends in managerial practice rather than on specific cases of misconduct that have been sufficiently spectacular to have attracted the attention of the national press. Appraising these trends, it appears that a number of the most important developments in management practice during recent decades are not only directly germane to our discussion but have positive implications for increasing ethical sensitivity in the business community.

THE HUMAN RELATIONS APPROACH

The development of the human relations approach in management, which began in the early 1930's, has been fundamentally a move toward improving the internal ethics of the firm. Though it originated mainly with social scientists who used industrial and business firms for their laboratories, its acceptance by management during the late forties and the fifties was so enthusiastic that its survival was for a while actually imperiled by overemphasis. A later generation of university-based consultants and advisors to management helped pull it back into focus and reassured managers that concern for the interests of the firm was quite as legitimate as for those of employees.[17] It appears now to be settling into a truly accommodative process within which managements sincerely look for solutions that will maintain the integrity of the interests of their firms and their work forces alike.

THE INCREASING PROFESSIONALIZATION OF MANAGEMENT

This movement contains two related but separate aspects: the emergence of the professional manager, and the desire of managers for truly professional stature. The first aspect is, of course, a result of the wide diversification of ownership of most modern corporations. Managerial staffs are largely made up of men for whom management is a vocation rather than an activity incidental to the expansion or preservation of personal or family fortunes. Since these men have been formally educated for management and because ownership of the enterprises they serve is ordinarily lodged with a vaguely defined and amorphous group of shareholders, their first loyalty is to the firm itself. They become concerned about the long-run survival of an enterprise rather than its short-run profit position. Thus they are likely to weigh very carefully the eventual socio-political consequences of short-run economic

---

[17] For good recent statements of the human relations approach, see Douglas McGregor, *The Human Side of Enterprise* (New York: McGraw-Hill Book Co., 1960), and Rensis Likert, *New Patterns of Management* (New York: McGraw-Hill Book Co., 1961). For its treatment with reservations, see George S. Odiorne, *How Managers Make Things Happen* (Englewood Cliffs, N.J.: Prentice-Hall, Inc., 1961). See also Glenn Gilman, "An Inquiry Into the Nature and Use of Authority," Mason Haire, ed., *Organization Theory in Industrial Practice* (New York: Wiley and Sons, 1962).

expediency. In other words, for what seem to them to be quite practical reasons their decisions are reached within a frame of reference that from another point of view is essentially ethical.

But professional managers are well aware that they are not yet members of "a profession" in the strictest sense of the word. There is by no means consensus among them that they would like to be.[18] Without going into the relative merits of professional stature for managers, the fact that there is a growing sentiment in its favor within the business community is significant to our discussion. A code of ethics policed by its own membership lies at the heart of every professional body, and it is this factor that appeals to those businessmen who would like to see management become truly a profession. Those who oppose the idea of a profession of management are not against the idea of a code of ethics. Their objection arises from certain difficulties they foresee in attempting to enforce one through a formal professional society, and in their belief that a manager as a risk-taker must be willing to assume personal liability for his failures even when they do not arise through mismanagement.[19]

RISE OF THE MARKETING CONCEPT

A change in the main orientation of managerial policy in our society also suggests that management decisions are increasingly being made along basically ethical lines. Until very recently most of our firms were product-oriented. They decided what they would produce in the way of goods or services and then used whatever means they could muster to gain public acceptance for their output. This worked very well in an economy within which scarcities in every direction could safely be assumed. But in our modern economy of at least quasi-abundance, product orientation has resulted in the development of unquestionably unethical means to force an unwanted product into a saturated market. The creation of psychological obsolescence, the "hard sell," hiding the true cost of "easy payments," and various other devices including such esoteric experiments as "subliminal advertising" are among them.

Many modern firms are abandoning product orientation in favor of consumer orientation, often referred to as "the marketing concept."[20] This consists quite simply of finding out first what the society wants, and only then determining the product or service to be offered for sale. This is, of course, sound business—but it is also ethical behavior in its most basic sense. The firm places itself truly in the position of serving the public rather than using it.

[18] The negative side of the argument is well presented by Paul Donham, "Is Management A Profession?" *Harvard Business Review*, September–October 1962, pp. 60–68.

[19] For a discussion of the double role of the manager as professional and risk-taker, see Peter Drucker, "Big Business and the National Purpose," *Harvard Business Review*, March–April 1962, pp. 52–59.

[20] See Peter Drucker, *The Practice of Management* (New York: Harper and Brothers, 1954), pp. 37–38.

THE CONCEPT OF THE CORPORATE COMMITMENT

A final indication of a fundamental shift in management philosophy is offered by a change in the role of public relations. In their first experiments, managers frequently relied on public relations men to "make the firm look good." When it became apparent that whitewash jobs and window-dressing were being greeted with mounting cynicism by the public, practitioners in the field—often out of conviction but sometimes in sheer self-defense—urged their manager clients to develop an acceptable "corporate image." The question so posed in the mind of the manager was "What can I do, or what can the company do, that will make it look good to the public?" This was an improvement over the earlier approach, a movement in the direction of an ethical relationship with the public, mainly through having abandoned one that was unethical. But though concern with one's corporate image was too self-conscious to be more than neutral in an ethical sense, it forced managers to take into account the attitude of the public toward their firms and thus laid a foundation for the next and present stage of public relations.

This concern created the kind of sensitivity among managers that encouraged them to co-operate with public relations counselors when the latter urged them to take the final and essentially ethical step of "defining the corporate commitment."[21] This task—closely tied in with the marketing concept, by the way—required that the manager ask quite a different question of himself than when he was attempting merely to develop an acceptable corporate image in the mind of the public. Now he had to ask "What are the obligations of my firm to the public?" The ethical implications of this question need no discussion.

THE ROLE OF ETHICS

Certainly some of us, on evaluating the practical reasons underlying managerial support for the policies noted above as suggesting increasing ethical sensitivity and improved ethical behavior among managers, are bound to say "But they prove nothing at all! Granted, they demonstrate significant trends in managerial policy. But these new policies were not developed for ethical reasons. They have been adopted for the simple reason that they are 'good business'!" Behind this judgment lies the uneasy feeling many of us have that if we behave in a fashion that can be described as ethical merely because there is some personal advantage in it for us, our behavior is not really ethical at all. There is merely an accidental similarity.

This assumption as to the nature of ethical conduct completely misses the role of ethics in a society. When a society begins to develop sufficient homogeneity for it to provide its membership with a way of life, a culture as well as formal organization, its ethical concepts begin to be internalized. Its mem-

21 See David Finn, "Struggle for Ethics in Public Relations," *Harvard Business Review,* January–February 1959, pp. 49–58.

bers come to think of certain decisions as being reasonable and natural in terms of their own self-interest, when actually they are being made within the ethical frame of reference that has been developed by the society. An effective ethical system, in other words, should neither lie heavily upon those who answer to it nor should it be self-consciously served. Its prescriptions and prohibitions should seem to the members of the society within which it operates as outlining the natural and proper way to behave, quite apart from any considerations of right or wrong.

The fact, therefore, that managers may behave ethically because "good ethics is good business" ought not give us any concern. On the contrary, we ought to be heartened by it. It suggests, as a matter of fact, that we are finally beginning to develop a national *ethos* sufficiently powerful so that those decisions which seem to be "good" from a personal point of view are held to be "right" as the total society looks at them.

A Positive Code of Ethics
Business Week

24

"There is no question but that five-percenters in Washington, the deep freeze and mink coats and oriental rugs for government employees, the payola in TV programs, the collusion of businessmen and union leaders with organized crime, the price-fixing cases in the electrical industry, and the conflict-of-interest revelations about business leaders have all raised public questions as to the standards of conduct of businessmen."

So spoke Prof. Robert W. Austin last Friday at the 31st annual National Business Conference of Harvard Business School, and when he was done, a thousand returning alumni gave him an ovation that old-timers said was unprecedented at these conferences.

Refusing to end their applause until Austin at last rose in acknowledgment, the homecoming executives made it plain they accepted the lesson as read by their former teacher.

SHOP TALK

Half a dozen eminent speakers had already broadcast their words of wel-

Reprinted from the June 17, 1961 issue of *Business Week* by special permission. Copyright © 1961 by McGraw-Hill, Inc.

come, their jokes, and their high regard for each other, for Harvard, and for business. For business conferences at Harvard in most respects do not differ from the pattern followed by hundreds of others across the country.

This meeting was devoted mostly to the topic of incentives for executives. Patrick E. Haggerty, president of Texas Instruments, Inc., and Thomas M. Ware, president of International Minerals & Chemical Corp., discussed their companies' plans. All day the audience listened to talk about stock options, profit-sharing, referred income, and other plans of reward. But it was Austin who gave the conferees something to think about beyond the carrot and the stick.

"More and more people are wondering," he said, "whether business leaders have a code of conduct other than that of making a profit."

POLICING A CODE

Top corporate leaders are being told they must set up high ethical standards and strict policies, and that they must then police these. Austin doubted that a code of "shalt nots," imposed from above, would act as a positive incentive for good.

They don't enlist psychological support, he said, and they leave a fallible individual to judge whether the "shalt not" applies to his particular situation.

Corporate morality and business ethics mean nothing as phrases, Austin said. The "concept of ethics or morals is one relating to right and wrong actions of individuals," not of artificial entities such as corporations. The public bases its opinion wholly on the actions of individual business managers.

AFFIRMATIVE CODE

In this dilemma, Prof. Austin offered business management a way out through continuing its own professionalization. Let it develop a simple and affirmative code of conduct, he said, and let it publicly profess that every business manager as an individual has an obligation to society that overrides any other obligation he may have.

This is the prescription that drew the applause last Friday:

The professional manager affirms that he will place the interest of his company before his own private interests.

He will place his duty to society above his duty to his company and above his private interest.

He has a duty to reveal the facts in any situation where his private interests are involved with those of his company, or where the interests of his company are involved with those of society.

He must subscribe wholeheartedly to the belief that when business managers follow this code of conduct, the profit motive is the best incentive of all for the development of a dynamic economy.

Prof. Austin might have found additional support for his case close at home. The 10th reunion survey of the Class of 1951 reveals that, among almost 300 men responding, 11% believe that they are under pressure to behave in "ethically repugnant" ways toward other members of their organizations. And 14% regard as unethical some of the business practices their organizations follow.

B.   Business and Religion

Capitalism and Christianity   **25**
Thomas C. Campbell, Jr.

Few theologians understand the fundamental goals of our free-enterprise system, and economists are rarely inclined to try to explain capitalism in the light of religious principles. An even greater gap is left between the pursuits of individual enterprisers and the basic objectives of religion. Consequently, more often than not, these businessmen who are such great contributors to the progress of our society wonder whether the economic system they serve is not, after all, really anti-religious.

What is the result of this suppressed but gnawing doubt? For one thing, many businessmen are troubled by a pessimism—an unusual emotion for most executives—or even a feeling of defensiveness when faced with the question of whether their work is truly Christian (in the broad sense of the whole Judaeo-Christian tradition). This distresses them; they wish to live and work in harmony with their religious beliefs, but they are constantly faced with the realities of a business world which demands certain actions commonly considered out of harmony with recognized religious goals.

Faced with this dilemma, businessmen are likely to take refuge in statements like, "Let's not mix religion with business"; or else they go to the other extreme of trying to equate the two, of seeking to prove to themselves —and others—that the practices and objectives of business and the church are identical. Neither way out of the problem is satisfying or satisfactory:

> Any thoughtful man interested in organized religion knows that religious ethics and religious living cannot be applied at certain times and places, only to be ignored at others. If such a "religion" does exist, it must be empty of content and meaning, for it will be observed only when convenient. A set of principles which are marked "For Sunday Only" is no religion at all.

Reprinted with permission from the *Harvard Business Review* (July–August 1957), pp. 37–44. Copyright © 1957 by the President and Fellows of Harvard College; all rights reserved.

On the other hand, it is unrealistic to claim that religion and business are essentially the same thing—that their goals, practices, and personnel are interchangeable. Each has its own role, each is a separate part of a whole. It would be equally useless to try to "prove" that the goals of a plumber and a painter are the same—though they may indeed have some common ends—and it would be equally unnecessary. To say the two are different is not to set them apart or put one above the other on some ultimate scale of values. It simply recognizes the bewildering variety of man's pursuits, talents, and objectives.

I do not think businessmen want to ignore this problem, as the easy alternative to forever doubting the worthiness of their chosen profession. So let us meet the issue head-on, and consider whether or not our capitalistic system is inherently or inevitably in conflict with religious goals and requirements. With this basic issue clarified, it will be far easier for each one of us to work out a system of values, as businessmen, which are both acceptable in a religious sense and practical as guides to our day-to-day professional lives.

CHURCH AND OFFICE

I do not believe that our capitalitic system is "bad," or that it cannot be reconciled with religion, as I shall indicate. But, unfortunately, many businessmen do not seem to agree with me, judging by their prevailing attitudes.

It is true, of course, that many businessmen are active workers in the religious institutions of the United States. They make financial and other contributions to the churches. By generally accepted standards of comparison, they are religious people. Yet these men, too, spend the greater part of their working hours in business, and in so doing make every reasonable attempt to meet competition and operate successfully as do their fellow businessmen who do not take an active part in organized religion.

The point is that business activity takes place on five or six days in the week while religious work is confined to Sundays and occasional evenings. It is not a common practice to engage in religious discussion or religious activity during the so-called working hours of the business day, and most businessmen make a sharp division between their church and their office. They commonly avoid any reference to the one when engaged in the other; seldom do they breach the wall they have built between the two.

As a matter of fact, many of them doggedly insist that the two must remain separate. Their contention is that efforts by clergymen, businessmen, or professional economists to consider the two at the same time do more harm than good, and that religious goals are in their place only when expounded by the clergy and by laymen while they are engaged exclusively in religious work. They further contend that economic goals are distinctly different from religious goals, which are by their very nature impractical and out of line with reality. This point of view is well illustrated by Josephus Daniels:

The pew wishes sermons that are redolent of the whole Gospel. They tire of essays, discussions on economics, solutions to social problems, and the like. They have a surfeit of these on weekdays. . . .[1]

CONTINUING DEBATE

Following this line of reasoning, much of the early criticism of Christian churches in the United States involved the question of whether religious groups should take any official position in regard to activities of organized labor and the attitudes of many industrialists toward organized labor. The question of church participation in social problems was debated vigorously by such well-known clergymen as Henry Ward Beecher and Washington Gladden, and covered extensively in articles and editorials of religious publications. This question has not been and probably never can be completely settled. The dispute still continues:

In recent years, the work of the Department of the Church and Economic Life of the National Council of Churches has uncovered—and unleashed—considerable disagreement as to whether the church should take any part in studying economic problems. A series of books published on *Ethics and Economics of Society* has been part of a major effort in this field, but it has met with vigorous criticism. Even those who have been otherwise active wth the Natonal Council could not agree on the advisability of sponsoring studies of this nature. Other organizations, too —like the American Council of Christian Laymen—have strongly opposed these studies.

This determined effort on the part of businessmen to divide God from Caesar both reinforces and gains strength from the idea that the two are irreconcilable. If we insist that the two "do not mix," we are driven to the assumption that one is good, and the other bad—that they are irreconcilable because they are out of harmony with each other, and that they are out of harmony because our economic system does not measure up to the standards and demands of our religion.

So the argument inevitably runs, and it leads straight to many of the attacks on our enterprise system which businessmen so deplore. Unless they join hands with the theologians and face up to the issues involved, the religiously based criticisms of which they complain—and many of the political criticisms as well—will continue to flourish. By ducking the tough ones, by subscribing to the idea that "business and religion don't mix," by telling the church to "tend to its own affairs," they perpetuate the notion that religion and capitalism are in conflict. On this assumed conflict rest many of the modern attacks on our enterprise system.

[1] Frank H. Knight and Thornton W. Marriam, *The Economic Order and Religion* (New York, Harper & Brothers, 1947), p. 129.

FOUR COMMON ACCUSATIONS

Let us now look at four of the more common misconceptions and traditional accusations which confuse the relationship between religion and business and tend to divide the two, setting one against the other.

"THE SCRIPTURES ARE NO HELP"

Possibly the first on the list is that "religious teachings just are not designed to apply to economic systems; they have no contribution to make, because they are concerned with a totally different phase of life." Anyone who takes this position overlooks the fact that all our basic religious teachings and philosophies are several centuries old. By comparison, our business system is extremely new. The illustrations used in early religious writings—the applications of fundamental teachings—were based on events and circumstances at the time in which the writings took place. The messages or principles involved are not necessarily dated or limited to the time of their origin; in fact, many of the messages apply to all times with absolutely no limit. But the particular implementations were better understood during early periods of history than in our present industrial society.

> During the time of most of the Biblical writings, contacts of human beings with one another were face-to-face; rarely were there sizable group meetings. As a result, religious ethics have been influenced by the absence of large group contacts and all the attendant problems such as beset an industrial society.
>
> The organization of these primitive communities was basically simple. Large, cooperative enterprises were unknown; the interdependence of management, capital, and labor on a massive scale was inconceivable.
>
> Life moved at a slow pace, and varied but little. When change did come, it was likely to be by upheaval, not evolution.
>
> The tremendous possibilities for an individual so characteristic of our world just were not available. The struggle for simple existence was a continuing and often futile effort; man's vision was limited both geographically and in scope of the problems he faced. Rigid stratifications of all kinds determined the pattern of a man's life, and those of his children.
>
> The state tended to be a hostile agent over which the individual had no control. Cooperative effort was rare; virtually no legal, accepted machinery existed for righting social and economic wrongs.
>
> The possibility of a life hereafter assumed high importance because life on earth presented so few possibilities. Man's origins, still mysterious, were then shrouded in complete darkness. Communications was undeveloped; mass education was impossible.

The impact of all these circumstances on the traditional applications of religion is incalculable. Take, for instance, the single problem of wealth. In the world of 2,000 years ago, distribution of one man's riches to the poor had a real impact on his society. The giver was not entangled in complicated effects on the economy of the community because of a sudden withdrawal of capital from an enterprise. He did not have to worry about the response of the recipients; the damage to personal dignity and initiative was not important in a civilization where individual enterprise was neither a factor nor a possibility.

Or look at automation—and the complex problems involved in displacement of workers by new machines as set against the increased productivity of the whole society. Is automation "good" or "bad"? The answer depends on the time scale you are using and the group about whom you are talking.[2] The ancient teachers were faced with no such paradoxes—or, at least, not in that form.

Though attempts have been made throughout the centuries to realign and reinterpret religious teachings with the economic facts of the time, these efforts seem to have ground to a halt within the last century or so. Thus we are left heirs to the confusion which is inevitable when the words of 2,000 years ago are sounded today.

"IT'S NEVER BEEN DONE"

The church, its critics say, is departing from its historical role when it becomes involved in the problems of the day. It should stick to a man's soul and his salvation, which is its order of business and always has been. Again, we hear the recurring theme that "religion and business don't mix."

But the facts of the case are quite the opposite. Jesus himself demonstrated a lively concern with the issues of his time; as I have just pointed out, that interest of his has contributed to our confusion about the Scriptures today. Churchmen through the ages have turned their eyes to current issues. St. Thomas Aquinas held strong views on wealth and property; the Puritans of New England were not the first people to build a society around what they considered religious truths; the Popes have spoken out on public issues, and continue to do so now.

Of particular significance, John Calvin sought to apply religious teachings to economic realities in the sixteenth century—and in so doing laid the basis for much of our current theology with his concept that it was man's duty to work diligently in whatever calling he might have chosen. Thus, acquiring wealth as a result of diligent work came to be looked on with favor and as the reward for Christian application to duty. The point of view that a life of poverty went hand in hand with piety gradually changed to the concept that a man should make the most of his God-given talents in his daily business.

There is no point in belaboring this matter; the record speaks for itself.

[2] See Abram T. Collier, "Faith in a Creative Society," HBR May–June, 1957, p. 37.

"JUST A FRONT GROUP"

Christianity, it has been said, is primarily concerned with the justification of the capitalistic system. The accusation is valid to the extent that certain individuals have used Christianity to justify certain activities of their own. Childs and Cater, referring to the ecclesiastical outlook of the late Middle Ages, said:

It had come to the point where the church (at least the Protestant Church) was considered as scarcely more than a ceremonial ratification of the morality that prevailed.[3]

Likewise, Henry F. May writes that "in 1876 Protestantism presented a massive, almost unbroken front in its defense of the social status quo."[4] Of a later period, he makes the following statement:

Despite recurrent disclosure of corporate robbery, openhanded and enterprising captains of industry remained heroes to most Americans throughout the century. A large faction of church opinion staunchly continued its unqualified defense of business and its leaders.[5]

Among the most severe critics of Christianity and its relation to the capitalistic system in this regard have been certain varieties of socialists. Their contention is that, because religious institutions receive a substantial portion of their financial support from property owners, "official church boards shape the policies of such organizations with an eye to continuing or increasing their receipt."[6]

The socialists further claim that religious institutions along with newspapers, radio stations, and universities have great influence on public opinion; therefore, the policies of these agencies "are designed to protect and foster those institutions from which they draw their sustenance."[7]

Professor John Ise has raised this same question in his recent book:

Since a few businessmen provide a considerable portion of the financial support of most churches, preachers often find it necessary to avoid discussion of problems of this earth, particularly labor problems; apparently our businessmen think it more important to prepare people for the next world than to make this one a more satisfactory place to live in.[8]

This interpretation of church-business relationships is held by many and denied by few. Any religious institution as well as any other institution with a major program must have financial support; and it is, likewise, logical to

---

[3] Marquis W. Childs and Douglas Cater, *Ethics in a Business Society* (New York, The New American Library of World Literature, Inc., 1954), p. 136.

[4] Henry F. May, *Protestant Churches and Industrial America* (New York, Harper & Brothers, 1949), p. 91.

[5] Ibid., p. 130.

[6] William N. Loucks and J. Weldon Hoot, *Comparative Economic Systems* (New York, Harper & Brothers, 1948), p. 309.

[7] Ibid.

[8] John Ise, *Economics* (New York: Harper & Brothers, 1946), p. 550.

assume that necessary financial support will not be forthcoming if the institution is constantly or even periodically criticizing the source of the support.

The weakness of both the socialist contention and that of Professor Ise is twofold:

1. They are based on the assumption that property owners in our capitalistic system are a separate and distinct class apart from the remainder of the population.

2. They assume there is a preferable system that could free the church from such control.

Property owners instead of being rare in the United States are a large portion of the entire population; and even those who do not own real estate or corporate stocks or bonds are not very different, for many of them have not acquired such items simply because of their personal choice to make other uses of their income and savings. Religious institutions in America receive their primary support from large numbers of small contributors; those receiving a substantial portion of their financial support from just a handful of very wealthy contributions are rare. Moreover, even in the case of those churches where most of the financial support comes from one or a few large sources, it is difficult to find definite indications that the basic policies followed differ much from the views of the smaller contributors.

But even if their criticisms are accurate, the socialists offer a still more unsatisfactory alternative. There is more likelihood of a close relationship between the expressions of religious institutions and their source of financial support when that support comes from the government. In such cases, coercive power is linked to financial control, and the effect is devastating. In countries where the church is state-supported, it is unlikely that its leaders will speak out against the government or against views held by political leaders for fear of retaliation.

Theoretically, it would be a good idea to have economic support of religious institutions completely independent of their teachings and policies, and we should surely try to divide the two as much as possible. But at the least we should seek to spread the burden of financial support over as wide an area as we can, calling on many different persons to contribute voluntarily.

Finally, I should point out that the fact that religious institutions exist and progress in a society in which the economic system is the capitalistic or free-enterprise system does not mean that the religious institutions must have—or do have—the justification of the economic system as a major purpose.

"GUILT BY ASSOCIATION"

A final accusation, related in some degree to the one which I have just discussed, is the so-called logic that declares, "Christianity and capitalism exist together; capitalism is bad; therefore Christianity is bad, too."

This "guilt by association" approach is typical of Karl Marx and his latter-day disciples. Marx, of course, was caustic about religion as such; it is "the opiate of the people," he solemnly declared. He complained that religion did not have a rational base. He was critical of the church for preaching about heaven in order to lessen the interest of people in improving worldly conditions. Marx contended that throughout the Middle Ages "the Church preached heaven, but strove to possess as much as possible of the earth."[9]

But the point is that Marx hated an economic system even more than he hated religion. His great antagonism to Christianity festered and grew because he associated it with an attempt to maintain an economic order which he wished to upset. In explaining the attitude of Marx toward Christianity, Professor Bober writes that Marx believed that "Christianity, when examined closely, is an earthly institution, and not the mother of elevated ethical ideals."[10] He states further that "as soon as it gained recognition by the state, the church eagerly joined the ranks of those engrossed in sordid affairs and enlisted itself as an agency of oppression."[11]

It is no surprise to anyone that Marx was not able to find in Christianity any help in bringing about the social order he advocated, or any support for the methods by which he urged that the new order be instituted. He wanted to destroy capitalism, and the methods he was willing to use meant that anything standing in the way had to be erased. Thus his real concern was with the economic system; his views on all else reflected his basic discontent with capitalism.

Unfortunately, Marx has no monopoly on accusations ostensibly hurled at religion but actually aimed elsewhere. How many people dislike a minister or a church or a doctrine and condemn the entire complex of tradition, aspiration, and belief! But our interest here is with the relationship between religion and an economic system.

Both have suffered from assaults on the other. We have witnessed attacks on the economic system which accuse it of being "un-Christian"; but when we probe, we find that the real issue is something altogether different. The accuser does not care much whether or not the system is Christian; he is disturbed because it is not doing its job of production and distribution as he thinks it should be done. By the same token, Christianity has been on the receiving end of assaults as "irrational" or "the front for the status quo" when the attacker did not really care about Christianity one way or the other; he was merely using this as one more weapon to club a social or an economic order.

What, then is the relationship between an economic system—especially

---

[9] M. M. Bober, *Karl Marx's Interpretation of History* (Cambridge, Harvard University Press, 1950), p. 152.
[10] Ibid., p. 151.
[11] Ibid.

capitalism—and religion? Are their objectives opposed to one another? Is the promotion of economic well-being a "materialistic," ungodly pursuit?

NO CONFLICT OF GOALS

There is not likely to be uniformity of agreement on the goals or objectives of our economic system. However, we can mark out several of its basic objectives which meet with general approval. One scholar has listed four objectives with which it is difficult to disagree:

1. A higher standard of living for all.
2. Economic security and freedom.
3. Production in accordance with consumer demands.
4. An equitable distribution of income.[12]

These interlocking objectives might be summarized as the greatest possible *economic* welfare, which includes both the highest standard of living achievable at the present time and even higher levels in the future. Each of these goals depends on and is related to the others, and one cannot be pursued to the exclusion of the rest.

Religion is much broader in scope than an economic—or political or social—structure, and religious goals are broader than economic. Without running the danger of unduly limiting them, the objectives of religion might be summarized as the greatest possible *human* welfare, as the fullest development of man, in all possible ways—physical, mental, *and* spiritual, economic *and* noneconomic—in accordance with the will of God. Must the goal of greatest possible economic welfare of society be in conflict with the non-economic aspects of human welfare? If economic advance is achieved at the expense of other aspects of human well-being, then economic goals are of necessity in conflict with religion. If, however, a higher living standard does not require the sacrifice of broader human values in general, economic objectives are in harmony with religious goals. For, after all, greater economic welfare is a part of greater human welfare.

If religion and capitalism are rated according to importance, religion must unquestionably be number one since it, not some economic system, is the chief guide in the determination of the vital goals of life. Therefore, capitalism must conform to religious principles and objectives. If it does not, capitalism, not religion, must go. It would be unthinkable to discard a religion for not doing an effective job in justifying an economic system. The basic question should be: Does this particular economic approach of capitalism enable us more nearly to achieve basic religious goals than any other economic system?

[12] George Leland Bach, *Economics, An Introductory Analysis* (New York: Prentice-Hall, Inc., 1957), p. 70.

A BETTER SYSTEM

The socialist would, of course, answer *no,* in chorus with all those who advocate some other system. He would point out that the objectives listed above could be the goals of other types of economic systems—*with* some modifications, particularly freedom of choice as to how to engage one's productive resources, and production in response to consumer demand.

But the point is that these goals are much more likely to be realized under a free-enterprise system. First, the capitalistic system affords the greatest stimulus to high and continuously increasing production. Therefore, it enables us to have a higher standard of living than would be attainable under any other system. It affords more freedom of choice in the use of productive resources and more freedom of choice on the part of consumers. No other system places as much emphasis on the freedom of the individual. In other words, capitalism is more harmonious with religion primarily because it works—because it does, in fact, advance human economic welfare.

It is true that capitalism has been widely criticized for its distribution of income. Undoubtedly certain other systems can provide for a more equitable distribution. After a formula for equity in distribution of income has been determined, several different systems might enable most of society to follow the formula at least as well—if not better—than free enterprise. But the great failure of other systems lies in the level of productivity they can achieve. Equitable distribution of less than a high and ever-increasing output of commodities and services inevitably leads to a low standard of living.

The mistake made by so many critics of our economic system is their failure to consider a combination of objectives, none of which should be ignored. Where these basic objectives have not been met, day-to-day operations have been to blame, not the system as such. It must be recognized, however, that these day-to-day failures are not unique to capitalism; they will be found anywhere. And free enterprise is more likely to correct such imperfections or breakdowns than is any other system yet devised.

Christianity and capitalism, then, are not in opposition to one another, although they are neither exactly parallel nor exact duplicates. Christianity is much broader in its approach to greater human welfare than is capitalism. While Christianity is concerned with the problem of the whole life of the individual and of better living for all mankind, capitalism is limited to the economc aspects of human society. The noneconomic aspects or phases of society are more extensive than are the economic. But since economic welfare is one important aspect of life, and a definite goal of the capitalistic system is greater economic welfare of all people, it is therefore not in opposition to Christianity and actually conforms to the basic religious goal of a better life for society as a whole.

Because the free-enterprise system produces greater economic progress than would be possible under any other economic system known at the present, it is doing more to advance the broader goals of Christianity than could any other existing arrangement. Furthermore, there is no inherent reason why economic welfare under capitalism must be in any way at the expense of the general welfare; as a matter of fact, just the opposite is increasingly true. Nor is there reason to believe that the general welfare of society must or even will likely be reduced as a result of economic progress or greater economic welfare.

CAPITALISM AND DEMOCRACY

In this discussion, I have been careful to differentiate between an economic system—capitalism—and a social and political system—democracy. Obviously they are closely related to one another in theory, in history, and in fact. But nevertheless they are separate in that capitalism is essentially a type of *economic* organization while democracy is a *political* organization.

If, through some unhappy mischance, capitalism became interwoven with a political system of oppression and provided a continuous improvement in the standard of living at the expense of the basic individual freedoms as outlined in our Bill of Rights, it might still be in harmony with religion. But the total society of which it was a part would not be.

As a matter of fact, however, none of the great strengths of capitalism— and an attribute adding to its acceptability in religious terms—is that it can add to the preservation and expansion of human freedoms. It is philosophically and practically consistent with a free political system and contributes its influence to the fashioning of a free society which permits and encourages each individual to fulfill and develop his own talents and his own personality.

CONCLUSION

Whatever may be said of religions—or interpretations of spiritual teachings of the past—it is clear that the predominant religions in the United States today do not spell out the specific nature of an economic organization.

The American enterprise system developed long after Judaism and Christianity had many adherents, and religious goals cover much wider areas than just economic activity. Thus they can provide only a framework within which several forms of economic organizations might possibly be able to operate.

The specific nature of an economic system, then, should not fall under the control of religion or of religious institutions such as churches and synagogues. By the same token, the system should not expect to be protected against all attacks and criticisms; it should not look to the church for justification, though it certainly has a right to expect sympathy with its objectives. The fact that religious institutions seem to be in harmony with capitalism constitutes a compliment to the system rather than an obligation on the church to justify it.

Our experience in this country has been that the free enterprise system most nearly complies with the religious principles and is at the same time the most productive. It is conceivable that one could describe a hypothetical system which might appear to operate more nearly in line with religious principles, but the weakness of the proposals made so far is that they do not work as well—do not turn out the goods. An economic system must work as well as conform to high ideals.

Incidentally, our critics frequently overlook the fact that many of the disadvantages they see arise from the degree of freedom inherent in our approach. Systems that do not provide economic and political freedom are unacceptable to us, and we are willing to put up with some shortcomings in order to protect that freedom. Further, it is imperative that any system which is in harmony with basic religious principles provide as much economic freedom as possible.

THE PRACTICING EXECUTIVE

The individual businessman is still left with the vitally important question: Can I be successful in business and at the same time work toward objectives which conform to my religious beliefs? It is difficult to see how we can expect full support of an economic system as a whole if we are unable to reconcile its day-to-day operation with our basic religious beliefs. Such support is seriously weakened by any widespread feeling that the activities of financial and industrial leaders are un-Christian. Consequently, the fact that we are following an economic system which conforms to the basic concepts of Christianity is not enough; we have to raise the question of whether the work of each businessman follows the same basic concepts.

It is, of course, perfectly possible for individual businessmen to ignore religious teachings in their quest for personal economic gain. It is, likewise, conceivable for this to be done even on a national basis. Though this may not be the fault of the system any more than it is Christianity's fault that at various periods of history certain individuals and groups have acted in an un-Christian way in the name of Christianity, it still poses a tough question: Is Christianity workable in the business world, or must we be content with saying that the objectives and general principles of free enterprise are in harmony with religion?

I believe that an executive can conduct his business in harmony with religious principles without subjecting it to undue risks. The religious teachings of Judaism and Christianity do not either of them provide specific answers to every business or economic problem any more than they offer clean-cut solutions to the many noneconomic problems. However, both religions provide a framework or set of principles and values in which successful businessmen may operate. Given a sense of confidence in the harmonious relationship between religion and our capitalistic system, each businessman can proceed to work out his own code and operating philosophy for his own situation.

"Skyhooks"   **26**
O. A. Ohman

During the last several years, while my principal job assignment has been management development, I have become increasingly impressed with the importance of intangibles in the art of administration. With the managerial revolution of the last generation and the transition from owner-manager to professional executive, there has appeared a growing literature on the science and art of administration. A shift in emphasis is noticeable in these writings over the past 30 years.

Following the early engineering approach typified by the work of Frederick Taylor and others, there next developed a search for the basic principles of organization, delegation, supervision, and control. More recently, as labor relations became more critical, the emphasis has shifted to ways of improving human relations. The approach to the problems of supervisory relationships was essentially a manipulative one. Textbooks on the techniques of personnel management mushroomed. Still later it became more and more apparent that the crux of the problem was the supervisor himself, and this resulted in a flood of "how to improve yourself" books. Meanwhile the complexities of the industrial community increased, and the discontents and tensions mounted.

It seems increasingly clear, at least to me, that while some administrative practices and personnel techniques may be better than others, their futility arises from the philosophical assumptions or value judgments on which this superstructure of manipulative procedure rests. We observe again and again that a manager with sound values and a stewardship conception of his role as boss can be a pretty effective leader even though his techniques are quite unorthodox. I am convinced that workers have a fine sensitivity for a boss who believes in something and in whom they can believe.

This observation leads me to suspect that we may have defined the basic purposes and objectives of our industrial enterprise too narrowly, too sel-

Reprinted with permission from the *Harvard Business Review* (May–June 1955) pp. 1–9. Copyright © 1955 by the President and Fellows of Harvard College; all rights reserved.

fishly, too materialistically. Bread alone will not satisfy workers. There are some indications that our people have lost faith in the basic values of our economic society, and that we need a spiritual rebirth in industrial leadership.

Certainly no people have ever had so much, and enjoyed so little real satisfaction. Our economy has been abundantly productive, our standard of living is at an all-time peak, and yet we are a tense, frustrated, and insecure people full of hostilities and anxieties. Can it be that our *god of production* has feet of clay? Does industry need a new religion—or at least a better one than it has had?

I am convinced that the central problem is not the division of the spoils as organized labor would have us believe. Raising the price of prostitution does not make it the equivalent of love. Is our industrial discontent not in fact the expression of a hunger for a work life that has meaning in terms of higher and more enduring spiritual values? How can we preserve the wholeness of the personality if we are expected to worship God on Sundays and holidays and mammon on Mondays through Fridays?

I do not imply that this search for real meaning in life is or should be limited to the hours on the job, but I do hold that the central values of our industrial society permeate our entire culture. I am sure we do not require a bill of particulars of the spiritual sickness of our time. The evidences of modern man's search for his soul are all about us. Save for the communist countries there has been a world-wide revival of interest in religion. The National Council of Churches reports that 59% of our total population (or 92 million) now claim church affiliation. The November 22, 1954, issue of *Barron's* devoted the entire front page to a review of a book by Barbara Ward, *Faith and Freedom*.[1]

Perhaps even more significant is the renaissance in the quality of religious thought and experience. Quite evidently our religion of materialism, science, and humanism is not considered adequate. Man is searching for anchors outside himself. He runs wearily to the periphery of the spider web of his own reason and logic, and looks for new "skyhooks"—for an abiding faith around which life's experiences can be integrated and given meaning.

WHY "SKYHOOKS?"

Perhaps we should assume that this need for "skyhooks" is part of man's natural equipment—possibly a function of his intelligence—or if you prefer, God manifesting Himself in His creatures. It seems to me, however, that the recent intensification of this need (or perhaps the clearer recognition of it) stems in part from certain broad, social, economic, political, and philosophical trends. I shall not attempt a comprehensive treatment of these, but shall allude to only a few.

[1] Barbara Ward, *Faith and Freedom* (New York, W. W. Norton & Company, Inc., 1954).

ABUNDANCE WITHOUT SATISFACTION

I have already indicated that on the economic front we have won the battle of production. We have moved from an economy of scarcity to one of abundance. We have become masters of the physical world and have learned how to convert its natural resources to the satisfaction of our material wants. We are no longer so dependent and so intimately bound to the world of nature. In a way we have lost our feeling of being part of nature and with it our humble reverence for God's creation.

While the industrialization of our economy resulted in ever-increasing production, it also made of individual man a production number—an impersonal, de-skilled, interchangeable production unit, measured in so many cents per hour. For most employees, work no longer promotes the growth of personal character by affording opportunities for personal decision, exercise of judgment, and individual responsibility. A recent issue of *Nation's Business* quotes the modern British philosopher, Alexander Lindsay, on this point as follows:

> Industrialism has introduced a new division into society. It is the division between those who manage and take responsibility and those who are managed and have responsibility taken from them. This is a division more important than the division between the rich and poor.[2]

Certainly the modern industrial worker has improved his material standard of living at the cost of becoming more and more dependent on larger and larger groups. Not only his dignity but also his security has suffered. And so he reaches out for new "skyhooks"—for something to believe in, for something that will give meaning to his job.

DISILLUSIONMENT WITH SCIENCE

A second trend which seems to bear some relation to our urgent need for a faith grows out of our disillusionment with science. As a result of the rapid advance of science, the curtains of ignorance and superstition have been pulled wide on all fronts of human curiosity and knowledge.

Many of the bonds of our intellectual enslavement have been broken. Reason and scientific method were called on to witness to the truth, the whole truth, and nothing but the truth. We were freed from the past—its traditions, beliefs, philosophies, its mores, morals, and religion. Science became our religion and reason replaced emotion.

However, even before the atom bomb there was a growing realization that science did not represent the whole truth, that with all its pretensions it could be dead wrong, and, finally and particularly, that without proper moral safe-

---

2 John Kord Lagemann, "Job Enlargement Boosts Production," *Nation's Business.* December 1954, p. 36.

guards the truth did not necessarily make men free. Atomic fission intensified the fear and insecurity of every one of us who contemplated the possibility of the concentration of power in the hands of men without morals. We want science to be in the hands of men who not only recognize their responsibility to man-made ethical standards (which are easily perverted) but have dedicated themselves to the eternal and absolute standards of God. Thus, while the evidence of material science has been welcomed, our own personal experiences will not permit us to believe that life is merely a whirl of atoms without meaning, purpose, beauty, or destiny.

TREND TOWARD BIGNESS

A third factor contributing to our insecurity is the trend toward bigness and the resulting loss of individuality. This is the day of bigger and bigger business—in every aspect of life. The small is being swallowed by the big, and the big by the bigger. This applies to business, to unions, to churches, to education, to research and invention, to newspapers, to our practice of the professions, to government, and to nations. Everything is getting bigger except the individual, and he is getting smaller and more insignificant and more dependent on larger social units. Whether we like it or not this is becoming an administrative society, a planned and controlled society, with ever-increasing concentration of power. This is the day of collectivism and public-opinion polls. It is the day when the individual must be *adjusted to the group*— when he must above all else be sensitive to the feelings and attitudes of others, must get an idea of how others expect him to act, and then react to this.

This is the insecure world which David Riesman has described so well in his book, *The Lonely Crowd*.[3] He pictures man as being no longer "tradition directed" as was primitive man, nor as in Colonial days is he "inner directed" as if by the gyroscope of his own ideals, but today he is "outer directed" as if by radar. He must constantly keep his antenna tuned to the attitudes and reactions of others to him. The shift has been from morals to morale and from self-reliance to dependence on one's peer group. However, the members of one's peer group are each responding to each other. Obviously these shifting sands of public opinion offer no stable values around which life can be consistently integrated and made meaningful. The high-water mark of adjustment in such a society is that the individual be socially accepted and above all else that he appear to be *sincere*.

This is certainly not a favorable environment for the development of steadfast character. It is essentially a neurotic and schizophrenic environment which breeds insecurity.

This socially dependent society also offers an ideal market for the wares

[3] David Riesman, *The Lonely Crowd* (New Haven, Yale University Press, 1950).

of the "huckster," the propagandist, and the demagogue. Lacking a religious interpretation of the divine nature of man, these merchants in mass reaction have sought the least common denominator in human nature and have beamed the movies and newspapers at the ten-year mental level. One wonders if this approach to people does not make them feel that they have been sold short and that they are capable of much better than is expected of them. Has this demoralizing exposure of the cheapness of our values not intensified our search for something better to believe in?

On top of all these disturbing socioeconomic trends came the war. This certainly was materialism, science, and humanism carried to the logical conclusion. The war made us question our values and our direction. It left us less cocksure that we were right, and more fearful of ourselves as well as of others. It made us fearful of the power which we had gained, and led us to search our soul to determine whether we had the moral strength to assume the leadership role that had been given to us. We have been humbled in our efforts to play god and are about ready to give the job back. Note, however, that this is not a characteristic reaction to war. Typically wars have been followed by a noticeable deterioration of moral standards, traditional values, and social institutions.

Perhaps none of these rationalizations for our return to religion is entirely valid. I suspect that the search for some kind of overarching integrative principle or idea is the expression of a normal human need. Certainly history would indicate that man's need for a god is eternal even though it may be more keenly sensed in times of adversity. A religion gives a point of philosophical orientation around which life's experiences can be organized and digested. Without the equivalent, a personality cannot be whole and healthy. Short-term goals which need to be shifted with the changing tide do not serve the same integrative function as do the "skyhooks" which are fastened to eternal values. I do not personally regard the current religious revival as a cultural hangover, nor as a regression. Being a mystic I prefer instead to view the need for such a faith as the spark of the Creator in us to drive us on to achieve His will and our own divine destiny.

WHY MONDAY THROUGH FRIDAY?

If we may grant for the moment that modern man *is* searching for deeper meanings in life, we may then ask, what has this to do with industry. If he needs "skyhooks," let him get them in church, or work out his own salvation. The business leaders of the past insisted that "business is business" and that it had little bearing on the individual's private life and philosophy.

There are several reasons why "skyhooks" must be a primary concern of the business administrator:

1. For the individual the job is the center of life, and its values must be in harmony with the rest of life if he is to be a whole and healthy personality.

2. This is an industrial society, and its values tend to become those of the entire culture.

3. The public is insisting that business leaders are in fact responsible for the general social welfare—that the manager's responsibilities go far beyond those of running the business. They have delegated this responsibility to the business executive whether he wishes to play this role or not.

4. Even if the administrator insists on a narrow definition of his function as merely the production of goods and services as efficiently as possible, it is nevertheless essential that he take these intangibles into account since they are the real secrets of motivating an organization.

5. Besides all this the administrator needs a better set of "skyhooks" himself if he is to carry his ever-increasing load of responsibility without cracking up. The fact that so many administrators are taking time to rationalize, defend, and justify the private enterprise system is an outward indication of this need for more significant meanings.

ANYTHING WRONG WITH CAPITALISM?

We may ask, then, what specifically is wrong with our capitalistic system of private enterprise. What is wrong with production or with trying to improve our standard of living? What is wrong with a profit, or with private ownership of capital, or with competition? Is this not the true American way of life?[4]

Nothing is necessarily wrong with these values. There are certainly worse motives than the profit motive. A refugee from communism is reported to have observed: "What a delight to be in the United States where things are produced and sold with such a nice clean motive as making a profit."

I am not an economist, and it is beyond the scope of this article to attempt a revision of our economic theory. I am tempted, however, to make a couple of observations about these traditional economic concepts:

1. That while the values represented by them are not necessarily wrong, they are certainly pretty thin and do not challenge the best in people.

2. That many of the classical economic assumptions are outmoded and are no longer adequate descriptions of the actual operation of our present-day economy.

For example, the concept of economic man as being motivated by self-interest not only is outmoded by the best current facts of the social sciences, but also fails to appeal to the true nobility of spirit of which we are capable.

The concept of the free and competitive market is a far cry from the highly controlled and regulated economy in which business must operate today.

---

[4] For a comprehensive treatment of the criticisms of business see J. D. Glover, *The Attack on a Big Business* (Boston, Division of Research, Harvard Business School, 1954).

General Motors does not appear to want to put Chrysler out of business, and apparently the union also decided to take the heat off Chrysler rather than to press its economic advantage to the logical conclusion. The assumption that everyone is out to destroy his competitors does not explain the sharing of technology through trade associations and journals. No, we also have tremendous capacity for cooperation when challenged by larger visions. We are daily denying the Darwinian notion of the "survival of the fittest" which, incidentally, William Graham Sumner, one of the nineteenth-century apologists for our economic system, used for justifying unbridled self-interest and competition.

Certainly the traditional concept of private ownership of capital does not quite correspond to the realities of today's control of large blocks of capital by insurance companies and trusteed funds.

The notion of individual security through the accumulation of savings has largely given way to the collectivist means of group insurance, company annuities, and Social Security.

The concept that all profits belong to the stockholders is no longer enthusiastically supported by either the government or the unions since both are claiming an increasing cut.

And so, while we may argue that the system of private enterprise is self-regulatory and therefore offers maximum individual freedom, the simple, cold fact is that it is in ever-increasing degree a managed or controlled economy—partly at the insistence of the voters, but largely as the result of the inevitable economic pressures and the trend toward bigness.[5]

Regardless of the rightness or wrongness of these changes in our system of enterprise, the changes have been considerable, and I doubt that classical economic theory can be used as an adequate rationale of its virtues. I am therefore not particularly optimistic about the efficacy of the current campaign to have businessmen "save the private enterprise system and the American way of life" by engaging in wholesale economic education, much of which is based on outmoded concepts.

Much as economic theory needs revision, I fear that this is not likely to cure our ills. Nor do I believe that profit-sharing or any other device for increasing the workers' cut (desirable as these efforts may be) will give us what we really want. It is rather another type of sharing that is needed, a sharing of more worthy objectives, a sharing of the management function, and a sharing of mutual respect and Christian working relationships.

GOALS AND PURPOSES

What is wrong is more a matter of goals and purposes—of our assumptions about what we are trying to do and how we can dignify and improve

[5] See John Kenneth Galbraith, *American Capitalism* (Boston: Houghton Mifflin Company, 1952).

ourselves in the doing. There is nothing wrong with production, but we should ask ourselves: *"Production for what?"* Do we use people for production or production for people? How can production be justified if it destroys personality and human values both in the process of its manufacture and by its end use? Clarence B. Randall of Inland Steel in his book, *A Creed for Free Enterprise,* says:

> We have come to worship production as an end in itself, which of course it is not. It is precisely there that the honest critic of our way of life makes his attack and finds us vulnerable. Surely there must be for each person some ultimate value, some purpose, some mode of self-expression that makes the experience we call life richer and deeper.[6]

So far, so good, Mr. Randall. But now notice how he visualizes industry making its contribution to this worthy objective:

> To produce more and more with less and less effort is merely treading water unless we *thereby release time and energy for the cultivation of the mind and the spirit* and for the achievement of those ends for which Providence placed us on this earth.[7]

Here is the same old dichotomy—work faster and more efficiently so that you can finish your day of drudgery and cultivate your soul on your own time. In fact he says: "A horse with a very evil disposition can nevertheless pull the farmer's plow." No, I am afraid the job *is* the life. *This* is what must be made meaningful. We cannot assume that the end of production justifies the means. What happens to people in the course of producing may be far more important than the end product. Materialism is not a satisfactory "skyhook." People are capable of better and want to do better. (Incidentally I have the impression that Mr. Randall's practices line up very well with my own point of view even if his words do not.)

Perhaps we should ask what is the really important difference between Russian communism and our system. Both worship production and are determined to produce more efficiently, and do. Both worship science. Both have tremendously improved the standard of living of their people. Both share the wealth. Both develop considerable loyalties for their system. (In a mere 40 years since Lenin started the communist revolution a third of the world's people have come to accept its allegiance.) True, in Russia capital is controlled by the state while here it is theoretically controlled by individuals, although in actual practice, through absentee ownership, it is controlled to a considerable extent by central planning agencies and bureaus, both public and private.

No, the real difference is in the philosophy about people and how they may be used as means to ends. It is a difference in the assumptions made about

[6] Clarence B. Randall, *A Creed for Free Enterprise* (Boston: Little, Brown and Company, 1952), p. 16.
[7] Ibid.

the origin of rights—whether the individual is endowed with rights by his Creator and yields these only voluntarily to civil authority designated by him, or whether rights originate in force and in the will of the government. Is God a myth, or is He the final and absolute judge to whom we are ultimately responsible? Are all standards of conduct merely man-made and relative, or absolute and eternal? Is man a meaningless happenstance of protoplasm, or is he a divine creation with a purpose, with potential for improvement, and with a special destiny in the over-all scheme of things?

These are some of the differences—or at least I hope that they still are. And what a difference these intangible, perhaps mythical, "skyhooks" make. They are nevertheless the most real and worthwhile and enduring things in the world. The absence of these values permitted the Nazis to "process" people through the gas chambers in order to recover the gold in their teeth.

THE ADMINISTRATOR CONTRIBUTES

This, then, is part of our general cultural heritage and is passed on to us in many ways. However, it really comes to life in people—in their attitudes, aspirations, and behaviors. And in a managerial society this brings us back to the quality of the individual administrator. He interprets or crystallizes the values and objectives for his group. He sets the climate within which these values either *do* or *do not* become working realities. He must define the goals and purposes of his group in larger and more meaningful perspective. He integrates the smaller, selfish goals of individuals into larger, more social and spiritual objectives for the group. He provides the vision without which the people perish. Conflicts are resolved by relating the immediate to the long-range and more enduring values. In fact, we might say this *integrative function* is the core of the administrator's contribution.

The good ones have the mental equipment to understand the business and set sound long-term objectives, but the best ones have in addition the philosophical and character values which help them to relate the over-all goals of the enterprise to eternal values. This is precisely the point at which deep-seated religious convictions can serve an integrative function since they represent the most long-range of all possible goals.[8] Most really great leaders in all fields of human endeavor have been peculiarly sensitive to their historical role in human destiny. Their responsibility and loyalty are to some distant vision which gives calm perspective to the hot issues of the day.

This function of the administrator goes far beyond being a likable personality, or applying correct principles of organization, or being skillful in the so-called techniques of human relations. I am convinced that the difficulties which so many executives have with supervisory relationships cannot

[8] For further elaboration see Gordon W. Allport, *The Individual and His Religion* (New York: The Macmillan Company, 1953).

be remedied by cultivation of the so-called human relations skills. These difficulties spring rather from one's conception of his function or role as a boss, his notion about the origin and nature of his authority over others, the assumptions he makes about people and their worth, and his view of what he and his people are trying to accomplish together. To illustrate:

> If, for example, my personal goal is to get ahead in terms of money, position, and power; and if I assume that to achieve this I must beat my competitors; that the way to do this is to establish a good production record; that my employees are means to this end; that they are replaceable production units which must be skillfully manipulated; that this can be done by appealing to the lowest form of immediate selfish interest; that the greatest threat to me is that my employees may not fully recognize my authority nor accept my leadership—if these are my values, then I am headed for trouble—all supervisory techniques notwithstanding.

I wish I could be quite so positive in painting the picture of the right values and approaches to management. I suspect there are many, many different right answers. No doubt each company or enterprise will have to define its own long-term purposes and develop its own philosophy in terms of its history, traditions, and its real function in our economy. I am also certain that no philosophy would be equally useful to all managers. The character of an organization is, to a large extent, set by the top man or the top group, and it is inevitable that this be the reflection of the philosophy of these individuals. No one of us can operate with another's philosophy. I have also observed that in most enterprises the basic faith or spirit of the organization is a rather nebulous or undefined something, which nevertheless has very profound meaning to the employees.

A SUCCESSFUL EXECUTIVE

Recognizing then the futility of advocating any one pattern of values, it occurs to me that it might, however, be suggestive or helpful if I told you something of the philosophy of one extremely successful executive whom I have pumped a good deal on this subject (for he is more inclined to live his values than to talk about them):

> As near as I can piece it together, he believes that this world was not an accident but was created by God and that His laws regulate and control the universe and that we are ultimately *responsible to Him.* Man, as God's supreme creation, is in turn endowed with creative ability. Each individual represents a unique combination of talents and potentials. In addition, man is the only animal endowed with freedom of choice and with a high capacity for making value judgments. With these gifts (of heredity and cultural environment) goes an obligation to give the best possible accounting of one's stewardship in terms of maximum self-

development and useful service to one's fellows in the hope that one may live a rich life and be a credit to his Creator.

This executive also assumes that each individual possesses certain God-given rights of self-direction which only *the individual* can voluntarily delegate to others in authority over him, and that this is usually done in the interest of achieving some mutual cooperative good. The executive therefore assumes that his *own* authority as boss over others must be exercised with due regard for the attendant obligations to his employees and to the stockholders who have temporarily and voluntarily yielded their rights in the interest of this common undertaking. (Notice that he does not view his authority as originating with or derived from his immediate superior.) This delegated authority must, of course, be used to advance the common good rather than primarily to achieve the selfish ambitions of the leader at the expense of the led.

He further assumes that the voluntary association of employees in industry is for the purpose of increasing the creativity and productivity of all members of the group and thus of bringing about increased benefits to all who may share in the ultimate use of these goods and services. What is equally important, however, is that in the course of this industrial operation each individual should have an opportunity to develop the maximum potential of his skills and that the working relationships should not destroy the individual's ability to achieve his greatest maturity and richness of experience. As supervisor he must set the working conditions and atmosphere which will make it possible for his employees to achieve this dual objective of increasing productivity and maximizing self-development.

These goals can best be achieved by giving employees maximum opportunity to exercise their capacity for decision making and judgment within their assigned area of responsibility. The supervisor is then primarily a coach who must instruct, discipline, and motivate all the members of the group, making it possible for each to exercise his special talent in order to maximize the total team contribution. Profits are regarded as a measure of the group's progress toward these goals, and a loss represents not only an improper but even an immoral use of the talents of the group.

There is nothing "soft" about his operation. He sets high quality standards and welcomes stiff competition as an additional challenge to his group. He therefore expects and gets complete cooperation and dedication on the part of everyone. Incidentally, he views the activity of working together in this manner with others as being one of life's most rewarding experiences. He holds that this way of life is something which we have not yet fully learned, but that its achievement is part of our divine destiny. He is firmly convinced that such conscientious efforts *will* be rewarded with success. He manages with a light touch that releases creativity, yet with complete confidence in the outcome.

This is probably a poor attempt at verbalizing the basic philosophy which this man lives so easily and naturally. I hope, however, that it has revealed something of his conception of his role or function as an executive, and his view of what he and his organization are trying to do together. With this account of his values I am sure that you would have no difficulty completing the description of his administrative practices and operating results. They flow naturally from his underlying faith, without benefit of intensive training in the principles and art of administration.

As you would suspect, people like to work for him—or with him. He attracts good talent (which is one of the real secrets of success). Those with shoddy values, selfish ambitions, or character defects do not survive—the organization is self-pruning. Those who remain develop rapidly because they learn to accept responsibility. He not only advocates but practices decentralization and delegation. His employees will admit that they have made mistakes, but usually add with a grin that they try not to make the same one twice. People respond to his leadership because he has faith in them and expects the best in them rather than the worst. He speaks well of the members of his organization, and they appear to be proud of each other and of their record of performance. He takes a keen interest in developing measurements of performance and in bettering previous records or competitive standards. He feels that no one has a right to "louse up a job"—a point on which he feels the stockholders and the Lord are in complete agreement.

While he does not talk much about "employee communications" nor stress formal programs of this type, his practice is to spend a large proportion of his time in the field with his operating people rather than in his office. He is "people oriented" and does a particularly good job of listening. The union committee members have confidence in his fairness, yet do a workmanlike job of bargaining. In administering salaries he seems to be concerned about helping the individual to improve his contribution so that a pay increase can be justified.

In his general behavior he moves without haste or hysteria. He is typically well organized, relaxed, and confident, even under trying circumstances. There is a high degree of consistency in his behavior and in the quality of his decisions because his basic values do not shift. Since he does not operate by expediency, others can depend on him; and this consistency makes for efficiency in the dicharge of delegated responsibility. Those operating problems which do come to him for decision seem to move easily and quickly to a conclusion. His long-term values naturally express themselves in well-defined policies, and it is against this frame of reference that the decisions of the moment easily fall into proper perspective.

In policy-level discussions his contributions have a natural quality of objectivity because "self-concern" does not confuse. Others take him at face value because his motives are not suspect. When differences or conflicts do arise, his approach is not that of compromise; rather he attempts to integrate the partisan views around mutually acceptable longer-range goals. The issues of the moment then seem to dissolve in a discussion of the best means to the achievement of the objective. I have no doubt that he also has some serious problems, but I have tried to give a faithful account of the impression which he creates. There is a *sense of special significance* about his operation which is shared by his associates.

THIS IS THE KEY

It is precisely this "sense of special significance" which is the key to leadership. We all know that there are many different ways of running a successful operation. I am certainly not recommending any particular set of administrative practices—although admittedly some are better than others. Nor am I suggesting that his set of values should be adopted by others, or for that matter could be. What I am saying is that a man's real values have a subtle but inevitable way of being communicated, and they affect the significance of everything he does.

These are the vague intangibles—the "skyhooks"—which are difficult to verbalize but easy to sense and tremendously potent in their influence. They provide a different, invisible, fundamental structure into which the experiences of every day are absorbed and given meaning. They are frequently unverbalized, and in many organizations they defy definition. Yet they are the most real things in the world.

The late Jacob D. Cox, Jr., formerly president of Cleveland Twist Drill Company, told a story that illustrates my point:

> Jimmy Green was a new union committee member who stopped in to see Mr. Cox after contract negotiations had been concluded. Jimmy said that every other place he had worked, he had always gone home grouchy; he never wanted to play with the children or take his wife to the movies. And then he said, "But since I have been working here, all that has changed. Now when I come home, the children run to meet me and we have a grand romp together. It is a wonderful difference and I don't know why, but I thought you would like to know."[9]

As Mr. Cox observed, there must be a lot of Jimmy Greens in the world who want an opportunity to take part freely in a cooperative effort that has a moral purpose.

[9] Jacob D. Cox, Jr., *Material Human Progress* (Cleveland, Cleveland Twist Drill Company, 1954), p. 104.

Cases

Nikipoulis Grocery Store

Mr. George Nikipoulis, owner of the Nikipoulis Grocery Store, located in a small city in a large mid-western state, has been approached by the local salesman for a large national dairy, Reliance Milk Company. If Nikipoulis promises to buy all his milk from Reliance, the salesman would give Mr. Nikipoulis a ten per cent rebate off the wholesale price of the milk. Mr. Nikipoulis would continue to be billed at the wholesale price by Reliance. However, he would receive a personal check from the salesman for the rebate each month. The salesman explained that he was willing personally to take a lower commission in exchange for getting all the milk business from the Nikipoulis Grocery Store. The salesman claimed that several other groceries had already accepted his proposal.

The state in which the Nikipoulis store is located, like many other dairy states, maintains fixed wholesale prices on milk to protect its dairy industry. In recent years, there has been considerable consumer protest as well as protest by the large dairies against these fixed prices. The dairy farmers, however, have a strong influence in the state legislature and successfully have prevented the ending of fixed prices. Mr. Nikipoulis has purchased all his milk from the Acme Dairy Company for the last three years. When told of the Reliance salesman's offer, the Acme salesman claimed it was illegal and said he would not be able to offer a similar rebate. The Acme salesman further claimed that the rebate was offered by Reliance itself and would not, in fact, be deducted from the salesman's commission.

Mr. Nikipoulis is wondering whether he should accept the Reliance salesman's offer. Mr. Nikipoulis runs his grocery with the help of his wife. The Nikipoulis store is currently faced with intense competition from large supermarket chains, as are other "mama and papa" stores. Mr. and Mrs. Nikipoulis are able to stay in business only through such services as staying open later than the chains on evenings and weekends, through granting

This case was prepared by Assistant Professor Donald Grunewald as a basis for class discussion within Rutgers, The State University. Cases are not designed to present illustrations of either correct or incorrect handling of administrative situations. Reprinted by permission of the author.

credit to customers, and through the reputation of friendliness and personal attention that has been built up after 34 years in the grocery business at the same location. Nevertheless, the business is marginal at best and furnishes the owners with but a small income. Mr. and Mrs. Nikipoulis have no other source of income apart from the grocery.

If Mr. Nikipoulis accepts the rebate he could reduce the retail price of his milk to the price charged by the supermarket chains or else pocket the rebate as an additional profit which he estimates to be in the neighborhood of ten to twenty dollars per week.

The Anatomy of a Price-Fixing Conspiracy

This is the case history of a price-fixing conspiracy. It took place in a small industry in a middle-sized town, but it has the same characteristics as conspiracies recently uncovered and made public that operated nationally and in major industries.

It is not worth notice simply because it operated in violation of the law, or because it is unusual. Federal antitrust enforcers acknowledge that conspiracies of this type probably function in dozens of industries and dozens of cities around the nation. Antitrust agents simply are not equipped to uncover them. Price-fixing conspiracies, after all, are conducted in secret.

But this case is noteworthy because price-fixing is a subject not often openly discussed. There is little understanding about what a price conspiracy is, even less about what goes into the start of a "fix" and what factors lead to its demise. This story is presented with the thought that better understanding of what makes otherwise honest businessmen take part in an illegal activity will benefit both the business community and the government agencies that watch out for such things.

SETTING THE SCENE

The industry involved here is ready-mixed concrete; the area, a medium-sized industrial city where construction has boomed for the last 15 years. The conspiracy is not operating now, but many of the factors that led up to its inception are appearing again. It could start up any day.

As it happens, the ready-mix industry is vulnerable to price-fixing. It is

From *Business Week,* September 8, 1962, pp. 72–73. Reprinted by the courtesy of the publisher.

essentially a local business; trucks can haul wet concrete within a radius of only 15 miles or so. It is a retail business—ready-mix producers, like supermarkets, set prices largely by what competition is charging. It is an easy industry to enter. A smart operator with a good credit line can set up a "portable" plant for only a few thousand dollars.

In the city where this story takes place there are more than a dozen competitors now. They have the typical small-business weakness of inadequate accounting facilities. Producers usually don't really know how much it costs them to sell, mix, and haul a yard of concrete, so prices often have no relation to costs.

HIGH OVERHEAD

It is an industry with high overhead costs. A truck fleet must be maintained to meet peak demand, and trucks cost up to $24,000 each. Volume is subject to extreme seasonal fluctuations. There is little business in winter, and in summer a couple of days of rain can transform a highly profitable week into a dismal one. It takes as much manpower to run a plant waiting for the weather to break, or waiting for contractors to get jobs ready to pour, as it does to man a plant operating full-tilt for a 15-hour day.

It is an industry of many small companies—this town's largest ready-mix producer grosses under $1-million a year. Producers and their principal customers, the contractors, are often good friends. Each producer knows what big jobs his competitors have.

Sighting a competitor's truck heading in the direction of one of his own big jobs causes momentary panic in a producer, and he'll give chase to find out where the truck is going. Contractors can be prima donnas and, almost on whim, cancel a big order from one producer and give it to another, with two quick phone calls.

THE FIX

Ready-mix producers in this town decided late in 1959 to "stabilize" their prices at $14.50 a yard. The "fix was on" for about 18 months. Last year, distrust among competitors led to its breakdown. The price, even while fixed, was not unreasonable; in some areas, concrete regularly sells for $16 or $17 a yard. But the factors that led up to the conspiracy, and to its end, make a fascinating story.

POSTWAR EXPERIENCE

Prior to World War II, this town had only a couple of producers, and only one of them, Smith, had a sizable operation. In those days, ready-mix was not as popular as it is now but each producer had a good business.

The postwar building boom made ready-mix more popular. In the late 1940s, producer Jones set up a sizable plant. There still was plenty of business for the first producer; indeed, contractors had to schedule pouring weeks ahead. If it happened to rain on your day, tough luck—get in line again.

Big contractors avoided this bottleneck by setting up their own concrete plants and buying transit-mix trucks. New competitors moved in, too.

By the mid-1950s, the building boom had slacked off. The independents were scratching for business. The contractor-owned producers, finding themselves with excess capacity, also were bidding for outside jobs. Since their overhead was at least partially absorbed by the larger contracting business, they could afford to go in with low prices. Prices weakened and, by the time the 1958 recession hit, nobody was making any profit.

TRADE GROUP ACTION

For some years, producers had sponsored a local trade association that served as a clearing house for credit ratings and worked on quality control. As prices plummeted, producers began to wonder if they could gain price stability through the association. All those who showed up for an association meeting in the fall of 1959 were disgruntled about prices, and when one of the small producers suggested it might be time to "stabilize," they were ready.

They all knew that Smith, still the largest, would have to agree before the fix could work. He did. They quickly hit on $14.50 because that was the price that had been "stabilized" in a nearby metropolitan area. Then, over drinks in a hotel room, they haggled for more than five hours how to do it, how to enforce it, how to avoid going to jail.

ETHICAL QUALMS

The thought of price-fixing went against the grain for most of the participants, though there was some debate as to whether such an agreement was legal or not. They concluded that it was not. But prices were weakening by the day, and their practical decision, somewhat overdramatized, was that they'd rather go to jail than starve. There was no effort to hit upon a system of bid rotations, because this practice was viewed as an out-and-out illegality.

"It was sort of like the difference between getting a ticket for parking and a ticket for speeding," says one.

It was probably this reluctance that eventually led to the end of the fix.

ADMINISTERING PRICES

The new price became effective in a couple of weeks. Jobs already contracted for were protected; each producer drew up a list of these protected jobs that was put in a sealed envelope and filed, to guard against later accusations of price-cutting.

A three-man "enforcement" committee also was appointed, but for the first several months it had little work to do. The association met weekly and reviewed "I know where I can get it cheaper" complaints from contractors. There were few charges of claim-jumping among producers themselves and, for the first year or so, the enforcement committee conducted only a couple of investigations into the alleged price-cutting. Producers were building trust among themselves, and the fix was, in fact, working well. Prices were "stabilized."

In practice, the committee could do little to enforce the price, as became obvious when the fix started to fall apart. Enforcement was based on personal relationships. If a rumor got about that a price had been cut, the suspected offender got a phone call from a member of the committee, who suggested that he stop. Says one participant: "I reckon everybody had some deals going, but they were all kept pretty quiet."

One producer, invited to lunch by a committee member, was charged with cutting his price on a big job. He had the foresight to bring with him his purchase order, proving he had not.

THE FALLING-OUT

After more than a year, Smith claimed he was losing jobs. He accused his smaller competitors of "chiseling." Maybe they were, maybe not; at any rate, they had become more aggressive and were selling harder.

There was no doubt that "deals" were worked out. A producer with excavating equipment, for example, would hold the price on concrete but give a lower bid for excavation work. Concrete forms, which contractors usually must rent or buy, were thrown in free. Discounts were offered on other supplies.

But there were two effective pressures against admitting to price-cutting: (1) producers did not want to be known as "chiselers," and (2) of course, they wanted to hold the $14.50 price.

During a long, ill-tempered lunch, Smith accused Jones of cutting prices and stealing a big job. Jones denied it. Smith made a similar accusation against another smaller producer, and this producer showed a purchase order proving he did not cut. Smith accused him of giving a kickback.

Smith was not the only dissatisfied producer; by this time there was a good deal of distrust among the group. Smith was angry, but he had been considering the situation coolly, too. He finally said he was "sick of the way you all are fooling around," and announced an across-the-board cut of 50¢ a yard. Without anyone saying so, everybody knew there was no longer any price agreement. Prices dipped to close to $13.75.

BACK TO FREE ENTERPRISE

Business so far in 1962 has been worse than last year, and producers are making less, or losing more. Producer Jones says his profit-and-loss sheet looks worse than in 1961, when his before-tax profit was $1,250. Jones figures that when he sells concrete at $12.50 a yard, he's just covering expenses and not paying for overhead, to say nothing of making a profit. He's making some sales at $12.50 right now, although maybe a slightly greater proportion of his sales now are at a higher price than last year after the price break.

For the last year or so, the association has continued to function, but not as a price-fixing vehicle. Lately, though, there has been some talk about this.

Jones' only objection to a new fix is that it probably won't work any better now than it did before. Establishment of a system of bid rotation or a central collection agency would be the only way to make it work, he feels. But he thinks producers simply would not consider rotating bids. And if a central collection agency was set up, it would mean no "deals."

Says Jones: "The only reason it worked for as long as it did before is because everybody had their deals going."

But things are tough. "Probably half of us are hanging on from day to day," says Jones. "And the more jobs you sell at $12, the worse it gets. I suppose the only way out of this fussin' is for some of the bigger men to buy up some of the smaller ones and either put them out of business or run them part-time."

Bibliography

A. The Ethical Aspects of Business

Adam, Paul J. "What Is a Conflict of Interest?" *Challenge* (June 1963), pp. 11–14.

Austin, Douglas. "A Defense of the Corporation Pirate," *Business Horizons* (Winter 1964), pp. 51–58.

Carr, Albert. "Is Business Bluffing Ethical?" *Harvard Business Review* (January–February, 1968), pp. 143–153.

Fair, William. "The Corporate CIA—A Prediction of Things to Come," *Management Science* (June 1966), pp. 489–503.

Graham, Billy. "The Answer to Corruption," *Nation's Business* (September 1969), pp. 46–49.

Hodges, Luther. "The Gray Areas in Business Ethics," *Management Review* (March 1963), pp. 40–50.

Little, Robert W. "The Hart Truth-In-Packaging Bill," *University of Washington Business Review* (April 1963), pp. 3–13.

"Low Marks in Ethics," *Business Week* (September 28, 1968), pp. 64–70.

Rostow, Eugene V. "The Ethics of Competition Revisited," *California Management Review* (Spring 1963), pp. 13–23.

B. Business and Religion

Broehl, Wayne. "Do Business and Religion Mix?" *Harvard Business Review,* (March–April, 1958), pp.139–152.

Ford, S. "What the Bible Tells the Businessman," *Business Management* (December 1969), pp. 48–51.

Johnson, Harold L. "Can the Businessman Apply Christianity?" *Harvard Business Review* (September–October, 1957), pp. 68–75.

Roalman, A. R. "PR Program for Religious Involvement," *Public Relations Journal* (October 1969), pp. 75–77.

Ward, L. B. "Ethics of Executive Selection," *Harvard Business Review* (March 1965), pp. 6–8+.

Worthy, James C. "Religion and Its Role in the World of Business," *Journal of Business* (October 1958), pp. 293–303.

————. "Does Religion Affect Media Habits?" *Media/Scope* (June 1967), p. 112.

PART SIX

Business Management Philosophies

The operation of business in a free enterprise society has naturally aroused certain conflicts. These issues have disclosed the businessman's lack of understanding of basic economic and social concepts and his failure to recognize and understand ethical and religious values of individuals and groups. In many situations, we have found apparent conflicts in the area of the rights and prerogatives of the parties. In order to resolve these conflicts of rights, we must identify their corresponding responsibilties. Any definition of rights and responsibilities should be comprehensive enough to include the problems of all groups and individuals with business. This will entail the development of a systematic body of principles capable of being integrated into a codified philosophy or creed. If such a philosophy can be formulated, management will then, and only then, be on the way to resolving its problems while satisfying its professional needs. Without such a philosophy, attempts to resolve these issues under the constantly changing conditions of our dynamic economy and society can never hope to achieve a uniformity and consistency of business practices compatible with the prevailing, social ideologies and mores.

A. Management Rights

Among the basic rights with which business is most concerned is the right to stay in business. Concomitant with this right is the right of management to control business operations and thereby achieve this survival objective. Immediately the question is raised as to which rights are exclusively managerial and inherently necessary to the survival and control of the business. In "Managers Have to Manage" [27] C. P. Ives delineates management's basic rights and absolute control needs. He tells us that the right to manipulate labor is derived from the private property right, through management's direction of employees in the organizational chain. Certain management prerogatives require absolute control over such issues as plant relocation, subcontracting, efficiency measures, wages and prices. Unfortunately, the legislation providing for collective bargaining stands to refute, or at least qualify, many of these rights or prerogatives. Ives delineates the most important managerial needs for management to survive in a competitive market, and grow in a profitable fashion. The other side of this issue has been stated by Neil Chamberlain in article 28, "What is Management's Right to Manage?" If, as Chamberlain contends, management's rights relate only to the control of property delegated to it by the stockholders, it actually has no rights over personnel other than those negotiated in the individual and union employment contracts. This point of view would identify the source of management's rights as the constitutionally protected right of private property plus the legislative provision for, and recognition of, collective and individual labor-contract agreements.

Individual managerial rights, insofar as legal ramifications are concerned, are generally limited by managerial job definitions and company policies. In addition, there is a most significant change which has occurred in business during this century. This change started from the original concept that employees were subject to the general authority of management in all areas of work activity. Today the employee is subject to management's authority only insofar as it affects the specific items contained in his job description. This can complicate problems in the future when we envision the needs of achieving employment stabilization through work changes resulting from automation and the necessity for retraining and transferring employees. With these impediments to the adaptation of business to a changing society and economy, the question of management's rights becomes a paramount issue of society as well as of business.

A test of management rights is presented in the Fisher Manufacturing Company case. A number of conflict incidents in the case illustrate the "absolute" perspective of management rights, and their conflicts with the views of other managers, employees, and owners of the company. While management can usually exercise its rights in an arbitrary, if not absolute, manner in the short run, the cost is often prohibitive. More importantly, if management can approach any conflicts of rights with the aim of establishing equitable resolutions, the benefits to the organization should definitely be significant. Both long- and short-run goals of the many individuals and groups will be maximized, thereby contributing to both management's long-run self-interest and justice for all concerned.

B. Business Philosophies and Objectives

The objectives of business have historically come in conflict with the objectives of our total society, particularly in the realm of aggregate economic activity. The roots of this conflict lie in the position of classical economic theory to promote profits as a primary, if not exclusive, objective for business and to oppose theories promoting the social responsibilities of business. Contemporary surveys of business objectives reveal an extensive variety of internally and externally oriented objectives by individual managers, firms, industries, and the total economy. In spite of this variety, there is a high degree of unanimity regarding profits as the primary, if not exclusive, objective of business, sometimes emphasized as the means of survival for the firm.

Peter Drucker emphasizes five survival objectives of business in article 29, "Business Objectives and Survival Needs. Notes on a Discipline of Business Enterprise." Drucker's objectives include: a human organization capable of perpetuating itself; an organization capable of effective adaptation with society and its economy; the supply of economic goods and services; adaptation to a changing economy and technology; and last, but certainly not least, profits. These objectives embody the critical factors required for business survival, but they fail to question the justification for the absoluteness of the survival objective. This concept is tested in the Anatomy of a Price-Fixing Conspiracy case in Part Five. We find the answer to the mutual survival of business, employees, customers, and other related groups in society in the balance of the needs, rights and prerogatives of all legitimate interest groups and individuals. The exclusive or absolute concern with any individual's or group's right in our pluralistic society cannot survive, including business' need and right to profits.

When the businessman approaches the essential issues involved in the determination of the objectives of business, he is confronted with the historical and contemporary purpose of the institution. As cited by Ralph C. Davis in "A Philosophy of Management" [30] if the primary objective of business is profits, then the service objective may become the means to that end and, therefore, subordinate to the profit goal. If, on the other hand, the service objective is deemed paramount, the profit objective may be relegated to a position of lesser importance. The determination of the priority of ends versus means in these two objectives will be ultimately decided by society, either in the exercise of its choices and options in the free marketplace or in the actions of particular interest-pressure groups seeking social controls through government regulations.

Since the profit and service objectives are so frequently pitted against each other, it would appear necessary to explain their essential relationships in a free enterprise society. Given the different frames of reference and interest of the two groups—business and society—the following theory is proposed. For society, the primary purpose and objective of business is service to society.

The best means or incentive for achieving this service objective has been the use of the profit motive in a free enterprise society. By using the profit motive to provide these services, society hopes not only to achieve the benefits of productivity and efficiency, but also the highest degree of freedom available in an alternative economic system. From the businessman's point of view, the primary purpose or goal of business is profits. The means of achieving these profits is the provision of goods and services to society in such a way that the highest degree of societal satisfaction and business profit are achieved. From this perspective, the service objective to society is the means to the end of profit for business.

The excessive or exclusive emphasis upon profit as the objective of business has often been called a philosophy of "individualism" or "Progressive conservativism." This philosophy tends to emphasize the protection and preservation of the private property right and the freedom of its use. It would curtail governmental controls, particularly from a centralized government. Other appeals are made for a philosophy which will not be excessively individualistic, but will be comprehensive in terms of integrating the objectives of the diverse groups. This latter philosophy would draw upon the knowledge accumulated from the art, science, and theories of management developed to date.

Remembering the preeminence of the value of freedom in the economic activities of our society, we see justification and grave necessity for preservation of our present system. On the other hand, when this system fails to achieve its objectives in meeting the needs and rights of respective business firms, individuals, and groups in society, its deficiencies must be corrected by socially responsible actions of all parties and groups. It would be preferable if these socially responsible actions be taken at levels of society lower than the federal government.

If professional management is to be achieved to guide business and resolve its problems and conflicts with society, it must somehow develop a comprehensive philosophy which will support the free enterprise system and also make it compatible with the American way of life. This philosophy must provide a code of ethics for professional managers which will clearly delineate their responsibility to society as well as their rights. It will also provide universally applicable principles by which claims upon our economic system can be equitably balanced and resolved.

A.   Management Rights

Managers Have to Manage   **27**
C. P. Ives

The main thing to remember about the price-wage-profit crisis in which the Kennedy Administration is now floundering is that on July 5, 1935, the Congress abolished the older power of business management to manage business in the United States. That is the date of the National Labor Relations (Wagner) Act. The express purpose of this act was to give trade unions *equal* bargaining power with management—that is, power to block or veto managerial decisions on wages and working conditions. But though abolishing the older power of management to manage, the Congress didn't assign managerial powers anywhere else. The result has been 27 years of continuous wage inflation powered by union monopoly and pro-union government.

Private management in the United States did retain the power to manage prices. It utilized this power as it had to—to inflate prices at approximately the rate of the wage inflation and as the shortest way to meet the wage demands which the inflation imposed. But the President's brusque intervention in the steel industry looked like formal notice that management is now to be deprived of its older power over prices. An industrial system in which management controls neither wages nor prices is like a case of cerebral palsy. It lacks essential coordination. Yet the American economy is now up against two rival systems in which price-wage coordination is still firm and industrial management still confident. In the friendly but competitive Common Market countries of Western Europe and Japan private management retains its old power to manage. In the deadly hostile Communist countries state power to manage, though clumsily and wastefully exerted, is without any limitation at all.

The fact is that since the thirties, the federal Administrations, with one or two exceptions, have been advised by academic economists almost exclu-

Reprinted with permission from the February 23, 1963 issue of the *National Review,* 150 East 38th Street, New York, N. Y., pp. 157–158.

sively; and as the late Joseph Schumpeter of Harvard wrote in the *American Economic Review,* "Many of the men who entered the field of [economics] teaching or research in the twenties or thirties had renounced allegiance to the bourgeois [private ownership] scheme of life, the bourgeois scheme of values. Many of them sneered at the profit motive and at the element of personal [especially managerial] performance in the capitalist process . . ." It was natural that such men should draw, consciously or unconsciously, on Lenin's notion that large industrial enterprise is largely automatic, that any clerk of average intelligence could preside over its day-to-day routine. In this view private managers were little more than parasites. To vest trade unions with power to counter and even immobilize such managers was in no sense to impair automatic prosperity and growth.

WHERE TO BEGIN

With the deepening wage-price-profit crisis of three decades later, the time has plainly come for a re-survey of the economic elementals. To be sure, the government can fiddle about at the edge of the economy with credit policy and tax manipulation. But these measures do not touch the economic elementals—the vital innards where paralysis and organic maladjustment lurk. The President himself has called for a re-survey of the elementals. He has not yet indicated that the obvious place to begin is with a reappraisal of the managerial function.

At the root the word management means the same as the word government. To govern is to manage and to manage is to govern. You manage or you govern a horse or a steel mill. In primitive societies now, and in the earlier history of all the Western countries, the government did indeed do the economic as well as the political governing and managing. In feudal times the king owned outright and absolutely (under God) all property—mainly land. He passed down its actual custody and management through a broadening pyramid of earls, barons and lesser nobility and gentry. Naturally this old-fashioned totalitarianism was tough on the common men at the bottom of the heap who didn't have anything at all except life and limb.

The remedy, worked out with much philosophizing and a fair amount of blood and tears over centuries, was a steady breaking-up and distribution among private men of the total property rights once enjoyed by the king alone. Just as the old king could do what he liked with his own, so could the new little kings of private property. That included the power to employ other men at whatever wages and working conditions the property-holders thought best, all things—including wage and price competition in the market—considered.

But why should anybody at all have the power to boss other men around? Why a thousand little kings any more than one big king? This is the heart of the matter, which seems to have eluded the Administration: there must be management because there must be discipline. Work is always more or less burdensome, involving exertion and fatigue. Organization of men and materials is not spontaneous, as Lenin thought: it requires rare and specialized managerial skills.

Once it was easy to see this. It was easy to see that a seventeenth-century locksmith must have authority to tell his journeymen and apprentices what to do. But as manufacture grew more sophisticated elemental relationships between discipline and production receded from easy view. When machinery proliferated and steam and then electricity did what human muscle used to do, production came to look more and more automatic. Well, if production really runs itself, why management? Enter Lenin and his clerk. And in the milder versions of the anti-management syndrome, here also enters the modern trade union power to veto management at will. More and more the union veto takes the form of the strike, and in nationally unionized industries, the nationwide paralysis strike. But the Kennedy Administration no more than its predecessors can tolerate these national paralysis strikes. Paralysis strikes in transport, in steel, are perilous enough. Paralysis strikes in the missile and space industries could jeopardize the physical survival of the nation itself.

The remedy to which the earlier Administrations have been forced again and again is the seizure of strike-bound industries and the return of the workingmen to work under any one of various forms of compulsion. Having destroyed the delicate private property mechanisms by which managerial discipline had been house-broken to freedom, the government men recaptured the function of economic discipline for themselves by reverting in a single lunge 500 years to the omni-managing kings of feudalism.

This route the Kennedy Administration has so far managed to avoid. The President has stated frequently that he wants no part of the job of fixing wages and prices in any general pattern of government take-over. With this view the unions themselves are now more sympathetic. In the beginning cheerful about their chances with friendly Administrations, they have gradually noted in successive seizures an unforeseen and ominous thing: the government does not displace the private managers when it seizes struck industries. It simply runs the Stars and Stripes up over the seized plants and commands workingmen more or less peremptorily to get back to their work, and no strike nonsense.

The brutal fact, now emerging again, is that managers are essential in any industrial system, free or slave, developed or undeveloped—but trade unions are not. The nature of management, after all, is to reduce costs and expand production, while that of unions is to increase costs at the risk of reducing production. It is not accidental that none of the mature industrial states had strong unions in the time of their development. They did have exceedingly tough and often very efficient managers—from the Scrooges of the early Industrial Revolution in England to the robber barons who industrialized the

United States and the totalitarian commissars who have built contemporary Sovietia. They had to have tough managers to enforce the rigorous discipline on which development depends—to keep wages, which is to say consumption, down and to push profits up because profits breed the investment of which development consists. Modern trade unionism is a hothouse growth, characteristic of a single type of industrialism in the easy years of its maturity and affluence—when, indeed, there may be economic virtue in combinations of workingmen which force purchasing power more broadly over the consuming public. But there have been only a handful of such economies in all recorded history. And just as these economies could not have industrialized had unions vetoed management in the time of their development, so even in the years of their strength they waver when unions veto management. The moral of a factual, one might even say a morphological, rethinking of the economic elementals seems clear enough: industry is less like Lenin's perpetual-motion machine and more like an army exercise. Firm management is as essential as firm generalship. True, there must be limits on the manager's power over the workingman, just as the military code prescribes to the generals in their command of personnel. The managerial limitations, moreover, are civilian, involving precious liberties, and so are rightly much broader and more restrictive: wage and hour laws, safety, health and sanitation regulations, workmen's compensation statutes, social security and appropriately qualified recognition of trade unions.

But within the scope of the limiting industrial laws, management must be free to manage, which means to control wages, to set prices and to command profits large enough to maintain and expand the productive plant. The peripheral manipulation of credit and tax policy is all well enough, but its aim is to influence management, and it must fail if management is denied the power to manage. Not until the President, his Labor Secretary and his New Frontier economists think their way back to these economic elementals, will the country begin to find its way out of the wage-price-profit crisis which now threatens all we have and can hope for.

What Is Management's Right to Manage?

28

Neil Chamberlain

The recent unpleasantness between the Ford Motor Co. and the United Automobile Workers about the speed of assembly lines provided the latest of a series of dramatic conflicts over the issue of managerial prerogatives in the automobile industry. Control over assembly-line speeds was also in dispute in the prolonged Chrysler strike of 1939, when Herman L. Weckler, Vice President in charge of operations, stated: "Management cannot abdicate its responsibility for any aspect of this business, whether it relates to labor, to engineering, to production or to selling. It cannot consent to sovietize the plants." And the General Motors shutdown in the winter of 1945–46 brought the pronouncement from H. W. Anderson, Vice President in charge of personnel, that the "functions of management cannot be delegated to anyone not responsible for the continuing of the business. They will not be surrendered to the union."

While the issue has thus been dramatized in the automobile industry, there are few companies in the U.S. in which it has not been raised at some time during the course of collective-bargaining negotiations. Indeed, the nature of the managerial prerogative in relation to the union was one of the points on which the President's postwar labor-management conference broke down, with union and management committee members rendering separate and diametrically opposed reports. Ira Mosher, then president of the National Association of Manufacturers, subsequently asserted: "Labor wouldn't even agree to an effort to define the functions of management, although we made a real effort to get that issue settled. We drew up a list of some thirty-odd specific acts, such as the determination of prices, accounting procedure, and so forth, which it seemed clear to us must be reserved to management. Labor refused to accept a single one, and we were told . . . the reason . . . was that at some future time labor may want to bring any one of these functions into the realm of collective bargaining." Mosher's statement points attention to one reason why the conflict remains unresolved. If the "right to manage" can be defined *only* by a listing of "specific acts, such as the determination of prices," no general principle is available to serve as the standard for inclusion or exclusion of such specific acts. Does any principle of management rights exist to provide the needed standards?

Reprinted from the July 1949 issue of *Fortune Magazine*, pp. 68–70, by special permission; © 1949 Time Inc.

There seems ample reason for believing that in the minds of many managers the right of management is virtually synonymous with their right to make business decisions. Weckler's concern for "responsibility" and Anderson's for "the continuing of the business" are in line with this view. If this is to be regarded as a principle, however, what can be said of management's willingness to bargain on wages, hours, layoffs, promotions, and the host of other matters that go into the modern collective-bargaining agreement? Consider wages, for example. Is not the size of the wage bill a business decision of first importance? Prior to the advent of the union in an industrial enterprise, is not one of management's chief problems—in charting the continuing success of the business—that of bringing its cost and price structures into line, with wages an important element of costs? Does the introduction of collective bargaining make this any less a business decision? Why is managerial prerogative not raised as a barrier to negotiation on the subject of wages? Is the size of the wage bill of different order of significance from the speed of assembly lines? What principle bars negotiation of rates of operation and permits bargaining on wages, if both are managerial decisions?

The answer appears to be that no principle is involved, but rather that the process of inclusion and exclusion suggested by Mosher is at work. Wages have become accepted as "legitimate" matters of collective bargaining, while production speeds have not. In 1851 the New York *Journal of Commerce* editorialized that it would not yield "the control of our business to the dictation of a self-constituted power outside of the office" in the matters of hours and apprenticeship. Today both of these subjects are commonly to be found in collective agreements. In 1945 Inland Steel and other companies fought the union's demand for a voice in a company pension plan. Today welfare programs, including pensions, have become rather widely accepted as a bargaining matter. Today Henry Ford II asserts, in his recent conflict with the U.A.W.: "I want to make it quite clear that this company now *and always* will hold to its right—fairly and firmly guaranteed under our contract—to establish work standards which will assure efficient operation without impairing in any way the health or safety of our employees." Are Ford's strong words to be taken as evidence only of *present* exclusion, or is he gifted with prophetic vision that this subject, unlike others before it, will *never* find acceptance as a "legitimate" matter for collective agreement?

At the root of the problem of management's right to manage is simply the increasing insubstantiality of management's ability to maintain it. It has been said that the right emerges from the laws of private property, in which management as the actual or representative owner has the privilege of determining the use to be made of its property. It was Justice McReynolds, dissenting in the Jones & Laughlin case, who objected to the National Labor Relations Act on the ground that "a private owner is deprived of power to manage his own property by freely selecting those to whom his manufacturing operations are to be entrusted." But it is sometimes overlooked that the property basis of management involves no duty on the part of others to be managed.

That is to say, the trouble with property ownership as a conferer of authority is that it gives command only over *things*. This involves no special difficulties in a society of small property holders and individual proprietorships, for control over things is all that is needed to produce for, and sell in, the market. But when business enterprise assumes a corporate form and requires the cooperation of large numbers of people performing specialized functions, control over things ceases to be sufficient.

Except for authoritarian relationships (for example, in the military services at home, and in totalitarian societies generally abroad), people can be managed and directed only with their own consent. While property rights carry with them a power of disposition of goods, they do not carry an equal power to use those goods *if* the cooperation of others is necessary to that use. Cooperation, without which the property right is reduced to a power of disposition, cannot be commanded. It can only be won by consent. The property rights of the stockholders, exercised for them by management, can be made meaningful only with the cooperation of all those who are actually needed to operate the business, including the workers.

But there is no legal compulsion upon the workers to cooperate. There is no legal statement of the terms on which cooperation must take place. The definition of those terms is left directly to the parties involved, and there is nothing in the law to stop the union from demanding as the price of the cooperation of its members a voice in some matter previously independently determined by management. Since property rights do not give command over others, management *may* find it essential to share its authority as a means of inducing cooperation, in order to maintain the value of a going business. Over a period of time it becomes customary to share authority, in order to win cooperation, in certain recognized areas of business decisions—wages, for example, or hours; perhaps someday the speed of assembly lines.

Thus the management and direction of others do not flow out of legal rights but must be granted by those very people who are managed and directed. And the price of the grant may be, in the words of the editorial writer for the New York *Journal of Commerce* in 1851, that management—and the owners—yields their independence in certain matters of business operation. *What* matters? Potentially none would seem to be excluded—whatever matters are deemed important to those whose cooperation is being sought.

What then is the managerial prerogative? The answer may come more easily if management is viewed as a function rather than as a group of people —the function of making and effectuating business decisions. This function is to be found at all levels of organization in an enterprise. It may be remembered, for example, that in recent years a drive has been under way to instill in foremen the feeling of being part of management. Any definition of the managerial prerogative would presumably, then, have to include within its scope the foreman as well as the president.

A good working definition of the management prerogative is, perhaps, that it is the power to make decisions and to see to their effectuation within whatever framework of discretion may exist. If the framework changes, so does the prerogative. The limits of the foreman's prerogatives are thus set for him by the decisions of higher management, within which his authority must be exercised. The extent of top management's prerogatives is defined by national and state legislation and by the decisions of the board of directors if the board functions *de facto* as well as *de jure*. But the power to make a decision is not the same as the power to carry it out. The power to decide the speed of assembly lines is not the same as the power to secure the operation of assembly lines at that speed. To tranlate decision into accomplishment requires the assent of those whose cooperation is essential.

In winning that assent it may be necessary to reach some agreement with the union that represents the employees. The decision becomes a collective decision, and establishes the framework within which the management prerogative at lower levels of organization must be exercised. It may thus be the case that the *management* prerogative (of determining the speeds of operation, for example) can be exercised *only* through union participation, if management is regarded as a function. Or to put the case another way, the management prerogative—in the sense of power to carry out decisions made—*may* in some instances be preserved only if the union joins in making the decision.

Looked at in this fashion, it becomes evident that *collective bargaining is in fact one method of management*. It is a process for making business decisions that can be carried out. It is no guarantee of good decisions or of proper effectuation—any more than any method of management can provide such a guarantee. But it may be, in specific instances, a more appropriate method of management than some other.

This view does not, of course, lead to the conclusion that management should necessarily accede to the union's demand for a voice in particular aspects of the managerial function. The Ford Motor Co. may have been well advised in making the stand that it did. Possibly it may not have been well advised. The exclusion of certain subjects from the process of collective agreement or the inclusion of other subjects within its terms must be justified on the basis of all the relevant facts. The only question involving any principle of the management prerogative, however, is whether the union's participation in the decision-making process is essential or conducive to the effectuation of the decision. Strike or threat of strike, if the union is not included in the making of a business decision, is not the only test. There is no necessary assurance that union participation in the matter of rates of operation will in fact secure compliance with the decision even though it is a collective one. If the union is torn with factionalism or controlled by a minority so that employee-union cohesion is weak and there is danger that joint no less than unilateral decisions will be disregarded or subverted, strong ground may be found for declining to share the management prerogative with the union.

There is thus perhaps some salutary effect in management's resistance to the union's expanding role in the making of business decisions. It may bring weight upon the unions to perfect their organizations so as to *improve* their business performance; and it may thus provide conviction to those now skeptical that sharing managerial authority with a union carries the advantage of inducing compliance with decisions once reached. No benefit would seem to inhere, however, in a doctrinaire conviction that certain areas of control must be preserved inviolate of union influence. On any particular subject, good management may someday if not now suggest an opposite conclusion.

This conception of the relationship between collective bargaining and the management prerogative suggests a further conclusion. For years schools of business administration have been preoccupied with teaching students improved methods of business management. Professional managers have likewise encouraged continued investigation of efficient business procedures. If it becomes evident that collective bargaining is in fact a method of management, there would seem to be some point in approaching it similarly, with the intent of improving it as a decision-making process in industry. The fact that conflict of interests is present in the process makes the problem difficult, but it is no secret that conflicts arise now within the so-called "family of management" and procedures must be found for resolving them. Techniques of management will not, of course, provide solutions in themselves, but they assist in arriving at decisions when needed. If collective bargaining *is* management—one form of it—business interests might well be persuaded that its improved practice will help rather than hinder business performance, and unions might be led to believe that increased participation will be facilitated by paying attention to the procedures they employ. The study of collective bargaining *as one method for making business decisions* might lead to conclusions for its greater effectiveness, which would benefit all concerned. In such an analysis unions would have to be viewed not as something falling outside of the structure and processes of management but actually included within its terms.

B. Business Philosophies and Objectives

Business Objectives and Survival Needs:
Notes on a Discipline of
Business Enterprise

29

Peter F. Drucker

The literature of business management, confined to a few "how to do" books only fifty years ago, has grown beyond any one man's capacity even to catalogue it. Professional education for business has become the largest and most rapidly growing field of professional education in this country and is growing rapidly in all other countries in the free world. It also has created in the advanced postgraduate education for experienced, mature, and successful executives—perhaps first undertaken in systematic form at the University of Chicago—the only really new educational concept in a hundred and fifty years.

Yet so far we have little in the way of a "discipline" of business enterprise, little in the way of an organized, systematic body of knowledge, with its own theory, its own concepts, and its own methodology of hypothesis, analysis, and verification.

THE NEED FOR A THEORY OF BUSINESS BEHAVIOR

The absence of an adequate theory of business enterprise is not just an "academic" concern; on the contrary, it underlies four major problems central to business as well as to a free-enterprise society.

1. One is the obvious inability of the layman to understand modern business enterprise and its behavior. What goes on, and why, "at the top" or "on

From the *Journal of Businesss* (April 1958) pp. 81–90. Reprinted with permission of the author.

the fourteenth floor" of the large corporation—the central economic and one of the central social institutions of modern industrial society—is as much of a mystery to the "outsider" as the magician's sleight of hand is to the small boy in the audience. And the "outsiders" include not only those truly outside business enterprise. They include workers and shareholders; they include many professionally trained men in the business—the engineers or chemists, for instance—indeed, they include a good many management people themselves: supervisors, junior executives, functional managers. They may accept what "top management" does, but they accept on faith rather than by reason of knowledge and understanding. Yet such understanding is needed for the success of the individual business as well as for the survival of industrial society and of the free-enterprise system.

One of the real threats is the all-but-universal resistance to profit in such a system, the all-but-universal (but totally fallacious) belief that socialism—or any other ism—can operate an industrial economy without the "rake-off" of profit, and the all-but-universal concern lest profit be too high. That the danger in a dynamic, industrial economy is that profit may be too low to permit the risks of innovation, growth, and expansion—that, indeed, there may be no such thing as "profit" but only provision for the costs of the future—very few people understand.

This ignorance has resisted all attempts at education; this resistance to profits has proved impervious to all propaganda or appeals, even to the attempts at "profit-sharing."

The only thing capable of creating understanding of the essential and necessary function of profit in an expanding, risk-taking, industrial economy is an understanding of business enterprise. And that for all without personal, immediate experience in the general management of a business can come only through a general "model" of business enterprise, that is, through the general theory of a systematic discipline.

2. The second problem is the lack of any bridge of understanding between the "macro-economics" of an economy and the "micro-economics" of the most important actor in this economy, the business enterprise. The only "micro-economic" concept to be found in economic theory today is that of "profit maximization." To make it fit the actual, observable behavior of business enterprise, however, economists have had to bend, stretch, and qualify it until it has lost all meaning and all usefulness. It has become as complicated as the "epicycles" with which pre-Copernician astronomers tried to save the geocentric view of the universe: "profit maximization" may mean short-run, immediate revenue or long-range basic profitability of wealth-producing resources; it may have to be qualified by a host of unpredictables such as managerial power drives, union pressures, technology, etc.; and it completely fails even then to account for business behavior in a growing economy. It does not enable the economist to predict business reaction to

public policy any more; to the governmental policy-maker business reaction is as "irrational" as government policy, by and large, seems to the businessman.

But in modern industrial society we must be able to "translate" easily from public policy to business behavior and back again. The policy-maker must be able to assess the impact of public policy on business behavior; and the businessman—especially in the large enterprise—must be able to assess the impact of his decisions and actions on the "macro-economy." "Profit-maximization" does not enable us to do either, as this paper intends to show, primarily because it fails to understand the role and function of profit.

3. The third area in which the absence of a genuine theory of business enterprise creates very real problems is that of the internal integration of the organization. The management literature is full of discussions of the "problem of the specialist" who sees only his own functional area or of the "problem of the scientist in business" who resents the demand that he subordinate his knowledge to business ends. Yet we will be getting even more specialized; we will, of necessity, employ more and more highly trained "professionals." Each of those must be dedicated to his specialty; yet each must share a common vision and common goals and must voluntarily engage in a common effort. To bring this about is already the most time- and energy-consuming job of management, certainly in our big businesses, and no one I know claims to be able to do it successfully.

Twenty years ago it was still possible to see a business as a mechanical assemblage of "functions." Today we know that, when we talk of a "business," the "functions" simply do not exist. There is only business profit, business risk, business product, business investment, and business customer. The functions are irrelevant to any one of them. And yet it is equally obvious, if we look at the business, that the work has to be done by people who specialize, because nobody can know enough even to know all there is to be known about one of the major functions today—they are growing too fast. It is already asking a great deal of a good man to be a good functional man, and, in some areas, it is rapidly becoming almost too much to ask of a man. How, then, do we transmute functional knowledge and functional contribution into general direction and general results? The ability of big business—but even of many small ones—to survive depends on our ability to solve this problem.

4. The final problem—also a symptom both of the lack of discipline and of the need for it—is of course the businessman's own attitude toward "theory." When he says, "This is theoretical," he by and large still means: "This is irrelevant." Whether managing a business enterprise could or should be a "science" (and one's answer to this question depends primarily on how one defines the word "science"), we need to be able to consider theory the foundation for good practice. We would have no modern doctors, unless

medicine (without itself being a "science" in any strict sense of the word) considered the life-sciences and their theories the foundation of good practice. Without such a foundation in a discipline of business enterprise we cannot make valid general statements, cannot therefore predict the outcome of actions or decisions, and can judge them only by hindsight and by their results—when it is too late to do anything. All we can have at the time of decision would be "hunches," "hopes," and "opinions," and, considering the dependence of modern society on business enterprise and the impact of managerial decisions, this is not good enough.

Without such a discipline we could also neither teach nor learn, let alone work systematically on the improvement of our knowledge and of our performance as managers of a business. Yet the need both for managers and for constant improvement of their knowledge and performance is so tremendous, quantitatively as well as qualitatively, that we simply cannot depend on the "natural selection" of a handful of "geniuses."

The need for a systematic discipline of business enterprise is particularly pressing in the underdeveloped growth countries of the world. Their ability to develop themselves will depend, above all, on their ability rapidly to develop men capable of managing business enterprise, that is, on the availability of a discipline that can be taught and can be learned. If all that is available to them is development through experience, they will almost inevitably be pushed toward some form of collectivism. For, however wasteful all collectivism is of economic resources, however destructive it is of freedom, dignity, and happiness, it economizes the managerial resource through its concentration of entrepreneurial and managerial decisions in the hands of a few "planners" at the top.

WHAT ARE THE SURVIVAL NEEDS OF BUSINESS ENTERPRISE?

We are still a long way from a genuine "discipline" of business enterprise. But there is emerging today a foundation of knowledge and understanding. It is being created in some of our large companies and in some of our universities. In some places the starting point is economics, in some marketing, in some the administrative process, in others such new methodologies as operations research and synthesis or long-range planning. But what all these approaches, regardless of starting point or terminology, have in common is that they start out with the question: What are the survival needs of business enterprise? What, in other words, does it have to be, to do, to achieve—to exist at all? For each of these "needs" there has, then, to be an "objective."

It may be said that this approach goes back to the pioneering work on business objectives that was done at the Bell Telephone System under the presidency of Theodore Vail a full forty years ago. Certainly, that was the first time the management of a large business enterprise refused to accept the old, glib statement, "The objective of a business is to make a profit," and asked instead, "On what will our survival as a privately owned business depend?" The practical effectiveness of the seemingly so obvious and simple approach is proved by the survival, unique in developed countries, of privately owned telecommunications in the United States and Canada. A main reason for this was certainly the "survival objective" Vail set for the Bell System: "Public satisfaction with our service." Yet, though proved in practice, this remained, until recently, an isolated example. And it probably had to remain such until, within the last generation, the biologists developed the approach to understanding of "systems" by means of defining "essential survival functions."

"Survival objectives" are general; they must be the same in general for each and every business. Yet they are also specific; different performance and different results would be needed in each objective area for any particular business. And every individual business will also need its own specific balance between them at any given time.

The concept of survival objectives thus fulfills the first requirement of a genuine "theory"—that it be both formal and yet concretely applicable, that is, "practical." Survival objectives are also "objective" both as to their nature and as to the specific requirements in a given situation. They do not depend on "opinion" or "hunch." Yet—and this is essential—they do not "determine" entrepreneurial or managerial decisions; they are not (as is so much of traditional economics or of contemporary behavioral science) an attempt to substitute formulas for risk-taking decision or responsible judgment. They attempt rather to establish the foundation for decision and judgment, to make what is the specific task of entrepreneur and manager possible, effective, and rational, and to make it understandable and understood.

We have reached the stage where we know the "functions" of a business enterprise, with "function" being used the way the biologist talks about "procreation" as a "function" essential for the perpetuation of a living species.

There are *five such "survival functions"* of business enterprise. Together they define the areas in which each business, to survive, has to reach a standard of performance and produce results above a minimum level. They are also the areas affected by every business decision and, in turn, affecting every business result. Together these five areas of "survival objectives" describe therefore (operationally) the "nature of business enterprise."

1. The enterprise needs, first, a *human organization designed for joint performance* and capable of perpetuating itself.

It is an assemblage not of brick and mortar but of people. These people must work as individuals; they cannot work any other way. Yet they must voluntarily work for a common result and must therefore be organized for joint performance. The first requirement of business is therefore that there be an effective human organization.

But business must also be capable of perpetuating itself as a human organization if only because all the things we decide every day—if, indeed, we are managers—take for their operation more time than the good Lord has allotted us. We are not making a single decision the end of which we are likely to see while still working. How many managerial decisions will be liquidated within twenty years, will have disappeared, unless they are totally foolish decisions? Most of the decisions we make take five years before they even begin to have an impact; this is the short range of a decision. And then they take ten or fifteen years before (at the very earliest) they are liquidated, have ceased to be effective, and, therefore, have ceased to be reasonably right.

This means that the enterprise as a human organization has to be able to perpetuate itself. It has to be able to survive the life-span of any one man.

2. The second survival objective arises from the fact that the enterprise exists in *society and economy.* In business schools and business thinking we often tend to assume that the business enterprise exists by itself in a vacuum. We look at it from the inside. But the business enterprise is a creature of society and economy. If there is one thing we do know, it is that society and/or economy can put any business out of existence overnight—nothing is simpler. The enterprise exists on sufferance and exists only as long as society and economy believe that it does a job and a necessary, a useful, and a productive one.

I am not talking here of "public relations"; they are only one means. I am not talking of something that concerns only the giants. And I am not talking of "socialism." Even if the free-enterprise system survives, individual businesses and industries within it may be—and of course often have been restricted, penalized, or even put out of business very fast by social or political action such as taxes or zoning laws, municipal ordinances or federal regulation, and so forth. Anticipation of social climate and economic policy, on the one hand, and organized behavior to create what business needs to survive in respect to both are therefore genuine survival needs of each business at all times. They have to be considered in every action and have to be "factored" into every business decision.

Equally, the business is a creature of the economy and at the mercy of changes in it—in population and income, ways of life and spending patterns, expectations and values. Again here is need for objectives which anticipate so as to enable the business to adapt and which at the same time aim at creating the most favorable conditions.

3. Then, of course, there is the area of the specific purpose of business, of its contribution. The purpose is certainly to *supply an economic good and service.* This is the only reason why business exists. We would not suffer this complicated, difficult, and controversial institution except for the fact that we have not found any better way of supplying economic goods and services

productively, economically, and efficiently. So, as far as we know, no better way exists. But that is its only justification, its only purpose.

4. There is another purpose characteristic which I would, so to speak, call the nature of the beast; namely, that this all happens in a *changing* economy and a *changing* technology. Indeed, in the business enterprise we have the first institution which is designed to produce change. All human institutions since the dawn of prehistory or earlier had always been designed to prevent change—all of them: family, government, church, army. Change has always been a catastrophic threat to human security. But in the business enterprise we have an institution that is designed to create change. This is a very novel thing. Incidentally, it is one of the basic reasons for the complexity and difficulty of the institution.

This means not only that business must be able to adapt to change—that would be nothing very new. It means that every business, to survive, must strive to *innovate*. And innovation, that is, purposeful, organized action to bring about the new, is as important in the social field—the ways, methods, and organization of business, its marketing and market, its financial and personnel management, and so on—as it is in the technological areas of product and process.

In this country industrial research expenditures have risen from a scant one-tenth of 1 per cent of national income to 1½ or 2 per cent in less than thirty years. The bulk of this increase has come in the last ten years; this means that the impact in the form of major technological changes is still ahead of us. The speed of change in non-technological innnovation, for instance, in distribution channels, has been equally great. Yet many businesses are still not even geared to adaptation to change; and only a mere handful are geared to innovation—and then primarily in the technological areas. Here lies therefore a great need for a valid theory of business enterprise but also a great opportunity for contribution.

5. Finally, there is an absolute requirement of survival, namely, that of *profitability*, for the very simple reason that everything I have said so far spells out *risk*. Everything I have said so far says that it is the purpose, the nature, and the necessity of this institution to take risks, to create risks. *And risks are genuine costs.* They are as genuine a cost as any the accountant can put his finger on. The only difference is that, until the future has become past, we do not know how big a cost; but they *are* costs. Unless we provide for costs, we are going to destroy capital. Unless we provide for loss, which is another way of saying for future cost, we are going to destroy wealth. Unless we provide for risk, we are going to destroy capacity to produce. And, therefore, a minimum profitability, adequate to the risks which we, by necessity, assume and create, is an absolute condition of survival not only for the enterprise but for society.

This says three things. First, the need for profitability is objective. It is of the nature of business enterprise and as such is independent of the motives of the businessman or of the structure of the "system." If we had archangels running businesses (who, by definition, are deeply disinterested in the profit motive), they would have to make a profit and would have to watch profitability just as eagerly, just as assiduously, just as faithfully, just as responsibly, as the most greedy wheeler-dealer or as the most convincedly Marxist commissar in Russia.

Second, profit is not the "entrepreneur's share" and the "reward" to one "factor of production." It does not rank on a par with the other "shares," such as that of "labor," for instance, but above them. It is not a claim *against* the enterprise but the claim *of* the enterprise—without which it cannot survive. How the profits are distributed and to whom is of great political importance; but for the understanding of the needs and behavior of a business it is largely irrelevant.

Finally, "profit maximization" is the wrong concept, whether it be interpreted to mean short-range or long-range profits or a balance of the two. The relevant question is, "What minimum does the business need?" not "What maximum can it make?" This "survival minimum" will, incidentally, be found to exceed present "maxima" in many cases. This, at least, has been my experience in most companies where a conscious attempt to think through the risks of the business has been attempted.

Here are five dimensions; and each of these five is a genuine view of the whole business enterprise. It is a human organization, and we can look upon it only in that aspect, as does our human relations literature. We can look at it from its existence in society and economy, which is what the economist does. This is a perfectly valid, but it is a one-sided view.

We can, similarly, look at the enterprise only from the point of view of its goods and services. Innovation and change are yet another dimension, and profitability is yet another. These are all genuine true aspects of the same being. But only if we have all five of them in front of us do we have a theory of business enterprise on which practice can be built.

For managing a business enterprise means making decisions, every one of which both depends on needs and opportunities in each of these five areas and, in turn, affects performance and results in each.

THE WORK TO BE DONE

The first conclusion from this is that every business needs objectives— explicit or not—in each of these five areas, for malfunction in any one of these endangers the entire business. And failure in any one area destroys the entire business—no matter how well it does in the other four areas. Yet these are not interdependent but autonomous areas.

1. *Here, then, is the first task of a discipline of business enterprise:* to

develop clear concepts and usable measurements to set objectives and to measure performance in each of these five areas.

The job is certainly a big one—and a long one. There is no area as yet where we can really define the objectives, let alone measure results. Even in respect to profitability we have, despite great recent advances in managerial economics, figures for the past rather than measurements that relate current or expected profitability to the specific future risks and needs. In the other areas we do not even have that, by and large. And in some—the effectiveness of the human organization, the public standing in economy and society, or the area of innovation—we may, for a long time to come, perhaps forever, have to be content with qualitative appraisal making possible judgment. Even this would be tremendous progress.

2. A second conclusion is hardly less important: *no one simple objective is "the" objective of a business; no one single yardstick "the" measure of performances, prospects, and results of a business; no one single area "the" most important area.*

Indeed, the most dangerous oversimplification of business enterprise may well be that of the "one yardstick," whether "return on investment," "market standing," "product leadership," or what have you. At their best these measure performance in one genuine survival area. But malfunction or failure in any one area is not counterbalanced by performance in any other area, just as a sturdy respiratory or circulatory system will not save an animal if its digestive or nervous system collapses. Success, like failure, in business enterprise is *multidimensional.*

3. This, however, brings out another important need: a rational and systematic approach to the *selection and balance among objectives* so as best to provide for survival and growth of the enterprise. These can be called the "ethics" of business enterprise, insofar as ethics is the discipline that deals with rational value choices among means to ends. It can also be the "strategy" of entrepreneurship. Neither "ethics" nor "strategy" is capable of being absolutely determined, yet neither can be absolutely arbitrary. We need a discipline here that encompasses both the "typical" decision which adapts to circumstances and "plays" the averages of statistical probability, and the innovating, "unique event" of entrepreneurial vision and courage breaking with precedent and trends and creating new ones—and there are already some first beginnings of such a discipline of entrepreneurship. But such a discipline can never be more than theory of composition is to the musical composer or theory of strategy to the military leader: a safeguard against oversight, an appraisal of risks, and, above all, a stimulant to independence and innovation.

Almost by definition the demands of different survival objectives pull in different directions, at least for any one time period. And it is axiomatic that the resources even of the wealthiest business, or even of the richest country, never cover in full all demands in all areas; there is never so much that there has to be no allocation. Higher profitability can thus be achieved only by taking a risk in market standing, in product leadership, or in tomorrow's human organization, and vice versa. Which of these risks the enterprise can take, which it cannot take, and what it cannot afford not to take—these risk-taking, value-decisions between goals in one area versus goals in others, and between goals in one area today versus goals in others tomorrow, is a specific job of the entrepreneur. This decision itself will remain a "judgment," that is, a matter of human values, appraisal of the situation, weighing of alternatives, and balancing of risks. But an understanding of survival objectives and their requirements can supply both the rational foundation for the decision itself and the rational criteria for the analysis and appraisal of entrepreneurial performance.

AN OPERATIONAL VIEW OF THE BUDGETING PROCESS

The final conclusion is that we need a new approach to the process in which we make our value decisions between different objective areas—the budgeting process. And in particular do we need a real understanding of that part of the budget that deals with the expenses that express these decisions, that is, the "managed" and "capital" expenditures.

Commonly today, budgeting is conceived as a "financial" process. But it is only the notation that is financial; the decisions are entrepreneurial. Commonly today, "managed" expenditures and "capital" expenditures are considered quite separate. But the distinction is an accounting (and tax) fiction and misleading; both commit scarce resources to an uncertain future; both are, economically speaking, "capital" expenditures. And they, too, have to express the same basic decisions on survival objectives to be viable. Finally, today, most of our attention in the "operating budget" is given, as a rule, to other than the "managed" expenses, especially to the "variable" expenses, for that is where, historically, most money was spent. But, no matter how large or small the sums, it is in our decisions on the "managed" expenses that we decide on the future of the enterprise.

Indeed, we have little control over what the accountant calls "variable" expenses—the expenses which relate directly to units of production and are fixed by a certain way of doing things. We can change them, but not fast. We can change a relationship between units of production and labor costs (which we, with a certain irony, still consider "variable expenses" despite the fringe benefits). But within any time period these expenses can only be kept at a norm and cannot be changed. This is of course even more true for the expenses in respect to the decisions of the past, our "fixed" expenses. We cannot make them undone at all, whether these are capital expenses or taxes or what-have-you. They are beyond our control.

In the middle, however, are the expenses for the future which express our risk-taking value choices: the "capital expenses" and the "managed expenses." Here are the expenses on facilities and equipment, on research and merchandising, on product development and people development, on management and organization. This managed expense budget is the area in which we really make our decisions on our objectives. (That, incidentally, is why I dislike accounting ratios in that area so very much, because they try to substitute the history of the dead past for the making of the prosperous future.)

We make decisions in this process in two respects. First, what do we allocate people for? For the money in the budget is really people. What do we allocate people, and energy, and efforts to? To what objectives? We have to make choices, as we cannot do everything.

And, second, what is the time scale? How do we, in other words, *balance* expenditures for long-term permanent efforts against any decision with immediate impact? The one shows results only in the remote future, if at all. The development of people (a fifteen-year job), the effectiveness of which is untested and unmeasurable, is, for instance, a decision on faith over the long range. The other may show results immediately. To slight the one, however, might, in the long range, debilitate the business and weaken it. And, yet, there are certain real short-term needs that have to be met in the business—in the present as well as in the future.

Until we develop a clear understanding of basic survival objectives and some yardsticks for the decisions and choices in each area, budgeting will not become a rational exercise of responsible judgment; it will retain some of the "hunch" character that it now has. But our experience has shown that the concept of survival objectives alone can greatly improve both the quality and effectiveness of the process and the understanding of what is being decided. Indeed, it gives us, we are learning, an effective tool for the integration of functional work and specialized efforts and especially for creating a common understanding throughout the organization and common measurements of contribution and performance.

The approach to a discipline of business enterprise through an analysis of survival objectives is still a very new and a very crude one. Yet it is already proving itself a unifying concept, simply because it is the first *general* theory of the business enterprise we have had so far. It is not yet a very refined, a very elegant, let alone a very *precise*, theory. Any physicist or mathematician would say: This is not a theory; this is still only rhetoric. But at least, while maybe only in rhetoric, we are talking about something real. For the first time we are no longer in the situation in which theory is irrelevant, if not an impediment, and in which practice has to be untheoretical, which means cannot be taught, cannot be learned, and cannot be conveyed, as one can only convey the general.

This should thus be one of the "breakthrough" areas; and twenty years hence this might well have become the *central* concept around which we can organize the mixture of knowledge, ignorance, and experience, of prejudices, insights, and skills, which we call "management" today.

A Philosophy of Management
Ralph C. Davis

30

The term "philosophy" means to the undersigned a body of related knowledges that supplies a logic for effective thinking for the solution of certain kinds of problems. A management philosophy supplies the basis for the solution of business problems. An executive without a philosophy can have only limited capability for creative thinking, regardless of his basic intelligence. The development of a sound philosophy of management for oneself is, consequently, the most practical self-developmental project that an executive can undertake.

The following is a highly condensed statement of the basis of a management philosophy that has been helpful to the undersigned. It has been suggested that it may be helpful also to executives and students in developing management philosophies of their own. It is with this purpose in mind that the following statement is made:

1. This management philosophy is based upon the right of private property and the concept of a "free" market economy. It is, accordingly, a philosophy of economic decentralism. This philosophy tends to be opposed, therefore, to:

 a. Philosophies of socialism,[1] since they are basically philosophies of economic and political centralism that tends to diminish the freedom of the individual and the exercise of individual initiative.

 b. Centralized controls of the economy by central government beyond the necessary minimums, since these weaken the right of private property.

Reprinted with permission from the *Advanced Management Journal* (April 1959) pp. 5–6.

[1] As used in this paper, the term socialism refers to any economic, political, and social system under which the means of production are owned or controlled by the State for the purpose of assuring a condition of production and distribution of goods and services that is thought to be "fair" by the political leaders of the State. It is based on a right of public property, rather than a right of private property. It is evident that a particular condition of socialism can exist anywhere along a continuous spectrum of varying degrees of "socialism."

c. Monopoly, either of capital or labor, since this monopoly tends to destroy a free market economy.

d. Any measures designed to prevent the formation of private capital, without which there can be no system of private capitalism.[2] These measures include confiscatory taxation, social pressures that are exerted deliberately to promote "dissaving," "planned inflation," and various others that tend to prevent private capital formulation. Such measures lead to the substitution of state capitalism for private capitalism and the development of a socialist economy. A "free" market economy can only operate effectively under a system of private capitalism.

2.   This philosophy emphasizes the prior obligation of private enterprises and their owners and employees to contribute significantly to a standard of living that is being augmented continuously through time. It is based, therefore, on the concept that the primary objectives of the business organization are those economic values that are needed or desired by its customers. This is, accordingly, a philosophy of economic service by private enterprise to the public interest.

3.   The acceptance of this service obligation by owners and managers is necessary for the validation of the concepts of private property and private profit. It is not necessary, however, that this acceptance be completely voluntary. It is sufficient that it be accepted under the duress of competition and a minimum of supporting governmental regulation. This philosophy recognizes that an earned profit depends on a prior, competitive accomplishment of a company's service objectives. Accordingly, this is a philosophy of intelligent selfishness.

4.   This philosophy commits owners and managers to the active promotion of social and economic progress. It is accordingly a philosophy of progressive conservatism:

a. It does not sanction attempts by owners or managers to "turn back the clock," since it recognizes the economic and social obligations of private ownership to contribute to progress in an expanding economy. It is therefore not a reactionary management philosophy.

b. This philosophy does not sanction attempts by politicians or academic theorists to bet the fruits of past technical and managerial achievements

---

[2] "Private capitalism" refers to any system for the production and distribution of goods and services in which the capital provided is the private property of citizens of the State or of corporate entities created by the State. It is not the property of the State. The productive process in an industrial economy is based on a cycle of conversion of capital into values that can satisfy consumer needs or desires. Consumer payments for these satisfactions complete the cycle of conversion, returning it once more to some form of capital. The use of capital in the productive process under a system of private capitalism is not controlled by the State, except as the economic, political, and social activities of private enterprises must conform to public policy.

of private enterprise on the nose of some untested economic, political or social hypotheses. Accordingly, it is not a radical management philosophy.

5. This philosophy recognizes the importance of big rewards for big results. It does not seek to chisel away the fruits of success, whether they be in the form of profits, bonuses, incentive pay, salaries, wages, fringe benefits, or various intangible values, provided that these are earned under competitive conditions. It is, accordingly, a philosophy of positive motivation. This philosophy recognizes, therefore, the validity of the profit objective in private enterprises, on the basis of:

a. The concept of a profit as a reward of private capital for the successful acceptance of business risk in the rendering of an economic service under competitive conditions in a free market. The hope of gaining a profit is the principal stimulus that motivates investors and entrepreneurs to risk capital for the purpose of expanding old businesses or founding new ones. This philosophy recognizes, consequently, that a profit is the principal objective of the businessman, even though customer service is the primary objective of the business organization.

b. The concept of profit-making as a necessary function in the processes for the formation of private capital. The growth of a business, and the growth of the Economy, depend greatly on the ability of Management to "plow back" a substantial proportion of its profits for purposes of expansion.

6. No organization can be better than its leadership, over a period of time. The work of management is the work of executive leadership. It is the mental work of planning, organizing, and controlling the activities of others in the joint accomplishment of a common objective. This common objective, in the case of the business organization, is service to the customer through the organization and its leadership. Each line or staff component of a business organization has its service objective accordingly. The executive head of an organizational component is or should be accountable for the accomplishment of its objectives. He must have the rights of decision and command that are necessary for an accomplishment of these objectives as well as those necessary for effective leadership anywhere. The executive has also the concomitant obligations of leadership. This philosophy recognizes, however, that an uncontrolled exercise of executive authority is neither in the public interest nor in the interest of private enterprise. It is a leadership philosophy in this respect.

7. This philosophy also emphasizes the importance of confidence in the purposes of executive leadership as a basic factor in the development of good organizational morale, and in the maintenance of sound business relations of all kinds. It emphasizes, therefore, the importance of ethical principles in the formulation of business policies. It is a moral philosophy in this respect.

8. This philosophy requires the recognition by owners and managers of labor's right of collective bargaining. It recognizes also the corresponding obligation of labor—the obligation to support management's right of executive leadership in the accomplishment of customer service objectives, when a satisfactory labor contract has been accomplished without the exercise of duress by either party. This is a labor-management philosophy in part.

  a. It recognizes that the loss of a property right in one's services is coincident with or follows the loss of property rights in one's goods. A denial of the right of collective bargaining, and its concomitant right to organize, leads to socialism. The socialist state owns or controls the means of production. These means include operative labor and management, as well as land and capital. There can be no true collective bargaining under socialism.

  b. It does not recognize any right of labor to a profit share because of the service obligations set up in a contract of employment. One cannot sell one's services, and retain title to them at the same time. It does recognize the right of capital to dispose of its profits or losses in any legitimate manner.

9. This philosophy emphasizes the concepts of delegation, decentralization, individual initiative, and individual accountability. It recognizes the obligation of the individual to contribute to the accomplishment of the primary service objectives of his organization, as well as his right to a reasonable satisfaction of his personal objectives. It emphasizes the importance of the individual, while recognizing the importance of group coordination and cooperation. In this respect, it is a philosophy of individualism.

10. This philosophy breaks down the problem of management in a free-enterprise economy into its basic elements. It analyzes the principal factors, forces, and effects in the management process. It develops a logic of effective thinking, in terms of business objectives, policies, functions, factors, and relationships, that is applicable to the solution of managerial problems anywhere. It is a scientific philosophy of management in this respect.

It is believed that any sound philosophy of management in a free enterprise economy must meet the above requirements.

There has been a continuous erosion of the right of private property over the past twenty-five years, or more. This has been a necessary effect, to some extent, of a rapid growth in the size and complexity of our Economy. It has reflected, in part, a distrust of business owners and executives, because of earlier abuses of economic power. It has been an effect, to some extent, of the successful attempts of some politicians to get themselves elected by promoting the short-run interests of voters at the long-run expense of the Economy. It has been an effect, to some extent, of the attempts of some individuals to promote a socialist economy.

It is a responsibility of American Business Leadership to take every legitimate step that will assure the adjustment of our "free enterprise" system to the changing needs of a growth economy. It must adjust its methods to changing political and social concepts when these changes do not weaken seriously the right of private property. It cannot compromise this responsibility because the right of private property underlies the liberties of the private citizen. It must oppose these changes when they do. Most employers' associations attempt to discharge these responsibilities by means of lobbying activities. Lobbying is a legitimate exercise of a constitutional right of petition. It is also a "rearguard" action for the protection of the right of private enterprise. Continuous lobbying suggests, therefore, that the forces of private enterprise are continuously in retreat. Observation of the passing scene over the past twenty-five years suggests that this has been the case. One cannot win a campaign while one is continuously on the defensive. Business Leadership cannot go on the offensive successfully until it has developed a simple statement of a management philosophy that is in consonance with the public interest. It cannot go on the offensive then, until the particular philosophy is known, understood and accepted by the public. The political climate would change, obviously, if this were to happen, and fast.

Many able executives and management scholars have published statements of management philosophies recently. There is a direct relation between a sound management philosophy and a community of ideas concerning the basic requirements for a successful operation of a system of private enterprise. It is suggested that these statements represent some recognition of this relation. It may be that none of the published statements will do the job that must be done. It is quite certain that out of them will come some statement that will. Such statements are a response to a vital need of he times; measures for the preservation of the free enterprise system, and the right of private property on which it rests.

Case

Fisher Manufacturing Company

In the early spring of 1964, The Fisher Manufacturing Company appeared to be on the verge of greatly increasing its sales and scope of operations. Since its organization by Mr. Leonard Fisher in 1955, the company realized profits from the manufacture and sale of wood-plastic building panels. In 1958, for instance, a profit of approximately $25,000 was earned, in addition to the approximately $15,000 drawings for that year by Mr. Fisher.

Since 1958 reported profits were not as substantial because much time and between $75,000 and $100,000 of funds were applied to research and development, and were considered expense items. Nevertheless, profits were shown in every year except 1961, when a loss of approximately $12,000 was incurred. This was in the midst of the development of the largest portion of the new products and manufacturing processes. During this period much of Mr. Fisher's time was devoted to research and development. The erstwhile profitable lines which were the basis of the 1955-58 substantial profits were not emphasized, but rather attention was centered on the development of the new products and new manufacturing processes. During the fiscal year ended June 30, 1963, the firm showed a profit of $17,500, in addition to officers' salaries.

On July 1, 1963, the company moved from the small southern town in which it was located to a larger town, in Mississippi, of nearly 40,000 population. To accommodate this greatly expanded scope of operations, the company was financially reorganized on October 1, 1963. At this time, the old stock was retired, and a new issue of 400,000 shares of $1 par value was authorized. Leonard Fisher was given $200,000 par value of the new stock in exchange for his old stock. It was anticipated that the $200,000 net capital that was authorized would help the firm in realizing growth due to its posi-

Reprinted with permission from Hargrove, Harrison and Swearingen, *Business Policy Cases with Behavioral Science Implications* (Rev. Ed., Homewood, Illinois: Richard D. Irwin, Inc.).

This case was prepared by Professor Herbert G. Hicks of Louisiana State University, a member of the Southern Case Writers Association, as a basis for class discussion. Southern Case Writers cases are not intended as examples of correct or incorrect administrative or technical practices. All names have been disguised.

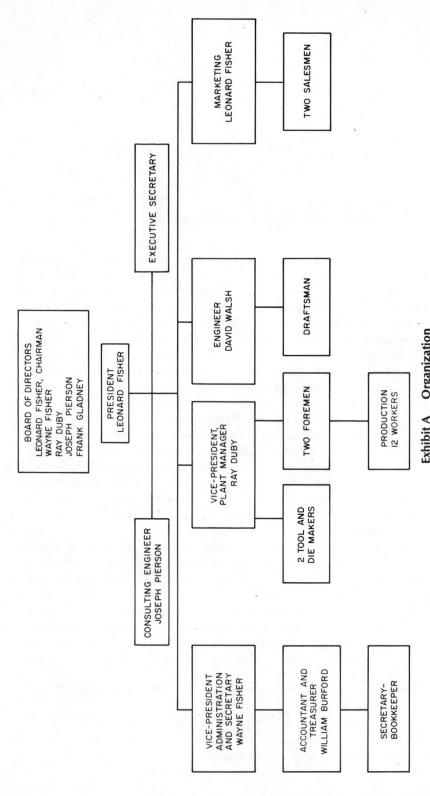

Exhibit A Organization

tion of having new products, new and efficient manufacturing processes, a new plant, a new qualified plant manager, and some of the best knowledge and experience in its field.

THE ORGANIZATION AND THE OFFICERS

An organization chart of the company (Exhibit A) shows the formal relationships which existed as of January 1, 1964, in accord with the established procedures in the company.

According to company literature, the president was the chief executive officer in the company and had final and complete authority and responsibility for all the operations. However, each manager was to make all practicable decisions in his area because of a policy of decentralized authority. Performance was to be measured primarily by pre-set goals and with data provided in systematic ways.

The officers were:

Leonard Fisher, founder of the company, Chairman of the Board, and President, age 45, was born near Baton Rouge, Louisiana. After completing high school in Baton Rouge, he worked in various construction jobs in Baton Rouge and New Orleans, with most of this work in the area of insulation. From 1941 to 1945, he served in the United States Army and rose to the rank of Sergeant in Armored Maintenance. During his last year in the Army, Mr. Fisher was in charge of a twelve man truck maintenance crew.

Leaving the Army in late 1945, Mr. Fisher entered his uncle's hardware and building supply business in central Louisiana. By 1946, his uncle had allowed him to buy into the business, which was experiencing rapid growth in the post-war boom. Although this business enjoyed considerable success and growth, Mr. Fisher decided in 1954 to start his own business for the manufacture of wood-plastic building panels, in which he had become interested as the answer to the demand for sturdy, durable panels that could be easily installed and would give good insulation performance. These panels were made by a technique which combined wood shavings and plastic materials in a molding process to produce panels of varying sizes and widths.

After completing arrangements for his new business, The Fisher Manufacturing Company, Mr. Fisher took the approximately $45,000 which he had accumulated during his association with his uncle and started the new venture. Under Mr. Fisher's careful and constant supervision, the company has grown to its present size. Although not trained formally, Mr. Fisher is recognized as one of the foremost authorities in the nation in insulation panel technology and applications. He has exhibited a high level of proficiency in all areas of the industry. His acceptance as an expert in the industry is reflected in the officer capacities which he holds in two national organizations and the number of addresses he has made to professional groups and other interested parties.

Throughout the growth of the company, Mr. Fisher has personally designed, engineered, and supervised the production of a wide range of the wood-plastic panels and related products.

Wayne Fisher, age 32, Leonard's younger brother, was the Vice-President of Administration and Secretary of the company, a position he had held since joining the firm in the fall of 1959. In this position, Wayne was in charge of personnel, planning and policy, accounting, motivation and incentives, and finance. Leonard's idea was to groom his younger brother to take over the presidency within the next four years, so that he, Leonard, might become a "super salesman" for the company and not be bothered with administrative details, although he would still retain his position as Chairman of the Board.

After graduating from Baton Rouge High School, Wayne attended Louisiana State University, where he received an undergraduate degree in mechanical engineering in 1954. After working for several months as a design engineer for a St. Louis firm, he entered the United States Air Force as an engineering officer. While in the Air Force he supervised up to 175 employees and was in charge of a power plant and other equipment worth approximately $18,000,000.

Resigning from the Air Force in 1957, Wayne entered Graduate School at The University of Texas, where he was awarded a Master in Business Administration degree in August of 1959. While in school in Austin, Wayne was employed part-time at The Balcones Research Center, working on government projects.

Ray Duby, Vice-President and Plant Manager, was 29 years old and a native of Natchez, Mississippi. He indicated in his resume that he had attended several different courses in production management, taught in high school and at one of the small Mississippi state colleges. He had also attended several management seminars held at Mississippi State University.

Prior to joining The Fisher Manufacturing Company in the spring of 1963, Ray was employed by Johnson & Johnson, Inc., a metal working firm located in New Orleans. With this company he was promoted from line foreman to plant superintendent, and was offered the position of plant manager when he advised his superiors of his plans to resign and join Fisher because he felt that his opportunities were greater there. At Johnson & Johnson Ray had up to 125 men under his supervision, and he was in full charge of all production facilities, buildings, and equipment. He had eight years of training in production cost control and budgetary controls. He also had considerable experience in the engineering of products, and was in charge of tooling and die programs at Johnson & Johnson.

The following quotation is from Ray Duby's resume which he sent to Leonard Fisher and the other company officers in early 1963.

In the future, I plan to actively try and work myself out of my present position. I expect to set a good example for my subordinates to do the

same, and thus have a rapidly growing organization which will stay ahead
of any competition.

My *ultimate goal is—the Presidency!*

Joseph Pierson, age 54, was a Director and Consulting Engineer for Fisher
Manufacturing Company. After receiving his mechanical engineering degree
from M.I.T. in Boston, Mr. Pierson was affiliated with several companies in
engineering design capacities; then he took a position with Boeing Aircraft in
1942. At Boeing, he was instrumental in designing several significant contributions to the war effort. He ended his career in the aircraft field as an
assistant plant superintendent.

After the war he acquired and directed an electric motor manufacturing
plant in New Orleans. Since that time he has expanded and consolidated his
operations to include multiple line electrical equipment. Although he still
maintains an interest in his business complex, the major part of his time for
the next few years will be spent in helping to increase production at Fisher.
In his words, "Fisher Manufacturing Company has the greatest potential of
any company with which I have ever been affiliated."

David Walsh, Production Engineer for the company, was 39 years old and
a native of the town in which the plant is located. He graduated from high
school in 1943 and entered one of the small state universities where he studied
electrical engineering for two years. Interrupting his education to serve in the
United States Navy for two years, he returned to finish his degree in electrical
engineering. After graduating, he was employed by an oil company and
eventually advanced to a position of heading up an oil exploration crew.
This job carried him to many foreign countries and gave him experience in
hiring, maintenance of equipment, purchasing and promoting good foreign
relations. In 1959, he left the oil company to be with his family more. His
next job as a research engineer with a national manufacturer of windows,
doors, and curtain walls carried him to the West Coast and the Middle West
operations of the company. He left this company in the fall of 1963 to join
Fisher Manufacturing Company because "I felt my new employer had greater
growth capacity than the company I was presently with."

William Burford, Accountant and Treasurer, was 32 years of age and a native
of Little Rock, Arkansas. After graduating from the University of Arkansas with
a Bachelor's degree in Accounting in 1954, he went to work for a national
accounting firm in their Dallas office, and was subsequently transferred to
their New Orleans office in 1957. In 1960 he joined Fisher Manufacturing
Company as their accountant because of the great potential which he felt
existed for the company. A statement in his resume read, "I feel that my past
experience will be an asset to the company in many ways, and that both
Fisher and I will be able to grow and mature together."

Frank Gladney, a Board member and old friend of Leonard Fisher, had purchased some of the stock of the company when it was organized in 1954. Al-

though he gave advice to the company on occasions about finances, his role in the company was largely passive.

Other employees in the company were:

Sam Clark .... assembler
William Cooper .... semiautomatic mold
David Cross .... die maker
Joe Panzica .... assembler
Rick Harrison .... semiautomatic mold
Joe Burke .... carpenter
Tom Patterson .... material control
Gil Thrasher .... toolmaker
Sherman Anderson .... assembler
Ronald Peacock .... foreman
Mike Williams .... salesman
Jerry Smith .... draftsman
Holt Kelley .... welder
Bill Davidson .... chemical mixer
Manuel Jordan .... semiautomatic mold
George Mason .... salesman
Curtis Hatcher .... assembler
Paul Davis .... foreman
Martha Roberts .... executive secretary
Sarah Edwards .... secretary-bookkeeper

Cooper, Anderson, and Jordan were Negroes and had been with the company longer than those in other positions.

THE PRODUCTS

The Fisher Manufacturing Company originally produced insulation panels for refrigerated storage units. These panels were made by a patented process, purchased by Leonard Fisher in 1953, that combined wood shavings and plastic foam. However, since 1960 the company had been pushing for expansion into nonrefrigerated building applications, which would include prefabricated convenience stores and service stations. Further, applications of the panels to interior curtain walls were being vigorously investigated. Even though these products constituted a lucrative market, Leonard Fisher has constantly stressed that the company must continue to innovate in order to continue to grow. Therefore, he states that the product line will include anything that the company is able to produce profitably, for to restrict the product line would restrict innovation and opportunity and lead to an early decline in sales when the competition in the present lines becomes intense. The prospectus of the company, as written by Wayne Fisher, stated:

A policy of the Company is to be market oriented. The functions of both marketing and production are to satisfy customer needs. More specifically, the function of marketing is not merely to sell what the production function can produce. Both production and marketing are to view themselves in the partnership of creating customer satisfactions.

The major products of the company fell into the classes described below.

NON-REFRIGERATED BOXES

Non-refrigerated boxes made from wood-plastic panels were a product that had such excellent insulation qualities that they could replace, for instance, refrigerated trucks used in the distribution of frozen food. The frozen items could simply be placed in the boxes in the morning, and without refrigeration they would stay frozen all day.

The company enjoyed a competitive advantage because of its pioneer production of the panels for the refrigeration industry.

Estimated sales were:

Fiscal Year Ended June 30	Amount
1964	600 boxes at $75 = $ 45,000
1965	2,000 boxes at $75 = $150,000
1966	3,000 boxes at $75 = $225,000

WOOD-PLASTIC ARCHITECTURAL BUILDING PANELS

These panels were the key to the Company's growth and profits because they were used in some form or another in every one of the Company's products. Because of the cost, insulating, and structural advantages over competing products, the situation was generally one where superior products to those presently on the market could be offered at lower prices than present products commanded.

The Company had invested very heavily in research, development, and engineering and had developed a manufacturing process superior and less costly than any other known process.

Present production capacity for these panels by the Company was easily 5,000,000 sq. ft. of panels per year. If pushed, the present facilities could produce 8,000,000 sq. ft. per year. With the investment of an additional ten thousand dollars, production could be increased to 15,000,000 sq. ft. per year.

Productive capacity for these panels appears virtually unlimited. Moreover, since this was a new product, the Company had not yet been able to find the demand limits of the market. Fisher executives strongly felt that in the areas of cold storage plants, refrigerated rooms and boxes, non-refrigerated boxes, prefabricated buildings and interior curtain walls, the product the Company had was superior to competing products and could be sold at lower than competitive prices at a profit.

However, the company could not make accurate estimates of the size of the market for these panels, but it was Leonard's opinion that the market was tremendously large. Very conservatively, he estimated that sales of panels, in addition to those used in their other products described above, would be:

Fiscal Year Ended June 30	Amount
1964	72,000 sq. ft. × $1.00 = $ 72,000
1965	240,000 sq. ft. × $1.00 = $240,000
1966	360,000 sq. ft. × $1.00 = $360,000

After returning from a mid-winter vacation-business trip to Trinidad, Leonard started pushing the idea that the company should use its knowledge and product resources to set up an outlet for its panels in the West Indies. He suggested to a Board meeting that since supermarkets were just beginning to develop in the Islands and since low cost, sturdy housing was also in demand, the company could find a profitable and extensive market for its products there. In order to acquaint the local businessmen with the advantages of the panels, he wanted to set up a mango juice processing plant made out of the panels as a model of their various uses. Further, he said the plant itself would be profitable since there would be a ready market for the juice in the States. The Board decided not to take any definite action on Leonard's latest proposal, but to keep the possibilities in mind.

PRE-FABRICATED STORES AND SERVICE STATIONS

As another end use of the panels, the Company was in a position to supply pre-fabricated stores and service stations. Like the panel sales, the size of this market was indeterminate, but it estimated from experience in this area that sales would be:

Fiscal Year Ended June 30	Amount
1964	20 stores @ $15,000 = $300,000
1965	40 stores @ $15,000 = $600,000
1966	60 stores @ $15,000 = $900,000

The Company felt that the construction of convenience and grocery stores would provide a means of capitalizing on some knowledge of store lay-out, design, and merchandising in the grocery field. Leonard Fisher was recognized as an authority in all these areas. He had twice addressed the Southern Association of Convenience Stores on these topics. Further, Wayne Fisher had extensive training in this area while in graduate school.

INCIDENTS AT FISHER MANUFACTURING COMPANY

The following incidents took place during the month of March 1964. Because many of the workmen had appeared uneasy with Leonard in an office which had a window looking directly into the plant area, Leonard had moved to an office in a Motor Hotel two blocks from the plant. During March, Leonard traveled on company business a great deal; consequently, with Leonard out of town and in line with Wayne's recent innovation of stressing the need for written communication instead of spoken (he had given out pads with the words DON'T SAY IT—WRITE IT! at the top), several memos appeared which might normally not be written.

INCIDENT

INTER-OFFICE CORRESPONDENCE   March 3, 1964
To: Leonard
By: Wayne

The following quote was interesting to me:

"The test of a good manager is not how good he is at bossing, but how little bossing he has to do because of the training of his men and the organization of their work."

INCIDENT

INTER-OFFICE CORRESPONDENCE   March 3, 1964
To: Ray
Subject: Panel Costs
By: Wayne

Please get me labor costs for our standard wall panels in the following quantities per month:

100
150
200
250

INCIDENT

INTER-OFFICE CORRESPONDENCE   March 5, 1964
To: Ray
Subject: When foremen are sick
By: Leonard

I thought I had made it clear that if a foreman is out for some reason that Cooper, Anderson, or Jordan are not to take over. Those niggers may be able to operate that complex machinery OK, but it just wouldn't look right or be right for them to operate people. With me going out of town tomorrow I don't want this to happen again.

INCIDENT

William Burford entered Wayne's office late in the afternoon on March 10, and the following conversation took place.

Fisher: "Hi, Bill, what's on your mind?"

Burford: "I've got those revised cost statements you wanted. The projections were really off. If Ray doesn't come a little closer, we're going to have to revise all our projections, 'cause it doesn't look like we'll hit anywhere near the sales level we need."

Fisher: "Yea, I know that things aren't going exactly to plan, but with a little bit of luck the adjustments won't be too significant. Besides, we can't do any juggling until Leonard gets back next week."

Burford: "True, but we've got another problem that's going to have to be solved right now."

Fisher: "How's that?"

Burford: "Well, Martha (Martha Roberts, executive secretary) called her lawyer this afternoon. She blew up when I asked her to clear her desk. You remember Leonard got on a "clean the office up" campaign before he left, and I finally got around to saying something to her. She said that if the company was too cheap to hire a janitor then she wasn't going to do that. And that not only was she not doing the work of an executive secretary, but that she had not seen any executives around this place."

Fisher: "What did you do?"

Burford: "I told her that we would try to work something out, but I heard her call some lawyer anyway after I left the office."

Fisher: "What do you think we should do?"

Burford: "I don't know. There's really not enough work to keep Martha busy all the time, but I hate to see her leave because Leonard will put Cynthia (Leonard's wife) in there and she'll be just like a spy when he's not around."

Fisher: "Now, Bill, you know that Cynthia won't be purposefully spying on anyone if she comes in."

Burford: "Hell, if I don't! Leonard's been complaining about Martha for a month now, and she's a damned good secretary regardless of what he says. Besides, now that he's exiled over at the motel he just wants someone here that'll tell him everything that happens."

INCIDENT

Martha called in on March 10 and said that she would not be returning to work, and asked that her final check be mailed to her.

INCIDENT

An excerpt from an Air Mail, Special Delivery letter to Wayne from Leonard at a manufacturers' conference in Chicago, dated March 10 and received March 11.

"... so in the light of the ideas an encouragement I've picked up here, I think that we should move up the time schedule for you to take over the operations and let me concentrate on selling. I think I can begin to build a really top-notch force right away. I showed some of our material to a salesman from Alcoa, and he said we had the hottest building material in the country and he would like to talk to us about joining up. And he wasn't the only one that's showed such enthusiasm."

INCIDENT

INTER-OFFICE CORRESPONDENCE March 13, 1964
To: Bill Burford
Subject: Source and Application of Funds Statements
By: Wayne

I have not yet received the statements which you promised to have in my office by today at noon. I had planned to work on them over the weekend. Perhaps it has been delayed in getting to me, if so please disregard the following.

I believe it is important that you keep your promises or at least let the other person know in advance that you can't.

INCIDENT

The following letter was written to Leonard on March 16. Carbon copies were sent to all members of the Board.

Dear Mr. Fisher:

This is to inform you of my resignation as accountant-office manager of your company.

I am truly sorry to bring this up at a time when we are just getting operations under control, but I feel that public accounting is more promising and suited for me.

I believe that we are able to say that the worst part is over and my resigning now will not affect operations.

I have gained valuable experience with this company during the short while employed, and want to personally congratulate all the men and yourself for the fine efforts and patience extended during this re-organization.

I hope that my resignation will not hinder our relations as professional men, but instead, improve them.

If ever I may be of assistance to you or any employee of your firm, you can be assured that the matter will receive my immediate attention.

Yours very truly,
s/William Burford

INCIDENT

INTER-OFFICE CORRESPONDENCE   March 19, 1964
To: Leonard
Subject: Bond Issue
By: Wayne

A bond issue for us might be a good idea. I have done most of the work already and will discuss it in detail at your house Sunday. I would estimate the cost of a $250,000 issue as follows:

$ 400   Printing
  300   Filing fee
  500   Selling costs
─────
$1200

Of course, I do not think it would be wise for you to spend too much time selling these if you could better spend your time on sales.

INTER-OFFICE CORRESPONDENCE   March 20, 1964
To: Leonard
Subject: Ideas to discuss as soon as we can
By: Wayne

I feel that the following ideas are helpful in the present stage of the development of *our* organization. It seems to me that a thing that we need in the organization is more discipline (not necessarily punishment, now, discipline). And discipline to do the following things:

1. Planning. Set up goals and objectives *in advance* and *stick* to them. (Unless there are very compelling reasons to change.)

2. Controlling. Comparing what *does* happen with what was *supposed to happen according to the plan*. Obviously, no real control can be done without good planning in the first place.

INCIDENT

On the afternoon of March 20 Wayne went into the plant area to talk to Ray about getting more realistic cost estimates on panels. The conversation eventually got around to the company as a whole.

Duby: "Frankly, Wayne, I don't think anyone pays any attention to what I have to say around here. I'm not paying my own way and Leonard won't sit down and talk things over with me. If things don't improve, then I'm going to leave this mess."

Fisher: "Ray, it's not all that bad. We're just going through some growing pains that all businesses have to experience when they move from small to large scale operations."

Duby: "That may be true, but why in the hell won't Leonard let me run the plant like I want to? After all, he hired me to make decisions, and now when he's around he tries to run the whole show. We're on an eternal merry-go-round; we're not moving, not making sales. Every time we get a new product all lined up, it's off on some tangent and the really good ideas are left by the wayside."

Fisher: "O.K., simmer down, Ray. Things may not be going very smoothly right now, but a lot of the trouble between you and Leonard can be traced to you. You're competitive with him too much—after all, this just adds fuel to any smoldering fires. And of course he's defensive about this company's operations, he did start the company you know."

Duby: "Well, you're right of course, but if things don't cool down, then Leonard's going to have a heartattack or something, and I'm going to get out of here but fast."

Fisher: "I promise I'll try to talk to Leonard about all this tension as soon as we get all the other matters taken care of. A lot has piled up while he's been away."

INCIDENT

Going through his desk late on the night of March 21 after returning from his business trip, Leonard found the following on top of a stack of correspondence.

INTER-OFFICE CORRESPONDENCE   March 20, 1964
To: Leonard
By: Wayne

I sincerely hope that we'll be able to sit down Sunday and work something out definitely about several problems.

On Sunday, after discussing Leonard's trip and some minor company problems, Wayne and Leonard had a long discussion about all the recent developments in the company. The following are excerpts from that conversation.

Leonard: "Well, it just seems like Duby's not panning out as we expected. I think he really sold us a bill of goods, and we believed that he'd produce a helluva lot better than he did. Don't you agree?"

Wayne: "Yes, but I don't think Ray's to blame alone. We've had an awful lot of tension and disruption in the plant recently, although he really has messed us up on those estimates about the panels."

Leonard: "Right! I'm going to call him in Monday and find out what his excuse is. I have several people in mind that I know can do his job, and probably all of them can do it better than him! In fact, the more I think about it, the more I know we can get along a lot better without Ray Duby."

Wayne: "Leonard, at least promise you'll give him a chance to explain. After all, several of his mistakes can be traced to your not bothering to write out a communication and then expecting him to remember a lot of details."

Leonard: "My failure to write everything out is beside the point. Besides you know I hate to write things out because of my poor grammar and spelling. After all, I can't have the employees thinking I'm an illiterate. You stick to the memos, Little Brother, and I'll stick to making the big decisions and pushing those sales up."

Leonard: "I'm sold on the idea that we're about to really get moving, and we'll pass up a golden opportunity if we don't go through with that idea of mine about setting up an operation in Trinidad. I want you to go down there with me as soon as we can get a new plant manager and get him squared away."

Wayne: "I thought we had decided not to do anything about that right now, until we sort of get firmed up in some other areas."

Leonard: "No, I'm sure this is the best thing right now. The other areas will take care of themselves. We just can't make the mistake of not taking advantage of all those sales waiting for us down there."

Wayne: "Leonard, don't you think we're jumping around too much? We just get going with one product, in one area, and then before things are really running smoothly, we jump into something else. There's a lot more to being a success than making sales, you know."

Leonard: "Hell, Wayne, if you can sell enough, you can cover up any managerial mistakes you make along the way—you don't have to go to college to know that. I want those sales. That's what'll make us a big company."

Wayne: "That may be your idea, but mine is different; and if we don't get some organization and cooperation here, then I'm pulling out. You might have built this company into what it is today, but you damn sure will never get any further with the attitude you have now. And I don't want to worry with it and then have the lid blow off in my face—and that's exactly where we're headed!"

INCIDENT

INTER-OFFICE CORRESPONDENCE   March 24, 1964
To: Mr. Ray Duby
Subject: Resignation
By: Leonard Fisher, President

After our talk yesterday, I'm sure the best thing for you to do is to resign.

Your failure to follow orders and the general mess in the plant and the poor estimates all show that you would be better off somewhere else, and we would too.

I expect you to turn your resignation letter in to Wayne by noon tomorrow. He'll give you a check for one weeks work. Good luck in finding a new job.

INTER-OFFICE CORRESPONDENCE   March 24, 1964
To: Wayne
Subject: Duby's Resignation
By: Leonard

Ray will never work out no better than he has. I told him to resign by noon Wednesday. Give him a check for one weeks wages. Better place an ad in the New Orleans paper for a new man. I'll interview applicants when I get back in town Friday. Sorry I won't be here until then, but am sure you can work things out OK.

Balance Sheet—December 31, 1963

Assets

Current Assets:				
Cash on Hand and in Bank			$ 2,075.91	
Accounts Receivable	$	50,620.01		
Less: Allowance for Doubtful Accounts		5,010.13	45,609.88	
Notes Receivable			1,451.73	
Inventories			83,071.07	
Prepaid Insurance			1,250.32	
Deposits on Notes Receivable Discounted			13,604.38	
Total Current Assets				$ 147,063.29
Other Assets:				
Telephone & Utility Deposits				$ 227.50
Fixed Assets:				
Land			$ 10,000.00	
Building	$	97,114.61		
Machinery and Equipment		77,990.14		
Automobiles and Trucks		14,015.19		
Furniture and Fixtures		5,121.61		
Total Depreciable Assets	$	194,241.55		
Accumulated Depreciation		29,881.97	164,359.58	
Total Fixed Assets				$ 174,359.58
Intangible Assets:				
Goodwill				$ 82,184.16
Total Assets				$ 403,834.53

Liabilities and Stockholders' Equity

Current Liabilities:

Accounts Payable	$	28,525.98	
Mortgage Payable—Sherman Building Co.		15,000.00	
Federal Income Taxes Payable		2,742.20	
Accrued Payroll and Other Taxes		3,056.37	
Accrued Payroll		1,149.13	
Accrued Expenses—Other		726.41	
Reserve for Warranty on Panels		7,072.75	
			$ 58,272.84

Long-Term Liabilities:

Mortgage Payable—Townson Building Assn.		$ 69,028.74
Total Liabilities		$ 127,301.58

Stockholders' Equity:

Capital Stock (Note)	$	273,100.00	
Surplus Arising from Re-evaluation of Fixed Assets		14,142.88	
Retained Earnings (Deficit)	(	10,709.93)	
Total Stockholders' Equity			$ 276,532.95
Total Liabilities and Stockholders' Equity			$ 403,834.53

Source: Fisher Manufacturing Company.

Statement of Income (Loss)
for the Six Month Period Ended December 31, 1963

Income:			
Sales	$	264,367.15	
Less: Sales Returns and Allowances		5,599.23	
Net Sales			$ 258,767.92
Cost of Sales			$ 233,175.08
Gross Profit on Sales			$ 25,592.84
Operating Expenses:			
Factory Selling Expenses	$	10,392.74	
Factory General Expenses		12,624.64	
Operating Expenses		30,722.73	
Total Operating Expenses			$ 53,740.11
Net Loss from Operations			($ 28,147.27)
Other Income:			
Discounts Earned	$	2,781.10	
Interest and Carrying Charges		2,108.41	
Miscellaneous		221.94	
Total Other Income			$ 5,111.45
Net Loss before Other Deductions			($ 23,035.82)
Other Deductions:			
Interest			$ 2,536.95
Net Loss for the Period			($ 25,572.77)

Source: Fisher Manufacturing Company.

Projected Statement of Income for the Year Ended June 30, 1964
(At June 30, 1963)

	Amounts		Percent to Sales
Sales		$838,000.00	100.00%
Cost of Goods Sold:			
Direct Material		$603,600.00	72.01%
Direct Labor		38,100.00	4.56%
Factory Overhead:			
Indirect Labor	$ 16,850.00		
Overtime Premium	10,700.00		
Factory Supplies	11,800.00		
Utilities	1,600.00		
Repair and Upkeep	3,700.00		
Employee Benefits	2,350.00		
Supervision	400.00		
Rent	7,900.00		
Engineering	5,500.00		
Depreciation	8,600.00		
Insurance	2,400.00		
Payroll Taxes	4,250.00		
Superintendent	13,000.00		
Miscellaneous	1,750.00	90,800.00	10.85%
Total Cost of Goods Sold		732,500.00	87.42%
Gross Profit on Sales		105,500.00	12.85%
Selling Expenses:			
Salesmen's Salaries & Commissions	$ 34,400.00		
Depreciation	300.00		
Insurance	825.00		
Payroll Taxes	625.00		
Salesmens' Travelling Expenses	6,275.00		
Advertising	1,175.00		
Rent	700.00		
Stationery and Printing	175.00		
Telephone	5,600.00		
Delivery Expense	1,500.00		
Miscellaneous	425.00		
Total Selling Expenses		52,000.00	6.20%
Net Profit on Sales		53,500.00	6.38%

General and Administrative Expenses:

Salaries	19,000.00	
Depreciation	300.00	
Insurance	425.00	
Payroll Taxes	1,150.00	
Travel and Entertainment	375.00	
Telephone	1,800.00	
Rent	375.00	
Utilities	100.00	
Repair and Upkeep	400.00	
Employee Benefits	350.00	
Engineering	625.00	
Experiments	375.00	
Professional Fees	8,500.00	
Stationery and Printing	1,025.00	
Miscellaneous	1,000.00	
Total General and Administrative Expenses	35,800.00	4.27%
Net Income from Operations	17,700.00	2.11%
Other Income:		
Discounts Earned	9,000.00	1.07%
Net Income before Other Deductions	26,700.00	3.18%
Other Deductions:		
Administrative Services	1,200.00	
Interest	4,500.00	
Total Other Deductions	5,700.00	.68%
Net Income for the Year	$21,000.00	2.50%

Source: Fisher Manufacturing Company

Projected Income Statements for Fiscal Years Ending June 30
(Thousands of Dollars)
(At June 30, 1963)

	1964	1965	1966	1967
Sales	$838	$3,000	$4,500	$5,500
Cost of Goods Sold (80%)	670	2,400	3,600	4,400
Gross Profit on Sales (25%)	168	600	900	1,100
Selling Expense (7.5%)	63	225	338	412
Net Profit on Sales (12.5%)	105	375	562	688
Gen. and Adm. Expense (2.5%)	21	75	112	138
	84	300	450	550
Less Expense for New Plant	61	—	—	—
Net Income before Taxes	24	300	450	550
Taxes	12	150	225	275
Net Profit after Taxes	$ 12	$ 150	$ 225	$ 275

Source: Fisher Manufacturing Company.

Bibliography

A. Management Rights

Bangs, John R. and Frank R. Fraser. "The Impact of the Courts on Arbitration and the Right to Manage," *California Management Review* (Summer 1963), pp. 51–60.

Denise, M. L. "Right to Manage: The Responsibility Lies with Management," *Iron Age* (January 3, 1963), pp. 122–125.

Derber, Milton, W. E. Chalmers and Milton Edelman. "Union Participation in Plant Decision-Making," *Industrial and Labor Relations Review* (October 1961), pp. 83–100.

Kuhn, James. "Encroachments on the Right to Manage," *California Management Review* (Fall 1962), pp. 18–23.

McGrath, William L. "Management's Right to Manage," *Supervision* (June 1960), pp. 4–6.

"Where Do the Rights of Management End?" *Business Week* (December 19, 1964), pp. 114–115.

Young, Stanley. "The Question of Managerial Prerogatives," *Industrial and Labor Relations Review* (January 1963), pp. 240–245.

B. Business Philosophies and Objectives

Bower, Marvin. "A New Look at the Company Philosophy," *Management Review* (May 1966), pp. 4–14.

Dent, James K. "Organizational Correlates of the Goals of Business Management," *Personnel Psychology* (Autumn 1959), pp. 365–393.

Jacobs, Laurence. "The Meaning of Goals," *Business Horizons* (Winter 1967), pp. 59–60.

Litzinger, W. D. and T. E. Schaefer. "Perspective: Management Philosophy Enigma," *Academy of Management Journal* (December 1966), pp. 337–343.

Nowotny, Otto H. "American vs. European Management Philosophy," *Harvard Business Review* (March–April, 1964), pp. 101–108.

Odiorne, George. "A Search for Objectives in Business—The Great Image Hunt," *Michigan Business Review* (January 1966), pp. 19–24.

Stull, R. A. "New Approach to a Philosophy of Management," *Advanced Management Journal* (October 1966), pp. 18–26.

PART SEVEN

Social Responsibilities of Business

A. The Social Responsibility Debate

A striking aspect of the social responsibility concept is the history of its evolutionary development over the past century. This development has been caused by changes in the values of society and by management's response to these changes. Similarities are found between the historical development of these social responsibilities, outlined by Morrell Heald in "Management's Responsibility to Society: The Growth of an Idea" [31], and by Robert E. Moore in the first article of the book in which he describes the evolution of capitalism. Both interpretations reveal a high degree of unanimity on the theory that management's social responsibilities must be directed toward those values of greatest emphasis in society at a given period. In his article, Heald emphasizes the many and varied types of social responsibilities accepted by business, ranging from industrial feudalism to total commitment to the service objective. For example, the failure of our economic system to meet its responsibilities during the depression of the thirties brought dissatisfaction and disillusionment with business to much of American society. These reactions, in turn, led to individual, group, and governmental pressures for the recognition of social responsibilities by the businessman.

The evolution of an increasing number of responsibilities for management and business has been accompanied by comparable trends in legal decisions of the United States Supreme Court in recent years. A survey of these decisions reveals an overwhelming trend toward subordination of the private property right of individuals and businesses to individual and group liberties when these two come into conflict. This trend constitutes a change in basic social philosophy which must be studied and understood by business.

Throughout this same period of change, persistent appeals have been made by business for a return to rugged individualism and laissez-faire capitalism. However, the changing values of our society indicate increasing emphasis on a political democracy. Business is generally faced with the choice either of assuming social responsibilities at the local, state and national level or of losing these functions and prerogatives to other power groups such as labor unions and governmental bodies.

The recent trend toward the recognition and acceptance of the social responsibility concept is still contested on many grounds. A recent survey of businessmen revealed the findings presented in article 32, "Where Do Corporate Responsibilities Really Lie?" Eighty-five percent of the businessmen surveyed answered that management is primarily responsible to the stockholder because: a) stockholders created the corporation to make a profit; b) management has a trust or stewardship to the owners; c) the interests of other groups in society are "automatically" protected if the interests of stockholders are safeguarded; and d) the corporation is an economic and not a social institution. Although the stockholders-owners deserve primary consideration by management, managers must also consider the legitimate interest groups with whom business is interdependent. These might be considered by business in the following order: the customers, employees, interrelated firms and institutions, the local, state, national and even the international community. Business will maximize its long-run interests by serving the interrelated interests of society, and society will best achieve its interests through the free enterprise system and the profit motive.

Given the economic function of, and the mandate for, maximum allocation of resources by society, business desires to operate in a free enterprise system with profits serving both as incentive and goal. The achievement of this goal will be conditioned by responses in the marketplace and by social controls in society. Another consideration of the dominant values of our society reveals maximum freedom for all individuals and groups as a corollary goal for business. Maintaining the highest degree of freedom normally requires checks and balances among power groups in society. If the acceptance of social responsibilities on the part of the businessman would be detrimental to these checks and balances, as cited by some writers, business as an institution would be forced to re-evaluate these responsibilities. But until this situation exists in fact, management faces the problem of recognizing and adapting to the current values emphasized by society.

While most businesses are justifiably accused of a lack of social concern, critics also suggest that a preoccupation with social concerns may be detrimental to the success of the firm. For example, in an article entitled "Should You Buy Stocks for Your Children?" which appeared in the April 21, 1968 issue of *Parade*, analysts warned readers against investing in companies whose concern for the profit motive was preempted by social concerns. These companies tended to show a slow profit. This analysis is, of course, correct. Social responsibilities must be delicately balanced in the light of a company's long-run self-interest and survival. In the Grafton case, a business faced with the economic necessity of changing its location is confronted with the virtual collapse of the community which depends upon it for the majority of its jobs, economic support, and long-term municipal bonded debt. This case dramatically portrays the rather frequent situation in which groups in society are almost totally dependent for their survival on one business firm's decisions.

B. Professional Responsibilities of Management

Management must recognize the effects of the specialization and division of labor in our economy resulting in increased types and levels of interdependence between individuals, groups and institutions. This interdependence leads to concomitant social responsibilities. Given these degrees of interdependence, business also must recognize its position as a dominant power group. The existence and use of this power is an issue of concern in the daily press, particularly insofar as it manifests economic monopoly or oligopolistic potentialities. In addition, business possesses social and human power in the local community and over individual employees in the organizaton. In article 33, "Can Business Afford to Ignore Social Responsibilities?" Keith Davis points out that if business uses its power in an irresponsible and arbitrary fashion, other forces and groups will meet the responsibilities due consumers and employees. The question is then raised: Could these power conflicts be minimized if professional managers formulated and met their social responsibilities at lower organizational levels in industry and society? This would be especially important if provided before these issues reached proportions requiring countermeasures by government or organized labor.

Considered from the standpoint of professional responsibility of business power groups, businessmen today have access to an increasingly standardized body of business-management knowledge to meet professional status criteria. In addition to a body of knowledge, two other criteria apply to professions in the classical sense—licensing by examination and the codification and enforcement of a code of ethics.

Licensing by examination is a very remote possibility, for it would tend to deter entrepreneurs, and would be impossible to apply to "qualified" managers. But "certification" on a voluntary basis could be substituted for licensing. The question of an enforced code of ethics appears to have both advantages and disadvantages. Howard R. Bowen contends in "Business Management: A Profession?" [34] that enforcement of such a code of ethics by professional groups in the economic realm could evolve into oligopolistic, if not monopolistic, practices. And we have but to look at the "classical" professions today to realize that social goals are not effectively sought, nor are professional members prosecuted under the codes. But this should not undercut the potential benefits of meaningfully stated and positively oriented codes of business and management ethics. These might, for example, take the form of business-society goals similar to the National Goals presented in Part Eight.

A. The Social Responsibility Debate

Management's Responsibility to Society: 31
The Growth of an Idea
Morrell Heald

In recent years we Americans have been engaging in a nationwide "name-the-product" contest: the object, a new, presumably, more accurate and more attractive term to describe the nature and performance of our economic system. The venture has, indeed, been something more than a public relations gimmick, more even than a tactical move on the ideological checkerboard of the cold war. While government officials and popular journalists seem, at least for the moment, to have settled upon the term "people's capitalism," social scientists have increasingly turned to the phrase "welfare capitalism" as expressing most adequately the character of contemporary American economic life. We still have our critics and skeptics who argue that the leopard has not changed his spots, but there is apparent a growing belief that the private enterprise system, American style, is a far cry from the laissez-faire capitalism of fifty, or even thirty, years ago.

A prominent aspect of the new capitalism, according to businessmen and nonbusinessmen alike, is the emergence of a "corporate conscience," a recognition on the part of management of an obligation to the society it serves not only for maximum economic performance but for humane and constructive social policies as well. Much has been written about the contemporary manifestations of this aspect of business thought; but relatively little attention, so far, has been paid to its origins and the factors which have contributed to its growth. It is with the history of this new approach on the part of management to its social relations that this article is concerned.

Reprinted with permission from the *Business History Review*, Vol. 31 (Winter 1957), pp. 375–384. Copyright by the President and Fellows of Harvard College; all rights reserved.

Like many other social phenomena it appears, on closer examination, to be not quite so new as the current upsurge of interest and comment may suggest.

In a notable effort to explain what they saw, in 1951, as the emergence of a humane and socially responsible economic system in America, the editors of *Fortune* magazine described business practices at the turn of the century: ". . . American capitalism seemed to be what Marx predicted it would be and what all the muckrakers said it was—the inhuman offspring of greed and responsibility. . . . It seemed to provide overwhelming proof of the theory that private ownership could honor no obligation except the obligation to pile up profits."[1] Yet, a severe contemporary critic of American business of that time, William J. Ghent, was less stringent in his condemnation. Ghent saw, in the large-scale combinations of the day, an economic feudalism comparable to that of the Middle Ages; but he grudgingly admitted that it was at least a "Benevolent Feudalism." He noted an increase in "conspicuous giving . . . always shrewdly disposed with an eye to the allayment of pain and the quieting of discontent." This took the form of contributions by wealthy businessmen to hospitals, colleges, libraries, the construction and maintenance of model industrial communities, and similar philanthropies. Such gifts Ghent attributed to a number of causes. Outstanding among them was a fear of the growing power of the labor movement and a desire to forestall public criticism and regulation of business in the age of Progressive reforms. Further, Ghent saw, growing hand in hand with the power of the industrial magnates, a greater self-consciousness of authority and responsibility. He anticipated that this paternalistic, "seignorial" attitude would ultimately be restrained by "a sense of the latent strength of democracy" and "a growing sense of ethics." He conceded that, ". . . the principle of the 'trusteeship of great wealth' has won a number of adherents. . . . A duty to society has been apprehended, and these are its first fruits. It is a duty, true enough, which is but dimly seen and imperfectly fulfilled."[2]

Most of the philanthropic activities upon which Ghent commented were, of course, those of wealthy individuals rather than of business corporations as such. These men were following the precepts of Andrew Carnegie, who for years had preached the gospel of the trusteeship of wealth on behalf of the rest of the community. To disarm the mounting criticism of great fortunes and aggregations of economic power which accompanied industrial expansion, Carnegie had proposed the devotion of surplus wealth to "the reconciliation of the rich and the poor—a reign of harmony" among men of all classes.[3] Yet corporations, too, were undertaking the work. During the 1880's and 1890's, the railroads had initiated a policy of financial support

---

[1] The Editors of *Fortune* in collaboration with Russell W. Davenport, *U.S.A. The Permanent Revolution* (New York, 1951), pp. 88, 67.

[2] W. J. Ghent, *Our Benevolent Feudalism* (New York, 1902), pp. 9–47, 59–64, 182ff., *passim*.

[3] Andrew Carnegie, *The Gospel of Wealth* (Garden City, 1933 ed.), p. 11.

for the activities of the Y.M.C.A. among their employees; and this support was gradually broadened to include contributions from other industries as well. Corporate donations to local charities of other types were few, but increasing in number, in the years before the First World War.[4] In many instances these activities and those described by Ghent filled a real need and represented a recognition on the part of employers of an obligation to, and a stake in, the well-being of their workers. Sometimes they were undertaken with even more ambitious objectives in view. The Colorado Fuel and Iron Company, for instance, announced that it was "the purpose of this corporation to solve the social problem."[5] Worthy as these goals might be, their weakness lay in the fact that both "the social problem" and its solution were often defined from the standpoint of the employer without true recognition of the needs and attitudes of others.

Of greater immediate value to the worker than these experiments in "enlightened absolutism" was the increase in interest and attention on the part of management to safety and sanitary conditions in its plants, to payments for accidents, retirement, and death. Such policies were the direct result of labor, public, and political pressures; but they at least implied an obligation on the part of management for the health and welfare of those most directly affected by its operations.

In addition to programs limited in their scope to industrial workers alone, there were a number of companies in the pre-World War I years whose rapid growth, great size, or unique characteristics created special problems of public relations and forced upon their managements the need to obtain the approval of the general public. One of these was the Bell System which, in combining a nationwide network of telephone facilities, had assumed many of the characteristics of a public utility. Recognizing the inevitability of government supervision of its business, the Bell management under the leadership of Theodore N. Vail publicly welcomed this regulation. So effective was the effort to humanize the corporation in the eyes of the public that Vail has been ranked as "one of the first leaders of American industry to appreciate the problems of public relations in a farsighted way and to find a basis for their long-term adjustment."[6] The Bell management believed that regulation need not mean direct interference with corporate policies. Through steady emphasis on efficient and economical service and through frequent reports to its shareholders, it strove to demonstrate a conviction on the part of management that, "We feel our obligation to the general public as strongly as to our investing public, or to our own personal interests."[7] A similar

---

4 Pierce Williams and Frederick E. Croxton, *Corporation Contributions to Organized Community Welfare Services* (New York, 1930), pp. 50–53, 76–79.

5 Ghent, *op. cit.*, p. 61.

6 Norton E. Long, "Public Relations Policies of the Bell System," *Public Opinion Quarterly*, Vol. I (Oct., 1937), pp. 6–19.

7 From the 1913 *Annual Report*, quoted in "Report of the Structure of the Bell System and Some of Its Fundamental Principals" (New York, 1922), p. 38.

policy of fuller reports to stockholders was pursued by the United States Steel Company, whose chairman, Elbert H. Gary, apparently sensed the quasi-public nature of an enterprise of such scope.[8] The Standard Oil management, too, began to modify its traditional position that economic performance alone was the measure of its obligation to society. Under steady attack, Rockefeller and his associates came to recognize that this policy neither convinced nor satisfied the public. Their efforts to win social approval through wider publicity, like those of other managements, were undoubtedly directed more toward public persuasion than toward self-examination. Nevertheless, a new sensitivity to community opinion had begun to take form.[9]

George W. Perkins, an outspoken director of U. S. Steel and International Harvester, held more advanced views. He argued in 1908 that "The larger the corporation becomes, the greater become its responsibilities to the entire community." Economic concentration meant for Perkins that "The corporations of the future must be those that are semi-public servants, serving the public, with ownership widespread among the public, and with labor so fairly and equitably treated that it will look upon its corporation as its friend. . . ."[10] He advocated profit-sharing, a national corporation law and at least limited government supervision of large-scale enterprises. Perkins became a close friend and adviser of Theodore Roosevelt and a leader of the conservative wing of the Progressive Party in 1912.

Underlying the appearance of this tentative, but recognizable concept of social accountability in the Progressive period were two major conditions. The first was the emergence of an economic order based increasingly upon large-scale enterprise with interests which affected an ever-widening circle of citizens. Secondly, popular reaction to this change and the resulting activities of state and national governments led business leaders to see their ultimate dependence upon a favorable social climate and the need for more than economic performance alone in order to maintain that climate.

To these forces a third was added by the advent of the First World War. Not only did the war call forth in extraordinary measure a spirit of self-sacrifice and service to the nation, it also imposed demands for massive social assistance programs. The care and maintenance of an Army, the dislocation of thousands of industrial workers, and the claims upon humanitarianism represented by the plight of many thousands of Europeans created an unprecedented need for organized welfare activities. Business contributions of leadership and funds were substantial and a practice of corporate giving for community welfare programs was firmly established. Even after the en-

---

[8] Ida M. Tarbell, *The Life of Elbert H. Gary: The Story of Steel* (New York, 1925), pp. 138–144; Arundel Cotter, *United States Steel, A Corporation with a Soul* (New York 1922), pp. 7, 106, 178.

[9] Ralph W. and Muriel E. Hidy, *Pioneering in Big Business, 1882–1911* (New York, 1955), pp. 209–218, 652–663.

[10] George W. Perkins, "The Modern Corporation" (New York, 1908).

thusiasm and need of the war years relaxed, such support remained a policy of many, though far from all business firms. Postwar conditions brought a decline but not an end to the acceptance of these new responsibilities.[11]

Once the attention of businessmen could be fully devoted to peacetime problems again, it appeared that still further social and economic changes pointed in the direction of new social relationships for management. Among these were the wider distribution of stock ownership and an accompanying increase of management's independence from stockholder control. By the time Berle and Means had produced their classic analysis of this evolution at the end of the 1920's, many businessmen had recognized it and begun to act upon it. Even more important was the acceptance and application of the principles of mass production and a growing awareness of their broader implications. The dependence of mass production on the creation and maintenance of a mass market had been dramatically demonstrated by Henry Ford. Widely preached by Ford, E. A. Filene, and others, it was somewhat less widely practiced—as later events were to show. Still, the need for an ever-widening market for American industry was sufficiently evident to spark a boom in management's interest in advertising and public relations. With the help of the publicity men, and with obvious intent to maintain the prestige and leadership regained during the war years, "service" became the motto of business in the twenties.

For each of the developments just mentioned precedents can be found in the prewar years. In one major respect, however, the climate of "normalcy" differed notably from the Progressive Era. Business in the twenties was seldom faced with the widespread, organized, and outspoken criticism to which it had been subjected by the age of the muckrakers. On the contrary, although businessmen may have feared a recurrence of government supervision and reform, and while the threat of Bolshevism loomed ominously on the horizons of the timid, for the most part the business community was relatively free in this peaceful decade from effective external pressures and criticisms. Management had the opportunity to define "service" largely in accordance with its own views of the nature and limits of its social obligations.

Speaking in the light of the war experience, John D. Rockefeller, Jr., in 1923 asked:

> Shall we cling to the conception of industry as an institution primarily of private interests, which enables certain individuals to accumulate wealth, too often irrespective of the well-being, the health, and the happiness of those engaged in its production? Or shall we adopt the modern viewpoint and regard industry as being a form of social service, quite as much as a revenue-producing process?

[11] Williams and Croxton, *op. cit.*, pp. 56–93.

For Rockefeller, the answer was clear; the old order was past. "To cling to such a conception is only to arouse antagonisms and to court trouble. In the light of the present every thoughtful man must concede that the purpose of industry is quite as much the advancement of social well-being as the production of wealth." As Rockefeller saw it, "The parties to industry are four in number; capital, management, labor, and the community." He was prepared to see all four represented in the councils of business.[12] Like Rockefeller, Judge Gary of U.S. Steel saw business as an institution in which each of the "parties" has a stake and an interest. Gary, as a representative of the emerging management class, however, placed his own group in a special relation to the other three. Management stood in a "position of balance" between the other claimants and must reserve to itself the final determination of their interests.[13] Owen D. Young of the General Electric Company, also, spoke of his position as "trustee" for the various interests affected by corporate policy in terms which anticipated the business outlook of the 1950's. In addition to the rights of stockholders and employees, "Customers have a right to demand that a concern so large [as General Electric] shall not only do its business honestly and properly, but further, that it shall meet its public obligations and perform its public duties . . . in a word, vast as it is, that it should be a good citizen."[14]

Henry Ford, too, emphasized service to the community, "service before profit"; but service to Ford meant primarily the increase of production and productivity. This was the greatest contribution business could make to the national welfare. Industry devoted to this kind of service, Ford wrote, ". . . removes the need for philanthropy. Philanthropy, no matter how noble its motive, does not make for self-reliance. We must have self-reliance. A community is the better for being discontented, for being dissatisfied with what it has."[15] The argument that mass production itself was the major contribution of business to social health was presented most persuasively by Edward A. Filene. Filene agreed that "Real service in business consists in making and selling merchandise of reliable quality for the lowest practically possible price, provided that the merchandise is made and sold under just conditions." Production for the masses forces recognition of the essential interdependence of business and society:

> We cannot distinguish between the old and the new capitalism by saying that one gives service whereas the other did not. Business has always

[12] John D. Rockefeller, Jr., *The Personal Relation in Industry* (New York, 1928), pp. 11–21.
[13] Elbert H. Gary, "Principles and Policies of the United States Steel Corporation" (n.p., n.d., 1921), pp. 5–6. See also Alfred P. Sloan, Jr., "Modern Ideals of Business," *World's Work* (Sept., 1926), pp. 694ff.
[14] Quoted in J. D. Glover, *The Attack on Big Business* (Boston, 1954), p. 338.
[15] Henry Ford in collaboration with Samuel Crowther, *My Life and Work* (New York, 1922), pp. 20, 206, 208–210.

given service to someone; and it has given some sort of service, often, even to those whom it robbed and cheated and exploited. It is the discovery that it pays to give service, and that it pays best to give the greatest possible service to the greatest possible number, which is now not only revolutionizing business but revolutionizing the whole world in which we live. . . . What is new is the discovery that the machinery of modern business does make the whole world one, that we are all "members one of another," that no individual and no group can be independent of others, but that we are mutually dependent and must, if we are to give expression to our very will to live, go in with all our heart for mutual service.

Service was, thus, not only a legitimate objective, it was the essential means to profit under mass production. Filene rejected "mere benevolence," yet, in almost the same breath, he found business committed to "the liberation of the masses . . . the inevitable goal of mass production. . . ."[16]

No doubt the ideas of those cited here were atypical of business thought in the twenties. Certainly these were men whose station and responsibilities made them especially conscious of their relationship to the public. Most businessmen probably thought of public relations in terms of convincing consumers of the merit of their products and citizens of the correctness of their economic views and practices. No clear and agreed-upon philosophy of corporate responsibility for community welfare had yet emerged, but new criteria for business policy were winning attention. As noted earlier, one of the conditions which characterized the predepression decade was the virtual absence of effective external criticism of business performance. The debate over the social consequences of business policy had become, in effect, a monologue. In part this was a tribute to the success of business statements and policies in persuading the public that the general interest was, in fact, being served under the new dispensation. In any case, the lack of external criticism was compensated for with a vengeance after 1929.

The depression of the thirties convinced many Americans, rightly or wrongly, that the new prescriptions for business responsibility had been largely intended for public consumption and "not to be taken internally." Dissatisfaction and disillusionment with business performance reached new levels of bitterness. And the public policies growing out of this climate of opinion have played a central part in the more careful examination of the issues which has characterized business thought in recent years. Without examining in detail the contemporary situation, we can safely assert that today we have more strongly entrenched potential critics of business performance than ever before—largely as a result of the public disenchantment of the New Deal days. Still, recently, the critical voices have once again

[16] Edward A. Filene, "A Simple Code of Business Ethics," *Annals of the American Academy of Political and Social Sciences,* Vol. CI (May, 1922), pp. 223–228; *Successful Living in This Machine Age* (New York, 1932), pp. 79 ff., 196.

seemed muted and restrained. Attacks on business and its policies are seldom heard, and still less frequently listened to.

Our review of a half century's evolution in the thinking of American businessmen on the subject of their social role and responsibilities has, I believe, shown that two chief categories of causes are involved. Primary, of course, have been the internal factors in industrial growth: the development of large-scale enterprise spanning the nation in its activities and concerns, the unification of the labor force, the application of mass production and the growing awareness of its dependence upon an ever-widening circle of willing and able consumers, and the capital requirements of an expanding economy leading to widespread stock ownership and a redefinition of the role of management. A second group of factors, external to the direct processes of industrial growth, has also been of major importance. Among these factors have been the traditional values of individualism and equality of opportunity which entered into the antitrust movement and the continuing suspicion of the power of collective wealth, the idealism and spirit of service growing out of wartime experience, the growing political power of organized labor and other nonbusiness groups, the acceptance of the principle of the ultimate responsibility of government for social welfare in those areas where private efforts fail, and the involvement of the United States in a world-wide struggle of democracy with totalitarianism in its various forms. It would take a fine scale, indeed, on which to weigh the relative importance of these two types of influences. But the record suggests that, in the past, external criticism, sometimes even irresponsible criticism, of the social consequences of business policies, has made a vital contribution to management's acceptance of a larger concept of obligation to the community.

In 1951, Frank W. Abrams, chairman of the board of Standard Oil of New Jersey and one of the most active and effective exponents of current management thought, wrote:[17]

> . . . management's responsibility, in the broadest sense, extends beyond the search for a balance among respective claims. Management, as a good citizen, and because it cannot function properly in an acrimonious and contentious atmosphere, has the positive duty to work for peaceful relations and understanding among men—for a restoration of faith of men in each other in all walks of life.

But is there not at least an equal grain of wisdom in Henry Ford's apparently cantankerous and self-centered statement: "A community is the better for being discontented, for being dissatisfied with what it has?"

---

[17] Quoted in Glover, *op. cit.*, pp. 338–339.

Where Do Corporate Responsibilities Really Lie?
32
Arthur W. Lorig

To whom do top corporate executives feel most responsible? To society, as some claim? Or to a lesser group such as employees, stockholders, creditors, or customers? Some writers and, university students—influenced, no doubt, by professors—insist that a corporation's chief responsibility is to society and that business decisions are made in accordance with that understanding. This is so contrary to my own belief and observations that I have undertaken to find the answer by going directly to those who administer corporations with a survey questioning where their chief loyalties do, indeed, lie.

The results of the survey were much as I expected: corporate executives do *not* feel their greatest responsibility is to society. Overwhelmingly, they reported that their chief responsibility was to stockholders as the owners of business. No other group was even a close second. Responsibility to society ranked at the very bottom, far below the closest group.

Furthermore, no real difference was found between the views of top executives (presidents and chairmen of boards of directors) and the controllers and financial executives. And, perhaps surprisingly, no discernible difference resulted from variation in size of corporations. The executives of corporations with annual sales of over $1 billion felt almost exactly as those of corporations with sales under $50 million. (Corporations with annual sales under $1 million were not included in the survey, for their executives are not likely to regard responsibility to society as an important consideration in their operations.)

THE SURVEY

Questionnaires were sent to 300 companies in the United States. (The companies selected were the odd-numbered ones in the list of 600 used by the American Institute of Certified Public Accountants in compiling its 1965 edition of *Accounting Trends and Techniques.*) The questionnaire listed groups interested in corporations (creditors, employees, society as a whole, stockholders, and others to be written in) and requested that responsibilities to them be ranked 1, 2, 3, and so forth. Groups of similar importance were to be given the same rank.

Reprinted with permission from *Business Horizons* (Bloomington, Ind.: The University of Indiana Press, Spring 1967), pp. 51–54.

One-half of the questionnaires were sent to the corporation presidents, who sometimes were also the chairmen of the boards of directors. In a few instances, answering the questionnaire was delegated by the president to another executive such as a vice-president or director of public relations. The remaining questionnaires were mailed to the controller or, if none was listed in *Poor's Register of Corporations,* to the treasurer or other chief financial officer. Two groups were used because it was thought that the officers dealing with finances might regard corporate responsibilities differently than do presidents. As mentioned previously, this was not the case.

To be certain that answers would be given freely and frankly, no identifying names or symbols were used on the questionnaires or return envelopes. Executives were invited to write out their views in letter form; some chose to do this, usually to explain their views at length or to state why they elected not to participate in the survey. The other respondents are unknown.

One hundred and fifty-two usable responses were received. An additional nine indicated the executives could not, or chose not to, rank their group responsibilities. Seven more ranked all groups equally and hence were omitted in the tabulation, and five came in after the tabulation was completed. It is significant that a total of 173 replies was received, constituting a 58 per cent response. Considering the work pressures, the response was gratifying.

RESULTS

The figures tell the story clearly. Table 1 presents the assignments of rank 1. The tally of rank I assignments in Table 1 is slightly greater than the number of responses used because some executives assigned rank 1 to more than one group. Some gave no ranking whatsoever to certain groups; hence, only one group, the stockholders, has a full 152 rankings. Customers as an important group were not included in the questionnaire list, but thirty-four executives added that group as a write-in. Other write-ins, such as suppliers and government, were very few and were ranked quite far down, none being ranked first.

With 84.2 per cent of the respondents ranking the stockholders as the group to which they owe greatest responsibility and only 2.4 per cent placing society as a whole in that rank, the evidence is conclusive that corporations are considered by the responding executives to be instruments of the stockholders, not society. However, several pointed out that providing a profitable operation for the stockholders served to benefit society as a whole. The reasoning usually was not given, but some hints appeared occasionally. For example, one executive stated that "no business can long expect to maximize profits [for the stockholders] unless it also consistently makes available to its customers products and services of competitive quality at competitive prices . . . and serves the basic interests of the society in which it is organized." Several mentioned that if the stockholders, employees, and customers were treated properly, society as a whole would be served. On

Table 1   Summary of Rank 1 Designations

	Times Group was Ranked	Times Group was Given Rank 1	Percentage of Responses Given Rank 1
	Chief Executives		
Stockholders	72	59	81.9
Employees	66	8	12.1
Customers	23	6	26.1
Creditors	51	6	11.8
Society	55	3	5.5
	Controllars and Finance Executives		
Stockholders	80	69	86.2
Employees	76	8	10.5
Customers	11	0	0.0
Creditors	73	8	11.0
Society	70	0	0.0
	Total		
Stockholders	152	128	84.2
Employees	142	16	11.3
Customers	34	6	17.6
Creditors	124	14	11.3
Society	125	3	2.4

Table 2   Average Ranks Assigned to Groups

	Times Group was Ranked	Average Rank
	Chief Executives	
Stockholders	72	1.28
Employees	66	2.20
Customers	23	2.22
Creditors	51	2.92
Society	55	3.78
	Controllers and Finance Executives	
Stockholders	80	1.20
Employees	76	2.16
Customers	11	2.55
Creditors	73	2.75
Society	70	3.91
	Total	
Stockholders	152	1.24
Employees	142	2.18
Customers	34	2.32
Creditors	124	2.82
Society	125	3.86

the other hand, a couple of warnings were given that management does not have the right to utilize the assets and power of the corporation to carry out personal, political, or social viewpoints that are not demonstrably in the best interests of the shareholders.

Much the same information and conclusions are obtained by comparing the average ranks assigned to the various groups. Table 2 presents this comparison. The average group rankings for different sizes of corporations were also determined; sizes were measured by the annual sales reported on the questionnaires. Table 3 compares these rankings and discloses no appreciable difference in rank assignments because of corporate size.

Table 3   Average Ranks by Size of Corporation as Determined by Sales

Sales ($ millions)	Stockholders	Employees	Customers	Creditors	Society
$5–50	1.25	2.05	2.00	2.85	3.79
50–500	1.23	2.18	2.56	2.80	3.95
500–1,000	1.33	2.29	2.60	2.68	3.70
Over 1,000	1.10	2.24	1.80	3.14	3.81
All corporations	1.24	2.18	2.32	2.82	3.86

REASONING BEHIND THE RANKINGS

The questionnaires invited the executives to give the reasons behind their selections for first rank; in most cases they complied. The reasons offered for ranking the stockholder group first were that (1) stockholders are the corporate owners; (2) stockholders, through their representatives the board of directors, hire the executives to run the business; (3) stockholders created the corporations to make a profit for them and they take the greatest risk; and (4) the executives hold a trust or stewardship relationship toward the stockholders' properties and are accountable for those properties. Several replies were to the effect that if the stockholders' interests were safeguarded properly, those of the other groups would automatically be taken care of.

Some interesting single reasons were given also: the corporation is an economic, not a social, institution—a pooling of resources for profit; stockholders have a responsibility to society, but the corporation does not; stockholders are the primary source of new funds; and, first responsibility to the stockholders is necessary in building the company image. Several vigorous declarations were received—it is inconceivable to rank stockholders other than first; it is the American way of life.

The reasons given by those ranking other groups first (such as creditors, customers, and employees) dwelt upon the importance of the group to the operation of the corporation. The few executives insisting that all groups should be ranked equally also used this line of thought—the essential nature of each group to the corporation's existence and successful operation. As one executive stated, "Which of your children do you love the most? It is like riding a bicycle—you must keep your balance."

Probably no better summarization could be found of the prevailing attitude of top executives toward groups of principal concern to corporations than the letter received from a vice-president of a corporation with multi-billion dollar annual sales. It accompanied the return of the questionnaire and is quoted with his permission.

> In the . . . Company, the stockholder is regarded as the owner of the business. Dividends are viewed as distribution of profits. While acknowledging our considerable responsibilities to all other groups our prime responsibility is still to the owners as it is in all other forms of business organization. Although the interests of the various groups occasionally conflict and the short-term resolution may appear to be inconsistent with stockholder interest, each decision is made with the long-term interest of the stockholder in mind.
>
> Every business enterprise is formed with one basic objective—to make a profit. The fundamental economics of capitalism is the formation of capital with the objective of producing a profit for the owners. This is undoubtedly more obvious in smaller corporations where owner and manager are the same. In our opinion, it becomes even more important that this fundamental be recognized as a company becomes larger. Profits benefit all other groups through the creation of jobs, payment of taxes, etc., but the stockholder is the prime beneficiary and is most directly interested in increasing the wealth position of the company. Other groups have their own interests and responsibilities which are naturally oriented toward self-interest. Creditors are interested in company well-being primarily from the standpoint of solvency. Employees are vital to the success of a business and their loyalty is coveted by management, but the majority of them are primarily interested in the preservation and security of their own jobs rather than in the creation of new ones. Society as a whole is a little remote from the individual company, and, of course, has many interests of which business is only one. Customers want high quality at the lowest possible cost and will go elsewhere, as they should, if the company cannot meet their requirements. Communities are interested in local purchases, job stability, and tax revenues and are fearful of volatile-type businesses. There is an interrelationship of all these interests and the corporation must be responsive and responsible to all of them within its own objectives and limitations. These responsibilities cannot be met without profits, and profits will not result unless corporate obligations are met.
>
> The stewardship function of management has tended to become somewhat blurred in the emphasis on the income statement, earnings per share, and 'growth,' but the preservation of capital is still a basic responsibility to the stockholder and almost all spending proposals consider return on investment and risk as major criteria. Motivations vary among individual managers, but our officers and directors recognize there are limitations to the risks that can be taken with company assets.

A principal criterion of success of a company is its ability to raise substantial amounts of long-term capital at favorable cost. The stockholder is the basic source of this capital. Unless his long-term objectives are met, there will be no funds and, hence, no fulfillment of other responsibilities and obligations of the corporation. In this particular area, the management and stockholders are particularly well attuned. Both are interested in long-term growth. Individual manager motivation may be prestige, personal reward, sense of accomplishment, or other things, but the basic objective is the same for both groups.

Last, but far from least, is that the stockholder has a recourse other than selling his stock to register dissatisfaction—the vote. This is not legal fiction. Even in the largest corporation, the proxy fight is not impossible. It happens just enough to sober any manager who may tend to identify the company as something separate from the stockholders. Stockholder relations activities are increasing throughout the country. More and more information about company activities is disbursed to stockholders.

This is partly because the stockholder has a right to know as an owner and partly because he can be a source of capital, may be a customer, and can be an ambassador of the company in the community, all of which contributes to the mutual objectives of the company and its owners and also to the special interests of other groups.

B. Professional Responsibilities of Management

Can Business Afford to Ignore Social Responsibilities?

33

Keith Davis

Few persons would deny that there are significant changes taking place in social, political, economic, and other aspects of modern culture. Some of these changes businessmen may want and others they may dislike, but in either instance the changes do exist and must be faced. As our culture changes, it is appropriate—even mandatory—that businessmen re-examine their role and the functions of business in society. One area undergoing extensive re-examination is the responsibility businessmen have to society in making business decisions. These are the questions that are being asked:

Why do businessmen have social responsibilities, if in fact they do?
How does a businessman know in what directions his social responsibilities lie?
If businessmen fail to accept social responsibilities incumbent upon them, what consequences may be expected?

It is my purpose in this article to discuss these questions in a very fundamental way. Without looking at specific company practices and without insisting upon a particular program of action, I wish to discuss three basic ideas which must underlie all of our thinking about social responsibility, regardless of what choices we eventually make. The first two ideas are constant and enduring, no matter what social changes occur. The third is more directly related to social changes today, but I believe it is just as fundamental as the others.

Social responsibility is a nebulous idea and, hence, is defined in various

Copyright © 1960 by The Regents of the University of California. Reprinted from *California Management Review* (Spring 1960), pp.70–76, by permission of The Regents.

ways. It is used here within a management context to refer to *businessmen's decisions and actions taken for reasons at least partially beyond the firm's direct economic or technical interest.*[1] Thus, social responsibility has two rather different faces. On the one hand, businessmen recognize that since they are managing an economic unit in society, they have a broad obligation to the community with regard to economic developments affecting the public welfare (such as full employment, inflation, and maintenance of competition). A quite different type of social responsibility is, on the other hand, a businessman's obligation to nurture and develop human values (such as morale, cooperation, motivation, and self-realization in work). These human values cannot be measured on an economic value scale. Accordingly, the term "social responsibility" refers to both socio-economic and socio-human obligations to others. Popular usage often omits or underplays the socio-human side, but I shall suggest later in this article that it deserves more emphasis.

Note that the importance of social responsibility in this context derives from the fact that it affects a businessman's decisions and consequently his actions toward others. Social responsibility has applied in any situation if it *influences* a businessman's decision even partially. It is not necessary that a decision be based wholly on one's attitude of social responsibility in order to qualify. For example, when a businessman decides to raise or lower prices, he is normally making an economic decision; but if the management of a leading automobile firm decided not to raise prices because of possible effects on inflation, social responsibility would be involved. As a matter of fact, *rarely* would social responsibility be the exclusive reason for a decision.

While it is true that only businessmen (rather than businesses *per se*) make socially responsible decisions, they decide in terms of the objectives and policies of their business institution, which over a period of time acquires social power in its own right. Thus each business institution and the entire business system eventually come to stand for certain socially responsible beliefs and actions. But in the last analysis it is always the businessman who makes the decision. The business institution can only give him a cultural framework, policy guidance, and a special interest.

RESPONSIBILITY GOES WITH POWER

Most persons agree that businessmen today have considerable social power. Their counsel is sought by government and community. What they say and

---

1 Some socially responsible business decisions by a long, complicated process of reasoning can be "justified" as having a good chance of bringing long-run economic gain to the firm and thus paying it back for its socially responsible outlook. This long-run economic gain is often merely rationalization of decisions made for non-economic reasons, and in any case the connection is so problematical that some social responsibility is bound to be present also. An example is a decision to retain a very old employee even though his productivity is low.

do influences their community. This type of influence is *social power*. It comes to businessmen because they are leaders, are intelligent men of affairs, and speak for the important institution we call business. They speak for free enterprise, for or against right-to-work policies, for or against their local school bond election, and so on, *in their roles as businessmen*. When they speak and act as citizens only, and those involved recognize this fact, then whatever social power businessmen possess is that of a citizen and is beyond the bounds of this discussion. In practice, however, it is often difficult to distinguish between these two roles, thereby further complicating the situation.

To the extent that businessmen or any other group have social power, the lessons of history suggest that their social responsibility should be equated with it. Stated in the form of a general relationship, it can be said that *social responsibilities of businessmen need to be commensurate with their social power*. Though this idea is deceptively simple on its face, it is in reality rather complicated and is often overlooked by discussants of social responsibility. On the one hand, it is argued that business is business and anything which smacks of social responsibility is out of bounds (i.e., keep the power but accept no responsibility). On the other, some would have business assume reponsibilities as sort of a social godfather, looking after widows, orphans, water conservation, or any other social need, simply because business has large economic resources. Both positions are equally false.

The idea that responsibility and power go hand in hand appears to be as old as civilization itself. Wherever one looks in ancient and medieval history—Palestine, Rome, Britain—men were concerned with balancing power and responsibility. Men, being something less than perfect, have often failed to achieve this balance, but they have generally sought it as a necessary antecedent to justice. This idea appears to have its origins in logic. It is essentially a matter of balancing one side of an equation with the other.

The idea of co-equal power and responsibility is no stranger to business either. For example, one of the tenets of scientific management is that authority and responsibility should be balanced in such a way that each employee and manager is made responsible to the extent of his authority, and vice-versa.[2] Although this tenet refers to relationships *within* the firm, it seems that it would apply as well to the larger society outside the firm. As a matter of fact, businessmen have been one of the strongest proponents of co-equal social power and responsibility, particularly in their references to labor unions.

Based upon the evidence, it appears that both business leaders and the public accept the idea of co-equal power and responsibility. Although businessmen accept the logic of this idea, their problem is learning to respect

[2] Harold Koontz and Cyril O'Donnell, *Principles of Management* (New York: McGraw-Hill Book Company, Second Edition, 1959), p. 95.

and apply it when making decisions. Granted that there are no pat answers, they still need some guides, else each shall take off in a different direction. At this point, the idea already stated continues to offer help. If "social responsibilities of businessmen need to be commensurate with their social power," then, in a general way, *in the specific operating areas* where there is power, responsibility should also reside. Let us take an example:

> Company "A" is the only major employer in a small town. It is considering moving its entire plant out of the area. Company "B" is considering moving its plant of the same size out of a large city where it is one of many employers. It would seem that, other things being equal, Company "A" should give more weight to social responsibilities to the community when considering its move.

Even accepting the greater responsibility of Company "A", and some would not go this far, we still do not know how much greater nor in what way Company "A" should let its decision be amended, if at all. Thus the principle of co-equal power and responsibility can at best serve only as a rough guide, but a real one. For example:

> Do businessmen by their industrial engineering decisions have the power to affect worker's feeling of accomplishment and self-fulfillment on the job? If so, there is roughly a co-equal responsibility.
> Do businessmen have power as businessmen to influence unemployment? To the extent that is so, is there not also social responsibility?
> Do businessmen have power to determine the honesty of advertising? To the degree that they do, is there also social responsibility?

One matter of significance is that the conditions causing power are both internal and external to the firm. In the example of advertising honesty, power is derived primarily internally from the authority structure of the firm and management's knowledge of product characteristics. In the case of Company "A" described earlier, much of its social power is derived from the external fact that it is the only employer in a small town. Each case is situational, requiring reappraisal of power-responsibility relationships each time a major decision is made.

There are, of course, other viewpoints concerning the extent of business social responsibility, and most of them offer a much easier path for businessmen than the one I have been describing. Levitt, in a powerful attack on social responsibility of businessmen, points out that if business assumes a large measure of social responsibility for employee welfare it will lead to a sort of neo-feudalism with all its paternalistic and autocratic ills. The result would be socially less desirable than in the days before businessmen were concerned with social responsibility.[3] Selekman, in an important new analysis,

[3] Theodore Levitt, "The Danger of Social Responsibility," *Harvard Business Review,* September–October, 1958, pp. 41–50.

suggests that attention to social responsibility will undermine the main objective of all business, which is to provide economic goods and services to society.[4] A collapse of business' basic economic objectives would indeed be a catastrophe. Certainly the primary economic objectives of business must come first, else business will lose its reason for existence. Selekman's solution is a form of constitutionalism in which the responsibility of the business, other than its economic goals, is to administer its affairs with justice according to a constitutional framework mutually established by all groups involved. These criticisms and others raise questions about putting much social responsibility into business' kit of tools, a fact which leads directly to the second fundamental point of this discussion.

LESS RESPONSIBILITY LEADS TO LESS POWER

Certainly, if social responsibilities could be avoided or kept to insignificant size in the total scheme of business, a weighty, difficult burden would be raised from businessmen's shoulders. Business progress would be a primrose path compared to the path of thorns which responsibilities entail. But what are the consequences of responsibility avoidance? If power and responsibility are to be relatively equal, *then the avoidance of social responsibility leads to gradual erosion of social power.* To the extent that businessmen do not accept social-responsibility opportunities as they arise, other groups will step in to assume these responsibilities. Historically, government and labor have been most active in the role of diluting business power, and probably they will continue to be the principal challenging groups.[5] I am not proposing that this *should* happen, but on basis of the evidence it appears that this will tend to happen to the extent that businessmen do not keep their social responsibilities approximately equal with their social power. In this same vein Howard R. Bowen, in his study of business social responsibilites, concluded, "And it is becoming increasingly obvious that a freedom of choice and delegation of power such as businessmen exercise would hardly be permitted to continue without some assumption of social responsibility."[6]

Admiral Ben Moreell, Chairman of the Board, Jones and Laughlin Steel Corporation, put this idea more dramatically:

[4] Benjamin M. Selekman, *A Moral Philosophy for Business* (New York: McGraw-Hill Book Company, 1959), especially chapter 27.

[5] For government's role, see George A. Steiner, *Government's Role in Economic Life* (New York: McGraw-Hill Book Company, 1953) and Wayne L. McNaughton and Joseph Lazar, *Industrial Relations and The Government* (New York: McGraw-Hill Book Company, 1954). For labor's role, see Neil W. Chamberlain, *Collective Bargaining* (New York: McGraw-Hill Book Company, 1951) and John A. Fitch, *Social Responsibilities of Organized Labor* (New York: Harper and Brothers, 1957).

[6] Howard R. Bowen, *Social Responsibilities of the Businessman* (New York: Harper and Brothers, 1953), p. 4.

I am convinced that unless we do [accept social responsibilities], the vacuum created by our willingness will be filled by those who would take us down the road to complete statism and inevitable moral and social collapse.[7]

History supports these viewpoints. Under the protection of common law, employers during the nineteenth century gave minor attention to worker safety. Early in the twentieth century, in the face of pressure from safety and workmen's compensation laws, employers genuinely accepted responsibility for safety. Since then there have been very few restrictions on business power in this area, because business in general has been acting responsibly. At the opposite extreme, business in the first quarter of this century remained callous about technological and market layoff. As a result, business lost some of its power to government, which administers unemployment compensation, and to unions, which restrict it by means of tight seniority clauses, supplemental unemployment benefits (SUB), and other means. *Now business finds itself in the position of paying unemployment costs it originally denied responsibility for, but having less control than when it did not pay!*

A current problem of social responsibility is gainful employment for older workers. The plight of workers in the over-45 age bracket is well known. In spite of public pronouncements of interest in them and in spite of their general employability, many of them find job opportunities quite limited or even nonexistent. I have said elsewhere that "unless management . . . makes reasonable provision for employing older persons out of work, laws will be passed prohibiting employment discrimination against older workers."[8] Just as a glacier grinds slowly along, the responsibility-power equation gradually, but surely, finds its balance.

In line with the foregoing analysis, Levitt's proposal of "business for business' sake" loses some of its glamor, because it means substantial loss of business power. Historian Arnold J. Toynbee predicts this result when he speaks of business managers being part "of a new world civil service," not necessarily working for government, but working under such stability and elaborate rules both from within and without that they form a relatively powerless bureaucracy similar to the civil service.[9]

It is unlikely that businessmen will concede their social power so easily, and I for one do not want them to do so. Businessmen are our most capable core of organization builders and innovators. We need them. In spite of pessimistic views, businessmen during the next fifty years probably will

---

7 Admiral Ben Moreell, "The Role of American Business in Social Progress" (Indianapolis: Indiana State Chamber of Commerce, 1956), p. 20.

8 Keith Davis, *Human Relations in Business* (New York: McGraw-Hill Book Company, 1957), p. 415.

9 Arnold J. Toynbee, "Thinking Ahead," *Harvard Business Review*, September–October, 1958, p. 168.

have substantial freedom of choice regarding what social responsibilities they will take and how far they will go. As current holders of social power, they can act responsibly to hold this power if they wish to do so. If their philosophy is positive (i.e., *for* something, rather than against almost any change) they can take the initiative as instruments of social change related to business. They will then be managers in the true sense of shaping the future, rather than plaintive victims of a more restrictive environment. The choice *is* theirs.

NON-ECONOMIC VALUES IN BUSINESS

Early in this discussion I distinguished two types of social responsibilities. One was socio-economic responsibility for general economic welfare. The other was socio-human and referred to responsibility for preserving and developing human values. Let us now further discuss this distinction as it relates to a third idea underlying the entire problem of social responsibility.

There is general consensus that the "economic man" is dead if, indeed, he ever did exist. Men at work, as customers, and as citizens of a plant community do expect more than straight economic considerations in dealing with business. Since man is more than an economic automaton computing market values, what will be the role of business in serving his other needs? My third basic idea is that *continued vitality of business depends upon its vigorous acceptance of socio-human responsibilities along with socio-economic responsibilities.* A number of people accept the general idea of social responsibility, but they argue that business is wholly an economic institution and, therefore, its responsibilities are limited only to economic aspects of general public welfare. Following this line of reasoning, businessmen might be concerned with economic costs of unemployment, but not with the loss of human dignity and the social disorganization that accompany it. They would be concerned with making work productive in order to better serve society's economic needs but not with making it meaningful in a way that provided worker fulfillment.

The idea of confining social responsibility within economic limits fails on several counts. In the first place, it is hardly possible to separate economic aspects of life from its other values. Business deals with a *whole* man in a *whole* social structure, and all aspects of this situation are interrelated. It is agreed that the economic functions of business are primary and the non-economic are secondary, but the non-economic do exist. Second, even if economic aspects of life could be wholly separated out, the general public does not seem to want business confined only to economics. They also have human expectations of business. Third, businessmen currently have socio-human power; hence, if they ignore responsibility in this area, they will be inviting further loss of power. On three counts, then, it appears unwise to equate social responsibility with economic public welfare.

As a matter of fact, it is not a question of "Will these non-economic values be admitted to the decision matrix?" but "To what extent will they be admitted?" Regardless of professions to the contrary, businessmen today are influenced by other than technical-economic values when making decisions. Businessmen are human like all the rest of us. They do have emotions and social value judgments. It is foolish to contend that they, like a machine and unlike other human beings, respond only to economic and technical data.

Businessmen in making decisions typically apply three separate value systems, along with overriding ethical-moral considerations. These are:

Technical—Based upon physical facts and scientific logic.
Economic—Based upon market values determined by consumers.
Human—Based upon social-psychological needs other than economic consumption needs. This value system often goes by the term "human relations."

In many business decisions all three of these value systems exert some weight upon the final decision. Because man is human this aspect of his life cannot be ignored by any institution that deals with him.

But there are dangers in generalizations which are too sweeping, such as, "Business is responsible for human values in general." What is needed is a concept which marks business as an instrument *for specific human goals* (along with technical-economic ones) in the life of man and his society— something which gives direction and hope to the climb of mankind from the depths of the Stone Age to the great potential which his Creator has given him. This kind of concept does not come easily but it must come eventually. By giving people motivation, social goals, and work fulfillment, business might over the long pull be termed a "movement" in the same way that history refers to the labor movement.

Certainly some major efforts at being explicit have been made recently. Theodore V. Houser, writing from the point of view of big business, stated five specific areas of social responsibility, ranging from employees to government.[10] Selekman's idea of constitutional justice was discussed earlier.[11] Crawford Greenewalt emphasized the importance of individual creativity and stated, "The important thing is that we bring into play the full potential of all men whatever their station."[12] And there are many others. For my own use I have summed these ideas into a single manageable phrase, as follows: *To fulfill the human dignity, creativity, and potential of free men.*[13] This

[10] Houser (see note 2), p. 2.
[11] Selekman (see note 2), p. 7.
[12] Greenewalt (see note 2), p. 2.
[13] One analyst has put this point even more strongly: "The making of goods is incidental and subordinate to the making of men." Raphael Demos, "Business and the Good Society," in Edward C. Bursk, Ed., *Business and Religion* (New York: Harper and Brothers, 1959), p. 190.

can be businessmen's long-run guide to socially responsible action in each situation they face. The term "fulfill" is used because business cannot award goals such as human dignity. It can only develop the proper climate for their growth. The term "man" is used because unless *man* is free, men cannot be free. Other institutions and groups will also be interested in this goal. Businessmen are not wholly responsible here, but only partially so, approximately to the extent of their social power.

AN IMPORTANT CHOICE AHEAD

The subject of social responsibility places business at an important crossroads in its history. Which way it will go is not known, but in any event social responsibility will tend to equate with social power, which means that avoidance of responsibilities as they develop will lead to loss of business power. Some hard thinking is needed so that the right course can be charted. This is not the time for pat slogans, clichés, and wheezes. Clearly, economic functions of business are primary, but this does not negate the existence of non-economic functions and responsibilities. The price of social freedom is its responsible exercise.

Because society is changing, evidence suggests that the continued vigor of business depends upon its forthright acceptance of further socio-human responsibilities. In spite of protestations of impending corporate feudalism and dilution of economic objectives, the trend in this direction is already apparent. Some of the more fruitful avenues of interest are: making work meaningful, developing persons to their fullest potential, preservation of creativity and freedom, and fulfillment of human dignity.

In summary, the *first* social responsibility of businessmen is to find workable solutions regarding the nature and extent of their own social responsibilities.

We can be confident that modern business leadership does have the capacity to deal with questions of social responsibility. Although the next fifty years will bring major social change, business should perform effectively in this instability because it is geared for change. Typically, during the last century it has had an unstable economic environment; yet it has learned to live and prosper therein. It can do the same during a period of social reevaluation by developing flexible responses to the needs of society. But if it does not do so, it will use up its capital in human and spiritual values, which is a sure way to go socially bankrupt.

Business Management: A Profession?   **34**

Howard R. Bowen

Walter Rauschenbusch, the great architect of the "social gospel," once wrote:

> Business life is the unregenerate section of our social order. If by some magic it could be plucked out of our total social life in all its raw selfishness, and isolated on an island, unmitigated by any other factors of our life, that island would immediately become the object of a great foreign mission crusade for all Christendom.[1]

That such words could be written by a responsible religious leader only forty years ago attests to the great progress in the mores and conduct of American business since the era of the "muckrakers." Whatever may be the faults and inadequacies of business today, words so extreme as these no longer fit. Business has unquestionably become more humane and more responsible than it was a generation ago.

At the very time Rauschenbusch was writing, the eminent jurist, Louis D. Brandeis, saw the possibilities of professionalism in business:

> . . . success in business must mean something very different from mere money-making. In business the able man ordinarily earns a larger income than one less able. So does the able man in the recognized professions—in law, medicine or engineering; and even in those professions more remote from money-making, like the ministry, teaching or social work. The world's demand for efficiency is so great and the supply so small, that the price of efficiency is high in every field of human activity.
>
> The recognized professions, however, definitely reject the size of the financial return as the measure of success. They select as their test, excellence of performance in the broadest sense—and include, among other things, advance in the particular occupation and service to the community. These are the basis of all worthy reputations in the recognized professions. In them a large income is the ordinary incident of success; but he who exaggerates the value of the incident is apt to fail of real success.
>
> To the business of to-day a similar test must be applied. True, in business the earning of profit is something more than an incident of success. It is an essential condition of success; because the continued absence

Reprinted with permission from the American Academy of Political and Social Science, *The Annals* (January 1955), pp. 112–117.

1 *Christianizing the Social Order* (New York: The Macmillan Company, 1914), p. 156.

of profit itself spells failure. But while loss spells failure, large profits do not connote success. Success must be sought in business also in excellence of performance; and in business, excellence of performance manifests itself, among other things, in the advancing of methods and processes; in the improvement of products; in more perfect organization, eliminating friction as well as waste; in bettering the condition of the workingmen, developing their faculties and promoting their happiness; and in the establishment of right relations with customers and with the community.[2]

This paper deals with two questions, both suggested by Brandeis' eloquent words: (1) Is business management in fact becoming a profession? and (2) Should business management take on the attributes of a profession? There are many who answer one or both of these questions in the negative. My conclusion is that both questions can be answered affirmatively—that business management is gradually assuming some of the marks of a profession and that this tendency is on the whole desirable.[3] But before taking up these questions directly, it is well to consider just what is meant by the word "profession."

A full-fledged profession is a vocation in which the following conditions exist: (1) pursuit of the vocation demands that practitioners acquire an intellectually based technique; (2) practitioners assume a relationship of responsibility toward clients; (3) practitioners are organized into responsible associations which set standards for admission to practice and exert control over the actions of their members through codes of ethics.[4] In most professions, the social control exerted by the association is reinforced by public licensing and supervision. Among the traditional professions in which these conditions are most fully realized are theology, law, and medicine. Later additions are, among others, dentistry, veterinary medicine, engineering, architecture, teaching, and accounting.

With these criteria in mind, let us now consider the extent to which the conditions of professionalism are fulfilled in present business management.

INTELLECTUALLY BASED TECHNIQUE

The art of management has increasingly become a subject for study and research by disciplined and disinterested investigators and scholars. The early work in this field is associated with the name of Frederick W. Taylor,

[2] *Business—A Profession* (Boston: Small, Maynard & Company, cop. 1914 and 1925), pp. 3–5.

[3] This paper is based in part on my book *Social Responsibilities of the Businessman* (New York: Harper & Brothers, 1953).

[4] Cf. Paul Meadows, "Professional Behavior and Industrial Society," *Journal of Business,* July 1946, p. 150. See also A. M. Carr-Saunders and P. A. Wilson, *The Professions* (London: Oxford University Press, 1933); R. H. Tawney, *The Acquisitive Society* (New York: Harcourt, Brace and Company, 1920), pp. 91–122; Talcott Parsons, "The Professions and the Social Structure," *Social Forces,* May 1939, pp. 457–467.

who made pathbreaking studies of efficiency, especially in the art of cutting metals. Taylor's most important contribution, however, was not the particular results of his studies but his approach. He showed that the problems of business might be studied with same objectivity, the same rigor, and many of the same methods as are common in the laboratories of physical sciences.

In time, many more investigators applied themselves to the problems of business, and their interests were eventually broadened to include not only productive techniques in the factory and offices but also problems of sales, advertising, finance, records, accounting, inventory control, quality control, employee selection and training, job analysis, worker morale, incentives, collective bargaining, public relations, and administrative organization. The effect of these studies, as they have accumulated from the modest beginnings of a half-century ago, is to persuade businessmen: (1) that there are efficient and inefficient ways not only of cutting metals but also of meeting problems of business relations; (2) that efficient methods are less costly and therefore more profitable than bad methods; and (3) that the efficient ways may be more easily and surely discovered through the proven methods of painstaking experiment and disinterested observation than through following rules of thumb or uninformed prejudice.

As a result of the development of an intellectually based technique, the practice of management is becoming an art for which one must prepare himself through education and experience. The education need not be formal education; yet increasing numbers of younger men are preparing themselves for managerial roles by study in schools of business, and more and more junior executives are studying for positions of greater responsibility by attendance at the many institutes, night classes, and company training programs now being provided. In short, there is a more or less systematic body of knowledge which one must acquire before one is qualified to fill a managerial position in a large corporation. This is not to say that one may learn to become a successful manager by reading books any more than one can become a great physician by reading books. In both cases, certain personal qualities and long years of experience are required. Nevertheless, formal knowledge is a practical necessity.

RESPONSIBILITY TO CLIENTS

Business is sharply distinguished from the traditional professions in the nature of its clientele and in the character of its relationships to that clientele.

In the traditional professions, the clients are primarily the persons or groups who are served by the practitioners—they are the "customers." And professional ethics are concerned primarily with the relationships between the practitioners and the customers. But the clients of business, that is, the persons who are affected by business operations and for whom business is therefore responsible, include not only customers but also stockholders, workers, suppliers, citizens of the communities in which business is conducted, and, in our interdependent world, the public at large. Responsibility toward all those persons whose lives are touched by business operations.[5] In this sense, the concept of professionalism as applied to business is even broader and more inclusive than as applied to medicine or law or theology.

In most of the traditional professions, the human relationships involved are distinctively *personal* relationships. They are primarily the relationships of individual practitioners to clients who are known face to face. But in business—particularly in the large corporation—the "practitioner" is a *group* of persons who jointly constitute "management" and who are collectively responsible for the conduct of the enterprise. And the clients, often, are known only vaguely and impersonally as "stockholders," the "market," "organized labor," the "public," and so forth.[6]

Because the clientele of business is so diffuse and ramified and distant, and because business relationships are so impersonal, it is much more difficult for businessmen, as compared with members of the traditional professions, to perceive their responsibilities and to respond to them. It is one thing for a physician to realize and accept his responsibilities toward a patient whom he knows as a fellow human being; and it is quite another thing for a business management to understand that its decisions may affect the lives of flesh-and-blood human beings and to act accordingly. Our whole ethical tradition is more immediately serviceable for direct interpersonal relationships than for the kind of impersonal and distant human relationships which are common to business. This means, on the one hand that it is unusually difficult for businessmen to acquire professional attitudes and practices, and on the other hand that businessmen deserve great credit for the substantial progress already achieved.

MANAGEMENT AS A BALANCE WHEEL

There is no doubt of an increasing acceptance among businessmen of important obligations toward their diverse clients. The concept of "stewardship" is, of course, an old one, and many businessmen have been thinking in this direction. Especially within the past few years, large numbers of business leaders have publicly acknowledged and actively preached the doctrine that they are servants of society and that management merely in the interests (narrowly defined) of stockholders is not the sole end of their duties.[7]

---

[5] This is, of course, not an absolute distinction. Practitioners of the traditional professions have responsibilities to the community—the physician for public health, the lawyer for justice, and so forth. Yet the emphasis in professional ethics is upon the relationship of the practitioner to the person served.

[6] Again this distinction is not absolute in a day of giant law firms and great medical clinics.

[7] In an earlier issue of The Annals, I tried to show in some detail the growing sense of social responsibility on the part of businessmen: "How Public Spirited Is American Business?" The Annals, Vol. 280 (March 1952), pp. 82–89.

The following are two examples (many more might be supplied) of statements by leading businessmen in which they acknowledge their role as trustees:

> Today, most managements, in fact, operate as trustees in recognition of the claims of employees, investors, consumers, and government. The task is to keep these forces in balance and to see that each gets a fair share of industry's rewards.[8]
> It is becoming clear that in our modern society top management has the opportunity—in fact, I should say the duty—to act as a balance wheel in relation to three groups of interests—the interests of owners, of employees, and of the public, all of whom have a stake in the output of industry. Management can best represent the interests' of ownership by acting fairly and wisely with respect to the claims of employees and the public as well. It is a difficult but vital role. It seems to me only too obvious that the very survival of private enterprise requires that private enterprise act to maintain a productive and equitable relation among these three elements: the individual's right to, and the social necessity for, profits; the economic and human aspirations of all workers; and the public's demand for an abundance of goods at low cost. The alternative is plainly intensified industrial conflict followed by increased government regulation forced by an impatient public.[9]

One must not, of course, exaggerate the extent to which businessmen and their corporations have disavowed their selfish impulses and turned their thoughts to the social welfare. And the progress that has occurred has been achieved primarily as a result of changes in the social climate of opinion, attitudes, and values within which business functions. Nevertheless, businessmen have made great progress in their responsiveness to their obligations to society.

PROFESSIONAL ASSOCIATIONS

The luxuriant growth of trade associations, better business bureaus, chambers of commerce, and service clubs suggests that business is in the proces of developing professional associations analogous to those in the traditional professions. These businessmen's associations do not presume to enforce standards of competence for entry into the practice of business management or to regulate the conduct of their members. But they are at least marginally concerned with formulating codes of ethics and with promoting consultation among businessmen on problems of mutual concern. In the past the orientation of these associations has often been toward the narrow interests of members, and the attitudes of association officials have frequently surpassed those

---

[8] Clarence Francis, Chairman of General Foods Corporation, address at the annual conference of the Harvard Business School Alumni Association, June 12, 1948.

[9] F. W. Pierce, Director of Standard Oil Company of New Jersey, address before the Cincinnati Chapter of the Society for the Advancement of Management, December 6, 1945.

of member businessmen in their reactionariness. Nevertheless, such associations have on the whole broadened the vision of members by focusing attention on the problems of the industry, business at large, or the community, as well as of the single enterprise.

Businessmen's associations have also been useful in providing the sense of group consciousness which is so essential a basis for ethical behavior.

HOW TO CONTROL BUSINESS?

We have now considered professionalism in business in terms of three criteria: (1) intellectually based technique, (2) responsibility toward clients, and (3) professional organization. With reference to each of these criteria, it can be said quite definitely that business has been moving in the direction of professionalism. Business management is clearly becoming a learned art for which the practitioner must prepare himself through education and experience. Businessmen are steadily becoming more conscious of the manifold consequences of their actions and more concerned about their social responsibilities. And business organizations are becoming increasingly interested in the ethical aspects of business operations. But it can be said with equal definiteness that business has by no means reached the advanced state of professionalism attained by, for example, the medical profession. And it seems most unlikely that it will (or should) ever attain that degree of professionalism.

The concept of "profession" implies, essentially, a particular form of *control* over the conduct of the practitioner. This control is through voluntary codes which have been formulated by his peers with primary concern for the public interest and which are enforced by these same peers. Professionalism means peer-group responsibility for the conduct of the individual practitioner of the learned arts. When we speak of professional conduct, we refer to actions of a practitioner which are consistent with the accepted code of his peer group. Professionalism is, in other words, a form of social control over the behavior of individuals. When we speak of professionalism with reference to business, we are in fact concerned about the questions, How should business be controlled? and, Is professionalism a feasible or desirable method of control over business?

There is no doubt that business must be subjected to some form of social control. Men cannot safely be turned loose in pursuit of self-interest without some method of ensuring that their behavior will be comfortable to the general welfare. In general, there are three types of control available for the purpose: (1) competition, (2) governmental regulation, and (3) professionalism.

The advocates of laissez faire proposed that detailed governmental control over business decisions should be minimized, and that the control, instead, should take the form of widespread and relentless competition. (The early proponents of laissez faire lived too early to consider professionalism as a form of control.) Later, when it became apparent that extreme laissez faire afforded insufficient control over business to prevent certain abuses or undesirable conditions, other forms of social control were advocated. One of these was governmental regulation. Extreme socialists proposed that this should be virtually the sole form of control. Another alternative was professionalism, or voluntary control under the aegis of a peer group to define social responsibilities and enforce "ethical" behavior.

There are few responsible persons in the Untied States today who believe that any one of the three forms of social control can be relied upon exclusively. There are few remaining advocates of extreme laissez faire, even fewer socialists, and almost no proponents of complete self-regulation by business.

Americans have strong faith in competition as a regulator of business conduct, yet they doubt its usefulness as a sole form of control. They feel that government—in the form of policemen, judges, and regulatory commissions—is useful in curbing the selfishness of men and directing their activities into socially desirable channels. At the same time, they are skeptical of the socialist model of all-pervasive governmental regulation. Americans feel that there is a place for professionalism or self-regulation, yet they do not have confidence in the wisdom and restraint of private businessmen to regulate themselves without external control.

The kind of economy we are evolving is a mixed economy in which control by competition, by governmental regulation, and by self-regulation are combined. Honest men differ as to the most desirable proportions of these three types of control, and when specific problems arise they differ as to which type of remedy is preferable. But they are generally agreed that some combination of the three is essential.

SIGNIFICANCE OF PROFESSIONALISM

The importance of professionalism (or voluntary regulation) for business is that it offers a type of control that is intermediate between competition and governmental regulation. In so far as businessmen can learn to perceive the social consequences of their actions and voluntarily act in terms of the social interest, the abuses of laissez faire and the dangers of excessive governmental regulation may both be avoided. In this respect, tendencies toward professionalism in business may be regarded as wholesome.

At the same time, it would be naïve and dangerous to assume that voluntary regulation could or should largely supplant competition and governmental regulation in the control of our economic life. Business is different from the traditional professions in the degree to which control through competition is possible or desirable. In the case of medicine, for example, control is achieved primarily through professional self-regulation supplemented by governmental regulation, and competition is obviously unsuitable as a major form of control. For business, on the other hand, competition is a workable form of control which, though it cannot be relied upon exclusively, is more efficient than either professionalism or government. Under these circumstances, business is unlikely ever to become a full-fledged profession, nor is such a development desirable. For professionalism in business is not without danger. The apparatus of organizations and codes that is characteristic of professionalism could easily become a mask for monopoly. The tendency toward professionalism in business may be regarded as socially desirable only if it becomes a means of lessening the need for governmental control—not if it becomes a device for stifling competition.

Case

Grafton

Grafton, a small town of about one thousand people, was located in the northwest corner of one of the northern United States. Its development began about 1922 with the discovery of several oilfields in the vicinity, and the subsequent need for facilities for refining and marketing the oil. Newton Oils, a major oil company chose Grafton for the site of a refinery with a total daily output of 1500 barrels.

Newton Oils did a great deal for the town during the following years. New homes were built for the employees and schools and churches were erected. Water works, installed outside of town by the oil company, provided water for both refinery and the town of Grafton. As the oil industry expanded and the number of oilwells in the district increased, Grafton boomed. To meet the problem of overcrowded schools, centralization took place over a radius of ten miles. In 1948, residents of the town voted for a new high school costing $750,000 and an elementary school costing over $100,000. Along with this, the establishment of a fire department and the installation of sewer facilities necessitated the expansion of the water supply. To pay for these, the town and district were bonded; that is, they pledged themselves to pay town and district taxes based on yearly assessments until all debts were paid.

Suddenly, in 1957, Newton Oils announced its intention to shut down their refinery in Grafton and to move its production to a more central location. Employees were to be included in the move—slightly more than one-half the total tax-paying population.

Grafton was faced with disaster. Of the money owned for the expanded facilities, little more than $260,000 had been paid, leaving $500,000 owing on the high school and $90,000 on the elementary school. Eleven percent of the total school taxes and more for the public utilities had been paid by Newton Oils. A number of homes owned and built by the oil company were to be moved, thus resulting in a direct loss in assessment. Businessmen in Grafton estimated that school taxes alone would increase 30 percent as a result of the loss of revenue from the refinery, and other town taxes would also balloon.

Reprinted with permission of the University of Alberta. Copyright © 1958, by the University of Alberta. The case authors are Professors Emmett Wallace and Wynn Carrick.

Added to these problems, was the danger that many other people would also leave Grafton—the merchants and others who depended on the refinery for their livelihood. A final crisis arose when the company gave no indication as to what was to be done with the water works, leaving the residents to wonder if these, too, would be removed, or whether they would be able to buy the machinery and pipes from the company, in either case burdening themselves with additional expenses.

In addition to the grave problems facing the town as a whole, individual groups were also affected. One of the churches had begun a much-needed expansion program. Now, with the advancing possibility of a ghost town, there was no need for the huge church which had been built. Members of one of the local service clubs had solicited funds and even begun construction on a modern swimming pool designed to serve the town of Grafton and the surrounding district. They realized that this would never be needed after the departure of Newton Oils. The quality of the education received by the children would experience a sharp decline, as the town would no longer be able to support the salaries of the present teachers, and also because it seemed illogical that good teachers would want to teach in a town which resembled a ghost town.

To defend itself, the company stated its main reason for leaving. Since it was at the northern end of its area of distribution, high freight rates to the markets had to be paid on all refined products. It had thus become economically necessary to move the refinery to a more central location.

Bibliography

A. The Social Responsibility Debate

Chamberlain, Neil W. "The Role of Business In Society's Perfectability," *Monthly Labor Review* (April 1967), pp. 41–43.

Champion, George. "Private Enterprise and Public Responsibility in a Free Economy," *Conference Board Record* (June 1966), pp. 18–22.

Dale, Ernest. "Trends In Management's Changing Responsibilities," *Steel* (January 17, 1966), pp. 27–28.

Finley, Grace. "Business Defines Its Social Responsibility," *Conference Board Record* (November 1967), pp. 9–12.

Johnson, Harold L. "Socially Responsible Firms: An Empty Box or a Universal Set?" *Journal of Business* (July 1966), pp. 394–399.

Martin, Edmund F. "Business Responsibilities Toward our Social Goals," *The Commercial and Financial Chronicle* (September 7, 1967), p. 8.

Phillippe, Gerald L. "In Defense of Corporations," *Duns Review* (February 1963), pp. 52–53, 98–100, 104.

Tead, Ordway. "Management's New Responsibility to Its Publics," *Advanced Management Journal* (July 1966), pp. 19–29.

Turner, W. Homer. "The Societal Role of the Corporation," *Conference Board Record* (January 1968), pp. 11–13.

B. Professional Responsibilities of Management

Busbey, Charles R. "What Would be Accomplished if Management was Made a Profession?" *Systems and Procedures Journal* (March 1965), p. 44.

Cordiner, Ralph. "Is Management a Profession?" *Advanced Management Journal* (October 1967), pp. 15–18.

Dutton, Richard E. "Business Management: A Profession?" *Advanced Management Journal* (April 1965), pp. 59–64.

Hall, Richard H. and James D. Thompson. "What Do You Mean, 'Business Is A Profession'?" *Business Horizons* (Spring 1964), pp. 39–44.

Klatt, L. "Professionalization of Everyone," *Personnel Journal* (September 1967), pp. 508–509.

Sacchetti, Richard V. "Professionalization of Management," *The Office* (April 1967), pp. 16–23.

Shay, Philip W. "Ethics and Professional Practices in Management Consulting," *Advanced Management Journal* (January 1965), pp. 13–20.

PART EIGHT

Business and
Its Environment

A. Immediate Challenges

Businessmen of the seventies are faced with a series of immediate challenges that may radically change the relationship of business and society. The decaying urban environment, the world population explosion, racial and international tension, and environmental pollution are realities with which both business and government must deal. The solutions to these crises must certainly be at the forefront of our nation's list of priorities in the present decade.

Three major problems associated with the urban environment which presently confront businessmen are delineated in "Business and the Urban Crisis" [35]. In the area of jobs, education and housing, U.S. cities are sorely in need of assistance. Recognizing that urban government cannot satisfy the needs of a growing urban population, the federal government has often interceded with manpower and money. Business, too, has demonstrated a growing interest in lending assistance and advice to cities in distress. The authors argue that the businessman is uniquely qualified to provide the leadership necessary to attack urban problems. In addition, the businessman will find it very much in his long-range, if not short-range, self-interest to resolve these problems. If he does not, the cost to society and to himself will be prohibitive. The responsibility of business to provide jobs for a growing urban population, and specifically for high unemployment groups, has been discussed in Part Four. But it should be noted here that the actual cost in tax money will surely increase if reasonable levels of employment are not achieved. The entrepreneurial expertise of the businessman in partnership with government will be required to attack these problems. Businessmen are, indeed, a community's greatest resource for change.

The varied responses of business to the threat of air and water pollution are presented in article 36, "Pollution Abatement in Industry: Policies and Practices." In facing the problems of pollution, businessmen have described pollution abatement as a "high priority goal" in the delineation of their business objectives and company policies. While only a few firms have at this point formulated written policies concerning pollution, a large number have expressed serious concern. But the complexity of this problem poses difficulties for both the businessman and government at the local, state, and federal levels. The cost of pollution abatement may be prohibitive for some industries and many firms. Technological breakthroughs will often be required. Economically feasible means for controlling pollution have not yet been developed on a widespread basis, and both the diversity and complexity of the problem appear to require assistance from all related segments of society. These segments, which to a certain extent define the parameter of the problem, include the individual business firm, the respective industry and trade associations of which it is a member, and federal, state, and local governmental units. Article 36 points out that governmental assistance might take the form of actual research, or government might offer accelerated depreciation, tax credit or construction grants, as incentives to business. Standards that are established by individual firms, industries, or government agencies must be formulated and enforced. Unfortunately, the businessman is not strongly motivated to establish and enforce standards. To avoid federal intervention, businessmen have requested that policy makers apply the "principle of subsidiarity" which states that the resolution of a problem be sought at the lowest jurisdictional level. That is, wherever possible, responsibility for pollution abatement should rest with the local authorities, or better yet, with the individual businessman. And furthermore, the businessman prefers his right to private initiative in the solution of pollution. In effect, the businessman seeks the preservation of his entrepreneurial "freedom" to resolve these problems and enforce certain industry-formulated standards.

The realities of the urban pollution problems are seen in the Mason Chemical Company case. Management is particularly concerned with its public relations image, and its relationship to industrial pollution. Management is also vitally concerned with the possibility of governmental action to enforce pollution control. As the company plans a major modernization and expansion program, it must consider the additional cost of pollution control. In this case, policymakers are faced with the alternatives of reducing pollution—perhaps at great cost to the firm—or moving to another location which will reduce the number of job opportunities and tax base of the local community. Obviously, the problem must be perceived and evaluated in terms of all alternatives and their effects upon the company and all segments of the local community.

Another major and immediate challenge to businessmen in the seventies is the operation of the multinational corporation in an era of "rising nationalism" abroad. In his article entitled "National Interests and Multinational Business" [37] Henry H. Fowler points out the most recent problems facing businessmen in the conduct of international business. Given the past performance of many American corporations overseas, host nationals are hostile or, at best, tolerant of American business enterprise. Too often, American businessmen have been negligent of host country sentiments and business interests. In order to improve relations between American business and host countries, businessmen are seeking a role in the formulation of American foreign policy that will be in harmony with American business interests and in the interest of host country nationals. The multinational business firm with its American base will, therefore, become increasingly interdependent with American foreign policy makers. It is interesting to note that this growing interdependence of business and government is a reversal of the "principle of subsidiarity" supported by businessmen in their attitude toward pollution abatement. Internationally, businessmen are eliciting the support and seeking the cooperation of American policy makers in the interest of improved international-business relations and for the betterment of the international environment.

The Lawrence Steamship Lines case is a good illustration of the problems facing American firms operating beyond our borders. The unfavorable political climate in Canada during the 1950s due to American domination of manufacturing and natural resources directly affects the business decisions made by Lawrence Steamship Lines, a Canadian subsidiary of an American firm. Lawrence managers must carefully weigh the alternatives of purchasing a new tanker from a Canadian or English shipbuilding company in the light of economic and social-responsibility factors: their interest in improving business and social relations with the Canadian public, their concern for sound financial planning, and changing Canadian-American trade regulations.

B. Responsibilities of the Future

The long-run projects of business-government relations in terms of the international community are illustrated for us in "The Environment and Corporate Change" [38] by Theodore H. Gordon. The author argues that business and government in dealing with national and international problems are indeed becoming increasingly interdependent. He expresses the notion that we are steadily moving toward a single world culture. But the road toward one world is filled with obstacles. All nations will be required to respond to changes in technology and increasing populations. Gordon contends that management will face greater social responsibilities as the demand for jobs and food continues to soar. Management will be asked to provide guidelines for the utilization of increased leisure time and must discover ways to increase productivity in response to growing consumer demands. Given these overwhelming responsibilities, the businessman of the future will become a business-statesman.

A comprehensive overview of the potential range of social responsibilities that may be assumed by the businessman in the immediate and long-range future is provided in article 39, "Business and Society: Contemporary Issues and National Goals." The issues facing the businessman in the past two decades are compared with the national goals formulated during the Eisenhower administration of the late 1950s. If we assume that roughly these same goals apply to the present Republican administration, we can then address ourselves to both the specific goals and their relative priorities. But first let us review some of the fundamentals of business-society relationships. The businessman is concerned with a great variety of interest groups. This is occasioned by varying degrees to which business is "vested with a public interest," and the varying degrees to which business is concerned with interest and pressure groups. Based upon the great variety and scope of these publics, business must take a much more comprehensive view of society to include all of its publics or interest groups, and attempt to develop not only a public relations image, but also an operating business philosophy that will more effectively relate business to society, and resolve their conflicts. This philosophy should result from a comparative analysis of business goals and social or national goals so that any potential conflicts may be reconciled. If the primary national goal is the maximum development of the individual, the concern of the individual businessman must be the individual manager-employee relationship as well as the aggregate relationship of business to society and its many groups and institutions. If business is to provide the type of leadership that will maximize the achievement of individual and group goals in society, managers must systematically delineate their rights and duties or responsibilities to society. They must then develop a comprehensive business-society philosophy with a positively stated code of ethics which will serve as guidelines in the conflicts that arise between business and society. These guidelines will also serve to maximize the achievements and attain the goals of individuals and groups—including business—in society.

A. Immediate Challenges

Business and   **35**
The Urban Crisis
Business Week

THE PROBLEM

"If you cats can't do it, it's never going to get done."

The speaker: Frank Ditto, a Black militant leader in Detroit.

The cats: a group of Detroit businessmen who visited Ditto's Voice of Independence headquarters after last summer's riots.

"The government can't lick this problem," Ditto added. "So business has to."

Of course, business *has* to do nothing of the sort. What's more, no one—business included—can expect to come up with a swift cure for the ills that plague the cities.

But, if only for intelligently selfish reasons, businessmen can't afford to ignore the urban crisis. Here's why:

If you ignore the crisis, no one else may be able to cool the anger that boils up in riots. So far at least, no one else has gotten more than token results—not the government, not the labor unions, not the churches, and not the civic organizations.

Make no mistake—the riots are not yet revolutionary, nor do they involve more than a tiny fraction of the Negro population. They are significant only as a headline-grabbing symbol that focuses attention on the resentment felt by Negroes, now 11% of the nation's population. The real problem is not the riots but the frustration that generates them.

That frustration often explodes in rioting just when conditions are improving. Reason: Deprived people feel most frustrated when their hopes and expectations have been raised but not completely satisfied.

Reprinted with permission from *Business Week* (February 3, 1968), pp. 57–72. Copyright © 1968 by McGraw-Hill, Inc. All rights reserved.

Detroit was a case in point. Its poverty programs were held up as models. Its mayor and police chief were sympathetic to Negroes. Detroit, in short, seemed well on its way to avoiding racial outbreaks. Yet Detroit was wracked by 1967's worst riot.

If you ignore the crisis, slums could siphon off more and more of your profits. Slums are a luxury few cities can afford, and much of what they cost is paid by taxes on business. Deterioration of the cities speeds up the flight of middle- and upper-income families (and some industries) to the suburbs. Result: Tax bases are reduced, retail trade slumps, and an increasing share of the tax burden falls on business.

New York City's annual slum bill, for example, is $3.2 billion. Welfare alone costs $1.5 billion—$1 billion in federal and state funds, plus $500 million raised by the city. To that, add a $1.7-billion subsidy in the taxes the slums don't pay, the extra fire and police protection they require, and the social and health problems they create.

But even that huge outlay isn't doing the job. Right now, according to the New York Regional Planning Association, the city needs another $1.1 billion —$300 million for educating slum children, plus $800 million for a host of poverty services.

Is New York an isolated example? Not really. It is simply an advanced case of what many other cities could experience in less than a decade.

If you ignore the crisis, you may be overlooking a big potential market. The city has always been a social and economic necessity for businessmen. Markets thrive in healthy cities, waste away in sick ones.

If today's sick cities can be cured—if ghetto dwellers can be better housed, better educated, and, above all, better employed—new and profitable markets will open up for business.

Even the very process of saving the cities creates opportunities for some industries—construction, for example. Between now and the year 2000, the city ghettos will need some 10 million new dwelling units. No matter who builds these units—private operators or public authorities—they will add up to $200 billion in today's dollars in new business for developers, contractors, and building-product manufacturers.

What's needed to open up this huge market, to begin cutting the high cost of slums, and to cool the anger that boils up in riots is to break down the barriers that trap Negroes in the ghettos.

Slums, of course, have always been a fact of U.S. life. The rural and immigrant poor moved in, found jobs (especially in unskilled and semi-skilled fields), and then moved up the economic ladder. Not so today. Now the poor (mostly non-whites) still move in, but that's as far as they can go.

Why? What traps the Negro in the ghetto? One barrier—both a cause and a result of the problem—stands out:

The income gap between this country's whites and non-whites is wide and getting wider. Today, in the midst of general prosperity, over 30 million Americans live in poverty (family incomes under $3,130), and almost 30 million more live in deprivation (incomes from $3,130 to $5,000). Roughly half of each group is clustered in the city slums.

To be sure, slum dwellers' incomes are rising—but not at the same pace as the incomes of everyone else. And in the worst slums, incomes are actually falling. In New York's central Harlem, for instance, the average dropped from $3,997 in 1960 to $3,907 in 1966. Meanwhile, consumer prices in the New York metropolitan area rose 12%.

Just how badly off is the typical Harlem family? A Bureau of Labor Statistics study, released last fall, shed some light on that one. Said BLS: A year's moderate living for a family of four in New York City costs $10,195—or almost three times the average income in Harlem.

The gap between white and non-white buying power is largely the result of a paradox: Advancing technology, a boon to most Americans, has made it steadily more difficult for the hard-core poor to find work. Mechanized farming has sped the migration of Southern Negroes to Northern cities. And in the cities, automation has wiped out the very jobs that untrained, rural-bred Negroes can handle. In 1950 one out of six Negro migrants failed to find jobs in Northern cities; by 1960 the figure had doubled to two out of six.

But the income gap is just one of the barriers that trap non-whites in the city ghettos. Here are four others:

1. Zoning bars low-income families from the suburbs—first, by stipulating lot sizes (and thus house prices) that are beyond their reach; second, by keeping out blue-collar industry that could provide jobs for people now living in the city.

2. Welfare often hinders more than it helps. First of all, the welfare burden (annual cost: $7 billion) falls heavily on the Northern cities and lightly on the areas where the bulk of the poor came from. Second, even states and cities with liberal benefits fail to meet federally defined minimum-income levels. Finally—and this is the crux of the matter—welfare practices kill the slum dweller's incentive to find a job and hold his family together. If the father of a family on welfare gets a job, whatever he earns is deducted from his family's welfare payments. In effect, he is taxed 100% on his earnings. So he may face a hard choice: Quit the job or abandon his family.

3. A new legislative coalition has little sympathy for the sick cities. In state legislatures and Congress, there has always been an understandable rivalry between representatives of the cities and the rural areas. Now—and for equally understandable reasons—the rural spokesmen have a potent new ally: representatives of the burgeoning suburbs. This new coalition reinforces suburban

zoning and limits the ability of urban-based legislators to put across programs aimed at solving the cities' problems.

4. Cities lack the financial base to do the job that must be done—to tackle adequate housing programs, for instance. The basic problem: Property taxation—source of most municipal revenue—is inequitable; it puts the biggest burden on business, the smallest on slum-housing owners. So, not surprisingly, many companies flee the city—which only loads a bigger burden on those who stay, puts the city in a worse financial bind than ever, and makes it less and less likely that slum problems will be solved with local money.

In theory at least, removing all those barriers is every American's problem. But this report is about what businessmen can do—if they get involved. And since this report stresses the purely practical reasons for business action, it goes without saying that getting involved invites economic risks.

When the president of Detroit's largest department store led a state open-housing fight last November, more than 10,000 customers closed out their accounts in 10 days. Every time Henry Ford II has made a pronouncement in behalf of Negro rights, Ford Motor Co. sales have tumbled in the South.

But Henry Ford still maintains: "People who don't face up to this issue are stupid. It's a great opportunity for business. It's shortsighted not to step in and do something to solve the problem."

What, then, can business do to ease the frustration of the ghetto dwellers? Business can turn the staggering need for low-rent city housing into a big and profitable market—if some of the government-imposed rules that now regulate housing construction are changed (see p. 464).

Business can also put its influence and special skills behind sorely needed changes in the city school systems (see p. 470).

And business alone holds one key to breaking the vicious slum cycle of unemployment, poverty, poor housing, poor education, and low productivity. That key is jobs.

JOBS

How many jobs are needed? Secretary Wirtz estimates a half-million for 100 city slums, another half-million for the rest of the country.

In a growing economy that produces a million and a half new jobs a year, the need to place half a million slum dwellers—or even a million—does not sound all that tough.

But it is. Business has found that hiring and training the people at the bottom of the ghetto barrel—"making the transition from the street corner to a job," as a Los Angeles training executive puts it—is tougher than it sounds.

Yet business must face up to it. President Johnson, for one, has issued a direct challenge: ". . . Help me find jobs for these people or we are going to have to offer every one of them a job in government."

Members of the Urban Coalition, which includes the nation's top industrialists, recently pledged a million jobs. And many businessmen cite practical
reasons for action.

Says Chester Brown, Allied Chemical's chairman: "Business can broaden
its markets by increasing people's purchasing power. One way to do this is
to lift the economic status of poverty-stricken slum dwellers."

Says H. C. (Chad) McClellan, who heads the Los Angeles-based Management Council for Merit Employment: "Shall we go on paying $400 million a
year in Los Angeles welfare costs, or shall we go down and take a realistic
look at the potential workers in the slums?"

Just who are these potential workers? Mostly they are the hard-core unemployed—unschooled, unskilled, and unmotivated. To turn them into productive workers, business must help them overcome handicaps that bar them
from good jobs: culturally impoverished lives, grossly deficient education,
poor health, fear of failure, the exodus of jobs to the suburbs, and finally
society's discrimination against them.

There is no clear-cut answer. Businessmen, in fact, are simply learning by
doing. Here are some of the things they have learned:

**No program to hire the hard-core poor will succeed unless top management
is totally committed.** "Any company that gets into this kind of project without the backing of the top man will fall flat on its face," says Richard Knapp,
personnel manager at Warner & Swasey, Cleveland. Kodak Chairman William
Vaughn says bluntly: "Unless top management lays it on the line, lower-
echelon people won't do it. Even then, they may not do it without follow-up."

Follow-up by top management is vital if a project is not to drift. Humble
Oil's recruitment coordinator, Harry G. Taylor, says: "We recently shook up
a lot of our people when we called them together and told them they weren't
doing as well as they should. Now those who have been taking it easy know
management is serious."

A firm stand also heads off possible resistance from other employees.

"You find some resistance among plant employees," admits Walter Maynor,
industrial relations director at Sherwin-Williams. "But we let them know in no
uncertain terms that this policy had been set by our top people and that they
intend to enforce it."

Martin Stone, president of Los Angeles' Monogram Industries, lost one
foreman who wouldn't go along with his program. "You've got to sell the
shop supervisors," Stone warns. "If you don't, the job will never get done—
and you'll never be able to pinpoint why."

**They won't come knocking at your door—recruiting may call for special
efforts.** You can't just hang out a sign and expect a flood of grateful, job-
hungry applicants.

"If we had waited for them to come to us," says Harry Taylor, recruitment coordinator at Humble Oil in Houston, "we might still be waiting." Humble even finds it difficult to convince college people that it really wants to hire Negroes.

"Pessimism pervades the entire minority," says Charles Rutledge, assistant to the president at Lockheed Missiles & Space. "They feel they've got as much chance getting to the moon as getting a job at Lockheed."

When Kaiser Industries started looking for "qualified" minority employees in Oakland, "most of the unemployed didn't even bother to apply," says Vice-President Norman Nicholson. Now Kaiser has a program for "qualifiable" people and cultivates contacts with Negro groups.

Candor is the best antidote to diffidence and distrust, Nicholson finds. "We're late in doing this, and it was under pressure," he tells Negroes. "But don't cry about past history. The door is open now."

To reach across the barriers of suspicion, companies can call on dozens of job-development groups in the Negro-employment field. The Urban League, for one, has had long experience.

Another notable Negro-led effort, the Opportunities Industrialization Centers, stresses enlisting business to help Negroes help themselves. Started in Philadelphia by the Rev. Leon H. Sullivan, OICs have spread to 65 cities.

The Twin Cities OIC in Minneapolis is typical. Launched a year ago with 75 trainees, it raised $80,000 from business, now has 1,100 trainees and 300 already on jobs. Like other OICs it devotes about half its training program to skills, office and shop work, and service trades—the other half to grooming, work habits, attitudes, and basic reading and arithmetic.

Other sources of help are community-wide groups that seek to reconcile disparate civic and racial organizations, moderate and militant alike, and to bring the jobless into contact with jobs.

Some of these groups—Cleveland's AIM-JOBS, St. Louis' Work Opportunities Unlimited, Los Angeles' Management Council—provide pre-job training, on-the-job counseling, and other aids. And they are getting results.

AIM has helped find jobs for some 600 applicants; WOU for 6,500; the Boston Community Development Corp. for 5,000; the Management Council for 18,000. And the new Detroit Committee, working with the Detroit Board of Trade, has spurred 20 companies into hiring 15,000 unskilled Negroes.

Such results call for special recruiting efforts. A few examples:

After the Watts riots in Los Angeles, some 50 companies sent recruiters directly into the district, and the Management Council induced the California Employment Commission to open a branch there.

In Rochester, N.Y., Kodak and other companies hold interviews at Negro neighborhood centers and take job referrals from 17 social agencies.

United Airlines sends Negro pilots, stewardesses, and ticket agents into the ghettos to talk with people. Says Daniel E. Kain, personnel director for field services: "These people have to taste it, feel it, see it. Otherwise it's a bunch of hot air."

You may have to relax your hiring standards and change your hiring practices. Most companies find they have to drop their hiring bars a bit or, if they are taking admittedly unqualified people, a lot. Intensive training projects like Whittaker Corp.'s "Instant Hiring" in Los Angeles ask for little except a will to work.

Warner & Swasey eliminated the usual hiring yardsticks, including testing. Pacific Telephone & Telegraph, along with other companies, has hired people with police records. Ohio Bell Telephone went back over its list of rejected applicants just to hire some who had been considered unqualified. And Lockheed Missiles went looking for high school dropouts—people with no marketable skills—for its VIP (Vocation Improvement Program). Of the first 100 applicants referred to the company by social agencies, only 11 were rejected.

Not everyone agrees, however, that lower hiring standards are a prerequisite. For instance, Chad McClellan of the Los Angeles Management Council tells companies: "Don't hire anyone who doesn't meet your standards. Don't lower your standards—raise theirs."

And while hiring requirements may be less stringent, there's no compromise on work performance. A Pacific Telephone & Telegraph executive speaks for most companies: "We would rather train than perpetuate the problems of unskilled labor."

You may also have to restructure some of your jobs to make them easier to master. Some companies have solved the work performance problem by redefining or restructuring jobs to bring them closer to the reach of unskilled people. Lockheed compares this to measures used to train wartime workers.

Buxton-Skinner in St. Louis established a category of "electrician's helper" one step below "electrical maintenance assistant" to provide niches for poorly skilled workers. To implement its nurse training project, the Kaiser Foundation in San Francisco created the job of "clinic assistant" to relieve nurses of such routine though important chores as weighing patients and taking temperatures.

But this approach may not appeal to every company. "McDonnell-Douglas in Los Angeles has never changed production procedures to fit trainees," says a company official. "We fit the trainees to our procedures."

McDonnell-Douglas doesn't think much of the war-period analogy, either. "The days of Rosie the Riveter are gone forever," its spokesman says. "The one-step assembly worker has given way to workers handling a series of operations on the line."

The key to success—and the toughest part of the whole program—is the right kind of training. "The first question an executive must ask himself is: 'Are we ready to spend the extra time to prepare these employees?' Unless the answer is a flat yes, the program wont' go."

This advice from an Emerson Electric executive in St. Louis is based on hard experience in training workers from scratch. It's more than a matter of teaching specific job skills. At the very least, companies must orient their trainees to a totally unfamiliar environment of shop or office. At the most, they must somehow plug up wide gaps in basic education. And they must grapple all along the line with problems of instilling motivation and a proper attitude.

It can be done. Business is already deep in the effort. Some 1,600 companies have contracts to offer training under the Manpower Training & Development Act, which turned out 140,000 trainees in the past fiscal year.

Westinghouse Electric is one large company that is training hard-core unemployed under a new Concentrated Employment Program. Raytheon is launching a special project at its Waltham (Mass.) plant for 100 hard-core people. Government is offering new lures to employers who will tackle the training of unskilled people. About $350 million in federal funds is available this fiscal year.

New training techniques are often needed. Emerson Electric, for example, uses closed-circuit TV to show clerical trainees their job operations in slow motion. Hoffmann-La Roche also uses audio-visual aids to train clerks in its Newark (N.J.) offices.

The results of a balanced program can be impressive. Of 111 in a Lockheed VIP training group, only four were fired—mostly for poor attendance—and 105 are working today. Lockheed bore down hard on teaching both skills and attitudes. "We overtrain," says Charles Rutledge, assistant to the president, "so the worker will be able to perform all his duties and get an immediate feeling of success."

The key to effective training is a job at the end of the training cycle. That's what community programs, however well-intentioned, cannot promise. Much of what passes for training in store-front settings has little relation to employer's needs. And trainees themselves sense this. "Training to be unemployed" is how one New York Negro put it.

Only business can provide both training and a job. What's more, most company training programs pay the trainee while he's learning.

Eugene Cox, who runs Whittaker Corp.'s "Instant Hiring" project, declares: "Nobody but business—not welfare, not the government, not charities—can offer green-power motivation."

Mayor Alfonso J. Cervantes of St. Louis notes that "private industry's training of the disadvantaged on the job is much more efficient than training by any public agency." And only industry, he adds, can give purpose to the training by providing a job at the end of the line.

But the mere existence of beginners' jobs is not enough. Trainees must also be able to see some chance to advance. Business, too, must count on an upgrading process. Unless trainees can advance, a Kodak executive points out, the bottom jobs will soon be clogged with unpromotable people.

Effective training isn't always limited to job skills—you may even have to teach the three Rs. Lee Gassler, industrial relations director at Kodak Park points out: "The under-educated worker is often unable to get over even the first hurdle in getting a job. A simple application form holds terror for him if he can neither read the questions nor write the answers."

Gassler speaks from experience. In 1964 Kodak began an experimental project to hire unskilled people and bring them up to the entry level for skilled apprenticeship training. Even though classes were small—no more than 15 each—the company found that classroom instruction was not enough. So the instructors—skilled men pulled off regular jobs—wound up giving almost individual tutoring.

The basic problem: Trainees were seriously deficient in reading, writing, and arithmetic. "We were surprised at how retarded they were," says a training executive. Even prior schooling was no guarantee. One trainee who had attended three years at a Rochester high school was told to drill a series of holes a foot apart. "What's a foot?" he asked. Another was given a job requiring measurement with a ruler. When the instructor found the job undone, the embarrassed trainee admitted he didn't know how to use a ruler.

Kodak's experience is hardly unique: A Los Angeles bus company recruiting in a ghetto area found few people who could make change for a dollar.

Kodak took steps to solve the problem in 1966. In the midst of a bruising battle with a militant Rochester group called Fight, the company reorganized its training. It now limits instruction by Kodak personnel to on-the-job programs and brings in outside experts—the board for Fundamental Education of Indianapolis—to teach reading, writing, and numbers. The unskilled are put in a job class and if they need it, in a BFE class. One BFE section raises basic education to the fifth-grade level, another from fifth to eighth.

Effective training may also immerse you in the personal problems of your trainees. Sometimes, in fact, the line between training and therapy gets very thin indeed. Fear of failure, for example, is widespread.

"These kids are oriented to failure," says an Inland Steel vice-president, William G. Caples. For that reason, Kodak's BFE classes aim as much at instilling confidence as at teaching facts. Says an instructor: "Most of these people have failed everywhere—in school, at home, in jobs. So we try to put them in situations where they'll succeed."

Since they fear failure, many trainees resist responsibility—at least at the start.

"We start them off where they make no decisions," says Training Dept. Manager R. H. Hudson of Lockheed-Georgia. "Then we slowly let them take on responsibility."

First-line supervisors get involved in mundane problems. Stanley W. Hawkins, training coordinator at Lockheed Missiles, points out: "We help with problems, on shift and off—getting people into hospitals and out of jail, getting gas and electricity turned back on, towing cars off the freeway, fighting off finance companies, arguing with car dealers."

How do you cope with problems like these? One way is to put qualified Negroes into supervisory and managerial jobs.

"You can use some white guys, but there's a real need for the worker to identify with the top guys, the upper echelon," says Leon Woods, the 24-year-old Negro general manager of Watts Mfg. Co. in Los Angeles. This is the highly publicized company that Aerojet-General started in the riot-torn Watts area to provide jobs for Negroes in their own neighborhood. One of Aerojet's aims was to eliminate a prime cause of absenteeism—long trips between slums and plants, often without public transportation.

Sometimes the waters are murky—you may have trouble communicating with your trainees. "Most jobs are lost by attitudes, not inability to do the work," says the Rev. Leon Sullivan of the Opportunities Industrialization Centers. A Kodak executive agrees. But, he adds, "It's often hard to know what their attitude is."

Many workers are reluctant to admit they don't understand. Verbal confusions crop up. A newly hired Negro clerk at a St. Louis company wanted to quit because she was "bored." A bit miffed, her supervisor was ready to let her go until he found she really meant she was perplexed.

At Lockheed Missiles, one instructor tries to anticipate poor understanding. Every day he reviews his material for "suspect words," then writes these on the blackboard and defines them whether anybody asks or not.

Clear communication is particularly important in the crucial process of motivating new workers. Training personnel tend to agree with Eugene Cox of Whittaker Corp. that motivation starts with showing people how they can get tangible rewards. "The best way to change attitudes about their future," he says, "is to show them what they can get if they apply themselves."

Frank Libby, vocational training supervisor at Kodak Park, puts it simply: "I try to get them addicted to the paycheck." And Frank S. Jabes, an employee relations executive at TRW in Cleveland, adds: "If you want to see some really motivated people, take a look at a guy who is having his first chance to make a living wage. You couldn't have a better employee."

This is no one-way street—you have to strike a balance between sympathy and firmness. Companies that hire hard-core unemployed minority people can expect them to behave differently from the corporate rank and file. Turnover is high—holding more than 50% of trainees is pretty good. Absenteeism, tardiness, a general lack of responsibility are common failings.

"Mondayitis is almost epidemic," says one supervisor.

"They have a tremendous number of grandmothers and grandfathers who keep dying month after month," another supervisor complains.

It doesn't help to be over-sympathetic, companies have found. In fact, a firm hand on the reins seems to work best.

A Kodak instructor, Frank Palmisano, explains why his company decided to take a firmer attitude toward absenteeism and tardiness in training classes: "We checked on former trainees and found that those with poor attendance records in training did no better on the job. So now we deal with absenteeism in training—ask the problem cases what's wrong and how we can help them. If they still goof up in spite of our efforts, we let them go."

Jack B. McCowan, vice-president of Firemen's Fund American Insurance in San Francisco, lets supervisors "spoonfeed" trainees for a while in work matters. But he makes it clear that he expects standards to be met on attendance and behavior.

A practical question: What will all this extra time and effort cost? It depends on what you have to start with—the background of your trainees—and on the level of skills you need from them. Experience indicates that the cost per trainee can range from a few hundred dollars to several thousands.

On the more modest level, IRC, Inc., a Philadelphia electronics company, spends between $300 and $400 per person; McDonnell Aircraft in St. Louis, $450. Leon Sullivan's OICs report an average $900 per trainee.

For harder cases and higher skills, the tab gets bigger. Lockheed-Georgia spends $700 of its own money plus $400 of government funds for each trainee. Humble Oil spends $1,200 per man. It cost Kaiser Engineering at total of $12,000 to train six draftsmen.

When you deal with badly underskilled people, you run into big money. Just how big is open to argument. And it's an argument that often involves the federal government, which pays part of the cost of these hard-case training programs.

Robert Scanlon, corporate training director at Whittaker Corp., says "Instant Hiring" costs two or three times as much as conventional industrial training.

Avco Corp. estimates it will cost $5,000 per man to train 230 hard-core unemployed, including ex-convicts, reformed drug addicts, and former alcoholics. The government will pick up two-thirds of the cost.

In the last analysis, are the extra training costs worth it? Most businessmen who have tackled the job problem think so. And Norman Nicholson of Kaiser Industries speaks for many of them when he says, "The costs of training are high. But riots and jails are also expensive."

Businessmen point out, however, that they are thinking primarily of long-range values rather than immediate pay-off. Kodak's Lee Gassler, for example, says his training program helps the company, the trainee, and the community, "but at the moment the trainee and the community are benefiting most."

More specifically, there are signs of real progress.

Says an auto company executive: "Some of the inner-city people we hired are working out better than the walk-ins."

Says Industrial Relations Manager Joe Flynn of Kaiser Aerospace & Electronics: "We've already upgraded 21 minority employees at our San Leandro plant. Our experience has been excellent."

Says the manager of a Philadelphia store that employs eight Philco-Ford trainees: "In the past we hired Negroes because we felt we had to. Now we feel these girls deserve to be hired on their own merits."

And that, of course, is the aim of every hiring and training program.

HOUSING

The problem of supplying housing in the cores of cities is not a problem of logistics or construction technology. It is purely a problem of economics.

Under present taxation and finance practices, no one can supply the volume of housing needed. But if the rules that force these practices are changed —if some new form of government subsidy is accepted and if red tape is trimmed from federal housing programs—a staggering need can be turned into a profitable market.

Business' stake in changing the rules is pretty simple and direct. Just replacing the substandard housing in cities would involve more new construction than the total volume of housing starts over the past five years.

The 1960 housing census uncovered more than 4 million urban dwelling units that were completely dilapidated, some 3 million more that were badly deteriorated, and another 2 million with serious code violations or serious overcrowding. If that is not a bad enough problem—or a big enough market—recent Census studies indicate the 1960 figures may have underestimated the number of dilapidated units by as much as one-third.

What's more, revitalizing the cities would encourage the return of hundreds of thousands of families who have fled to the suburbs—and thus would generate new demand for middle- and upper-income housing.

So sitting right there in the city slums is a market for well over 7 million new and rehabilitated housing units and all the building products that go into them—everything from flooring and dry-wall to lighting and plumbing fixtures. And, points out Raymond H. Lapin, president of HUD's Federal National Mortgage Assn.: "The profit earned on a sheet of gypsum board is the same whether the board is used in a low-rent apartment or a $50,000 house."

Key problem: the gap between what housing costs and what low-income families can pay. New housing in multi-family buildings—the kind needed in most city slums—costs from $17,000 to $22,000 a unit, even with an urban renewal land write-down. Rehabilitated housing, in any volume and in the densities desirable, cost at least as much, and sometimes more.

This means the monthly rent for a $20,000 unit with one bedroom would be roughly $150. That figure would include (1) maintenance, (2) operating costs, (3) amortization and interest on a subsidized loan with interest a few points below market yields and a term up to 40 years, (4) partial realty-tax abatement (about 50%), and (5) a two-thirds write-down of the land cost.

Yet half the low-income families in the slums can afford to pay only $65 to $110 a month for rent. And the other half cannot afford more than $35 to $60 a month.

Government programs to fill the gap have been too small, under-financed, and over-complicated. Congress has created one program after another—FHA's Section 221d3 and public housing and urban renewal, for example—with enough visibility to persuade voters that something is being done. But most of these programs are too poorly funded to have any impact on urban problems. Many of them overlap and even conflict with earlier programs. So each new program adds chaos to the already chaotic machinery of federal, state, and local governments. In retrospect, it is easy to see why the programs tried so far have not worked:

Until fairly recent years, the public housing idea was unacceptable to most Americans—"Why should I pay part of somebody else's rent?" Congressional authorizations for low-rent public housing have permitted only a fraction of what is needed. And, with some notable exceptions, the quality of public housing has been bad: monolithic, prison-like structures, stripped of such "frills" as doors on the closets. In short, super-slums.

Urban renewal has not solved the problem. Most localities have used renewal programs to broaden their tax base with new commercial development or upper-middle-income housing rather than to provide low- and middle-income housing.

FHA's 221d3 program, greeted in 1961 as the answer to low-income housing, has virtually ground to a halt because of too-low mortgage limits ($17,500 in high-cost areas) and the fantastic red tape involved in getting projects through local FHA offices.

The 221d3 program was designed to provide new and old rehabilitated rental and co-op housing for low- and moderate-income families. In some cases it permits a below-the-market interest rate of only 3% on mortgages. But as Jason Nathan, head of New York City's Housing & Development Administration, pointed out last fall: "Six years after the program was started, it had provided only 4,350 rehabilitated apartments—and 1,500 of them are in New York City."

Most other FHA programs were never intended to provide low-income housing. In fact, the agency's original purpose in the 1930s was to get money moving again. Built into its legislative history is the requirement that mortgage insurance be placed only on economically sound properties. Since it is hard to argue that a slum area is economically sound, slum properties were automatically ruled out.

"FHA is the easy and popular target for all our frustrations," says New York City's Nathan. "But to blame FHA alone is not the whole truth. Their reluctance is not simply a matter of inertia. It also arises out of a schizophrenic Congress. One segment of Congress blasts FHA for failure to provide socially motivated housing. Another segment almost gleefully seeks out a few cases of mortgage defaults and scorches FHA for its radicalism and lack of sober conservatism."

But, Nathan adds, "Even if existing programs were adequately financed and enthusiastically administered, there would be enormous problems."

The myth that new technology can cut costs continues to confuse the issue. It is unrealistic to count on some magical breakthrough in technology to solve the cost problem.

It is unlikely that research will find new materials cheaper than wood and brick and cement and gypsum. It is equally unlikely that labor practices can be changed in any effective way. Yet industry leaders and government officials from HUD Secretary Robert Weaver on down keep calling for the breakthrough—thus delaying a commitment to solve the problem with the building tools already at hand.

For years one innovator after another—often aided by federal grants—has tried to put housing on the assembly line. And for years these attempts have failed to cut costs.

Reason: Most innovators have concentrated on the shell of the building—the bare walls, floor, and roof. And the shell is the cheapest part—if the walls were simply eliminated, the total price would be cut by less than 5%. The bulk of the cost is in land, financing, overhead, profit, interior finishes, and mechanical equipment.

Rehabilitation of slum housing is a highly publicized solution—but hardly a cure-all. It does indeed improve housing in what is usually a rather limited rehabilitation area. But, so far at least, it has fallen short on other counts.

Rehab has not added to the supply of housing units. Except in a few neighborhood-wide ventures, it has not performed the social function of rehabilitating a community. And, despite such rarities as New York City's 48-hour "Instant Rehab" (new units were dropped into the shells of gutted tenements), it has not solved the problem of relocating slum families while the job is being done.

In slum areas, where tenements brought up to a "safe and sanitary" standard are at best a minimum goal, rehab does buy time while better plans are made. But a big question remains: Is rehab housing really cheaper than new housing? Many experts do not feel it is—especially when the high costs of planning and managing a rehabilitation job are counted in.

What's more, there is still no evidence that rehab can be profitable. A number of major corporations—including Alcoa, Armstrong Cork, Rockwell Mfg., Reynolds, U.S. Steel, and Smith, Kline & French—have made small experimental forays into rehabilitation. On a larger scale, several companies in Pittsburgh—Westinghouse, National Gypsum, Pittsburgh Plate Glass, and others—have teamed up to form a limited-profit rehab corporation.

The best-known effort is U.S. Gypsum's rebuilding of several hundred units in New York City's Harlem and its plans for similar work in Chicago and Cleveland. But USG has yet to say how its venture is faring financially.

Whether a businessman sets out to fix up old apartments or build new ones, he faces two harsh realities:

Harsh reality No. 1: a shortage of money to finance low-rent city housing.

There is no magic way to finance housing. Housing must draw on the same capital pool that business, industry, and the consumer draw on. Any investment in housing must match the market yield of other segments of the capital pool.

Ray Lapin of the Federal National Mortgage Association puts it this way: "Let's admit at the outset that there are no new sources of mortgage funds. There is no money tree—not the Federal Reserve, not the U.S. Treasury, not FNMA, and certainly not the treasuries of the nation's corporations."

Lapin points out that the traditional sources of mortgage money—life insurance companies, mutual savings banks, savings and loan associations, and, more recently, the commercial banks—have invested about as much as they can afford.

"From now on," he says, "the volume of mortgage lending by these institutions will be limited to the future course of savings—and to the choice between mortgages and other investments."

Harsh reality No. 2: the red tape that strangles government housing programs.

Government-assistance programs won't work unless some way can be found to eliminate the time-consuming rules and procedures that confront—and frustrate—every prospective builder or developer.

In New York City it takes at least two years to process the average FHA 221d3 project—and by that time, costs have risen 10%. Furthermore, builders often run into delays before their proposals even reach FHA. A case in point: Late last year a 1,450-unit project, proposed by HRH Construction Co. in 1961, was still awaiting approval by the New York City Board of Estimate.

But, notes HRH Vice-President Richard Ravitch, there are signs that federal administrators are finally bending their rules and speeding up their procedures. Last fall, for example, HUD Assistant Secretary Philip N. Brownstein told his district directors: "Slash through red tape, indecision, and pussyfooting. . . . Set rigid time goals and see that they are met. . . . Be prudent as well as urgent, but be prepared to take the risks necessary to get the job done."

Brownstein's conclusion was most direct: "You should work at this task as though your job depended on it—because it may!"

Several ways to provide more mortgage money have been proposed. Three recent ones:

FNMA's Lapin has suggested a government-backed mortgage market. He hopes such a market would offer the investor a competitive yield and give the mortgage borrower access to all parts of the savings pool—not just the "compartmented, specialized part of the capital market" now available.

A group of 348 life insurance companies has pledged to invest $1 billion in new and rehabilitated slum housing within the next year. It should be noted, however, that these mortgages will carry the peak FHA rate of 6%. And to insure them, FHA must substitute a policy of social benefit for its traditional policy of economic soundness.

A task force of the National League of Insured Savings & Loan Associations has recommended that the S&Ls put $5 billion a year for the next 12 years into renewing the city slums. Bart Lytton, the task force chairman, says this can be done if the government permits a combination of federal loan guarantees, tax-free interest on investments in risky "improvement districts," and terms of up to 60 years to reduce monthly mortgage payments.

New federal programs may provide more money and loosen the stifling rules. Perhaps the most important—if it is adequately funded—is the Model Cities program. In the first round, it provides $11 million for planning and $300 million for construction (by paying 80% of what, under normal urban-renewal procedures, is the one-third local contribution to a project's cost).

Another program, launched in 1966 and now beginning to accelerate, is the so-called "Turnkey." Designed to involve private enterprise to a degree rare in government-sponsored work, this program gives a developer an almost-free hand to proceed as he would with a private project. It simplifies the approval process and permits the developer to build low-rent public housing on his own land, to his own plans and specifications, and then to sell the project to a local housing authority. Early experience leads government officials to believe that public housing built this way can be completed in two or three years' less time and at cost savings ranging from 10% to 15%.

In the wings is legislation that may involve business much more deeply in urban housing. Best known are the Percy and Kennedy proposals.

Sen. Charles Percy would set up a quasi-public agency capitalized with up to $2 billion in government-guaranteed debentures at market interest rates. The agency would offer 30-year mortgages to non-profit housing corporations at subsidized interest rates.

Sen. Robert Kennedy's proposal calls for a tax credit of up to 30% accelerated depreciation on a sliding scale (from 20 years down to 7 years) and an insurance fund to protect capital investment. For 100% equity in a project, an owner would get a 22% tax credit and 10-year depreciation.

Early this year President Johnson was expected to propose an omnibus housing bill, including requests to continue urban renewal, public housing, and other major programs through 1973. The Administration bill will probably overlap one proposed by Sen. John Sparkman and his housing subcommittee. The most significant change urged by the Sparkman committee is to raise the 6% statutory ceiling on interest rates for FHA and VA mortgages. This would stimulate the flow of money into construction, but, politically, it is a hot potato.

Do all the difficulties faced so far rule out adequate housing for slum families? Not if one idea—admittedly distasteful to some businessmen—is accepted:

Any solution to city housing problems must involve some form of government subsidy. Subsidies now look like the one way to span the gap between what low-income families can pay for housing and what private enterprise can supply at a reasonable profit.

The subsidy idea is hardly new. It was the aim, if not the result, of many existing federal housing programs. It is also the basic tool of the Kennedy and Percy proposals. What's more, many businesses—from farming and oil to autos and aerospace—benefit from subsidies, open or hidden. One example: The U. S. government finances irrigation projects for agriculture to the tune of $1 billion a year on 50-year, zero-interest loans.

Some of the required housing subsidy can continue in the form of below-the-market interest rates and long-term mortgages. But this alone is not enough. Bolder forms of subsidy will also be needed. The most obvious possibilities: total land write-down (in essence, state or municipal ownership of the land) and total tax abatement on dwelling units for at least as long as they are occupied by low-income families.

Yet no major city could afford to write down land entirely and lose all taxes on the property. This suggests the oft-mentioned possibility that the federal government relieve the cities of all welfare, health, and education costs, on the ground that these services are a national concern.

Whatever form the expanded subsidies take, the government must be prepared to provide them without insisting on over-complicated procedures. The government has a right to regulate what it subsidizes, but rules that keep every conceivable wrong-doer out of a program make it almost impossible for right-doers to get in.

Finally, as business and government work together on new rules to make the needed housing possible—by making it possible for private enterprise to earn a profit building it—one often-overlooked principle must be kept in mind:

While the most urgent need is to replace the slums, the cities also need the kind of housing that will attract and hold a middle class. It makes no sense simply to reinforce the ghettos, to freeze the trend that populates the cities only with the very rich and the very poor. Socially, politically, and economically, cities need a broader base of people.

This country is a long way from President Johnson's dream of "cities of spacious beauty." But if business and government face some hard facts, at least a start can be made.

EDUCATION

At the U.S. Office of Education, Commissioner Harold Howe II spells out the problem: "There is a vast psychological gap between the clientele of today's city schools (students and parents) and the suppliers of education (teachers, administrators, and school board members.)"

This gap is steadily widened by the spreading Negro ghettos, the flight of white families to the suburbs, and the mushrooming non-white population of city schools.

An example that scares everybody is Washington, D.C., where 93% of public-school pupils are Negroes and the percentage is still rising. Elsewhere, worried school administrators watch the trend and see their systems as "Washington minus five years" or "Washington minus three years." In Detroit, non-whites represent 57% of the school population, in Chicago, 54%, in Cleveland, 53%, in St. Louis, 62%.

When the Negro school population reaches such high levels, the quality of education suffers. Negro pupils begin to feel segregated and lose their motivation to learn. Teachers have to spend more time keeping order than teaching. So, not surprisingly, the most-experienced teachers tend to shun the very schools that most need them.

Total solution of the educational problem may not be possible. But ghetto schools can be vastly improved—if there are major changes in attitude and action not only among educators but also among businessmen.

Educators must become more flexible and more responsive to the pupils' needs. Critics claim that an entrenched bureaucracy, unmoving and un-responsive, has fought bitterly against changes in some cities.

"Our urban public school systems seem musclebound with tradition," says Dr. Kenneth B. Clarke, a Negro sociologist and president of the Metropolitan Applied Research Center. "They seem to represent the most rigid forms of bureaucracies, which are paradoxically most resilient in their ability to resist demands for change."

Bureaucracy strait-jackets not only some school systems but also many government officials. So businessmen emerge as one force that can bring about change.

Businessmen must understand education, support it, and even get directly involved. Specifically:

Businessmen will have to alter their traditional opposition to more spending for schools, and face up to higher taxes. Almost every suggestion to improve the ghetto schools takes enormous sums of money. One federal act alone, authorized $6.1 billion for fiscal 1967 and 1968 to help elementary and secondary education; and the figure is over $9 billion for 1969 and 1970.

Some businessmen have already changed their stance on school spending. In Detroit last year the usually conservative Board of Trade raised $60,000 to campaign for higher school taxes that would bring in an additional $25 million a year.

Businessmen will have to speak out on school improvements, many of which are controversial. In Pittsburgh, for example, businessmen have allied themselves with educators and civic and religious groups to support a revamped educational system that includes replacing all the city's high schools with five super high schools—a move to aid integration.

Businessmen will have to work more with professional educators. When the Hartford (Conn.) Board of Education and Common Council reached an impasse on what should be done about the city's schools, the Chamber of Commerce persuaded both parties to bring in an outside consultant to recommend action. The New Detroit Committee, formed mainly of businessmen after last summer's rioting, is pressing Detroit's school system to adopt consultants' recommendations that had been ignored by the city's educators.

More businessmen should also turn to education for a career. In Philadelphia, for example, an enlightened school administration has gone to business rather than traditional educational circles for two new associate superintendents. One, a former partner in a large accounting firm, is in charge of finance; the other a professional planner, heads the school system's planning.

Finally, businessmen need to make one other contribution to education: Using skills perfected for business—such as marketing, engineering, and management—they can help frame creative proposals for new educational programs.

If educators and businessmen are to work together to upgrade the city schools, what changes and improvements should they seek? Here are five suggestions by men who have already been deeply involved in the problem:

1. Change the ghetto schools to gear them more closely to the right culture. Harold B. Gores, president of Educational Facilities Laboratories Inc., a non-profit corporation established by the Ford Foundation, blames a lot of the schools' troubles on the existence of two cultures in the cities. And, he says, many schools are geared to the wrong one.

"That culture," Gore explains, "is white, middle-class, Anglo-Saxon, Protestant. The children attuned to it are success-oriented and have strong family ties. In contrast, the Negro child in a ghetto doesn't know or appreciate the standards, values, or morals of the middle-class family. He may have no father. His only close relative, his mother, may raise him to live for the pleasure of the moment. For such a child, there is no tomorrow to worry about or plan for."

Kenneth Mines, a Negro lawyer in Detroit, describes an added handicap: "Every Negro child realizes he is different, that there is something wrong with him. This builds an inferiority complex. Some children react negatively; some react violently; some just drift down and become inferior."

So the ghetto school has to be both school and family for many Negro pupils. That is the reasoning behind some of the compensatory programs that have been started.

The Preschool Project in Ypsilanti, Mich.—a program that included home visits, psychological consulting, medical services and a special task-oriented curriculum—produced a consistent jump in intellectual ability among disadvantaged Negro children—but at a cost of $1,500 per pupil.

Frustratingly, high cost doesn't guarantee success. Three years after New York City started the More Effective Schools program that raised instructional costs from $434 to $994 per pupil, The Center for Urban Education concluded: "The MES program has not had any significant . . . effect on children's performance in arithmetic . . . [nor has it] stopped the increasing retardation of children who began it in grades two or three."

The same charge of ineffectiveness has been leveled at Headstart, the Office of Economic Opportunity's $1.5-billion-a-year program for pre-school children. Although it is still too early for a complete evaluation, critics maintain that the children lose their headstart soon after leaving the program. Apparently, the government sees some truth in the charge, because it is now adding a "Follow Through" program to continue up through the third grade.

2. Change the school curriculums to make them more realistic than they are now. Even if a young Negro now makes it through early grades, he's likely to fall afoul of a curriculum that bears little resemblance to real life around him.

No part of the curriculum is held in lower regard by the average ghetto dweller than vocational training, which is supposed to turn out graduates ready to step into jobs in industry. Negroes claim that many vocational programs teach trades oriented to the '30s and '40s rather than the '60s. Negro students now want to learn telephone installing, business-machine repair, computer programming, and television maintenance instead of traditional woodworking, metal working and automobile repair.

Ghetto leaders hope that business, prompted by its need for better employees, will force a change to more useful training. In fact, only business can make vocational training more realistic, according to Robert Potts, of the Virginia Park Rehabilitation Citizens Committee, which is trying to rebuild the area where Detroit's 1967 riots started.

"Private industry will have to contribute people and equipment and help plan the curriculum," says Potts. "School administrators don't know what kinds of jobs industry has today."

Exactly what can industry do? Here is one example: Michigan Bell Telephone Co. adopted a heavily Negro Detroit high school whose students went on strike last year to oust the principal. The company sends its personnel people to the school to teach weekly classes on how to get a job—what to wear, how to act and what the interviewer is looking for.

"Only eight students showed up for the first class," says Michigan Bell President William Day, "but when the others heard via the grapevine that it was for real, more started to attend. Now the classes are jammed."

3. Consider a whole new approach to the design of school buildings.   Too many city school buildings are old and outmoded. In Boston, for example, a third of the schools were built more than 100 years ago. Even worse in the minds of architects, most of today's school design still stems from a 120-year-old idea first applied at Boston's Quincy school, which is still in use. It treats a school as an egg crate that seals the pupils into compartments, each with a teacher.

"Today's schoolhouse is monastic, antiseptic, and unattractive," says Harold Gores of the Educational Facilities Laboratories. "Its only benefit is that it is nearly indestructible." More to Gores' liking are wide-open spaces, now starting to show up in suburban schools, that allow team teaching and greater flexibility.

4. Bring more Negro teachers and administrators into the city school systems.
"Negro pupils would be more motivated to learn," says Ernest Brown, a personnel executive with the Michigan Consolidated Gas Co., "if they had models to look up to. Since the first person of stature a Negro child

meets may well be his teacher, there should be more Negro teachers in ghetto classrooms."

That's easier said than done, according to many school officials. Not enough Negroes are qualified, and business often snaps up those who are.

True enough—but only to a degree. It's also true that some school systems have not been sympathetic to hiring Negroes, and others have simply not thought about it. In Detroit's system, for example, where enrollment is more than 50% Negro, there is not a single Negro athletic director.

5. Take a new look at the thorny question of integration.   With the fast-rising Negro population in so many cities and the equally fast white exodus, the integrated school's ideal racial mix—70% white and 30% Negro—is no longer physically possible in more and more schools. Result: Some of the first integration efforts—busing, educational parks, and metropolitan schools —don't look so effective anymore.

Now the most promising efforts seem to be aimed at upgrading the city schools enough to lure whites back. That means adding a lot of educational services once considered frills: extensive counseling, extracurricular remedial programs, smaller classes, and higher salaries for teachers.

But integration is no longer the chief concern of militant Black leaders like James Del Rio, a Michigan state legislator.

"We don't want integration," he says bluntly. "We want to improve the education in our Black schools." Del Rio's goal is also the goal of some more-moderate Negroes and whites—at least as a realistic first step toward solving the problem.

For the long pull, however, the best solution still seems to be the old Horace Mann concept of a common school where the banker's daughter and the blacksmith's son attend classes together. In a well-publicized study (the so-called Coleman report), two Johns Hopkins professors found that mixing students of all classes and races was a more effective way to improve education in ghetto schools.

Pollution Abatement in Industry: Policies and Practices

36

National Industrial Conference Board

Replies from 441 companies in a recent Conference Board survey[1] show that most of those whose operations tend to contribute to air or water pollution generally consider its abatement as one of their top community responsibilities and are doing something about it. As in other recognized business functions, responsibility for action has been assigned and standards and procedures established to ensure that pollution-control equipment is designed into new operations and upgraded in old, and that laws and regulations are observed. Company standards sometimes exceed those prescribed by government.

The cost of pollution-control equipment is high, and only a few surveyed companies have succeeded in recovering effluents whose value is a significant offset to the costs incurred. For these reasons, most survey respondents would welcome government incentives, particularly accelerated depreciation.

Progress would be further hastened, they say, if the Federal Government would step up its research for more effective and less-costly equipment. Cooperators predict that the need for such equipment will become increasingly acute as the industrial expansion continues amidst public clamor for cleaner air and water. It is the consensus of the surveyed companies, however, that the setting and enforcement of standards is better in all respects when handled at the lowest possible level of government.

A COMMUNITY RESPONSIBILITY

Most of the companies surveyed recognize their community responsibility for pollution control and are taking steps to conserve our air and water resources. In several cases, such efforts extend back several decades to the founding of the company. While the concern of most of the companies is of more recent origin, and at times in the nature of a "catch-up" program,

Reprinted with permission from the Conference Board *Record* (December 1966), pp. 35–38. Copyright © 1966 the National Industries Conference Board. This survey was financed by the National Pollution Control Foundation.

[1] The material analyzed in this survey is drawn from replies to an August, 1966 Conference Board inquiry directed to some 700 companies who, in reporting to NICB in an earlier public affairs study, identified pollution control as a business objective. A total of 527 responses was received from a wide cross-section of business firms, including both heavy and light industry and the service fields. Of these, 86 had to be eliminated from analysis because of incomplete response. Subsequent *Record* articles offer more detailed information on an industry-by-industry basis.

there are numerous instances in which pollution-abatement policies were enunciated well in advance of the heightened interest of the general public in the subject and the attendant spate of legislation.

It is company policy to regard the management of air and water as a basic community responsibility. It is basically no different from providing financial support to local charities or taking part in the solution of local civic problems, for the aim is a better community. Company beliefs and objectives concerning pollution abatement are sprinkled with such expressions and phrases as, "a civic obligation," . . . "community obligation," . . . "a responsible corporate citizen wherever we are," . . . "always a good neighbor." For example, a producer of primary metals writes that the rationale behind his company's pollution control is to be found in its credo, which reads: "We strive to be a good neighbor in communities in which the company is located, and we will foster and support civic activities directed at the fundamental improvement of these communities." Other companies see their pollution-abatement activities as an ethical obligation and at times a moral one. A textile company, for instance, comments: "We have no right to destroy or pollute air or water which belongs to all our citizens."

But companies are not wholly altruistic as they move to meet their civic responsibilities: Being a good citizen is good business. They are quick to point out that creating a nuisance, inconveniencing a neighbor, or endangering the health of local inhabitants will reflect adversely upon the company. Some are concerned lest the company receive a bad name. Others look upon pollution abatement as an opportunity to attract "qualified employees" to their community.

ABATEMENT, A HIGH-PRIORITY GOAL

For most companies faced with the problem, pollution abatement is not just another community responsibility—it receives special attention. There is an urgency about it that is not present to the same extent in other civic activities. This sentiment is expressed by a textile executive who writes: "Government and public pressures make pollution abatement a demanding community responsibility. We are giving more time and attention to this than to other equally important but less pressing matters in the community."

In rating pollution control with their other local commitments, the vast majority of cooperators to the survey give it equal importance; and many rank it among their top-priority responsibilities. Some companies in the paper, oil refining, chemical, and utility fields, for example, view their control efforts to be of "major," . . . "prime," . . . "serious," . . . "critical," or "paramount" importance. Nor is the policy of considering pollution abatement essential in the planning and engineering of a company's activities restricted to those companies only in which contamination is a major problem. Many other companies regard abatement as a "routine responsibility."

One reason for attaching special importance to pollution abatement is the deep-rooted feeling that the environment of the community should be preserved. There is a general feeling that a company's obligation extends to virtually all society—other members of industry, the government, and the private citizen. Another reason is cited by a chemical executive who sees companies in his industry subjected to public scrutiny to an unprecedented degree. He writes: "Pollution control is a prime element in our planning, particularly today when the public is highly sensitized to both the real and imaginary problems associated with chemical plants."

In several instances companies are of the opinion that the health hazards of contamination will impose major restrictions on growth if industry does not arrest pollution.

Several company officials view the pollution problem in a somewhat broader context than their community responsibilities. A utility company sees pollution removal as second only to the company's prime responsibility of supplying dependable and economic electric service to its customers. A member of the food industry regards the management of air pollution as an aspect of his company's safety program. "We selfishly hold our grain and flour dust to a minimum," he writes, "as a critical mixture of dust and air will cause an explosion."

Companies are ever on guard against incurring needless expenditures for

---

Policy on Air and Water Control

(From a food company's operations bulletin)

"We recognize the responsibility of maintaining facilities that are assets to the communities in which they are located.

"This responsibility includes taking every practical step to avoid contaminating air and water resources with industrial waste materials.

"In constructing new facilities, special attention will be given to inclusion of the most appropriate pollution control equipment.

"We also accept the responsibility of continuing to review existing facilities in order to assure ourselves that these plants are operating within acceptable standards.

"If sources of pollution from company facilities are discovered which are contrary to community or state standards, it will be our policy to develop a program of improvement to bring such operations to an acceptable level within a reasonable length of time."

equipment which, although it is constantly being improved, is still inadequate for solving certain abatement problems. This reservation applies particularly to control of air pollution. Comments generally draw attention to the economic aspects of abatement and the technical know-how which is called for. This stipulation found in the policy of a paper producer is typical: "We shall correct this (pollution) by taking steps which are technically proven, physically possible, and at a rate as rapid as is economically feasible." A chemical producer says: "Our effluents are as pure as technical know-how and adequate expense can produce."

Few companies have formal written policies on pollution abatement; only nineteen were reported in the entire survey (for one, see box on p. 477.)

Of course, pollution is not a problem faced by all companies. The Board survey shows that in some companies—particularly in the electronics and communication industries, air transportation, and electric utilities with hydroelectric operations—contamination problems are minimal or nonexistent. Even companies located in rural areas where the problem is less pressing are taking action to clean up their environment. Some have become involved in committee work sponsored by industry trade associations and government groups. In one instance, a food executive's interest was sparked by the belief that his company's research and development staff may make a contribution to pollution-control-and-abatement techniques.

INCENTIVES

Like other company policies dealing with an organization's basic beliefs and long-term objectives, those on pollution control are almost invariably either silent or indefinite when it comes to the timing of company goals. Obviously, the timing will be influenced by the trend of legislation. But in the opinion of virtually all cooperators in this survey, government incentives could significantly accelerate the pollution-abatement efforts now underway in industry. Of the 235 companies discussing incentives, all but 14 say that such assistance would remove a major economic obstacle.

Most companies would welcome financial assistance because of the high cost of pollution-abatement equipment, which is characterized as "nonproductive" since it is usually not expected to pay for itself in terms of dollar income. Some executives see the stimulus to company action provided by incentives as sufficiently strong to reduce the pressures for further legislation and regulation significantly.

In several instances, companies that see huge expenditures ahead view incentives as "imperative." A Los Angeles manufacturer, who recently installed abatement systems that doubled operating costs, and who faces still more newly enacted regulation, states: "We will have to have a very careful look at the economics to determine if we would wish to continue manufacturing in the Los Angeles area under the conditions as set forth by the new regulations. This is not to indicate that we disagree with the policy; it is merely a statement of the economic facts of life."

Cooperators offer a variety of suggestions involving all three levels of government. The most frequently mentioned incentive is accelerated depreciation. A number of companies also favor a tax credit on their capital investment for pollution-abatement purposes.[2] A rubber company, for example, would like to see a tax credit of 20% with an option to amortize the expenditure over a period of one to five years. A few companies speak of construction grants similar to those enjoyed by municipalities. One executive finds such grants a happy alternative to further complicating the tax structure. Loans with low interest rates would also help ease the financial strain.

Many companies would also like relief at the state and local levels. Mentioned is relief from sales and use taxes, and from ad valorem levies. Land occupied by pollution-abatement equipment, respondents hold, should be tax exempt so long as it is used for that purpose. An electric power company believes that state and local redevelopment funds for industrial location should be made available for industrial relocation within the state in the event that waste treatment cannot be properly accomplished at a company's present location.

A few cooperators favor incentives on a restricted basis only. A number would apply incentives only to equipment used in connection with existing company installations; in the words of an oil executive, we should "use incentives to remove the big backlog of pollution problems." Another oil official is inclined to exclude new plants because it is often difficult to segregate the expense for such facilities.

A food executive would have incentives in force "when new knowledge shows a need for drastic change involving unusual costs," while several other cooperators would limit incentives to nonproductive equipment.

Of the few respondents who do not favor incentives, some maintain that community and public pressures will bring about the necessary remedial measures, while others point to their accomplishments without benefit of incentives. A chemical company expresses an entirely different viewpoint, however, suggesting that the problem is not a financial one: "What is needed is not incentives but a clear quantification of objectives for air and water purity so that technical developments will be expedited."

PENALTIES

Judged by the smaller number of companies (155) commenting upon penalties, it would seem that industry prefers the carrot to the stick. These

---

[2] The new legislation suspending the 7% investment tax credit on capital expenditures specifically excludes investment in pollution-abatement equipment.

companies are sharply divided: 89 favor penalties and 66 reject them.

With few exceptions, however, they hold that penalties are to be applied, "after all else fails," . . . "as a last resort," . . . "to gross polluters only," . . . "only after the company had been given the widest latitude in taking corrective measures." Only two companies suggest drastic, across-the-board penalties.

Those opposing forfeitures often give the reasons for their stand in considerable detail. The major argument they put forward concerns the influence of penalties on pollution abatement. The penalties might be construed as a "license to pollute for a fee," an attitude that would hinder, rather than expedite, industry's efforts. Thus, these cooperators reason, fines would not be in the public interest.

But others have misgivings about the technical problems involved in administering penalties. Several companies share the view of a primary metals producer who, discussing the administration problems of such a system, says "it would require costly and perhaps unsavory bureaucratic operations." A chemical producer rejects the idea of penalties "because it implies measurement of materials used which we regard as proprietary." Yet another company wonders if penalties would be applied to municipalities and other sources outside the business community. And a drug company will withhold decision pending the results of its investigation of the Ruhr plan for penalties.[3]

GOVERNMENT RESEARCH

Some cooperators feel that more technical advice and counsel on the part of government would be a powerful spur to pollution removal. They believe that the Federal Government should concentrate its pollution-abatement efforts on research and development. In the opinion of many executives, progress is being impeded by a critical lack of information about technically and economically feasible methods for abatement. As a member of the paper industry sees it: "Pollution must be more clearly defined in terms of what constitutes pollution, allowable quantities, and effective means of testing." And several respondents conclude that, without such knowledge, the chances of formulating reasonable and effective legislation are slim.

[3] The Ruhr River Basin in West Germany contains half of that country's industrial capacity and has a small stream flow. However, according to all accounts, the Ruhr River is clean enough to swim in, for fish to live in, and even to provide drinking water with only mild treatment. The antipollution program is carried out by the Ruhr Associations or semi-governmental organizations. Instead of establishing treatment requirements, or effluent standards, and trying to enforce them, the Ruhr Associations, simply charge every town and every industrial plant a stiff levy proportional to the amount of pollution they deliver to the river. The effluent assay is based on the single measurement of "biochemical oxygen demand" (BOD), which is equivalent to the organic waste load in the water.

Companies frequently find government agencies cordial and cooperative but offering little concrete help in solving specific problems concerning controls and standards. Exchanges often prove to be one-sided, with most of the information originating in industry rather than government.

THE ROLE OF GOVERNMENT

While advocating an active role for the Federal Government in furthering our store of scientific knowledge about pollution, respondents also give their views of the responsibilities each level of government might best assume for cleaner air and water. Their philosophy is much the same for the control of pollution as for the regulation of other business activities, namely, that responsibility should rest with the lowest level of government capable of doing the job. This concept is sometimes referred to as the principle of subsidiarity.

Few cooperators question government involvement. Since government is charged with the protection of the public health, safety, and welfare as well as the preservation of our natural resources, government action on pollution is regarded by most respondents as a proper function.

Some companies even see a positive need for government intervention. Without some kind of ground rules, they state, good corporate citizens would be penalized should their competitors elect to do nothing. Legislation, among other things, will force laggards to act.

Even national standards, however, would not alleviate the problem of one machinery manufacturer who says that expenditures made to control air and water pollution "have made us less competitive in our world markets. Many of our foreign competitors appear to be less concerned with these controls and therefore have lower costs through no capital expenditures for control equipment."

National Interests and Multinational Business

37

Henry H. Fowler

The major premise of this article is that the resolution of the conflict between national interests and those of the multinational corporation requires
the earnest attention of government and business in the free world. What
is needed is a pooling of numerous impressions of the nature of this conflict
and the studied formulation of an enlightened policy for free world governments and multinational business to follow in their mutual interest. Thus,
a basis can be provided to answer two vital and interrelated questions:

Will the economic recovery that has characterized the developed countries of the free world since World War II founder on the shoals of nationalism?

Will the multinational corporations—those mighty engines of enlightened
Western capitalism—be permitted to play their vital role in the less-developed countries?

The answers to these questions will depend in large measure upon the
reconciliation of national interests with those of the multinational private
business corporation. Both interests are essential elements in a future that
must have both freedom and a healthy, dynamic economic environment for
the free world. But the harsh reality is that they seem at times to be
moving on a collision course.

The expansion of international trade, the freedom of money to flow across
national boundaries, the welcome extended to foreign business units, the
stimulating effects of broadened competition, and the spread of technical
and organizational knowledge—all these conditions, hallmarks of multinational business, have helped to bring an expanding, more integrated, and
more efficient economic structure to the West since World War II. And
there is no doubt that, given these same conditions, plus some reasonable
assurance against state confiscation, state competition, and discrimination
against foreign enterprise, the multinational corporations of the West could
make a significant contribution to the emergence of viable and free economic societies in the less-developed countries.

Reprinted from the *California Management Review*, Vol. VIII, No. 1 (Fall) 1965, pp. 3–12.
Copyright © 1965 by The Regents of the University of California.

This article was based upon a paper prepared by the author for the UCLA-INSEAD seminar
at Fontainebleau, France in September 1964. The author would like to acknowledge the
numerous direct quotations from *International Business: Principles and Problems*, by
Professor Howe Martyn.

But certain facts must be faced. The postwar revival of capitalism in Western Europe and Japan resulted in large measure from the tendency of national governments to lessen their interference with international business. Bretton Woods, GATT, currency convertibility, the emergence of the European Common Market with its limitations on certain aspects of national sovereignty in economic matters, the hospitable reception to any influx of outside capital and enterprise—these all played a part in avoiding a clash between national interests and multinational business.

Now the winds of change seem to be blowing the other way, and there is a questioning calm in the attitudes of the developed countries that have been so congenial to the multinational company in the past. And in many of the less-developed countries, the rising tide of nationalism, mixed with state intervention in varying degrees up to outright confiscation, has created an uncongenial atmosphere for multinational private business. So today in 1965 with multinational business at an all-time peak, and the multinational corporations of the Organization for Economic Cooperation and Development countries possessed of the greatest potential for international economic development in history, the dangers and opportunities match each other in challenge.

MUTUAL RECOGNITION

Is there no final or definitive solution? There does not appear to be. But one proposition is clear. A wholesome relationship between national interests and multinational private business requires an increasing concern of those responsible for the welfare of one for the needs of the other. A first step toward mutual concern is mutual recognition. For that reason, the coming together at Fontainebleau (joint UCLA-INSEAD research seminar at the Palais de Fontainebleau, France, in September 1964) of representatives of various nation states and those responsible for long-range corporate planning was a good omen. It marked the recognition by those engaged in long-range corporate planning that national interests must be taken into account, and that leaders of business must share in the education of governments on the true role of multinational business.

However, more than recognition of the problem is needed. The growth and development of multinational business, as is true of business generally, will depend on a large measure of freedom to innovate in organization and policies, as well as in products. Common purposes between national interests and multinational business must be identified and pursued. Confusion and misunderstanding concerning the relations of multinational business to the political principles and social values of both base and host countries must be dispelled. Specific areas of actual or potential conflict must become the subject of thoughtful and temperate policies by governments and business rather than arenas of arbitrary conduct.

An improved institutional environment will be necessary for the growth and development of multinational business to its full potential in a manner consistent with legitimate and proper national interests. There are both public and private imperatives in this institutional environment. They must be determined.

INTERDEPENDENCE

Those responsible for government policies in both developed and less-developed countries may ask why they should be concerned with the effect of national interests on multinational business. A short answer is that freedom of opportunity for the multinational corporation will greatly serve the free world for decades ahead.

The multinational corporation today is a key part of the free world economic picture as it moves goods, capital equipment, skills, and know-how to places where they are needed. It serves national interests in many economic patterns. Beyond that it is an important link in the chain of interdependence that promises peace, stability, and dynamic development.

The extension of operations of the multinational corporation is designed to take a profitable advantage of trading or market opportunities. Sometimes tariff and exchange controls and nontariff trade barriers give such major advantages to goods produced in a given market that the only way for an outside entity to compete effectively in that market is to establish an operating unit there. Sometimes there are distinct economic benefits in producing in, or closer to, a foreign market. There can be considerable cost advantages, especially where raw materials or components are available or transportation is a major factor. Sometimes natural consumer preference for locally produced products is a factor. No matter what the rationale, the utilization of resources to earn a profit is the end objective.

Whatever the mix of private economic motivation, it has grown considerably since World War II, creating new institutions and generating new forces. For example, nearly 3,000 United States firms have foreign subsidiaries and their sales are double what the United States exports. These American-based companies that operate on a multinational basis conduct manufacturing enterprises abroad, extract and process natural resources, provide services, and market the resulting goods and services on an international scale. Indeed, in the tradition of some of the earlier great companies of other nations, many of them think of themselves as, and have in fact and spirit become, worldwide or truly international corporations instead of United States companies operating abroad.

The extent of United States interest in multinational corporations is revealed in the value of United States direct investments abroad (excluding portfolio and short-term holdings). These increased from $11.7 billion in 1950 to $37.1 billion in 1962. In the manufacturing category alone, the increase was from $3.8 billion to $13.2 billion.

In this process of extending corporate business on a multinational scale, much more is involved than the economic advantages of investors of capital and the return of profits, although it must never be forgotten that this is always the controlling rationale. Multinational companies are playing an increasingly important role in the expansion of world trade, in serving the interests of the less-developed countries, and in providing capital, knowledge, industrial know-how, and useful employment in countries other than the base country, as well as increased employment, assets, and profit returns for the base country.

ROLE IN FOREIGN POLICY

Since I am not an authority on what serves the national interests of other countries, I will only venture an assessment of the areas of common purpose of the United States and United States-based corporations, other than the private commercial advantages of its citizens. Transcending the private commercial importance of the foreign operations of United States multinational corporations is their significance and role in a United States foreign policy that has met with general approval by the Atlantic countries. Since World War II, every President, practically every Congress, and numerous public and lay leaders of national and international thought have emphasized the importance to national interests of the role of these private companies operating on a multinational basis.

For example, the various foreign aid enactments beginning with the Marshall Plan in 1948 have all stressed the importance of promotion of United States private investment abroad, in their provisions for investment guaranties and other means of encouraging foreign investments by American business. The importance of the foreign operations of United States-based companies in lending momentum to the economic and industrial development of the free world during the reconstruction of Western Europe and Japan, and now to the continents of Asia, Africa, and Latin America, has been acknowledged for some years.

Moreover, in dealing with the United States balance of payments problem, recent examination of the sources of national wealth and power has focused attention on the long-term importance to the United States of income from and participation in the industrial development of other nations by United States private corporations. For example, from 1950 through 1962, $29 billion was received in earnings, interest payments, management fees, and royalties from direct investments overseas. This compares with the $16 billion capital outflow from the United States for direct investment abroad in the same period. Furthermore, additional exports have been generated in the form of capital equipment, materials, parts, and services required to support these investments.

The developed countries of the free world have a collective national interest in the growth of the less-developed countries. The private, multinational corporation has a most important role to play in furthering this collective national interest. But the areas of common purpose between national interests and the multinational corporation go far beyond either private commercial advantage or sharing in the economic fruits of the developing markets. Indeed, there is much to support the thesis of a distinguished American industrial leader, Mr. Roger Blough, Chairman of the Board of the United States Steel Corporation, who remarked recently that:

> . . . the multinational corporation may ultimately prove to be the most productive economic development of the twentieth century for bringing the people of nations together for peaceful purposes to their mutual advantage; and . . . it can thus provide the adhesive which can do more to bind nations together than any other development yet found by man in his pursuit of peace.

The operations of modern multinational corporations contribute to rising incomes and economic progress in both the home country and abroad. By bringing together human and natural resources from a number of countries, they contribute to the well-being of the countries receiving the investment as well as the country supplying it. From the standpoint of the receiving country, these corporations provide an investment of capital and an infusion of know-how, technique, and skills. In many cases, these resources could not be otherwise obtained. Good jobs are created for people who might otherwise be less productively employed, and private and governmental incomes gain. Products are supplied which might otherwise not be available. Domestic productivity is enhanced and the export capacity of receiving countries is increased.

Through its plants and marketing operations, the multinational or international corporation has a stake in many countries and, conversely, many nations of these same countries have a continuing stake in the corporation. Many close relationships are developed between the businesses and citizens of all the countries concerned—producer to customer, employer to employee, purchaser to supplier, etc. Indeed, it is difficult to imagine a more promising basis for understanding and a common economic interest among the peoples of free nations than the multinational corporation.

THE RISING TIDE

Although I have no desire to exaggerate the potential conflict, I cannot join those who would ignore or minimize the tensions between national interests and the multinational corporation. More than at any time since the end of World War II, the rising tide of nationalism in all countries is generating public attitudes and policies that could obstruct the growth of multinational corporations and the atmosphere of greater freedom that is conducive to their proliferation. This situation requires the attention of political scientists, economic theorists, officials, and journalists, as well as businessmen.

Of course, national interests will assert themselves in the area of business and commerce, whether local or multinational. Senator Sherman, a sponsor of the famed United States legislation that bears his name, once observed:

> If we will not endure a king as a political power, we should not endure
> a king over the production, transportation, and sale of any of the necessities of life.

Today, in the treatment of multinational business, a strong exercise of national sovereignty is the prevailing mood. Realism requires us to recognize it. In many developed countries, there are signs that their political leaders believe they have a diminishing need for foreign capital, technology, or management.

In a number of the less-developed countries, new political leaders manifest a distinct preference for government-to-government grants and loans for local or state-owned enterprises over direct foreign private investment. As the number and size of foreign private firms in both developed and less-developed nations continue to increase conflicts between the policies of these countries and guest corporations often follow. Tension often develops between host countries and the home governments of the corporation concerned. Efforts are made to discriminate against foreign firms already established or to force them to become policy instruments of the host countries. Criticism is specifically directed against the extent of foreign control in what are termed "key sectors" of local economies. New discriminating laws or regulations devised in one country quickly spread among others. Dissatisfaction is especially vented against the larger international corporations. Complaints made against foreign ownership include the loss of locally earned profits, with resultant balance of payments problems; remoteness of decision making which lessens the effectiveness of local political and economic controls; loss of flexibility for local operations, which affects the market for local employment and exports; and a narrowed scope for potential local top management on the world scene.

AREAS OF CONFLICT

A brief review of some of the specific areas where thoughtful and temperate policies by both government and business are necessary to minimize potential conflict would include at least five:

> Trade.
> Balance of payments.
> Conditions of entry and regulations.
> Confiscation and state operation.
> Transfers of production and employment.

TRADE

The ability to export goods and services to a given country without excessive obstruction from tariff, exchange controls, and nontariff trade barriers is required to create a market in a country. The degree of freedom here requires considering if a given market can be more efficiently serviced from a local plant than from the base country. Additionally, the larger the market, both in size and population, the greater the likelihood of local production. Hence, the movement toward the general lowering of trade barriers and the creation or enlargement of regional marketing areas, encompassing many countries in which goods move relatively freely, is conducive to the infusion of capital, initiative, and technology from both external and internal sources.

It follows that the success of the Kennedy Round and the elimination or reduction of trade barriers that tend to compartmentalize countries into small units for market purposes will improve the outlook for the future of the multinational corporation. Conversely, the failure of the Kennedy Round, or a cessation of efforts of many countries to dispense with trade and customs barriers through larger marketing or regional groupings, will bring the multinational corporation in conflict with national or larger regional interests seeking self-containment and self-sufficiency.

MONETARY SYSTEM

BALANCE OF PAYMENTS

A second area of potential conflict between national interests and the multinational corporation arises from the international monetary system requirements that governments maintain sufficient reserves of gold and foreign exchange or credits to meet external payments. Multinational business may be affected by these requirements in either base or host countries.

Balance of payments difficulties in host countries often lead to stringent regulation of the repatriation of profits of multinational corporations. This dampens incentive and discourages further investment when most needed, creating an additional hazard that tends to restrain company managements from venturing even when the normal commercial risks are acceptable.

By the same token, the damaging effect of a drastic policy of disinvestment by the multinational company through the wholesale transfer of funds out of the host country must be taken into account if there is a serious balance of payments situation in that country.

Balance of payments difficulties in base countries may lead to the regulation of investment flows which confines or inhibits management initiative. While substantial progress has been made in removing exchange controls in many of the developed countries which have the resources to serve as base countries for generating business, only the United States, Canada,

Germany, and Switzerland are free from exchange controls. Although aiming for full liberalization, France, Italy, the Benelux countries, and Austria have preserved certain restrictions. A third group of countries, including the United Kingdom, Ireland, Japan, Australia, Spain, and the Scandinavian countries, retains a wide range of controls for balance of payments and monetary policy reasons.

The impact of exchange controls on multinational companies varies. In general, direct investment is treated the most liberally. The importance of leaving private industrial and commercial interests free to make capital investments abroad through the multinational corporation was demonstrated recently in the United States in connection with its balance of payments problems. At all stages of policy development, up through the so-called Interest Equalization Tax, President Kennedy, President Johnson, and the United States Treasury have strongly opposed any restraint, direct or indirect, on the flow of direct investment abroad through the multinational corporation.

New developments in the evolution of the International Monetary Fund and the related international financial cooperation now under consideration could serve to diminish the potential conflict that can arise from balance of payments restraints between national interests and the multinational corporation.

NATIONAL SOVEREIGNTY

CONDITIONS OF ENTRY AND REGULATION IN THE NATIONAL INTEREST

There is no international law applicable to business because there is no supranational authority to issue and enforce it. Thus the conditions and circumstances of entry and the regulation of the operations of the subsidiary, affiliate, or branch of a multinational corporation chartered in a given country are subject to the laws of the country where it operates. National sovereignty covers corporations as well as people. When corporations or businesses become resident in a country, they become subject to its laws.

These truisms describe an area of give and take between sovereign national interests and the multinational company that will continue as long as both endure. Only applied good will, mutual understanding, and equal treatment under the law for foreign and domestic enterprises can minimize conflict.

The doctrine that domain follows property has for all practical purposes ceased to exist. It no longer can be used to excuse interference by strong nations in the internal affairs of weaker countries when their business interests are mistreated. With the disappearance of this doctrine, there was a turn to treaties that bind governments to maintain indefinitely the terms and privileges granted to each other's investors and otherwise protect them from arbitrary acts. For example, treaties of Friendship, Commerce, and Navigation with a number of countries include pledges designed to secure fair treatment for United States property, direct investment, and attendant operations. However, treaties can be denounced. And without actually flouting a treaty there are many ways in which ingenious governmental officials can discourage foreign entry, indirectly diminish the rights and privileges of foreign corporations, or discriminate severely against them.

Friction may also arise from special aspects of national corporation or business laws. Some host countries may favor certain types of products which are the special province of domestic companies. Others may deny foreign concerns entry to certain types of industries because national interests are said to require that these industries remain in the full control of nationals. Freedom of competition may be limited by licensing requirements which fix determined quotas to foreign affiliates. Even concessions such as special tax considerations to induce entry that brings scarce foreign currency and equipment can be administered so as to be discriminatory to existing units or prejudicial to investment decisions.

Another source of friction arises because the business laws of some countries in which multinational companies are based may be either more comprehensive or substantially different from the laws in host countries. For example, the gap between the laws and regulations applied to business in the United States and legal controls in many countries where American branches or subsidiary companies operate is often so large as to be unbridgeable to American legislators and enforcement agencies. Attempts to make American laws applicable to subsidiaries or affiliates in other countries may create serious difficulties for the governments of host countries.

Sometimes the situation works in reverse. One of the major antitrust cases pending in the United States Supreme Court involves a situation in which a trade association in a given industry in a given country is charged with the attempt to restrict business in the United States as a condition for the continued right to operate in that country. This situation can occur even without the direct exercise of national sovereignty when the laws of the country permit trade associations, as private bodies, to regulate various aspects of commerce and industry and also make membership therein compulsory.

A very special problem arises out of differences in the regulation of business according to varying conceptions of what the national interest requires with regard to trusts, monopolies, restraints on trade, and similar business practices. The extraterritorial application of the United States antitrust laws may bring the United States-based multinational corporation into conflict with national sovereignties which have a differing conception and application of antitrust principles, and under which its subsidiaries or affiliates must operate.

The need for a clarificaton and revision of the United States antitrust laws as they affect foreign trade and investment has long been recognized. This need will increase as differing concepts of undesirable business practices emerge in areas such as the European Common Market with the application of the pertinent articles in the Treaty of Rome to United States companies operating in the market. This need is already recognized in the United Kingdom and Canada.

During the past decade, positive recommendations have been made by committees of the American Bar Association, the New York City Bar Association, and many business organizations. In 1962, a report by a Joint Committee of the Antitrust Section and the Section of International and Comparative Law of the American Bar Association concluded that new legislation was needed to restate and harmonize our foreign antitrust policy with other foreign policies. The Committee concluded:

> The time has come when Congress must modernize our antitrust procedures to conform to a mid-twentieth century world, in which every nation has a stake in international trade, and unilateral action by the United States is inconsistent with our own objective of inducing even greater international cooperation.

One of the major deterrents to the full performance of their vital role by the multinational corporations is the pattern of taxation and regulatory discrimination that is often visited against foreign-based enterprises. Even in the United States, there is widespread belief that many of the current patterns of state taxation against interstate corporations are discriminatory and that there is grave need of some form of national harmonization if interstate companies are not to be affected by serious discrimination. Particularly in the so-called advanced countries, the more detailed and comprehensive tax laws and regulatory exercises of police power afford opportunities for national officials to favor preferred local interests over the foreign-based concern.

A COMMON THREAT

CONFISCATION AND STATE OPERATION OF COMPETITIVE UNITS

In the less-developed countries, perhaps the most serious deterrent to the multinational private corporation is the specter of state confiscation and state operation of competitive units. A growing tide of nationalism in the less-developed countries does not necessarily spell increasing freedom of opportunity for private business. Indeed, state confiscation, either direct or indirect, through excessive regulation and harassment, state operation of competitive units, or threats of these actions from political parties out of power, has become as commonplace as the daily newspaper.

Perhaps of equal significance is the growing tendency, best exemplified in the so-called Final Act of the United Nations Conference on Trade and Development, to couple proposals for promoting foreign private investment in developing countries with rather generalized plans for state ownership or operation of productive enterprise. This trend, especially when accompanied by direct participation by government trade organizations in foreign trade, without any clear delineation of the areas to be reserved for private commercial activity, betrays complete ignorance of the dynamics of foreign private investment.

The judgment of an outsider as to the proper course for assuring the development of local resources in a given country may not always be welcome. However, outside opinion should make certain truths about the stages of development clear beyond doubt. One in particular needs to be drummed home to governments and peoples of less-developed countries through chanceries and international agencies concerned with government-to-government loans and grants. This truth is that the multinational corporation cannot and will not play its proper role in developing countries in an institutional environment that accepts state confiscation or state operation of competitive units on an unrestricted basis as a national policy. Toleration of unrealistic delusions in this area is a disservice to those whose sensibilities are being spared.

FACTORS OF TIMING

TRANSFERS OF PRODUCTION AND EMPLOYMENT

Another extremely troublesome area of conflict between national interests and the multinational corporation concerns decisions that result in the transfer of production and employment from one country to another. If these decisions, resulting in a loss of jobs or exports, coincide with substantial unemployment or a serious loss of an export market, then repercussions from the political authorities are to be expected. The reaction is doubled if the plan is for the production unit to which work is transferred to ship its output back into the market which lost the production.

Managements of multinational companies are prone to be impatient with politicians who ignore the requirements of economics. Equally, politicians will be severe with managements that flout the canons of politics and public relations. When transfers of production are inevitable, factors of timing must be considered and, where at all possible, measures should be taken by management and public officials to minimize to the fullest the creation of any lasting unemployment. Failure to do so places a great strain on the government-corporation relationship.

Something more than temperate treatment of specific areas of conflict is needed if national interests and multinational corporations are to live together harmoniously. I suggest we should be searching for an improved institutional environment.

In this search, Americans naturally look for guidance to their own experience with the gradual submergence of tension between the individual states and interstate corporations. The same currents of thought that gave rise to the credo of political freedom in the Declaration of Independence in 1776 produced that same year a statement of economic freedom in Adam Smith's *Wealth of Nations*. A few years later, the Constitutional Convention of 1789 responded to the demands for a larger market economy and free competition. Indeed, it was to secure freedom of commerce—to break down the structure of interstate barriers being erected against multistate business operations— that the drive was initiated which led to the Constitution.

The commerce clause in the Constitution gave protection from state legislation inimical to national commerce on the basic principle that our economic unit was a nation. For the first hundred years, the overwhelming proportion of cases in the Supreme Court involving this clause concerned state legislation which, it was claimed, unconstitutionally curtailed commerce by entrepreneurs organized in one state attempting to extend their business to others.

Beginning with the famous case of *Dartmouth College* v. *Woodward*, the United States Supreme Court also gave a measure of protection to the corporation from the vagaries of a state chartering authority under the constitutional principle regarding the sanctity of contracts. Later, the Court utilized the "due process of law" clause of the 14th Amendment to strike down forms of state and local harassment of interstate business units deemed unreasonable.

Given these protections from abuse by public authority, the interstate corporation became a great force in the United States economy. This development was feasible because the people and their representatives felt that the interstate corporations served the needs and desires of the society better than solely relying on local capital, know-how, and organizational initiative. Equally important was the fact that the management of interstate corporations, exercising good long-range corporate planning principles, developed a tradition and practice of good corporate citizenship in the areas where the company conducted substantial producing or selling operations.

The result of this combination of legal protection against abuses by state authority and good corporate citizenship is well know. The corporation chartered in New York or Delaware—or in any of the fifty states—is relatively free to establish branch, subsidiary, or affiliated operations in any or all other states. From them it may service local or national markets, or export. For these operations, it may employ local personnel or bring in technicians who become a part of the community. It operates relatively free from state or local discrimination. Indeed, most consumers and public officials are unaware whether a given company is a domestic one incorporated in their own state or a so-called "foreign" corporation which has qualified to do business there.

This system has produced a great measure of economic development, reasonably well balanced between regions, and a considerable degree of political unity. Had it been fully developed by the mid-nineteenth century without the dependence of one predominantly raw material economy on slave labor, there would have been no war between the states. Since this system has matured, the United States does not easily accept any section or area as less developed.

What lessons, if any, does this experience have for creating a better institutional environment for the multinational corporation as it deals with nationalism and national sensibilities?

Clearly, the development and observance of a Code of Good Corporate Citizenship by multinational corporations is essential. Basic to this objective is the recognition that this is a task for individual and collective long-range strategic corporation planning. Equally fundamental is the requirement for an adequate two-way flow of realistic information. This must flow from the branch or subsidiary or affiliate to the main office and be reinforced by travel of home office executives to the field and of field staff to the home office. This information must disclose realistically the standing of the company with all segments of the population, not just government officialdom. This information flow must anticipate problems rather than report on crises.

The employment of citizens of the host country in line management, accounting, marketing, and technical areas as well as lesser positions is of great importance. The upgrading of citizens of the host country to positions leading to advancement and influence in the top management of the parent is equally significant, giving the company the flavor of being a truly international, rather than just a multinational firm. These policies place a high premium on training. Somewhat related is the widening of the corporate research base, wherever practicable, through the foreign subsidiary in cooperation with local educational institutions.

INTERNATIONAL OWNERS

An even more challenging vista has been opened in recent years by two leading United States executives, Frederic Donner, Chairman of General Motors, and Roger Blough, Chairman of United States Steel, who advocate ownership participation. Mr. Donner states:

> Hasn't the time come when thought should be given to making the ownership of these international corporations also truly international? In other words, should it not be possible for investors in the countries in which international corporations operate plants to participate directly in the ownership of these international corporations?

This does not necessarily mean direct local participation in the ownership and earnings of the local subsidiary. It may take the form of ownership of stock of the parent. Mr. Donner envisaged this as more desirable in cases where unified ownership interest is necessary because of the close business relationships between parent and subsidiary or between subsidiaries of the same parent.

On the same subject, Mr. Blough recently said:

In addition to an open-minded attitude regarding employment, the multinational corporation should also have an open-minded attitude regarding investments in the enterprise by nationals of the host nation. This investment may be done in many ways—in the parent company or through a joint venture with nationals of the host nation, or by some other method designed to permit nationals to keep a continuing interest in the enterprise.

Although pointed toward another objective, the recent Report to the United States President by a Task Force on Promoting Increased Foreign Investment in United States Private Securities set forth a series of recommendations on ways and means of promoting ownership participation.

Of course, one of the attributes of good corporate citizenship is the willingness to pay a fair share of taxes. Tax avoidance or corporate effort to minimize taxes wherever proper is understandable and expected. But when tax avoidance leaves off and intolerable tax evasion through the abuse of tax havens begins is a serious question for farsighted management. I am fully cognizant of the opposition of many United States multinational companies to efforts in the United States Revenue Act of 1962 to curb tax haven abuses. However, this effort was most sympathetically received, if not formally cheered, by tax authorities in many countries who felt that the time had come for someone to halt such abuses.

A related question concerns charitable efforts, such as the donation of funds, management, and leadership to hospitals, orphanages, youth centers, and facilities for rehabilitation of the less fortunate. Corporations are likely to accept these responsibilities and community activities automatically in their home country. They are all the more important in a host country where the multinational corporation is engaged in substantial operations, provided, of course, they are welcome.

A keen sense and practice of good public relations will disclose many other attributes of good corporate citizenship and measures to discharge this citizenship that will avoid offense to national sensibilities. I have already referred to transfers of production. Some consideration should also be given to avoiding acquisitions or engaging in ventures, particularly in developed countries, which tend to increase the proportion of foreign investment in a key sector of industry or trade and thus to raise questions of economic or political self-determination.

COOPERATIVE PLANNING

These are a few of the many phases of good corporate citizenship in which long-range corporate planning—strategic and tactical—can play a vital role for the multinational corporation. Policies of the base or home country government can supplement these efforts. The home government can eschew utilizing the multinational company as an instrument of national policy to obtain political influence in foreign activities. It can insure firms against losses from political disturbances and currency devaluations which sometimes invite corporate intervention in political affairs. It can review its tax laws and regulations to make sure there are incentives for private investment in less-developed countries where external capital flows are badly needed. It can make sure that there are no legal obstacles to joint ventures with nationals of the host country if these are appropriate business courses.

FUTURE PROSPECTS

But in the final analysis, the prospect for an improving institutional environment for multinational companies depends primarily on the willingness of potential host countries as a matter of national policy to forego voluntarily the exercise of extremes of nationalism. This gives rise to three questions:

1. What particulars should this substantive abnegation take to provide assurance against serious discrimination, confiscation, and unfair government competition?

2. What forms and procedures should be established by the host countries to secure enforcement of their own self-made and self-imposed rules of conduct?

3. To what multilateral outside tribunal will the host countries voluntarily confide jurisdiction to arbitrate or make decisions?

The very statement of these questions suggests that a multilateral effort to answer them collectively at some international round table might be more fruitful than reliance upon individual wisdom. Yet these are questions, particularly significant for the less-developed countries, which were not answered at the recent United Nations Conference on Trade and Development. But these are questions that must be answered satisfactorily if the signatories to the so-called Final Act adopted there are really, in the words of the Preamble to the United Nations Charter, "to employ international machinery for the promotion of the economic and social advancement of all peoples."

In conclusion and by way of summary, coordination between national interests and multinational business with great dividends for freedom and a healthy economic development of the free world would be served by:

Frank recognition that mutual concern for the needs of the other is a prerequisite to temperate, constructive policies by both.

Continued lowering of trade barriers and an enlargement of free trading areas.

Development of national and international monetary policies and machinery that will lessen restraints both on repatriation of profits from host countries and on direct investment from base countries imposed by balance of payments stringencies.

Assiduously avoiding discrimination against foreign corporations both in the conception and in the administration of national business laws conditioning entry or regulating business.

Embodying a high degree of comity in any extraterritorial application by base countries of laws regulating business so as to avoid placing multinational companies in a cross fire of conflicting authority.

In connection with public grant or loan programs, emphasizing more effectively to less-developed countries the truth that multinational business will not risk capital, initiative, and technology in a nation that adheres to a national policy of state confiscation and state competition in certain prescribed areas, further emphasizing the necessity of enforcing self-imposed rules of conduct.

Given these initiatives, the future of the multinational corporation in the free world is a bright one. More important, the future of the free world economy will promise the increasing interdependence that is our best assurance of peace with freedom and a healthy, dynamic economic society.

B. Responsibilities of The Future

The Environment and Corporate Change

38

Theodore J. Gordon

What responses in the nature and form of the corporation, what changes in its rules, may be likely as its environment changes in the decade ahead? For, like other human institutions, it will change, responding to its demanding environment. And the changing environment itself will largely be the product of business, since business produces many of the technological advances which mold the course of society.

Forecasting of this sort is not merely an idle intellectual exercise. It is becoming increasingly apparent that future-directed studies can contribute significantly to the goal-selection process of a free society by stating explicitly potential problems which might lie in our paths and then by testing alternative courses of action which might limit or eliminate these problems. In other words, forecasting can make informed choice possible, and in this age when the time between invention and potential catastrophe is so small, it is essential that the problems and choices be stated as clearly and as early as possible.

The RAND Long Range Forecasting Study resulted in some substantive predictions about possible technological advances and other features of our world which might occur before the middle of the next century. The new world foretold by the study would be characterized by:

Reprinted with permission from the Conference Board *Record* (June 1967) pp. 40–44. Copyright © 1967 the National Industrial Conference Board.

Adapted from a speech before the public affairs conference of The Conference Board in New York City, April 20, 1967. Mr. Gordon is director, Space Stations and Planetary Systems, Douglas Space Center, Huntington Beach, California. He wishes to acknowledge the assistance and criticisms of several colleagues, including: R. D. Stowell, O. Helmer, and A. Anderson. Portions of this article are based on an earlier work of the author, "Future Needs for Engineering Research," presented to the faculty of the Department of Engineering, University of California, Los Angeles.

Automated production techniques and large-scale computers performing tasks of increasing importance.

Expanding population and urbanization.

Sharpening of biological skills.

Possession of weapons of increasing efficiency, but with no cure for war in sight; a world characterized by innovation and social challenge.

Clearly, the RAND study was not exhaustive, yet even this brief glimpse implied the tremendous range of options which will exist in products, methods, and functions of business; the possible consequences of corporate action or inaction; and the various responsibilities which the corporation may assume toward the society it will affect so importantly.

MAKING CHANGES

The technological changes we are witnessing and the social changes which accompany them are penetrating the fiber of our existence. Ours is the age of innovation. Our economy feeds on innovation—devouring new ideas and transforming them into the seeds of national security, or consumer comforts. The forces we command have begun to match those of nature; yet we need more innovation, used effectively and quickly, or we will perish.

Change is the norm, and mainstream developments now in progress will be important to the world order of tomorrow. These include:

The new biology, which offers man for the first time in his history the ability to control his evolution, influence his genetic destiny, and control his health and age absolutely; yet it raises to unflattering visibility his absolute unpreparedness for the task.

Behavior control, by which man will be able to control his fellows with certainty, accuracy, and according to his aims.

Information technologies, which add to our ability to process large amounts of data, to make this data accessible in a number of ways in essentially real time, and to use this data to solve analytical and intellectual problems, but which may, in the process, cause unemployment, corporate restructuring, and social upheavals.

Space enterprises, which by virtue of their scientific and technological challenge, add to our competence in earthbound endeavors, create new heroes and goals for youth, and promise the excitement of the next great exploration.

Population growth, which illustrates the success of man as a species on earth, but threatens in its success to cause calamities with proportions hard to imagine and, because of its dissymmetry, threatens to increase the real and imagined disparities between economies and races.

Internationalism, which marks the shifting tides of political alliances, man's propensity to war and at the same instant his longing for peace, and the emergence of a single culture spanning the world, based on the rapid spread of information and the diffusion of technology.

What can these trends mean to the corporation and its business over the next 50 years? The immersion of the corporation in a new society, "the post-industrial society"; with new values, which Kenneth Boulding calls the super-culture (meaning the unification of cultures through the use of common technology); and with new problems.

FOOD PRODUCTION

Barring a major unforeseen catastrophe, world population will expand to over 6 billion shortly after the turn of the century. Producing food for these people will represent an engineering challenge of the greatest magnitude. New lands will have to be opened to cultivation; lands already under the plow will have to be raised to ultimate productivity. Yet, even if farm acreage increases by 25% and all the world's farmers achieve crop production equivalent to Western European yields in the next 35 years, the world's population will still be as undernourished as today, and a large segment will still exist at only starvation levels. Before this problem is solved, it may be important to devise new means of food production.

But even if we can achieve a food production level which will meet the demands of over 6 billion people, there remains the greatest challenge of all: devising an acceptable social means for its distribution.

UNWANTED LEISURE

Automation brings with it the specter of unemployment. The issue is highly charged and competent economists have forecast either social catastrophe resulting from very widespread unemployment, or labor scarcity in a time of unmatched productivity several decades from now. Both points of view are sometimes supported by the same sets of data. The fact is that either position might be correct; the forecast of whether we have gross unemployment or labor scarcity depends very sensitively on guesses about the growth rate of the Gross National Product, the increase in labor productivity, and the number of people who will be in our working force.

The question is whether the GNP will increase fast enough to absorb both our extra productivity and our increasing work force. A little arithmetic shows that a GNP growth rate of about 4.75% per year would be required to keep unemployment at its current level.

Happily, there is good reason to anticipate a continued long-term growth of our GNP. Economic growth is a bootstrap operation. As production increases, so does affluence and with affluence, the demand for leisure-time services, recreation, transportation, and material possessions.

In addition, our government is likely to continue to undertake large-scale projects designed to press the frontiers of science and demonstrate our technological preeminence. These projects, inevitably, feed back into industry skills born of challenge and exploration. New businesses which will add significantly to our GNP will be conceived: nuclear power; automation itself, which will support a new industry of hardware and softwear suppliers; electric automobiles; education for the masses; transportation; the new biology. All of these and others will stimulate the nation's economic growth.

The scope of services offered by individuals and corporations will expand greatly. In the future, we might expect to see corporations which provide specialized educational services; insurance companies might offer complete medical, dental, psychiatric, and hospital care; housewives might even subscribe to a dietary planning service which would deliver daily balanced menus, tailored to the tastes of the family.

Even if this potential growth is not sufficient to absorb the output of our work force with its growing production capacity, remedial action is possible, including measures which will reduce the effective working force or create new tasks for their labors. Retraining will permit some increased mobility of the labor force and help offset technological unemployment. Shortening of the work week, more and longer vacations, compulsory education past high school, and massive public works projects which might involve cooperation of many governments can absorb the shock of increased productivity.

Some of the anti-unemployment measures which have been suggested will increase leisure time. If GNP continues to grow, this leisure, presumably, need not be accompanied by economic need. The issue would be whether people could endure their "no-work" status.

If our population feels unneeded, unwanted, and frustrated, the conversion to a hedonistic, degenerate leisure will be easy. Indeed, the use of leisure has been posed as the most significant problem facing us in the future, outweighing in importance food production and potential war. Leisure can be a boon to man, or a curse. The choice largely rests with the ingenuity of our planning.

OVER-POPULATION

We can expect to see continuous evolution in the industrialization processes of all countries. Every nation of the world seems to have, as a part of its unwritten national goals, the simple statement, "for all, more." The surest way that it can be implemented is through industrialization and economic growth.

The population expansion of many countries works contrary to this goal. Stated simply, the more people there are, the lower the per capita GNP, at least over a short period of time. Therefore, for nations to realize their goals of productivity clearly, means for limiting population must be discovered and utilized.

Is population expansion a problem which will affect business? Increasing population levels assure increasing numbers of consumers. Thus, a world of expanding population is suited to the concept of expanding corporations.

There is, however, the possibility that a very effective contraceptive might be developed, and population could stabilize quite rapidly. If population were to stabilize, increased markets could be obtained only through planned obsolescence or increased perceived needs, which would increase the rate of durable goods production.

While population is expanding, business has the challenge of producing enough to meet the effective demand, not only in our country, but throughout the world. Food and the implements and services needed to manufacture it, transportation, education, waste disposal, production of raw materials, medicine—all of these will tax production as the world's population grows.

As population expands, there will probably be racial, ethnic, and geopolitical disparities in the rate of acceptance of birth control measures. The population imbalances will intensify differences between economies.

PRESERVING FREEDOM

Science is taking us headlong into a society for which we have only moderate preparation, into a society which has not demanded the innovations it is being handed. Behavior control drugs, electronic stimulation of the cortex, genetic manipulation, bureaucracy made more efficient through automation—all of these may become available to a society not trained to use them. All of these devices can limit individual freedom. All of these can drive us toward the anti-utopias of Orwell's *1984,* or Huxley's *Brave New World,* and the specter is real.

Automation can limit liberty too. It is not inconceivable that all data related to a given individual will be on a data drum, filed neatly under his social security number; records of his birth, all of his grades, his predilections, military service, his employers' recommendations, his tax structure, his fingerprints will all be available for instant recall. Will the citizen in a free society accept this?

STRUCTURAL CHANGES

The technology which bears these changes will also change the way a corporation is structured and functions. First, life in the factory and its headquarters is changing and will change even further as a result of the introduction and use of the new information technologies which place large masses of data at easy reach and almost as it happens. Properly prepared, this data will tell anyone who knows how to ask the amount of plasma in the corporate inventory, the rate of its metabolism, and through feedback with the marketplace, the effectiveness of its energies. The revolution is not only in the increasing sophistication of the tools, but in the sophistication of the users. Information technology is a new medium, and in McLuhanian terms, the medium *is* the message.

A new class of industrial employees—information experts—has already formed which knows how to prepare the machines and the data so that other employees, equally specialized, can get the correct answers to questions they pose. This second level of specialization, the question askers, are specialized because their questions must be tailored to machine knowledge and capacities. These stratifications are forming in operations, technical, marketing, manufacturing, distribution; in fact, throughout all business disciplines. In companies which have rigidly centralized these skills, paths must open to the potential horizontal users, or the unnatural isolation will nullify any advantages which might result from the new medium.

This central reality leads to a conceptual restructuring of the firm. Span of authority can increase because information synthesis is quicker, more precise, and particularized. Increasing span of control results in recentralization, in which top executives can logically reserve for themselves a deeper level of decision-making. Middle management splits; those managers who can, move to the ranks of question askers, others move to data collectors. A new language arises, tuned to the machines: PERT, modeling, gaming, linear programming, minimax, cost benefits; communications between people and between people and machines take place in these terms.

But decisions will still be made by men, perhaps teams of synergistic men with insightful judgment. Machines can present alternatives and probabilities, not certainties. Somewhere, man must still weigh, judge, and bear the responsibility for action. Successful firms will reach their achievements through men of knowledge and courage, at all levels in the organization.

The requirements for labor skills will also change in character as automation progresses. First of all, machines will take over an increasingly large segment of the unskilled tasks. The laborers displaced will have to be retrained or employed in massive public works tasks. Because the information sciences will provide fast feedback from the marketplace, it will not be uncommon for corporations to change products rapidly, and adaptability and versatility of the labor force will therefore become very important.

New tools will also be at hand for matching men to their roles. Psychological tests of increasing accuracy will measure men not only for intelligence, but for inventiveness, authority, creativity, and compatibility with their team members or colleagues. These assessments will be used in making job assignments; promotions; transfer, particularly to remote locations; and retirement candidacy.

The new information devices will also encourage geographic decentralization. Managers might meet with staffs at other locations by closed circuit television. The data systems of all divisions might be linked together in vast information networks. These same information networks could be used to unify the functions of ownership and management. A stockholder of the future might exert management control by plugging his stock certificate-key into the owners' network to participate in real-time corporate voting—sort of an automated board of directors. Automation might return to the owners some of the decision-making reserved today for management.

CORPORATE RESPONSIBILITY

Public problems, such as crime, diminishing privacy, and poverty are apparent today; these, in changing dimensions, and new problems such as leisure and behavior control, will exist tomorrow. What is the responsibility of the firm toward these issues?

For today, and increasingly in the future, the manufacturers and the innovators will maintain the responsibility for their products. This responsibility will extend beyond the safety of foods and drugs or honesty in packaging and labeling; it will include an in-depth understanding of the uses, proper and improper, which can be made of the product, and the effect of those uses. Shoddy products may still be sold, but dangerous products will be controlled. What's more, the definition of dangerous products will be extended beyond food and drugs. Products will be reviewed for potential effects, not on the user alone, but on his progeny or society as a whole. And the extent of governmental control, it seems to me, depends on the measures which industry itself adopts for insuring safety.

Safety will probably be interpreted as more than just the preservation of life and health; it may include value preservation as well. For example, advertising may be required to adhere to certain codes of acceptable behavior control; certain courses of programmed instruction may be subjected to political review; personality control drugs might be analyzed for moral as well as health effects. In the coming age of enlightened productivity, business will carry responsibility for what it sells and how it sells its products.

Marshalling our increasingly available forces to solve increasingly important public problems, in a manner which subordinates political power to public good and yet preserves the spark of creativity and enterprise which has made our economy the greatest in the world—this will be one of the major political and business problems of the next decade.

Finding the means to apply our energies, using the new tools of man's inventiveness, to the humanitarian problems of the coming societies, is at once the challenge and promise of our business future.

Business and Society: Contemporary Issues and National Goals
39
William T. Greenwood

Issues of conflict have arisen between business and society because of out-side pressures from individuals and groups. Most *conspicuous* among pres-sure groups are labor and government. The constant increase in the number and variety of these issues reveals the urgent necessity for resolving them in some systematic and comprehensive manner.

But labor and government are not the only pressure groups interested in the objectives and practices of business. The contemporary scene has pro-duced many other group and individual pressures. This fact is supported by business literature in the decade of the fifties. A survey of business periodicals between 1950 and 1963 reveal over 1,000 articles discussing these issues ex-ternal to the firm. In the majority of these discussions, pro and con positions were presented treating these controversial topics, and the balance of other approaches constituted new trends of thought and action for the business-man. The issue-topics discussed most frequently in the business periodical literature of the past decade are grouped and classified in Table 1. It will be noted that the problems of business size, freedom, competition, profits, profit-sharing, anti-trust actions, and the legitimacy of free-enterprise capital-ism have been treated as major issues of the day in spite of the many de-bates and dissertations on these same issues in prior decades and, in some cases, centuries of time.

The public relations function of business has undergone revolutionary changes in this period. New trends creating corporate images provide sys-tematic guides and controls in coping with external pressures on the firm. This trend developed in response to influences designed to guide the political activities and charitable functions of business. The human relations problems of the businessman have been dominant in the period following World War II, especially in delineating problems and developing methods for their reso-lution in the period of the fifties. The conflict between the individual em-ployee, the firm, and traditional management practices is now waged over the necessity for organizing work around people as opposed to the traditional pattern of people around work.

Other problems of participative versus autocratic leadership and individual versus conformity practices have assumed a position of prominence in the literature. Labor-management issues have been reduced from an infinite

Reprinted with permission from *Issues in Business and Society: Readings and Cases* by William T. Greenwood (First Ed., Boston: Houghton Mifflin Company, 1964) pp. 512-536.

Table 1　Comparison of Contemporary Business and Society Issues with National Goals

Contemporary Issues	National Goals	National Goals Essays
I. Our Free Enterprise Society	I. Goals at Home	I. American Fundamentals
A. Capitalism and Freedom	1. The Individual	1. The Individual
B. Business, Competition, and Government	2. Equality	2. The Democratic Process
C. The Role of Profits	3. The Democratic Process	II. Goals at Home
II. Business and Its Publics	4. Education	3. National Goals in Education
A. Public Relations and the Corporate Image	5. The Arts and Sciences	4. A Great Age for Science
B. The Political Role of the Businessman	6. The Democratic Economy	5. The Quality of American Culture
C. The Problem of Business Giving	7. Economic Growth	6. An Effective and Democratic Organization of the Economy
III. Business and the Individual in Society	8. Technological Change	7. High Employment and Growth in The American Economy
A. Human Relations and Leadership	9. Agriculture	8. Technological Change
B. For Business: Conformity or Individualism	10. Living Conditions	9. Farm Policy for the Sixties
IV. Labor-Management Relationships	11. Health and Welfare	10. Framework for an Urban Society
A. Labor Relations and Collective Bargaining	II. Goals Abroad	11. Meeting Human Needs
B. Management's Employment Responsibilities	12. Helping to Build an Open and Peaceful World	III. The Role of Government
C. Fair Employment Practices	13. The Defense of the Free World	12. The Federal System
V. Ethics, Religion, and Business	14. Disarmament	13. The Public Service
A. Ethical Aspects of Business Practice	15. The United Nations	IV. The World We Seek
B. Business and Religion		14. The United States Role in the World
C. Management Philosophy		15. Foreign Economic Policy and Objectives
VI. Trends Toward a Philosophy of Management		16. A Look Further Ahead
A. Management Rights		
B. Business Objectives		
C. Management Philosophy		
VII. Social Responsibilities of Business		
A. The Social Responsibility Concept		
B. Professional Responsibilties of Power Groups		
C. Responsibilities of the Future		

The American Assembly Goals for Americans, The Report of the President's Commission on National Goals and Chapters Submitted for the Consideration of the Commission (New York: Prentice-Hall, 1960), p. 4.

variety of problems to fundamental underlying issues relating to the success of our collective bargaining system, management's assumption of employment opportunity responsibilities, and external pressures for consideration of fair-employment practices as opposed to arbitrary managerial decisions. These issue have motivated the search for new labor-management relationships to provide harmony and peace in achieving economic and social objectives in society.

Common to the afore-mentioned problems of business with individuals and groups in society have been the questions of morality and ethics in business-mangement practices. Business has been increasingly buffeted by criticisms for its failure to meet the moral-ethical-religious needs of our society and the apparent lack of reconciliation of business goals and philosophies with those of individuals and groups in society. The new developments in all of these areas have created a cumulative pressure for the business firm to reconcile these conflicts in some uniform and consistent way. These pressures have evolved into increasing demands for business creeds and philosophies by which the issues can be resolved. Diverse and unclassified business and man-agement philosophies of the past have contributed little toward a universally applicable systematic approach. Attrition of management prerogatives and rights has demanded a redefinition of conflicting rights. Business objectives have often been exclusive, creating new pressures from outside groups whose objectives come into serious conflict with those of business.

These developments have culminated in the expression of expectations for management in the form of social responsibilities. While yet in the debatable or issue stage, increasing demands have been made for business to equate its powers with social responsibilities in our society. As business managers are forced to take on the role of professional men, their responsibilities will have to be defined in order to provide uniform ethical standards that can be en-forced by the profession.

The traditional goals and practices of the businessman are finally chal-lenged for their limited scope in developing solutions for the economic prob-lems of our age. Business objectives and policies not only fail to assess the international ramifications of our domestic economic issues, but, in many cases, are seriously detrimental to total economic development. Humanitarian, philosophical, religious, and foreign policy problems confront the business-man because his objectives and practices frequently come into conflict with societal goals.

Resolution of these many issues of the 1950's and 1960's is the dominant challenge to business today. The evolution of these issues indicates the need for an over-all solution which must come from a systematic and comprehen-sive set of values, a philosophy that will define universally acceptable objec-tives which, in turn, can be manifested in specific responsibilities for business managers. Such a set of objectives and values might have as its first considera-tion the Goals for Americans defined by President Eisenhower's Commission on National Goals for the 1960's. A comparison of these goals with the issues of the 1950's as found in the survey of business literature for that period are outlined in Table 1.

Fifteen national goals are concisely defined for Americans, eleven for domestic problems and four for foreign issues. The goals are supplemented and amplified in sixteen essays on the relevant points of each. A significant correlation may be noted between the issues of the 1950's and the goals of the 1960's. Because of this correlation, the goals provide an initial means of formulating a more universally applicable structure of business goals, philosophies, and creeds. These national goals will be discussed in the sequential structure of the contemporary issues of business and society.

OUR FREE ENTERPRISE SOCIETY

Among the issues facing business and society during the 50's, the one relating to our free enterprise society is the most fundamental of all. Laissez-faire capitalism is defended on one hand as necessary to maintain political freedoms, achieve our national economic goals, and as a dependable trustee for society by assumption of its professional responsibilities. At the same time, its critics deplore the overprivileged position of management resulting in the loss of social and political values in our democracy. These losses have resulted from the existence and use of excessive power of large business firms and conflicting objectives and practices inherent in the competitive process. The increase in frequency and types of these conflicts relating to our free enterprise society is indicative of underlying issues which have not yet been resolved. For example, the basic concepts of freedom and capitalism or free enterprise have meant different things to different people. These concepts have taken on different meanings at different points of time in the evolution of our capitalistic system, and the failure of business management to understand and to adapt to these changes has further complicated the issue. These problems have been compounded by the increasing role of government at federal, state, and local levels. It is also contended that the underlying cause of the entry of government into these areas of business activity has been the failure of business to develop either the ability or the willingness to resolve them. This failure to meet business responsibilities has created a vacuum into which government and labor have entered to assume these responsibilities to society.

The resolution of these problems may be enhanced by a consideration of the correlated national goals. In this instance, Goal No. 3, The Democratic Process, suggests that the:

> degree of effective liberty available to its people should be the ultimate test for any nation. Democracy is the only means so far devised by which a nation can meet this test.[1]

[1] *Goals for Americans* (New York: Prentice-Hall, 1960), p. 4.

This plea for maximum use of the democratic process provides a guide for business in avoiding the pursuit of objectives and methods that may take the form of rugged individualism and greedy (or unethical) laissez-faire capitalism. These types of business practices have historically led to social-government controls.

Government's regulation of business during the fifties manifests the continuation of increasing social controls. Whether this is due predominantly to irresponsible business practices or excessive government zeal and bureaucratic growth is a moot question. Both business and government should be alerted to their mutual responsibilities. Business must openly recognize and cooperate with legitimate external interest groups and:

> Government participation in the economy should be limited to those instances where it is essential to the national interest and where private individuals or organizations cannot adequately meet the need.[2]

On the other hand, business must recognize that capitalism is only one of many functions and value-goals of our democratic society. It must realize that:

> The Bill of Rights was not designed for corporations; free enterprise is only one fruit of liberty, not its root. Property and business exist for the benefit of individuals and have no inherent rights.[3]

This quotation from Essay No. 1, The Individual, succinctly states the essential relationship of business to the individual and society. A reconsideration of the fundamental concepts defining the relative positions of business and other individuals and groups in society must therefore start with an analysis of the original meaning of these terms.

The inherent complexity of many of the goals of society sometimes leads to positions that appear contradictory. For example, Goal No. 7, Economic Growth, provides directives for the businessman, by saying that:

> The economy should grow at the maximum rate consistent with primary dependence upon free enterprise and the avoidance of market inflation.[1]

Conflicting with these goals are pressures for corporate taxation, government regulations, and policy directives affecting existing concentrations of power under the anti-trust laws. The goal of economic growth also embraces the objective of full employment through the determination of unacceptable unemployment levels ranging between 3.4 and 6 per cent.

Business has much to gain from these national goals in its search for support of its own growth goals. Desirable tax programs, increased depreciation allowances, and minimum interference in the free-market mechanism by

2 *Ibid.*, p. 9.
3 *Ibid.*, p. 52.
4 *Ibid.*, p 10.

governmental activity are sought by both business and the President's Commission. This is qualified to some extent by approval of governmental action where serious imbalances and inequities are incurred in the maximum economic growth quest. Dr. Clark Kerr in his Essay No. 6, An Effective and Democratic Organization of the Economy, states that:

> Governmental action cannot, of course, be called upon to redress all imbalances which are bound to occur from time to time in a dynamic economy. It should be reserved for cases where the imbalance of power is serious and continuing.[5]

Dr. Kerr also desires that:

> The role of government should be restricted to clear cases of national interests which cannot be served by private means, and the government should withdraw whenever its participation is no longer essential—when the particular public need no longer exists or when it can be adequately met by private economic activity.[6]

The latter idea of withdrawal has yet to be successfully voiced by the business community or considered in a general way by government or society. This, therefore, offers an area of potential significance as business attempts to achieve both its economic and social goals in society.

In its maintenance of a free enterprise society, business can greatly enhance the increased freedom of activity in the economic realm by changing its attitude toward the legitimate co-existence of business and government. While much is gained through the exercise of countervailing power, especially by the dominant groups in our society, an admission by business that many government controls and services need not be reserved to the private sector of the economy would be a helpful starting point. Dr. James P. Dixon, Jr., states this position in Essay No. 11, Meeting Human Needs, when he says:

> Society as a whole has two functions. It can develop ways by which people can meet their own needs more readily and fruitfully, and it can develop ways by which society as a whole can meet needs that would otherwise be unmet. There are individuals who will not meet their own needs, and others who cannot.[7]

Business, contrary to the position advocated in this quotation, has generally taken the position that government intervention in meeting social needs in the economic realm is undesirable. When the statements of Dr. Kerr and Dr. Dixon are combined, the legitimacy and desirability of government involvement should be better understood and also advocated by business leaders in our society. In this form of cooperation and collaboration with other groups in society, business not only can more successfully achieve its goals, but also

[5] *Ibid.*, p. 154.
[6] *Ibid.*, p. 160.
[7] *Ibid.*, p. 249.

can reduce animosity held by many groups toward the historical business image of arbitrary power decisions.

Another issue of increasing interest to both the businessman and the President's Commission is the role of profits in our society. Nothing could be more fundamental to the businessman in terms of our free enterprise society than the profit motive. On the other hand, an increasing number of new issues have developed in the past decade concerning the proper role of profits and their rightful distribution. Economic growth goals desire levels of reinvested profits which often negate other claims made upon them, notably those of the stockholder, society via government taxation, and recent labor union claims. More basic than this, profits as the primary incentive and regulator of our economic system have been de-emphasized in recent theory and practice. Theories of satisfactory returns and workable competition have supplanted the classical theory of profit maximization. Many theorists and business managers have voiced alarm at this transition with claims that under-utilization of economic resources must result. Continuing arguments have been maintained by both sides. This contemporary issue is considered in Goal No. 7, Economic Growth, when it is advocated that:

> Public policies, particularly an overhaul of the tax system, including depreciation allowances, should seek to improve the climate for new investment and the balancing of investment with consumption. We should give attention to policies favoring completely new ventures which involve a high degree of risk and growth potential.[8]

New perspectives toward profits are difficult to conceive by the businessman. A further study of this concept within the framework of all national goals may help to illuminate the many facets of the problem and clarify the action that may be taken toward its resolution.

In addition to the changing role of profits in our society, profit-sharing claims have also established a beachhead on the collective bargaining scene. While the rights of labor to share in profits has not been resolved, precedents have been set recently in the American Motors-United Auto Workers contract and in the Kaiser Steel Fontana Plant contract in California. The question of consumer and society interests in profits is also being increasingly voiced today. Added to this is the variety of humanitarian, philosophical, theological, and foreign policy claims for participation by underdeveloped countries in our economic bounties. Both theoretically and pragmatically, the problem has been compounded for the businessman. If business is to reconcile these conflicts, it must first understand the nature of the democratic society within which it operates. The relative priority of the conflicting claims between business and other groups and individuals in society will ultimately be decided through democratic procedures. As Dr. Kerr says in Essay No. 6:

8 *Ibid.*, p. 10.

The problem becomes one of balance, as is always true of the operation of a pluralistic society such as our own. The public objectives which we may select for our economy must be weighted against their cost in the area of individual rights.[9]

BUSINESS AND ITS PUBLICS

Business has historically shown a high degree of personal interest in its public relations functions. These functions have in the past been related particularly to the consumer groups with whom business dealt. In recent years, other groups have increased in size and numbers and have brought pressures of opposition to the goals and objectives sought by business. The broad institutional groups of labor and federal, state, and local governments have been most important in this respect. In dealing with an increasing variety of social and institutional groups, business has been forced to develop a many-faceted image to represent its goals and operating practices to each of them.

In performing the public relations function in the past, business has often been condemned by society for unethical practices that approach manipulation; and society has sought in many cases to bring counteracting pressures. One aspect of this relationship of business to society is considered by Mr. August Heckscher in Essay No. 5, The Quality of American Culture, wherein he states:

> An industrial civilization, brought to the highest point of development, has still to prove that it can nourish and sustain a rich, cultural life. In the case of the United States, it is evident that cultural attainments have not kept pace with improvements in other fields. . . . The ethic of the contemporary economic system emphasizes consumption, with 'happiness' and 'comfort' as the objectives to be sought. The end product seems to be a great mass prepared to listen long hours to the worst of TV or radio and to make our newsstands—with their diet of mediocrity —what they are.[10]

In his concluding remarks, Mr. Heckscher questions the advances of materialism, the type of materialism promoted by business in its public relations programs. He is concerned with the exclusive interest in economic satisfactions and implies responsibility for the considerations of a way of life that will emphasize more the qualities and ideals of our humanity. The degree to which business public relations influence public opinion toward values of a low order to the detriment of higher cultural goals may confront business leadership with new responsibilities in the future. These admonitions of Mr. Heckscher should direct us to the ideals and values that affect our society,

[9] *Ibid.,* p. 159.
[10] *Ibid.,* p. 127.

particularly insofar as business influences them. It would appear that if business is to be successful in dealing with its many publics, it probably will have to consider them in some hierarchical sequence. For example, it could classify them by a) size—international, national, industry, state, community, etc., b) special interests—consumers, suppliers, employees, government, related firms, etc.; and c) philosophies, ideals and values—religious, cultural, economic, political, etc. Based upon these classifications, business could then consider when and where its exclusive pursuit of the profit objective may come into serious conflicts with other societal goals.

The point of greatest conflict for most firms in handling public relations problems is at the community level. Given the highest degree of interdependence between business firms and communities, the pressures upon business and the variety and degree of activities in which business is involved in the community and political life become most significant. Also, the expectations of society for business leadership and support are manifold in these communities. In Goal No. 10, Living Conditions, these expectations are pronounced for the need of private leadership to aid in procuring improved community services and renewal programs. Community interest in industrial development and location are the order of the day and the degree of social and community dependence on industrial and economic growth can only increase these expectations in the future. Goal No. 10 supports this need with a plea for greater industry-municipal cooperation in experimenting with new ideas and programs for community development. This call for business leadership is further emphasized in Essay No. 10, Framework for An Urban Society, wherein it is stated that:

> The goals and means for metropolitan progress include all the proposals in earlier sections, but the key instruments may be outlined: 1. Stronger civic, business, and political leadership at the metropolitan level, willing to accept the need for innovation.[11]

The increasing number of business-society issues found in the business literature testify to the increasing demands being made upon businessmen. With this wave of externally created problems, business is faced with the necessity of making the most delicate decisions as to which claims and groups are both legitimate and deserving of business support. The legitimacy of the activities of these interest groups in our society is established for us by Mr. Rossiter in Essay No. 2, The Democratic Process, wherein he says:

> This leads us naturally to consider the thousands of interest groups, no less fondly as pressure groups or lobbies, and more fondly as civic groups, that form one of the continuing wonders of American life. Whatever we call these groups, we are aware that they swing a sizable amount of persuasive power over the men who make and execute policy in all

[11] *Ibid.*, p. 243.

governments in all parts of the land, and that the democratic process would be very different without them. They do not have a high standing in the mythology of American democracy. Indeed, they are often represented as the worst enemies of democracy. Yet they are natural products of an open, plural, energetic society, serving effectively to institutionalize two of our most precious liberties: freedom of association, and the right of petition. They, like the parties, can be no better, no more honest, no more broad-minded than the men who direct or support them. Laws that seek to regulate them can reach only a small way; most hopes for cleansing their methods and raising their sights begin and end with educating the active citizenry.

The one large objection that we might keep in view as we strive to make the interest groups a healthier feature of American democracy is to give them a broader, more democratic character to the influence they exert. The serious doubts we have about these groups arise out of contemplation of their purposes as well as of their methods. Too many of them have too much energy to burn, money to spend, and thus influence to peddle in behalf of highly special and selfish interests. What the democratic process needs is the strengthening of existing organizations (and perhaps creation of new ones) that are broad rather than narrow in scope, general rather than particular in interest, public rather than private in operation.[12]

If the businessman is given this fuller perspective of the legitimacy, and even the necessity, of these conflicting interest and pressure groups, he should be better able to adapt himself to his environment and resolve these conflicts with opposing interest groups.

Of the number of increasing roles assumed by the businessman in society today, his role as a political leader in the community is probably the most controversial. Specific political activities are prohibited the businessman by law, such as contrbutions to particular political organizations. On the other hand, business is compelled with a high degree of responsibility to represent the legitimate interests of its stockholders, business, industry, and free-enterprise system. Conflicting with these responsibilities are claims made by opposing power, pressure, and interest groups. Beyond protecting his own individual interests, he also assumes a leadership role, particularly in the community in which he operates. This leadership role often takes the form of active public service as has been exemplified for us by many business leaders assuming these roles at great personal sacrifice, the best example being the position of Secretary of Defense in our national government. This participation by businessman is not only desirable for business as an institution in society, but also contributes to an ideal representation, a goal advocated by Mr. Wallace S. Sayre in Essay No. 13, The Public Service. Mr. Sayre's concern includes a fair share of our nation's skills and talents at all levels of government.

[12] *Ibid.,* p. 71.

One of the most significant claims of the various pressure and interest groups is for contributions to a variety of community, charitable, and philanthropic causes. Unfortunately, business has yet to formulate an effective philosophy and policies for systematically handling these requests, and in most cases adapts itself to the relative degrees of pressure and influence forced upon it. One area of increasing demand is the appeal for funds for education, particularly private higher education, in our society. In addition to these private requests, Goal No. 4, Education, recommends that

> Greater resources—private, corporate, municipal, state, and federal—must be mobilized. A higher proportion of the gross national product must be devoted to educational purposes. This is at once an investment in the individual, in the democratic process, in the growth of the economy, and in the stature of the United States.[13]

It is further stated that not only should greater proportions be devoted to this purpose, but that for business these contributions should be doubled by the year 1970. (Essay No. 3, National Goals in Education, by John W. Gardner.)

A consideration of these goals and essays offers the individual businessman an opportunity to gain a wider perspective of his public relations problems and to more effectively relate himself to these publics. By anticipating the expectations of the pressure-interest groups in the future, business is forewarned and should be able to accomplish a more effective job of public relations by relating its objectives to broad national goals, particularly those strongly advocated by the most significant groups in society.

BUSINESS AND THE INDIVIDUAL IN SOCIETY

Interest in the relationship of business to the individual in society has shown a dramatic increase since the end of World War II. This interest has been primarily in the consideration of human relations problems, types of managerial leadership, and the effects of these two activities on the controversial position of individualism and conformity within business organizations. These problems have caused a debate over ends and means within the business firm and economic system in ascertaining the sources and limits of managerial rights and responsibilities as they operate toward business or individual goals. The President's Commission on National Goals puts the position of the individual in context in the introduction to its report when it states:

> The paramount goal of the United States was set long ago. It is to guard the rights of the individual, to insure his development, and to enlarge his opportunity. It is set forth in the Declaration of Independence drafted by Thomas Jefferson and adopted by the Continental Congress on July 4, 1776. The goals we here identify are within the framework of the orig-

[13] *Ibid.*, p. 6.

inal plan and are calculated to bring to fruition the dreams of the men who laid the foundation of this country.[14]

The human relations problem is also considered in Essay No. 11, Meeting Human Needs, by Dr. James P. Dixon, Jr.:

> We have a strong desire to help persons in need. We believe that the individual is central to our society, that the principal asset of human society is human life itself, and that society must therefore help to protect the lives and interests of every individual. . . .
> At the same time, deep conviction that the individual and his productivity are basic to our free society makes us reluctant to meet human needs in a fashion which might reduce individual initiative and self-reliance.[15]

If management perceives the individual as does the Commission on National Goals, that is, central and primary to our whole society, it is highly questionable whether improper human relations practices would be as likely to occur. In fact, it is questionable whether the findings of recent behavioral science studies relevant to leadership and conflicts between the individual and business organizations would have been necessary to bring these problems to the attention of business managers. Instead, those problems which seriously conflict with the basic aims and goals of the individual in our society would have been detected and resolved at much earlier dates. A philosophical consideration of the rights of the individual within the full context of society including the free enterprise system should mitigate the tensions and conflicts now researched in such great detail by these behavioral scientists.

The broad view of business-individual-society relations is considered in Goal No. 6, The Democratic Economy, by emphasizing freedom for individuals in the economic realm. A high priority is implicitly assigned to this goal when the responsibility for adaptation is placed on our economic system in making necessary adjustments to the needs of our political system. The relative importance of political and individual as opposed to economic rights is elaborated on by Mr. Henry M. Wriston in Essay No. 1, The Individual.

> The economic argument is not primary, but it is exceedingly strong. Endless talk of the need for capital and machinery obscures the far more vital need for brains. To promote economic growth, it is necessary to think not only in terms of what the federal government can do or what private capital can do, not merely in terms of law and regulation and investment. Far more vital is the development and exploitation of the innate capacities of people to the fullest degree. The most severe limitations upon the expansion of the economy are deficiency and rigidity in the skills of the work force.[16]

[14] *Ibid.*, p. 1.
[15] *Ibid.*, p. 249.
[16] *Ibid.*, pp. 53, 54.

The effect of this interpretation is to add a new dimension to the role of business leadership in a democratic society. This position has also been increasingly taken in recent business literature wherein the preferable types of managerial leadership are discussed. Mr. Wriston on this subject decries the pattern of centralized autocratic leadership and recommends instead a more democratic distribution of management decision making and leadership. These considerations of the type of leadership that management must adopt in the individual firm and in the total economic system should provide strong guides toward the elimination of autocratic types of leadership: leadership in which arbitrary decisions result in inequitable effects on individuals within the organization. The whole question of leadership relates to the problem of conformity and the opposing degree of individualism sought by personalities within business organizations. Given the image of the organization man and the research findings of behavioral scientists revealing serious conflicts between the individual and the organizational structure-authority system, business is hard-pressed to reconcile these two opposing goals in a balanced and mutually satisfactory way. The question is, what is the acceptable degree of conformity necessary within a business organization to meet its goals and policies, as opposed to the social and political mandate for the highest degree of individualism? As Mr. Wriston says in Essay No. 1:

> A business corporation may become so bureaucratized that only an 'organization man' can survive. Corporate policy may oppose taking 'controversial' positions on public questions or actively participating in a political party, particularly one not favored by the management. In dozens of intangible ways it may restrict freedom. All sorts of devices, even including 'benefits,' may reduce the mobility of the individual, and virtually tie him to his place of occupation. The tendency of every organization to eat up its members is perennial and must be fought every step of the way.[17]

It is noteworthy to recognize that Goal No. 1, At Home, as established by the President's Commission is "The Individual." This goal initially states that:

> The status of the individual must remain our primary concern. All our institutions—political, social, and economic—must further enhance the dignity of the citizen, promote the maximum development of his capabilities, stimulate their responsible exercise, and widen the range and effectiveness of opportunities for individual choice.[18]

If business is to effectively synthesize and apply the findings of the behavioral scientists to human relations problems within the business organization, it must also consider the correlation of these findings with the goals defined for our nation and the philosophical principles underlying them.

[17] *Ibid.*, p. 52.
[18] *Ibid.*, p. 3.

Given the mandate from society for an efficient utilization of the economic responsibility for allocation of resources in a free society, business must meet this mandate through efficient and effective operations in meeting both the needs of individual firms and the ever-changing needs of our pluralistic society. This means that while the problems of democratic participation of the individuals in the economic sphere are severely limited in terms of their frequent incompatibility with the achievement of the prime mandate of economic and efficient production goals, there must nevertheless be the over-riding consideration of the individual and the democratic process in the daily routine of business operations. One of the best means of adopting objectives and policies that will reduce the conflicts between the individual and the organization is to relate the organization to broader national, social, and individual goals whereby a higher degree of harmony and equitable balance of these goals can be achieved by the various competing claimants.

LABOR-MANAGEMENT RELATIONSHIPS

The best-known conflict area of business and society is that of labor-management relationships. With the legislatively established institutions of union recognition and collective bargaining, labor and management are engaged in a continuous power struggle for the achievement of their respective goals. Today this problem has taken on new emphasis because of strikes, featherbedding practices, and the relative inability of labor and management to resolve their differences without serious adverse effects on society. The emergence of government as a final arbitrator through increasing legislation and regulations raises the serious question of the maintenance of the desired freedom in the resolution of these conflicts. Goal No. 6, The Democratic Economy, recommends that:

> Collectve bargaining between the representatives of workers and employers should continue as the nation's chief method for determining wages and working conditions.
>
> Conferences among management, union leaders, and representatives of the public can contribute to mutual understanding of problems that affect the welfare of the economy as a whole.
>
> Corporations and labor unions must limit the influence they exert on the private lives of their members. Unions must continue to develop adequate grievance procedures and greater opportunities for legitimate opposition. Professional organizations and trade associations should conduct their affairs on a democratic basis.[19]

Collective bargaining agreements have affected the competitive position of American business abroad, a fact which has been cited repeatedly in our daily press. The effect of these agreements on total national growth is also

[19] *Ibid.*, p. 9.

cited in the concluding notes for the national goals. In order to avoid these undesirable effects, business must develop a broader perspective of the collective bargaining process—a societal perspective. This perspective reveals initially a high degree of interrelationships between these groups. This interrelationship in turn can be interpreted as interdependencies between the institutional forces of business, labor, government, and society. It makes all the more pressing the consideration of the need for governmental participation, mediation, and, if necessary, arbitration to resolve these conflicts which seriously affect the national interests. At the same time, the overriding consideration of resolving these conflicts freely rather than arbitrarily by some governmental body evoked the following statement by Dr. Clark Kerr in Essay No. 6, An Effective and Democratic Organization of the Economy:

> In the area of national emergency strikes, the government might enter earlier into potentially difficult situations and play a more aggressive role in making settlement proposals, but collective bargaining still works best when it is left to the parties. Compulsory arbitration leads automatically to wage-fixing, as in Australia. And the Australian situation also indicates that it is very difficult, in a democracy, to make such arbitration really compulsory. There are several alternative courses to compulsory arbitration, including different degrees of mediation and a fact-finding and voluntary arbitration. Experience has shown that it is better to have several such courses of action available, to be chosen in accordance with the situation, rather than to rely on a single rigid course of action. The greater use of independent third parties to assist in collective bargaining, for example, has been helpful in several instances when major changes and rules and arrangements were involved.[20]

Foremost among labor-management issues today is the problem of job security, levels of unemployment, and, implicitly, the employment responsibilities of our economy in general and of individual firms in particular. With the present rate of technological advance, displacements of personnel, persistent levels of unemployment, and the view of business from the trustee concept of serving society in providing employment opportunities, serious consideration must be forthcoming for achieving these goals of job security in the present and in the future. Dr. Clark Kerr in Essay No. 6 explains this in these terms:

> A concept of public responsibility for the effectiveness of the economic organization was gradually taking shape. This concept received perhaps its most conscious and formal recognition in the Employment Act of 1946. The act set forth 'the continuing policy and responsibility of the federal government' as follows: 'to coordinate and utilize all its plans, functions and resources for the purpose of creating and maintaining in a manner calculated to foster and promote free competitive enterprise and the general welfare, conditions under which there will be afforded

[20] *Ibid.*, p. 161.

useful employment opportunities, including self-employment, for those able, willing and seeking work, and to promote maximum employment, production and purchasing power.[21]

Other statements are made in the national goals essays supporting this position. For example, Dr. James P. Dixon, Jr. points out the fact that unemployment insurance is not the answer to the problem, but rather, more jobs (Essay No. 11, Meeting Human Needs). Also in Essay No. 8, Technological Change, Mr. Thomas J. Watson, Jr. indicates an increasing acceptance of responsibility for full employment by the American businessman.

The causes of unemployment are difficult to enumerate and assess, and the variety of corrective actions which can be taken too easily allow for shifting of the responsibility. The effects of the problem resulting from technological developments and persistent unemployment levels in particular industries and regions of our country emphasize a shifting downward of the responsibility from the national levels to particular industries, areas, and individual firms. A hope for the future may be contained in the remarks of Mr. Warren Weaver in Essay No. 4, A Great Age for Science, when he says:

> An energetic development of science is absolutely essential to the continuing flow of new knowledge which leads to new inventions, new materials, new procedures, new industries, new opportunities for employment, and, in total, to a sound and vigorous economy. . . .
> Rather spectacular evidence may be found by observing that the rapidly developing portion of our economy—one could even say the fast-moving stocks on the exchange—are those based upon relatively new scientific advances, such as in solid state physics, (transistors, etc.), electronics, computors, and automation, etc.[22]

The consideration of these national goals should help to provide some guidelines and portents of the future for management in meeting these increasing employment responsibilities.

Another contemporary problem of labor-management relationships has been created by the efforts of unions and governmental bodies to offset management's arbitrary decisions affecting individual personnel. When these arbitrary decisions take on the form of discrimination in terms of race, color, creed, and other nonessential reasons, grievances often blossom into widespread movements resulting in such activities as governmental legislation for fair employment-practices commissions. As stated in Goal No, 2. Equality:

> Vestiges of religious prejudice, handicaps to women, and, most important, discrimination on the basis of race must be recognized as morally wrong, economically wasteful, and in many respects dangerous. In this decade we must sharply lower these last stubborn barriers. . . .

[21] *Ibid.*, p. 158.
[22] *Ibid.*, pp. 112, 113.

Respect for the individual means respect for every individual. Every man and woman must have equal rights before the law, and an equal opportunity to vote and hold office, to be educated, to get a job, and to be promoted when qualified, to buy a home, to participate fully in community affairs. These goals, which are at the core of our system, must be achieved by action at all levels.[23]

This responsibility harks back to the type of managerial leadership employed to develop and utilize human potentials to the fullest. A failure to maximize this potential not only affects individuals and minority groups, but also is a waste of manpower resources and skills needed for productivity goals (Goal No. 5, The Arts and Sciences). Dr. Clark Kerr also emphasizes the importance of failing to provide the "equality of opportunity" through discriminatory practices because of its negative effects on the basic nature of the economic process. Mr. George Meany of the AFL-CIO expresses his disappointment at the failure of the President's Commission to support a national fair employment-practices law which would complement state and local laws of the same type. These citations not only serve to establish goals for the businessman, but also establish the fact that they can be best achieved within the traditions of our free enterprise society through responsible and perfectly legitimate management and governmental actions. They establish specific goals for the consideration of the businessman and enhance the reasonable expectations that these goals may be achieved with due regard for freedom of all groups and individuals operating within our capitalistic system.

ETHICS, RELIGION AND BUSINESS

Business has in recent years been condemned for unethical practices such as price-fixing, sweetheart contracts, business espionage, and particularly for misleading and untruthful public relations practices. The role of business in our free-enterprise society has even been cited in some cases as a moral failure. Some go further and say that it is inherently in contradiction to the religious, ethical, and moral principles of our society. From all of these contentions, one fact is made clear: business faces the problem of developing an ethic compatible and operative with the many ethics in society. Given the community ethic, the Judaeo-Christian ethic, the Ten Commandments, and the Golden Rule, many tenets are found common to all of these, but there is nevertheless extreme difficulty in making applications of their principles in specific business conflict situations. Goal No. 2, Equality, emphasizes the moral wrong involved in religious and racial prejudice, for example, and for other arbitrary practices that create serious inequities for individuals and groups in our society.

The question of ethics for business, or any other group in society, readily

---

23 *Ibid.,* pp. 3, 4.

evolves into a question of its identification with a given religion or set of values. Since religions are the major value-forming institutions in our society, any set of values to be used for the determination of right and wrong moral actions will probably find some identification with particular religious ethics. While businessmen face the difficulty of relating business to religious principles, it is nevertheless recommended that they draw upon this framework in order to establish their own individual ethics that will provide guides for their contacts with the many groups in society. The businessman has been challenged in the literature to effectively relate the meaning and significance of work to spiritual principles in order to enhance the dignity and self-fulfillment of the men involved in the enterprise. This is further supported by Essay No. 1, The Individual, wherein Henry M. Wriston says:

> This goal touches the foundations of democracy. From the first it was realized that popular government required an educated citizenry. The declaration in the Northwest Ordinance of 1787 is classic: 'Religion, morality, and knowledge being necessary to good government and the happiness of mankind, schools and the means of education shall forever be encouraged.' What was necessary then is doubly essential today.[24]

In the concluding remarks on the National Goals, it is stated that:

> The very deepest goals for Americans relate to the spiritual health of our people. The right of every individual to seek God in the well springs of truth, each in his own way, is infinitely precious. . . .
> Our faith is that man lives, not by bread alone, but by self-respect, by regard for other men, by convictions of right and wrong, by strong re-religious faith.[25]

In order to effectively relate the goals, policies, and operations of a business enterprise to those higher values held by our society, the businessman must first reach the conviction of Mr. Wriston that:

> Dignity does not derive from a man's economic situation, nor from his vocation. It does not require a white-collar job or any other status symbol. It rests exclusively upon the lively faith that individuals are beings of infinite value.[26]

Business is therefore pressed to re-examine its goals, policies, and operations in light of existing ethical and religious values in our society. This should include consideration of those components of a value system that result from the conviction that:

[24] *Ibid.*, p. 53.
[25] *Ibid.*, pp. 22, 23.
[26] *Ibid.*, p. 49.

The humanities, the social sciences, and the natural sciences, all are essential for a rounded, cultural life. Literature and history are vital to understanding, the capacity to feel and communicate, to a sense of values.[27]

Given the relationship between the objectives and goals of business and the broader objectives and goals emphasized in our present-day society, business is provided with the means of establishing a more comprehensive code of ethics with which it can contribute to the development of a profession for its managers. In turn, this profession can develop and implement a philosophy which will be comprehensive enough to effectively relate the whole system of business to the broader system of society.

TRENDS TOWARD A PHILOSOPHY OF MANAGEMENT

The persistently increasing number of issues and conflicts between business and society has been attributed to the many individual and group interests that relate significantly to business. By identifying the most important value-goals of these groups and individuals, the seriousness of these conflicts is indicated by their ethical and religious implications. The great variety of, and degree of differences between, these issues requires the formulation of a comprehensive approach with a more universal application, a new philosophy for business-management and society. This philosophy will serve to reconcile the conflicts of rights, identify and relate the respective objectives, and, in the process of its formulation, identify those factors integral to a philosophy for business management. It will serve as a framework for the professionalization of business managers, and will provide a type of professional leadership that can give a positive orientation to the consideration of these problems.

Most areas of conflict, when reduced to their essential features, relate to the rights of the individuals and groups concerned. Business has historically regarded its prerogatives as exclusive and unilateral. The exercise of the private-property right by business is certainly a legitimate right to be protected by our society. On the other hand, these rights come into increasing conflict, particularly with the institutional power group of labor. With the significant attrition of traditional management prerogatives through the collective bargaining process, management is now hard pressed to arrest this trend by a well-reasoned and documented statement of its necessary and legitimate rights.

The opposition of labor and other groups in society to the arbitrary use of managerial prerogatives is supported in Goal No. 3, The Democratic Process, wherein it is stated that:

27 *Ibid.,* p. 8.

Private interest groups exemplify the rights of assembly and petition. Thus, the functioning of pressure groups of many kinds has become a part of our democratic process. Special interest groups must operate legitimately. The program of any particular group can be opposed most effectively by the formation of a counter group. There is need for more which represent broader interests such as consumers and taxpayers.[28]

To put the issue into a fuller context, Mr. Wriston in Essay No. 1, The Individual, states that:

Each person has both particular and general interests, individual wants and social needs. When the general interest is over accentuated, freedom declines and may disappear; first controls, then paternalism supervene. On the other hand, if individual interests utterly neglect social needs, anarchy is the end result. The consequence of either extreme is loss of liberty.[29]

The rights of management, labor, and all individuals and groups in society find their legal source in the Constitution of the United States, but prerequisite to its adoption was the promise of a Bill of Rights to protect the individual. This Bill of Rights amplified in principle form the basic rights of life, liberty, and the pursuit of happiness initially considered in the Declaration of Independence. If management is to delineate its rights, particularly on those issue areas wherein their rights come into conflict with those of labor or other individuals or groups in society, it must go back to these basic documents to establish a priority of rights. Quite often the rights with which management is most concerned are those that have been traditionally regarded as managerial prerogatives over time, in light of the accepted objectives sought by the business firm. In this respect, the dependability and applicability of these rights will relate to the legitimacy of the objectives which they seek to achieve.

There is probably no greater or more significant point of conflict between business and society than the debate over the purpose and objectives of business itself. Classical economic theory advocating profit maximazation comes into conflict with the new concept of economics emphasizing social responsibility and satisfactory profits. A study of business in America reveals a tremendous variety of goals sought by business firms and a pattern of both similarities and differences in terms of the priority of these goals. Unquestionably, the goal of profits has been paramount in most cases. On the other hand, the new philosophy is quoted by an increasing number of writers relegating profits to a satisfactory level in order to achieve a more equitable allocation of earnings to other individuals and groups in society. It is precisely at this point that the National Goals defined by the President's Commission appear to have their greatest application as an aid in the resolution of

---

[28] *Ibid.*, p. 5.
[29] *Ibid.*, p. 48.

business-society conflicts. If business will relate the goals which it has traditionally sought to these national goals, the opportunity will be created for achieving maximum collaboration and equity with society. This should result in some redefinition of their goals and respective priorities on the part of business managers. Dr. Clark Kerr provides an interrelationship of these goals in Essay No. 6 when he says:

> In today's world, our economic system must continue to serve the individual directly by providing opportunities for his material well being and advancement. But this alone is not enough. Our economy must also serve the individual indirectly by enabling the nation to meet such challenges as the maintenance of an adequate, diversified, enormously expensive defense system; the acceptance of broad responsibility in the area of international cooperation, including especially assistance to under-developed counties; the maintenance and expansion of an educational system far greater in scope and quality than ever before envisioned, to meet the demands of the modern world; the provision of public services required by rapid and extensive urbanization and by rising standards regarding the minimum requirements of life in a civilized community—in short, the whole range of endeavors suggested throughout this volume as essential steps toward the continuing fulfillment of our basic national purpose.[30]

The effects of not working for these public as well as individual business goals are also described by Dr. Kerr when he says:

> The present economic process, developed over the decades after so much discussion, is geared to maximizing the freedom of individuals and private groups to make their own decisions. But these decisions have yielded depressions in earlier years and in recent years constant inflation, not stability; moderate rates of growth, not forced draft advances; strikes, not uniform industrial peace; additional durable consumer goods more readily than a new school, a new park, a new concert hall; an apparent sense of purposelessness, instead of visible public objectives.[31]

To make business goals both legitimate and more meaningful, they can be related to these other goals in society, giving mutual achievement and satisfaction to the groups and individuals concerned. For example, Thomas J. Watson, Jr., recommends in Essay No. 8, Technological Change, three basic national goals in the technological area.

> Technological change should be used to improve men's lives. . . . Technological change should be encouraged to meet our own increasing industrial needs, to stimulate our social and economic progress, and to face successfully the long-term challenge of international communism. Technological knowledge should be shared so that people throughout

30 *Ibid.*, p. 150.
31 *Ibid.*, p. 158.

the world, particularly in the under-developed nation countries, may improve their lives and benefit from up-to-date technology.[32]

A study in depth relating business and national goals can contribute also to the formulation of a philosophy which will have a mutuality of application to individuals, groups, and business in our society. Looking at perhaps the most fundamental conflict between business and society, that of the individual exercise of the private property right as opposed to individual and group liberties in our society, we detect a significant trend of judiciary decisions and executive policy statements supporting liberty when these rights come into conflict. But with the variety of goals and conflicts in our society, Messrs. Stein, and Denison, in Essay No. 7, High Employment and Growth in the American Economy, explain that:

> There is a limit to the number of goals that the American people or any people can pursue, the number of crusades they can engage in. There is a limit to our supply of leadership for 'pointing the way' and to the supply of attention and followership. In this sense, any goals proposed at the expense of others that are or might have been advanced, and the cost of elevating accelerated economic growth to the front rank of goals is that something else is deprived of that position. . . .
> There may be value in having a 'national goal' aside from the benefits of achieving any particular goal and almost without regard to what the goal is. The goal may be inspiring, give 'point' to life, and serve as a common bond holding the society together. This may be a benefit even though at the present stage of history a psychological need would be better served by a goal less materialistic and less parochial than the growth of the American economy.[33]

In the discussion of business-society issues and conflicts today, the end result most often sought is a recommendation for the definition and acceptance of greater social responsibilities on the part of the businessman. Therefore, the definition and implementation of a comprehensive philosophy for business management to effectively relate itself to its society will inherently contain a definition of business rights and duties, the latter now referred to as social responsibilities.

SOCIAL RESPONSIBILITIES OF BUSINESS

While discussion of social responsibilities for business managers has increased tremendously in the literature and at the dinner table in our society, the concept nevertheless remains a very controversial one. One point of view would reassign to business the economic function with profit orientation as its sole goal. Classical economic theory claims that the maximum allocation

[32] *Ibid.*, p. 196.
[33] *Ibid.*, p. 190.

of resources, and therefore maximum benefit to society, will be achieved by following this goal exclusively. A resolution of this debate might be enhanced by recommendations made by the President's Commission on National Goals. For example, Dr. Clark Kerr in Essay No. 6, says:

> Industrialization has brought the individual rich benefits in health, material goods, and the leisure and means important to individual fulfillment. But it has also created large and powerful private organizations whose influence over the individual gives rise to new and often subtle questions of democratic procedure. And it has made individuals increasingly interdependent in many spheres. The economic success or failure of an individual or a private group today may depend upon or may affect many others. The complexities and costs of many desirable projects are completely beyond the scope of private individuals. Industrialization is resulting in new concepts of public responsibility and of public endeavors.[34]

The axiom that responsibility must always equal the degree of power in our socety also finds application to this issue. Mr. Clinton Rossiter, in Essay No. 2, The Democratic Process, says:

> This fact of power puts a new strain on all Americans, but especially on those who hold public responsibilities. . . . the men to whom we assign control of our finances, public services, and schools, of our factories, fields, and facilities of transportation. They, too, hold far too much power over the lives of other men ot be exempted from the growing demand for decision-makers and administrators who are first of all mature and prudent. What we might call the 'imperative of responsibility' must pervade and stiffen the whole spirit of democracy.[35]

Control of power, individuals, and groups in society has been provided in our democratic system by the development of checks and balances within the political system. Business power has been checked particularly by organized labor, but much more so by social controls at all levels of government. Dr. Clark Kerr warns against failures of existing checks and balances to control collusion of these power centers, for example, business and labor in the collective bargaining process. Collusion has also been found between institutional power groups, as well as within them. The effects of these practices have been to pass on to society the unnecessary, often illegal, and certainly unethical costs that defeat the achievements of our free enterprise society; the most efficient allocation and utilization of resources.

If business management is to professionalize its role in society, it must formulate in great detail its social responsibilities. This is particularly applicable to those areas where large degrees of power and interdependence exist between industries, business firms, individuals, and groups in the local or

---

[34] *Ibid.,* p. 150.
[35] *Ibid.,* p. 76.

even international community. Commitment on the part of professionalized management groups to the achievement of corporate, economic AND broader national goals of our society-economy should and can enhance business' position in both the short and long run. Relating business to society, particularly from the standpoint of the public relations function, has typically been to consider those societies upon whom business depends, such as customers, stockholders, and employees. Of late there has been an increasing trend toward recognizing other publics because of increasing degrees of interdependent relationships with supplier firms, service industries, etc. This trend, in many instances, has reached the point where giant corporations have assumed responsibilities not normally considered within the baliwick of traditional business functions. This has applied, for example, in situations where either extensive international operations or degrees of monopolistic control over skills and capital resources affecting other nations in the world made the assumption of these responsibilities both desirable and, in some instances, necessary.

It is significant to note that a recent consensus of fifty of the world's top thinkers revealed an almost unanimous conclusion that the prime problem facing America in the next twenty years is that of assisting the under-developed nations to emerge as free, strong, democratic societies. They also cited the national problems of inflation and full employment.[36] There is a comparable priority assigned in the goals cited by the President's Commission wherein 4 of the 15 goals established for Americans for the decade of the 1960's relate to activities abroad. These goals provide for assisting the underdeveloped countries, defending the free world, achieving disarmament, and supporting the United Nations. In the introduction to these "goals abroad" it is stated:

> The basic foreign policy of the United States should be the preservation of its own independence and free institutions. Our position before the world should be neither defensive nor belligerent. We should cooperate with the nations whose ideals and interests are in harmony with ours. We should seek to mitigate tensions, and search for acceptable areas of accommodation with opponents. The safe-guarded reduction of armaments is an essential goal.[37]

The types of assistance recommended by the Commission reveal an overwhelming emphasis upon trade rather than aid. Starting with the premise that a free-world economy will also be the healthiest economy, appeals are made for systematic tariff reductions to preserve a vital national economy (Goal No. 12, Helping to Build an Open and Peaceful World). These actions would be accompanied by similar support fror other healthy free-world

[36] "The Next Twenty Years," *Fortune* (January 1958), pp. 110–111, 188–191.
[37] *Goals for Americans, op. cit.,* p. 15.

nations for the purpose of creating strong and free nation-economies in the under-developed countries.

Mr. John J. McCloy in Essay No. 15, Foreign Economic Policy and Objectives, establishes the primary principle upon which these international goals are based. Since our country has been the dominant world exporter of industrial goods and since we depend significantly upon critical materials and other goods as the major world importer, an inherent economic interdependency has been created. This interdependency is increasing rather than decreasing, and, therefore, a philosophy of mutual rights and duties in the international political economy is required to regulate these relationships. This interdependency between our country and other nations in the world, politically, economically, etc., creates a uniformity of interests and goals that can be best understood through the common denominator of all human beings and societies throughout the world. The difficulty for the businessman is in establishing the relative degree of legitimate interdependency when claims are made upon business for support and in the resolution of conflicts that are occurring increasingly between business and other groups. In support of this basic common denominator, Mr. McCloy tells us that:

> At the same time there is in the American character a broad streak of humanitarianism, an instinct of generosity toward those who are less fortunate. If for no other reason than that it is in keeping with our ingrained habits and values, we are bound to come to the aid of peoples in the less-developed lands.[38]

Mr. McCloy refers us to some specific actions and considerations when he explains the relationship and justification for economic assistance to the less-developed lands. He says:

> In the highly industrialized states, economic advance is so rapid that the standard of living may rise 100 per cent within a generation. The tendency therefore is for the gap in living standards between the industrialized and the under-developed regions to widen rather than narrow. . . . The United States, with the highest standard of living ever attained by mankind, cannot safely shirk a leading role in making available to the economically under-developed nations the benefits of the industrial and technological revolutions. In the interests of its own peace and progress it must assume a heavy burden, for it cannot hope to prosper in isolation. Its goals must be the creation of a world order compatible with American traditions as well as with American interests in security, one in which all nations will have a reasonable opportunity for economic progress and social well-being.[39]

38 *Ibid.*, p. 343.
39 *Ibid.*, p. 317.

American interests in security referred to by Mr. McCloy are made evident by the dominant expenditures in the U.S. national budget—appropriations for national defense. The twentieth century has negated the concept of isolationism. It is economically and militarily unfeasible and also immoral, according to most moral and religious ethics in American society. Therefore Goal No. 13, The Defense of the Free World, develops our responsibilities in the world order by making recommendations for counter-measures to meet the Soviet and Communist China threats. This goal asks for continuing support for military alliances and also for programs that may ultimately achieve independence for countries now subject to communist influence and domination.

If the variety and significance of goals already cited to this point have not convinced the individual businessman, Goal No. 14 on Disarmament should be considered. This goal contends that:

> Since a major nuclear war would be a world catastrophe, the limitation and control of nuclear armament is imperative. Disarmament should be our ultimate goal. It cannot be attained without eliminating the sources of distrust and fear among nations. Hence, our immediate task must be the step-by-step advance toward control of nuclear weapons and their means of delivery, with effective international inspection.[40]

Concomitant with the achievement of disarmament is the support of the organization through which its accomplishment must come. Goal No. 15, The United Nations, recommends that:

> A key goal in the pursuit of a vigorous and effective United States foreign policy is the preservation and strengthening of the United Nations. Over the next decade, it will be under tremendous strain. However, it remains the chief instrument available for building a genuine community of nations.[41]

While it may not be expected that all of these national goals will be achieved simultaneously or to the degree which is believed desirable by the President's Commission, it is nevertheless inconceivable to move in any direction other than toward their achievement. The greatest contribution of the national goals may rest in their consideration by the United States businessman in order to see in total perspective the many conflicting values, goals, interests, and pressures that are legitimately sought by individuals and groups in the American and world societies. In summary, the individual businessman must widen his perspective in considering his goals and practices in a free enterprise society. This perspective must include a recognition of the many goal-seeking groups and individuals in society. It will require

40 *Ibid.,* p. 19.
41 *Ibid.,* p. 20.

assessments of the legitimacy of the increasing interdependency of business with these groups and individuals. Finally, it must seek through involvement with all groups and individuals a national consensus on the goals most important to our society as a whole. In this way a statement of national goals can be translated into a positive philosophy and ethic to which a professional commitment can be made.

Cases

Mason Chemicals, Inc.

Early in February, 1965, U. S. Secretary of Health, Education, and Welfare Anthony Celebrezze, called for a public conference to consider the problem of water pollution in the Chicago area. The conference, called under legislative authority granted in 1948 and amended in 1956, was to convene March 2 at McCormick Place, Chicago, and run for four days.

A few days before Secretary Celebrezze's action, the U. S. Public Health Service had issued a special report stating that dangerous amounts of sewage and industrial wastes were being discharged into Lake Michigan and the Calumet River system in Indiana and Illinois. Public Health Service officials, whose concern in the matter was based on the fact that the pollution moves across state boundaries, said that the Grand Calumet River and Indiana Harbor Canal are grossly polluted, and that the southern end of Lake Michigan was becoming seriously affected by pollutants.

Lake Michigan provides the water supply for nearly five million people in Chicago, its suburbs, and the Indiana cities of Gary, Hammond, Whiting, and East Chicago. The lake also is a source of water for industrial processes and cooling purposes in dozens of major industrial plants in the area, and is used for swimming, boating, water skiing, and fishing. The rivers and canals in the area are used primarily for shipping, but also somewhat for recreational boating.

Among the business firms called to appear at the anti-pollution conference was Mason Chemicals, Inc., a medium-sized producer of heavy industrial chemicals. Its diversified line of specialty chemicals includes those used in petroleum refining, metal processing and coating, and the production of such diverse products as iron and steel, automotive and refrigeration equipment, and insulation and building materials. Over 80% of the company's production occurs at its large plant in East Chicago, Indiana, and most of its sales are made to other industrial firms located in Indiana, Illinois, Wisconsin, Ohio and Michigan.

This material was prepared by Professor Richard W. Barsness utilizing public sources and a student report by Charles Henning. Northwestern University cases are prepared to stimulate class discussions. No judgments about the described events are intended nor should any be implied from their use here. Reprinted with permission of the author.

The firm's sales for the past five years have averaged about $120 million, and in fiscal 1965 the company had sales of $146,700,000, and a net operating profit of $17,764,000. Sales and operating profits for 1965 were both about 6% higher than in 1964. Other income (from investments, real estate, patent royalties, etc.) totaled $1,931,000. As a result of certain business deductions and special tax credits, Mason Chemicals paid only $6,919,000 in Federal and state income taxes on its total income of $19,695,000.

With a net income of $12,776,000, the company paid $4,373,000 in common share dividends (no preferred stock is outstanding), and added $8,403,000 to its retained earnings. The addition of this sum brought its retained earnings to a total of $50,834,000 at the end of fiscal 1965. The stockholders' equity in the company at the end of 1965 was approximately $90 million.

Property, plant, and equipment were valued at a cost of $120 million, less accumulated depreciation of $65 million. Annual depreciation charges have averaged about $6 million. In recent years new capital expenditures by Mason Chemicals for plant and equipment have varied greatly, but have averaged about $8 million per year. Long-term debt at the end of 1965 stood at $25 million, and is being reduced at a rate of from $3,500,000 to $4 million per year.

FEDERAL CONCERN OVER WATER POLLUTION

The Public Health Service report issued in February, 1965, declared that large quantities of municipal sewage and industrial wastes, "treated to varying degrees," are discharged into the area's waters. As a result, the streams are discolored, often smelly, and marked by floating debris and oil. "Along the shores of Lake Michigan, in Indiana and the southern shore in Illinois, the waters are discolored by suspended and dissolved waste materials, in sharp contrast to the pleasing appearance of the rest of Lake Michigan," the agency said.

United States Steel Corporation, Youngstown Sheet and Tube Co., and Inland Steel Co., were cited by the report as the largest sources of waste in the river and canal, and three petroleum refineries (Cities Service Petroleum Co., Sinclair Refining Co., and Mobil Oil Co.) were listed as "lesser but still major sources of waste."

The principal sources of waste discharged directly into Lake Michigan were identified by the Public Health Service as Union Carbide Chemicals Co., American Oil Co., American Maize-Products Co., United States Steel Corporation, and Mason Chemicals, Inc.

Communities in the area, however, were equally at fault, the agency said. It cited ineffective disinfection in municipal waste disposal systems, the prevalence of combined storm-sanitary sewage systems that discharge untreated sewage during and after heavy rains, and the increasing number of small treatment plants that discharge into ditches and small streams.

The public conference called by Secretary Celebrezze involved sewage and industrial wastes from about 35 municipalities and 40 plants. Under Federal law, the participants in a water pollution conference are expected to draw up a program to improve their local situation. If this fails, then the Secretary of Health, Education, and Welfare may convene a hearing at which sworn testimony is given, following which the hearing board makes recommendations and the Secretary orders specific action. If local governments and plants still do not cooperate, then the Secretary has authority to take the matter to court.

Use of this three-step enforcement machinery, with its emphasis on giving the contributors to water pollution ample opportunity to remedy the situation voluntarily, has accelerated considerably in recent years. And Federal action seems likely to continue to grow since public concern over both air and water pollution has risen sharply in the past three years, and President Johnson has committed his Administration to work toward effective remedies. The Chicago area conference represented probably the most complex water pollution problem tackled thus far by the conference approach, and much depended, of course, on the attitude and degree of cooperation shown by the participating municipalities and companies.

BACKGROUND OF MASON CHEMICALS AND THE PROBLEM OF WATER POLLUTION

The history of Mason Chemicals, Inc. in the matter of waste disposal is fairly typical of other firms in the industrial region at the south end of Lake Michigan. Prior to 1940, there were no sewage treatment facilities of any nature in this plant. The entire effluent was discharged into Lake Michigan, which the plant had access to by means of some large private sewers. In 1940, sanitary sewage facilities were made available to the plant by the East Chicago, Indiana Sanitary Board. At that time, sanitary sewage was separated from the cooling waters that were being returned to Lake Michigan.

In 1944 an extensive six-month survey and study of all industrial wastes was initiated by the company for the following purposes:

1. to classify the pollution load of industrial wastes on the basis of individual sources

2. to determine the basic characteristics and magnitude of waste from each source

3. to determine seasonal fluctuations affecting each waste

4. to develop methods to reduce and control the strength of these wastes.

On the basis of the findings obtained in this survey, Mason Chemicals, Inc. embarked on a waste abatement program which was completed in 1950. Through this program the daily plant sewer loadings to Lake Michigan were

reduced from 61,148 pounds of BOD (bio-chemical oxygen demand, a meas-
sure, of pollution) to 3,200 pounds. This was accomplished by the isolation
of all waste-bearing waters, the re-use of process waters, the recovery of all
solids possible, and the reduction of considerable volatile organic matter.
To accomplish this reduction in pollution the company spent approximately
$8 million.

In 1952 Mason Chemicals began a modernization and expansion program,
the most important feature of which was the shift from a batch operation
process to continuous process production of most chemicals. This change
resulted in more waste waters than could be handled by the existing waste
abatement program. In order to cope with the larger volume of waste
waters and provide a "permanent" type system for controlling pollution,
Mason Chemicals built a lagoon treatment system.

Chemical production capacity at the East Chicago plant has increased
38% since 1952, and the pollution load is currently 6,076 pounds of BOD
per day. Presently some twelve million gallons of water are pumped from
the lake each day and about ten million gallons are returned as cooling
water. The two million gallons retained by the plant are treated in its waste
abatement facilities before being discharged into the lake again. The water
returned to Lake Michigan is chlorinated, and is sampled on a frequent basis
seven days a week. A complete analysis is made each day of the samples
taken. Capital expenditures by Mason Chemicals, Inc. for industrial waste
control from 1940 through 1962 totaled approximately $14,327,000. The
operating cost of the waste abatement program currently is about $1,225,000
annually.

Up to the early 1960's, the anti-pollution controls placed on firms such
as Mason Chemicals were relatively lax. Only occasionally did either state
or Federal authorities take action to reduce water pollution. Such action
typically was in the form of setting minimum standards of waste abatement
to be achieved by individual firms by a certain date, with court action to
be brought against those failing to comply. A shortcoming of this approach,
however, was the fact that any *relative* improvement in the quality of each
gallon of industrial water returned to Lake Michigan often was more than
nullified by the fact that increased production required more and more
water, hence increasing the *absolute* total of pollutants.

Although Mason Chemicals, Inc. did not find it a hardship to meet such
standards as government imposed in the past, the company realized early
in 1965 that the "good old days" were all but past regarding water pollution,
and that the firm would have to devote serious attention to shaping new
policies to meet new conditions. One aspect of the new situation, of
course, was the Federal Government's call for a public conference on water
pollution in the Chicago area, and the increasing likelihood of extensive
Federal activity in the future. A second aspect of the problem for the company was how to handle the growing volume of complaints by East Chicago

residents about both the company's role in water pollution of the lake, and the objectionable odors which originate in its waste treatment facilities and pervade a considerable portion of the city.

If Mason Chemicals were forced to meet the water standards which some Federal officials apparently had in mind for Lake Michigan, the company knew that it would be faced with a difficult problem both technically and financially. The cost could easily run in the neighborhood of $25 million, and depending upon the time limit involved, such a requirement would have a profound effect on the future course of the company's business. In particular, management at Mason Chemicals had been giving serious consideration to a series of steps to modernize and expand production facilities at the East Chicago plant, and whatever position the company took in the proceedings at the Federal anti-pollution conference would have to be made in this light.

MASON CHEMICALS' PLANNED EXPANSION

The firm's desire to modernize and expand had its origin in the prosperity of the early 1960's. Sales, profits, and tax considerations were favorable, and the prolonged period of prosperity was accompanied by an expanding demand for heavy industrial chemicals, especially in the Midwest, where steel producers, auto manufacturers, and other major industrial chemical users were experiencing rapid growth.

As a well-established firm with excellent access to this market, Mason Chemicals believed it would be desirable to modernize and expand the productive capacity of its East Chicago plant by about 30% over the next five years, providing suitable financing could be arranged. A variety of considerations precluded the issuance of additional common stock, thus any new capital investment would have to be financed by retained earnings and long-term borrowing. Depending upon the specific facilities to be included in such an expansion program, the cost was estimated at between $70 million and $85 million. These figures, when contrasted with the cost of previous major expansions in the company's history, emphasized the steady inflation which had occurred in the absolute dollar cost of expansion, but more troublesome than this observation was the fact that the cost of such major expansion would not fall evenly over the whole five-year period. The principal burden of the necessary capital expenditures would come in a twenty-month period during the third and fourth years.

Furthermore to achieve the desired increase in the capacity of the East Chicago plant, it would be necessary to utilize virtually all remaining vacant land at the site. As far as efficiency in production was concerned, this made good sense, but it presented two unattractive prospects with respect to waste abatement. First, it would prevent any additional land from being devoted to waste treatment facilities; second, it would increase the demand on existing waste treatment facilities by at least 30%, and Mason Chemicals was already being criticized by the Federal Government and local residents for the inadequacy of its waste abatement program.

The only available alternatives for boosting the capacity of the present space devoted to waste abatement were: (1) to deepen the existing settling lagoons (an expensive process which promised diminishing returns in terms of keeping pace with the increased quantity of pollutants accompanying any plant expansion); (2) the development of some entirely new technology to cope with the company's particular pollution problems. The latter certainly was not inconceivable, but even if successful, the time and money required for a technological breakthrough were quite unpredictable.

Thus the spatial demands and cost of more extensive waste treatment facilities seemed directly opposed to the spatial and financial requirements of plant modernization and expansion. And along this line, Mason Chemicals was troubled by some information concerning its strongest competitor in the heavy industrial chemical market in the Midwest.

This competitor also was known to be considering expansion to strengthen its position in the growing market, and while it had some financial problems of its own to contend with, it did not face any spatial problems, since its plant site in neighboring Hammond, Indiana, contained a substantial quantity of unused acreage. Furthermore, in reference to the forthcoming Federal anti-pollution conference, at which this firm also was to appear, one of the firm's vice-presidents said in a newspaper interview that the Public Health Service had "grossly misinterpreted the facts" about water pollution in the area, and that the company had no intention of disclosing the amounts and types of materials in its industrial wastes, since such information would aid its competitors.

Mason Chemicals recognized that to some extent their competitor was correct in suggesting that information about industrial wastes could be of assistance to a competitive firm. Set against this, however, was the fact that government officials and the public generally were likely to regard this viewpoint simply as a corporate refusal to admit guilt in the matter of water pollution, and a rejection of any responsibility to help correct the situation.

As the date for the Federal anti-pollution conference neared, the management of Mason Chemicals recognized that they faced two problems of differing magnitudes which called for some decisive action on the part of the company. The lesser of these was the problem of community relations involving the objections being raised by some residents of East Chicago. These complaints were regarded by the company as somewhat contradictory, since they criticized the company both for its contribution to water pollution in Lake Michigan, and for the strong odors which emanated from the company's efforts to treat waste in its lagoon system. Nonetheless, they could not be lightly dismissed.

The greater problem facing management concerned the position the company should take at the forthcoming anti-pollution conference. The considerations here were: what water quality standards should the company support as a satisfactory compromise between its own interests and the public interest; how much information should the company make public regarding its past and present waste abatement program; how could the firm reconcile its desire to modernize and expand its East Chicago plant with its future policy in regard to waste abatement; and finally, what type of public relations effort, if any, should accompany the decisions which the company reached in these matters?

Lawrence Steamship Lines

In September, 1956, Mr. Donald Brown of the Lawrence Steamship Lines was trying to decide where the company's order for an oil tanker should be placed. Mr. Brown had a choice between Ship Construction, Ltd., in Shoreside, England, and the Thompson Shipyards, Ltd., at Prescott, Ontario, Canada.

The Lawrence Steamship Lines was a Canadian subsidiary of an American transportation holding company. The company operated oil tankers on the Great Lakes and the St. Lawrence River System. The tankers which sailed on the Great Lakes were too wide and long to pass through the locks and canals between Prescott, Ontario, and Montreal, Quebec, and consequently the Lawrence Lines operated several tankers which met the 14-feet depth, 43-feet width and 250-feet length requirements. The 2,100-ton tanker to be purchased would be of these general width and length dimensions, and with a 14-foot draft, it would carry 18,000 barrels of oil. Fully loaded with 24,000 barrels, it would have a deadweight of 3,200 tons and would draw 16 feet.

The Lawrence Lines intended to place the new tanker in service from Toronto to Montreal to carry heavy Bunker C fuel oil. The company could also use the tanker for the delivery of refined petroleum products from Montreal to small ports on the St. Lawrence River and Gulf of St. Lawrence. At the existing cargo rates and expense levels, the Lawrence Lines expected the new tanker to earn $190,000 before depreciation, interest, and income taxes. The vessel's revenues would run about $1,445 daily, and the ship's crew, fuel,

Reprinted with permission of Professor Emeritus George Baker, the Harvard University Graduate School of Business. Copyright © 1957 by the President and Fellows of Harvard College; all rights reserved.

and general overhead expenses would average $640 a day. The shipping season on the Great Lakes and the St. Lawrence River usually lasted about 235 days from the middle of April to early December.

SHIPBUILDING NEGOTIATIONS

The sequence of events leading to the determination of a price for a ship were the submission of the general specifications to several shipyards; the selection of the most attractive bid; the detailed blueprinting of the specifications; the letter of intent; and the modification of the plans and final bargaining. When a new tanker was to be constructed, the management of the Lawrence Lines would decide on the vessel's size and weight, the hull shape, cargo-carrying configuration, type of motor power, and the auxiliary equipment. Mr. Brown would then contact several yards in Canada and the United Kingdom for bids, and would eliminate the less attractive ones. The Lawrence Lines had narrowed their consideration down to Ship Construction and Thompson Shipyards.

Upon selection of the yard to build the tanker, the marine engineers of the Lawrence Lines and those of the shipbuilding company would proceed with the drawing of the ship's plans. Decisions would also be made on the suppliers for the engines and mechanical equipment; electrical cable, and pipe fittings, and upon completion of this phase of the work, Mr. Brown would forward a letter of intent authorizing the project and agreeing on a total price. The shipyard's original price could be significantly changed as a result of detailing the vessel's requirements. To keep the price close to the original agreement, representatives of both companies generally proposed modifications, and these would be negotiated until agreement on a price was reached. The shipyard would require an escalator clause to cover increases in the price of steel, other purchased items, and wages, and they would demand progress payments during the eight months the vessel was expected to be under construction. Although projects usually proceeded with the same shipyard after the letter of intent was submitted, contracts had been occasionally broken off by mutual consent when agreement could not be reached in negotiations on changes and the cost thereof.

ADVANTAGES IN HAVING THE TANKER BUILT AT THE
THOMPSON SHIPYARD

An earlier delivery date, easier supervision of the project and negotiation of changes, as well as future yard relations were some of the important factors favoring a decision to buy in Canada. The Lawrence Lines could expect delivery of the new 2,100-ton tanker in time for the 1957 shipping season if the order were placed with the Thompson yards at Prescott, Ontario. Ship Construction, Ltd., was unwilling to quote a delivery sooner than November,

Exhibit 1 Lawrence Steamship Lines
Return on Investment Calculations

Tanker Built in Canada for $1,150,000

	Year 1	Year 2	Year 3	Year 4	Year 5	Year 6	Year 7	Year 8	Year 9	Year 10	Total
Annual Operating Profit	$190,000	$190,000	$190,000	$190,000	$190,000	$190,000	$190,000	$190,000	$190,000	$190,000	
Depreciation	127,000	133,300	139,600	145,900	152,200	158,500	164,800	128,700	0	0	
Interest at 6%	63,000	56,700	50,400	44,100	37,800	31,500	25,200	18,900	12,600	6,300	
Profit Before Tax	0	0	0	0	0	0	0	42,400	177,400	183,700	
Tax 47%	0	0	0	0	0	0	0	19,928	83,378	86,339	
Net After Income Tax	0	0	0	0	0	0	0	22,472	94,022	97,361	
Depreciation Added Back	127,000	133,300	139,600	145,900	152,200	158,500	164,800	128,700	0	0	
Cash Flow	127,000	133,300	139,600	145,900	152,200	158,500	164,800	151,172	94,022	97,361	
Discounted at Cash Flow at 4%	127,000	128,235	129,130	129,705	130,131	130,287	130,192	114,891	68,730	68,445	$1,156,746

Tanker Built in United Kingdom for $850,000

	Year 1	Year 2	Year 3	Year 4	Year 5	Year 6	Year 7	Year 8	Year 9	Year 10	Total
Annual Operating Profit	$190,000	$190,000	$190,000	$190,000	$190,000	$190,000	$190,000	$190,000	$190,000	$190,000	
Depreciation	127,500	108,375	92,119	78,301	66,556	56,572	48,087	40,874	34,742	29,531	
Interest at 6%	45,000	40,500	36,000	31,500	27,000	22,500	18,000	13,500	9,000	4,500	
Profit Before Tax	17,500	41,125	61,881	80,199	96,444	110,928	123,913	135,626	146,258	155,969	
Tax 47%	8,225	19,329	29,084	37,694	45,329	52,136	58,239	63,744	68,741	73,305	
Net After Income Tax	9,275	21,796	32,797	42,505	51,115	58,792	65,674	71,882	77,517	82,664	
Depreciation	127,500	108,375	92,119	78,301	66,556	56,572	48,087	40,874	34,742	29,531	
Cash Flow	136,775	130,171	124,916	120,806	117,671	115,364	113,761	112,756	112,259	112,195	
Discounted at Cash Flow at 10%	136,775	118,325	103,181	90,725	80,369	71,641	64,161	57,844	52,425	47,571	$ 823,017
at 8%	136,775	120,538	107,053	95,920	86,488	78,563	71,669	65,737	60,620	56,098	879,461
Book Value–15% Declining Balance	722,500	614,125	522,006	443,705	377,149	320,577	272,490	231,616	196,874	167,343	

Notes:

1. A ship built in Canada can be depreciated up to 33⅓% a year until written off. If vessel's earnings do not cover the 33⅓% charge, the difference can be taken against the company's over-all earnings.

2. Ships purchased in the United Kingdom are written off on 15% of the declining balance method.

3. Assumed $1,050,000 borrowed on a ship built in Canada, $750,000 on a ship built in the United Kingdom.

Source: Company records.

1958, but hoped, nevertheless, that the tanker could be delivered by April, 1958. Ship Construction was already five months late with a tanker which was to have been delivered to the Lawrence Lines in April, 1956.

By building the tanker in Canada, the Lawrence Lines' engineers would be able to visit the Thompson yard at little expense, and they would be able to check on the workmanship and material going into the ship. If necessary the engineers could make last minute changes in the plans, and the negotiations on the cost of these modifications could be carried on without the time and expense difficulties that great distance would impose on a project with Ship Construction.

The Thompson yard needed business badly to keep its steel fabricating and machine shop facilities operating at an economical volume. The yard's management was also fearful of losing its trained labor force of 1,400 if the men had to be laid off. Mr. Brown felt that by giving Thompson business in a time of need Thompson might give the Lawrence Lines' vessels priority over other work when repairs were needed and the yard might be operating at capacity. The Thompson yard would install in the tanker Canadian-built Fairbanks-Morse diesel engines and other Canadian equipment which could be serviced or repaired by the manufacturers' representatives almost immediately when breakdowns occurred. Ship Construction would probably use German or Swiss diesels. Canadian yards generally did not have a complete inventory of replacement parts for foreign-built equipment, thus the Lawrence Lines would have to invest in them if the tanker were bought in England.

THE ADVANTAGES OF SHIP CONSTRUCTION, LTD.

A better-built ship and a higher return on investment were the basic advantages of buying the 2,100-ton tanker in England. Workers at Ship Construction's yards had been steadily employed for many years, and their shipbuilding skills had been passed down from one generation to the next. Mr. Brown and the Lawrence Lines' officers felt the result of the workers' accumulated experience was a better-built vessel. This belief had been proven over the years by their infrequent hull repairs, and many of the line's captains thought they "handled better than ships built elsewhere." Many of the vessels of the "canaller" class in the Lawrence Lines' fleet had been built by Ship Construction, Ltd., at the Shoreside Yard.

The return on investment by purchasing the tanker in England was estimated by the Lawrence Lines' management to be 9% compared to 4% on the purchase in Canada. The company's calculations are presented in Exhibit 1. The physical life of the tanker was expected to be 20 years. A 10-year period of comparison was chosen, however, because Mr. Brown wished to see what the return would be in a shorter period of time. There was a possibility that the opening of the St. Lawrence Seaway might make the tanker competitively uneconomical and obsolete.

The Lawrence Lines had $100,000 cash to invest in the 2,100-ton tanker. Mr. Brown planned to borrow the remaining balance of the purchase price by means of 10-year, 6% first mortgage bonds which would require equal annual repayments. These bonds would be sold over-the-counter to the general public. Mr. Brown did not anticipate any trouble in borrowing the additional $300,000 if he decided to have the tanker built in Canada.

PROGRESS PAYMENTS

The final contract with either yard would call for construction advances or progress payments when certain stages of the tanker's hull and fittings had been completed. If the purchase were made at Ship Construction this provision would introduce either a risk that the cost of the vessel might increase or an opportunity to save an additional $17,000–$34,000 depending upon the trend in exchange values between the Canadian dollar and the sterling pound. If the Lawrence Lines could be reasonably certain of the dates the progress payments would be due, Mr. Brown could contract to buy sterling at an agreed price at specific dates in the next three months. Thus the Lawrence Lines could minimize fluctuations in the price of the ship and reduce a loss if an unfavorable trend developed in the exchange rates. The market was currently discounting the stated value of the sterling pound, and this would allow a saving of one to two cents per pound if the sterling was purchased in the New York market.

Recent quotes in foreign exchange rates are presented in Exhibit 2. Mr. Brown was watching the Suez crisis and wondering what effect it would have on the value of the pound as well as on the United Kingdom's ship-building requirements—especially for tankers. In the event of war or in-ability to use the canal, Mr. Brown felt the Lawrence Lines' tanker might be completed and impressed into service for the British Government, although it was more likely that it's completion would be delayed to permit the con-struction of tankers which would be put on the route around the Cape of Good Hope.

THE POLITICAL ATMOSPHERE IN CANADA IN 1956

Canadian elections were to be held in 1957. Two proposals to change regulations on coasting trade and the role of United States investment in Canada were issues in the summer of 1956 which could affect the Lawrence Lines' decision.

The St. Lawrence Seaway was expected to open by 1960, and its comple-tion was expected to quadruple the volume of traffic moving on the St. Lawrence River. Canadian operators hauling commodities between two ports on Canadian soil were becoming fearful of new foreign competition, and they requested legislation which would permit trading between Canadian ports by Canadian-flag ships only. The Canadian Government established a Royal Commission on Coasting Trade in 1955 to holding hearings and make recommendations on the evidence. By the summer of 1956, the briefs of the more than 100 interested groups had been published. The Royal Commis-

Exhibit 2

Lawrence Steampship Rates

Foreign Exchange Rates

Years	United Kingdom	Canada
	(in cents)	(in cents)
1934	503.93	101.01
1935	490.18	99.49
1936	497.09	99.91
1937	494.40	100.00
1938	488.94	99.42
1939	443.54	96.02
1940–1945	403.50	90.91
1946	403.28	95.20
1947	402.86	100.00
1948	403.13	100.00
1949	368.72	97.49
1950	280.07	90.91
1951	279.96	94.94
1952	279.26	102.15
1953	281.27	101.65
1954	280.87	102.72

Source: *The Economic Almanac*, 1956, p. 525.

Exchange Values—July 31, 1956
(in cents)

	High	Low	Final
Canadian Dollar	101.890	101.859	101.89
Sterling $2.80 Per Pound			

	Tuesday	Monday	Week Ago	Year Ago
Cables	278 13/32	278 11/32	279 5/16	279 7/32
30 Days	277 7/8	277 27/32	278 13/16	278 1/4
60 Days	277 3/8	277 11/32	278 15/16	277 11/16
90 Days	276 7/8	277 13/16	277 13/16	277 1/4
Transferable	27615	27620	27730	

Source: *New York Times*, August 1, 1956.

sion, however, had not made its recommendations public. The maritime provincial governments, the coasting and inland waterway operators, and the shipbuilders were the major proponents of the legislation. The opposition to the amendment originated with a small number of Canadian-flag ocean operators and the agricultural provinces interested in the development of the export of Canadian grains. Mr. Brown said it was difficult to forecast, at this time, which of the groups had the greatest legislative strength.

An amendment to the registration regulations, which would permit only Canadian-built vessel in Canadian-flag trades, was also being considered with the coasting trade legislation. Although the proposed law would not affect the purchase of this tanker, the opportunity to buy a second or additional ships in the same class was important because their construction cost was generally lower than that of the initial vessel. This was possible because dies, machine shop fixtures, and welding patterns and templates could be used over again. This second amendment lacked the support of many ship operators because they had purchased the majority of their vessels from United Kingdom yards and they wished to continue to be able to buy less expensive ships abroad. The Lawrence Lines' management shared this view, and the company was against this amendment because the St. Lawrence Seaway would make it possible, for the first time, for the Lawrence Lines to build its big lake tankers away from the American and Canadian shipyards located on the Great Lakes.

During the political debate of the summer of 1956, American domination of Canadian manufacturing and natural resources had become a political issue. "Dollar diplomacy" and "economic colonialism" were terms being used by critics of Canada's current unfavorable balance of trade, the predominantly foreign ownership of industrial concerns, the investment of Canadian wealth outside the country and the practice of many American or United Kingdom owned corporations in Canada to finance with debt rather than equity capital. Being the subsidiary of an American corporation, Mr. Brown was keenly aware that the Lawrence Lines' stand on national issues should be carefully formulated and stated to maintain good relations with the Canadian public. The 2,100-ton tanker project would be financed almost entirely with debt capital—currently one of the "hottest" issues. The high interest rate of 6%, on prime security, was indicative of the acute shortage of credit which existed in the fall of 1956.

CONFERENCE WITH GOVERNMENT OFFICIALS

Mr. Brown had conferred with officials of the government department of Trade and Commerce about where the purchase of the 2,100-ton tanker should be made. The officials had told Mr. Brown that they hoped the Lawrence Lines would build in a Canadian yard because of the depressed condition of the shipbuilding industry. Exhibit 3 gives a summary of Canadian shipbuilding activity from 1946 to 1953. Post-World War II shipbuilding activity had been considerably below wartime levels, and Mr. Howe was interested in keeping the shipyards' employment high and facilities in good operating condition for national defense purposes.

Some Canadian shipyards had turned to subcontracting work in an effort to keep their businesses operating; however, Mr. Brown felt the majority of them had not tried to organize for competitive operation with foreign yards. He also felt they were content to live on vessel construction orders from the Canadian Navy which acted as an indirect subsidy. Mr. Brown knew orders from the Lawrence Steamship Lines alone could not support the Canadian shipbuilding industry, but, as the officer responsible for equipment and financial decisions, he was wondering how much importance he should place on national defense and public relations in making his selection of a builder for the 2,100-ton tanker.

Exhibit 3

Lawrence Steampship Lines								
Dollar Value of Ships Delivered, Vessel Repairs and Conversions								
Shipbuilding Area	1946	1947	1948	1949	1950	1951	1952	1953
	($000,000 omitted)							
Great Lakes Shipbuilding	$ 6.7	$ .1	$ 8.9	$ 5.2	$ 7.0	$ 8.3	$31.1	$ 3.5
Repairs and Conversions	2.2	2.7	2.9	4.3	3.1	4.6	4.7	5.9
Total	$ 8.9	$ 2.8	$ 11.8	$ 9.5	$10.1	$12.9	$35.8	$ 9.4
Total All-Canada* Shipbuilding	$30.0	$44.5	$ 87.3	$31.7	$26.3	$12.9	$42.0	$44.4
Repairs and Conversions	24.1	27.7	22.6	18.0	17.1	24.3	37.8	51.1
Total Billings	$54.1	$72.2	$109.9	$49.7	$43.4	$37.2	$79.7	$95.5

* There are four shipbuilding areas in Canada: Atlantic Coast, Great Lakes, Pacific Coast (the smallest), and St. Lawrence (the largest).
Source: *Seventh Report of the Canadian Maritime Commission*, June 24, 1954.

Question: With which company should the Lawrence Lines place the contract to build the 2,100-ton tanker? Why?

Bibliography

A. Immediate Challenges

"Cleaning Up the Nation's Air," *Business Week* (July 23, 1966), pp. 89–96.

"Crisis in the Cities: Does Business Hold the Key?" *Duns Review* (November 1967), pp. 31–35.

Demaree, Allan T. "Business Picks Up the Urban Challenge," *Fortune* (April 1969), pp. 103–104, 174, 179–180, 184.

Diamond, Robert S. "What Business Thinks," *Fortune* (February 1970), pp. 118–119, 171–172.

Faltermayer, Edmund K. "We Can Afford Clean Air," *Fortune* (November 1965), pp.159–163.

———. "How To Wage War on Ugliness," *Fortune* (May 1966), pp. 160–165.

Moore, I. W. "Urban Unrest—Whose Problem Is It?" *California Management Review* (Summer 1969), pp. 7–10.

Robbins, L. C. "The Role of Management in Economic Development," *Advanced Management Journal* (July 1965), pp. 24–33.

Smith, Larry. "Business Can Save American Cities," *Nation's Business* (November 1965), pp. 38–39, 50–55, 122.

B. Responsibilities of the Future

Austin, Robert W. "Who Has The Responsibility for Social Change—Business or Government?" *Harvard Business Review* (July–August, 1965), pp. 45–53.

Bright, James R. "Opportunity And Threat In Technological Change," *Harvard Business Review* (November–December, 1963), pp. 76–86.

"From Now to 1980: Amazing Growth," *Business Week* (October 16, 1965), pp. 57–60.

"Herman Kahn's Thinkable Future," *Business Week* (March 11, 1967), pp. 114–118.

"How Industry Will Find the World in 1986," *Iron Age* (January 5, 1967), p. 23.

Irwin, Patrick H. and Frank W. Langham, Jr., "The Change Seekers," *Harvard Business Review* (January–February, 1966), pp. 81–92.

Silberman, Charles E. "Is Technology Taking Over?" *Fortune* (February 1966), pp. 112–115, 212, 217–222.

Ways, Max· "The Era of Radical Change," *Fortune* (May 1944), pp. 113–115, 210, 215–216.

ABCDEFGHIJ— RM —76543210